FASHION & LUXURY Marketing

Sara Miller McCune founded SAGE Publishing in 1965 to support the dissemination of usable knowledge and educate a global community. SAGE publishes more than 1000 journals and over 800 new books each year, spanning a wide range of subject areas. Our growing selection of library products includes archives, data, case studies and video. SAGE remains majority owned by our founder and after her lifetime will become owned by a charitable trust that secures the company's continued independence.

Los Angeles | London | New Delhi | Singapore | Washington DC | Melbourne

FASHION & LUXURY Marketing

Michael R. Solomon and Mona Mrad

SAGE

Los Angeles | London | New Delhi
Singapore | Washington DC | Melbourne

SAGE Publications Ltd
1 Oliver's Yard
55 City Road
London EC1Y 1SP

SAGE Publications Inc.
2455 Teller Road
Thousand Oaks, California 91320

SAGE Publications India Pvt Ltd
B 1/I 1 Mohan Cooperative Industrial Area
Mathura Road
New Delhi 110 044

SAGE Publications Asia-Pacific Pte Ltd
3 Church Street
#10-04 Samsung Hub
Singapore 049483

Editor: Matthew Waters
Editorial assistant: Charlotte Hanson
Assistant editor, digital: Mandy Gao
Production editor: Katherine Haw
Indexer: Charmian Parkin
Marketing manager: Kimberley Simpson
Cover design: Francis Kenney
Typeset by: C&M Digitals (P) Ltd, Chennai, India
Printed in the UK

Library of Congress Control Number: 2021946025

British Library Cataloguing in Publication data

A catalogue record for this book is available from the British Library

ISBN 978-1-5264-1924-8
ISBN 978-1-5264-1925-5 (pbk)

At SAGE we take sustainability seriously. Most of our products are printed in the UK using responsibly sourced papers and boards. When we print overseas we ensure sustainable papers are used as measured by the PREPS grading system. We undertake an annual audit to monitor our sustainability.

Praise for the book

"What a fantastic book! All key fashion marketing concepts, models and strategies are covered and directly applied to the contemporary fashion industry, making it a rare and valuable resource. A must-have for all students and lecturers across all fashion business courses"
Dr Rosy Boardman, Senior Lecturer of Fashion Business, Department of Materials, University of Manchester

"This book is a *tour de force* in explaining and framing the specificities of fashion and luxury consumption. It combines classic marketing frameworks, such as the 4Ps, with ones specific to the industry, such as the Fashion Marketing Mix. The book features a wealth of case studies that reflect a diverse cultural landscape of fashion and luxury consumption practices"
Professor Benjamin G. Voyer, Cartier chaired Professor of Behavioural Science, ESCP Business School

"Solomon and Mrad do an excellent job of distilling the complex, global fashion system through clear examples and case studies. Readers will come away with a focused understanding of the nuances of fashion industry within the context of marketing."
Joshua Williams, President, Fashion Consort, Assistant Professor, Parsons School of Design

"Written in an accessible style and illustrated throughout with examples and case studies, this book covers a wide range of business strategy and consumer behaviour content across historical and contemporary fashion and luxury, providing insights into fashion as both a dynamic global industry and a significant cultural phenomenon. The authors' approach reinforces the need to continually analyse the marketing environment by highlighting shifting industry and consumer trends and provides discussion starters on how consumers think about fashion's contemporary issues including sustainable fashion, ethical business, technological innovations and data privacy"
Professor Natascha Radclyffe-Thomas, Professor of Marketing and Sustainable Business, British School of Fashion, Glasgow Caledonian University London

"The fashion system has its own rules of communication and marketing and, moreover, is subject to rapid changes and transformations. This book explains the intrinsic link between fashion and luxury both by explaining it from a historical point of view, also through case studies, and by dealing with contemporary changes. The result is an in-depth work from a historical, cultural and sociological, as well as marketing, point of view. A section entirely dedicated to consumer choices and their motivations completes the panorama of topics covered. In short, a work that sheds precious light on the crucial sectors of the fashion system and luxury."

Mauro Ferraresi, Associate Professor of Sociology of Communication, Director of the Master Made in Italy, Iulm University

"Finally, a fashionable book about fashion: a must read for those aiming for a career in the industry, but not only!"

Roberto Donà, Professor of Practice in Management, Associate Dean for Corporate Engagement, International Business School Suzhou (IBSS), Xi'an Jiaotong-Liverpool University

"This textbook is born canonical since it very successfully reconciles fashion and luxury marketing that have long been viewed as opposite if not contradictory. It provides extremely powerful insights to both students and practitioners since it covers with precise examples and illustrations all the stages of fashion marketing. By embracing the many sides of this complex phenomenon called fashion, this book invites the reader on an a rich historical, sociological, behavioural and managerial journey. A real tour de force that should be praised since it fills an obvious gap in the literature."

Professor Benoît Heilbrunn, Professor of Marketing, ESCP Business School

Contents

Table of Contents

List of Case Studies

About the Authors

Michael Solomon "wrote the book" on understanding consumers. Literally. Hundreds of thousands of business students have learned about Marketing from his 30+ books including *Consumer Behavior: Buying, Having, and Being*—the most widely used book on the subject in the world. He is Professor of Marketing in the Haub School of Business at Saint Joseph's University in Philadelphia.

Michael's mantra: We don't buy products because of what they do. We buy them because of what they mean. Michael helped to develop the first system to test consumers' responses to apparel and footwear styles online for the National Textile Center, U.S. Department of Commerce and his text *Consumer Behavior: In Fashion* is widely used in university merchandising programs. He edited the first multidisciplinary book on *The Psychology of Fashion*, which was published in 1985.

He advises global clients in leading industries such as apparel and footwear (Calvin Klein, Levi Strauss, Under Armour, Timberland), financial services and e-commerce (eBay, Progressive, McKinsey), CPG (Procter & Gamble, Campbell's), retailing (H&M), sports (CrossFit, Philadelphia Eagles), manufacturing (DuPont, PP&G) and transportation (BMW, United Airlines) on marketing strategies to make them more consumer-centric. Michael is a regular Contributor at Forbes.com, where he writes about retailing, consumer behavior and branding. His latest book, co-authored with Brandon Roe, host of The Fashion Consumer podcast, is Why Fashion Brands Die & How to Save Them.

www.michaelsolomon.com

Mona Mrad is an Assistant Professor in Marketing at the American University of Sharjah. She holds a PhD in Marketing from the University of Manchester, UK. She has also obtained a degree in fashion design from ESMOD and attended fashion courses at the London College of Fashion in the UK. Mona's research interests fall in the general area of consumer behavior, technology and innovation, and fashion/luxury marketing. She is particularly interested in researching the consumer-brand relationship, as well as the excessive buying behavior phenomena toward brands and products, in particular toward fashion and luxury brands. Her research has appeared in academic journals such as the *Journal of Business Research, European Journal of Marketing, Journal of Retailing and Consumer Services, Journal of Brand Management, Technology Analysis & Strategic Management* and *Qualitative Market Research*.

Online Resources

Fashion & Luxury Marketing is supported by online resources to help instructors incorporate the text in their teaching, which are available for access at **study.sagepub.com/solomon**.

For Instructors

- **An Instructor's Manual** will help you encourage discussion in class and provide links for useful multimedia resources across the Internet to help further reading and engagement with the subject.

- **PowerPoint slides** prepared by the authors will allow you to seamlessly incorporate the chapters into your weekly lessons.

SECTION I

Introduction to Fashion Marketing

CHAPTER 1

Fashion Marketing: An Introduction

LEARNING OBJECTIVES

After you read this chapter, you will understand the answers to the following:

1. What is fashion marketing?

2. Who are the players in the fashion industry?

3. What career opportunities are there in the fashion industry?

Mia groans as the alarm on her iPhone jolts her awake. Oh no, she's overslept again for her early Accounting class! What a mistake to stay out late last night at that fashionable new restaurant. Well, she still has half an hour to make the lecture, so it's time to step lively. She jumps out of bed, and races to the kitchen to insert her life-saving Nespresso. As the brew pours into her mug Mia thinks about what she has to do to get ready. She takes a big sip and smiles as she feels at least some of her brain cells waking up. Mia grabs the mug and races into the bathroom to do her make-up. Fortunately, her years of practice pay off as she almost automatically applies moisturizer and her red lipstick. Yes, she thinks as she checks herself out in the mirror, maybe I do look a bit like Staz Lindes when I use this lipstick. Now, on to the closet for the really hard choices. "What kind of a day do I want it to be?" she thinks. "Should I go into slouch mode and just throw on some sneakers and jeans? On the other hand, I'm going to need to look well put-together so I'm confident when I give my presentation later today—maybe I should go for it and rock it with a nice scarf and even that new pair of Balacienga shoes I've been saving." Oh, and probably a good idea to wear the ring that her friend gave her; that always brings good luck. A mere 10 minutes later, miraculously Mia is racing out the door. As she starts the engine of her car and turns up the volume as the radio plays Blackpink K-Pop, she wonders if all of her hard prep work will be enough to keep her awake during the accounting lecture.

What is Fashion Marketing?

As Mia's mad dash to get ready for class shows us, fashion influences many parts of our lives. Whether it's what we wear, eat, drive, or listen to, it's likely that fashion processes play a role—even if we're not aware of it at the time.

The **fashion system** includes all the people and organizations that create symbolic meanings and transfer them to goods and services. Those "hidden" meanings are all around us! Mia believed (as do many of us) that the outfit she chose for an important presentation would help her to come across to the audience as competent, and she also wore a ring as a superstitious "good luck" charm just in case. The material objects that surround us brim with symbolic meanings, so a lot of what we're going to discuss about fashion marketing relates to how organizations create goods and services that provide us with the "ammunition" we need to live our daily lives.

And—this is important: when we hear the word "fashion," many of us are likely to think of a glamorous model parading down a Paris catwalk or an influencer posing on Instagram. That's part of the picture, but a fairly small part. In fact, fashion processes affect all types of cultural phenomena, including products such as toys, electronics, games, cars, furniture, and kitchen appliances in addition to music, plastic surgery, food options, art, architecture, and TV shows, movies, books and plays. Fashion also influences the world of ideas; we see its impact in politics, religion, and even science (i.e., certain research topics and individual scientists are "hot" at any point in time—maybe even your professor!).

At the outset, let's distinguish among some terms. **Fashion** is the process of social diffusion by which some group(s) of consumers adopts a new style (see also[1]). In contrast, *a fashion* (or style) is a particular combination of attributes (say, a slim fitting bodysuit with palazzo trousers). To be *in fashion* means that some individuals, groups, or organizations are popular at that moment (e.g., *Vogue* endorses this look as "in" for this season).[2] Fashion is closely linked to the individual, self-identity and image—this is what makes fashion distinct.

The creation and spread of fashion is a $2.5 trillion global industry.[3] The products and services that are "in fashion" are a kind of looking glass that reflects how members of a culture define themselves and the world in which they live. Remember, this looking glass includes a lot more than "just" clothing—we call upon a huge range of things to help us to define these meanings that also include cosmetics, food/beverage, home furnishings, cars, travel choices, and many more.

We can think of fashion as a *code*, or a language, that helps us to decipher these meanings.[4] Unlike a language, however, fashion is *context-dependent*. This means that people might interpret the same item differently, and in different situations.[5] In *semiotic* terms (how we interpret the meanings of symbols) the meaning of a fashion product often is *undercoded*—that is, there is no one precise meaning but rather plenty of room for interpretation among perceivers that varies based upon their own frame of reference. For example, if you start with a basic apparel item such as a pair of Levi's jeans, the impression it imparts to others differs based upon what you pair it with: if you wear the pants with a blazer and a scarf it means something much different than when the same item appears beneath a black leather motorcycle jacket.

What is Marketing?

Now that we've made a start at explaining fashion, let's do a brief recap of what we mean by marketing in this context.

When you ask people to define the term marketing, you get a lot of different answers. Many of these responses are something like, "marketing is advertising," or "marketing is selling." Neither are correct, though in both cases these definitions cover a piece of what marketing is. But the marketing process is much bigger than either some cool ads or some pushy salespeople!

As a **consumer**—the ultimate user of a good or service—you of course experience aspects of marketing all the time—just as Mia did during her busy day. Indeed, consumers like you (and your humble authors!) are at the center of all marketing activities. By the way, when we refer to consumers, we don't just mean individuals like you or us. Many organizations such as design houses, fabric suppliers and advertising agencies also are consumers and customers as well.

So, what is marketing? The easy answer is that marketing is about satisfying needs and thus creating value. We like to say that the consumer is king (or queen), but it's important not to lose sight of the fact that the seller also has needs—to make a profit, to remain in business, and even to take pride in selling the highest-quality products possible. Here's a more formal (and longer!) definition, according to the American Marketing Association:

> Marketing is the activity, set of institutions, and processes for creating, communicating, delivering, and exchanging offerings that have value for customers, clients, partners, and society at large.[6]

And when we check the British definition, the Chartered Institute of Marketing decrees,

> Marketing is the management process responsible for identifying, anticipating and satisfying customer requirements profitably.[7]

Notice that the AMA definition includes the words "exchanging offerings." That's a crucial part because what we call an "exchange relationship" is key to every marketing act. An **exchange** occurs when a person gives something and gets something else in return. The buyer receives an object, service, or idea that satisfies a need, and the seller receives something they feel is of equivalent value. Thus, today's marketers are likely to focus upon the benefits a customer receives when he or she consumes a product or service, rather than merely keying in on the objective attributes of what people buy. So, while Lululemon might describe one of its garments as a "...limited-edition Nulu™ Fold Crop Tank—featuring unique seam detailing on buttery-soft, nearly weightless Nulu™ fabric,"[8] a loyal customer (who might even describe herself as a "Lulu") buys and wears the product because it helps her to feel comfortable, relaxed, stylish, and even blissful as she moves to her crow pose (Kakasana) during the yoga class she takes in her local Lululemon store.

The Marketing Mix

In order to appeal to the changing needs and wants of consumers, marketers of any product or service need to find the right combination of elements to convince the buyer that they will receive value in exchange for the money or other resources they will pay. In the marketing discipline, these elements are called the **marketing mix**. This label refers to the "Four Ps":[9]

1. **Product:** What is the specific good or service that will convey value?

2. **Price:** What should be the cost of the good or service that customers believe to be a fair amount for the value they receive?

3. **Promotion:** How should we inform the customer of what we are selling, and persuade them that it is something they need or desire?

4. **Place:** Where should the good or service be delivered?

Wants versus Needs

We also said that satisfying needs is core to the marketing concept. The needs we satisfy range from hunger and thirst to love, status, and even spiritual fulfillment.

This begs the question of just what a need is. That issue is especially relevant in fashion marketing, where the plain truth is that many of the products on offer do not necessarily satisfy a need—or at least a basic one. Do you really *need* that ridiculously expensive Christian Dior scarf and handbag?

That's why it's important to distinguish between needs and wants. In the strict sense, a *need* is something we must have to survive such as clean water or adequate shelter. In contrast, a *want* is a specific solution our culture has taught us to satisfy a need. So, marketers often focus on translating a generic need into a specific want that a shopper can satisfy by purchasing their brand rather than a competitor's. For example, two women may both experience a need for positive recognition from their peers. But the one who lives in a rural area in France buys an IKKS bag while the other who lives in Paris craves that pricey Louis Vuitton bag to satisfy the same underlying desire.

As much as some die-hard *fashionistas* may object, a lot of the goods and services within the realm of fashion marketing are not necessities. They are not "must haves," they are "nice to haves," which means that

Woman Wearing a Christian Dior Scarf and Handbag

Image courtesy of Patrick Sawaya Photography

we may choose to devote some of our discretionary income (money we have available after paying for necessities) to acquire them.

Having said that, of course "one man's meat is another man's poison"; each person has their own set of values and priorities. We know of some struggling university students who largely subsist on a diet of cheap ramen noodles, yet they choose to splurge on the occasional Ladurée macaron! As we'll see later, many players in the fashion industry have to stay on top of changing consumer priorities—for example, a lot of fashion customers who went into lockdown during the pandemic began to rethink what they actually needed in order to be happy.

So, how do marketers learn about a brand's target consumers and their deep desires? The direct answer is *data*. Marketers rely on several forms of data collection such as sales tracking, media coverage, focus groups, surveys, along with other viable options, as a way to unlock their consumers' preferences and buying patterns in order to communicate these to their designers and manufacturers. The feedback includes the type and quantity of goods to be produced. We'll go into more depth on how to collect data in Chapter 5.

Is Fashion Marketing Different?

At one level, there's not that much that's different about marketing a can of peas, a dance company, an "in" restaurant, or a designer suit. But the devil is in the details, and many of these distinguish fashion marketing from other kinds of marketing. **Fashion marketing** is the process of designing, producing, communicating, supplying, and exchanging fashion products and services that have value for customers, retailers, partners, and the society at large. The whole process is built around the deep understanding of consumers' needs and desires so that brands can provide its target market with the right and appropriate product and services.

The types of goods and services we deal with in the fashion industry typically are a bit different than many other products. Fashion by definition is dynamic and constantly changing which differentiates it from **FMCG (fast-moving consumer goods)**. Think for example about the kinds of FMCG that marketing giants like Unilever and Procter & Gamble sell. This large category includes products that have extremely high demand, sell very quickly at reasonable and affordable prices, and are largely available to everyone with at least modest economic resources who wants them. Examples include packaged food and beverages, toiletries, beverages, stationery, over-the-counter medicines, cleaning and laundry products, plastic goods, and personal care products.

Consumers use these products on a regular basis, and they tend to shop for them frequently. They're called "fast-moving" because they usually leave a store's shelves very quickly and they must be restocked immediately to avoid a shortage in supply. Some of these products, like meat, dairy products, baked goods and vegetables are highly perishable so they either sell quickly or they have to be discarded. Small price changes, such as a small discount that a store coupon offers, tend to impact sales pretty dramatically, and the demand for these goods may change based upon seasons or holidays.[10]

How do FMCGs differ from most fashion products? One contrast is that FMCG products typically do not undergo major transformations over the years. Think of the Dove Beauty Bar. This bar of soap has been in the market for almost 60 years and is well-known for cleansing the face while restoring the skin with similar lipids that have been lost during the washing process. This simple product is a favorite for many consumers. Sure, it has undergone some minor changes; over the years Dove has launched line extensions such as the "Gentle Exfoliating Beauty Bar" and the "Relaxing Lavender Beauty Bar".[11] But the basic product is largely unchanged.[12]

Now, compare Dove soap to a pair of Balenciaga sneakers. An FMCG product doesn't usually respond to changes in the market every time a company introduces a slight modification. However, when it comes to fashion, the fashion industry is very dynamic and fast-paced. As we like to say, "the only thing in fashion you can count on to stay the same is that nothing stays the same."

Constant change occurs because these products and services are strongly influenced by different seasons, fashion and color trends. Contrary to most fast-moving consumer goods, fashion items include a strong creative and design element. But you might object: "Aren't luxury products resistant to change as well? They are classic styles that seem timeless." A good point! But, even high-end luxury has been impacted by pressure from avid collectors to offer both well-known styles and new variations, including new ready to wear collections each season, to satisfy customers' desires for novelty and stimulation.

Who Sells, and Who Buys?

A blouse, a high heel shoe, a manicure, and a poké bowl all have something in common: In each case, someone has to create the good or service and someone has to buy it. But that's where the similarities end, because there are huge differences in the process that moves the object we purchase from the manufacturer to the consumer. In some cases, the transfer is direct: the manicurist applies the polish to your nails. In others, there may be several intermediaries who transfer the item until it reaches you: those heels may have started with a designer in Italy who ordered leather from Australia, which was shipped to a factory in China to be crafted into a shoe and then delivered to a department store in London.

Channels of Distribution

A **channel of distribution** is the series of firms or individuals that facilitates the movement of a product from the producer to the final customer. This channel at minimum consists of a producer—the individual or firm that manufactures or produces a good or service—and a customer. But most channels involve more players than that; they often include one or more channel intermediaries—firms or individuals, such as wholesalers, agents, brokers, and retailers, who in some way help move the product to the consumer or business user. After all, even that manicurist we referred to earlier has to purchase her beauty supplies from one or more vendors, and they each have to acquire raw materials—nail polish is made from nitrocellulose (cellulose nitrate); a combustible liquid (also used to make dynamite!) that is mixed with tiny cotton fibers and other ingredients, and of course they need the bottles to put the polish in, etc.

Each partner in the channel (hopefully) adds some kind of value—but also *cost* as each one takes some profit as they mark up the price before they transfer the item to the next partner in the chain.

So, for example if you buy a pair of ALDO heels from a factory outlet store at a discount, that's because you cut out some middlemen such as retailers that usually sell them at a higher price. However, this doesn't mean that those middlemen don't also add value! For example, it's likely that the pair of heels you bought are not from the manufacturer's current collection or licensed seller, and they may even be damaged in some way. On the other hand, if you buy a different pair—probably at a higher price—from Hermès or a retailer such as theoutnet.com, you will know that you have the more current version and that you can return them if you discover a flaw. Again, value is in the eye of the beholder so if you don't care about having the latest style, this "value" may not be worth the money to you.

We find many different channels of distribution in the fashion industry, and these evolve all the time as companies jockey to keep up with their customers' shifting demands for lower prices, exclusivity or a more unique range of merchandise. A lot of this change is being driven by several underlying factors, including:

1. An increased focus on sustainability and fashion's impact on the environment.

2. A re-examination of values (especially post-pandemic) that lead some shoppers to reconsider their buying priorities.

3. An acceleration of the movement toward online shopping.

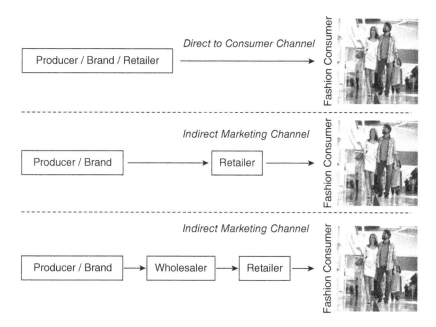

FIGURE 1.1 Fashion distribution channels

Image courtesy of Freepik.com

Fashion companies need to decide about the form of retail store through which they would like to appeal to their target market. Are their shoes going to be available at department stores, where a wide range of merchandise is sold across various sections? Will you be able to find their artisan chocolates at supermarkets where an extensive selection of edible and household goods is available? Can a sunglass shopper find that pair of Féroce shades she's been looking for at a franchise operation like Sunglass Hut? Some fashion brands may also choose to offer their products at discount stores, where their goods are sold at a lower price than the normal retail price, or at an off-price retailer that focuses on offering national brands, designer brands or promotional goods with high quality goods at lower prices. Or they may turn to outlet stores that sell slow moving and out-of-date goods at heavily discounted prices.

You need to keep in mind that we need to make marketing decisions at both the wholesale and retail levels. What differs is that wholesalers sell their products to retailers, which include boutiques, department stores, and online retailers. To do this, they rely upon fashion shows, catalogs, and a sales force to provide the sample products in order to match the products offered by the manufacturer with the needs of the retailer's customers. On the other hand, some brands sell their own products at their own stores; their primary concern is finding a match between their products and end consumers. Both of these levels of channel activity involve promotional efforts such as advertising, public relations, direct marketing, sales promotion and personal selling that help to establish brand recognition and enhance a brand's reputation concerning some characteristics like the quality, price, or trendiness offered.

Elements of the Fashion Marketing Mix

So, back to the famous "Four Ps." Let's take a quick look at how these elements of the marketing mix apply to fashion marketing. As we make our way through the book, we'll do a deeper dive into each of these important components.

Fashion Products

The fashion product is the most important element in the marketing mix. Without a proper product, no price, place or good promotion will be effective. Products—whether they are automobiles, phones, apparel, accessories, shoes, or cosmetics—involve a *lot* more than the physical items. They also include services, events, people, locations, firms, ideas or a combination of these. A **fashion product** consists of quality, design, style, brand name, package, features, values, color, size, material, logos, and trademarks etc.; features that allow the actual product to be marketable. Broad categories of fashion products include the following:

- **Fashion services** includes cosmetic surgery, styling, image consultancy, personal shopping, cosmetic dentists, tanning salons, hair transplants, personal fitness training, clothing repair, hairdressing and make-up salons, and rental shops.

- **Fashion goods** include all types of clothing from basics (e.g., underwear) to more luxury apparel such as suits, skirts, jackets, T-shirts); cars, trendy food, phones and other tech items like sound systems, furniture and home furnishings, and other items that express elements of aesthetics or culture. We can also add shoes, fragrances, accessories (e.g., scarves, hats, belts, bags, sunglasses...), cosmetics, cooking equipment, and watches to the mix. As a reminder: Fashion encompasses much, much more than clothing!

Fashion Prices

Pricing is considered as one of the most challenging areas for fashion firms given the stock-keeping unit complexity of numerous style *variations, and the continuous* development of new collections.

Traditionally, pricing was more related to art than science, as marketers simply set an amount they thought would attract buyers without "giving away the store." More recently, many companies turn to statistical techniques to price seasonal items such as swimwear, or luxury goods such as shoes; these can yield much greater sales and profits.

However, while these more sophisticated techniques have been available for a long time, the reality is that most general fashion firms still rely upon the amount individuals are willing to pay, to competitive benchmarking, and to margin contribution.[13]

Luxury brands take a different approach by adopting a tactic called prestige or **premium pricing**. Contrary to the classic *Law of Supply and Demand* you learned about if you took a course in Economics, for these products we often find that shoppers actually are more willing to buy a product as the prices go up, rather than down!

An effective strategy to price fashion products is one that has to be justified based on the brand name, quality of products, location, competition and many other factors. In fashion, price doesn't constitute the only reference to the amount of cash that should be charged for a given product. Consumers' perceptions of the "value equation" set the ceiling for the product price. As a consumer you will want to know: for the $1000 you pay for a handbag, what kind of benefits and practical utility are you going to receive? Is it the style, prestige, quality, convenience? Again, one person may never consider spending so much on a container for her wallet and other personal items, while another may derive great satisfaction (and maybe even ecstasy!) that to her is well worth the high price.

There are other reasons that pricing fashion products tends to be a real challenge. For one, a price that may work well in one environment may not be competitive in others. That is why retailers need to consider the economic situation in certain markets; for example, if a region of the world is going through a bad economic period, or if the entire world's economy is severely slowed by a pandemic. They may also need to think of price-positioning considerations that could change the price and make it lower or even higher. Notice that Rolex and Chanel keep increasing their prices in order to enhance the value of their items.

Finally, fashion brands introduce products designed in a way to serve different customer needs through different price points ranging from lower prices to more expensive ones. Yes, you can buy something from Louis Vuitton for around $200—if it's a candle you want. At the same time, you can buy the company's Stellar Sneaker Boot for about $1,070 or an LV Escale OnTheGo GM handbag for $2,860 to put the candle into. We'll talk more about pricing in Chapter 10.

Fashion Promotion

The promotion of the fashion product describes the different techniques that the brand will use to effectively connect customers to its products and communicate with its target market. There are different ways to market fashion brands, ranging from more traditional forms to more modern communication tools.

Chanel Fashion Show

Image courtesy of Patrick Sawaya Photography

One of the most traditional tools is advertising, which can take the form of TV, radio, printed messages, and online ads. Public relations are another important promotional tool; it usually occurs in the form of fashion shows that create a lot of buzz, celebrity endorsements, and product placements. Sales promotion is more of an effective promotion technique for mass fashion brands; this approach includes discounts, coupons, displays and demonstrations. Personal selling is a technique luxury fashion brands primarily use; the brand's salesperson directly interacts with the final consumer to finalize a transaction and build long-term customer relationships. Finally, direct and digital marketing (e.g., websites and social media) are the best ways for the fashion or luxury company to directly engage with its target audience and build better relationships with them—especially if its' clientele skews younger. In Chapter 11, we will discuss in detail the different promotion mix strategies that fashion brands use.

Fashion Place

A "place" refers to how and where the fashion product will sell. Fashion brands follow different sales strategies in order to reach consumers. As we've seen, Nike is currently trying to adopt a **direct-to-consumer (DTC) strategy**, while apparel giant Levi Strauss is steadily moving toward selling less of its products in stores and more DTC.[14] Some luxury brands also apply DTC sales channels (exclusive physical store or a commerce-enabled website) in order to maintain a luxury image.

It is important to keep in mind that some luxury brands such as Chanel are still reluctant to sell most of their products online for fear of diluting their elite images. Other fashion brands follow a multichannel approach that allows them to reach a wider audience. This can take different forms: from the brand directly to consumer (online or through physical stores), from the brand to a retailer (e.g., Macy's, Selfridges, Harrods, Nordstrom or **pure play** retailers that only sell online such as ASOS and then to consumer, or from the brand to different levels of wholesalers to retailer and finally to the consumer. We'll flesh out these options in Chapter 10.

We Call it a *Mix* for a Reason

We like to talk about the Four Ps as separate elements, but in reality, they're often related to one another because decisions about one tend to affect decisions about the others. That's why we refer to a strategy that combines elements from each of The Four Ps as a marketing *mix*.

For example, what if Fenty Beauty by Rihanna decides to introduce a more luxurious product that is higher end than the ones it manufactures now? If the company uses more expensive materials to make this item, it has to boost the selling price to cover these higher costs; this also signals to consumers that the cosmetic is more upscale. In addition, Fenty Beauty would have to create advertising and other promotional strategies to convey a top-quality image. Furthermore, the firm must include high-end retailers like Net-a-Porter in its distribution strategy to ensure that shoppers who seek out high-end items will come across the product. Thus, all the pieces in the puzzle we call the 'marketing mix' work together.

Dress as Nonverbal Communication

We express a great deal of information through our appearance, dress, accessories, and actions. We process detailed visual information in a short amount of time—that is, we make first impressions about others and things very quickly.

Dress is one form of nonverbal communication that serves as background for other forms of communication. Some theorists describe dress as a **nondiscursive behavior** (which doesn't relate to a language or discourse), since dress is unchanging for many hours of the day, unlike other dynamically changing behavior.[15]

Sociologists known as **symbolic interactionists** describe appearance as a sign (something that has social meaning).[16] They discuss the concept of a **code** (or rule) that can be manipulated by an individual to produce their own message through apparel or fashion. A **signifier** is a vehicle through which a sign conveys its message. Clothing and elements of appearance become the signifiers (or the channel). Signifiers can gain and lose meaning over time, which is certainly important in the realm of fashion.[17] It is important that marketers understand the meanings that consumers attach to such items. Think of the example of a white dress which is the conventional outfit for a wedding ceremony in Western culture; whereas the same color is linked to death in an Asian culture and is usually used for funerals.

Appearance communication can be quite complex given the many variables involved with all the components of communication: sender, message, channel, and receiver. We normally think of communicating appearance through the visual channel; however, we also use the senses of hearing, touch, and smell (as discussed in Chapter 7). We hear the rustle of taffeta, we touch soft velvet, we smell someone's perfume or cigar.

Figure 1.2 below outlines some of what occurs in the complex process of appearance communication. The sender can manipulate cues or signs (to manage their appearance) to create a certain impression on the receiver. Often people engage in a process of **impression management**, where they consciously manipulate aspects of themselves (such as their wardrobes) in order to influence what others think of them.[18] We get advice from wardrobe experts and others on how to dress or how to make a good impression; that is manipulation of cues. We often know what others are looking for and try to dress to impress or to fit in—whatever our goal might be. We can control the situation with appearance, but some people are more skilled in this area than others.

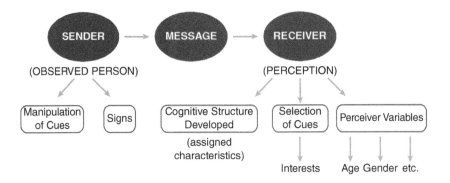

FIGURE 1.2   Appearance communication process

- Sender (Observed Person) may engage in impression management

- Receiver relies on appearance to understand sender; interprets signs

- Receiver develops cognitive structure assigned to person

- Receiver may concentrate on selected cues

- Receiver's unique characteristics influence perception

Fashion versus Luxury

So far, we have talked mostly about fashion. Do you think there is difference between fashion and luxury? Do fashion and luxury overlap?

According to some researchers "Luxury is in fashion."[19] Brands such as Louis Vuitton, Balenciaga, Christian Dior, Burberry are all fashion brands that adopt a **luxury market position**. Their strategies focus on exclusivity, heritage, country-of-origin, timelessness, craftsmanship, prestige etc., to generate the highest brand value and pricing power.[20] These luxury brands help to set fashion trends when they include hot colors and styles in their fashion shows.

The nature of luxury is currently changing as luxury brands are striving to attract younger consumers, particularly those who live in non-Western countries like China. This generation is more interested in innovations in design, and they look for exclusive collections that can express their individuality and values.[21] Many luxury brands today try to adopt or even set fashion trends such as streetwear style by forming limited edition collaborations with streetwear companies. While streetwear was initially a subculture born out of a need for an antidote to fashion trends, its incorporation into mainstream fashion has seen it become a major trend of the past few years. Think of Louis Vuitton and Supreme, Valentino and Birkenstock, Valentino and Moncler, Moschino for H&M. We'll take a closer look at different kinds of fashion brands–including luxury brands–in Chapter 2.

Players in the Fashion Industry

The fashion industry involves a huge number of employees across an extensive range and depth of occupations working together all over the globe to operate effectively. Also, the items are usually designed in one country, produced in a different one, and then distributed in numerous countries around the globe. The fashion industry also builds ties across related industries around the world in order to bring fashion goods to the doorsteps of the final buyer.

It Takes a Village to Sell a Dress

Think for example about all the collaborations that are necessary just to design, produce and sell a simple blouse. Fashion brands cannot operate without photographers, illustrators, models, fashion influencers, artists, marketing logistics specialists, and organizations that source and procure the raw materials they need, and often these different experts are located all around the world. For instance, the Levi's jeans that you see on the shelf were designed in the U.S., produced in Vietnam, and then sold in France, the UK, and many other countries.

Levi's Jeans

Image courtesy of Pixabay

Here are a few examples of industry components that ultimately affect what you buy at Macy's, Harrods, Net-a-porter, ASOS, Tesla or even IKEA:

• Research and Development (R&D):

Fiber research on natural and synthetic fibers; fiber marketing. For example, Evolved by Nature is a company that penetrated the fashion industry in early 2019 when Chanel acquired a marginal stake. By harnessing technology to address fashion's toxic chemical issues, the company has received much praise for its innovative research. It pioneered a high-performance yarn made from regenerated fibers and Activated Silk called CircleMade™.[22]

R&D companies often create new entries such as Banana fiber, one of the world's strongest natural fibers. These forms take a great deal of technology to perfect and much marketing to introduce to fabric companies, designers, and consumers. It takes years to bring a new product to the consumer. Generally, fibers and fabrics companies deal directly with manufacturers. And remember, it's not just about creating apparel: for example, as a step toward becoming more sustainable, the luxury car maker Tesla recently patented a new fabric it calls "fibrous foam architecture." This fabric will provide a new, more comfortable and recyclable material that is soft and durable for Tesla's electric vehicle seats.[23]

• Color and fashion forecasting:

Many brands across different industries work with forecasting houses such as Promostyl and Pantone, trade associations such as Cotton Incorporated that perform extensive research to help predict what consumers will want approximately eighteen to twenty months before they buy a new product. IKEA, for example, integrated "living coral", which was forecast to be the color of the year in 2019 by Pantone, into many of its furniture items like sofas, lamps, scented candles and cushion covers.[24] Zara partnered with Pantone to create a new color palette made of the natural shades that were forecasted to be stylish for the brand's spring 2020 collection, that is all about sustainability and customization.[25]

- Fabric mills, knitting and weaving:

China is currently the largest producer and exporter of textiles in the world. This industry has contributed greatly to the country's economy; textile exports are valued at around $119 billion per year.[26] Other than China, many designers feel they need to go to Europe or Japan for the availability of distinctive, high-quality fabrics in smaller lots. An example is Hosoo; a Kyoto-based textile company that is 327 years old and has supplied huge luxury brands like Chanel, Louis Vuitton and Dior with exceptional fabrics of high quality. Hosoo also supplies for brands that are involved in art and interiors.[27]

Fabric or textile suppliers differ according to whether they sell to a mass-market fashion retailer or a luxury brand. Marks and Spencer, which lies on the mass end of the continuum, is very popular for its lint cotton used for clothing and home accessories. It sources the cotton fibers sustainably from all around the world including India, China, Pakistan, Turkey, Brazil, USA, Africa and Australia. The brand does not own any farms or factories and it sources its raw materials in a global market.[28] Luxury fashion brands, known for their exquisite high-quality materials, mostly source their fabrics from Europe. For example, Hermès owns several tanneries in France and Italy in order to ensure a constant supply of its famous calf leather. Some luxury brands are vertically integrating and choosing to own parts of their production process as they acquire the suppliers of their unique raw materials, while others continue to work closely with small artisan suppliers that they have worked with for generations.[29]

- Converters:

Converters are responsible for finishing the fabric with dyes, prints, and finishes. Examples of converters are Accentex, Blocks Fashion Fabrics and Noveltex, who specialize in various products such as bridal and evening wear fabrics, linen and heat transfer prints and novelty brocades.[30]

China Textiles is a famous fabric wholesaler that has been operating since 1999. The company performs extensive research, designs and sells many types of fabrics and previously established a partnership with two fabric producers in Italy and Spain.[31]

- Designers and manufacturers:

More and more of the garments as well as other products we buy are manufactured in developing countries and imported to other countries. A good example is Apple, which designs its products in California and produces them in China.[32] Nike and Adidas have been producing their sneakers in Vietnam after gradually shifting their production from China. The brands chose to undergo such a change since Southeast Asia is known for being a lower wage region, however, they still rely on China for the production of their clothes because it offers more efficient infrastructure and skilled workers.[33]

- Support services:

  o This includes trade publications such as *Women's Wear Daily*, advertising agencies such as Interpublic Group, Omnicom Group, Publicis Groupe, and Dentsu that work with brands, in addition to retail and economics analysts, trade associations, import specialists, and brokers.[34]

  o Representatives for the manufacturers and designers who sell to retail buyers. Reps show their lines at **Market Weeks** (a specified time for buyers and sellers to get together) at hotels and apparel marts all across the world and at huge trade shows. **Fashion trade shows** are events where fashion designers and brand owners from around the world reveal their new collections and designs to potential clients and retailers.

An example is Première Vision, which takes place for three consecutive days in Paris-Nord Villepinte twice a year. At this event, six major industries that supply materials and services to the fashion industry come together.[35] The UK, popular for its trade shows, hosts Pure London that takes place in London Olympia where emerging designers showcase their collections.

Other important trade shows include MAGIC (for menswear) in Las Vegas, the International Apparel & Textile Fair (Dubai), MICAM Milano and Texworld Paris and USA.[36] Due to the coronavirus pandemic, some of these shows were cancelled in 2020 and were rescheduled for new dates.

At the end of the selling season, reps sometimes have sample sales (at wholesale prices or less) directed at consumers who live in apparel market centers such as New York, Los Angeles, Dallas, Chicago, and Atlanta. There are also several other smaller regional centers.

- Consumer magazines:

These are publications that advertise and editorialize the fashions, for example *Vogue, Elle, Harper's Bazaar* and *GQ*. Some consumer magazines are only digital now, but we still include them in this category.

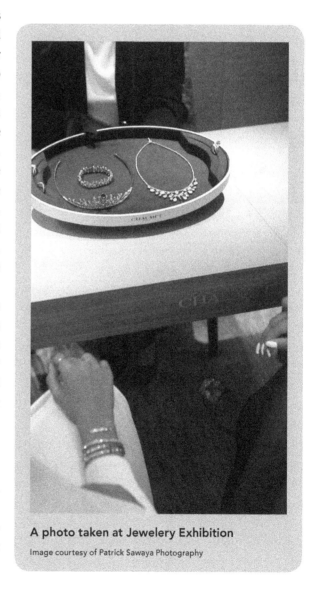

A photo taken at Jewelery Exhibition
Image courtesy of Patrick Sawaya Photography

- Retailers:

Offline and online stores (including but not limited to brand showrooms, department stores and boutiques) of all types that sell the merchandise to the ultimate consumer. According to the National Retail Federation, Inditex; the owner of Zara, scored the highest sales in 2019 with $28.89 billion. This figure puts it ahead of its major competitor Hennes and Mauritz, also known as H&M.[37] However, sales figures have changed after the Covid 19 pandemic. Zara's sales decreased by 24.1% as the company shut down 4,000 stores globally[38] with a permanent move to online for a large percentage of those remaining retailers.

Careers in the Fashion Industry

Although professions such as fashion designer, model, or fashion editor are very common and popular within the industry, they only represent a small part of this ever-changing industry. Due to its continuous evolution, the fashion industry has witnessed a lot of emerging trends and shifting consumer needs and preferences that in turn create new job opportunities in previously unexplored fields.[39] For example, the industry is steadily moving toward a much more pronounced digital presence, so job applicants who have a background in technology are in high demand. Here is an overview of careers that dominate the fashion industry today.

Garment and Textile Technologist

The person taking this job would act as the liaison between fashion brands' design teams and factories where the production takes place. The textile technologist is responsible for making sure that the basics of the product/fabric, like its fit and performance, are well-aligned with the fashion brand's goals and vision, and that the whole manufacturing process runs smoothly. The garment technologist also communicates garment measurements and construction to allow the making of samples and then relays feedback to the factories.

In order to become a clothing or textile technologist, you should consider studying textile engineering or chemistry or undertake an apprenticeship. Gaining some experience in pattern cutting is crucial for a clothing technologist. You may also need to familiarize yourself with the different body types, fabric performances, and construction in addition to basic math.[40]

Fashion Trend Forecaster

The role of trend forecasters has definitely accelerated due to social media. In addition to this, some aspects of this role have also been integrated into other roles within the industry with the growth of digitalization.

Think of this: you are scrolling on your Instagram feed and you spot a famous celebrity wearing a really trendy outfit. Then in less than a month you find a very similar outfit at Zara, Boohoo, FashioNova or NastyGal. This is where the notion of trend forecasting has really shifted in an era of digitalization where the most important weapon to possess is your phone. Today, influencers and celebrities can create trends with just one click of a button, which has made the job of trend forecasters easier and faster.[41] They check out the latest collections of designers and fashion houses and then predict which items will be the trendiest in the upcoming season and would create the biggest influence in the market. Forecasters also analyze the market conditions and consumers' buying behaviors to point their clients in the right direction when they provide them with their **trend reports**. Some fashion brands have their own in-house forecasting team, while others rely on an external party to deliver the insights regularly.[42] For this position, staying on top of the latest fashion trends and getting hands-on-experience, such as through a media or marketing internship, is crucial.[43]

Fashion Designer

The role of a fashion designer is very volatile and complex. Designers may work in different industries such as manufacturing, apparel companies, and design firms. In order for a person to become a successful designer, they must show an appreciation for *fashion* and possess the knowledge to create products that the target audience will love. Designers must involve themselves in research, creative concepts, technical drawings and creating prototypes of garments.

Recently, designers have been expected to know how to use Adobe Photoshop, InDesign, and computer-aided design and other creative software. Some fashion designers also have become the creative directors of their own brand or the fashion brands where they worked.

Surprisingly, not all designers studied fashion design in college. Raf Simmons and Virgil Abloh actually graduated with degrees in interior design and civil engineering and architecture respectively. But one way to increase the odds of success in this highly competitive field is to graduate from a top fashion school in one of the main fashion capitals (e.g., Central Saint Martins, ESMOD International, Institut Français de la Mode, Instituto Marangoni, Parsons School of Design, China Academy of Art) with a degree in fashion design. Internships while pursuing the degree are also highly recommended.[44] In addition to this small set of schools, there are many other attractive possibilities as interest in this field grows.

Jean Paul Gaultier, a Fashion Designer
Image courtesy of Patrick Sawaya Photography

Fashion Buyer

A fashion buyer is typically responsible for all the products sold in fashion stores, so this is a very important job. One of the tasks is to supervise the progress of the apparel aimed toward a specific market and price range. For that, buyers usually work alongside the merchandising team, fashion designers and department managers in order to help decide on the right quantity and prices to sell each item.

Buyers also need to have a forecasting vision when it comes to creating the budget and the profits that the fashion company will make. They also help to monitor which current fashion trends and classic traditional items are selling the most to make sure that these items are always available in stock and avoid shortages. They do this by constantly following up with the suppliers to make sure that they deliver all items in a timely manner. Fashion buyers constantly communicate with internal and external stakeholders to make sure that all processes are running smoothly.

The buying job involves a lot of traveling, visiting production sites and attending fashion shows and showrooms. Having a degree in Fashion Design and Fashion Merchandising is great if you are interested in working as a fashion buyer. Business degrees in Marketing, Public Relations, Promotions and Merchandise Planning are also great for this job. And of course, a little retail experience in a fashion boutique or shop as a salesperson or buyer are a plus.[45]

Fashion Merchandiser

Fashion merchandisers work alongside the buying team and support the analysis process. While fashion buyers are more future-oriented, merchandisers use the past as a tool to identify previous buying patterns and consumer buying behavior. There are also fashion merchandisers who are considered to be more product-oriented. These merchandisers aid the design team in creating and shaping the collections. Their job includes envisioning the collection plan and then building the actual framework from which creativity can grow. As you can tell, the role of a fashion merchandiser is to combine instinct with data to create the perfect collections that consumers would want to buy.[46]

Anna Wintour, editor-in-chief of *American Vogue*

Image courtesy of Myleskalus and Daniel Case via WikiMedia Commons. Shared under the CC BY-SA 4.0 license.

Fashion Writer/Editor

Fashion writers or editors usually work through a publication to cover all the latest stories in the fashion world. They can either specialize in a certain area of fashion or cover all types of stories as they arise. A big part of the job involves arranging interviews with designers, models and celebrities in order to gain valuable insight and translate the information into writing that readers can easily understand. They also cover fashion shows in order to get a sneak peak of the latest trends, help with photoshoots and work closely with some fashion designers. Fashion writers or editors also work with public relations firms so that they can establish good relationships with them that will help their stories get published and earn more coverage.

Some of the tasks that fashion writers perform include working late hours to meet very tight deadlines, editing their work in addition to other writers' articles in certain situations, connecting and networking with prominent figures in the fashion world as a way to build credibility, and learning how to write articles proficiently in a way to convey their ideas properly and clearly. A relevant bachelor's degree in journalism is required for this fast-paced job.[47] Anna Wintour, who is the editor-in-chief of *American Vogue* and the artistic director of Condé Nast, started out at a London shop called Biba, then she completed her training program at Harrods. Her first fashion writer job was a junior fashion editor at *Harper's Bazaar*, and today she is one of the most influential figures in fashion globally.[48] As the industry has developed, this route and the requirements for a career in fashion journalism may have changed.

Fashion Sales Associate

With the rise of the Internet and the Covid-19 virus lockdown, shopping online has never looked more convenient. While bricks-and-mortar shopping remains a beloved pastime for many, some customers today prefer to scroll through retailer websites and apps from the comfort of their own environment. During the Covid lockdowns, this method also allowed people to buy, try and return if needed, as changing rooms were closed for use. This is why the rise in online shopping has definitely brought further challenges to brick and mortar stores, which led many retailers to cut their costs and hire only a few sales associates. For example, in 2019 (pre-pandemic), online apparel sales already accounted for roughly 40% of total U.S. apparel sales.[49] This profession may become obsolete for some retail categories over time, but it remains important in the luxury sector where the human touch will always be required.[50] Fashion sales associates are responsible for selling clothing in stores, greeting customers, offering their help and services, answering any questions or concerns from the customer's end, increasing in-store sales, and at times taking over the cash register and managing financial transactions.

The key to this job is providing excellent customer service, which helps to form tight-knit bonds with the customers and encourages them to return. It is also very important for sales associates to be extremely familiar with the fashion brand's products in order to relay their knowledge to the customer and make their shopping experience worthwhile.

As a fashion sales associate, you can eventually get promoted to a fashion retail manager if you prove yourself and excel in your work within a certain period of time – and you will probably make faster progress if your employer offers a graduate management training program. A fashion retail manager is responsible for running the store and making sure that all goals and rules are being met. One of the main tasks is to maximize profits and ensure that the customer service principles are being fully met by maintaining close contact with the customers and the sales personnel.[51]

Personal Stylist

Online shopping has become much more common these days. About 2.14 billion people worldwide shopped online in 2021.[52] Due to this dramatic shift, there has to be a position that caters to the tech-savvy shopper and provides expert advice mixed with the human touch as a way of preserving the personal experience in shopping.

The perfect solution? Online styling services. These services rely on intelligent algorithms to help offer personal styling sessions to shoppers. The job revolves around a combination of technology with a team of actual stylists. Many fashion retailers have taken up this opportunity and invested in good personal stylists who have a drive for fashion and a passion for truly helping others along with sophisticated artificial intelligence (AI) software to provide personal styling advice to consumers. An example of a fashion brand that uses a personal stylist is Keaton Row; the company creates **look books** of outfit inspirations from several online retailers like ASOS. The brand Everywhere is also known for recommending outfit ideas for customers based on what's already in their closets and then goes on to share the insights with other fashion shops so that they can understand why certain items or trends are successful while others aren't.[52] There is also the traditional stylist who works offline with either regular customers or celebrities. Monica Rose is a very famous personal stylist well-known for her work with big celebrities like Kendall Jenner and Gigi Hadid.[53]

Chapter Summary

Now that you have read the chapter, you should understand the following:

1.   What is fashion marketing?

Fashion is the process of social diffusion by which some group(s) of consumers adopt a new style. Now that we've explained fashion, then what is marketing? Marketing is all about satisfying consumers' needs through exchanging offerings whereby a buyer receives an object, service, or idea that satisfies a need, and the seller receives something he or she feels is of equivalent value. In order to satisfy consumers' needs, marketers usually refer to their marketing mix toolbox, which includes the product itself, the price of the product, the promotional activities (such as advertising) that introduce it to consumers, and the places where it is available. While marketing in general can encompass different product categories such as fast-moving consumer goods (e.g., detergents, food), fashion marketing is more category-specific. It is the process of designing, producing, communicating, supplying, and exchanging fashion products and services that have value for customers, retailers, partners, and society at large. The whole process is built around the deep understanding of consumers' needs and desires so that brands can provide its target market with the right and appropriate product and services.

2.   Who are the players in the fashion industry?

The fashion industry needs a large number of workers who are scattered across an extensive range and depth of occupations working together worldwide in order to function effectively. Products are usually designed in one country, produced in a different one, and then distributed in numerous countries around the globe. The fashion industry also builds ties across related industries around the world in order to bring fashion goods to the doorsteps of the final buyer. For instance, research and development, color and fashion forecasting, converters, manufacturers and designers are all involved in the development of an individual fashion product. In order to launch and to communicate the products, the media is highly needed. Finally, in order to make the products available to consumers, representatives for the manufacturers and designers who sell to retail buyers, online and offline retailers all play an important role.

3. What career opportunities are there in the fashion industry?

Although professions such as fashion designer, model, or fashion editor are very popular within the industry, they only represent a small part of this ever-changing industry. The fashion industry has witnessed a lot of emerging trends and shifting consumer needs and preferences that in turn create new job opportunities in previously unexplored fields. Some of these careers that dominate the fashion industry today are garment and textile technologist, fashion trend forecaster, fashion designer, fashion buyer, fashion merchandiser, fashion writer/editor, fashion sales associate, personal stylist...

DISCUSSION QUESTIONS

1. The chapter discusses a recent trend of luxury brands partnering with other kinds of companies (like streetwear designers) to remain current. What is a luxury partnership you would like to see? Why does it make sense, and how would you start to think about using the marketing mix to help this new entity succeed in the market?

2. List four brands from which you would like to buy. What are the marketing mix elements each of the brands uses in order to make you loyal to them?

3. Select a fast-moving consumer good and a fashion product. What are the important differences between these products?

4. How important are the four elements of the marketing mix for the development of a fashion item?

5. Why do you think that marketing for fashion products is different than marketing for a fast-moving consumer good?

EXERCISES

1. Select a new fashion company that wants to engage in a business to consumer retailing. What are the different channels through which the company can reach its customers? Explain why.

2. Even words come and go in fashion, such as "extra", "snatched," "fire," and "JOMO." JOMO (Joy of Missing Out) is considered as a relative of FOMO (Fear of Missing Out) and is all about living in the present moment and being content with your current position in life. JOMO is a term created to encourage people to control their inner voice or conscience that is constantly telling them that they could have done something differently or better.[54] "Extra" is a slang term that is often used when someone is acting in a dramatic manner while "snatched" is used to describe someone who is very fashionable. "Fire" is similar to "snatched" and is used to refer to something or someone who is very cool and amazing.[55] Indeed, new words (and their definitions) continually enter our language. Identify a term that's currently in fashion and write a brief history about it.

3. Form a small group. For every fashion career, try to find some influential people and interview them via email or LinkedIn. What were their main success factors?

4. Conduct an in-group discussion and ask your colleagues to mention the career that they would like to take in the context of fashion. Ask them why they would choose this career, and what competitive advantage they would have over others.

5. Form a small group and think of a need or want that has not been satisfied by an existing fashion product in the marketplace. Come up with ideas on how you would develop a product to satisfy these needs and wants.

CASE STUDY: PRADA'S PLACES – BRAND IDENTITY AND ARCHITECTURE

Abby Lillethun, Montclair State University

Prada stands apart in the landscape inhabited by luxury fashion brands due to its continuous and high-profile engagements with cultural creation through architectural collaborations for its headquarters, numerous retail stores, and other related activities. Of course, other luxury brands hire architectural firms to design groundbreaking retail buildings and art museums. One notable example is the LVMH group's collaboration with Frank Gehry for the Louis Vuitton Foundation, a contemporary art museum and cultural center described as a "cloud of glass" that opened in Paris in 2014. Another example is Maison Hermès, the "magic lantern" in Tokyo's Ginza district designed by Renzo Piano that opened in 2001. The Prada Group markets its relationships with architecture and architects, by foregrounding them, featuring them prominently in corporate web pages.

Prada, which originated as a family company, reached $3.2 billion in revenue in 2019. In 2011, one-fifth of the shares were listed on the Hong Kong Stock Exchange with the code *1913*. Mario Prada opened Prada in 1913 as a high-quality leather goods store in Milan's elegant, vaulted glass-ceilinged shopping arcade, the Galleria Vittorio Emanuele II. His daughter Luisa took over the business, and in 1979 her daughter Miuccia Prada did the same. She met Patrizio Bertelli, who was also in the leather goods industry. Today, as a married couple, they serve as the co-CEOs and Executive Directors for the Prada Group. Miuccia Prada maintains her role as head designer and creative director. Headquartered in Milan, the company includes Prada, the lead brand, Miu Miu, a brand focused on a youthful customer, Church's, a fine men's shoe brand; and the Car Shoe brand. Leather goods currently comprise 55% of revenue. Footwear is 30%, ready-to-wear is 23%, and licensing of food, fragrance, and eyewear trail at 2%. However, a 2019 agreement with L'Oréal Group for a Prada beauty line promises new markets. The global sales profile by region is Europe at 39%, Asia-Pacific at 32%, the Americas at 14%, and Japan at 12%.[56]

Prada Group defines its brand as "synonymous with innovation, transformation, and independence."[57] Divergent pairings inhabit the brand identity—unexpected and familiar, quirky and classic, contingent and long-lasting, material and intellectual—that emanate from Miuccia Prada's design aesthetic. Its contemporary cutting-edge retail buildings and their interior designs uniquely re-produce the brand identity, in part by providing evocative experiences, both visceral and intellectual, to Prada's customers as they enter a retail location to shop.

Several architects have collaborated with Prada, but Herzog & de Meuron and Office for Metropolitan Architecture (OMA) emerge as primary. Each has engaged with Prada for numerous projects, and both are award-winning firms with undeniably contemporary approaches unrestrained by tradition. Jacques Herzog, a partner at Herzog & de Meuron, designed the glass Prada Epicenter Aoyama, as the store is named, that opened in Tokyo's high-end Aoyama district in 2003. The multi-level building concept combines the façade and the weight-bearing structure into one element instead of two. The exterior of smokey glass diamond shapes that are framed in black steel reflects the city environment in visual undulations resulting from the light on bulging and flat glass diamonds. While the exterior exudes a green-tinged murkiness mixed with reflected light, the creamy-white interior, from carpet to curved stairwells to upholstered seating areas to the molded product zones, soothes the visitor. Consciousness of the building's structure, which is entirely visible and transparent, becomes superseded by the monochromatic interior's luxurious effect, which punctuates the color story of the shoes, bags, and apparel on view. Herzog & de Meuron also designed Prada's New York headquarters that utilize a renovated Manhattan piano factory.

(Continued)

The firm also created a production and shipping facilities in Italy, and it has designed exhibition spaces and a pop-up store for Prada.

Rem Koolhaas founded OMA with partners Elia Zenghelis, Madelon Vriesendorp, and Zoe Zenghelis. OMA designed the Prada Epicenter in New York and the Prada Epicenter Rodeo Drive in Los Angeles. The firm also designed the highly innovative Prada Transformer, a cultural venue in Seoul, Korea, and the Prada Foundation (art museum) campus in Milan. Prada often engages OMA to create fashion show settings and to collaborate on a variety of small projects. In Soho, New York City, the Prada Epicenter, completed in 2001, opens to the street fully across the front span, gently beckoning the consumer-visitor down below street level via a broad stairway. The open entry and interior subvert shopping, temporarily, placing the individual in a finely honed ambiance where inner thoughts and stillness are welcomed, as if in a museum rather than a store. Similar to the experience in the Prada Epicenter Aoyama, the experience in Soho invites the consumer to feel exceptional in having ease and calmness within the bustling city.

Values of exclusivity and uniqueness, which are vital and fundamental to luxury fashion retailing, rely on impressions of luxury retail as an intimate and exclusive experience. However, Prada retail spaces also encourage explicit contemplation of the architecture that one is in, that is to say to experience the space and one's understanding of it somewhat like the experience of visiting a great monument or museum. In this way, the Prada stores invite a state of self-discovery, even if it is one in which the company calculates, through design, to benefit from purchases of its merchandise. Prada banks upon its spatial marketing, its architecture that displays the brand value of innovation, while implying that the brand identity elements of transformation and independence can be, indeed are, present within the consumer of their products.

Miuccia Prada's first big success was a pocone nylon backpack called Vela in 1984. The novel use of this durable, water resistant textile proved prescient and the brand continues to use the tent material to make handbags and backpacks. For the Fall 2018 menswear collection, Prada asked Rem Koolhaas, Herzog & de Meuron, and additional architects to collaborate with them by designing a pocone nylon accessory for the collection. Koolhaas even moved the backpack to a bag the user wears on his or her chest instead. Jacques Herzog designed a printed shirt, invoking the loss of printed texts in contemporary life.[58] This clever marketing move gave Prada menswear, Prada pocone products, and all the involved architects a boost!

DISCUSSION QUESTIONS

1. Collaborations between luxury fashion companies and artists, architects, and celebrities are frequent in the twenty-first-century environment of cross-over linkages that seek to grow exposure across consumer segments. What are potential pitfalls and opportunities in these partnerships, which are in the end, marketing tools?

2. The Prada case study mentions two contemporary art museums created by fashion luxury brands, Louis Vuitton Foundation and Prada Foundation. Investigate current exhibitions at contemporary art museums and develop a plan for a collaborative project between an artist you have learned about and a luxury fashion brand.

3. Examine a luxury fashion brand that needs a fresh approach to its retail space. While being true to the brand identity, propose three ideas for an innovative design change to their present location that will amplify the consumer's internal experience of merely being in the space.

NOTES

1. Jansen, M.A. (2020) 'Fashion and the phantasmagoria of modernity: An introduction to decolonial fashion discourse', *Fashion Theory*, 24 (6): 815–36.
2. Wallendorf, M. (1980) 'The formation of aesthetic criteria through social structures and social institutions', *ACR North American Advances*, 7: 3–6.
3. Amed, I., Balchandani, A., Jensen, J.E., Berg, A., Hedrich, S. and Rölkens, F. (2021) *The State of Fashion 2021: In Search of Promise in Perilous Times. The Business of Fashion*/McKinsey. www.mckinsey.com/industries/retail/our-insights/state-of-fashion (accessed August 2, 2021).
4. Auty, S. and Elliott, R. (1998) 'Fashion involvement, self-monitoring and the meaning of brands', *Journal of Product & Brand Management*, 7 (2): 109–123.
5. Davis, F. (1985) 'Clothing and fashion as communication', in M. Solomon (ed.). *The Psychology of Fashion*, Abingdon: Routledge. pp. 15–27.
   Karunaratne, P. (2017) 'Meanings of fashion: Context dependence', *International Journal of Multidisciplinary Studies*, 3 (2): 35–44.
6. American Marketing Association (2017) *Definitions of Marketing*. www.ama.org/the-definition-of-marketing-what-is-marketing/ (accessed August 2, 2021).
7. The Chartered Institute of Marketing (CIM) (2015) *Marketing and the 7Ps: A Brief Summary of Marketing and How It Works*. Maidenhead: CIM. www.cim.co.uk/media/4772/7ps.pdf (accessed August 2, 2021).
8. Milled (n.d.) Our limited-edition Nulu Fold collection has arrived. https://milled.com/lululemon/our-limited-edition-nulu-fold-collection-has-arrived-TGGSHE3yBbYS_qum (accessed October 12, 2021).
9. Solomon, M.R., Marshall, G. and Stuart, E. (2020) *Marketing: Real People, Real Choices*, 11th ed., Hoboken, NJ: Pearson Education.
10. Hoskins, J. D. and Griffin, A. (2019) 'New product performance advantages for extending large, established fast moving consumer goods (FMCG) brands', *Journal of Product & Brand Management*, 28 (7): 812–29.
11. Dove (2021) 'Beauty bars', www.dove.com/arabia/en/washing-and-bathing/beauty-bar.html (accessed August 2, 2021).
12. Dove (2021) 'Beauty bars', www.dove.com/arabia/en/washing-and-bathing/beauty-bar.html (accessed August 2, 2021).
13. Dwivedi, A., Nayeem, T. and Murshed, F. (2018) 'Brand experience and consumers' willingness-to-pay (WTP) a price premium: Mediating role of brand credibility and perceived uniqueness', *Journal of Retailing and Consumer Services*, 44: 100–7.

14. Nishimura, K. (2020) 'Levi's leaders reveal most effective pandemic pivots', *Sourcing Journal,* November 10. https://sourcingjournal.com/denim/denim-brands/levis-omnichannel-stores-iab-brand-disruption-summit-dtc-harmit-singh-243888/ (accessed August 2, 2021).

15. McCracken, G.D. (1990) *Culture and Consumption: New Approaches to the Symbolic Character of Consumer Goods and Activities* (Vol. 1). Bloomington, IN: Indiana University Press.

16. Guercini, S. (2012) 'Integrating design and fashion marketing', *Journal of Global Fashion Marketing*, 3 (1): 1–4.

    Khare, A., Mishra, A. and Parveen, C. (2012) 'Influence of collective self esteem on fashion clothing involvement among Indian women', *Journal of Fashion Marketing and Management: An International Journal*, 16 (1): 42–63.

17. Kaiser, S. B. (1996) *The Social Psychology of Clothing: Symbolic Appearances in Context.* New York, NY: Fairchild Books.

18. Loureiro, S.M.C., Jiménez-Barreto, J. and Romero, J. (2020) 'Enhancing brand coolness through perceived luxury values: Insight from luxury fashion brands', *Journal of Retailing and Consumer Services*, 57: article #102211.

    Richey, M., Ravishankar, M.N. and Coupland, C. (2016) 'Exploring situationally inappropriate social media posts: An impression management perspective', *Information Technology & People*, 29 (3): 597–617.

    Shukla, P., Singh, J. and Banerjee, M. (2015) 'They are not all same: Variations in Asian consumers' value perceptions of luxury brands', *Marketing Letters,* 26 (3): 265–78.

19. Kapferer, J.N. and Bastien, V. (2012) *The Luxury Strategy: Break the Rules of Marketing to Build Luxury Brands.* London: Kogan Page.

20. Cristini, H., Kauppinen-Räisänen, H., Barthod-Prothade, M. and Woodside, A. (2017) 'Toward a general theory of luxury: Advancing from workbench definitions and theoretical transformations', *Journal of Business Research*, 70: 101–7.

    Fionda, A.M. and Moore, C.M. (2009) 'The anatomy of the luxury fashion brand', *Journal of Brand Management*, 16 (5): 347–63.

    Ko, E., Costello, J.P. and Taylor, C.R. (2019) 'What is a luxury brand? A new definition and review of the literature', *Journal of Business Research*, 99: 405–13.

21. Danziger, N.P. (2019) 'Three ways millennials and Gen-Z consumers are radically transforming the luxury market', *Forbes,* May 29. www.forbes.com/sites/pamdanziger/2019/05/29/3-ways-millennials-and-gen-z-consumers-are-radically-transforming-the-luxury-market/?sh=2bc455b2479f (accessed August 2, 2021).

22. Evolved by Nature (n.d.) 'All the ingredients of an evolution: From all-natural silk protein', www.evolvedbynature.com. www.evolvedbynature.com/applications (accessed August 2, 2021).

23. Klender, J. (2019) 'Tesla patents "fibrous foam architecture", hinting at new seating material and interior trim to come', Teslarati, November 15. www.teslarati.com/tesla-patent-fibrous-foam-architecture-interior-seats-dashboard/ (accessed August 2, 2021).

24. Garneau, A. (2018) '13 ways IKEA is "already" rocking the Pantone 2019 color living coral', *Brit+Co,* December 10. www.brit.co/ikea-home-decor-pantone-living-coral/ (accessed August 2, 2021).

25. Pantone (2020) 'Pantone x Zara: The custom color collection by Zara', *Pantone.* www.pantone.com/articles/color-palettes/pantone-x-zara (accessed August 2, 2021).

26. Sabanoglu, T. (2020). 'Value of the leading global textile exporters in 2019, by country', *Statista,* November 30. www.statista.com/statistics/236397/value-of-the-leading-global-textile-exporters-by-country/ (accessed August 2, 2021).

27. Macalister-Smith, T. (2015) 'Inside Hosoo, the 327-year-old textiles mill supplying Chanel and Dior', *Business of Fashion,* July 2. www.businessoffashion.com/community/voices/discussions/how-can-traditional-craftsmanship-survive-in-the-modern-world/inside-hosoo-the-327-year-old-textiles-mill-that-supplies-chanel-and-dior (accessed August 2, 2021).

28. Marks and Spencer (2021) 'Cotton', *Marks and Spencer.* https://corporate.marksandspencer.com/sustainability/clothing-and-home/product-standards/raw-materials-commodities/cotton#51234fabb33d4fd1988af9d4d0ffe011 (accessed August 2, 2021).

29. Reuters Staff (2013) 'Hermes buys d'Annonay tannery to secure supplies', Reuters, January 10. www.reuters.com/article/hermes-tannery-idUSL5E9CA7TG20130110 (accessed August 2, 2021).

30. Fashiondex (2020) 'Converters', *Fashiondex.* https://fashiondex.com/aisb/converters/ (accessed August 2, 2021).

31. Marsia, A. (2018) '15 best wholesale fabric suppliers in UK/China/USA/India [pro tips]', *China Brands,* November 7. www.chinabrands.com/dropshipping/article-best-wholesale-fabric-suppliers-14908.html (accessed August 2, 2021).

32. Jourdan, A. (2018) 'Designed in California, made in China: how the iPhone skews U.S. trade deficit', *Reuters,* March 21. www.reuters.com/article/us-usa-trade-china-apple/designed-in-california-made-in-china-how-the-iphone-skews-u-s-trade-deficit-idUSKBN1GX1GZ (accessed August 2, 2021).

33. Bain, M. (2018) 'To see how Asia's manufacturing map is being redrawn, look at Nike and Adidas', *Quartz,* May 10. https://qz.com/1274044/nike-and-adidas-are-steadily-ditching-china-for-vietnam-to-make-their-sneakers/ (accessed August 2, 2021).

34. Graham, M., and Pasquarelli, A. (2018) 'LVMH chooses dentsu AEGIS network for its North American media business', *AdAge,* August 16. https://adage.com/article/agency-news/lvmh-taps-dentsu-aegis-network-n-america-media-biz/314638 (accessed August 2, 2021).

35. Première Vision Paris (2021) 'The Concept', *Première Vision Paris.* https://paris.premierevision.com/en/the-show/the-concept (accessed August 2, 2021).

36. Sewport Support Team (2021) 'Top fashion trade shows to attend & how to prepare for an exhibit', *Sewport,* August 4. https://sewport.com/fashion-trade-shows (accessed August 2, 2021).

37. Sabanoglu, T. (2021) 'Sales of selected fashion manufacturers/retailers worldwide in 2020', *Statista,* May 17. www.statista.com/statistics/242114/sales-of-the-leading-10-apparel-retailers-worldwide/ (accessed August 2, 2021).

38. Business Today (2020) 'Coronavirus impact: Zara owners shut down 4,000 stores worldwide', *Business Today,* June 10 www.businesstoday.in/current/world/coronavirus-impact-zara-owners-shut-down-4000-stores-worldwide/story/398717.html (accessed August 2, 2021).

39. Chitrakorn, K. (2016) 'Six fashion careers of the future', *Business of Fashion,* November 14. www.businessoffashion.com/articles/workplace-talent/six-fashion-careers-of-the-future (accessed August 2, 2021).

40. Yu, A. (2019) 'Fashion careers: What exactly does a garment technologist do?', *Fashion United,* March 29. https://fashionunited.uk/news/fashion/fashion-careers-what-exactly-does-a-garment-technologist-do/2019032942447 (accessed August 2, 2021).

41. Soar, S. (2018) 'How I became… a trend forecasting director at WGSN', *Business of Fashion,* September 24. www.businessoffashion.com/articles/careers/how-i-became-a-trend-forecasting-director-at-wgsn (accessed August 2, 2021).

42. Seto, F. (n.d) 'How does trend forecasting really work?', *Highsnobiety.* www.highsnobiety.com/p/trend-forecasting-how-to/ (accessed August 2, 2021).

43. Soar, S. (2018) 'How I became… a trend forecasting director at WGSN', *Business of Fashion,* September 24. www.businessoffashion.com/articles/careers/how-i-became-a-trend-forecasting-director-at-wgsn (accessed August 2, 2021).

44. Business of Fashion (n.d.) 'Working as a fashion designer', *Business of Fashion.* www.businessoffashion.com/education/collection/working-as-a-fashion-designer (accessed August 2, 2021).

45. FS Staff (2011) 'Fashion buyers – fashion career profile', *Fashion Schools,* July 6. www.fashion-schools.org/fashion-buyer.htm (accessed August 2, 2021).

46. BOF Team (2018) 'How to become a successful buyer or merchandiser', *Business of Fashion,* April 16. www.businessoffashion.com/articles/education/how-to-become-a-buyer-or-merchandiser (accessed August 2, 2021).

47. Careers (2021) 'Fashion writer/fashion editor job description, career as a fashion writer/fashion editor, salary, employment', *stateuniversity.com.* https://careers.stateuniversity.com/pages/7796/Fashion-Writer-Fashion-Editor.html (accessed August 2, 2021).

48. Business of Fashion (2021) 'Anna Wintour Biography', *Business of Fashion.* www.businessoffashion.com/community/people/anna-wintour (accessed August 2, 2021).

49. Berthene, A. (2020) 'E-commerce is 46% of all apparel sales', *Digital Commerce 360,* August 4. www.digitalcommerce360.com/article/online-apparel-sales-us/ (accessed August 2, 2021).

50. Chen, C. (2020) 'How to build the retail customer service dream team', *Business of Fashion,* January 8. www.businessoffashion.com/articles/professional/retail-customer-service-sales-associates (accessed August 2, 2021).

51. Fashion and Retail Personnel staff (2021) 'Store manager', Fashion and Retail Personnel. https://www.fashionpersonnel.co.uk/jobseekers/retail-job-sectors/store-manager (accessed August 2, 2021).

52. Coppola, D. (2020) 'Number of digital buyers worldwide from 2014 to 2021', *Statista,* November 27. www.statista.com/statistics/251666/number-of-digital-buyers-worldwide (accessed August 2, 2021).

53. Chitrakorn, K. (2016) 'Six fashion careers of the future', *Business Of Fashion,* November 14. www.businessoffashion.com/articles/workplace-talent/six-fashion-careers-of-the-future (accessed August 2, 2021).

54. Monica Rose Team (2021) 'Monica Rose'. www.monicarose.com/ (accessed August 2, 2021).

55. Cording, J. (2018) 'Is the joy of missing out the new self-care', Forbes, July 21. www.forbes.com/sites/jesscording/2018/07/21/jomo-self-care/?sh=3aafcc27be7a (accessed August 2, 2021).

56. Davis, D.-M. (2020) '24 slang words teens and Gen Zers are using in 2020, and what they really mean', *Insider*, December 24. www.insider.com/24-slang-words-teens-are-using-2020-what-they-mean-2020-12 (accessed August 2, 2021).

57. Prada Group (2021) 'Prada and L'Oréal: long-term license agreement'. www.pradagroup.com/en/news-media/news-section/prada-and-loreal.html#:~:text=Prada%20S.p.A.%20signed%20with%20L,each%20of%20their%20own%20sectors (accessed December 1, 2021).

58. Prada (2019) *Prada Annual Report 2019*. www.pradagroup.com/content/dam/pradagroup/documents/Shareholderinformation/2020/inglese/april/e-prada%202019AR.pdf (accessed August 2, 2021).

59. Rysman, L. (2018) 'Architects and designers reinterpret a prada classic: Nylon', *New York Times*, January 18. www.nytimes.com/2018/01/18/t-magazine/fashion/prada-rem-koolhaas-herzog-and-de-meuron.html (accessed August 2, 2021).

CHAPTER 2

The BIG Picture of the Fashion Industry

LEARNING OBJECTIVES

After you read this chapter, you will understand the answers to the following:

1. How has fashion evolved over the years?

2. What are the different domains of fashion?

3. Are fashion products only related to apparel?

Peter is a normal enough guy when he's hanging out with his friends, but he has a rather unusual hobby. Peter delights in carefully posing food items and taking pictures that he can post and share with his fellow *aficionados*. He's closing in on one of his fantasies: the perfectly cooked and displayed cheeseburger, lounging on a colorful Michael Aram designer plate and surrounded by glistening French fries. Peter meticulously lays out the meat patty and adorns it with dabs of ketchup, then he adds a layer of tomato so that only parts of the burger peek out to tempt the viewer. Once he's got just the look he was going for, he grabs his iPhone, snaps the pic, and posts it for his fellow enthusiasts to share. Then, back to reality as he rejoins his mates to watch a football game.

Peter is hardly alone in his pursuit of the ultimate food photo. Due to the influx of celebrity chefs, cooking shows, Instagram pages that extol the virtues of veganism and sustainability, designer restaurants, and even the boredom of pandemic lockdown, many consumers have become transfixed in the hunt for the perfect food photo.[1] Legions of voracious fans are devoted to finding the next poké bowl, avocado toast or other food sensation that will rock

(Continued)

the culinary world. A comment by one enthusiast to an interviewer in a recent study is typical of this passion: "Later, another guest pulled out her phone to show me photos of every meal she had eaten in the last few years. 'I don't know why I do this,' she confessed, but there was evident joy and satisfaction on her face as she scrolled through the many moments of gustatory bliss."[2]

Food products, whether mundane or exotic, seem poised to become the newest fashion.

The Evolution of Fashion: A Brief History

Archaeologists have unearthed beads, pendants, and other ornaments that people more than 40,000 years ago may have used as a form of communication. They suggest that our ancestors could have used them to let strangers know about their gender, age, marital status, and the tribes they belonged to.[3] Fashion has been a part of our lives for a really long time.

People create fashion products to help them to communicate political, economic, and social dimensions of their lives. The apparel and jewelry that individuals wear and the type of furniture they buy reflects their social status, occupation, and even political points of view. In order to identify fashion in its current state and predict the prevailing fashions of the future, you need to understand how each adopted fashion trend reflects the state of the time. Let's dive together into the history of fashion and briefly learn how fashion has changed in recent years (no, not 40,000 years ago!) due to different circumstances.

Louis XIV of France

Image courtesy of wartburg.edu via Wikimedia Commons. Shared under the public domain.

Fashion and Luxury in the 18th Century: The Birth of *Couture*

Fine clothing has always been an indicator of wealth. During the reign of Louis XIV, French aristocrats looked up to members of royal court as a reference of taste and fashion.

Louis XIV fancied himself as the referee of fashion and he also represented the Palace of Versailles, where he was based, as a center of power, luxury, fashion and lifestyle for Europe and beyond. The Versailles courts were famous for their magnificence, wealth, and luxury tastes as the elite reveled in apparel made from lavish materials.[4]

Louis XIV established a luxury industry comprising furniture, apparel, jewelry and fabric that accounted for one third of the employment in Paris. The French court set firm rules that determined the suitable kind of dresses, fabrics, and accessories to be adopted for a given season and occasion. It also encouraged the regeneration of fashion two times a year, which set the stage for today's fashion shows. Paris became the home of fashion in the world, and people around the world tried to copy the French style in costume, language and cuisine.[5]

The modern fashion industry was born during the 19th century. Charles Frederick Worth, known as the father of **haute couture** (a term that refers to very high-quality, custom-made, or made-to-measure clothing), was the first English designer to set up his own fashion house in 1858 in France. He converted a rather decentralized industry made up of many individual designers working in small shops into an industry employing a massive number of people. He helped to establish the *Chambre Syndicale de la Haute Couture*, the regulating commission, which decides the designer houses that are entitled to be real haute couture houses.

Worth established the tradition of the fashion house, and he decreed new styles and silhouettes to suit his wealthy clientele. He fused fabric procurement with manufacturing, which changed clients' habits of bringing their own fabrics to designers. He was also the first to employ live models to showcase and market his designs to clients so they could see what they would look like after they bought them. His fashion house became a society meeting point, where customers were able to socialize while they tried on lavish ball dresses in lighting conditions that were similar to what they would encounter during the events.

Worth also had several important contemporaries in Paris. These designers included Jeanne Paquin, Louise Chéruit, Jacques Doucet, John Redfern, the Callot sisters and Jeanne Lanvin. These **couturiers** were the key power in fashion design for more than 100 years.

PRESENT DAY. *1894*

Charles Frederick Worth, the Father of *Haute Couture*

Illustration to "Paris Dressmakers" by M. Griffith, published in *The Strand Magazine* no. 48, Vol. VIII, July to December 1894. Text and images reproduced at http://www.avictorian.com/fashion_paris_dressmakers. html. Shared under the Public Domain.

The Industrial Revolution: The Development of the Modern Fashion Industry

One of the major developments during the 18th century took place with the Industrial Revolution in Britain, which quickly spread throughout the rest of Europe and North America. This movement involved numerous changes in technology that impacted the fashion industry. Garments, food products and other items that had to be made by hand could now be made rapidly and more economically by machines.

The creation of the *flying shuttle* in England is considered one of the major developments during that period. The invention of this machine reflected a main move towards automatic weaving devices. Patented in 1733 by John Kay, this shuttle helped produce more textile in less time, doubling the quantity a weaver could make. Later, in 1769, Richard Arkwright patented the *water frame*, a machine that allows 96 strands of yarn to spin at the same time.

England set very strict laws to prevent other countries from acquiring advanced technology. But Samuel Slater, a British-American, was able to memorize the designs of these machines and he secretly escaped with them to America in 1789. Known as the "Father of the American Industrial Revolution," Slater's pirated designs allowed the USA to supplant England as the world's foremost textile center.

The Emergence of the Middle Class: A Growing Demand for Luxury

The introduction of modern manufacturing technologies created a new middle class. This allowed many people to become successful merchants who thrived as they churned out mass-produced items for a growing market. As a result, more people had more leisure time, as well as more money to spend on luxurious items including apparel, and new styles become a visible status symbol of wealth.

The Development of the Modern Apparel Industry

The Industrial Revolution transformed the way goods are made and gave birth to mass production. This change started with the invention of the sewing machine in the USA by Elias Howe in 1846. Run by hand, this new machine made apparel manufacturing much easier and faster, so that companies could start to produce ready-made clothing for the masses. While Elias Howe retained his sewing machine patent, in the early 1850s, Isaac Singer designed a more practical sewing machine. This ingenious innovation that added more power and speed to the device made Singer a household name as he sold millions of machines around the world.

Ironically, it took the American Civil War in the 1860s to really kick-start this business. The war created a huge need for military uniforms, which led to the sale of 20,000 machines a year. The development of standardized uniform sizes stimulated the mass manufacturing of menswear after the war. However, the complexity in women's sizes and fittings made it less feasible to mass produce womenswear until the end of the 19th century.[6]

Fashion and Luxury During the 19th Century

Changes in fashion trends became much faster during the 19th century, especially with the emergence of the specific press, the Industrial Revolution, and the foundation of *Haute Couture*.[7] As Western societies moved in a more democratic direction following the American and French Revolutions, luxury became accessible to a larger number of people. At this time, we also saw the beginnings of the movement toward women's liberation, although significant changes in cultural expectations regarding the role of women didn't occur until the middle of the 20th century.

The Emergence of Fashion Retailing

- In the mid-19th century, industrialization allowed companies to offer wider assortments of consumer goods, such as jewelry, furniture, and mass-produced apparel, in stores. Retailers emerged to cater to the needs of well-off women (not just members of the aristocracy). For the most part until that time, women didn't venture into commercial establishments. They needed a different type of venue where it was socially acceptable for them to congregate outside the home, so new department stores rose up to fill this vacuum. Unlike many other stores that were dirty, unattractive and populated only by men, these environments were clean, spacious and aesthetically pleasing.[8] In the 19th century, department stores emerged as symbols of contemporary living and upward mobility.

Harrods Department Store

Image courtesy of Diliff via WikiMedia Commons. Shared under the CC BY-SA 3.0 license.

Here are four of the most famous retail emporia from this era:

- Lord & Taylor was one of the world's oldest department stores that was established in New York in 1826 by two English immigrants, George Washington Taylor and Samuel Lord.[9] The stores used to sell hosiery, misses' wear, and cashmere shawls. During the American Civil War in the 1860s, this department store launched a division to sell mourning clothing for widows.

- Harrods department store was founded in 1849 by Charles Henry Harrod in London. The store only used to have one room that offered tea and groceries. As the business grew, by 1880 Harrods had become a prosperous department store that sold a wide range of items such as medicine, fragrances, apparel and food to affluent shoppers.[10]

- In Paris, Le Bon Marché was the first department store. It was established in 1852 by Aristide Boucicaut, a fabric merchant, who noticed the new emerging trend of offering shoppers wider assortments of merchandise. He and his wife expanded it into an exceptional Parisian department store, with an extensive variety of items. In 1984, The LVMH Group acquired Le Bon Marché and turned it into the most exclusive department store in Paris.[11]

- Founded in 1909, Selfridges in London provided its customers with a number of departments in addition to restaurants, a roof garden, reading rooms, reception spaces for international visitors and a number of well-informed floor-walking assistants to assist shoppers.[12]

The Effects of World War I on Fashion

One of the major changes that took place during the First World War in Britain was that women started to work at traditionally male jobs because the men had to join the military. Before this time, women had few and hard-won rights. The disruptions in society began to change that, and women played greater roles in the workplace, in the arts and in society overall (including improving the right to vote).

As they moved into factory jobs, women now had to shed their jewelry and put on uniforms. This change prompted the movement away from the extravagant (and often uncomfortable) styles of the Edwardian period. It was pretty difficult to wear a restraining corset when you are on the assembly line! Dresses became more minimalistic, and skirts were shortened, making them more suitable to physical labor. Transportation had also a key impact in shifting fashion at the start of the 20th century. With the introduction in 1913 of the world's first moving assembly line for automobiles by Ford, the fashion industry had to also adapt to this trend by manufacturing apparel that was convenient for women who would use this new mode of transportation—not to mention bicycles that were growing in popularity.

The practical working apparel worn by women had a pronounced influence on the fashion industry. "Now that women work," *Vogue* reported in 1918, "working clothes have acquired a new social status and a new chic."[13] Consequently, the market for ready-to-wear apparel increased, making this industry become more and more acceptable.

Gabrielle Chanel

Image courtesy of Ctruongngoc via WikiMedia Commons. Shared under the public domain.

Some fashion designers were influenced by this trend to simplify styles. Gabrielle Chanel popularized the idea of trousers for women. She made this boyish style even more popular and introduced revolutionary pieces that combine comfort and elegance; a symbol of modern women who are active, glamorous and liberated. Due to the war, lavish fabrics were unavailable, so Chanel was the first brand to introduce jersey to its collection, a material that had been used primarily to make men's underwear. While this fabric was considered as cheap by the elite, it became very popular as it allowed women to move easily. The result was that apparel producers took notice of Chanel's fashion trends and the jersey style started to be adopted by the general public.

The Effects of World War II on Fashion

During World War II, many people existed under destitute conditions, with very limited access to fabrics, accessories, heat and even food. Like the after-effects of the pandemic in modern times, most fashion designers were hardly able to sustain their businesses. A lot of fashion companies had to shut down at that time or had their production moved to the war effort. These restrictions further accelerated the trend toward classic, simple styles and away from the elaborate gowns of earlier times. Nylon and wool were reserved for the military, so rayon became the new man-made material that factories used to make women's apparel during the war. Trousers became an essential for women employed in factories and rapidly obtained extensive acceptance as a casual wear item. As a great example of how styles in one sphere of culture affect others, the glamorous actress Katherine Hepburn played a major role in legitimizing the idea of trousers for women when she wore them in her movies.

Fashion and Luxury During the 20th Century

After the end of the Second World War, women were happy to welcome their husbands and sons back home, and by and large they reverted to their traditional feminine roles as men resumed work in the jobs they had left. At that time, Paris regained fashion dominance. Christian Dior was the designer who reenergized and revolutionized the fashion industry, creating a new look with a dominant feminine silhouette that merged the traditional models that were adopted before World War I and took a war-torn world into an era of extravagance and luxury.

Along the commercial boom that took place in the U.S. after the war, fashion consumption in the U.S. increased. Fashion designers responded to market demands. They began to create a unique American style such as Ivy League suits for men by Brooks Brothers, modest feminine appearances by Claire McCardell, and chic dresses by Charles James and Gilbert Adrian.[14]

The 1960s was a time for change in the U.S. with the profusion of children born after World War II, the Baby Boomers. This generation had a huge impact on popular culture. Firm rules that governed appearance started to disappear as "do your own thing" became the battle cry. By the end of the 1970s, the culture began to emphasize the importance of exercise and an active lifestyle for women. This created a new category of sportswear.[15]

Also, this period marked the attempt of women to achieve an equal position with men in the workplace. The concept of "dress for success" became very common, where women tried to copy traditional men's business attire as a path to gain more credibility in offices.[16] Giorgio Armani pioneered the power suit of the 1980s. He launched drape cuts jackets that were mainly inspired from menswear collections; they were meant to be worn as a badge of success.[17] During this period, status dressing became vital. Labels of fashion goods became more important than their aesthetics.

Ralph Lauren was the leader in the phenomenon of "status dressing" produced for the masses, and he was joined by other prominent designers such as Donna Karan and Calvin Klein.[18] Rolex watches, Gucci shoes, and Louis Vuitton handbags became status accessories as people wanted to let others know that they had achieved success (even if they hadn't!).[19]

However, in the 1990s, individuals were no longer interested in designer names as much to express their individuality. They began to look for items that were affordable and convenient. This is when the concept of "Casual Friday" (largely boosted by Levi Strauss in order to encourage people to buy more of its Dockers line) was introduced to the workplace in America and England.[20] By the end of the 20th century, maximalism directed the fashion cycle, according to Bain's data, which monitored the adoption of different styles at different periods of the luxury industry evolution. This stage was named "sortie du temple," a time when luxury brands started to launch lower-priced collections and appealing to a mass market whereby logo goods became very common.[21] This was at a time when a number of diffusion brands were introduced to the market like Versus by Versace, D&G by Dolce & Gabbana, and Cheap & Chic by Moschino, of which some have been either been discontinued today or renamed differently.

Fashion and Luxury in the 21st Century

As we have seen in the previous sections, the fashion and luxury industry has always been affected by political, social or even economical changes. The museum at New York's Fashion Institute of Technology notes that "…every fashion movement is a response to what came before it, perpetuating a design cycle that alternates between exuberant and restrained."[22]

At the beginning of the 21st century, up until 2007, an era of "democratization," took place, whereby luxury brands expanded around the world, prevailing icons and logos in a maximalist form.[23] Then in 2008 the Global Recession rocked the whole luxury and fashion industry as millions of employees lost their jobs. A large number of consumers started to spend less, and sales of fashion items plummeted. Retailers such as Saks Fifth Avenue, Barneys, and Neiman Marcus all reduced their prices by 70% in an attempt to clear out their excessive stock.

During this crisis, brands adopted a minimalistic approach. For example, Bottega Veneta offered a "stealth wealth" logo-free Intrecciato handbag for brand fans who didn't want to advertise their ability to afford such an item while others were suffering financial hardship.[24] Some consumers reconsidered the purchases of some luxury brands (for example, Chanel, Hermès, Rolex) as investments as they avoided goods that might lose their value with every change in the winds of style.

But then in 2015, the maximalist style prevailed when the luxury brand Gucci launched its collection with the new creative director Alessandro Michele. The collection focused on excessive looks filled with prints, ruffles, colors, and logos.[25] Following the revival of '90s logo trends, luxury brands such as Prada, Balenciaga, Burberry, Valentino and Chanel have jumped into this trend, by having their monograms engraved on all their offerings, which range from hats, apparel, handbags and shoes.[26]

In the music world, hip hop became the dominant force, and this helped to propel the **streetwear** concept. This trend boosted the brands of emerging brands such as Off-White, Supreme and Vetements and in turn created more demand for luxury products that sported bold and huge logos. Another reason that helps to explain the resurgence of prominent logos is the explosion of social media. During a period where a well taken photo is considered more valuable than verbal messages, logos are an outstanding way to make an item more recognizable. Also, big logos are a guarantee that selfies can serve as an effective marketing vehicle as people post millions of pictures of themselves standing in front of huge billboards in Times Square and elsewhere.[27]

According to Bain's 2017 study, starting 2018 the world has moved into a new era,

Valentino Shirt with Brand Logo
From Poise Design

a period termed as a "post-aspirational" era, the era of self-expression.[28] This shift is related to the retailers getting more insights about what their target market is looking for via large scale data gathering. They had accustomed their communication by focusing less on craftsmanship and heritage and more on the values they provide.[29] In 2020, with the coronavirus pandemic and the lockdown hitting the world, it left millions of people unemployed, and an expanding recession has obliged shoppers to rethink their consumption priorities.

The most likely shift is going to be oriented toward value. Consumers are expected to move to casual wear and to return to core basics instead of seasonal items.[30] While people are predicting that the coronavirus will force shoppers to reassess their values and alter their consumption away from fast-fashion and luxury brands, and become more focused on quality and sustainability, a recent report by *Business of Fashion* indicated that this is not true. By going back to historical events that took place earlier such as the economic crisis of 2008, after few years of refraining from shopping people went back to their normal consumption patterns. Also, another reason why the report claims that individuals are not expected to continue to focus on sustainability is based on

Off-White Streetwear

andersphoto / Shutterstock.com

research that reveals that although Millennials show high concern for this value, many of them do not purchase sustainable items since they are more expensive than fast-fashion brands and less fashionable and trendy.[31]

Traditional Fashion Categories

Many people use the terms fashion and style interchangeably, but they mean quite different things. Each of us has our own personality and our own "style" in our manner of living, speaking, and dressing. Certain celebrities who have distinctive styles also come to mind: Katy Perry, Rita Ora, Lady Gaga, Justin Bieber, Cara Delevingne, Miley Cyrus, Rihanna, and Emma Watson, Yang Mi, Beyoncé, or Victoria Beckham. We also think about hairstyles and furniture styles. There certainly are styles also in apparel, art, music, and politics.

In the domain of apparel, a style is a particular combination of attributes that distinguishes it from others in its category. For example, there are many styles of skirts: mini, midi, long, dirndl or gathered, pleated, A-line, circle, bell, and so on. Think about a style as having a characteristic that does not change; however, designers create new styles, and they can adapt old styles. From time to time, a style can become a fashion if enough consumers adopt it. For example, tailored jackets became fashionable (that is, accepted by many) in the 1970s as more women entered professional careers. In 2018, the power suit was on trend again to accentuate women's empowerment.[32] Today, we're less likely to spot this style, and more likely to see a more casual approach to officewear as many people got used to wearing athleisure during the lockdown.[33]

The fashion industry divides itself into different levels based upon the price points and uses of the garments. Let's review the most important ones:

High Fashion or *Haute Couture*

As we saw earlier in the chapter, *Haute Couture* originated in France during the 19th century, when designers made custom-made clothing for their private clients. This term translates as 'fine sewing'; it refers to very high-quality, custom-made, or made-to-measure clothing. Today it generally describes new styles that are very expensive and often exaggerated or extreme in style from designers or design houses such as Yves Saint Laurent, Valentino, Chanel, Dior, Maison Margiela, Armani, Versace, Gucci, Dolce & Gabbana, Prada, Alexander McQueen, Vivienne Westwood, Zuhair Murad, Sabyasachi, and so on.

Haute Couture involves the creation of **bespoke clothes** (apparel completely manufactured from scratch based on a consumer's preferences) that are hand-sewn with extreme attention to detail and finishing. But the label goes farther than that: for to be officially considered as *Haute Couture*, it must meet the specifications of the French Ministry of Industry. True *couture* or *Haute Couture* comes with a high price of at least $10,000 and more, a limited market to be sure. These items are purchased by a limited number of fashion leaders who want to be first to have the new items. These limited designs often provide the inspiration for mass-market styles, although as we'll see later this dynamic is shifting as designers increasingly shift their focus to what is happening on the streets rather than in exclusive couturiers.

Luxury Fashion

This market level comprises brands that provide high quality products, and boasts brand heritage, prestige, rarity, and craftsmanship[34] (see also[35]). For example, the Hermès brand prides itself on the principles of "heritage" and "exclusivity". Luxury brands are generally owned by three global groups: Maisons LVMH, Kering, and Richemont. Other independent luxury brands include Hermès, Chanel, Prada, Elie Saab, and promising Asian brands such as Mimpi Kita, Lantern Sense, and Rokh.[36]

Unlike *Haute Couture*, luxury fashion products are not custom-made. They take the form of **ready-to-wear lines** called **prêt-a-porter** (or pret for short) instead of custom-made items for particular people. Ready-to-wear refers to factory made apparel produced in standardized sizes to fit most people, instead of being manufactured exceptionally for one specific person.

Couture dresses by Rami Kadi
Image courtesy of Patrick Sawaya Photography

Standard patterns and faster manufacturing methods allow companies to provide them at a lower cost as compared to a custom-made goods of the same design.

Yves Saint Laurent was the first French designer to create a ready-to-wear collection. He opened his ready-to-wear fashion house in 1967, as he expanded his offerings beyond the more exclusive *haute couture* market.[37] These lines are still expensive by average consumer standards despite not being mass-manufactured, so they still hold the exclusive desirability effect since they are usually offered in limited quantities. Today the French brand Louis Vuitton dominates the luxury market; it is ranked as the top luxury brand in the world with a $32.223 billion brand valuation and 14% year-over-year growth in 2019.[38]

Not all luxury brands operate at the same level. In 2014, Rambourg developed a **luxury pyramid** that classifies luxury brands into different levels:

- *Everyday luxury* for less than $100 USD (e.g., artisan chocolates, wines, and designer fragrances)

- *Affordable luxury* for less than $300 USD (e.g., luxury designer eyewear, Tiffany silver jewelry)

- *Accessible core* for less than $1500 USD (e.g., designer accessories and apparel)

- *Superpremium* for less than $50,000 USD (e.g., Patek Philippe, Bottega Veneta, Harry Winston)

- *Ultra-high-end* for more than 50,000 USD (e.g., Leviev, Graff).[39]

The original meaning of luxury lies in its exclusivity, scarcity, and the inability of the masses to acquire it.[40] However, today, a lot of fashion brands are extending the restrictions of access to luxury,

Louis Vuitton
Vietnam stock photos / Shutterstock.com

by offering huge quantities of items to the masses as exclusivity and scarcity has changed with the rise of internationalized retail and ecommerce. This strategy refers to what we call **Masstige**, which refers to offering products that are "premium but attainable", usually priced between the middle class and the super-premium.[41] This strategy amplifies the democratization of luxury goods. Typical masstige brands include Lancôme, Michael Kors, Coach, The Kooples, All Saints and Massimo Dutti.

If they choose to offer lower-priced products, luxury brands should be very cautious. Designer brands that are made too accessible are becoming less attractive to very wealthy consumers. For example, the Louis Vuitton brand is perceived by wealthy Chinese to be more of a "brand for secretaries". Gucci also faces an image problem, whereas bespoke items and less common labels such as Bottega Veneta are rising.[42]

Diffusion Designer Brands

Some designers develop secondary lines, or **diffusion lines**, that also carry their names. These are often interpretations of their primary lines in a less expensive execution, perhaps made of lesser-quality fabric or licensed to another manufacturer for production (see also[43]). Examples of diffusion lines are Yeezy Gap, CK (Calvin Klein), Red Valentino by Valentino, and DKNY (Donna Karan).

Diffusion lines merge the aura of a luxury brand with more accessible manufacturing and lower price levels in order to attract younger shoppers and generate more revenues for the designer. However, lately changes in the market have exerted major pressures on diffusion lines. In particular, they are being challenged by the upsurge of emerging brands such as 3.1 Phillip Lim and Alexander Wang, in addition to luxury brand partnerships for limited edition collections with mass fashion retailers such as H&M.

In response to market changes, a number of fashion brands have redesigned their strategies regarding diffusion lines for the sake of maintaining a good luxury image. For instance, Prada Group decided to reposition the Miu Miu label, which was thought to be a diffusion line to become a sister brand to the luxury brand Prada. Other brands have instead decided to discontinue their diffusion lines such as Kors by Michael Kors and Burberry Sport by Burberry, D&G by Dolce & Gabbana, and Marc by Marc Jacobs.

Bridge Brands

Bridge brands comprise brand names that are positioned below luxury but above mass fashion (see[44]). These brands have been introduced in order to appeal to buyers who want garments that are high quality but still available at more affordable prices than are luxury brands. This concept started in the 1970s, when a need was recognized in the market for items with high quality but without the price points being connected to a designer name. For instance, think of Reiss, Sandro, Maje, Whistles, Ted Baker, COS and many more. These brands sell items that emphasize the highest quality possible within a more affordable price range.

Mass Fashion

Mass fashion accounts for the majority of fashion sales in the world. Mass fashion products are those that consumers perceive as more affordable and stylish in contrast to more traditional fashion styles.

They reflect popular trends and are intended for mass-market distribution. These are styles produced in large quantities and sold at Gap, Primark, Banana Republic, Uniqlo and in department and discount stores throughout the world. Similar copies are produced by many competing companies. Much of mass fashion today is made in developing countries using low-cost labor. Mass fashion is what one writer calls '…the bread and butter of the fashion banquet."[45]

Mass fashion brands follow different strategies. For instance, there are brands that are considered as fast fashion. **Fast-fashion brands** are characterized by low priced items manufactured rapidly in response to the most up-to-date fashion trends[46] (see also[47]). These brands have the ability to offer to the masses the newest and the trendiest products that copy and replicate the most up-to-date luxury fashion brand designs, via celebrity and social media trends, on a continuous basis with little or no replenishment.[48] This means that when these brands sell out quickly, they are not replaced, but rather newer styles come in instead. If you shop at Zara for example, you may have noticed that the chain refills its stores with new designs *twice a week*—unlike some fashion retailers that only update their stocks once in a season.[49] Other examples of fast-fashion brands include H&M, Boohoo, Shein etc.

So how does fast-fashion work? It is mainly characterized by **lean manufacturing;** this refers to the philosophy that seeks to identify every possible way to improve efficiencies in the textile and clothing industries.[50] The goal is to reduce production and distribution lead times and permit close matching of supply with market demand, decreasing the chance for inventory termination at a clearance price.[51] QR processes focus on using technology to develop lightning-fast communications among textile producers, clothing manufacturers, and retailers.[52] Normally, a fast-fashion brand is recognized for its ability to create a new fashion item and make it available in its stores ready to be bought by the final consumer within four weeks, while other mass fashion retailers may take up to several months.

Although fast-fashion has been a major force in the industry for a long time – largely due to its popularity among young shoppers who crave a constant flow of new, affordable styles, this approach is starting to hit some major roadblocks. Many consumers (and some people in the industry and other stakeholders such as NGOs and governments) are increasingly concerned about the environmental impact of this throw-away culture that clogs landfills with barely-worn garments.

For this reason, an approach called **slow fashion** is becoming more noticed by the mainstream now, in opposition to fast-fashion. This philosophy is defined as a way "…of identifying sustainable fashion solutions, based on the repositioning of design, production, consumption, use and reuse strategies that emerge alongside the global fashion system and pose a potential challenge to it"[53] (see also[54]). In contrast to fast-fashion, slow fashion designers emphasize the durability of their apparel and they reduce waste by incorporating used garments into their designs.

For instance, Eileen Fisher is an ethical and sustainable fashion label. In 2009, the brand launched its first eco-friendly initiative, "Green Eileen". The brand focuses on apparel recycling, sourcing sustainable textiles, and combating unfair working conditions. It won the Positive Change Award at the 2019 CFDA Fashion Awards.[55] Patagonia was one of the initial protectors of environmental ethics in the activewear market, and this brand is considered as the first to use recycled materials and organic cotton during its manufacturing process. Patagonia is increasing its commitment to labor ethics and produces as much as possible with American factories including in Texas and North Carolina.[56]

And, in another domain of fashion-related consumption we see a similar rise in popularity of the Slow **Food Movement** that advocates local and sustainable eating habits.[57]

The Collab

Recently, an era of collaborations between luxury and mass-market brands has emerged; this continues to be among the hottest trends in retail. These partnerships made the world of luxury fashion more accessible to lower-income shoppers.[58] This strategy aims to tap the spillover effect of the positive associations between the two partnering brands to boost both brand image and brand awareness.[59] Research supports the idea that these brand alliances can influence the images that shoppers have of both brands—but this can work both ways. In many cases the partnership results in greater media attention and buzz that generates more interest in the luxury brand among shoppers who were not aware of it before. However, there is the potential to dilute the brand's luxury image because people see it as going "down-market."[60]

Back in 2005, the activewear retailer Puma started a collaboration with the luxury designer Alexander McQueen that lasted for more than a decade. McQueen was a renowned "sneakerhead" and his partnership with Puma was identified as one of the initial remarkable alliances between sportswear and luxury. Since that time, luxury sportswear has become a main performer in the typical market. The year 2019 alone saw the takeoff of several noteworthy partnerships. For example, Dior declared that it would collaborate with Nike's Air Jordan to launch an exclusive edition "Air Dior," projected to sell for around $2,000. The luxury brand Balmain also announced its partnership with

H&M and Moschino
BOOCYS / Shutterstock.com

the sportswear retailer Puma, which is co-created by Olivier Rousteing, the creative director at Balmain and the fashion model Cara Delevingne.[61]

The fast-fashion brand H&M also collaborates with numerous luxury designers, including Karl Lagerfeld, Stella McCartney, Viktor and Rolf, Roberto Cavalli, Comme des Garçons, Jimmy Choo, Sonia Rykiel, Lanvin, Versace, Maison Margiela, Marni, Isabel Marant, Alexander Wang, Balmain, Kenzo, Erdem, Moschino, Giambattista Valli, Simone Rocha…

Collaborations went beyond brand-to-brand collaborations to reach collaborations between brands and influencers. For instance, in 2019, Chiara Ferragni, one of *Forbes'* "top fashion influencers", has formed a partnership with Lancôme for the creation of her first make-up collection.

Fashion Products: Beyond Apparel, Footwear and Jewelry

We noted early on that fashion is about more than a glitzy runway show where razor-thin women with haughty looks on their perfect faces wear outlandish styles as they parade in front of magazine editors and store buyers. Yet we've mostly talked about apparel so far. That's because for the most part the world (especially marketing executives!) continues to think that the drivers of *haute couture* are somehow different from the other kinds of products and services they sell. What can an automaker or a computer tablet manufacturer, a philanthropic organization, or even an accountant possibly learn from Supreme, H&M or Dior?

The answer is: a lot! No matter what line of business you're in, you still need to attract and retain customers. And the people or organizations that buy what you sell still have to learn about your brand and decide whether they prefer it over all the other options out there. In addition, over time these buyers tend to become tired of their current choices and they decide to try others—even if that means replacing a perfectly competent accountant or writing a check to a new charity.

Fashion and Art

Many people who design and buy fashion products consider their passion to be about art, rather than business. That's why we have apparel collections; much like art collections. It's also why there is sometimes a conflict between "pure" designers and those who view fashion as a business that needs consumers' acceptance in order to succeed. Some feel that the most effective link between art and fashion was during the 1930s when the designer Elsa Schiaparelli joined with surrealists, particularly Salvador Dali. Her designs included surreal decorative detail such as a piece of witty *trompe l'oeil* beading on a jacket, or a hat in the form of a vegetable.[62]

Fashion as Art

Fashion has often been represented as an art form and showcased in art museums and at times is coupled with other art pieces (see also[63]):

- The Saks Fifth Avenue's Project Art and Art Collection initiative, which seeks to combine the worlds of fashion, art, and design in an accessible way for the public. The Art Collection includes more than a thousand permanently installed artworks on display in Saks Fifth Avenue stores nationwide. Project

Art uses storefront windows as gallery space with works of photographer William Wegman, sculptor Charles Long, and painter-sculptor Kenny Scharf showcased in their store windows. Madison Avenue stores in New York including Ralph Lauren and Versace teamed up with artists for a promotion of the area called "Where Fashion Meets Art". Local gallery art was displayed next to fashion items.[64]

- Christian Dior transformed his childhood home in Granville, France into a beautiful museum, which holds a selection of the designer's work including the iconic "New Look" collection.[65] Many of his creations, in addition to other exquisite pieces—like Charlize Theron's Swarovski crystal gown, which we have seen in the 2008 famous J'Adore campaign—have also been displayed in the *Dior Designer of Dreams* exhibition[66] at the Victoria and Albert Museum in London, which was curated by Oriole Cullen.

- Giorgio Armani established an exhibition space, Armani/Silos, in the Zona Tortona of Milan, which displays many collections including daywear and suits. The space also has a whole floor comprised of the designer's "Color Schemes" and a research space completely dedicated to Armani's digital archives.[67]

- The iconic Louis Vuitton Foundation opened its doors in Paris in 2014. The fascinating architecture of the building creates the illusion of floating on water as if it were a ship. This museum includes a restaurant, an auditorium, and a gallery to be used for live fashion shows. The whole purpose behind this foundation is to support art and creation by showcasing collections of modern and contemporary art, organizing numerous events, designing educational programs and meeting up with some of the most exceptional artists.[68] Definitely a place to add to your bucket list.

Some feel *haute couture* can be considered art, because a $30,000 one-of-a-kind creation from a top designer is comparable to a painting hanging in someone's living room. Museums do display some one-of-a-kind gowns behind a thick shield of glass and certainly a lot of exquisite necklaces spend most of their time in secure safes rather than adorning their owners' necks. However, most fashion products probably can be considered a craft—they are valued to the extent that they do a job like covering our bodies—but do it beautifully. Fashion by definition is designed and produced with the purpose of selling to a mass market for profit. It is not considered art.

The age-old tension in fashion between art and commerce was highlighted when Jil Sander resigned from the Prada Group in early 2000 over a dispute related to creativity versus cost control. Designers fear losing control over their creative endeavors when they join a mass market group. On the other hand, large design houses (more and more prevalent today with mergers and takeovers) have the capital to offer their top designers the freedom to live out their fantasies.[69] That appears to be the case with Maria Grazia Chiuri, designer for Dior (part of LVMH), and Alessandro Michele for Gucci who both offer edgy to extreme collections. Some say that the big luxury houses like LVMH and Prada Group provide these pricey, edgy looks to build hype so that they can eventually sell logo products at the lower end. Donna Karan, although she has mass merchandised lines such as DKNY, is not ready to "go Gap". She says, "I couldn't live without the artistic hand in fashion... for me, fashion is sculpture for the human body."[70] But fashion is a business, and its bottom line is selling clothes.

The French designer Christian Lacroix put the issue this way: "... a dress which isn't worn doesn't exist for me. If I want to go even further in my fantasies, I turn to the theater so that these kinds of creations can exist on stage... or I look toward conceptual art, presenting myself to galleries to present my most radical ideas."[71] Thus, he sees fashion and art as a continuum. Rei Kawakubo said, "Fashion is not art. Art is for museums, galleries or the home. Fashion is living and is to be worn. What I find interesting is the synergy that can occur when different kinds of creation come together. This is the beauty of collaboration and the meaning of the meeting of art and fashion or art within fashion.[72]

Peter Wollen notes that "the design and making of garments has traditionally been viewed as artisanal (craft) rather than artistic... its status, however, has continued to rise during the last 200 years."[73] Not every art critic agrees, as the commercial character of fashion in constant change is the antithesis of what art represents. Inspiration from art such as Saint Laurent's 1965 Mondrian couture dresses, Versace's 1991 Andy Warhol's polychrome portraits of James Dean and Marilyn Monroe, Stephen Sprouse's Pop Art prints, or Karl Lagerfeld's Watteau collections are thought of by some as not just inspiration from history, but cannibalizing. Although many fashion designers are inspired by art, others believe that if you take it too literally you will only sell a piece of it.

Fashion and Food

Oreo, the cookie brand, has revealed its first-ever fashion collection, produced in partnership with three European influencers, Samantha Faiers from the UK, Anne-Laure Mais Moreau from France and Yvonne Pferrer from Germany, with the purpose of increasing cookie sales and engagement in European markets.[74] If a cookie can team up with stars, that's a clue that things are changing, and the domain of traditional fashion is expanding.

While cakes and luxury may appear an unusual combination, food is evolving as a new frontier for luxury goods.[75] It seems that many fashionistas in recent years have started to diversify from *haute couture* to a keen interest in *haute cuisine* as well. According to Stefano Cantino, strategic marketing director at Prada, "Food is luxury as much as fashion". The "haute café" (a term that refers to a luxury café) culture attracted the attention of Prada's owners who decided in 2014 to acquire the Milanese coffee and pastry shop Marchesi, established in 1824, which opened its second shop in London.[76] In the UK, venerable stores including Harvey Nichols, Harrods and Selfridges sell upscale food products as well as designer clothing.

A number of luxury brands have jumped into this bandwagon and have launched their own coffee shops or restaurants:

- Gucci opened Gucci Osteria restaurant in Florence in 2017 in collaboration with the Three-Michelin-star chef Massimo Bottura and more recently opened its second restaurant in Beverly Hills, with a third location scheduled for Tokyo.

- Luxury group LVMH launched its second high-end food hall in Paris, betting on a growing appetite from residents for gourmet groceries.[77]

- Members of the Ferragamo brand have established wine brands Il Borro and Castiglion del Bosco.

- The owner of the lingerie chain Calzedonia launched a chain of wine shops known as Signorvino.[78]

- The luxury brand Louis Vuitton newly launched its restaurant in Osaka, Japan, with the chef Yosuke Suga.

- The luxury jewelry brand Tiffany, responding to the diminishing appetites of young consumers for diamonds and capitalizing on the trend set by the movie *Breakfast at Tiffany's*, is diversifying into the food industry with its first Blue Box Café in New York, followed by another one in Hong Kong and a third inside Harrods, London.

Other Domains as Fashion

Have you ever thought of trains as art deco canvases? In 1930, as passenger railroads were striving to continue to exist during the Great Depression, a number of firms created sleek looking trains to lure riders. The period between 1930s and 1940s was exceptional when it came to streamlining trains. One of the most recognized industrial designers of the American railroads during that period was Otto August Kuhler. His widespread models for the "modernization of the American railroads" have impacted the global railways until our time. Another reputable designer of the time was Raymond Loewy who developed steam, electric and diesel trains for the Pennsylvania Railway. He also created the color patterns and interior designs for the Northern Pacific Railway's North Coast Limited.[79] Other examples of fashion in other domains include the crossover of luxury fashion houses with interior design, creating items such as exclusive wallpapers and furnishings such as Versace, Fendi, Roberto Cavalli.

Recently, traveling is not only being linked to reach a certain destination, but it has also been associated with the experience itself. Have you ever heard of Japan's *Seven Stars luxury sleeper train*? This cruise train is meant to bring new life to train travel, to make the travel itself an integral part of a Kyushu vacation. The plush, classic décor harkens back to bygone days, while the technological advancements and large, picturesque viewing windows push the comfort of travel by train to new heights.[80] Luxury traveling is not only restricted to trains, but it also encompasses yachts. Ritz Carlton yachts for example offer customized service, in addition to prominent dining and luxury amenities.[81] And we see a similar pattern in high-end residences that boast a fashionable signature. For example, the powerhouse developer Emaar Properties collaborated with the renowned fashion designer Elie Saab to build a residential tower in Dubai, expected to be completed by 2023.[82]

Chapter Summary

Now that you have read the chapter, you should understand the following:

1. How has fashion evolved over the years?

The evolution of fashion has been a response to changes in the environmental pressures such as political, economic, and social ones. During the 18th century, Louis XIV established a luxury industry comprising furniture, apparel, jewelry and fabric, making Paris the center of fashion in the world. The couture industry saw its birth during the 19th century.

(Continued)

The Industrial Revolution was one of the most important events of the 18th century, impacting different industries such as food, fabric, and apparel and leading to the creation of a middle class with a lot of money to spend on luxury. The invention of the sewing machine during the Industrial Revolution transformed the way goods were made, thus giving birth to mass production. With the availability of more consumer goods, fashion retailing emerged in the 19th century.

At the beginning of the 20th century, during World War I, women joined the workforce, replacing men. While most jobs required women to wear uniforms and trousers, this led to a more minimalistic lifestyle. During World War II, under manifested limitations and deprivation, most fashion designers were barely able to sustain their businesses, and some were forced to shut down. Materials restrictions led to more simplicity in women's apparel and resulted in the development of new man-made materials. Trousers became an essential for women employed in factories. After World War II, a dominant feminine silhouette was adopted with women welcoming back men from war.

In 1970s, physical activity became a routine part of life. "Dress for success" also emerged as women attempted to achieve equal position with men in the workplace. In the 1990s, individuals were no longer interested in designer names. By the end of the 20th century, maximalism directed the fashion cycle. At the beginning of the 21st century, up until 2007, an era of "democratization," took place, with luxury brands displaying icons and logos in a maximalist form. In 2008, the Global Recession rocked the whole luxury and fashion industry, forcing brands to adopt a minimalistic approach. From 2010 to 2014, an upsurge in maximalism and minimalism took place with a flow of new Chinese shoppers. Starting 2018, the world has moved into a new era of self-expression. During the 21st century, a number of trends have emerged such as food as luxury, gender neutral fashion, diversity and inclusivity, empowerment of women, hybrid products such as tech wearables and smart textiles.

2.   What are the different domains of fashion?

Fashion terminology is often used by consumers in overlapping ways. A style of apparel is defined by distinctive attributes that distinguish it from others in its category, such as different types of skirts; a fashion is a style that has been accepted by many people. Classification of fashion include the following: *High fashion* or *haute couture*, which refers to new styles that are very expensive and custom-made from design houses; *luxury fashion* refers to brands that provide high quality products, and which have brand heritage, prestige, rarity, and craftsmanship; *diffusion designer brands* are usually interpretations of the designers' primary lines in a less expensive execution, perhaps made of lesser-quality fabric or licensed to another manufacturer for production; *bridge brands* sell a variety of unsophisticated and minimalistic items that emphasize the highest possible quality within an affordable price range; *mass fashion products* are those that consumers perceive as more affordable and stylish. Recently, an era of collaborations between luxury brands and mass-market ones has emerged, which continues to be among the hottest trends in retail, making the world of luxury fashion becoming more accessible than ever.

3.   Are fashion products only related to apparel?

Fashion is about more than wearing eccentric styles. Fashion is about art. Many people who design and buy fashion products consider their passion to be about art, rather than business, which is why apparel collections are much like art collections. Fashion has for long been represented as an art form and has been showcased in art museums and at times is coupled with other art pieces. Museums do display some one-of-a-kind *haute couture* gowns behind a thick shield of glass and certainly a lot of exquisite necklaces. Fashion is not only linked to apparel; however, it encompasses so many other different categories such as food, automotive, yachts, trains, and restaurants.

1. What is the difference between an art and a craft? Where would you characterize fashion within this framework? What about advertising?

2. What are the pros and cons of apparel labels diversifying into food? Do they have the expertise to accomplish this? Will customers go for it?

3. What will fashion look like when the Covid-19 crisis is over?

4. Do you think that luxury brands should diversify into diffusion brands? Why or why not?

5. What are the pros and cons of fashion brands collaborating with external designers?

EXERCISES

1. In groups, think of diffusion designer lines that a luxury brand has lately created in order to appeal to a different target market. Do you think that this might work? Do you think there are any risks related to this decision?

2. Select a fashion brand. After doing some research, suggest a brand it can collaborate with from a different domain. What product would you launch with this collaboration?

3. Imagine that you are the marketing manager of Maserati. You want to collaborate with a well-known apparel brand. Who would you select, and why?

CASE STUDY: MANU ATELIER – A TURKISH BRAND IN THE 'TOP' FASHION FIELDS

Nazlı Alimen, Birmingham City University

THE FIELD(S) OF FASHION

Sociologist Pierre Bourdieu's framework of 'field' is "useful for understanding how fields of cultural production, such as fashion, operate" (Entwistle, 2015: 213). For Bourdieu, fields are "social microcosms" (Bourdieu and Wacquant, 1992: 97), "informed by specific rules of

(Continued)

functioning which shape the trajectories and practices of the agents that belong to [them]" (Rocamora, 2016: 234).

Bourdieu (2007) states that capital determines one's position in a field and identifies four forms: Economic, social, cultural and symbolic. Economic capital is monetary/financial assets, social capital one's contacts and networks, cultural capital consists of cultural resources, which can be cognitive, embodied, objectified, and institutionalized, such as bodily manners (e.g., air-kiss in the fashion field [Entwistle and Rocamora, 2006]), art works, degrees, and certificates. Symbolic capital can be defined as the amount of (social) status one holds. All these forms are unevenly distributed within and across fields and can be transformed from one to another (Bourdieu, 2007).

Capital specific to each field can be named after the field and consist of some or all four forms. Additionally, each player in a field possesses different levels of field-specific capital. Players of the fashion field, for example, such as fashion designers, photographers, buyers, models and social media influencers, possess different levels of fashion capital, and therefore different levels of power and status in the field.

There is a multiplicity of 'fashion fields', such as the French, Japanese and modest fashion fields (see, e.g., Alimen, 2018), and a hierarchy among them. This hierarchy largely emanates from the fact that fashion as a cultural industry was formed in Europe, particularly France, and was later joined by New York. Consequently, the fashion fields centered in Paris, London, Milan, and New York are at the top. Their players and institutions (e.g., retailers, media outlets, fashion schools) as well as capital possessed in those fields are placed above all others, such as the Chinese, Bhutanese and Turkish (see, e.g., Alimen and Kütük-Kuriş, 2020; Jansen and Craik, 2016).

Moreover, since fashion has long been regarded as a phenomenon specific to western societies (this is contested in contemporary fashion scholarship; see, e.g., Jansen and Craik, 2016), it is not easy for those fashion fields at the lower levels of the hierarchy and their players and institutions (e.g., designers and brands) to be recognized in the fashion fields at the top. In order to enter and succeed in those 'top of the hierarchy' fields, they need to fight harder "for the power to define what can be acknowledged as legitimate practice, aesthetic, taste or norm" (Rocamora, 2016: 234). The following is an example of a successful entrant (and seemingly long-term player) into the 'top' fashion fields.

Manu Atelier

Manu Atelier is a Turkish brand founded in 2014 in Istanbul by two sisters, Beste and Merve Manastır, who targeted the rapidly growing market for affordable designer bags with high quality materials and production (Goldstone, 2018). Their father, Adnan Manastır, began his leather production artisanship career as an apprentice in Istanbul and established a leather bags and accessories company, Yeşim Çanta, in 1976. Inherited cultural and social capital, i.e., the utilization of their father's expertise and experience in leather goods production and networks in the sector (e.g., suppliers), informed the sisters' design process and facilitated the production of their designs. This, along with the availability and relatively lower costs of high-quality raw materials and production in Turkey, enabled them to create and run a brand offering handcrafted designer bags at accessible prices. In early 2021 their bags cost from £180 ($246) to £495 ($677) (https://manuatelier.com).

Manu Atelier's first collection consisted of eight styles, three of which were "repurposed from their father's back catalogue and modified for the market", including their signature Pristine bag (Mellery-Pratt, 2015). The brand achieved rapid success in Turkey because Merve's schoolfriend, working as a senior buyer at high-end department store Vakko, saw Manu Atelier bags on Instagram (Mellery-Pratt, 2015). Consequently, Vakko bought 400 units outright (Mellery-Pratt, 2015). As the first order sold out in two weeks, Vakko ordered 1000 units more to be sold in all its 24 stores (Mellery-Pratt, 2015), thus becoming the brand's first bricks-and-mortar stockist.

When Eva Chen, director of fashion partnerships at Instagram, posted a photo of the brand's Pristine bag in June 2014, Manu Atelier stock at Vakko began selling even faster, leading the store to restrict consumers to "a maximum of three items per month" (Mellery-Pratt, 2015). Nonetheless, Beste notes, all Vakko's stock was sold out quickly, mainly to Chinese and Turkish consumers (Mellery-Pratt, 2015).

As retailers abroad, including Selfridges, Stylebop and Net-A-Porter, began contacting the sisters, they decided on a global strategy and hired Luisa de Paula as their global sales agent (Mellery-Pratt, 2015); she was crucial in the brand's global success (Goldstone, 2018). Following extensive market research, the brand was benchmarked with See by Chloé, Marc by Marc Jacobs, Mansur Gavriel, Philip Lim and Alexander Wang (Mellery-Pratt, 2015).

Manu Atelier chose to grow organically on social media and thus keep the momentum going (Goldstone, 2018). It introduced a hashtag family, #ManusPeople, creating a social media ripple effect. However, the sisters note that social media's effect on expanding a brand needs to be supported with design, quality and functionality (Goldstone, 2018). In addition to introducing new bag styles, Manu Atelier launched its footwear line in October 2018. Luisa de Paula points to the importance of an omni-channel approach and highlights the need to have the right mix of physical touchpoints and digital presence (Theodosi, 2017). Therefore, Manu Atelier products are sold through the brand website and in department stores and boutiques, both offline and online, in numerous countries (https://manuatelier.com).

Manu Atelier continues to be worn by celebrities (e.g. Bella Hadid and Kate Middleton), covered in leading media outlets (e.g. *The Times* and *Vogue UK*), and sold globally by renowned

(Continued)

retailers, such as Browns and Moda Operandi. The brand's Pristine bag was included in the Victoria & Albert Museum's 'Bags: Inside Out' exhibition (December 2020–September 2021) (V&A Museum, 2020a, 2020b). All this indicates that the Manastır sisters are highly likely to sustain Manu Atelier's global success by utilizing the fashion capital acquired through their family and business.

DISCUSSION QUESTIONS

1. When developing and launching the Manu Atelier brand, what forms of capital (economic, social, cultural and symbolic) have the sisters possessed and used?

2. What forms of capital have the sisters utilized and acquired as they entered the top fashion fields?

3. Do you think social media has a significant impact on the acquisition and spread of 'fashion capital' in the fashion fields? Discuss how and to what extent.

REFERENCES

Alimen, N. (2018) *Faith and Fashion in Turkey: Consumption, Politics and Islamic Identities*. London: I.B. Tauris.

Alimen, N. and Kütük-Kuriş, M. (2020) 'A snapshot of the fashion field in contemporary Turkey', *International Journal of Fashion Studies*, 7 (2): 133–45. doi.org/10.1386/infs_00023_2.

Bourdieu, P. (2007) 'The forms of capital', in R. Sadovnik (ed.), *Sociology of Education: A Critical Reader*. Abingdon: Routledge. pp. 83–95.

Bourdieu, P. and Wacquant, L.J.D. (1992) *An Invitation to Reflexive Sociology*. Cambridge: Polity.

Entwistle, J. (2015) *The Fashioned Body: Fashion, Dress and Modern Social Theory* (2nd ed.). Cambridge: Polity.

Entwistle, J. and Rocamora, A. (2006) 'The field of fashion materialized: A study of London Fashion Week', *Sociology*, 40 (4): 735–51.

Goldstone, P. (2018) 'From SJP to Eva Chen & Bella Hadid: How Manu Atelier became the new 'it' bag', *Marie Claire*, 16 February. www.marieclaire.co.uk/fashion/shopping/manu-atelier-578739 (accessed August 6, 2021).

Jansen, A.M. and Craik, J. (eds) (2016) *Modern Fashion Traditions: Tradition and Modernity through Fashion*. London: Bloomsbury.

Mellery-Pratt, R. (2015) 'Manu Atelier and the Eva Chen effect', *Business of Fashion*, 25 November. www.businessoffashion.com/articles/news-analysis/manu-atelier-and-the-eva-chen-effect-2 (accessed August 6, 2021).

Rocamora, A. (2016) 'Pierre Bourdieu: The Field of Fashion' in A. Rocamora and A. Smelik (eds), *Thinking Through Fashion*. London: I.B. Tauris. pp. 233–50.

Theodosi, N. (2017) 'Turkish accessories label Manu Atelier expands globally in a fragile economy', *WWD*, 2 March. wwd.com/accessories-news/handbags/turkish-istanbul-accessories-label-manu-atelier-expands-globally-10826704/ (accessed August 6, 2021).

V&A Museum (2020a) 'Bags: Inside out', vam.ac.uk, www.vam.ac.uk/exhibitions/bags (accessed August 6, 2021).

V&A Museum (2020b) '"Mini Pristine" bag by Manu Atelier', vam.ac.uk, https://collections.vam.ac.uk/item/O1512138/bag/mini-pristine-bag-by-manu-bag-manu-atelier/ (accessed August 6, 2021).

NOTES

1. Kozinets, R., Patterson, A. and Ashman, R. (2017) 'Networks of desire: How technology increases our passion to consume', *Journal of Consumer Research*, 43 (5): 659–82.

2. Kozinets, R., Patterson, A. and Ashman, R. (2017) 'Networks of desire: How technology increases our passion to consume', *Journal of Consumer Research*, 43 (5): 659–82.

3. Wong, K. (2001) 'Archaeologists home in on body ornament origins', *Scientific American*, June 5. www.scientificamerican.com/article/archaeologists-home-in-on/ (accessed August 6, 2021).

4. Okonkwo, U. (2016) *Luxury Fashion Branding: Trends, Tactics, Techniques*. London: Springer.

5. DeJean, J. (2007) *The Essence of Style: How the French Invented High Fashion, Fine Food, Chic Cafes, Style, Sophistication, and Glamour*. New York, NY: Simon & Schuster.

6. Blanco, J., Hunt-Hurst, P.K., Lee, H.V. and Doering, M. (eds) (2015) *Clothing and Fashion: American Fashion from Head to Toe* [4 volumes]. Santa Barbara, CA: ABC-CLIO.

7. Merlo, E., and Belfanti, C.M. (2019) 'Fashion, product innovation, and consumer culture in the late 19th century: Alle Città d'Italia department store in Milan', *Journal of Consumer Culture*, 21 (2): 337–58.

8. Stevens, L. and Maclaran, P. (2005) 'Exploring the "shopping imaginary": The dreamworld of women's magazines', *Journal of Consumer Behaviour: An International Research Review*, 4 (4): 282–92.

9. Benson, S.P. (1986) *Counter Cultures: Saleswomen, Managers, and Customers in American Department Stores, 1890–1940* (Vol. 314). Chicago, IL: University of Illinois Press.

10. BBC (2010) 'History of Harrods department store', *BBC News*, May 8. www.bbc.com/news/10103783 (accessed August 6, 2021).

11. 24S (n.d.) 'The History Of Le Bon Marché', 24S.com. www.24s.com/en-be/le-bon-marche/history (accessed August 6, 2021).

12. Glancey, J. (2015) *A History of the Department Store*. BBC Culture. www.bbc.com/culture/bespoke/story/20150326-a-history-of-the-department-store/index.html (accessed August 6, 2021).

13. Vogue (1918) 'What war has done to clothes', *Vogue Archive*, October 15. https://archive.vogue.com/article/1918/10/what-war-has-done-to-clothes (accessed August 6, 2021).

14. Blanco, J., Hunt-Hurst, P.K., Lee, H. V. and Doering, M. (eds) (2015) *Clothing and Fashion: American Fashion From Head to Toe* [4 volumes]. Santa Barbara, CA: ABC-CLIO.

15. Reddy, K. (2020) Fashion history timeline 1970–1979. https://fashionhistory.fitnyc.edu/1970-1979/ (accessed October 14, 2021).

16. Molloy, J.T. (1975) *Dress for Success*. New York, NY: Peter H. Wyden

    Molloy, J.T. (1977) *The Woman's Dress for Success Book*. New York, NY: Warner.

    Nava, M., Blake, A., MacRury, I. and Richards, B. (eds) (1997) *Buy This Book: Studies in advertising and consumption*. London: Routledge.

17. Hill, D.D. (2007) *As Seen in Vogue: A Century of American Fashion in Advertising.* Lubbock, TX: Texas Tech University Press.

     Tungate, M. (2008) *Fashion Brands: Branding Style from Armani to Zara.* London: Kogan Page.

18. Sterlacci, F. and Arbuckle, J. (2017) *Historical Dictionary of the Fashion Industry.* Lanham, MD: Rowman & Littlefield.

19. Stephens, F.G. (2002). *Fashion: From Concept To Consumer*, 7th ed. Chennai: Pearson Education India.

20. Sterlacci, F. and Arbuckle, J. (2009) *The A to Z of the Fashion Industry.* Lanham, MD: Rowman & Littlefield.

     Garber, M. (2016) 'Casual Friday and the "end of the office dress code"', *The Atlantic,* May 25. www.theatlantic.com/entertainment/archive/2016/05/casual-friday-and-the-end-of-the-office-dress-code/484334/ (accessed August 6, 2021).

21. D'Arpizio, C., Levato, F., Kamel, M.-A. and de Montgolfier, J. (2017) *Luxury Goods Worldwide Market Study, Fall–Winter 2017.* Bain & Company. www.bain.com/contentassets/913fa48282034511b178b0f4b7cc3d9a/bain_report_global_luxury_report_2017.pdf (accessed August 6, 2021).

22. Bain, M. (2020) 'The battle between minimalist and maximalist fashion has reached a new equilibrium,' *Quartz,* January 10. https://qz.com/1762078/growth-of-fashion-minimalism-has-caught-up-to-maximalism/ (accessed August 6, 2021).

23. D'Arpizio, C., Levato, F., Kamel, M.-A. and de Montgolfier, J. (2017) *Luxury Goods Worldwide Market Study, Fall–Winter 2017.* Bain & Company. www.bain.com/contentassets/913fa48282034511b178b0f4b7cc3d9a/bain_report_global_luxury_report_2017.pdf (accessed August 6, 2021).

24. Fernandez, C. (2020) 'As a global recession looms, quiet luxury returns', *Business Of Fashion,* March 18. www.businessoffashion.com/articles/luxury/the-return-of-quiet-luxury (accessed August 6, 2021).

25. Perino, M. (2019)' 'A chief marketing officer who works with 12,000 luxury brands says consumers are caught up in "logo-mania," and it's helped a famously flashy brand make a huge comeback', *Insider,* February 20. www.businessinsider.com/gucci-logo-mania-fashion-trend-luxury-brand-comeback-modesens-2019-2 (accessed August 6, 2021).

26. La Ferla, R. (2018) 'What gives the logo its legs', *The New York Times,* November 7. www.nytimes.com/2018/11/07/fashion/logos-gucci-fendi-supreme.html (accessed August 6, 2021).

27. Lau, S. (2013) 'The logo strikes back', *Business Of Fashion,* October 17. www.businessoffashion.com/opinions/news-analysis/susie-bubble-kenzo-opening-ceremony-homies-the-logo-strikes-back (accessed August 6, 2021).

28. D'Arpizio, C., Levato, F., Kamel, M.-A. and de Montgolfier, J. (2017) *Luxury Goods Worldwide Market Study, Fall–Winter 2017.* Bain & Company. www.bain.com/contentassets/913fa48282034511b178b0f4b7cc3d9a/bain_report_global_luxury_report_2017.pdf (accessed August 6, 2021).

29. Bain, M. (2020) 'The battle between minimalist and maximalist fashion has reached a new equilibrium', *Quartz,* January 10. https://qz.com/1762078/growth-of-fashion-minimalism-has-caught-up-to-maximalism/ (accessed August 6, 2021).

30. Bhattarai, A. (2020) '5 ways the pandemic is changing fashion and beauty trends', *The Washington Post,* June 15. www.washingtonpost.com/business/2020/06/15/fashion-beauty-trends-coronavirus/(accessed August 6, 2021).

     Testa, J. (2021) Schedule an Appointment With Those Clothes You Haven't Worn in a Year, *New York Times.* www.nytimes.com/2021/04/10/at-home/virus-clothes.html (April 10, 2021) (accessed August 6, 2021).

31. Rabkin, E. (2020) 'Op-Ed: An enlightened post-pandemic consumer? Don't count on it', *Business Of Fashion,* April 15. www.businessoffashion.com/articles/opinion/op-ed-an-enlightened-post-pandemic-consumer-dont-count-on-it (accessed August 6, 2021).

32. Hanbury, M. (2018) 'Ivanka Trump is ushering in a new fashion trend—and it shows how great people feel about the American economy', *Insider,* February 26. www.businessinsider.com/power-suit-back-in-style-2018-2 (accessed August 6, 2021).

33. Bottomley, T. (2021) 'Athleisure orders rise by 84 since start of pandemic', *The Industry.Fashion,* February 17. www.theindustry.fashion/athleisure-orders-rise-by-84-since-start-of-pandemic/ (accessed August 6, 2021).

34. Kapferer, J.N. and Bastien, V. (2012) *The Luxury Strategy: Break the Rules of Marketing to Build Luxury Brands.* London: Kogan Page.

     Ko, E., Costello, J.P. and Taylor, C.R. (2019) 'What is a luxury brand? A new definition and review of the literature', *Journal of Business Research*, 99: 405–13.

     Nieroda, M.E., Mrad, M. and Solomon, M.R. (2018) 'How do consumers think about hybrid products? Computer wearables have an identity problem', *Journal of Business Research*, 89: 159–70.

35. Chailan, C. (2018) 'Art as a means to recreate luxury brands' rarity and value', *Journal of Business Research*, 85: 414–23.

Dion, D. and Borraz, S. (2017) 'Managing status: How luxury brands shape class subjectivities in the service encounter', *Journal of Marketing*, 81 (5): 67–85.

Kapferer, J.N., Kernstock, J., Brexendorf, T.O. and Powell, S.M. (eds) (2017) *Advances in Luxury Brand Management*. Berlin: Springer.

Kapferer, J.N. and Valette-Florence, P. (2019) 'How self-success drives luxury demand: An integrated model of luxury growth and country comparisons', *Journal of Business Research*, 102: 273–87.

Shimul, A.S., Phau, I. and Lwin, M. (2019) 'Conceptualising luxury brand attachment: Scale development and validation', *Journal of Brand Management*, 26 (6): 675–90.

36. LLM Reporters. (2020) '5 Luxury Asian fashion brands set to make waves in the industry this year', *Luxury Lifestyle Magazine*, January 5. www.luxurylifestylemag.co.uk/style-and-beauty/5-luxury-asian-fashion-brands-set-to-make-waves-in-the-industry-this-year/ (accessed August 6, 2021).

37. Waddell, G. (2013) *How Fashion Works: Couture, Ready-to-wear and Mass Production*. New York, NY: John Wiley & Sons.

38. Davis, D. (2020) 'The 9 most valuable luxury brands in the world', *Insider*, January 28. www.businessinsider.com/most-valuable-luxury-brands-in-the-world (accessed August 6, 2021).

39. Rambourg, E. (2014) *The Bling Dynasty: Why the Reign of Chinese Luxury Shoppers has Only Just Begun*. New York, NY: John Wiley & Sons.

40. Dubois, B. and Paternault, C. (1995) 'Observations: Understanding the world of international luxury brands: The "dream formula"', *Journal of Advertising Research*, 35: 69–76.

Beauloye, F.E. (2020) 'The Future of luxury: Six Trends to Stay Ahead in 2021' *Luxe Digital*. https://luxe.digital/business/digital-luxury-trends/luxury-future-trends/ (accessed August 6, 2021).

41. Kim, J.E., Lloyd, S., Adebeshin, K. and Kang, J.Y.M. (2019) 'Decoding fashion advertising symbolism in masstige and luxury brands', *Journal of Fashion Marketing and Management: An International Journal*, 23 (2): 277–95.

Kumar, A., Paul, J. Unnithan, A.B. (2020) '"Masstige" marketing: A review, synthesis and research agenda', *Journal of Business Research*, 113: 384–98.

Paul, J. (2015) 'Masstige marketing redefined and mapped', *Marketing Intelligence & Planning*, 33 (5): 691–706.

Quach, S. and Thaichon, P. (2017) 'From connoisseur luxury to mass luxury: Value co-creation and co-destruction in the online environment', *Journal of Business Research*, 81: 163–72.

Kumar, A., Paul, J. and Starčević, S. (2021) 'Do brands make consumers happy? A masstige theory perspective', *Journal of Retailing and Consumer Services*, 58: article #102318.

Paul, J. (2018) 'Toward a "masstige" theory and strategy for marketing', *European Journal of International Management*, 12 (5–6): 722–45.

Paul, J. (2019) 'Masstige model and measure for brand management' *European Management Journal*, 37 (3): 299–312.

Wang, Y. and Qiao, F. (2020) 'The symbolic meaning of luxury-lite fashion brands among younger Chinese consumers', *Journal of Fashion Marketing and Management: An International Journal*, 24 (1): 83–98.

42. Willett-Wei, M. (2015) 'Here's the hierarchy of luxury brands around the world', *Business Insider*, March 23. www.businessinsider.com/pyramid-of-luxury-brands-2015-3 (accessed August 6, 2021).

43. Arora, A.S., McIntyre, J.R., Wu, J. and Arora, A. (2015) 'Consumer response to diffusion brands and luxury brands: The role of country of origin and country of manufacture', *Journal of International Consumer Marketing*, 27 (1): 3–26.

Phau, I. (2010) 'An Australian perspective of the effects of brand image and product quality on diffusion brands of designer jeans', *Journal of Global Business and Technology*, 6 (1): 41–51.

Phau, I. and Cheong, E. (2009) 'How young adult consumers evaluate diffusion brands: Effects of brand loyalty and status consumption', *Journal of International Consumer Marketing*, 21 (2): 109–23.

44. Ling, W., Taylor, G. and Lo, M.T. (1998) 'From designer brand to bridge line: Brand differentiation, brand strategies and customer purchasing behaviour in Hong Kong fashion retail operation', *Journal of Fashion Marketing and Management*, 2 (4): 361–68.

45. Stone, E. and Farnan, S.A. (2018) *The Dynamics of Fashion*. New York, NY: Bloomsbury.

46. Amatulli, C., Mileti, A., Speciale, V. and Guido, G. (2016) 'The relationship between fast fashion and luxury brands: An exploratory study in the UK market', in F. Mosca and G. Gallo (eds), *Global Marketing Strategies for the Promotion of Luxury Goods*. Hershey, PA: IGI Global. pp. 244–65.

Cachon, G. P. and Swinney, R. (2011) 'The value of fast fashion: Quick response, enhanced design, and strategic consumer behavior', *Management Science*, 57 (4): 778–95.

Shen, B., Choi, T.M. and Chow, P.S. (2017) 'Brand loyalties in designer luxury and fast fashion co-branding alliances', *Journal of Business Research*, 81: 173–80.

47. Bonilla, M.D.R., del Olmo Arriaga, J.L. and Andreu, D. (2019) 'The interaction of Instagram followers in the fast fashion sector: The case of Hennes and Mauritz (H&M)', *Journal of Global Fashion Marketing*, 10 (4): 342–57.

Camargo, L.R., Pereira, S.C.F. and Scarpin, M.R.S. (2020) 'Fast and ultra-fast fashion supply chain management: An exploratory research', *International Journal of Retail & Distribution Management*, 48 (6): 537–53.

Coskun, M., Gupta, S. and Burnaz, S. (2020) 'Store disorderliness effect: Shoppers' competitive behaviours in a fast-fashion retail store', *International Journal of Retail & Distribution Management*, 48 (6): 763–79.

Rese, A., Schlee, T. and Baier, D. (2019) 'The need for services and technologies in physical fast fashion stores: Generation Y's opinion', *Journal of Marketing Management*, 35 (15–16): 1437–59.

48. Amatulli, C., Mileti, A., Speciale, V. and Guido, G. (2016) 'The relationship between fast fashion and luxury brands: An exploratory study in the UK market', in F. Mosca and G. Gallo (eds), *Global Marketing Strategies for the Promotion of Luxury Goods*. Hershey, PA: IGI Global. pp. 244–65.

Christopher, M., Lowson, R. and Peck, H. (2004) 'Creating agile supply chains in the fashion industry', *International Journal of Retail & Distribution Management*, 32 (8): 367–76.

Sull, D. and Turconi, S. (2008) 'Fast fashion lessons', *Business Strategy Review*, 19 (2): 4–11.

Barnes, L. and Lea-Greenwood, G. (2006) 'Fast fashioning the supply chain: Shaping the research agenda', *Journal of Fashion Marketing and Management*, 10 (3): 259–71.

49. Lutz, A. (2013) 'Why the retail industry can't keep up with Zara', *Business Insider,* November 19. www.businessinsider.com/zaras-genius-business-model-and-retail-2013-11 (accessed August 6, 2021).

50. Azuma, N. and Fernie, J. (2003) 'The changing nature of Japanese fashion: Can Quick Response improve supply chain efficiency', *European Journal of Marketing*, 38 (7): 790–808.

51. Cachon, G.P. and Swinney, R. (2011) The value of fast fashion: Quick response, enhanced design, and strategic consumer behavior', *Management Science*, 57 (4): 778–95.

Caro, F., and Martínez-de-Albéniz, V. (2015) 'Fast fashion: Business model overview and research opportunities', in N. Agrawal and S.A. Smith (eds), *Retail Supply Chain Management: Quantitative Models and Empirical Studies*. Boston, MA: Springer. pp. 237–64.

Moon, K.L.K., Lee, J.Y. and Lai, S.Y.C. (2017) 'Key drivers of an agile, collaborative fast fashion supply chain', *Journal of Fashion Marketing and Management: An International Journal*, 21 (3): 278–97.

52. Caro, F. and Martinez De Albeniz, V. (2014) 'How Fast Fashion works: Can it work for you too?', *Harvard Business Review*, 21: 58–65.

53. Clark, H. (2008) 'SLOW+ FASHION–an oxymoron—or a promise for the future...?', *Fashion Theory*, 12 (4): 427–46.

54. Casto, M.A. and DeLong, M. (2019) 'Exploring aesthetic response to classic as a means to slow fashion', *Fashion Practice*, 11 (1): 105–31.

Jung, S. and Jin, B. (2014) 'A theoretical investigation of slow fashion: Sustainable future of the apparel industry', *International Journal of Consumer Studies*, 38 (5): 510–19.

McNeill, L.S. and Snowdon, J. (2019) 'Slow fashion—Balancing the conscious retail model within the fashion marketplace', *Australasian Marketing Journal (AMJ)*, 27 (4): 215–23.

Overdiek, A. (2018) 'Opportunities for slow fashion retail in temporary stores', *Journal of Fashion Marketing and Management: An International Journal*, 22 (1): 67–81.

Pookulangara, S. and Shephard, A. (2013) 'Slow fashion movement: Understanding consumer perceptions—An exploratory study', *Journal of Retailing and Consumer Services*, 20 (2): 200–6.

55. Rasool, A. (2019) 'How Eileen Fisher is the ultimate sustainable label', *CFDA* , May 30. https://cfda.com/news/how-eileen-fisher-is-the-ultimate-sustainable-label (accessed August 6, 2021).

56. Sonsev, V. (2019) 'Patagonia's focus on its brand purpose is great for business', *Forbes*, November 27. www.forbes.com/sites/veronikasonsev/2019/11/27/patagonias-focus-on-its-brand-purpose-is-great-for-business/?sh=264ec21554cb (accessed March 1, 2022).

Barnes, A., Woulfe, J. and Worsham, M. (2021) *A Legislative Guide to Benefit Corporations: Create Jobs, Drive Social Impact, and Promote the Economic Health of Your State,* Patagonia. www.patagonia.jp/static/on/demandware.static/-/Library-Sites-PatagoniaShared/default/dw1b80705a/PDF-US/Legislative-Guide-B-Corps_Final.pdf (accessed August 6, 2021).

57. Slow food (2015) www.slowfood.com/about-us/ (accessed August 6, 2021).

58. Sherman, L. (2019) 'High-low collaborations democratised fashion. But what did they do for the designers?', *Business of Fashion,* September 19. www.businessoffashion.com/opinions/news-analysis/high-low-collaborations-democratised-fashion-but-what-did-they-do-for-the-designers (accessed August 6, 2021).

59. Oeppen, J. and Jamal, A. (2014) 'Collaborating for success: Managerial perspectives on co-branding strategies in the fashion industry', *Journal of Marketing Management,* 30 (9–10): 925–48.

    Xiao, N. and Lee, S.H.M. (2014) 'Brand identity fit in co-branding', *European Journal of Marketing,* 48 (7/8): 1239–54.

60. Balachander, S. and Ghose, S. (2003) 'Reciprocal spillover effects: A strategic benefit of brand extensions', *Journal of Marketing,* 67 (1): 4–13.

    Geylani, T., Inman, J.J. and Hofstede, F.T. (2008) 'Image reinforcement or impairment: The effects of co-branding on attribute uncertainty', *Marketing Science,* 27 (4): 730–44.

    Mrad, M., Farah, M.F. and Haddad, S. (2019) 'From Karl Lagerfeld to Erdem: A series of collaborations between designer luxury brands and fast-fashion brands', *Journal of Brand Management,* 26 (5): 567–82.

    Shen, B., Choi, T.M. and Chow, P.S. (2017) 'Brand loyalties in designer luxury and fast fashion co-branding alliances', *Journal of Business Research,* 81: 173–80.

    Rollet, M., Hoffmann, J., Coste-Manière, I. and Panchout, K. (2013) 'The concept of creative collaboration applied to the fashion industry', *Journal of Global Fashion Marketing,* 4 (1): 57–66.

    Voss, K.E. and Mohan, M. (2016) 'Corporate brand effects in brand alliances', *Journal of Business Research,* 69 (10): 4177–84.

61. Davis, D.M. (2019) 'Puma and Balmain's limited edition collection features an $8,000 sequined kimono and a $250 pair of shorts, and it proves the luxury sportwear market is here to stay', *Business Insider,* December 28. www.businessinsider.com/balmain-puma-collection-luxury-sportswear-is-here-to-stay-2019-12 (accessed August 6, 2021).

62. Kim, S.B. (1998) 'Is fashion art?', *Fashion Theory,* 2 (1): 51–71.

63. Chailan, C. (2018) 'Art as a means to recreate luxury brands' rarity and value', *Journal of Business Research,* 85: 414–23.

    Jelinek, J.S. (2018) 'Art as strategic branding tool for luxury fashion brands', *Journal of Product & Brand Management,* 27 (3): 294–307.

    Joy, A., Wang, J.J., Chan, T.S., Sherry Jr, J.F. and Cui, G. (2014) 'M (Art) worlds: Consumer perceptions of how luxury brand stores become art institutions', *Journal of Retailing,* 90 (3): 347–64.

    Logkizidou, M., Bottomley, P., Angell, R. and Evanschitzky, H. (2019) 'Why museological merchandise displays enhance luxury product evaluations: An extended art infusion effect', *Journal of Retailing,* 95 (1): 67–82.

64. Women's Wear Daily Staff (n.d.) 'Fashion meets art on madison', *Women's Wear Daily.* https://wwd.com/fashion-news/fashion-features/fashion-meets-art-on-madison-1213593/ (accessed August 6, 2021).

65. Stodola, S. and Marcus, L. (2015) 'The art of style: 16 of the world's greatest fashion museums', *Conde Nast Traveler,* November 9. https://www.cntraveler.com/galleries/2013-10-12/fashion-designer-museums-italy-spain-south-korea (accessed August 6, 2021).

66. V&A (2019) Inside the Christian Dior: Designer of Dreams exhibition. www.vam.ac.uk/articles/inside-the-christian-dior-designer-of-dreams-exhibition. (accessed August 6, 2021).

67. Vernose, V. (2019) 'The most iconic fashion exhibits of all time: Is fashion truly museum art', *CR Fashion Book,* March 28. www.crfashionbook.com/fashion/a26950328/the-most-iconic-fashion-exhibits-of-all-time/ (accessed August 6, 2021).

68. Mun-Delsalle, Y.J. (2014) 'The long-awaited fondation Louis Vuitton will open its doors in Paris on October 27', *Forbes,* October 7. www.forbes.com/sites/yjeanmundelsalle/2014/10/07/the-long-awaited-fondation-louis-vuitton-will-open-its-doors-in-paris-on-october-27/?sh=1f4831824bfb (accessed August 6, 2021).

69. Socha, M. (2000) 'Art vs. commerce: Is the bottom line what drives the line?', *Women's Wear Daily,* February 10. https://wwd.com/fashion-news/fashion-features/article-1203998/ (accessed August 6, 2021).

70. Socha, M. (2000) 'Art vs. commerce: Is the bottom line what drives the line?', *Women's Wear Daily*, February 10. https://wwd.com/fashion-news/fashion-features/article-1203998/ (accessed August 6, 2021).

71. Socha, M. (2000) 'Art vs. commerce: is the bottom line what drives the line?', *Women's Wear Daily*, February 10. https://wwd.com/fashion-news/fashion-features/article-1203998/ (accessed August 6, 2021).

72. Edelson, S. (1998) 'Fashion and culture: An artful combination adds a marketing spin', *Women's Wear Daily*. https://wwd.com/fashion-news/fashion-features/article-1099900/ (accessed August 6, 2021).

73. Kim, S.B. (1998) 'Is fashion art?', *Fashion Theory*, 2 (1): 51–71.

74. Wightman-Stone, D. (2020) 'Oreo launches first fashion collection', *Fashion United*, January 14. https://fashionunited.com/news/fashion/oreo-launches-first-fashion-collection/2020011431663 (accessed August 6, 2021).

75. Sanderson, R. (2014) 'Food the new frontier for Italian luxury', *Financial Times*, December 23. www.ft.com/content/e1ec6362-86d6-11e4-982e-00144feabdc0 (accessed August 6, 2021).

76. Sanderson, R. (2015) 'Bar Luce: The devil drinks at Prada', *Financial Times*, June 12. www.ft.com/content/6395dd52-0fae-11e5-b968-00144feabdc0 (accessed August 6, 2021).

77. Segreti, G. (2018) 'Feeding the fashionistas: Gucci turns to fine dining', *Reuters*, January 9. https://www.reuters.com/article/us-luxury-food-gucci/feeding-the-fashionistas-gucci-turns-to-fine-dining-idUSKBN1EY1VV (accessed August 6, 2021).

78. Sanderson, R. (2014) 'Food the new frontier for Italian luxury', *Financial Times*, December 23. www.ft.com/content/e1ec6362-86d6-11e4-982e-00144feabdc0 (accessed March 1, 2022).

79. Grace, M.L. (2018) 'Kuhler, Dreyfuss, and Loewy, modernism, streamliners, and art deco trains', *Cruise Line History*, July 15. www.cruiselinehistory.com/kuhler-dreyfuss-and-lowey-modernism-streamliners-and-art-deco-trains/ (accessed August 6, 2021).

80. J Rail Pass (2019, October 23) *Seven Stars Kyushu: Riding the Luxury Train*. www.jrailpass.com/blog/seven-stars-kyushu-luxury-train (accessed August 6, 2021).

81. Ritz-Carlton (2021) 'The Ritz-Carlton yacht collection, *Ritz Carlton*. www.ritzcarlton.com/en/yachts (accessed August 6, 2021).

82. Chamberlayne, C. (2019) 'Romance has a new address: Elie Saab is building apartments in Dubai', *Harper's Bazaar Arabia*, April 7. www.harpersbazaararabia.com/fashion/the-news/elie-saab-apartments-in-dubai (accessed August 6, 2021).

CHAPTER 3

Understanding Fashion Change

LEARNING OBJECTIVES

After you read this chapter, you will understand the answers to the following:

1. What are the different theories of fashion?

2. What is the cultural production process?

3. What is the current state of fashion?

4. What are the major drivers of fashion today?

Søren is so excited—after waiting 16 long years, his very first trip to London from his home in Denmark! After he quickly gets the obligatory visit to Buckingham Palace out of the way, he heads over to the Peckham area where he strolls through the streets to watch the "natives." As a "*fashionista*-in-training," he's keen to see what new styles are popping up on the Bohemian types who inhabit the cafes and bars in sections of the city like this. Sure enough, he sees several blokes who are wearing clashing colors and statement-making printed T-shirts, which he's never seen before. After paying close attention to the details, he pops into a few shops and procures his own version of this innovative style. As Søren sits at Heathrow waiting his for his flight home to be called, he smiles to himself as he thinks of all the admiring—and some quizzical—looks he's going to get from his friends at school when he shows up sporting his latest fashion catch.

Theories of Fashion

Søren's London odyssey illustrates how a new style spreads. A fashion is adopted by a small group of consumers before the mass market tunes in to it. Because a fashion operates at both the individual level and at broader levels of society, it's not surprising to find that there are as many theories about it as there are social science disciplines (and even more!).

You may have heard the story of the seven blind men and the elephant: each described the animal differently, depending upon where they touched him. Similarly, different social sciences focus on varied aspects of fashion due to the types of analyses they perform. For example, psychological approaches tend to concentrate upon individual factors that determine fashion adoption, while broader-based disciplines such as sociology and anthropology see the "elephant" in terms of social and cultural factors that influence large numbers of people. All of these perspectives are valuable; their usefulness partly depends upon which part of the animal *you* need to understand. Let's review the most important approaches to understanding fashion.

Psychological Fashion Theory

Many psychological factors help to explain why people are motivated to be in fashion. These include conformity, variety seeking, personal creativity, and sexual attraction. For example, many consumers seem to have a "need for uniqueness"[1] (see also[2]): They want to be different, but not too different. For this reason, people often conform to the basic outlines of a fashion but try to improvise and make a personal statement within these general guidelines.

One of the earliest theories of fashion proposed that shifting **erogenous zones** (sexually arousing areas of the body) accounted for fashion changes and that different zones become the object of interest because they reflect societal trends. J.C. Flügel, a disciple of Sigmund Freud, proposed in the 1920s that sexually charged areas wax and wane in order to maintain interest and that clothing styles change to highlight or hide these parts. Interest in the female leg in the 1920s and 1930s coincided with women's new mobility and independence, whereas the exposure of breasts in the 1970s signaled a renewed interest in breastfeeding. Breasts were deemphasized in the 1980s as women concentrated on careers, but some analysts have theorized that a larger bust size is now more popular as women try to combine professional activity with child rearing. Some contemporary fashion theorists suggest that the current prevalence of the exposed midriff reflects the premium our society places on fitness.[3]

Economic Fashion Theory

Economists approach fashion in terms of a model of supply and demand. Items that are in limited supply have high value, while those readily available are less desirable. Rare items command respect, prestige, and generally high prices. Thus, we see high fashion in limited supplies at very expensive prices (see also[4]).

Scarcity even enhances the values of everyday items. We saw a great example of this during the Beanie Babies craze in the late 1990s or the collection of rare baseball cards. The manufacturer Ty Inc.

limited the number of a particular style it sent to retailers, but they were supposed to sell at regular prices (normally something in limited supplies can fetch high prices). However, after-market sellers skyrocketed. Limiting the supply kept the demand high, such that collectors called stores daily and even sent a list of those styles they wanted to buy. We see a similar phenomenon at work today when designers "drop" a new style in limited quantities to increase demand.

Another economic perspective comes from Thorsten Veblen's notion of **conspicuous consumption**, which proposed that the wealthy deliberately consume in excess to display their prosperity, for example, by wearing expensive (and at times impractical) clothing (see[5]).

This approach is somewhat outdated, since upscale consumers often engage in **parody display**, where they deliberately adopt formerly low-status or inexpensive products, such as Jeeps or jeans or shop at cheap-chic stores such as Target or even fast fashion retailers such as Zara. Other social factors also influence the demand curve for fashion-related products. These include a **prestige-exclusivity effect**, also called the *Veblen effect*, where high prices create high demand (for exclusive groups, high prices actually increase the demand, as they can show off their wealth through expensive purchases), and a snob effect, where lower prices reduce demand ("If it's that cheap, it can't be any good.").[6]

Sociological Fashion Theory

The fashion system embraces all the individuals and groups that form symbolic meanings and assign those connotations to cultural goods. While we frequently associate fashion with apparel, remember that fashion practices impact all forms of cultural phenomena, such as music, art, architecture, and even science (i.e., some research issues are "hot" at any point in time).

When (as we saw in the last chapter) the Industrial Revolution made it possible for many people to acquire mass-produced and distinctive products, the young field of sociology tuned in to this phenomenon to try to understand the forces at that time that drove a process of imitation from upper social classes to lower income classes.

Trickle-down theory was an early perspective; it states that two conflicting forces drive fashion change. First, subordinate groups adopt the status symbols of the groups above them as they attempt to climb up the ladder of social mobility. Dominant styles thus originate with the upper classes and trickle down to those below.[7]

Now the second force kicks in: those people in the superordinate groups keep a wary eye on the ladder below them to be sure followers don't imitate them. When lower-class consumers mimic their actions, they adopt new fashions to distance themselves from the mainstream. These two processes create a self-perpetuating cycle of change—the machine that drives fashion.

Cultural Movement

The forces of imitation still are powerful—that's why so many *fashionistas* eagerly copy the new styles they see influencers post on Instagram and other platforms. But today, the movement is less about moving in a downward direction, and more about moving in both upward and horizontal directions. In other words, while wealthy people may still be tastemakers, they tend not to be the forces of fashion they used to be. In fact, many new styles "trickle up" from lower social class or marginalized groups (think about tattoos, which were often associated with criminals and sailors). And the power of word-of-mouth alters the landscape so that a lot of what we learn about new fashions no longer comes just from "experts," but also from others who are roughly our equals in the social system—in particular, our "friends" and members of our social networks who may be similar to us in terms of age, income, etc. Thus, today fashionistas are probably as likely to get their style ideas from a fashion blogger or influencer as from the images they see of their favorite celebrity's most current looks.

But, that movement of ideas from one group to another still is vitally important. Leopard-skin pants, nipple rings, platform shoes, sushi, high-tech furniture, postmodern architecture, double decaf cappuccino with a hint of cinnamon. We inhabit a world brimming with various styles and options. The clothes we wear, the type of food we eat, the cars we drive, the locations where we live and work, the songs we listen to—all are affected by the movement of popular culture and fashion.

The culture in which we live creates the meaning of everyday products. A good question would be: how do these meanings move through a society to reach consumers? The advertising and fashion industries help to transfer meaning by associating functional products with symbolic qualities such as sexiness, sophistication, or being just plain "cool." These goods, in turn, impart their meanings to consumers as they use these products to create and express their identities (see Figure 3.1).[8]

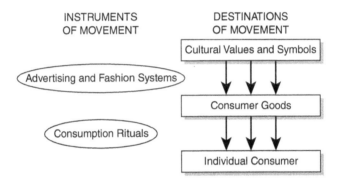

FIGURE 3.1   The movement of meaning

SOURCE: Adapted from McCracken, G. (1986) 'Culture and consumption: A theoretical account of the structure and movement to the cultural meaning of consumer goods,' *Journal of Consumer Research*, 13 (June): 72. Reprinted with permission of The University of Chicago Press.

Shoppers may sometimes feel overwhelmed by the big assortment of options in the marketplace. An individual trying to purchase something as basic as a pair of socks has many hundreds of choices. Regardless of this apparent abundance, nevertheless, the options available to shoppers at any point in time actually make up only a small portion of the whole set of possibilities.

The selection of particular options over others—be it apparel, cars, electronics, recording artists, political candidates, religions, or even scientific methodologies—is the culmination of a complex filtration process that is similar to a funnel as shown in Figure 3.2. A number of options primarily compete for adoption, and these are steadily winnowed out as they make their way down the path from conception to consumption through a practice known as **cultural selection**.

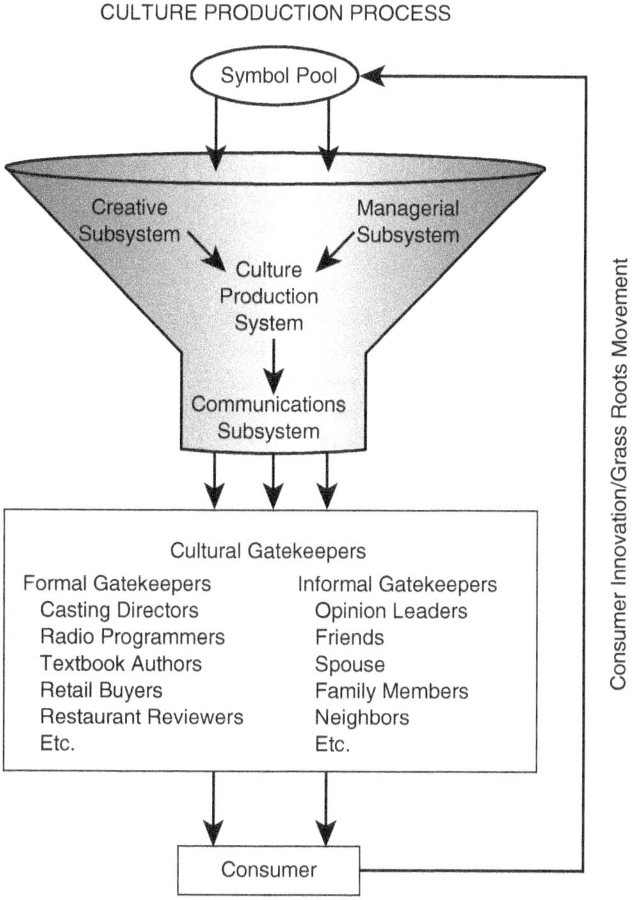

CULTURE PRODUCTION PROCESS

FIGURE 3.2 The culture production process

SOURCE: Adapted from Solomon, M.R. (1988) 'Building up and breaking down: The impact of cultural sorting on symbolic consumption,' in J. Sheth and E.C. Hirschman (eds), *Research in Consumer Behavior,* Kidlington: Elsevier. pp. 325–51, with permission from Elsevier Science.

We don't form our tastes and product preferences in a vacuum. Our selections are determined by what we see in mass media, by our observations of those around us, and even by our desires to live in the fantasy worlds marketers create. These options are constantly evolving and changing. A clothing style or type of cuisine that is "hot" one year may be "out" the next. Also, a style may fall out of favor with early adopters, but it may be eventually picked by laggards e.g., cold shoulder tops.

Below are some of the characteristics of fashion and popular culture:

- Fashions often are a reflection of deeper societal trends (e.g., politics and social conditions).

- A fashion often begins as a risky or unique statement by a relatively small group of people and then spreads as others increasingly become aware of it and feel confident about trying it.

- Fashions usually originate as an interplay between the deliberate inventions of designers and businesspeople and spontaneous actions by ordinary consumers who modify the fashion to suit their needs. Designers, manufacturers, and merchandisers who can anticipate what consumers want will succeed in the marketplace. In the process, they also help to fuel the fire by encouraging mass distribution of the item.

- These cultural products can travel widely, often across countries and even continents.

- Influential people in the media play a large role in deciding which fashions will succeed.

- Most fashions eventually wear out, as individuals frequently pursue different ways to express themselves and marketers struggle to keep pace with these needs.

- The cultural selection process is never discontinued, therefore when styles reach a stage where they become obsolete there is a demand to replace them with new ones (that may be modified from earlier popular styles).

There is no one designer, firm, or advertising agency that is totally responsible for creating popular culture. Every product, whether a new clothing style, a hit record, or a car, requires the input of many different participants. The set of individuals and organizations responsible for creating and marketing a cultural product is a **culture production system**.[9]

The nature of these systems helps to determine the types of products that eventually emerge from them. Factors such as the number and diversity of competing systems and the amount of innovation versus conformity that is encouraged are important. For example, apparel is an industry comprised of many companies with a great deal of competition. Designers and manufacturers strive to create uniqueness as a way to differentiate themselves from others, thus creating a unique image for which they become known.

A culture production system is composed of three important subsystems:

1. A *creative subsystem* to create new symbols and goods.

2. A *managerial subsystem* to choose, make tangible, create, and organize the diffusion of new symbols and goods.

3. A *communications subsystem* to provide meaning to the innovative goods and arrange for a symbolic set of features.

An example of the three components of a culture production system for a fashion item such as a perfume would be 1) a designer or a brand (e.g., Valentino = a creative subsystem); 2) a company (e.g., a company that manufactures and distributes this perfume (L'Oréal) = a managerial subsystem) and 3) the advertising or publicity agencies (agencies hired to promote the perfume = a communication subsystem).

Many judges or "tastemakers" influence the products that are generally provided to shoppers. These **cultural gatekeepers** are responsible for filtering the overflow of information and materials intended to consumers. Gatekeepers include magazine editors, retail buyers, movie and restaurant reviewers, and interior designers.

The Meme Theory of Fashion

In 2012, Angelina Jolie dressed in Versace at the Oscars and flashed her right leg, a posture that created unforgettable memes such as "Jolie'ing" and leg-bombing. And at the 2015 Met Gala, the singer Rihanna famously wore a bright yellow garment that was quickly labeled "the omelet dress" due to its similarity to eggs. This meme rapidly went viral, and it put the outfit's designer Guo Pei on the fashion map.[10]

Why did this designer become known across the globe so quickly? **Meme theory** can explain this. The term **meme**, coined by Richard Dawkins in 1976, refers to a unit of cultural infor-

Memes of Rihanna's Met Gala Dress

Instagram / henryholland

mation transferable from one mind to another. According to Dawkins, examples of memes are tunes, catchphrases ("OK Boomer"), or clothing fashions (see also[11]).

A meme propagates itself as a unit of cultural evolution analogous in many ways to the gene, the unit of genetic information. Memes spread among consumers in a geometric pattern, just as a virus (as we've seen first-hand unfortunately) starts off small and steadily infects increasing numbers of people until it becomes an epidemic. The diffusion of many products and fashions seems to follow a similar path. A few people initially use the product, but change happens in a hurry when the process reaches the moment of critical mass—what Malcom Gladwell calls the **tipping point**.[12] Cell phones, and microwave ovens followed such a path: a few early adopters, then suddenly almost everyone had one.

With the fashion scene being so competitive, memes have also attracted the attention of fashion brands. Today, some of the most popular designers are trying to produce products that can be meme-friendly, an "it" piece that stimulates consumers' interest and sets the Internet on fire. For instance, think of what Gucci did when the models during the fashion runway of Spring/Summer 2018 were carrying casts of their own heads, scenes that were perhaps more unforgettable—and surely more memeable—than the items themselves.[13]

Who Creates Fashion Trends?

Fashion trends are usually affected by social or subcultural changes such as women's empowerment or Black Lives Matter, economic factors such as the global recession due to the Covid-19 pandemic or even technological developments such as synthetic fibers, wearable computers, and many others.

Karl Lagerfeld

Image courtesy of Patrick Sawaya Photography

When it comes to premium fashion, it's more likely to be established by fashion leaders who play a role in creating new trends. These leaders can be:

- Fashion designers such as Elie Saab, Ralph and Russo, Donatella Versace, Alexander McQueen or creative directors such as Karl Lagerfeld, Olivier Rousteing, Raf Simons, Hedi Slimane, Virgil Abloh, or Maria Grazia Chiuri.

- Fashion opinion leaders such as celebrities or influencers also play a significant role in setting trends, and consumers are more likely to demand items like the ones worn by those leaders.[14] Think of how Kim Kardashian made contouring a vibrant makeup method.[15] The new technique steered cosmetic firms to create kits specially for contouring. Also, we cannot ignore the influence of Kanye West along with his friend Virgil Abloh, the creator of the Off-White brand. Both influencers made it easier for streetwear to be perceived as high fashion.

When fashion trends and styles are set by fashion leaders, be it a celebrity, a designer or a social influencer, this creates a great opportunity for apparel manufacturers who can take advantage and imitate these lines by creating different versions at a lower price and quality. This movement is best explained by the traditional "trickle-down effect" that provides a direct way of predicting the fashion diffusion process. This is how fashion trends and styles trickle down from luxury houses to mass and fast fashion brands to reach people with less disposable income who might be looking for similar styles at cheaper prices. The styles are copied again and again at much lower prices so that they become acceptable to mass-market consumers. We'll go into more detail about the trickle-down effect in Chapter 9.

Who Consumes These Trends?

The fashion trends that are transmitted and communicated by fashion leaders are usually consumed by **fashion followers.**[16] This term describes a large number of individuals who accept and adopt the trends that were communicated to them.[17] Fashion followers make mass fashion possible.

Some consumers are interested in outfits as seen on opinion leaders

Image courtesy of Century Black via Flickr. Shared under the public domain.

If fashion followers refrain from admiring and imitating fashion leaders, the fashion industry would be at risk, since this is where the bulk of the work in the industry resides.[18] An example of a fashion follower may be a person who sees a belt bag worn by Rihanna and then decides she has to have it as well.

The State of Fashion Apparel Today: Shifting Fashion Centers

Traditional Fashion Capitals

When you think of glamorous fashion, what places come to mind? The first locations that will probably pop up are Paris, London, Milan and New York. These four cities have been named as the main **fashion capitals** for as long as we can remember. Every single year, one of those cities takes precedence over the others and steals the number one ranking spot among the traditional fashion capitals. In 2020, New York was elected as the "Top Global Fashion Capital of the Decade".[19]

Paris

In order for a city to be named as a fashion capital, it must be home to designers, runway shows, showrooms, fashion schools, media companies and of course fashion consumers and buyers. One cannot talk about Paris without mentioning fashion and *haute couture* and paying tribute to the innumerous trends that were born in this fashion hub. Paris holds one of the most important events twice a year; Paris Fashion Week. La Ville Lumière houses some of the top fashion schools including ESMOD International, Institut Français de la Mode and the International Fashion Academy. Not to mention that some of the most reputable and famous fashion designers in the world hail from the region; Christian Dior, Christian Louboutin, Jean-Paul Gaultier and Coco Chanel are of French origin. Additionally, *Elle*; the world's best-known fashion magazine, was established in Paris in 1945.[20]

Yves Saint Laurent Show in Paris

Image courtesy of Patrick Sawaya Photography

London

London has always been a part of the four fashion capitals due to many reasons, including the origination of the Mod movement there in the 1960s. London Fashion Week is a bi-annual event begun by the British Fashion Council in 1984, which draws the biggest fashion names and brands every year. The London College of Fashion and Central Saint Martins are among the most prestigious fashion schools in the world. Stella McCartney, Alexander McQueen, John Galliano and Christopher Kane are some of the renowned fashion designers born in this fashion capital.[21]

New York

One cannot deny the major contributions that the city of New York has made to the fashion industry. To this day, it is still considered as the heart of fashion globally. New York Fashion Week, which launched in 1943 and is held bi-annually, continues to be considered as one of the most glamorous events, bringing together important figures of fashion worldwide. Numerous significant fashion schools like the Fashion Institute of Technology and Parsons School of Design are situated in

New York, in addition to some of the biggest fashion designers like Ralph Lauren, Tom Ford and Tory Burch.[22]

Milan

This majestic Italian city produces many of the complementary accessories that complete the whole fashion look, including handbags, sunglasses and shoes. Milan Fashion Week, held semi-annually, is one of the hottest events to take place annually in the fashion industry. It is also a center for the menswear industry. Milan also houses a number of major fashion schools. Examples are Accademia Costume & Moda in addition to the Instituto Marangoni. Italian fashion designers who are known for their superior craftsmanship and quality include Giorgio Armani, Gucci, Gianni Versace, Domenico Dolce and Stefano Gabbana (Dolce & Gabbana), Miuccia Prada, and the long list goes on.[23]

Tom Ford during New York Fashion Week

Ovidiu Hrubaru / Shutterstock.com

Emerging Fashion Capitals

Paris, New York, London and Milan do hold the spots for the big four fashion capitals; however, this does not mean that there is no room for other cities around the world to be referred to as fashion hubs. The list of cities that have made progressive changes in the fashion industry is very long and includes Shanghai, São Paulo, Berlin, Saint Petersburg and Antwerp.[24]

Tokyo also is an important emerging fashion capital. Known for its weird trends

Giorgio Armani posed during the Milan fashion week

DELBO ANDREA / Shutterstock.com

and unconventional fashion, this city has definitely made the cut and is gaining momentum as each year goes by. Tokyo Fashion Week has been known to display the exotic fashion trends and looks, making it one of the most anticipated events in this versatile industry. Tokyo is also the city where many fashion schools have helped to train some of the best fashion designers, like Kenzō Takada, founder of the famous brand KENZO.[25]

Going back to Europe, Barcelona is making headlines and creating lots of buzz. It has one of the fastest growing fashion industries due to its massive production of textiles. Some of the known fashion brands are Spanish in origin, like Balenciaga, Zara, Massimo Dutti and Mango. Not to mention that Barcelona Fashion Week is slowly gaining more popularity and attracting bigger fashion names.[26]

Another city that may belong on the emerging fashion capitals list is Copenhagen, however, it comes with a twist. The capital of Denmark is hoping to differentiate itself as the fashion capital of *sustainability*. In 2020, Copenhagen Fashion Week set goals on cutting its carbon footprint and notifying participating fashion brands that they have only until 2023 to meet the new sustainability requirements as part of the new action plan. Will it succeed in this new step? The answer remains unknown since this would be the first time any Fashion Week has attempted such a major and positive change.[27]

Another potential fashion capital candidate is, surprisingly, Kyiv. Ukraine has been pretty well-known for its sophisticated embroidery, which has made it onto runways and has acted as a source of inspiration to some top fashion brands including Valentino. Also, the fashion media has been booming in Kyiv with *Vogue Ukraine*, *Elle Ukraine* and *L'Officiel Ukraine*, allowing many designers to be featured in editorials.[28]

The list goes on and on, but the question to keep in mind is: Which of these cities do you think will earn the title of a fashion capital and potentially overthrow one of the main four?

Major Drivers of Fashion Now

Gender-Neutral Fashion

Today, fashion apparel retailers are trying hard to meet the demands of a shifting consumer market that increasingly is interested in gender-bending, gender-fluid and genderless products and services.[29] Market studies report a shift in the way Gen Z consumers (born after 1995) perceive gender. 38% of this generation in one survey stated that they highly agree that gender no longer describes an individual the way it used to in the past.[30] Recent findings of a study performed on Gen Z indicated that 56% of these consumers already purchase products that are not linked to their biological gender, and they express little interest in apparel that companies classify into traditional, gendered categories.[31]

In recent fashion seasons, some luxury brands such as Gucci, Saint Laurent and Haider Ackermann have merged menswear and womenswear in their fashion shows. Other brands like Proenza Schouler have displayed their womenswear pre-collections at the time when the industry traditionally previews menswear. Fast fashion retailers like Zara are starting to launch genderless collections, where they feature models of both genders who appear in the same outfit. Also, Uniqlo and Muji offer more gender-free looks. Adidas even launched a new gender-neutral collection in collaboration with the singer Beyoncé that comprises jumpsuits, asymmetric dresses, cargo pants, hoodies and cycling shorts, typically highlighting signature Adidas triple stripes.[32]

The move toward genderless collections also has expanded into the kids' market. For instance, Abercrombie & Fitch launched its first collection of gender-neutral apparel for kids in 2018. The strategy of eliminating gender labels was stimulated by customer feedback, which revealed that parents and their kids do not want to be confined to a particular style or colors based on sexes. Accordingly, Abercrombie Kids has customized a unisex collection to appeal to this shifting consumer demand.[33]

The department store chain John Lewis was the first in the UK to announce that it was removing gender labels from its kids' apparel. Their division will refer instead to "Girls & Boys" or "Boys & Girls." Caroline Bettis, the head of kidswear at John Lewis, stated the following: "We do not want to reinforce gender stereotypes within our John Lewis collections and instead want to provide greater choice and variety to our customers, so that the parent or child can choose what they would like to wear."[34]

Modest Fashion

Modest fashion refers to a fashion trend among religious females who cover their bodies in a stylish way so that they can remain fashionable without violating their religious or personal preferences to avoid body-baring clothing.[35] The precise meaning of 'modest' differs across cultures and countries. Dressing modestly but in a stylish way is already very common among young women, but it's not limited to individuals who belong to one particular religion.[36] For a lot of people, modest fashion is a personal choice that only signifies dressing in more conventional ways such as longer hemlines or higher collars. These styles formerly considered "less cool" attires are currently *en vogue*. Although modest fashion has always been linked to religious adherence, it is getting more response among nonreligious people as well. The online modest fashion retailer ModLi earns 90% of its sales from the US market.[37]

Muslim consumers' clothing purchases are expected to reach more than $368 billion by 2021.[38] A number of fashion retailers are trying to take advantage of this market opportunity. For example, H&M and Uniqlo are including models who wear veils in their current campaigns. Nike has lately launched a performance Hijab—a garment that permits Muslim women to take part in sports while diminishing the everyday challenges of wearing a religious item of apparel in a swimming pool or on an athletic field.[39] Other fashion brands, such as DKNY, Burberry, Tommy Hilfiger, Oscar de la Renta, Zara and Mango, have created Ramadan and Eid collection lines. Dolce & Gabbana also launched a collection of hijabs and luxury abayas.[40]

Diversity and Inclusivity

For several years, diversity in fashion meant that from time to time, a brand would include a non-white model in a photoshoot. But today, these token acknowledgments that not every woman is a six-foot-tall blonde Caucasian are no longer adequate. The industry is quickly making strides to get in step with a global trend toward inclusivity. This is driven by shoppers' desires to see people who look like them on the runways and in stores, and by employees and stakeholders advocating for change.[41] Nike, Macy's, Burberry, and Chanel have all hired diversity officers over the past several years. And other brands have appointed black creative directors such as Olivier Rousteing, Shayne Oliver, and Virgil Abloh, a sign that the fashion industry is becoming more inclusive of individuals of color. Virgil Abloh is the first black Men's Artistic Director of Louis Vuitton across the history of the French fashion house.[42]

One practical factor that is driving this change is simple, yet powerful: Consumers are pushing back against brands that do not incorporate the principles of diversity. Victoria's Secret faced a huge backlash over the refusal to include transgender or plus-size models in its fashion runway show, stating that the brand was founded more on fantasy rather than being "politically correct".[43] A year after that initial confrontation, Victoria's Secret formally recruited its first transgender model.[44]

Other brands also have had to change their tune as they created tone-deaf advertisements that were unflattering to minority consumers. A few recent notable examples include:

- In 2019, H&M Group hired its first-ever worldwide leader of diversity and inclusion, Annie Wu. This happened in the aftermath of an embarrassing misstep, when the company included a photograph of a Black child wearing a sweatshirt with the caption, "Coolest Monkey in the Jungle".[45]

- Gucci appointed its first chief diversity officer after it got caught up in its own misstep; an ad featured a black balaclava jumper with a cut-out mouth resembling oversized red lips that sparked outrage over social media.[46] Prada set up a diversity and inclusion council following a Manhattan window display presenting monkey figures that was associated with blackface stereotypes.[47]

- In 2018, Dolce & Gabbana launched an ad showing a Chinese woman eating pasta with chopsticks, which provoked public outrage in China.[48]

Gucci ad featuring a black balaclava jumper causing public outrage

NurPhoto / Contributor

Fashion brands are not only focusing on diversity and inclusion in relation to color, but also to sizes and disabilities. For instance, Anthropologie, has created items in sizes ranging from 00P to 26W, while Tommy Hilfiger has designed a specific collection of apparel for individuals with disabilities. The online retailer ASOS is also selling apparel specially introduced for people with disabilities.[49] With the adaptive-apparel market projected to reach almost $400 billion by 2026, a number of brands are designing adaptive-apparel collections, such as Zappos and Target.[50]

Christian Dior for Women Empowerment

Image courtesy of Patrick Sawaya Photography

Empowerment of Women

Inequality in the workforce has been a common practice, and the fashion industry is no exception. For example, British companies have an average median gender gap of 9.7% of hiring men over women in the workplace. Such disparities have been thrown into the spotlight along with the increase in reported sexual assault and harassment claims in the office. This phenomenon led to the boom of the #MeToo movement where activists all around the world demanded equality for women and fought to enforce gender diversity across all levels of business. In addition, fashion retailers were asked to start reporting their salary data to reveal which companies contribute to this gender pay disparity.

The movement didn't end here. The fashion industry felt responsible to use its influence to positively impact women, and the only way to achieve this goal is if every brand and company shifts its whole lens towards women's empowerment. Many fashion brands have participated in this initiative, including Christian Dior who kick-started Paris Fashion Week with the display of its new collection by Maria Grazia Chiuri. The collection revolved around the themes of feminism and women's empowerment and the venue was filled with graphic signs displaying eye-catching slogans like 'Consent', 'Women raise the uprising' and 'Patriarchy'. Dior also showed signs of solidarity when it designed Natalie Portman's ensemble for the Oscars and the cape had all the names of female directors who were *not* nominated for the Academy Awards.[51]

A number of fashion designers have also made it a point to emphasize the comeback of female power suits in their newly launched collections. Celine and Victoria Beckham are among those designers who created 1970s inspired suits with broad shoulders and high-waisted wide-leg trousers.

As more women join the workforce and dominate the industry, they are continuously seeking professional attire with a fashionable twist. Zara has also designed more affordable female power suits, allowing this trend to be even more accessible in the market.

This movement has also been making headlines in the Middle East. A Saudi Arabian designer, Arwa Al Banawi was inspired by female empowerment for her Spring/Summer 2020 collection titled "A'Lasafar", which included boxy suits and pop-color trench coats. Al Banawi chose the theme of travel as a reflection of independence and its relation to making your own decisions while navigating through life.[52]

Computer Wearables and Smart Textiles

It is an understatement to claim that technology plays an increasingly important role in our lives. We have even started to witness its gradual integration into the fashion industry. The **wearables** industry, which includes smart watches, is expected to reach $27 billion by 2022.[53]

Many fashion brands, including luxury brands, have taken advantage of this trend and have worked hard in order to appeal to a new tech-savvy generation. Think for example of the Louis Vuitton Tambour Horizon smart watch. The watch's leather strap features the brand's famous Monogram as a default band. In order to make it more versatile and convenient to different consumers' lifestyles and outfits, the luxury giant launched a variety of straps that match diversified tastes and budgets. But most importantly, all of these luxury timepieces are fully-loaded to provide the user with fitness tracking, world clock and alerts for text and emails.[54] Fossil, another fashion brand, has also created a smart watch that combines both style and technology.

A number of collaborations have also been established between luxury brands and tech companies. For instance, Apple and Hermès announced a partnership for a smart watch with a selection of elegant bands.[55] Another noteworthy collaboration took place between Tory Burch and Fitbit. The collection included silicone and metal bracelets with Tory Burch's signature print and colors, which can be paired with the Fitbit Flex activity device.[56] These partnerships have given high-tech companies the chance to penetrate the fashion and luxury market and appeal to a whole new target audience, thus increasing the future growth of this market.

But the fusion between fashion and technology goes well beyond watches. Aesthetic **smart textiles** include materials that can light up or change color by responding to energy from the atmosphere in the form of vibrations, sound and heat.[57] For example, Rainbow Winters used photochromic materials that change colors in the sunlight. Are you ready to wear their Petal Dress which changes color from pink to purple when exposed to the sun?[58]

Performance-enhancing smart textiles are used primarily in the athletic and military industries. Such materials have the ability to control body temperature, decrease wind resistance and regulate muscle vibration. Sports fashion brands like Stella McCartney for Adidas have designed workout gear from fast-drying textiles that keep athletes cool and dry during high temperatures.[59] Other sports brands such as Nike and Puma relied on smart textiles to create shoes with an advanced power-lacing system.[60] Athletes wearing the shoes can control and customize the fit either by manually touching the shoe or through the brand's mobile application.

One of the latest developments in smart textiles is microencapsulated fabrics. **Microencapsulation** involves a procedure whereby small active substances or droplets are bounded by a coating to provide small capsules, of countless useful characteristics.[61] This process has been used in sportswear for the sake of removing bacteria from apparel. The technique obstructs the cell walls of the bacteria and make them starve, therefore keeping apparel fresh and hygienic.[62]

Anti-Materialism and Sustainability

Before we talk about fashion as a massively profitable business, we have to recognize that at its core, fashion is all about people and the cultures in which they live. Two of these effects relate to 1. The widespread use of "luxury" brands as status symbols; and 2. The wide availability of relatively inexpensive fashion products and the social pressures that encourage consumers to constantly replace their inventories in order to be *au courant*.

Certainly, social media have contributed to the need for constant, new stimulation. Platforms like Instagram, some argue, have a detrimental effect on the fashion landscape because they encourage a throwaway fast fashion culture, where people feel the need to constantly alter their outfits in order to post the coolest selfies.[63] The fast fashion movement has been both a blessing and a curse: it slakes our thirst for constantly new, affordable items but at the same time it encourages us to dispose of them very quickly to the detriment of the environment.

The two fashion giants Zara and H&M are the leaders of the fast fashion movement. These companies improved their revenues by manufacturing cheap apparel in high quantities while continuously providing innovative items. Recently, a movement known as "**slow fashion**" that we discussed in Chapter 2 has risen to oppose the fast fashion mentality. This label refers to the process of finding sustainable fashion solutions, developed through changing the design, manufacturing, consumption, use and reuse tactics that develop alongside the overall fashion system and pose a possible threat to it.[64]

The movement is backed up by the new values of Millennials. Millennials, individuals born between 1981 and 1996, represent the biggest percentage of the world's population and display dissimilar traits compared to other generational cohorts. They progressively defend their beliefs regarding their consumption practices, selecting brands that are associated with their values and eschewing those that do not.[65] Millennials are dedicated to fulfilling Sustainable Development Goals (SDGs), such as gender equality, climate change, peace, justice, and poverty. They have distinctive consumption fashions that make SDGs objectives more achievable.[66]

One way to support sustainability is through the adoption of the **sharing economy**, a movement that has developed very fast. New technologies create platforms for different online marketplaces that enable consumers to "borrow" (i.e., rent) outfits from specialized companies like Rent the Runway or in some cases to exchange their used clothing for other people's castoffs (e.g, the "swishing party" is a popular social activity that facilitates this sharing process).

Think about it: now you can hire an electric scooter with Lime, rent a spare room or a luxury villa with Airbnb, rent an evening dress from Rent-the-Runway, borrow an item from H&M, or get a ride with Uber. Will this trend spell the end of ownership? Are we ever going to reach the point where we all just "lease" our clothes instead of buying, storing and then disposing of them?

Apart from the fast fashion and slow fashion movements, the way individuals consume or want to consume luxury today is different. Luxury consumers are becoming more and more demanding, and they are not being simply fascinated by "shiny baubles" as they used to be in the past.[67] For this reason, luxury brands are changing their strategies in order to meet the new market trends by promoting **"alpha" growth**, which is the capability to develop quicker than competitors. Think of how the luxury Group LVMH has been collaborating with a number of mass brands. For example, Louis Vuitton, the world's most valuable luxury brand, has collaborated with the brand Supreme by launching a capsule collection of clothing, leather goods, accessories and jewelry. Lately, the brand announced its first-time collaboration with a sport; the NBA (National Basketball Association).

The priorities of Millennials appear to have changed: they are mostly interested in experiences more than possessions. So, for them, instead of buying cars, apartments or luxury jewelry, they are tending to invest more in forming experiences by engaging in activities like traveling, cooking, and attending music festivals. For this reason, some luxury fashion brands are trying to appeal to new audiences in different ways by diversifying their businesses and creating novel experiences for customers. Think of the Blue Box Cafe that was launched by Tiffany & Co in order to increase foot traffic for example. Or, what about Le Café V by Louis Vuitton in Japan, Vivienne Westwood café in Shanghai; House of Dior by Pierre Hermé in Tokyo, the Emporio Armani caffè and ristorante in Milan, or the Gucci Osteria in Florence?

Exploring all the strategies that prominent fashion brands are designing, we need to understand that if a fashion brand wants to remain in the market, it should completely adapt to all changes in market trends and shifts in consumer behavior. Like any good marketing organization, a fashion brand cannot rest on its laurels; it has to constantly innovate and stay on top of important changes in values and preferences. As we said earlier, the only constant in fashion is change!

Chapter Summary

Now that you have read the chapter, you should understand the following:

1. What are the different theories of fashion?

Fashion tends to be adopted by many people simultaneously in a process known as collective selection. Perspectives on motivations for adopting new styles include psychological, economic, and sociological models of fashion. Psychological theories explain the reason why individuals are motivated to adopt fashion styles by referring to conformity, variety seeking, personal creativity, and sexual attraction. Economist theories view fashion in terms of a model of supply and demand. Items that are in limited supply have high value, while those readily available are less desirable. Finally, the sociological model of fashion explains the motivations to adopt fashion from the perspective of the individuals and groups impact on forming symbolic meanings and assigning those connotations to cultural goods.

2. What is the cultural production process?

The styles prevalent in a culture at any point in time often reflect underlying social and political conditions. The set of agents responsible for creating stylistic alternatives is termed as a culture production system. Factors such as the type of people involved in the system and the amount of competition by alternative product forms influence the choices of styles that eventually make their way to the marketplace for consideration by end consumers. An important gatekeeper in the fashion industry are blogs that provide positive and negative reviews of designers' works.

3. What is the state of fashion today?

Paris, London, Milan and New York have been known as the main fashion hubs or capitals. Every single year, one of those cities takes precedence over the others and steals the number one ranking spot among the traditional fashion capitals. While these cities do hold the spots for the big four fashion capitals, this does not mean that there is no room for other cities around the world to be referred to as fashion hubs. The list of cities who have made progressive changes in the fashion industry is very long and includes Tokyo, Shanghai, Barcelona, Sao Paulo, Berlin, and Saint Petersburg.

4. What are the major drivers of fashion today?

Given the major shift in consumer markets toward emerging trends, there are new major drivers that affect the fashion world today. For instance, fashion companies need to start looking into the new emerging market trends such as gender-neutral fashion, modest fashion, diversity and inclusivity, anti-materialism, computer wearables and smart textiles, as well as women's empowerment.

DISCUSSION QUESTIONS

1. Choose a cultural product, such as music or one you are familiar with, and identify the components of the culture production system including the creative subsystem, managerial subsystem and communications subsystem.

2. What is the difference between the sociological and the economic theory of fashion? Provide examples.

3. Which city do you think will earn the title of "a fashion capital" and potentially overthrow one of the main four fashion capitals?

4. What do you think is the future of fashion shows after the pandemic?

5. How important do you think is modesty when it comes to fashion selection? What are the elements that may impact this selection? Do you believe that there is an international market for modest apparel?

6. How important is diversity in fashion? Explain your answer.

EXERCISES

1. A meme propagates itself as a unit of cultural evolution. Can you identify additional memes other than the ones the chapter discusses?

2. Form a group and identify additional drivers of fashion from the ones described in the chapter. How can fashion marketers benefit from these market shifts?

3. Go online and read some reports on changing market trends due to Covid-19. Choose a fashion brand and discuss how it can keep up with the shifting trends, and respond to new needs.

4. In groups, select a fashion brand from any product category. As fashion marketers, identify the strategies you would apply to make sure that everyone feels included.

CASE STUDY: RIHANNA, FENTY AND THE EMERGENCE OF INCLUSIVE LUXURY

Nacima Ourahmoune, KEDGE Business School

The fashion line Fenty was created by the singer Rihanna in partnership with LVMH in 2019—the top French multinational luxury goods conglomerate headquartered in Paris. This has attracted much attention from the public and from the industry.

This event was perceived as important because it deconstructs many mottos of luxury marketing management practically and symbolically.

First, luxury conglomerates build on heritage versus new houses as a barrier for new entrants. This also represents a limitation for luxury conglomerates bound to search for brands to revitalize. Second, to ensure control over profitability and attract the most charismatic designer, luxury houses two powerful figures, the designer and CEO versus the classic model where power is concentrated in one person: the founder/designer/CEO. For instance, if Marc Jacobs was offered to join the LVMH group to expand his label, he is not the CEO. Rihanna in this case was presented by Arnaut and in the media as both CEO and designer, stressing her business skills. Third, as a human brand, Rihanna is a worldwide celebrity and a digital influencer, the model is reversed as it is likely that LVMH is willing to learn how to maximize a digital presence for their portfolio. Fourth, as many mentioned, Rihanna has become the first woman to create an original brand with LVMH. She is also the first woman of color.

The focus of this case study will be on diversity aspects and the birth of an oxymoron: inclusive luxury. Many brands struggle to resonate authentically with consumers in the digital era. Luxury brands are also pressured to address causes critical for consumers like gender, racial and social justice. This is particularly salient after the spread of global social movements such as #MeToo, Time's Up, or Black Lives Matter.

Especially Millennials and Generation Z are becoming key targets for luxury and they do challenge the traditional concepts of luxury founded on exclusion, European taste regimes, or the American idea of self-reward as defined by white elites. Rihanna's biography and vision of the Fenty brand as an 'extension of herself' reconciles fashion and diversity, feminism and racial justice ideals through what has been recently coined inclusive luxury.

To understand this oxymoron—inclusive luxury—we will first introduce Rihanna, second explain the concept of Fenty the fashion house and why it is relevant to diversity, and third we will illustrate the success and embodiment of the inclusive luxury concept through the cosmetic line Fenty Beauty and the Fenty Savage lingerie.

Who is Rihanna?

Robyn Rihanna Fenty, known as Rihanna, was born in 1988 in Barbados (Caribbean). Her "Good Girl Gone Bad" album and the hit "Umbrella" made her an international star in 2007. A series of hits followed. In her ten-year-career Rihanna has surpassed 60 million albums sold world-wide and 210 million singles, she has many distinctions like the Grammy Awards and is one of the most influential celebrities online with over 90 million followers on social media.

Very committed—Rihanna notably created the Clara Lionel Foundation, for the development of education and health among the most disadvantaged—Rihanna was elected "Humanitarian of the Year" in March 2017 by Harvard University. After collaborations with Armani in 2011 and the London Fashion Week in 2013, Rihanna emerged as an impressively successful Creative Director/Brand Ambassador for Puma. In the media, Rihanna is depicted as a strong black woman or an "island woman", a committed feminist especially referring to her experience of gender-based violence, an artist with a strong personality, and a shrewd businesswoman.

Fenty at LVMH: the first black woman head of a luxury *maison*

By building this 360-degree fashion project around Rihanna, since Fenty will offer ready-to-wear, shoes and accessories, LVMH hoped to capitalize on the singer's power of influence and to repeat the success she has carried out so far. From magazine covers to socks, everything Rihanna touches turns to gold. Puma, Stance, Manolo Blahnik, but also Dior (an important brand in LVMH's portfolio) and the Fenty cosmetic line distributed by Sephora (LVMH) proved Rihanna's vision to be successful in different areas.

With the appointment of Virgil Abloh as artistic director of the men's collections of Louis Vuitton, the only black designer to date at the head of a global luxury brand, LVMH had already taken a step in favour of diversity and openness. With Rihanna, the group is projected into the market of the future, drawing closer to communities and other cultural universes as well as to an ever-younger clientele.

Black in an industry where white men dominate, she is also young, she is new to the family, she is not trained in a prestigious fashion/design school or university, but what makes Rihanna

(Continued)

special in the eye of the consumer is that she is unapologetic. She turns all these elements into resources to break the dominant luxury code with an authentic will to make inclusion matter. The first Fenty release draws inspiration from the 1960s Black-is-beautiful movement elevating the aesthetics of the culture of Harlem's African-American community to a suitable heritage to express luxury today.

Rihanna embodies this new ideal to perfection. She has consistently valued her diversity, drawing millions of fans in her wake. Moreover, her personality, her strengths, but also her grey areas only made the pop star more authentic and credible to the public, more "human" and more relatable. Unfortunately, in February 2021, LVMH and Rihanna have agreed to suspend the fashion line Fenty less than two years after its launch. The coronavirus had negative impact on fashion and further examination of the failure is needed. According to the statement, the goal is to support the Fenty ecosystem, focusing on lingerie, cosmetics and skincare.

Fenty beauty and Fenty Savage underwear: Radical inclusion

Rihanna did shake the beauty industry as she launched a cosmetic line in 2017 with a foundation line that extends to 40 skin tones (now 50). Immediately, this innovation became successful and set an obligation for competitors to enlarge their assortments. She marked the field with a bold positioning. To come up with this idea of 40 shades to be launched at the same day and time around the world for all women, Rihanna explained she realized there was a sort of tax for girls with specific needs or darker skins to find the right product. She wanted girls with darker skin not to pay higher prices than white girls. She also did not want girls with very fair skin or any other skin condition to feel this is only good "on the model", not for them. Identifying these gaps, she really addressed a need in the market. She also signaled luxury as a positioning through the collaboration with Sephora, but the price tag that was lower than the top luxury brands ensured also a message of inclusiveness regarding socioeconomic aspects. Results: in the first year, the Fenty Beauty brand experienced the best beauty launch in YouTube history. It has generated huge commercial success and was among the top 25 inventions of 2017, according to the *Time Magazine*.

The next project of radical inclusion by Rihanna went through 'fentifying' lingerie, a sector hit hard by #MeToo and traversed by a demand from consumers for more meaningful body-positivity, more ethnic and sexual diversity. This is at odds with the previously successful Victoria's Secret shows visible in 192 countries that drew inspiration from sexualized empowerment limited to white skinny models... Instead, Fenty x Savage is about radical inclusion. It succeeds where many fashion brands fail because it promotes political connotations of empowerment that resonate with consumers. In the era of woke marketing, Fenty x Savage's show and brand imagery presents a festival of all kind of flesh and skin tones, life stages (pregnancy) and sexual identities. The public and commentators most often note the authentic take on diversity. It is not staged as a stereotype imposed trick to please consumers; it is imbued with both the experience of Rihanna as a Caribbean aware of colorism issues, but also her willingness to see every person embrace their sexuality, no matter their body type. Also, Rihanna has the power to provoke and she is using it. Fenty Savage displays an extension of the icon's fearless and confident personality to empower others.

To conclude, the luxury market has lagged behind in embracing the conversations around diversity, inclusivity and meaningful body-positivity. Rihanna's inclusive vision of luxury is radical and efficient in times of political movements, which are key to fashion consumers' identity construction.

DISCUSSION QUESTIONS

1. How is the Rihanna/LVMH agreement changing the usual luxury business model?

2. Which elements of Rihanna's biography feed the concept of the brand Fenty?

3. Why is Rihanna's radical vision of inclusion successful, both in the beauty and lingerie line?

POTENTIAL LARGER DISCUSSION

1. Discuss how today, conversations around diversity and branding are met with skepticism just like unsubstantiated ecological claims made by brands 10 years ago lead to green washing.

NOTES

1. Snyder, C.R. and Fromkin, H.L. (2012) *Uniqueness: The Human Pursuit of Difference.* Berlin: Springer.
2. Choi, J. and Kim, S. (2016) 'Is the smartwatch an IT product or a fashion product? A study on factors affecting the intention to use smartwatches', *Computers in Human Behavior*, 63: 777–86.

   Latter, C., Phau, I. and Marchegiani, C. (2010) 'The roles of consumers need for uniqueness and status consumption in haute couture luxury brands', *Journal of Global Fashion Marketing*, 1 (4): 206–14.
3. Dyett, L. (1996) 'Desperately seeking skin.', *Psychology Today.* www.psychologytoday.com/gb/articles/199605/desperately-seeking-skin (accessed August 9, 2021).
4. Adams, R.D. and McCormick, K. (1992) 'Fashion dynamics and the economic theory of clubs', *Review of Social Economy*, 50 (1): 24–39.

   Coelho, P.R. and McClure, J.E. (1993) 'Toward an economic theory of fashion', *Economic Inquiry*, 31 (4): 595–608.
5. Bagwell, L.S. and Bernheim, B.D. (1996) 'Veblen effects in a theory of conspicuous consumption', *The American Economic Review*, 86 (3): 349–73.

   Fassnacht, M. and Dahm, J.M. (2018) 'The Veblen effect and (in) conspicuous consumption—a state of the art article', *Luxury Research Journal*, 1 (4): 343–71.

Kastanakis, M. and Balabanis, G. (2011) 'Bandwagon, snob and Veblen effects in luxury consumption', *ACR North American Advances*, 38: 609–11.

Veblen, T. (2005 [1899]) *The Theory of the Leisure Class: An Economic Study of Institutions*. Delhi: Aakar Books.

Woodside, A.G. (2012) 'Economic psychology and fashion marketing theory appraising Veblen's theory of conspicuous consumption', *Journal of Global Fashion Marketing*, 3 (2): 55–60.

6. Leibenstein, H. (1976) *Beyond Economic Man*. Boston, MA: Harvard University Press.

7. Atik, D. and Fırat, A.F. (2013) 'Fashion creation and diffusion: The institution of marketing', *Journal of Marketing Management*, 29 (7–8): 836–60.

    Bonenberg, W. (2015) 'The trickle-up fashion effect in forecasting new trends in architecture', *Procedia Manufacturing*, 3: 1611–17.

    Law, K.M., Zhang, Z.M. and Leung, C.S. (2004) 'Fashion change and fashion consumption: The chaotic perspective', *Journal of Fashion Marketing and Management: An International Journal*, 8 (4): 362–74.

8. McCracken, G. (1986) 'Culture and consumption: A theoretical account of the structure and movement of the cultural meaning of consumer goods', *Journal of Consumer Research*, 13 (1): 71–84.

9. Giesler, M. (2008) 'Conflict and compromise: Drama in marketplace evolution', *Journal of Consumer Research*, 34 (6): 739–53.

    Hirschman, E.C. (1990) 'Resource exchange in the production and distribution of a motion picture', *Empirical Studies of the Arts*, 8 (1): 31–51.

    Peterson, R.A. (1976) 'The production of culture: A prolegomenon', *American Behavioral Scientist*, 19 (6): 669–84.

    Solomon, M.R. (1988) 'Building up and breaking down: The impact of cultural sorting on symbolic consumption', *Research in Consumer Behavior*, 3 (2): 325–51.

    Peñaloza, L. (2001) 'Consuming the American West: Animating cultural meaning and memory at a stock show and rodeo', *Journal of Consumer Research*, 28 (3): 369–98.

10. Ferrier, M. (2019) 'What does it meme? The rise and rise of the fashion viral', *The Guardian*, February 16. www.theguardian.com/fashion/2019/feb/16/what-does-it-meme-the-rise-and-rise-of-the-fashion-viral (accessed August 9, 2021).

11. Dawkins, R. (1999) 'The selfish meme', *Time*, 153 (15): 52–53.

    Laurent, J. (1999) 'A Note on the Origin of "Memes"/"Mnemes". *Journal of Memetics*, 3 (1): 20–1.

12. Gladwell, M. (2006) *The Tipping Point: How Little Things Can Make a Big Difference*. New York, NY: Little, Brown.

13. Ferrier, M. (2019) 'What does it meme? The rise and rise of the fashion viral', *The Guardian*, February 16. www.theguardian.com/fashion/2019/feb/16/what-does-it-meme-the-rise-and-rise-of-the-fashion-viral (accessed August 9, 2021).

14. Lee, S.H. and Workman, J.E. (2021) 'Trendsetting and gender matter: Brand loyalty, perceived quality, and word-of-mouth', *Journal of Global Fashion Marketing*, 12 (1): 16–31.

    Beaudoin, P., Moore, M.A. and Goldsmith, R.E. (1998) 'Young fashion leaders' and followers' attitudes toward American and imported apparel', *Journal of Product & Brand Management*, 7 (3): 193–207.

15. Vogue Editorial Team (2018) 'Everything you need to know about Kim Kardashian's KKW Beauty line', *Vogue France*, February 14. www.vogue.fr/beauty-tips/on-trend/story/everything-you-need-to-know-about-kim-kardashians-kkw-beauty-line/1153 (accessed August 9, 2021).

16. Beaudoin, P., Moore, M.A. and Goldsmith, R.E. (1998) 'Young fashion leaders' and followers' attitudes toward American and imported apparel', *Journal of Product & Brand Management*, 7 (3): 193–207.

17. Makkar, M.and Yap, S.F. (2018) 'The anatomy of the inconspicuous luxury fashion experience', *Journal of Fashion Marketing and Management: An International Journal*, 22 (1): 129–56.

18. Khurana, P. and Sethi, M. (2007) *Introduction to Fashion Technology*. New Delhi: Firewall Media.

19. Fashionating World (2020) 'New York named "top global fashion capital of the decade"', *Fashionating World*, February 10. www.fashionatingworld.com/new1-2/new-york-named-top-global-fashion-capital-of-the-decade (accessed August 9, 2021).

20. Fashion Schools Staff (2021) 'Top 10 global fashion capitals', *Fashion Schools*. www.fashion-schools.org/articles/top-10-global-fashion-capitals (accessed August 9, 2021).

    Forster, M. (2019) 'Fashion today: Top 5 fashion capitals of the world', *Tydlos*, August 16. https://tydlos.com/blogs/news/fashion-today-top-5-fashion-capitals-of-the-world (accessed August 9, 2021).

21. Fashion Schools Staff (2021) 'Top 10 global fashion capitals', *Fashion Schools*. www.fashion-schools.org/articles/top-10-global-fashion-capitals (accessed August 9, 2021).

Forster, M. (2019) 'Fashion today: Top 5 fashion capitals of the world', *Tydlos*, August 16. https://tydlos.com/blogs/news/fashion-today-top-5-fashion-capitals-of-the-world (accessed August 9, 2021).

22. Fashion Schools Staff (2021) 'Top 10 global fashion capitals', *Fashion Schools*. www.fashion-schools.org/articles/top-10-global-fashion-capitals (accessed August 9, 2021).

Forster, M. (2019) 'Fashion today: Top 5 fashion capitals of the world', *Tydlos*, August 16. https://tydlos.com/blogs/news/fashion-today-top-5-fashion-capitals-of-the-world (accessed August 9, 2021).

23. Fashion Schools Staff (2021) 'Top 10 global fashion capitals', *Fashion Schools*. www.fashion-schools.org/articles/top-10-global-fashion-capitals (accessed August 9, 2021).

Forster, M. (2019) 'Fashion today: Top 5 fashion capitals of the world', *Tydlos*, August 16. https://tydlos.com/blogs/news/fashion-today-top-5-fashion-capitals-of-the-world (accessed August 9, 2021).

24. Alyaka (2019) 'The emerging beauty and fashion capitals of the world', *Alyaka*, April 4. www.alyaka.com/magazine/emerging-beauty-fashion-capitals-world/ (accessed August 9, 2021).

25. Fashion Schools Staff (2021) 'Top 10 global fashion capitals', *Fashion Schools*. www.fashion-schools.org/articles/top-10-global-fashion-capitals (accessed August 9, 2021).

Forster, M. (2019) 'Fashion today: Top 5 fashion capitals of the world', *Tydlos*, August 16. https://tydlos.com/blogs/news/fashion-today-top-5-fashion-capitals-of-the-world (accessed August 9, 2021).

26. Fashion Schools Staff (2021) 'Top 10 global fashion capitals', *Fashion Schools*. www.fashion-schools.org/articles/top-10-global-fashion-capitals (accessed August 9, 2021).

Forster, M. (2019) 'Fashion today: Top 5 fashion capitals of the world', *Tydlos*, August 16. https://tydlos.com/blogs/news/fashion-today-top-5-fashion-capitals-of-the-world (accessed August 9, 2021).

27. Kent, S. (2020) 'How Copenhagen became fashion's sustainability capital', *Business of Fashion*, January 28. www.businessoffashion.com/articles/sustainability/how-copenhagen-became-fashions-sustainability-capital (accessed August 9, 2021).

28. Rabimov, S. (2015) 'Will Kyiv become a global fashion capital', *Forbes*, June 19. www.forbes.com/sites/forbesinternational/2015/06/19/will-kyiv-become-a-global-fashion-capital/?sh=49486d2d1a4f (accessed August 9, 2021).

29. Salam, M. (2019) 'Finding clothes, and identity, outside men's and women's wear', *The New York Times*, February 19. www.nytimes.com/2019/02/19/style/gender-neutral-clothing.html (accessed August 9, 2021).

30. Salam, M. (2019) 'Finding clothes, and identity, outside men's and women's wear', *The New York Times*, February 19. www.nytimes.com/2019/02/19/style/gender-neutral-clothing.html (accessed August 9, 2021).

31. (2019) 'The decline of gendered retail spaces', *Business of Fashion*, December 6. www.businessoffashion.com/articles/news-analysis/someday-there-might-not-be-a-menswear-department (accessed August 9, 2021).

32. Harper's Bazaar (2020) 'Beyoncé's new Ivy Park x Adidas gender-neutral collection is here', *Harper's Bazaar*, January 18. www.harpersbazaar.com/uk/fashion/fashion-news/a30575175/beyonce-ivy-park-adidas-collection-gender-neutral/ (accessed August 9, 2021).

33. Sanicola, L. (2018) 'Abercrombie is rolling out gender-neutral children's clothes', *CNN Business*, January 18. https://money.cnn.com/2018/01/18/news/companies/abercrombie-gender-neutral/index.html (accessed August 9, 2021).

34. Hosie, R. (2017) 'John Lewis gets rid of "Boys" and "Girls" labels in children's clothing', *The Independent*, September 2. www.independent.co.uk/life-style/john-lewis-boys-girls-clothing-labels-gender-neutral-unisex-children-a7925336.html (accessed August 9, 2021).

35. Adewunmi, B. (2011) 'Women faith-based fashion takes off online', *The Guardian*, June 16. www.theguardian.com/lifeandstyle/2011/jun/16/faith-based-fashion-online (accessed August 9, 2021).

36. Lawton, M. (2019) 'Modest fashion: "I feel confident and comfortable"', *BBC News*, November 13. www.bbc.com/news/newsbeat-50067975 (accessed August 9, 2021).

37. Weinswig, D. (2017) 'Is modest fashion the next big thing?', *Forbes*, March 31. www.forbes.com/sites/deborahweinswig/2017/03/31/is-modest-fashion-the-next-big-thing/?sh=6ca3fcb99e97 (accessed August 9, 2021).

38. Business of Fashion (2018) 'Op-Ed, the muslim fashion market is not a monolith', *Business of Fashion*, February 3. www.businessoffashion.com/opinions/news-analysis/op-ed-the-muslim-fashion-market-is-not-a-monolith (accessed August 9, 2021).

39. Dawling, E. (2018) 'The sports hijab dividing opinion', BBC, January 10. www.bbc.com/culture/article/20180110-the-sports-hijab-dividing-opinions (accessed August 9, 2021).

40. Alleyne, A. (2016) 'Dolce & Gabbana debuts line of hijabs and abayas', CNN *Style*, August 26. https://edition.cnn.com/style/article/dolce-gabbana-muslim-hijab-abaya/index.html (accessed August 9, 2021).

41. Business of Fashion Team & Mckinsey (2020) 'The year ahead: The business of inclusivity', *Business of Fashion*, January 2. www.businessoffashion.com/articles/news-analysis/the-year-ahead-the-business-of-inclusivity (accessed August 9, 2021).

42. Rasool, A. (2018) 'What Virgil Abloh's new appointment really means for black designers', *Teen Vogue*, March 27. www.teenvogue.com/story/virgil-abloh-louis-vuitton-black-designers (accessed August 9, 2021).

43. BBC News (2018) 'Halsey criticises Victoria's Secret over transgender comments', *BBC News*, December 3. www.bbc.com/news/newsbeat-46423671 (accessed August 9, 2021).

44. Carras, C. (2019) 'Valentina Sampaio makes history as first transgender Victoria's Secret model', *Los Angeles Times*, August 5. www.latimes.com/entertainment-arts/story/2019-08-05/victorias-secret-transgender-model-valentina-sampaio (accessed August 9, 2021).

45. Lieber, C. (2020) 'H&M's global leader for inclusion and diversity on the company's next steps', *Business of Fashion*, January 14. www.businessoffashion.com/articles/workplace-talent/hms-global-leader-for-inclusion-and-diversity-on-the-companys-next-steps (accessed August 9, 2021).

46. Chua, J.M. (2019) 'Why fashion needs chief diversity officers', *Vogue Business Talent*, November 21. www.voguebusiness.com/talent/articles/chief-diversity-officers-inclusion-burberry-gucci-hm/ (accessed August 9, 2021).

47. Ly, L. (2018) 'Prada pulls products after accusations of blackface imagery', *CNN Style*, December 15. https://edition.cnn.com/style/article/prada-pulls-products-blackface-imagery/index.html (accessed August 9, 2021).

48. Xu, Y. (2018) 'Dolce & Gabbana ad (with chopsticks) provokes public outrage in China', *NPR*, December, 1. https://www.npr.org/sections/goatsandsoda/2018/12/01/671891818/dolce-gabbana-ad-with-chopsticks-provokes-public-outrage-in-china (accessed August 9, 2021).

49. Larbi, M. (2018) 'ASOS is selling clothes specially designed for people with disabilities', *Metro*, July 4. https://metro.co.uk/2018/07/04/asos-selling-clothes-specially-designed-people-disabilities-7683519/ (accessed August 9, 2021).

50. Business of Fashion Team & Mckinsey (2020) 'The year ahead: The business of inclusivity', *Business of Fashion*, January 2. www.businessoffashion.com/articles/news-analysis/the-year-ahead-the-business-of-inclusivity (accessed August 9, 2021).

51. Business of Fashion Team (2014) 'Tory Burch: A culture of women's empowerment', *Business of Fashion*, May 20. www.businessoffashion.com/articles/workplace-talent/tory-burch-culture-womens-empowerment (accessed August 9, 2021).

52. Sunilkumar, K. (2020) 'Exclusive: Arwa Al Banawi's S/S20 collection celebrates female empowerment', *Harper's Bazaar Arabia*, March 16. www.harpersbazaararabia.com/fashion/featured-news/interview-with-saudi-arabian-star-designer-arwa-al-banawi (accessed August 9, 2021).

53. Lamkin, P. (2018) 'Smart wearables market to double by 2022: $27 billion industry forecast', *Forbes*, October 23. www.forbes.com/sites/paullamkin/2018/10/23/smart-wearables-market-to-double-by-2022-27-billion-industry-forecast/?sh=2bccbc9b2656 (accessed August 9, 2021).

54. Stafford, T. (2017) 'Louis Vuitton's first smartwatch has the one thing most other smartwatches don't', *GQ*, August 3. www.gq.com/story/louis-vuitton-tambour-horizon-smartwatch-review (accessed August 9, 2021).

55. Huen, E. (2015) 'What the Apple Watch Hermès tells us about the future of tech and luxury', *Forbes*, September 17. www.forbes.com/sites/eustaciahuen/2015/09/17/what-the-apple-watch-hermes-tells-us-about-the-future-of-tech-and-luxury/?sh=7606a402b228 (accessed August 9, 2021).

56. Levy, K. (2014) 'For $195, your Fitbit flex can look like a fancy piece of jewelry', *Business Insider*, July 16. www.businessinsider.com/tory-burch-fitbit-2014-7 (accessed August 9, 2021).

57. Castano, L.M. and Flatau, A.B. (2014) 'Smart fabric sensors and e-textile technologies: A review', *Smart Materials and Structures*, 23 (5): article #053001.

58. Winters, R. (2013) 'Chromic phenomena – colour and light manipulation in materials inspired by nature', *Hello Materials Blog*, May 13. https://hellomaterialsblog.wordpress.com/2013/05/13/chromic-phenomena-colour-and-light-manipulation-in-materials-inspired-by-nature/ (accessed August 9, 2021).

59. Fitzgerald, B. (2015) *5 fashion labels using smart textiles in activewear. SynZenBe,* May 14. www.synzenbe. com/blog/5-fashion-labels-using-smart-textiles-in-activewear-510/510 (accessed August 9, 2021).

60. Newcomb, T. (2019) 'Nike debuts self-fitting smart-sneaker technology as business model of future', *Forbes,* January 15. www.forbes.com/sites/timnewcomb/2019/01/15/nike-debuts-self-fitting-smart-sneaker-technology-as-business-model-of-future/?sh=6bd911a51c9b (accessed August 9, 2021).

61. Fu, F. and Hu, L. (2017) 'Temperature sensitive colour-changed composites', in M. Fan and F. Fu (eds), *Advanced High Strength Natural Fibre Composites in Construction.* Kidlington: Woodhead Publishing. pp. 405–23.

62. Winters, R. (2013) 'Chromic phenomena – colour and light manipulation in materials inspired by nature', *Hello Materials Blog,* May 13. https://hellomaterialsblog.wordpress.com/2013/05/13/chromic-phenomena-colour-and-light-manipulation-in-materials-inspired-by-nature/ (accessed August 9, 2021).

63. Halliday, S. (2018) 'Social media fuels fast fashion throwaway culture – survey', *Fashion Network,* October 9. https://uk.fashionnetwork.com/news/Social-media-fuels-fast-fashion-throwaway-culture-survey,1022355.html (accessed October 17, 2021).

64. Clark, H. (2008) 'SLOW+ FASHION—an Oxymoron—or a Promise for the Future…?', *Fashion Theory,* 12 (4): 427–46.

65. Amed, I., Balchandani, A., Beltrami, M., Berg, A., Hedrich, S. and Rölkens, F. (2019) *The influence of 'woke' consumers on fashion.* Mckinsey & Company, February 12. www.mckinsey.com/industries/retail/our-insights/the-influence-of-woke-consumers-on-fashion (accessed August 9, 2021).

66. Cheng, M. (2019) '8 characteristics of millennials that support sustainable development goals (SDGs)', *Forbes,* June 19. www.forbes.com/sites/margueritacheng/2019/06/19/8-characteristics-of-millennials-that-support-sustainable-development-goals-sdgs/?sh=6202f06729b7 (accessed August 9, 2021).

67. Falk, N. (2018) 'What you need to know about changing luxury consumer trends for 2019', *Forbes,* December 31. www.forbes.com/sites/njgoldston/2018/12/31/what-you-need-to-know-about-changing-luxury-consumer-trends-for-2019/?sh=d9470725e9d4 (accessed August 9, 2021).

CHAPTER 4

Ethical and Sustainable Fashion

LEARNING OBJECTIVES

After you read this chapter, you will understand the answers to the following:

1. What are consumer and business ethics?

2. What is corporate social responsibility in fashion?

3. What is the dark side of consumer behavior?

Just as the Covid-19 pandemic destroyed many fashion businesses, in the years after the Global Recession of 2008 a lot of apparel companies were in dire straits. In the face of this crisis, one company actually prospered – and it did so by telling its customers *not* to buy its products! Patagonia made headlines in 2011 when the outdoor products company ran an ad that proclaimed, "Don't Buy This Jacket." The message bemoaned the environmental cost of producing one of its best-selling fleece jackets, and asked shoppers to think twice before they bought it rather than getting a used Patagonia product. Lo and behold: The company's revenues actually grew by 30% in the following year, and by 2017 Patagonia reached $1 billion in sales.

How did it do so well during tough times? One important reason is that the company doesn't just talk the talk on ethics and sustainability. It walks the walk by donating a portion of its revenues to environmental causes. It only uses recycled, Fair Trade certified and organic material, and it even powers its California HQ on solar energy.[1] In addition to this, even though they update their ranges seasonally, Patagonia position themselves as an apparel company rather than a fashion brand.

In the wake of the coronavirus pandemic, Patagonia was one of the first to shutter its store for health reasons, and sales plummeted. Nonetheless, the company maintained connections with its avid followers by offering a variety of online courses to help people weather the

(Continued)

storm such as yoga and gardening classes. Despite the hits that Patagonia took, its CEO claims that in the long-term Patagonia will benefit because the pandemic will encourage people to buy items that last. She says that the crisis has reminded people "...of the value of wild and open spaces and clean air and clean water and if we can channel that to some good, all is not lost."[2] Patagonia is one of the most notable companies that thrive on the maxim, "Doing well by doing good."

Consumer and Business Ethics

In business, conflicts often arise between the goal to succeed in the marketplace and the desire to maximize the well-being of consumers. Marketers wrestle with these questions all the time: how do I maintain a competitive edge while at the same time providing safe and effective products and services that meet my customers' needs and are beneficial (or at least not harmful) to society? Where is the social or moral line when producing, promoting, and selling products? Sometimes personal ethics clash with business ethics, which can be problematic for employees who feel that their company is not being ethical. And consumers are by no means perfect either; sometimes they do things that cross the line.

Do you think consumers are usually concerned about who made the shirt they are likely to buy? Or how much they got paid to make it? Or how much profit the company made from it? Certainly, awareness is growing about these concerns.[3] For example, at numerous universities around the world students are demonstrating against their university's role in selling sweatshop-made apparel in their campus store.[4]

Business and Personal Ethics: *Doing Well by Doing Good*

Business ethics are rules of conduct that guide what companies do in the marketplace—the principles most individuals in a culture view as being right, wrong, good or bad, socially acceptable or unacceptable.[5] **Personal ethics** are similar codes of conduct that guide our daily living as individuals.[6] These universal standards or values include honesty, trustworthiness, fairness, respect, justice, integrity, concern for others, accountability, loyalty, and responsible citizenship. However, while "everyone" supports these ideas, their definition of just what constitutes abstract values like fairness and integrity may differ.

Industry is increasingly coming to realize that ethical behavior is also good business in the long run, since the trust and satisfaction of consumers translate into years of loyalty from customers whose needs have been met. Consumers think better of products made by firms they feel behave ethically.[7] In fact, social responsibility regarding issues such as labor practices and environmental issues is now the most important criterion consumers use when they decide which companies to patronize.[8] That helps to explain why a lot of companies today try to follow a new mantra: *Doing well by doing good.*

Sometimes, ethical decisions can be costly for businesses in the short term when they result in lost revenue. For example, when Kim Kardashian launched her first fashion brand named Kimono, she faced a backlash from Japanese consumers over the use of the brand name. They accused her of **cultural appropriation**. Following this, Kim had to rename the brand "SKIMS".[9]

Whether purposely or not, some companies do infringe their pledge of trust with shoppers. Table 4.1 illustrates some unethical business conduct. Production of flammable apparel and of toys with an excessive amount of chemical plasticizers that may cause poisoning to kids, excessive price mark-up, exaggerated claims and deceptive ads illustrate examples of what some people feel are unethical business behaviors. In certain situations, these activities may be illegal, as when a firm intentionally mislabels the ingredients of a package or a company implements a "bait-and-switch" selling strategy, whereby shoppers are enticed into the store with promises of cheap items in order to make them convert to higher-priced products.

TABLE 4.1 Unethical business conduct

Product	Example
Safety	Production of flammable apparel
	Production of toys with an excessive amount of chemical plasticizers that may cause poisoning to kids
Poor-quality items	Items that cannot withstand ordinary wear and tear
Environmental pollution	Using polluting dyes and chemicals in apparel and fabric manufacture
Mislabeled products	Identifying the wrong fiber content or country of origin on apparel
Brand counterfeits	Counterfeit goods labeled and sold as the genuine brand
Price	
Excessive markups	High prices used by retailers to connote quality
Price comparisons	False original price for sale price to appear as a bargain
Promotion	
Exaggerated claims	Cosmetic ads claiming to change skin structure
Tasteless advertising	Sexual innuendos and gender disparagement
Deceptive advertising	Lose pounds with no diet or exercise
Captive audiences	Mandatory TV commercials for schools subscribing to closed channel newscasts

Ethical Pain Points for the Fashion Industry

Use of Fur and Exotic Skins

Some consumers feel strongly that the use of animal fur is not ethical or moral. The antifur movement has been the most visible arm of the **animal rights movement**. Up until the 1980s, fur was synonymous with luxury, signifying a status symbol for a lot of women. After many years of activists protesting the use of animal fur to decorate consumers in the form of fashion (and the protests still continue today),[10] there is a concurrent resurgence in the interest in using furs.[11]

Animal Rights Movement

Gustavo Pantano / Shutterstock.com

The early 1990s saw a low point for the fur industry; many consumers felt it was politically incorrect to wear fur, and fur salons in upper-end department stores closed. In 1994, Calvin Klein refrained from using fur in its collection, the year during which PETA launched a campaign including renowned top models such as Naomi Campbell, Claudia Schiffer, and Christy Turlington, who stated they would "rather go naked than wear fur".[12]

Over the last few years, animal rights activists were able to force quite a lot of high-end luxury labels to stop using fur. For instance, brands like Stella McCartney, Donna Karan/DKNY, Gucci, Michael Kors, Vivienne Westwood, Jimmy Choo, The Kooples, Donatella Versace, Burberry, Maison Margiela, Phillip Lim, Coach, DVF, and Prada have stopped using real fur in their collections.

In addition to the use of fur, consumers concerned about animal welfare are also calling upon companies to stop using exotic skins. In 2018, the luxury brand Chanel decided to ban the use of exotic skins (e.g., snakes, crocodilians, lizards and galuchat) given that it was hard for the company to find responsibly sourced skins.[13] In 2020, Selfridge's department store banned items such as watches, luggage and handbags that are produced from python, alligator, crocodile or other exotic animal skins. The retailer committed to only offer items with leather obtained from agricultural livestock.[14]

Animal Testing

Perfect365, a free make-up and beauty platform with more than 100 million users, conducted a cruelty-free beauty survey with 15,000. The results showed that 36% of the respondents will only purchase products from cruelty-free beauty brands.[15] Given this growing sentiment, it's not surprising that the industry is scrambling to make changes in its long-established practice of safety testing on animals before they launch their products.

Many companies have changed their policies over the past years to reassure consumers that they are adhering to rigorous cruelty-free standards. Already, the prominent retailers The Body Shop and Lush are "**cruelty-free**". And many renowned brands have announced bans on animal testing, such as Illamasqua, BareMinerals, Fenty Beauty, Charlotte Tilbury, Urban Decay, NYX Cosmetics, Marc Jacobs Beauty, and Anastasia Beverly Hills.[16] In addition, some governments are stepping up: bans on animal testing are now in effect in the European Union, India, and Norway.[17]

Estée Lauder stated that it was expanding its collaboration with the Humane Society International and entering into a new agreement with Cruelty Free International. These activities denote an important move towards animal welfare, as the company is considered one of the leaders in the beauty and cosmetic industry. With this, the Humane Society International promises to "bring an end to cosmetic testing on animals by 2023."[18]

Offensive Fashion Advertising and Products

Until the early 1960s, fashion magazines did not give advertising or editorial space to underwear because the items were too personal in nature and made consumers uncomfortable.[19] But as society's attitudes toward sexuality changed, so too did fashion advertising. A controversial 1980s campaign for Calvin Klein featured the actress Brooke Shields saying, "Nothing comes between me and my Calvins." That imagery may actually seem tame to some of us today, as standards of "decency" continue to evolve. Calvin Klein's overly sexualized advertising campaigns during the 1990s were denounced for encouraging sexual promiscuity, teenage sex, and anorexia.[20] In 2007, Tom Ford's for Men fragrance campaign was banned as one of its photos featured a bottle wedged between a female model's naked breasts.[21] However, attitudes towards offensiveness differ across regions and cultures,

as evidenced by attempts to export overly provocative fashion advertising imagery to conservative regions like the Middle East where they are typically not accepted.[22]

But standards appear to be moving in the opposite direction more recently, as women have begun to push back against overtly sexual advertising messages that they find objectionable. For example, American Apparel has long been known for its provocative and controversial campaigns, featuring young-looking models including pornographic actresses, such as Charlotte Stokely. In 2014, the British Advertising Standards Authority (BSA)

Estée Lauder partners with Humane Society International and commits to Cruelty-Free Testing
ARTFULLY PHOTOGRAPHER / Shutterstock.com

Karlie Kloss, the top model who left Victoria's Secret

"146030_13488" by Walt Disney Television is licensed under CC BY-ND 2.0

banned the company's advertising in the UK, stating that "We considered the images were gratuitous and objectified women, and were therefore sexist and likely to cause serious and widespread offence." Victoria's Secret in particular has seen its business suffer dramatically due to what many consider an outmoded view of female sexuality. In 2019, Karlie Kloss, the top model and previous Victoria's Secret Angel commented, "The reason I decided to stop working with Victoria's Secret was I didn't feel it was an image that was truly reflective of who I am and the kind of message I want to send to young women around the world about what it means to be beautiful."[23]

Why is sex so common in fashion advertising? The answer is twofold: 1. It quickly establishes a daring or cutting-edge image for a brand; and 2. It gets our attention. However, research shows that female nudity in ads generates negative feelings and tension among female consumers, so the tactic can be counterproductive.[24] And ironically, a provocative picture can be *too* effective; it can attract so much attention that it hinders processing and recall of the ad's contents. Sexual appeals appear to be ineffective when marketers use them merely as a "trick" to grab attention. They do get noticed—but many viewers don't recall what the ad was plugging![25]

Not only ads but sometimes products can be offensive to consumers. T-shirts with offensive sayings glorifying drunkenness or mocking minorities have prompted many complaints to companies such as Abercrombie & Fitch, Urban Outfitters and Topman among others.[26] Adidas and Prada were both forced to make an apology and remove items criticized as racist. The upsetting Prada product was a monkey keychain criticized as resembling blackface imagery.[27] As for Adidas, the offensive product was a white pair of shoes in a collection of apparel and sneakers inspired by the Harlem Renaissance movement, and aiming to pay tribute to Black History Month. One analyst described the product as "a swing and a miss".[28]

Consumer Data Privacy

We might remember 2018 as the Year of Privacy: The GDPR (General Data Protection Regulation) became official, California signed into law its Consumer Privacy Act, Equifax discovered a huge consumer data breach, and Facebook was discovered to be mismanaging personal data.[29] Under Armour, the athletic clothing producer—that acquired MyFitnessPal in 2015 for $475 million—also suffered from a massive data breach in 2018, with stolen information involving account usernames, email addresses and passwords for the MyFitnessPal mobile app and website.[30]

Consumer data privacy is a hot topic today. Studies indicate that more than 90% of shoppers are worried about their privacy when they buy online and almost 50% have restricted their online activity as a result of privacy concerns.[31] The misuse of data security is no longer something that the public will tolerate.[32] Consumers are becoming very vocal, and they are more and more willing to take actions against brands that violate their trust. Today, a growing number of consumers are trying to protect their privacy by becoming privacy enforcers—notifying regulators of companies' misconduct, signing up for class-action lawsuits, and boycotting firms that fail to protect their privacy.[33]

While gathering consumer data is a normal practice nowadays, firms should use this information with caution. A lot of firms collect this information in order to better understand their customers, be able to satisfy their needs and wants, and provide them with a better experience. What is more important in this case is the reason for gathering the data, how it is to be protected, and whether people accept the way the data is used. New laws set by the European Union's GDPR and the California Consumer Protection Act (CCPA) require firms to implement ethical data procedures. "Businesses in those jurisdictions are now obligated to disclose all the information they have collected about a person upon that person's request, including a complete list of third parties with whom the data has been shared. Perhaps most importantly, when a consumer demands their data be erased, a company must comply or face legal ramifications."[34]

Corporate Social Responsibility

Corporate Social Responsibility (CSR) describes activities that organizations perform to benefit society and to "give back" to their stakeholders in the community.[35] The three pillars of CSR are: Profit, People and Planet, which refer to the economic, social and environmental consequences of corporate behavior.[36] The best ways to practice CSR include making charitable contributions, encouraging employees to volunteer for philanthropic activities, and of course to be responsible corporate citizens that minimize their negative impact on the environment. In this section we will cover the social aspect. In the next section we will cover the environmental aspect of CSR.

Companies recognize that socially responsible activities can improve their image among consumers and stockholders, and consequently influence purchasing decisions.[37] This road is a bit tricky, as many of today's consumers look closely at companies to decide whether they are walking the walk, rather than just talking the talk, when they say they really want to improve their business practices.[38]

Today, luxury and fashion companies are working hard to promote their CSR practices through philanthropic practices supporting the community while designing programs that are particularly associated with children's welfare and facing unemployment.[39] Some companies create special products to sell in support of a designated charity. For example, sales from a special Michael Kors' "Watch

Hunger Stop" T-shirt supports the World Food Programme (WFP) and fights the worldwide Covid-19 pandemic. Another example is Louis Vuitton which, in 2021, created a new silver Lockit bracelet and Doudou Teddy Bear to commemorate its partnership with UNICEF. When consumers buy these products, they contribute to UNICEF's work on giving access to water, sanitation, nutrition, education and more to children who are in need around the globe.[40]

Many companies promote causes because it is good for business as well as improving our lives—we call such actions "doing well by doing good." A case in point is breast cancer. This deadly disease affects 2.1 million women every year, and women are the main consumers of fashion, so the industry has rallied to support this cause.[41] Many apparel companies, manufacturers, and retailers have become well known for their work in many social causes:

- Rihanna's Savage x Fenty lingerie brand is giving profits from the sales of its pink lingerie styles to the Clara Lionel Foundation in order to support young women who are fighting aggressive types of breast cancer.

- Levi Strauss has a Foundation whose mission is to improve lives in communities where Levi's has employees. For more than 65 years, the foundation has been involved in creating advance revolutionary social change in the areas of HIV/AIDS, worker rights, worker well-being and social justice.[42]

- The Selfridges Group Foundation, established in 2015, contributes to a number of charitable practices with one focus on funding scientific studies that help to treat neurodegenerative, Alzheimer, and Parkinson diseases.[43]

- In order to fight Covid-19, the luxury Group Kering contributed three million surgical masks to the health service in France.[44]

- Brands like Balenciaga and Yves Saint Laurent converted their workshops in 2020 into the production of surgical masks to combat the coronavirus.[45]

Labor Issues and Exploitation

Global sourcing, or manufacturing in countries around the world, has stimulated much interest and concern among the public regarding human rights. Consumers and critics are showing their displeasure over what is perceived as a lack of ethics, social responsibility, and conscience of large fashion companies and those who produce their products in developing countries for wages as low as 51 cents an hour such as in Bangladesh and Vietnam.[46] Some consumers are aware of this and will not purchase products made in these countries.[47] However, many others are unaware of the controversy; perhaps they assume that if their favorite retailer offers a garment in its inventory, the company must have chosen suppliers that exhibit responsible labor practices.[48]

Some major companies are responding to these concerns although there is much more to do. Adidas and Lululemon stopped working with suppliers that rely on recruitment agencies to hire new employees. They are requesting these factories to directly hire their employees to control or reduce labor exploitation.[49]

However, difficulties remain, mainly at the bottom of the supply chain, where a lot of firms have minimal visibility. Many companies outsource the actual manufacturing to factories in developing countries where wages (but also oversight) are dramatically lower.

Child Labor and Human Trafficking

Concerns about working conditions in manufacturing facilities extend beyond long hours and poorly ventilated areas. There is also a lot to be done to combat the problem of human trafficking, where underage workers labor against their will.[50] For example, the production of raw materials such as cotton and silk remains a main threat for firms as these materials are usually supplied from countries such as India, where the use of child labor is common.[51] Other main resources needed in the fashion industry and which are thought to be extremely risky for child labor are cash-

Child Labor

Jahangir Alam Onuchcha / Shutterstock.com

mere originally produced in Mongolia and rubber sourced from Indonesia, Malaysia and Thailand. Wool is considered the only raw material that is not plagued by problems with child labor.[52]

Although many of these violations occur in factories that produce high volumes of inexpensive garments to feed the fast-fashion machine, there also are some luxury brands that have their own problems. According to the nonprofit group KnowTheChain, some luxury companies such as Prada, Salvatore Ferragamo, Fendi, and Christian Dior are more likely to hire employees who are vulnerable to abuse in textile workshops.[53]

While a number of brands focus on their Tier 1 suppliers and producers (the companies that supply directly to the brand), a number of orders are subcontracted through Tier 2 suppliers (for example those companies who manufacture the raw materials to be used in the finished item). According to journalist Shraysi Tandon, "...the people putting on the buttons or putting on the soles to your $500 shoes are often trafficked and invisible."[54]

One problem with analyzing compliance with labor laws in overseas apparel production is the lack of a standard, recognized evaluation model. However, improvements are occurring in the industry with audits being conducted by companies such as SGS, largely due to increasing public awareness of the deplorable conditions in such factories. Pressure comes from grassroots activism, shareholder activism, and media attention to get companies to take responsibility for their supply chains.

For example, for at least the past decade both Nike and Gap have been criticized for their use of sweatshops. Due to such social pressure, both have recently taken the important step toward taking responsibility for suppliers by releasing detailed supplier and audit information.[55] After more than 1,100 employees

Dhaka garment factory collapse in Bangladesh
Image courtesy of Sharat Chowdhury via WikiMedia Commons, shared under the CC BY 2.5 license.

died in an apparel manufacturer's building collapse at the Rana Plaza in Bangladesh in 2012, more pressure has been exerted on Western companies to become more transparent about their supply chain.

Marks & Spencer even allows its customers to see its supply chain by placing a factory map on its website, posting where exactly its different product categories are produced including apparel, home furnishings and food. Indeed, according to the Global Fashion Agenda (GFA), around 12.5% of the international fashion market, as well as giant retailers such as Nike, Adidas, Levi's and Gap, have committed themselves to achieve sustainability targets, which also comprises listing all the suppliers they partner with.[56] For instance, for its online shopping, the brand Arket provides full details for each item such as the type of material in addition to the factory that has produced the item. "When we communicate that, customers have the option to make more sustainable choices," says Karin Brinck, sustainability manager at Arket. "We see transparency as one of the means for our industry to drive positive change through increased openness."[57]

College students have also organized some movements such as United Students Against Sweatshops and have pressured university officials to take a tougher stand against sweatshop labor by joining the Fair Labor Association (FLA). The FLA was formed as part of the Apparel Industry Partnership, a White House task force set up in 1996 to combat sweatshop conditions internationally. Student protests appear to have had an effect. For example, the University of California (UC) added provisions to its code-of-conduct policy requiring a living wage and disclosure of names and addresses of its manufacturing plants, and it added protection for female employees working for contractors that produce university-logo products.[58]

Cultural Exploitation and Appropriation

One of the reasons for controversies in the apparel industry is that it is a global industry. Each country has its own mix of customs, laws, values, and ways of doing business. However, the companies that commission many of the products that are made in developing countries generally try to apply a common perspective when they formulate their codes of conduct. For example, some firms commit to the principles of the United Nations Sustainable Development Goals that address major societal issues such as ending hunger, poverty, and labor exploitation.[59]

Fair Trade Fashion

Fair Trade is defined by the World Fair Trade Organization (WFTO) as "...a trading partnership, based on dialogue, transparency and respect, that seeks greater equity in international trade."[60] A global movement toward acceptance of this standard was accelerated by the fallout from the terrible factory collapse of the Rana Plaza in Bangladesh we referred to earlier, an industrial disaster that killed 1,134 employees. This prompted the filming of the movie *The True Cost*, which increased people's awareness of the high level of continuing abuses of workers' rights in the developing world and the lack of environmental regulations imposed upon fashion firms and suppliers. Fair Trade fashion moves beyond only showing where the item is made. It requires ensuring producers are paid fairly and clearly revealing to the final consumer who is the real manufacturer of an item.[61] For example, the manufacturer Fair Indigo (www.fairindigo.com) uses Latin American suppliers that pay more than the minimum wage and offer other benefits such as medical treatment to their workers.

Fair Indigo provides "...sustainable lives for the world's garment workers. Our artisans and operators in Peru are paid a fair and living wage and treated like family, giving them the means to a healthy, happy life".[62]

Consumers increasingly look for a "Fair Trade" label when they choose a garment to ensure that it has been manufactured using acceptable standards.[63] For example, one study reported what it called a "fair-trade halo effect"; 81% of American respondents said they would view a brand they already buy more favorably if it carried a fair trade label.[64]

Fair Indigo

Myriam B / Shutterstock.com

This movement toward **ethical fashion** is gaining traction among both new and mainstream companies such as Nike. In 2013, the World Fair Trade Organization developed a new Fair Trade production labelling scheme that assures Fair Trade principles are reached across the supply chain, a guarantee that firms are meeting their ethical standards. Insertion of a World Fair Trade Organization label on a fashion good confirms to the user and consumer that the producer obeys the following principles of Fair Trade:

- Generating opportunities for economically disadvantaged producers

- Transparency and accountability

- Fair trading practices

- Payment of a fair price

- Ensuring no child labor and forced labor

- Commitment to non discrimination, gender equity and women's economic empowerment and freedom of association

- Ensuring good working conditions

- Providing capacity building

- Promoting Fair Trade

- Respect for the environment.[65]

Fashion Sustainability

The textile and fashion industry makes up a big portion of the world's most polluting industries. Apparel is usually produced from oil-based materials or resource-intensive agricultural goods such as cotton. Production practices often include harsh chemicals and huge volumes of water; millions of tons of apparels end up in landfill on a yearly basis.[66] Many feel the textile and fashion industries pose a serious threat to the environment due to the chemicals and finishes they use in fabric production; the pollutants in detergent consumers use to launder their clothing; and, most important, the underlying principle of the fashion industry—encouraging people to replace their clothing as frequently as possible.[67] These factors combine to make the fashion industry a huge global polluter. It's estimated that 6.3% of all waste buried in landfills around the world is made up of postconsumer textiles.[68] In fact, the global apparel sector has the fourth largest environmental impact after housing, transportation and food.[69] Around 90% of old clothes are either thrown away or burned rather than recycled in some way.[70]

But is it possible to be both fashionable and environmentally friendly?

Fashion sustainability is becoming more and more important, and consumers are forcing fashion brands to become more environmentally responsible, even as they move away from the waste of fast-fashion and show more interest in buying second hand.[71] Sustainability refers to using natural, biodegradable textiles in apparel, decreasing water use, or starting recycling programs.[72] Many retailers and manufacturers are currently attempting to meet the needs of consumers while at the same time staying true to their values of adhering to strict sustainable practices in the production of their product. It is not always easy being "green", as some companies and consumers have discovered. It's a balancing act for many companies, between profit and green policies. Many apparel, fashion, and catalog companies have attempted to offer consumers green alternatives. The following are just a few:

- Body Shop is a London-based cosmetics specialty chain that sells natural cosmetics and promotes saving the rain forest, protecting whales, and warning against the dangers of acid rain. None of the company's products are tested on animals and are labeled as such. It encourages customers to return empty containers for a refill at a reduced cost.

- Adidas uses plastic recovered from the ocean to form the upper parts of shoes and clothing, such as jerseys. It also has the Parley collection which is made from almost 75% captured marine trash. Presently, more than 40% of Adidas' apparel is produced from recycled polyester and the brand aims to replace all virgin polyester with recycled polyester by 2024. Adidas is also working on creating a 100% recyclable shoe to be released in 2021; the Futurecraft Loop. The concept behind this shoe is that it can be broken down and transformed into a brand-new pair if returned.[73]

- Rens, a Finnish footwear brand, launched its Kickstarter campaign in order to fund the manufacturing of their sustainable waterproof footwear. Every pair of sneakers is made from 300g of coffee waste and six plastic bottles, is 100% waterproof, and has built in odor-proof, moisture-wicking, and UV-resistant properties. This brand's shoes also follow an animal free design, and it avoids using polyurethane or virgin plastics.[74]

- Zara announced that it aims to source and produce more sustainable items. It recently launched a collection made from sustainable raw materials and all items will have a "join life" tag on them. The collection includes puffer jackets made from stuffing from retrieved textile products as a way to eliminate waste, and knitwear made from 100% recycled cashmere.[75]

- Burberry decided to refrain from destroying unsold fashion goods for the sake of protecting its brand image after the brand became a symbol of the industry's wasteful performers, destroying almost $40 million worth of stock in 2018, resulting in a controversy over waste in the fashion industry.[76]

- The Giving Movement, a Dubai based company is committed to the use of recyclable material produced from waste of water bottles and certified organic bamboo. For its packaging, the company makes use of bio-degradable plant starch.[77]

Upcycling

It is definitely time for the fashion industry to start making a change when it comes to its wasteful production processes. While the fashion industry produces a lot of waste that ends up in landfills, what's even worse is that less than 1% of discarded apparel products are reused to produce new clothes.[78]

Vanina

Vanina / Marya Ghazzaoui

That's why sustainable fashion is becoming more relevant and common with brands trying to use recycled materials in their collections. Some fashion companies decided to take it a step further and rely on **upcycling** throughout their production.

It is important to distinguish between upcycling and recycling. Upcycling, also known as *creative reuse*, is the process of reusing existing products or waste and transforming them into new products, like converting an old shirt into a dress. Recycling is using materials that have been previously broken down.[79] Here are some examples of companies that followed this approach:

- For its ReCrafted line, Patagonia manufactured around 10,000 jackets, sweaters and bags upcycled from old clothes. Alex Kremer, who is Patagonia's director of corporate development, observed that it was a very challenging task to work and repurpose old garments because the process consumed a lot of time and effort especially when trying to come up with creative ways to transform old fabrics into new clothes. Despite the hardships that the brand faced, Kremer said that the most important thing to focus on is reducing waste and engaging in a more circular economy for the sake of the environment.[80]

- Burberry also tackled the issue of waste by partnering with the luxury brand Elvis & Kresse in order to make use of its leather offcuts and potentially transform them into brand new handbags and accessories.[81]

- Reformation is an LA fashion brand that also implemented upcycling by salvaging fabric that hasn't been used or sold from other fashion companies, in addition to using eco-friendly fabrics and transforming them into vintage clothing items that even include glamorous wedding gowns. The brand newly created a mobile application that informs you how much water and energy you would be saving if you purchase from their stores since all of their business operations are sustainable in nature.[82]

- Vanina, a brand based in Beirut, worked on creating unique and youthful accessories inspired by art and nature using upcycled materials and relying on zero-waste methods for the production process. You can consider this brand as the perfect blend of craftsmanship coupled with a lot of environmental awareness.[83]

One can only wonder what's next for upcycling. Who knows, maybe the nearest item to you right now has the potential to be completely transformed into a one-of-a-kind masterpiece.

Is Fast-Fashion Dead?

The slow fashion movement is part of the sustainable fashion we discussed earlier.[84] This movement appeared as a response to Fast-fashion cycles and the "unsustainable" business evolution.[85] While fast-fashion has transformed the retail landscape over the past few years, some are questioning whether its death is imminent. Fast-fashion emphasizes short production times and cheap prices for the sake of creating new collections inspired by the fashion runway; nonetheless, its practices are harmful to the environment. Criticisms of fast-fashion are related to its environmental impact, water pollution, and its usage of toxic chemicals and growing amounts of fabric waste.[86] Can sustainable fashion be the reason for the death of fast-fashion?

According to an article in Drapers, "Jonathan Reynolds, associate professor in retail marketing at Saïd Business School, University of Oxford, says the demise of fast-fashion is 'a matter of when, rather than whether'. [...] Achim Berg, senior partner and global leader of the apparel, fashion and luxury group at McKinsey & Co, believes fast-fashion is likely to survive, but with different dynamics".[87] So how can fast-fashion retailers fashion a new business model that will allow them to survive?

Some fast-fashion companies are exploring the new dynamics that could lead to the idea of a **circular economy**, a concept related to redefining growth and focusing on creating positive benefits for businesses, the environment and society at large. It involves the slow disassociation of economic activity from the consumption of limited resources. This model is based upon three principles:

1. Design out waste and pollution

2. Keep products and materials in use

3. Regenerate natural systems.[88]

When it comes to the fashion industry, a circular economy is generally attained by creating enduring, timeless items (as opposed to seasonal items) and a number of "Re-s:" such as *repair, reuse, recycle, refurbish* to lengthen the lifetime of a certain good. A number of fast-fashion brands have in fact initiated collection and recycling programs, whereby consumers can drop off fabric and apparel that they do not want any more for other companies to recycle. A good example is H&M's recycle bins that were a part of the "H&M Conscious" campaign. Customers were encouraged to drop off their old clothes in the recycling bins found in stores in exchange for a 15% discount code on their next purchase. H&M recently created the Conscious Collection, a limited collection that informs shoppers where the items are made, the specific textiles that were used in production, and the names of the suppliers that were involved.[89] However, the "H&M Conscious" campaign has been highly criticized as consumers have questioned the extent to which the company can lessen the enormous and mounting impact it has on the environmental. Some advocate that this campaign was just "**greenwashing**," diverting from the degree of the damage the company does, and even enhancing sales.[90]

Further to this, H&M is investing in innovative firms that are leading the movement toward circularity such as re:newcell, Worn Again, and Treetotextile.[91] Inditex, the owner of Zara, has also followed this market demand, whereby the firm announced that all apparel will be manufactured with the use of 100% sustainable or recycled materials by 2025.[92]

However, with no clear messaging around how they will achieve this, it's one thing to talk the talk, and quite another to walk the walk. How might you help to track the industry's progress, or even encourage change yourself?

The Dark Side of Consumer Behavior

Despite the best efforts of researchers, government regulators, and concerned industry people, sometimes consumers' worst enemies are themselves. Individuals often are depicted as rational decision makers, calmly doing their best to obtain products and services that will maximize the health and well-being of themselves, their families, and society. In reality, however, consumer desires, choices, and actions often result in negative consequences to the individual and/or the society. Some consumer activities stem from social pressures, and the cultural value placed on money can encourage activities such as shoplifting or fraud. Exposure to unattainable media ideals of beauty and success can create dissatisfaction with the self.

Addictive Consumption

Consumer addiction refers to a physiological and/or psychological dependency on goods or services. While most people equate addiction with drugs, virtually any product or service can be seen as relieving some problem or satisfying some need to the point where reliance on it becomes extreme. Indeed, some psychologists even raised concerns about "Internet addiction," in which people (particularly college students) became obsessed by online chat rooms to a point that their virtual lives took priority over their offline lives.[93]

Compulsive Consumption

For some individuals, the term "born to shop" is taken quite literally. These individuals engage in buying since they feel compelled to do so rather than because buying is a pleasurable or functional activity. **Compulsive consumption** refers to regular and excessive buying, as a result of tension, anxiety, low self-esteem, depression, feelings of guilt or even boredom.[94] "Shopaholics" become obsessed and dependent on shopping in a similar way to people who are addicted to drugs or alcohol.[95]

Compulsive buying is particularly different from impulse buying. The impulse to purchase a precise good is momentary, and it mainly focuses on a given item at a certain time. However, compulsive buying is a lasting behavior that revolves around the practice of buying instead of the purchased items themselves. Have you ever heard of the lady who owns 1200 pairs of lavish shoes? Beth Shak is an American lady who owns this huge footwear collection. She confessed that she had never got close to wearing them all frequently. "Like any woman, I end up going for my ten favorite pairs," she says.[96]

In certain situations, it is equally safe to state that the shopper, similar to a drug addict, has little to no control over buying. The goods usually control the individual, be it drugs, alcohol, cigarettes, fashion goods, or even chocolate. Much negative or damaging consumer behavior can be described by three general features[97]:

1. The individual may not engage in the behavior by choice.

2. The individual experiences short-term gratification.

3. The individual may experience feelings of guilt and depression after being involved in compulsive buying.

Cosmetic Surgery Addiction

Can you be addicted to getting facelifts or nose jobs? **Cosmetic surgery** involves the "maintenance, restoration or enhancement of one's physical appearance through surgical and medical techniques".[98] These surgeries include liposuction, breast augmentation (the single most popular procedure), breast reduction, nose or eyelid reshaping, face lifting, and other procedures. Some of the most common non-surgical aesthetic procedures include Botox, hyaluronic acid, and laser hair removal.[99] Perhaps as a reflection of the power of some celebrities like Kim Kardashian to "break the Internet" with images of prominent derrieres, the number of patients who had elective buttocks surgery almost doubled in about five years.[100]

Studies attribute people's interest in cosmetic surgery by both men and women to high media exposure/consumption and a need for the enhancement of self-esteem, especially as they compare their appearance to others including glamorous celebrities and social media influencers.[101] Indeed, according to the American Academy of Facial Plastic and Reconstructive Surgery, 40% of surgeons believe that the motivation to enhance appearance is driven by the desire to look better in selfies that patients post on social media sites![102] Not only women seem to be fascinated by cosmetic surgeries, however nowadays, but a greater number of men are also embracing these procedures for the sake of lifting their confidence and enhancing their physical appearance.[103]

Eating Disorders

Have you ever heard of any person who passed away from complications arising from eating disorders? The fashion industry creates severe competition, and supermodels are under constant pressure to maintain a desirable body shape that will keep them employed—especially by the high-end designers who (with some exceptions) continue to promote rather unrealistic expectations about what glamorous women should look like. Fashion designers know that their apparel looks much better in smaller sizes, so thinness for models is typically a major requirement. This has led to numerous top high fashion models developing eating disorders such as anorexia or bulimia.[104]

This disorder obsession with thinness is not only affecting models but is even becoming more prevalent among everyday women consumers, especially younger ones. A recent study indicated a relationship between social media use and body image issues among adolescents.[105] Research findings revealed that adolescents reporting increased usage of social media are at risk of developing amplified body image concerns, which may result in poor psychological adjustment.[106]

A number of fashion firms have decided to join the battle and help those who are struggling with anorexia in response to the criticisms on how the industry encourages people to starve themselves in the pursuit of beauty are portrayed and treated. The magazine *Vogue* has stopped featuring fashion models who appear to have an eating disorder in 2012. Also, since 2017 the two renowned luxury groups Kering and LVMH have stopped recruiting models who wear smaller than a US size 2 (which means French size 34, UK size 6).[107] This has followed the new rules issued by the French government that forbid the use of ultra-thin models in 2015.

Consumer Theft

Shrinkage refers to the industry inventory and cash losses that may be attributed to issues such as workers' theft, shoplifting, administrative error, vendor fraud, damage, and cashier error. This is a huge issue for retailers that is passed on to shoppers through higher prices. Based on a 2018 survey by the National Retail Federation (NRF), shoplifting costs US retailers $46.8 billion.[108]

Shoplifting still is one of the most serious financial issues that retailers face. 60% of recognized shoplifters were identified going into at least two distinct stores of the same retail chain or brand in the US.[109]

Most shoplifting is *not* done by professional individuals or by those who really need the stolen goods.[110] In fact, it's common among adolescents. Previous research has shown that adolescent shoplifting is affected by social factors such as an individual' peers who shoplift as well. Adolescents also tend to steal if they don't perceive this practice to be morally wrong.[111] Sneakers, logo and brand-name clothing, denims, and undergarments are among the most commonly stolen items in the UK.[112] Cosmetics may be added to that list, with the trend toward open-selling merchandise formats (a hands-on tactic that permits buyers to play and experience the items) led by Sephora, a French cosmetics company with stores worldwide.

Retailers have taken measures to help fight shoplifting, but some stores do not want to use heavy sensor tags that make it hard for customers to try on clothing and give the impression that the store does not trust the consumer. Good customer service is the best defense against shoplifting; a sales associate who acknowledges customers and is aware of their moves deters such illegal behavior. Also, another effective way to reduce shoplifting is to implement good retail store design. For instance, the store can be configured to reduce the number of hidden corners that might allow potential shoplifters to load up their backpacks or purses.

Other retailers have relied on technology in order to prevent shoplifting. For example, **Radio Frequency Identification (RFID) tags** use electromagnetic fields within radio frequencies to distinctively detect items, such as apparel, accessories or shoes. Most of the retailers today such as Macy's, Lululemon, and Kohl's use this technology in order to reduce losses from stealing.[113] Many retailers also install closed-circuit television (CCTV) cameras in order to stop employee and consumer theft. **Facial recognition technology** can be adopted to recognize known shoplifters at the time they come to the shop in order to protect shops and their consumers against shoplifting crimes. The device scans the face of each individual who arrives to the store, and if a former thief walks in, the technology can detect them based on its database and warn store security to observe the customer and prevent further theft.[114]

Anti-consumption

Some forms of damaging consumer behavior take the form of **anti-consumption**, which is the practice of "intentionally and meaningfully excluding or cutting goods from one's consumption routine or reusing once-acquired goods with the goal of avoiding consumption".[115] In some cases, acts of anti-consumption are a form of cultural resistance, whereby consumers who are alienated from mainstream society (such as juvenile delinquents) single out objects that represent the values of the larger group and modify them as an act of rebellion or self-expression.[116] In the hippie culture of the 1960s and 1970s, for example, many antiwar protestors began wearing cast-off apparel, often replacing insignias of rank with peace signs and other symbols of "revolution."

FOMO

The acronym **FOMO** has become immensely popular today. FOMO, or the *fear of missing out*, is defined as feeling anxious or stressed over the possibility of missing out on an event or opportunity.[117] In other words, FOMO is characterized by a psychological state in which people fear missing out on social events, experiences, and interactions.[118] It's a great—and very current— example of the (potentially) negative dimensions of consumer behavior.

Critics argue that FOMO is caused by excessive smartphone and social media usage, which is very similar to addiction.[119] A recent study showed that almost 48% of Millennials have spent money they didn't have or have even gone into debt so that they can keep up with and imitate what their friends are doing and posting about.[120]

This concept is also becoming more relevant in the fashion industry. Consumers who suffer from **Fashion FOMO** are easily spotted and identified due to displaying certain "symptoms", which include checking the "new in" website sections of their favorite brands every single day, signing up to multiple newsletters in order to receive daily updates, queuing in front of fashion stores for hours just to get their hands on the latest and trendiest items and following large numbers of fashion influencers on social media, and checking their pages daily.[121]

Chapter Summary

Now that you have read the chapter, you should understand the following:

1. What are consumer and business ethics?

Business ethics essentially are rules of conduct that help in taking action in the marketplace. Universal standards or values include honesty, trustworthiness, fairness, respect, justice, integrity, concerns for others, accountability, loyalty, and responsible citizenship. Cultural differences exist in how ethics are defined.

Ethical decisions when it comes to the fashion industry include the use of fur and exotic skins, animal testing, offensive advertising and consumer privacy data.

2.   What is corporate social responsibility in fashion?

Socially responsible companies go beyond what is legal to do what benefits society. Many fashion companies engage in cause marketing in which marketing efforts are linked to charitable causes. The fashion industry should ensure that ethical standards are being followed and the rights of their workers are being protected throughout their supply chain. Many consumers are today aware of and concerned about exploitation issues related to labor in global apparel production. Fashion sustainability is becoming more and more important, and consumers are actually forcing fashion brands to become more environmentally responsible.

3.   What is the dark side of consumer behavior?

While textbooks often paint a picture of the consumer as a rational decision maker, calmly doing their best to obtain products and services that will maximize the health and well-being of themselves, their families, and society; the reality is that consumer desires, choices, and actions often result in negative consequences to the individual and/or the society. The dark side of consumer behavior includes the following: addictive consumption, which refers to a physiological and/or psychological dependency on goods or services; compulsive consumption, which refers to regular and excessive buying, as a result of tension, anxiety, low self-esteem, depression, feelings of guilt or even boredom; fear of missing out, which refers to psychological state in which people fear missing out on social events, experiences, and interactions; unnecessary cosmetic surgeries, and which refers to the preservation, restoration or improvement of one's physical appearance through surgical and medical methods; and eating disorders.

DISCUSSION QUESTIONS

1.   What are business ethics? To what extent do you believe that a fashion brand's marketing practices may be unethical?

2.   What are the main corporate social responsibilities for a fashion brand?

3.   Do you believe that human rights should be interpreted culturally? Explain why or why not.

4.   Facial recognition technology has been used to facilitate the recognition of shoplifters. How ethical is it to adopt this technology?

5.   Do you feel that government interferes too much with businesses producing and selling apparel or not enough for the sake of the consumer?

EXERCISES

1. Select a jewelry brand, a leather good and an apparel luxury brand. Discuss the major ethical concerns that might be related to these brands.

2. In groups, list a few charities. Then research the campaigns launched by these charities. Are they effective?

3. Identify some of the signs that indicate a person suffers from the fear of missing out.

4. Search online for jewelry brands. Explore how ethical their material sourcing is.

5. Conduct an online search of companies that are applying some sustainable practices. Choose one brand that you believe is the most credible and transparent. Explain why, and identify areas of improvement.

CASE STUDY: SUSTAINABILITY IN FASHION
Patsy Perry, Manchester Metropolitan University

Sustainable fashion should maximize positive and minimize negative environmental and social impacts along the supply chain from production, manufacture, transportation, and retail to end-of-life management, conserving an ecological balance by avoiding depletion of natural resources and supporting social justice across the supply chain. However, perfect sustainability is impossible and there are trade-offs between environmental and social issues. This was seen during the Covid-19 pandemic in 2020, when the halting of global supply chains led to a reduction in environmental pollution but also had a detrimental impact on many of the world's most vulnerable workers who lost wages or jobs as global retailers attempted to cancel orders placed with developing country suppliers. Further challenges to sustainability in fashion are presented by the increasing speed of change in trends and complexity of global supply chains, and the increasing levels of production and consumption across the world. In the marketplace, fashion brands and retailers address various aspects of sustainability through material selection or supply chain configuration. However, there is often no clear-cut answer as to which the most sustainable option is, as shown in the following examples.

(Continued)

Sustainable material selection

Chinese luxury brand Icicle's 'Made in Earth' philosophy underpins its approach to sustainability by seeking harmony with nature, so the brand uses organic cotton and other natural fibers in its collections. In contrast, outdoor brand Patagonia uses mostly recycled polyester in its T-shirt range, in recognition of recycled polyester's lower water and carbon footprint, compared to cotton. Recycled polyester saves natural resources and makes valuable use of plastic waste, but garments release millions of plastic microfibers when laundered. Cotton is a biodegradable fiber, but needs vast amounts of land, water, and pesticides to grow. 'Organic' is a powerful marketing term but organic cotton needs more water and land to yield the same amount as conventionally grown cotton. There are pros and cons to all fiber types and fiber choice is only one part of a complex picture. Fibers must be spun, knitted or woven, dyed, finished, sewn, and transported – all of which have different environmental and social impacts in each part of the process.

Sustainable supply chain configuration

Community Clothing sells an affordable and ethical range of durable modern basics through a direct-to-consumer supply chain, which is configured to source material inputs and manufacture products locally in the UK. This helps to reduce its carbon footprint as well as preserve skills and contribute to economic prosperity in deprived areas, as all staff are paid at least the national living wage. Social justice and sustainability may also be achieved by globally dispersed supply chain configurations. Australian premium denim brand Outland Denim is a certified B Corp that puts purpose, not profit, at the center of its operations and provides training, support, and employment opportunities to victims of sex trafficking in Cambodia. By providing a sustainable career path for vulnerable women to craft premium denim from the world's finest raw materials, the brand enables true social change for workers, their families and communities. Both local and global supply chain configurations can achieve positive social impacts, some of which may outweigh the environmental impacts of global sourcing.

Promoting sustainability in marketing communications

Fashion marketing communications aim to drive consumer purchase intention and increase sales, which contradict sustainability goals to reduce overproduction and consumption. Sometimes brands may send mixed messages in their marketing activities, which questions their commitment to sustainability. UK online fast-fashion retailer Pretty Little Thing launched a collection made from recycled polyester and waste materials to help create a more sustainable future, but also ran a Black Friday sales promotion offering a 99% discount. Some dresses were offered for as little as 15 pence, which promotes overconsumption and waste. There are very few brands (apart from Patagonia and Vivienne Westwood) that encourage consumers to buy less, buy used or repair what they already have as revenue streams in most fashion businesses are based on producing and selling more items.

DISCUSSION QUESTIONS

1. Is it possible for fashion brands and retailers to balance a sustainability agenda alongside the pressure to release new collections and grow their business? Explain your reasoning and provide examples to support your opinions.

2. Is it possible to balance social and environmental sustainability goals? Discuss examples of fashion brands and retailers and make suggestions for improvement.

3. Discuss the social and environmental sustainability performance of fast-fashion, mass market and luxury fashion brands—which group do you think is most/least sustainable and why?

4. Discuss examples of contradictions between sustainability goals and marketing strategies of fashion brands and retailers in your region.

NOTES

1. Thangavelu, P. (2020) 'The success of Patagonia's marketing strategy', *Investopedia*, February 3. www.investopedia.com/articles/personal-finance/070715/success-patagonias-marketing-strategy.asp (accessed August 13, 2021).

2. Maheshwari, S. (2020) 'Patagonia, quick to close, could be last to reopen', *The New York Times*, May 12. www.nytimes.com/2020/05/12/business/patagonia-reopening-coronavirus.html (accessed August 13, 2021).

3. Han, J., Seo, Y. and Ko, E. (2017) 'Staging luxury experiences for understanding sustainable fashion consumption: A balance theory application', *Journal of Business Research*, 74: 162–7.

   Henninger, C.E., Alevizou, P.J., Tan, J., Huang, Q. and Ryding, D. (2017) 'Consumption strategies and motivations of Chinese consumers: The case of UK sustainable luxury fashion', *Journal of Fashion Marketing and Management: An International Journal*, 21 (3): 419–34.

   Kong, H.M., Ko, E., Chae, H. and Mattila, P. (2016) 'Understanding fashion consumers' attitude and behavioral intention toward sustainable fashion products: Focus on sustainable knowledge sources and knowledge types', *Journal of Global Fashion Marketing*, 7 (2): 103–19.

   McNeill, L.S., Hamlin, R.P., McQueen, R.H., Degenstein, L., Garrett, T.C., Dunn, L. and Wakes, S. (2020) 'Fashion sensitive young consumers and fashion garment repair: Emotional connections to garments as a sustainability strategy', *International Journal of Consumer Studies*, 44 (4): 361–8.

   McNeill, L. and Moore, R. (2015) 'Sustainable fashion consumption and the fast fashion conundrum: Fashionable consumers and attitudes to sustainability in clothing choice', *International Journal of Consumer Studies*, 39 (3): 212–22.

   Ritch, E. L. (2015) 'Consumers interpreting sustainability: Moving beyond food to fashion', *International Journal of Retail & Distribution Management*, 43 (12): 1162–81.

4. Zager, D.S., Solis, A. and Adjroud, S. (2017) *These Georgetown Students Fought Nike—and Won*, September 15. Retrieved from The Nation: www.thenation.com/article/archive/these-georgetown-students-fought-nike-and-won/ (accessed August 13, 2021).

5. Beversluis, E.H. (1987) 'Is there "no such thing as business ethics"?', *Journal of Business Ethics*, 6 (2): 81–8.

    Joyner, B.E. Payne, D. (2002) 'Evolution and implementation: A study of values, business ethics and corporate social responsibility', *Journal of Business Ethics*, 41 (4): 297–311.

    Lewis, P.V. (1985) 'Defining "business ethics": Like nailing jello to a wall', *Journal of Business Ethics*, 4 (5): 377–83.

6. Quinn, J.J. (1997) 'Personal ethics and business ethics: The ethical attitudes of owner/managers of small business', *Journal of Business Ethics*, 16 (2): 119–27.

    Turnipseed, D.L. (2002) 'Are good soldiers good?: Exploring the link between organization citizenship behavior and personal ethics', *Journal of Business Research*, 55 (1): 1–15.

7. Mohr, L.A., Webb, D.J. and Harris, K.E. (2001) 'Do consumers expect companies to be socially responsible? The impact of corporate social responsibility on buying behavior', *Journal of Consumer Affairs*, 35 (1): 45–72.

8. Grazzini, L., Acuti, D. and Aiello, G. (2021) 'Solving the puzzle of sustainable fashion consumption: The role of consumers' implicit attitudes and perceived warmth', *Journal of Cleaner Production*, 287: article #125579.

    Lundblad, L. and Davies, I.A. (2016) 'The values and motivations behind sustainable fashion consumption. *Journal of Consumer Behaviour*, 15 (2): 149–62.

    Šontaitė-Petkevičienė, M. (2015) 'CSR reasons, practices and impact to corporate reputation', *Procedia-Social and Behavioral Sciences*, 213: 503–508.

9. Ilchi, L. (2019) 'The biggest fashion and beauty brand controversies of 2019', WWD, December 24. wwd.com/fashion-news/fashion-scoops/biggest-brand-controversies-2019-fashion-beauty-gucci-blackface-kim-kardashian-kimono-louis-vuitton-michael-jackson-1203241522/ (accessed August 13, 2021).

10. Foley, B. (2018) 'The fur debate', WWD, April 26. https://wwd.com/fashion-news/fashion-features/the-fur-debate-1202660445/ (accessed August 13, 2021).

11. Ely, M. (2019) 'Real fur to see resurgence in Canada amid perception shift: Opinion', *Retail Insider*, December 13. https://retail-insider.com/retail-insider/2019/12/real-fur-to-see-resurgence-in-canada-amid-perception-shift-opinion/ (accessed August 13, 2021).

12. O'Connor, T. (2018) 'Why fashion's anti-fur movement is winning', *Business of Fashion*, October 15. www.businessoffashion.com/articles/news-analysis/why-fashions-anti-fur-movement-is-winning (accessed August 13, 2021).

13. BBC News (2018) 'Chanel ends use of exotic skins in its fashion range', *BBC News*, December 4. www.bbc.com/news/world-europe-46449396 (accessed August 13, 2021).

14. Kent, S. (2019) 'Selfridges will ban exotic skins in 2020', *Business of Fashion*, February 26. www.businessoffashion.com/articles/news-bites/selfridges-will-ban-exotic-skins-in-2020 (accessed August 13, 2021).

15. Business Wire (2018) 'New survey from Perfect365 reveals 36% of women prefer to purchase cruelty-free beauty', *Business Wire*, March 29. www.businesswire.com/news/home/20180329006014/en/New-Survey-Perfect365-Reveals-36-Women-Prefer (accessed August 13, 2021).

16. Elle Beauty Team (2021) '14 cruelty-free make-up brands to invest in right now', *Elle*, April 20. www.elle.com/uk/beauty/make-up/articles/a31152/11-cruelty-free-makeup-brands/ (accessed August 13, 2021).

17. Humane Research Australia (2019) 'Australian cosmetic animal test ban bill passes Senate after government commits additional reinforcement measures to Humane Society International', *Humane Research Australia*, February 14. www.humaneresearch.org.au/australian-cosmetic-animal-test-ban-bill-passes-senate-after-government-commits-additional-reinforcement-measures-to-humane-society-international/ (accessed August 13, 2021).

18. Kushwaha, B. (2019) 'Estée Lauder expands commitment to cruelty-free testing', *L'officiel USA*, June 25. www.lofficielusa.com/beauty/estee-lauder-cruelty-free-testing-2019 (accessed August 13, 2021).

19. Swanson, K.K. and Everett, J.C. (2015) *Promotion in the Merchandising Environment*. New York, NY: Bloomsbury.

20. Bae, S.Y., Rudd, N. and Bilgihan, A. (2015) 'Offensive advertising in the fashion industry: Sexual objectification and ethical judgments of consumers', *Journal of Global Fashion Marketing*, 6 (3): 236–49.

    Business Insider (2014) 'Britain bans 'offensive and irresponsible' American Apparel ads', *Business Insider*, September 3. www.businessinsider.com/britain-bans-american-apparel-ads-2014-9 (accessed August 13, 2021).

21. Schneier, M. (2017) 'Tom Ford, where the rich and famous go to look rich and famous', *The New York Times*, August 15. www.nytimes.com/2017/08/15/fashion/tom-ford-store.html (accessed August 13, 2021).

22. Cader, A.A. (2015) 'Islamic challenges to advertising: A Saudi Arabian perspective', *Journal of Islamic Marketing*, 6 (2): 166–87. doi.org/10.1108/JIMA-03-2014-0028

23. Gorman, A. (2019) 'Victoria's Secret cancels annual televised fashion show as viewers turn off', *The Guardian*, November 22. www.theguardian.com/fashion/2019/nov/22/victorias-secret-cancels-annual-televised-fashion-show-as-viewers-turn-off (accessed August 13, 2021).

24. Belch, G.E., Belch, M.A. and Villarreal, A. (1987) 'Effects of advertising communications: Review of research', *Research in Marketing*, 9: 59–117.

    Wartella, E. (1985) 'Sex Stereotyping in Advertising', 10 (Spring): 583–5.

    LaTour, M.S. (1990) 'Female nudity in print advertising: An analysis of gender differences in arousal and ad response', *Psychology & Marketing*, 7 (1): 65–81.

    Yovovich, B.G. (1983) 'Sex in advertising: The power and the perils', *Advertising Age*, 54 (19): 12–15.

    Elliott, R. and Ritson, M. (1995) 'Practicing existential consumption: The lived meaning of sexuality in advertising', *ACR North American Advances*, 22: 740–5.

    Sengupta, J. and Dahl, D.W. (2008) 'Gender-related reactions to gratuitous sex appeals in advertising', *Journal of Consumer Psychology*, 18 (1): 62–78.

25. Wirtz, J.G., Sparks, J.V. and Zimbres, T.M. (2018) 'The effect of exposure to sexual appeals in advertisements on memory, attitude, and purchase intention: A meta-analytic review', *International Journal of Advertising*, 37 (2): 168–98.

26. Griffiths, J. (2017) 'Frown To A Tee. Are these the most offensive tops ever sold? From a blood-stained student sweater to a T-shirt asking women to "eat less"', *The Sun,* August 16. www.thesun.co.uk/fabulous/4256907/most-offensive-tops-ever-sold/ (accessed August 13, 2021).

27. Bloomberg (2018) 'Prada will stop selling $550 monkey figure decried as racist', *Business of Fashion*, December 14. www.businessoffashion.com/articles/news-analysis/prada-will-stop-selling-550-monkey-figure-decried-as-racist (accessed August 13, 2021).

28. Hsu, T. and Paton, E. (2019) 'Gucci and Adidas apologize and drop products called racist', *The New York Times,* February 9. www.nytimes.com/2019/02/07/business/gucci-blackface-adidas-apologize.html (accessed August 13, 2021).

29. Forrester (2018) 'Ethics and consumer action will transform privacy', *Forbes*, November 14. www.forbes.com/sites/forrester/2018/11/14/ethics-and-consumer-action-will-transform-privacy/?sh=4e5d9bae12c1 (accessed August 13, 2021).

30. Reuters (2018) 'Under Armour says 150 million MyFitnessPal accounts breached', *Business of Fashion,* March 30. www.businessoffashion.com/articles/news-analysis/under-armour-says-150-million-myfitnesspal-accounts-breached (accessed August 13, 2021).

31. Byer, B. (2018) 'Internet users worry about online privacy but feel powerless to do much about it', *Entrepreneur*, June 20. www.entrepreneur.com/article/314524 (accessed August 13, 2021).

32. Hedencrona, S. (2018) 'How data privacy is evolving and what it means for brands', *GreenBook,* May 21. www.greenbook.org/mr/insights/how-data-privacy-is-evolving-and-what-it-means-for-brands/ (accessed August 13, 2021).

33. Ritter, S. (2020) 'The ethical data dilemma: Why ethics will separate data privacy leaders from followers', *Forbes,* March 31. www.forbes.com/sites/forbestechcouncil/2020/03/31/the-ethical-data-dilemma-why-ethics-will-separate-data-privacy-leaders-from-followers/?sh=7f1dc9db14c6 (accessed August 13, 2021).

34. Ritter, S. (2020) 'The ethical data dilemma: Why ethics will separate data privacy leaders from followers', *Forbes,* March 31. www.forbes.com/sites/forbestechcouncil/2020/03/31/the-ethical-data-dilemma-why-ethics-will-separate-data-privacy-leaders-from-followers/?sh=7f1dc9db14c6 (accessed August 13, 2021).

35. Vitell, S.J. (2015) 'A case for consumer social responsibility (CnSR): Including a selected review of consumer ethics/social responsibility research', *Journal of Business Ethics*, 130 (4): 767–74.

36. Księżak, P. and Fischbach, B. (2017) 'Triple bottom line: The pillars of CSR', *Journal of Corporate Responsibility and Leadership*, 4 (3): 95–110.

37. Hagtvedt, H. and Patrick, V.M. (2016) 'Gilt and guilt: Should luxury and charity partner at the point of sale?', *Journal of Retailing*, 92 (1): 56–64.

    Minor, D. and Morgan, J. (2011) 'CSR as reputation insurance: Primum non nocere', *California Management Review*, 53 (3): 40–59.

38. Hodge, A. (2021) '5 Examples of brand authenticity to help you make a profit', *Instapage.com*, June 14. https://instapage.com/blog/building-brand-authenticity (accessed August 13, 2021).

39. Carcano, L. (2013) 'Strategic management and sustainability in luxury companies: The IWC case', *The Journal of Corporate Citizenship*, 52: 36–54.

40. Louis Vuitton (2021) 'Louis Vuitton for Unicef', *Louis Vuitton*. https://eu.louisvuitton.com/eng-e1/magazine/articles/lv-for-unicef (accessed August 13, 2021).

41. World Health Organization (WHO) (2021) 'Preventing cancer', *World Health Organization*. www.who.int/activities/preventing-cancer (accessed August 13, 2021).

42. Levi Strauss (2021) 'The Levi Strauss Foundation's philanthropic work is grounded in the company's values of originality, integrity, empathy and courage', *Levi Strauss*. www.levistrauss.com/values-in-action/levi-strauss-foundation/ (accessed August 13, 2021).

43. Selfridges (2021) 'Supporting our communities', *Selfridges*. www.selfridges.com/GB/en/features/events/supporting-our-communities/ (accessed August 13, 2021).

44. Kering (2020) 'Kering contributes to the fight against COVID-19', *Kering*, March 22. www.kering.com/en/news/kering-contributes-to-the-fight-against-covid-19 (accessed August 13, 2021).

45. Williams, R. (2020) 'Balenciaga, Saint Laurent to make masks in french workshops', Bloomberg, March 22. www.bloomberg.com/news/articles/2020-03-22/balenciaga-saint-laurent-to-produce-masks-in-french-workshops (accessed August 13, 2021).

46. McVeigh, K. (2019) 'Cambodian female workers in Nike, Asics and Puma factories suffer mass faintings', *The Guardian*, June 25. www.theguardian.com/business/2017/jun/25/female-cambodian-garment-workers-mass-fainting (accessed August 13, 2021).

   Kashyap, A. (2018) 'When clothing labels are a matter of life or death,' Daily Beast, May 2. www.hrw.org/news/2018/05/02/when-clothing-labels-are-matter-life-or-death (accessed August 13, 2021).

47. Phau, I., Teah, M. Chuah, J. (2015) 'Consumer attitudes towards luxury fashion apparel made in sweatshops', *Journal of Fashion Marketing and Management*, 19 (2): 169–87.

48. Han, J., Seo, Y. and Ko, E. (2017) 'Staging luxury experiences for understanding sustainable fashion consumption: A balance theory application', *Journal of Business Research*, 74: 162–7.

   Kapferer, J.N. and Michaut-Denizeau, A. (2020) 'Are millennials really more sensitive to sustainable luxury? A cross-generational international comparison of sustainability consciousness when buying luxury', *Journal of Brand Management*, 27 (1): 35–47.

   Rolling, V. and Sadachar, A. (2018) 'Are sustainable luxury goods a paradox for millennials?', *Social Responsibility Journal*, 14 (4): 802–15.

49. Zilber, A. (2018) 'Did "Slave Labor" make your designer bag? New report finds luxury brands like Prada, Fendi and Dior rank among the worst retailers for protecting workers from exploitation', *The Daily Mail*, December 16. www.dailymail.co.uk/news/article-6500211/Luxury-fashion-brands-like-Prada-Fendi-use-exploited-factory-workers-make-products.html (accessed August 13, 2021).

50. Suhrawardi, R. (2019 'The big issues facing fashion in 2019', *Forbes*, January 16. www.forbes.com/sites/rebeccasuhrawardi/2019/01/16/the-big-issues-facing-fashion-in-2019/?sh=31a7bd4723a9 (accessed August 13, 2021).

51. Kent, S. (2019) *The Fashion Supply Chain is Still High Risk for Child Labour. Business of Fashion*, May 30. www.businessoffashion.com/articles/sustainability/the-fashion-supply-chain-is-still-high-risk-for-child-labour (accessed August 13, 2021).

52. Kent, S. (2019) *The Fashion Supply Chain is Still High Risk for Child Labour. Business of Fashion*, May 30. www.businessoffashion.com/articles/sustainability/the-fashion-supply-chain-is-still-high-risk-for-child-labour (accessed August 13, 2021).

53. Jestratijevic, I., Rudd, N.A. and Uanhoro, J. (2020) 'Transparency of sustainability disclosures among luxury and mass-market fashion brands', *Journal of Global Fashion Marketing*, 11 (2): 99–116.

54. Suhrawardi, R. (2019 'The big issues facing fashion in 2019', *Forbes*, January 16. www.forbes.com/sites/rebeccasuhrawardi/2019/01/16/the-big-issues-facing-fashion-in-2019/?sh=31a7bd4723a9 (accessed August 13, 2021).

55. Stauffer, B. (2017) 'Follow the thread', *Human Rights Watch*, April 20. www.hrw.org/report/2017/04/20/follow-thread/need-supply-chain-transparency-garment-and-footwear-industry (accessed August 13, 2021).

56. Chitrakorn, K. (2018) 'Can transparency solve the consumer trust deficit?', *Business of Fashion*, December 10. www.businessoffashion.com/articles/sustainability/consumers-are-distrusting-transparency-matters-in-fashion (accessed August 13, 2021).

57. Chitrakorn, K. (2018) 'Can transparency solve the consumer trust deficit?', *Business of Fashion*, December 10. www.businessoffashion.com/articles/sustainability/consumers-are-distrusting-transparency-matters-in-fashion (accessed August 13, 2021).

58. University of California (2018) 'Trademark licensing code of conduct', *University of California*. https://policy.ucop.edu/doc/3000130/TrademarkLicensing (accessed August 13, 2021).

59. UN Department of Economic and Social Affairs (2021) 'The 17 Goals', *United Nations*. https://sdgs.un.org/goals (accessed August 13, 2021).

60. World Fair Trade Organization (WTFO) (2021) 'About us', *World Fair Trade Organization*. https://wfto.com/who-we-are (accessed August 13, 2021).

61. Minney, S. (2015) 'Op Ed: Fair trade goes beyond "made in"', *Business of Fashion*, June 18. https://www.businessoffashion.com/opinions/news-analysis/op-ed-fair-trade-goes-beyond-made-in (accessed August 13, 2021).

62. Fair Indigo (2021) 'About Fair Indigo', *Fair Indigo*. www.fairindigo.com/pages/about-fair-indigo-our-mission (accessed August 13, 2021).

63. Di Benedetto, C.A. (2017) 'Corporate social responsibility as an emerging business model in fashion marketing', *Journal of Global Fashion Marketing*, 8 (4): 251–65.

    Hwang, C.G., Lee, Y.A. and Diddi, S. (2015) 'Generation Y's moral obligation and purchase intentions for organic, fair-trade, and recycled apparel products', *International Journal of Fashion Design, Technology and Education*, 8 (2): 97–107.

64. Fairtrade America (2018) 'Majority of Americans trust fairtrade label', *PR Newswire*, February 28. www.prnewswire.com/news-releases/majority-of-americans-trust-fairtrade-label-300605879.html (accessed August 13, 2021).

65. WFTO Europe (2013) 'The 10 principles of fair trade', *World Fair Trade Organization*, August 12. https://wfto-europe.org/the-10-principles-of-fair-trade/ (accessed August 13, 2021).

66. Kent, S. (2013) 'What's stopping the fashion industry from agreeing on climate action?', *Business of Fashion*, May 23. www.businessoffashion.com/articles/sustainability/whats-stopping-the-fashion-industry-from-agreeing-on-climate-action (accessed August 13, 2021).

67. Perry, P. (2017) *'Read this before you go sales shopping: the environmental costs of fast fashion'*, *The Conversation*, December 28. https://theconversation.com/read-this-before-you-go-sales-shopping-the-environmental-costs-of-fast-fashion-88373 (accessed August 13, 2021).

68. United States Environmental Protection Agency (EPA) (2020) 'National overview: Facts and figures on materials, wastes and recycling', *United States Environmental Protection Agency*. www.epa.gov/facts-and-figures-about-materials-waste-and-recycling/national-overview-facts-and-figures-materials (accessed August 13, 2021).

69. Shurvell, J. (2020) 'The rise of upcycling: Five brands leading the way at London men's fashion week 2020', *Forbes*, January 8. www.forbes.com/sites/joanneshurvell/2020/01/08/the-rise-of-upcycling-five-brands-leading-the-way-at-london-mens-fashion-week-2020/?sh=445a5c4250a (accessed August 13, 2021).

70. H&M (2021) 'Reuse and recycling', *H&M*. https://hmgroup.com/sustainability/circular-and-climate-positive/recycling/ (accessed December 1, 2021).

71. Achabou, M.A., Dekhili, S. and Codini, A.P. (2020) 'Consumer preferences towards animal-friendly fashion products: An application to the Italian market', *Journal of Consumer Marketing*, 37 (6): 661–73.

    Blasi, S., Brigato, L. and Sedita, S.R. (2020) 'Eco-friendliness and fashion perceptual attributes of fashion brands: An analysis of consumers' perceptions based on Twitter data mining', *Journal of Cleaner Production*, 244: article #118701.

    Ritch, E.L. (2015) 'Consumers interpreting sustainability: Moving beyond food to fashion', *International Journal of Retail & Distribution Management*, 43 (12): 1162–8.

    Howland, D. (2021) 'Fast fashion faces steep declines in the next decade or sooner, UBS warns', *Retail Dive*, April 12. www.retaildive.com/news/fast-fashion-faces-steep-declines-in-the-next-decade-or-sooner-ubs-warns/598215/ (accessed August 13, 2021).

    Khusainova, G. (2021) 'The secondhand market is growing rapidly, can challengers like Vinokilo thrive and scale? *Forbes.com*, January 28. www.forbes.com/sites/gulnazkhusainova/2021/01/28/the-secondhand-market-is-growing-rapidly-can-challengers-like-vinokilo-thrive-and-scale/ (accessed August 13, 2021).

72. Brydges, T. (2021) 'Closing the loop on take, make, waste: Investigating circular economy practices in the Swedish fashion industry', *Journal of Cleaner Production*, 293: article #126245.

    Fletcher, K. (2013) *Sustainable Fashion and Textiles: Design Journeys*. Abingdon: Routledge.

Henninger, C.E., Alevizou, P.J. and Oates, C.J. (2016) 'What is sustainable fashion?', *Journal of Fashion Marketing and Management: An International Journal*, 20 (4): 400–16.

73. Morgan, C. (2020) 'How Adidas is turning plastic ocean waste into sneakers and sportswear', *Business Insider,* October 27. www.businessinsider.com/adidas-sneakers-plastic-bottles-ocean-waste-recycle-pollution-2019-8 (accessed August 13, 2021).

74. Rens (2021) 'Rens the first coffee sneakers'. www.kickstarter.com/projects/rens/rens-the-totally-waterproof-sneaker-made-from-coffee (accessed October 17, 2021).

75. Davis, J. (2019) 'Zara has released a new eco-friendly collection', *Harpers Bazaar*, December 2. www.harpersbazaar.com/uk/fashion/fashion-news/a30070234/zara-eco-friendly-collection/ (accessed August 13, 2021).

76. Kent, S. (2019) 'What fashion can learn from a decade of disasters', *Business of Fashion*, December 4. www.businessoffashion.com/articles/sustainability/end-of-the-decade-fashion-moral-sustainability-climate-labour (accessed August 13, 2021).

77. The Giving Movement (2021) 'Sustainability, responsibility and the fabrics we use', *The Giving Movement.* https://thegivingmovement.com/pages/sustainability (accessed August 13, 2021).

78. Kent, S. and Nanda, M.C. (2019) 'The future of upcycling: from rags to riches', *Business of Fashion,* December 4. www.businessoffashion.com/articles/sustainability/the-future-of-upcycling-from-rags-to-riches (accessed August 13, 2021).

79. Petro, G. (2019) Upcycling Your Way to Sustainability. *Forbes.* www.forbes.com/sites/gregpetro/2019/02/08/upcycling-your-way-to-sustainability/?sh=7b9bc0b058e2 (accessed August 13, 2021).

80. Patagonia (2021) 'How we turn scraps into new gear', Patagonia. www.patagonia.com/stories/second-stories/story-74520.html (accessed October 17, 2021).

81. Kent, S. and Nanda, M.C. (2019) 'The future of upcycling: from rags to riches', *Business of Fashion,* December 4. www.businessoffashion.com/articles/sustainability/the-future-of-upcycling-from-rags-to-riches (accessed August 13, 2021).

82. Small, D. (2020) '10 luxury fashion brands that upcycle', *Eluxe Magazine*, December 18. https://eluxemagazine.com/fashion/fashion-brands-that-upcycle/ (accessed August 13, 2021).

83. Salonga, B. (2020) 'Clean, conscious retail choices at net sustain', *Forbes,* February 13. www.forbes.com/sites/biancasalonga/2020/02/13/clean-conscious-retail-choices-at-net-sustain/#291e06001db9 (accessed August 13, 2021).

84. Battaglia, M., Testa, F., Bianchi, L., Iraldo, F. and Frey, M. (2014) 'Corporate social responsibility and competitiveness within SMEs of the fashion industry: Evidence from Italy and France', *Sustainability*, 6 (2): 872–93.

85. Henninger, C.E., Alevizou, P.J. and Oates, C.J. (2016) 'What is sustainable fashion?', *Journal of Fashion Marketing and Management: An International Journal*, 20 (4): 400–16.

86. Niinimäki, K., Peters, G., Dahlbo, H., Perry, P., Rissanen, T. and Gwilt, A. (2020) 'The environmental price of fast fashion', *Nature Reviews Earth & Environment*, 1 (4): 189–200.
    Zhang, B., Zhang, Y. and Zhou, P. (2021) 'Consumer attitude towards sustainability of fast fashion products in the UK', *Sustainability*, 13 (4): 1646.

87. Drapers Editor (2019) 'Is fast fashion dead?', *Drapers Online*, September 30. www.drapersonline.com/business-operations/special-reports/is-fast-fashion-dead/7037750.article (accessed August 13, 2021).

88. Ellen MacArthur Foundation (2017) 'The circular economy in detail', *Ellen MacArthur Foundation*. www.ellenmacarthurfoundation.org/explore/the-circular-economy-in-detail (accessed August 13, 2021).

89. Khusainova, G. (2019) 'Why the circular economy will not fix fashion's sustainability problem', *Forbes,* June 12. www.forbes.com/sites/gulnazkhusainova/2019/06/12/why-the-circular-economy-will-not-fix-fashions-sustainability-problem/#1d5143dc4d05 (accessed August 13, 2021).

90. Bain, M. (2016) 'Is H&M misleading customers with all its talk of sustainability?', *Quartz*, April 16. https://qz.com/662031/is-hm-misleading-customers-with-all-its-talk-of-sustainability/ (accessed August 13, 2021).

91. Lundvall, Å. and Söderlund C. (2018) *Sustainability Report 2018*. H&M. https://about.hm.com/content/dam/hmgroup/groupsite/documents/masterlanguage/CSR/reports/2018_Sustainability_report/HM_Group_SustainabilityReport_2018_%20FullReport.pdf (accessed August 13, 2021).

92. Cooper, R. (2019) 'Zara clothing to be made from 100% sustainable fabrics by 2025', *Climate Action*, July 23. www.climateaction.org/news/zara-clothing-to-be-made-from-100-sustainable-fabrics-by-2025 (accessed August 13, 2021).

93. Kuss, D. J., Griffiths, M. D. and Binder, J. F. (2013) 'Internet addiction in students: Prevalence and risk factors', *Computers in Human Behavior*, 29 (3): 959–966.

    Yellowlees, P.M. and Marks, S. (2007) 'Problematic Internet use or Internet addiction?', *Computers in Human Behavior*, 23 (3): 1447–53.

94. Black, D.W. (2007) 'A review of compulsive buying disorder', *World Psychiatry*, 6 (1): 14.

    Cui, C.C., Mrad, M. and Hogg, M.K. (2018) 'Brand addiction: Exploring the concept and its definition through an experiential lens', *Journal of Business Research*, 87: 118–27.

    Faber, R.J. and Christenson, G.A. (1996) 'In the mood to buy: Differences in the mood states experienced by compulsive buyers and other consumers', *Psychology & Marketing*, 13 (8): 803–19.

    Horváth, C. and Adıgüzel, F. (2018) 'Shopping enjoyment to the extreme: Hedonic shopping motivations and compulsive buying in developed and emerging markets', *Journal of Business Research*, 86: 300–10.

    Mrad, M. (2018) 'Brand addiction conceptual development', *Qualitative Market Research: An International Journal*, 21 (1): 18–38.

    Mrad, M. and Cui, C.C. (2017) 'Brand addiction: Conceptualization and scale development', *European Journal of Marketing*, 51 (11/12): 1938–60.

    Mrad, M. and Cui, C.C. (2020) 'Comorbidity of compulsive buying and brand addiction: An examination of two types of addictive consumption', *Journal of Business Research*, 113: 399–408.

95. Faber, R.J. and O'Guinn, T.C. (1988) 'Compulsive consumption and credit abuse', *Journal of Consumer Policy*, 11 (1): 97–109.

    Mrad, M. and Cui, C.C. (2020) 'Comorbidity of compulsive buying and brand addiction: An examination of two types of addictive consumption', *Journal of Business Research*, 113: 399–408.

96. Mulkerrins, J. (2012) '$1 million shoe lady Beth Shak: I really put Louboutin!', *Daily Mail,* August 12. www.dailymail.co.uk/home/you/article-2185043/The-1-million-shoe-queen.html (accessed August 13, 2021).

97. Mrad, M. and Cui, C.C. (2020) 'Comorbidity of compulsive buying and brand addiction: An examination of two types of addictive consumption', *Journal of Business Research*, 113: 399–408.

98. Swami, V., Chamorro-Premuzic, T., Bridges, S. and Furnham, A. (2009) 'Acceptance of cosmetic surgery: Personality and individual difference predictors', *Body image*, 6 (1): 7–13.

99. International Society of Aesthetic Plastic Surgery (ISAPS) (2018) *ISAPS International Survey on Aesthetic/ Cosmetic Procedures*. ISAPS. www.isaps.org/wp-content/uploads/2019/12/ISAPS-Global-Survey-Results-2018-new.pdf (accessed August 13, 2021).

100. Cision PR Newswire (2020) 'Latest global survey from ISAPS reports continuing rise in aesthetic surgery worldwide', *Cision PR Newswire,* August 12. www.prnewswire.co.uk/news-releases/latest-global-survey-from-isaps-reports-continuing-rise-in-aesthetic-surgery-worldwide-896115156.html (accessed August 13, 2021).

     Hershkovits, D. (2014) 'How Kim Kardashian broke the Internet with her butt', *The Guardian,* December 17. www.theguardian.com/lifeandstyle/2014/dec/17/kim-kardashian-butt-break-the-internet-paper-magazine (accessed August 13, 2021).

101. Furnham, A. and Levitas, J. (2012) 'Factors that motivate people to undergo cosmetic surgery', *Canadian Journal of Plastic Surgery*, 20(4): 47–50.

     The Aesthetic Society (2020) 'The Aesthetic Society unveils 2020 plastic surgery predictions', The *Aesthetic Society,* January 29. www.surgery.org/media/news-releases/the-aesthetic-society-unveils-2020-plastic-surgery-predictions (accessed August 13, 2021).

102. Roberts, N.F. (2018) 'Our addiction to selfies means big business for plastic surgeons', *Forbes,* April 10. www.forbes.com/sites/nicolefisher/2018/04/10/our-addiction-to-selfies-means-big-business-for-plastic-surgeons/#573099d02786 (accessed August 13, 2021).

103. The Aesthetic Society (2020) The Aesthetic Society unveils 2020 plastic surgery predictions', *The Aesthetic Society,* January 29. www.surgery.org/media/news-releases/the-aesthetic-society-unveils-2020-plastic-surgery-predictions (accessed August 13, 2021).

104. Bogar, N., and Tury, F. (2018) 'Abusing the body: Psychological abuse. The bioethical aspects of the fashion model profession', *Journal of Obesity and Eating Disorder*, 4 (1): 1–4.

105. Salomon, I. and Brown, C.S. (2019) 'The selfie generation: Examining the relationship between social media use and early adolescent body image', *The Journal of Early Adolescence*, 39 (4): 539–60.

106. Marengo, D., Longobardi, C., Fabris, M.A. and Settanni, M. (2018) 'Highly-visual social media and internalizing symptoms in adolescence: The mediating role of body image concerns', *Computers in Human Behavior*, 82: 63–9.

107. CBC (2017) 'Fashion giants LVMH and Kering ban size 0 models', *CBC*, September 6. www.cbc.ca/news/health/fashion-size-zero-1.4276814 (accessed August 13, 2021).

108. McCue, T.J. (2019) 'Inventory shrink cost the US retail industry $46.8 billion', *Forbes*, January 13. www.forbes.com/sites/tjmccue/2019/01/31/inventory-shrink-cost-the-us-retail-industry-46-8-billion/#479af686b701 (accessed August 13, 2021).

109. Face First (2021) 'New face recognition data on shoplifting reveals extent of organized retail crime', *Face First*. www.facefirst.com/blog/new-face-recognition-data-on-shoplifting-reveals-extent-of-organized-retail-crime/ (accessed August 13, 2021).

110. Cole, C.A. (1989) 'Deterrence and consumer fraud', *Journal of Retailing*, 65 (1): 107.

    Cox, D., Cox, A.D. Moschis, G.P. (1990) 'When consumer behavior goes bad: An investigation of adolescent shoplifting', *Journal of Consumer Research*, 17 (2): 149–59.

    Grove, S.J., Vitell, S.J. and Strutton, D. (1989) 'Non-normative consumer behavior and the techniques of neutralization', In *Proceedings of the 1989 AMA Winter Educators Conference* (Vol. 131). Chicago, IL: American Marketing Association. p. 135.

    Krasnovsky, T. and Lane, R.C. (1998) 'Shoplifting: A review of the literature', *Aggression and Violent Behavior*, 3 (3): 219–35.

111. Cox, A.D., Cox, D., Anderson, R.D. and Moschis, G.P. (1993) 'Research note: Social influences on adolescent shoplifting—Theory, evidence, and implications for the retail industry', *Journal of Retailing*, 69 (2): 234–46.

    Vermeir, I., De Bock, T. and Van Kenhove, P. (2017) 'The effectiveness of fear appeals featuring fines versus social disapproval in preventing shoplifting among adolescents', *Psychology & Marketing*, 34 (3): 264–74.

112. Centre for Retail Research (2019) 'The shoplifters' hit parade', *Centre for Retail Research*. www.retailresearch.org/shoplifters.html (accessed August 13, 2021).

113. HS Brands Global (2020) *The Five Pillars of Loss Prevention*. September 2. https://hsbrands.com/resource-center/articles/8-retail-loss-prevention-technology-trends (accessed August 13, 2021).

114. Miranda, L. (2018) 'Thousands of stores will soon use facial recognition, and they won't need your consent', *Buzz Feed*, August 17. https://www.buzzfeednews.com/article/leticiamiranda/retail-companies-are-testing-out-facial-recognition-at (accessed August 13, 2021).

115. Makri, K., Schlegelmilch, B.B., Mai, R. and Dinhof, K. (2020) 'What we know about anticonsumption: An attempt to nail jelly to the wall', *Psychology & Marketing*, 37 (2): 177–215.

116. Ozanne, J.L., Hill, R.P. and Wright, N.D. (1998) 'Juvenile delinquents' use of consumption as cultural resistance: Implications for juvenile reform programs and public policy', *Journal of Public Policy & Marketing*, 17 (2): 185–96.

117. Carducci, V. (2006) 'Culture jamming: A sociological perspective', *Journal of Consumer Culture*, 6 (1): 116–38.

    Abel, J.P., Buff, C.L. and Burr, S.A. (2016) 'Social media and the fear of missing out: Scale development and assessment', *Journal of Business & Economics Research (JBER)*, 14 (1): 33–44.

    Good, M.C. and Hyman, M. R. (2020) '"Fear of missing out": Antecedents and influence on purchase likelihood', *Journal of Marketing Theory and Practice*, 28 (3): 330–41.

    Przybylski, A.K., Murayama, K., DeHaan, C.R. and Gladwell, V. (2013) 'Motivational, emotional, and behavioral correlates of fear of missing out', *Computers in Human Behavior*, 29 (4): 1841–8.

118. Wegmann, E., Oberst, U., Stodt, B. and Brand, M. (2017) 'Online-specific fear of missing out and Internet-use expectancies contribute to symptoms of Internet-communication disorder', *Addictive Behaviors Reports*, 5: 33–42.

119. Hodkinson, C. (2019) '"Fear of Missing Out" (FOMO) marketing appeals: A conceptual model', *Journal of Marketing Communications*, 25 (1): 65–88.

    Riordan, B.C., Flett, J.A., Hunter, J.A., Scarf, D., and Conner, T.S. (2015) "Fear of missing out (FoMO): The relationship between FoMO, alcohol use, and alcohol-related consequences in college students', *Annals of Neuroscience and Psychology*, 2 (7): 1–7.

120. Frazier, A. (2020) 'What are FOMO and YOLO teaching us about our money?', *Forbes*, April 23. www.forbes.com/sites/forbesmarketplace/2020/04/23/what-are-fomo-and-yolo-teaching-us-about-our-money/#1c126f712dd8 (accessed August 13, 2021).

121. Edwards, J. (2015) '22 signs you suffer from fashion FOMO', *Cosmopolitan*, Ausgust 28. www.cosmopolitan.com/uk/fashion/style/a38215/signs-you-suffer-from-fashion-fomo/ (accessed August 13, 2021).

SECTION II

Fashion Marketing Strategy

CHAPTER 5
Strategic Planning and Marketing Insights

LEARNING OBJECTIVES

After you read this chapter, you will understand the answers to the following:

1. How do you analyze the marketing environment?

2. How do you gather market insights and trend forecasting?

3. How do you design the right fashion product?

For about 150 years, Louis Vuitton has been quite sure about what business it's in. The venerable French company has produced exquisite luggage, shoes, bags, and other luxury goods since 1854 and it was one of the jewels in the crown of the LVMH Group, which also owns other upscale labels including Christian Dior Couture, Loewe, Celine, Kenzo and Tiffany.[1]

Disaster struck in early 2020, and the mighty fashion industry stood still as the Covid-19 crisis slammed the brakes on sales of almost everything except essentials. In March of that year, retail sales fell by over 50%.[2] And that looked to be just the beginning as deaths soared, consumers lost their jobs, and all the places you wear your expensive luxury products to were shuttered.

For a short time, just about everyone in the fashion industry reacted like a deer in the headlights as the enormity of the situation became clear. But some companies reacted faster than others to "The New Normal." Their business radar still functioned adequately, as they continued to monitor the environment to try to make sense of it all.

Rather than shut their doors and go home, management at Louis Vuitton resolved to do what they could to help fight the pandemic—and also keep afloat. They thought about what they were

(Continued)

capable of doing when their production lines that normally turn out luxury products were idled. One much-needed option was hospital gowns to protect workers at French hospitals, who were being exposed on a daily basis to hundreds if not thousands of infected patients. The company shut down its ready-to-wear atelier in its Paris headquarters, refitted its machinery, and reopened to produce the gowns. Some employees volunteered to make the garments at the facility, and other pattern cutters were given their own machines so that they could work from home. Before long, the gowns were being delivered to six hospitals in the city.

Analyzing the Marketing Environment

Even in normal times, fashion brands can't afford to rest on their laurels. As we've said before, the only thing we can count on in the fashion world is that we can't count on anything (and the Covid pandemic certainly underscored that!). Strong brands and new entrants alike need to understand what is going on around them in order to stay current and continue to create products that will keep their customers coming back for more. This means, of course, that they have to be very aware of who their competitors are and what they're up to all the time. But it also means that marketers need to fine-tune their strategies as the world changes around them. Some of these changes are rather gradual, like an increase of consumers' interest in wellness products.

But others are quite sudden, like the onset of a pandemic that almost overnight decimated the entire fashion industry. In that case, some businesses were quick to pivot. In addition to Louis Vuitton's temporary transformation, for example, the fashion conglomerate LVMH converted three of its facilities that normally make perfume for its Guerlain, Givenchy and Christian Dior brands to produce hand sanitizer.[3] Some fast-fashion brands were also able to pivot to making loungewear with the data they had from the online searches that consumers made for "athleisure", "joggers" and related terms.[4]

This quick transition illustrates why it's so important for a fashion marketer to constantly keep its finger on the world's pulse—to understand and anticipate what changes might occur in technology, politics, consumer values, and other factors that could impact demand (in good or bad ways) for the brands it sells. That's why the process of **marketing planning**—the systematic tracking of both internal capabilities and external conditions and setting objectives for future growth—is so important.

The marketing environment comprises the forces that affect a fashion and luxury brand's capability to deliver products and services to its target market and controls the brand's capability to create and maintain flourishing relationships with its consumers. A variety of external and internal actors influence a brand's marketing planning. Some of them may be manageable while others are uncontrollable. A brand's marketing managers must adjust the company's strategies as changes occur. These environmental forces fall into two broad categories: The macro-environment and the micro-environment. Let's take a look at each.

The Macro-Marketing Environment

The macro-environment refers to all the factors external to the company that affect its operations. A thorough analysis typically involves what is sometimes called a PESTLE analysis. **PESTLE** is a mnemonic; in its expanded form it reminds us to pay attention to these dimensions:[5]

- Political
- Economic
- Social
- Technological
- Legal
- Environmental

The Natural Environment

Concerns about the impact of the fashion industry on our natural environment continue to climb– along with rising sea levels and temperatures. The McKinsey Fashion on Climate report found that the fashion industry is responsible for about 2 billion metric tons of GHG (greenhouse gas) emissions per year. Consider that this is equivalent to the annual emissions from the economies of France, Germany and the UK combined. Much of this comes from textile manufacturing–especially of synthetic fibers such as polyester. But even natural cotton production has its perils because the fertilizer farmers use releases nitrous oxide, a greenhouse gas with 300 times more warming power than CO_2. And while we're witnessing an uptick in the reuse and resale of used clothing, it's still the case that only 15% of clothing is recycled and less than one % of garments get turned into new clothes. The rest of what we wear and discard (quickly, if we're into fast fashion) winds up in landfills or it is incinerated (where the smoke also contributes to air pollution).

Especially after the pandemic, environmental issues are top-of-mind for an increasing number of consumers. In response, in 2018 a coalition of major fashion brands signed on to the Fashion Industry Charter for Climate Action, under the auspices of the United Nations. They pledged to reduce GHG emissions by 30% over the next decade and to develop a common messaging strategy to communicate the importance of climate action within the industry. It's clear that environmental sustainability will continue to play an outsized role in many consumers' choices going forward. A recent survey revealed that over 80% of consumers now say they prefer to buy sustainably. Will the fashion industry rise to the challenge? We all have a stake in the outcome of this transformation.

The Political and Legal Environment

The **political and legal environment** describes the local, state, national, and global laws and regulations that may impact a fashion brand. Legal rules can be crucial factors for countless business decisions. While some fashion brands decide to stay local, the majority need to consider international laws and regulations if they want to go global. Marketers of global fashion brands also need to take into consideration the major political factors that can impact how they operate their business internationally.

Companies need to keep an eye on the relevant **legislation**, taxation, and trade tariffs across their markets. For example, Norway's government has committed to ban all fur farms by 2025.[6] This new decision will shut down nearly 250 fox and mink farms in Norway. More and more fashion companies will be forced to go fur-free in the future. Even the content that people post may be subject to different laws in different countries. For example, in the US, the Federal Trade Commission states that online influencers must reveal their relationships with brands when they post about them.[7]

International companies are aware that when governments put some political constraints on trade, this can radically impact their business functions. At the extreme, of course, when two countries engage in a trade war the whole business environment will be affected. In some cases, countries may decide to enforce some tariffs on others. In 2019, fashion retailers raised their concerns and worries considering the trade war between China and America. Since few items are locally manufactured, American fashion retailers are highly dependent on trading imported items; 41.6% of all apparel imports come from China. Following the increased tariffs on imported items from China, some fashion retailers such as Levi's, Calvin Klein and Tommy Hilfiger shifted some of their production base outside of China.[8]

The Economic Environment

The **economic environment** refers to the economic factors, that, either in the immediate marketplace or in the global economy, may impact consumers' purchase behaviors and spending power. As the economy improves, people have more disposable income, thus they are more likely to purchase fashion and luxury items. However, during periods of recession and uncertainty consumers seem to be more careful about their buying.[9] Fashion retailers may be stuck with huge amounts of inventory left over at the end of the season, forcing them to sell these items at very reduced prices or in some cases to destroy them.

The 2008 recession caused a financial shock that had a very negative impact on consumer demand for products.[10] Luxury department stores such as Saks Fifth Avenue and Neiman Marcus faced a bleak situation, with sales plummeting 25% in 2009 and resulting in early markdowns of 70% due to inventory surplus.[11] The industry's recovery from the 2008 recession was helped by the high spending power of Chinese consumers[12] while luxury brands such as Hermès and LVMH that target ultra-wealthy American consumers prospered by providing a higher quality of products.[13] Further to this, off-price, outlet and resale stores had a great opportunity since mass market shoppers usually try to distribute their spending during hard economical periods. For example, off-price retailers such as TJ Maxx and Ross outstripped fashion retail sales during that time.

The Covid-19 pandemic in 2020 made the Global Recession of 2008 look like a day at the beach for many fashion companies. Companies are working feverishly to figure out how to adapt to the huge drop in sales that forced many companies into bankruptcy.[14] Many long-established retailers and manufacturers including Neiman Marcus, J.C. Penney, Brooks Brothers, Ascena (owner of Ann Taylor, Lane Bryant, and several other brands), Sur La Table, G-Star Raw, Lucky Brand, J. Crew, True

Religion, Pier 1, the Arcadia Group (owners of Topshop, Debenhams, Warehouse), Ralph & Russo and Oasis have gone into administration.

Of course, in the business world when one door closes, often another opens. Other retailers did quite well during the pandemic. This was especially true for companies with a big online presence, such as Walmart and Amazon, as well as for those that happened to be in a merchandise category that consumers craved during lockdown such as groceries (including toilet paper!), home office furnishings, loungewear, and cosmetics.[15]

The Sociocultural Environment

The **sociocultural environment** describes the characteristics of a society, the people who live in that society, and the culture that includes their values, customs and beliefs. Fashion marketers need to understand and adapt to customs and practices of the members of a society since changes to the society values can greatly impact the firm's marketing effort; thus presenting opportunities or posing threats. These factors include how members of a culture think about gender, racial and ethnic identity, or the value they place on practicing sustainability.

Some of these factors such as racial identity and inequality have been the impetus for major social movements like Black Lives Matter, as well for numerous entrepreneurs of color who challenge the *status quo*. This growing list includes Aurora James, Kerby Jean-Raymond of Pyer Moss, whose fashion shows have celebrated Black history, as well as Rihanna, who made history when she created Fenty as the first Black woman to create an original brand for LVHM.[16]

Barbie collection

Catherine Zibo / Shutterstock.com

Every culture has **norms** that dictate (whether formally or informally) the rules of behavior that people should follow. These include dress codes that most people follow when they decide what to wear to work or play. Obviously, these norms change over time within a culture (nowadays we see a lot more professional women with tattoos in Western society), but they also vary across cultures at any point in time. So, for example, expectations about the amount of bare skin or body outline for women to show are quite different in the Middle East compared to Western Europe. As we've discussed elsewhere, luxury brands like Dolce and Gabbana, Oscar de la Renta, Tommy Hilfiger, DKNY and Mango have responded to this sociocultural difference by creating separate collections for Muslim women. They were able to jump onto this new opportunity by staying abreast of environmental trends; this market estimated to reach USD 88.35 billion by 2025.[17]

One of the most important characteristics of a society is to examine its **demographics**. Demographics are statistical data concerning observable aspects of a given population such as population size, age, gender, race, ethnical group, income, education, occupation, and marital status. Fashion marketers find great value in examining demographics, especially when they want to estimate the size of markets for various products and services, ranging from cars to apparels and accessories, to restaurants and fashion-related services.

For example, while Millennials form the biggest generational cohort in history, many are postponing childbearing until their late twenties. By the time Millennials start to have children in greater numbers, the number of kids is estimated to be lower than for previous generations. For this reason, fashion retailers targeting kids are recommended to take into consideration the decrease in births when they estimate the size of this future market.[18]

Each society possess a combination of **cultural values**; core principles and ideals about what is right and wrong in life that it conveys to its members.[19] Those principles impact almost every aspect of our lives. For example, over many decades Mattel's popular Barbie doll has come under fire for encouraging little girls to buy into an ideal of a blonde, thin and buxom woman. Mattel responded by offering a more diverse set of dolls that include a range of skin shades, eye colors, hairstyles, and apparel. They introduced a Barbie wearing a Hijab, a Barbie with a prosthetic leg, and a Barbie in a wheelchair. Further to this, they introduced Barbies for different races, ethnicities (multiple skin tones) or body shapes (curvy and tall).[20]

The Technological Environment

The **technological environment** strongly impacts a fashion brand's marketing activities. An obvious example is the Internet, which changed the way that businesses function and the way shoppers buy. Technological change offers risks, opportunities and threats to businesses. Advancements in e-commerce technology for example have been disruptive to brick-and-mortar stores. Some more traditional fashion businesses find it very hard to enter the online business and compete with large e-commerce websites such as Amazon. This form of technological development might force some small fashion businesses to go out of operation.

Artificial Intelligence (AI), which refers to leveraging computers and machines to mimic the problem-solving and decision-making capabilities of the human mind is another game changer for the industry.[21] In 2019, *The Business of Fashion* (BoF) and McKinsey launched a report, *The State* *of Fashion 2018*, which showed that 75% of fashion retailers intended to adopt AI in 2018/2019.[22]

Fashion brands are gradually implementing AI technology and machine learning to boost the customer experience and enhance the efficiency of sales processes using predictive analytics.[23] **Predictive analytics** is a computing system that utilizes machine learning to evaluate data and generate forecasts[24] (see also[25]). Nike acquired Celect, a demand forecasting and inventory optimization company, to better predict the styles of shoes and clothing that customers want, when they want to buy and where they want to shop, as the company hopes to reduce out-of-stock rates.[26] Another example is True Fit, a company whose role is to collect global footwear and clothing data, collaborate with top retailers and brands, understand buyers' preferences and product features to better predict what buyers want, and finally build and offer an AI-driven platform.[27]

Fashion and luxury brands also recognize the importance of **chatbots** in online commerce.[28] These are automated programs

Balmain's creative director, Olivier Rousteing

Kathy Hutchins / Shutterstock.com

that simulate real people online; as they interact with shoppers, they collect data by asking questions, analyzing customer buying patterns, and proposing related and add-on items. Many fashion apparel and beauty brands use this technology such as Burberry, Louis Vuitton, Tommy Hilfiger, H&M, Sephora, Victoria's Secret, and Estée Lauder. "Fashion brands are also starting to leverage conversational assistants through chatbots and voice assistant devices such as Amazon Alexa, Apple Siri, Google Home, and Microsoft Cortana. For example, when a customer needs new shoes or a dress, instead of interacting with a website or mobile app, they can simply have a conversation with an intelligent conversational agent. Through back and forth dialog, the customer can find the optimal fashion product or accessory item". [29]

Extended Reality (XR) is a new term that combines all new and emerging technologies (virtual, augmented, and mixed reality) to generate more immersive digital experiences.[30] **Virtual reality** (VR) refers to an entirely digitally immersive experience where the shopper puts on a headset and experience technologically blended 'real-use' experiences of products and services.[31] The luxury brand Balmain adopted virtual reality to take its customers into "The City of Lights" creative journey, showing them the dream-like inspirations behind the designs of its creative director Olivier Rousteing.[32]

In response to the Covid-19 pandemic, a number of fashion brands have moved into digital fashion shows. For example, for its Spring/Summer 2021 collection, Louis Vuitton designed a virtual reality experience for its fashion show allowing consumers to view the show from home.[33]

Augmented reality (AR) superimposes a computer-generated image onto the real world through the use of smartphone screens or displays. Unlike VR, AR is not completely immersive—the shopper sees a digital "layer" of information that appears in conjunction with what they see in the real world. This technology is really promising, because it allows consumers to "try on" clothing, cosmetics, eyewear, etc. in a risk-free and hassle-free environment.[34] No more struggling in and out of a dozen pair of pants to find a style that suits you or holding ten eyeglass styles in front of your face to figure out which is the most flattering.

Several progress companies are experimenting with AR applications, for example:

- The Gap chain launched an augmented reality dressing room that gives consumers the option to try on its collections digitally by layering them over an image of the shopper's body.

- Sephora and Rimmel have both designed augmented reality applications that give customers the ability to try on products through filters while using their mobile phones.[35]

- The Tenth Street Hats brand launched a "Virtual Try-On" option that allows customers to virtually try the hats and see how they look on them.

- The luxury brand Dior gives customers the chance to try on sunglasses using their smartphones through a new filter on Instagram.

Mixed reality (MR) is an extension of AR, the combination of *real* and *virtual* world whereby physical and digital items exists together, allowing users to interact with the real world. A perfect example for this was the Three partnership with London Fashion Week. To launch its 5G service, the company decided to produce the first 5G mixed-reality catwalk in 2019, where the audience could view collections with holographic animations in real time.[36]

The Micro-Marketing Environment

A big part of marketing planning is not just about figuring out how to adapt to changes in the world. It's also about identifying how your organization is best able to respond to these changes. For example, LVMH was able to "pivot" to making hand sanitizer because it already had production facilities that could be reengineered to produce these liquids—just as the Ford Motor Company was able to figure out how to adapt some of its auto factories to produce respirators for virus patients.[37] Obviously, that would be a much bigger stretch for a luxury brand like Louis Vuitton—but it found its own new competency by making hospital gowns and masks.[38]

The **microenvironment** refers to the organization's own strengths and weaknesses. This kind of analysis is crucial, because you need to have a realistic picture of what you are capable of doing—and doing well—in response to external opportunities and threats. The idea is to identify your **competitive advantage**, or what you can do better than your competitors.

Generally, this advantage comes in one of two forms: a cost advantage or a differential advantage. You have a **cost advantage** when you can produce a good or service at a lower cost than your rivals and compete on price. You have a **differential advantage** when you make a product that buyers see as significantly different or (hopefully) superior to what others make. For example, H&M is able to sell items in its stores at a much lower price point than many other clothing retailers. On the other hand, Philip Plein has a differential advantage because its customers truly believe that the T-shirts it sells are of superior quality. In either case, the key is to analyze your organization's structure and do a good job of matching your strengths to the opportunities that may be out there.

Company and Departmental Structure

All departments in the company are responsible for understanding customers' needs and creating value for them. This involves groups such as top management, finance, research and development (R&D), purchasing, operations, marketing, and accounting.

For example, the management department is the backbone of every fashion brand. It is responsible for handling the business, planning and making the right strategic decisions. The operations department (the department responsible for efficient and profitable production) cannot function without being in line with the decisions taken by top management and with customer needs and wants that are usually gathered by the research and development department. In order to oversee design and control the whole manufacturing process of fashion products, the operations department should also be in touch with the purchasing department whose role is to procure the needed raw materials and machines.

Also, this department should always report to top level management and inform them about any changes in price or material availability that might affect the fashion company's operations. For instance, a change in the price of cotton will greatly impact the final price of a T-shirt. The purchasing department should in this case inform the marketing department, the design department and other top-level managers who will then come up with different strategies to deal with the raw material price increase.

Customers

Customers are considered the most important factor since *every* business revolves around understanding and satisfying their customers' needs and wants. After all, that's why you are reading this book!

Fashion brands should be customer-oriented and offer the right products and services to its target market. Customers of today are more sophisticated and knowledgeable; this means they also are much more demanding. Changes in consumers' tastes and lifestyles should be continuously monitored in order for fashion brands to be able to supply its target market with the right product, at the right time and with the right price.

For example, today's consumers like to support brands that understand their individual uniqueness. They are more likely to discard the brands that push them into a standard definition of beauty. Therefore, consumers expect to buy from fashion brands that offer more diversity and inclusivity in terms of their product lines, the models they use, and their advertising.[39]

Employees

Employees are the core constituent of a fashion business; they are the ones who considerably contribute to its success. In the bricks-and-mortar world, ironically a store is only as good as its worst employee—we've all had a bad experience with a sales associate who is nasty or uneducated about the products in the store. On the other hand, the Nordstrom chain is famous for its great service ethic; "Nordies" will routinely go out of their way to provide superior service to shoppers.

The fashion industry does not rely on solo individuals to perform a certain task. Instead, it relies upon a range of employees that include designers, production experts, and sales associates. The performance of employees greatly depends on the training methods, motivation programs, and promotion opportunities given to them. For example, Gucci offers support to its craftsmen through its training program called "École de l'Amour," or School of Love, which "[...] is aimed at teaching and passing down the luxury company's artisanal skills and its know-how to the next generation of workers, as well as to its current employees"[40] In the luxury industry, salespeople are trained to provide a high level of personalized service in order to exceed customers' expectations and delight them. The LVMH group has created the LVMH House, whose role is to train senior executives. Every employee at LVMH is supposed to go through an in-house training program, whereby a variety of themes are involved such as culture, business challenges, "métiers", management, and products.[41]

Suppliers

Suppliers are the entities that provide the raw material (e.g., fibers, machinery and chemicals; clothing and textiles, including technical textiles) to make a finished good or the initial production of fashion items.

A supplier's behavior will highly influence the fashion business. For example, if a supplier provides inferior raw materials, this can affect the final product quality. Also, a significant rise in the price of raw material prices can impact the brand's strategy and may push them to set higher prices on the final products. Part of an organization's internal competency is its ability to maintain a solid and reliable network of suppliers. This often takes many years to develop.

Competitors

Keeping a close eye on competitors' activities is of upmost important as it allows the company to plan and modify its marketing strategy based on current market trends. For example, H&M and Shein are fast-fashion competitors that appeal to almost the same target market, so obviously each is quite interested in the moves that the other makes.[42]

However, every retailer employs a different strategy to manage the distribution of their product lines. H&M has lately faced a lot of issues related to its unsold stock and inability to keep pace with technological changes. However, this is not the case of its competitor Zara, who, has managed to maintain very low inventory levels.

Another example is the context of luxury watches. Luxury brands have ignored the second-hand market for luxury watches for a long time. However, today many brands are now looking to get into this market, since they are worried about their slow-moving primary market and they are cautious of conceding too much ground to third-parties (who are considered as their competitors). Since watchmakers might lose crucial market share if they do not embrace this change, the luxury group Richemont—which owns luxury brands like Cartier, Officine Panerai, Piaget, and Baume & Mercier—has lately acquired the online retailer Watchfinder, which buys and sells premium pre-owned watches.[43]

Marketing Intermediaries

Marketing intermediaries are independent groups that link the producer or other members of the distribution channel to the end consumer. For example, fashion retailers such as Macy's, Selfridges and Harrods are all intermediaries that purchase and resell products. Further down in the channel, of course we cannot overlook the growing importance of fashion bloggers and other influencers who today play a very significant role in determining the options that the end consumer considers.

Agents are entities that form an extension of the production firm. Their key role is not to take ownership of the purchased goods but to represent the manufacturer to the final consumer in selling a certain product, while receiving a commission for every performed transaction. Fashion producers use raw materials and fabrics to manufacture a finished fashion product, which may be delivered directly to the retailer, or less often, to the consumer. However, other fashion finished goods move from the producer to one or more wholesaler before they finally get to the retailer and then, the consumer. Fashion companies do have an extensive number of distribution channels to work with; choosing the right channel to deal with is one of the brand's most crucial marketing decisions. The selection of marketing intermediaries greatly depends on the level of fashion brand. For instance, a luxury fashion brand may have a different distribution strategy than a mass fashion brand. For example, for some products such as nail polish, intermediaries are crucial since they offer greater efficiency in letting these products become widely available and accessible to final users all over the world.

However, this is not the case for luxury fashion brands. Luxury brands generally prefer to operate their own stores, since they can take full control over the products, prices and brand image. To overcome the luxury brand's concern for the allocation of intermediaries, Amazon launched its own luxury website. It will mimic the business process of the concession model implemented in department and specialty stores, whereby luxury brands successfully rent a given space or pay a percentage of sales to run their private stores within the department store. Amazon will allow brands to take full control over the look of their online space, which products they decide to sell and at what price. Customers will be offered the Amazon customer service and a fast delivery.[44]

Publics

Publics are entities that may have a substantial influence on the company's marketing activities and ability to attain its goals in serving customers. These are the major publics where a brand needs to have a good relationship:

- *Financial publics* impact the brand's ability to get funds. For example, the fashion sportswear brand Adidas secured €3 billion in coronavirus funding from a German bank.

- *Media publics* convey fashion news, features, and editorial opinions. Fashion brands and retailers need to know how to manage media to promote positives instead of negative events that may ruin the brand's reputation. Many fashion editors boycotted Dolce and Gabbana when it launched an advertising campaign that has been denounced as racist against Chinese people.[45]

- *Government publics* are the legislative bodies that can influence how the brand is allowed to conduct business in different countries. For example, France has issued a new law banning fashion brands from destroying unsold items.[46]

- *Citizen-action publics*—a fashion brand's activities can be sometimes challenged by consumer organizations such as environmental groups. For example, watchdogs in the United Kingdom and Norway have warned fashion brands against over-stating their sustainability claims.[47] Also, consumer pressure forced some fashion retailers like Nike and H&M to reveal plans to reduce carbon emissions or use more recycled materials during production.[48]

- *Local publics*—includes neighborhood residents and community organizations. For example, local residents and farmers near the Jian River in China suffered when textile factories nearby illegally discharged poisonous waste into the water.[49]

- *General publics*—a fashion company must be aware about the general public's attitude toward its brand, products and services. For example, the celebrity Katy Perry recalled two products from her shoe range after she received criticism that one of the designs was racist.[50]

- *Internal publics*—workers, managers, volunteers, and the board of directors. For example, at the beginning of 2019, 50,000 female employees at apparel manufacturers in Bangladesh, the second-largest apparel exporter in the world, were involved in a series of strikes for higher wages.[51] Fashion brands such as Gap, H&M, and even Beyoncé's Ivy Park have encountered similar complaints over harmful working conditions and low wages for employees.

A SWOT Analysis for Fashion

As you go through the process of understanding all the positives and negatives both within your organization and external to it, what do you do with all that information? Many companies combine all of this information into what is commonly called a **SWOT Analysis**. **SWOT** stands for strengths, weaknesses, opportunities, and threats. The intelligence about both internal and external factors gets combined to help an organization where it stands on each of these dimensions:

Strengths and *weaknesses* refer to internal aspects, which are the resources, assets, processes and experience that have to do with the company. Strengths refer to the company's internal abilities that can allow it to achieve its goals, while weaknesses refer to internal problems that can get in the way.

Opportunities and *threats* are external uncontrollable aspects that can be either good or bad for the organization. Opportunities refer to the external factors that the fashion company may be able to exploit to its advantage. Threats refer to the current and emerging external factors that may challenge the fashion brand's performance.

The main goal of this analysis is to use the collected information in order to take advantage of the company's strengths, apply them to generate new opportunities or to decide how your fashion brand's strengths could best be used so that you can avoid market threats. You'll see an example in Table 5.1.

TABLE 5.1   A sample SWOT analysis of a fashion brand

Internal	Strengths	Weaknesses
	Fashion brand image	Dependence on physical shops
	Good contact with PR companies	Inability to expand to other markets
	High quality of production	Lack of control over production or too much dependence on third-party suppliers
	Exclusive products	Weak relationships with customers
	Unique designs	Low quality
	High levels of craftsmanship	Less professional employees
	Collection variety	Inability to run next day deliveries
	Speed in manufacturing	Inability to cope with sustainability
External	**Opportunities**	**Threats**
	Adopting new forms of technologies	Economic instability
	More flexible government trades	Online retailing for luxury brands
	Emerging global markets	Coronavirus crisis
	Online shopping	Political instability
	Delivery within 90 minutes	Governmental rules for fashion brands
	Potential to diversify into different categories	Changing consumer tastes
	Lifestyle changes allowing to expand	Rising taxation
	Fully benefit from the digital revolution	Changes in legislation

After you are done with this analysis, your objective should be to link your firms' strengths to available market opportunities while at the same time reducing the weaknesses and lessening the threats. This marketing analysis should assist you in developing an effective market strategy.

Developing Strategies for Growth and Downsizing

Marketing is mainly concerned with attaining profitable growth for the company. Fashion marketers should recognize, assess and choose market opportunities and establish strategies to seize them. One suitable tool for identifying growth opportunities is the **product-market expansion grid** (see Figure 5.1). This grid is a portfolio planning device that pinpoints four different strategies that fashion companies can use for future expansion: market penetration, product development, market development and diversification. Each carries its own kind of risk; there's the real possibility of entering a new, unfamiliar market and failing spectacularly. One unfortunate example was when Mattel took its hugely popular Barbie doll to China. An all-too-common story: the brand didn't pay enough "attention to local consumer tastes. Chinese women tend to like cutesy, girlish pink clothes (think Hello Kitty), not the sexy and skimpy kind that Barbie wore".[52] Each strategy has its pros and cons, depending upon the local conditions:

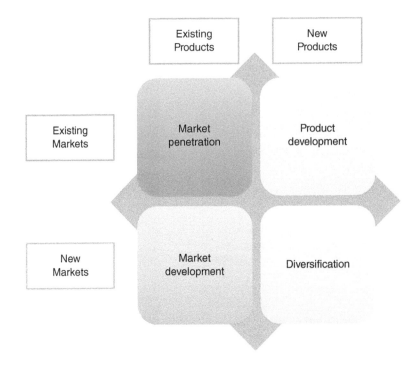

FIGURE 5.1   A product-market grid

Market Penetration occurs when a company sells existing products within its current market. The goal is to increase the number of customers, increase the average sale per visit, and enhance the fashion product's mix and range. For example, River Island has two stores on Oxford Street in London.

Market Development refers to entering a new market with an existing product. This strategy is commonly used by fashion brands. For example, the fashion brand Primark expanded from the UK to the American market by opening its first flagship store in the US back in 2015. The British luxury retailer Flannels originally opened in the North of England in 1976 and then expanded into different markets. In 2019 it opened its first London flagship store.[53]

Product Development is a strategy used by fashion brands in order to offer an existing modified product to the market or launch a new individual product or collection such as a diffusion line targeting the same market segment. Think of Porsche, which has introduced a new electric car, the Porsche Taycan.

Diversification is a strategy that is used to increase a company's growth by opening up or acquiring companies that are different from the company's existing products and markets. For example, Farfetch acquired the sneaker and streetwear retailer Stadium Goods for $250 million in its most important move since going public in September 2018.[54] Several luxury fashion houses are currently diversifying into restaurants. Tiffany opened a Blue Box Café in its New York flagship store and one in Harrods in London. The luxury brand Gucci opened its first ever restaurant in Florence, and in 2020 it opened its new location in Beverly Hills on the top floor of the brand's Rodeo flagship.[55]

Marketing Insights and Trend Forecasting

In recent times, some fashion companies are facing decreased sales volumes. The question is, why is this happening? Of course, we can trace a lot of this decline to the impact of the coronavirus, but even before the lockdown hit, we saw that many consumers were starting to rethink the value of frequent clothing purchases for various reasons including economic hardship, concerns about sustainability, and a shift toward allocating more discretionary income to experiences (like travel) rather than goods (like the latest Prada garment).[56] Indeed, all of the factors we've been discussing usually require some effort to compile the information an organization needs for intelligent decision-making.

Answers to these challenges can be acquired through the collection of accurate and systematic **customer insights**, which is the basis of all effective business ventures since it generates a wealth of information about potential and current customers, competitors, and the fashion industry in general. Every fashion company should continuously research the market by identifying or resolving challenges that it may be facing, understanding the needs of existing or potential customers, identifying new market opportunities, and anticipating shifting and new market trends for the sake of improving its decision-making process, and controlling the marketing of its products and services. Marketing research is an integral part of the business planning process.

Where do these insights come from? A lot of fashion companies use a **marketing information system (MIS)** to gather information. MIS is a tool that collects, categorizes, analyses and stores the type of information fashion marketers need to enable suitable marketing decision-making. Information can be collected from three different types of data: internal company data, market intelligence, and market research.

Internal Data

Internal company data involves the collection of information from within the firm's internal sources to develop reports on the outcomes of sales and marketing activities. It includes a company's sales records related to current and prospective customers—such as data related to which shoppers purchase which fashion goods and in what amounts and at what time intervals, which products are in store and which are currently out of stock, the time when products were delivered to shoppers, and which products have been returned and for what reason.

This information can be collected from various sources such as the marketing department (e.g. customer characteristics and profiles, sales records per customers, consumer behavior, website visits and level of consumer engagement), customer service department (e.g. customer satisfaction or complaints records and customer service issues), operations department (e.g., fashion products manufacturing, shipments, inventories), financial department (e.g. cash-flow reports and budgets), and sales data (e.g., revenue, profitability, marketing channels).

Internal data can assist fashion companies that seek to advance efficiency and productivity and fashion companies that fail to produce sufficient revenues. Marketing managers can periodically check the day-to-day or weekly sales data for a specific brand or product category from internal data-sources. They can rely on the monthly sales reports to assess how much they are progressing towards achieving sales and market share goals.

For example, Zara relies on the information obtained inside the store to guide new product design and adapt its offerings to consumer preferences. The information collected in-store is aggregated at the company's headquarters in Spain and if feedback from a big number of stores is consistent, this data is usually shared with the in-house designers who are requested to create new items based on this feedback. The marketing team is also responsible for assessing and analyzing the sales data collected from the stores and discuss them with the designers as well, thus allowing Zara to continuously create value by providing collections based on consumers' demand.[57]

Market Intelligence

In order to make effective decisions in a competitive market, marketers need to investigate the external environment and stay up-to-date with all the changes that are happening in the marketing environment. Therefore, a different way to gather data is through a **market intelligence system**, which requires the gathering and analysis of publicly available data related to consumers, competitors and changes in the marketplace that can be relevant to their firm. This information can be obtained from a company owned e-commerce website, monitoring Internet buzz (Internet forums, blogs, and social media networks), benchmarking competitors' products, industry trade publications, market share information, interrogating the company's own employees or direct field observations of the competitive marketplace.

Fashion companies greatly depend on their sales associates as a rich source of data in relation to consumers, distributors or possible customers. Fashion retailers usually recruit people who are tasked to go to their stores or to competitors' stores by taking the role of a potential customer and then are requested to report back on their experience of customer service and other retail activities. This technique is known as **mystery shopping**.

Marketing managers may also use market intelligence information in order to forecast variations in sales as an outcome of a range of macro-environmental factors such as the ones described at the beginning of this chapter including economic, political, sociocultural, and technological issues. In addition to this, fashion companies need to analyze trends that may impact consumers and predict colors and trends that they may want to buy in the future, approximately two years ahead, in order to implement the right strategies in their future collections.

Color Forecasting

Color forecasting is the "the practice of predicting the colors and color stories that consumers will want to purchase in the near future". These predictions are not limited to apparel; companies in the automotive, furniture, consumer goods, textiles, and even food industries rely on this as well. For instance, Samsung is basing its 2022 color palette on "'Fiery Dusk,' which was designed from the worldwide obsession with space exploration and Mars mission".

As we will see in Chapter 7, color is an important feature in the branding, designing and packaging of fashion and luxury goods because it has a huge impact on consumers' perceptions of the brand. For this reason, fashion brands work hard to anticipate consumers' tastes in colors ahead of time. These estimates impact the development of new products, allowing fashion companies to plan ahead of time and produce products based on consumers' demand and expectations. It also guides them with the color directions required to create matching products and services. Hence, if rose gold is *"en vogue* color", a lot of consumers will then want to get products with this color. They may want to buy a phone case, wearable, bracelet, and even cars or furniture in that color.

There are several color forecasting associations and groups whose primary purpose is to present colors to the industry that they feel will be successful in future years. In the apparel industry, early decisions in both the fiber and fabric markets are based on color, and therefore designers and retailers work closely with specialized forecasting houses.

The most prominent of these groups are the Color Marketing Group, International Color Authority (ICA), the Color Association of the United States, and the Color Box. Color forecasts are also included as a part of trend forecasts from forecasting services such as Promostyl (www.promostyl.com), the forecasting division of Doneger Group (www.doneger.com), and textile trade associations including Cotton Incorporated (www.cottoninc.com). Pantone conducts periodic research on consumer color preferences as well.

How does color forecasting work? The forecasting process comprises collecting a range of data from field reports, consumer studies, fairs, pop culture, press and more in order to come-up with color stories for the upcoming two years. The forecasters generate **mood boards**, whereby an assortment of photos, texts, or materials are collected to induce a specific idea or concept that backs up the evolving color's story. Numerous **color stories** emerge along this procedure. After stories are deliberated, colors types, shades and labeling are set as color directions that reinforce the story.[58]

Often, these predictions link specific hues to guesses about the "moods" that people will be in. For 2020, Pantone announced the color of the year was Pantone 19-4052 Classic Blue. The forecasters explain their choice this way: "Instilling calm, confidence, and connection, this enduring blue hue highlights our desire for a dependable and stable foundation on which to build as we cross the threshold into a new era."[59] The forecasts aim to sync with the moods that the company believes consumers will experience in the coming year. Most are fairly uncontroversial, though a recent choice did raise some eyebrows: Pantone introduced a new shade it calls "Period red" that focuses on the taboos around menstruation.[60]

Mood Board

Image courtesy of Xoyos.com via Flickr. Shared under the CC BY-ND 2.0 license

These forecasts do have a bit of a "self-fulfilling prophecy;" as numerous manufacturers cali-brate their palette choices to be in line with the predictions, it's perhaps not so surprising to find that the colors they choose do actually wind up in stores. Even so, it's important for companies to be aware of these forecasts so they can be sure to align their new products with the "hot colors" everyone will be looking for.

Trend Forecasting

If a fashion marketer could see into the future, they would obviously have an enormous advantage when developing products and services that would meet the needs of consumers next year, in five years, or in ten years. No one is able to do that, but a number of marketing research firms try very hard to predict social trends, or broad changes in people's attitudes and behaviors.

As the fashion industry changes so fast, it is imperative for marketers to keep on top of trends. Lifestyle forecasting gives hints of new product acceptance, but most apparel manufacturers and retailers also do more specific forecasting. One way is to subscribe each season to such services as Promostyl, Nigel French or Doneger Group forecasting, among others. Other industry sources including fiber companies and trade associations like Cotton Incorporated produce trend books for clients or members. Employees travel the world, visit the hot spots, photograph street fashion and anything edgy, and upon returning back, put together themes for manufacturers and retailers that subscribe to their services.

In addition to these services there are several online fashion trend sites for up-to-the-minute fash-ions. Examples are Women's Wear Daily, The Fashion Spot, Instyle, Vogue.com, Harper's Bazaar... WGSN (Worth Global Style Network), lets you walk in other worlds virtually. Walk down King's Road in London, see what's happening at the Paris flea markets, take a virtual tour of practically any trade show, and see what everyone else is looking at, all with a click of your mouse.

These sites give you information as opposed to analysis. That part is up to you. WGSN continu-ously monitors the signs of change that will influence the way people think, feel and act. The company has a team of 200 creative and editorial experts whose job is to connect the dots to precisely forecast the products, experiences and services that consumers will want in the coming years, guiding brands in how to stay up-to-date and prosper in the future.[61] They report on evolving trends mounting glob-ally from things taking place in the most advanced cities to interviews with prominent futurists in design, architecture and consumer culture.

Marketing Research

Marketing research is the practice of gathering, analyzing, and interpreting data related to prod-ucts or service offered to a market, to existing or potential customers, competitors, and the industry as a whole in order to improve marketing effectiveness. While firms gather market intelligence data incessantly to keep managers well-informed of changes in the marketplace, marketing research is also necessary when fashion marketers are searching for specific types of information to assist them in making accurate decisions.

No matter what kind of fashion goods these firms are offering, in order to succeed fashion com-panies need to understand what customers want, where they want to get it from, at what time or occasion they want it, and benchmark against their competitors. Depending upon the size and resources of the company, it may conduct the research itself. But it's likely that it will hire a professional marketing research firm to do the work. However, even if you don't do the actual research yourself, it's important for you as a consumer of this information to understand how it was collected.

There are different stages to conduct a research study:

Marketing Research

MIND AND I / Shutterstock.com

Step 1: Identify the Research Problem

The initial stage in the marketing research process is to clearly help the researcher define the problem in order to understand the type of information needed. At this stage, the researcher needs to specify the proper research objectives.

Let's say H&M wants to understand the reason why its sales decreased over the past few years. The research objective may include finding answers to many potential questions: Is the brand's communication strategy failing to appeal to the correct target market? Are the company's products having any particular defect or quality features that turn customers away? Are competitor brands offering products that are more fashionable and convenient? Are customers having problems with the company's customer service? Do consumers feel that they are getting the right value?

Step 2: Select the Research Design

After marketing managers pinpoint the specific objective, the next stage of the research process is to choose the research design that precisely identifies the type of information that should be gathered and the kind of research to perform. Not all marketing problems need to be answered through the same research practices, and fashion marketers resolve many issues most effectively by using a mixture of methods.

Research with Secondary Data

The primary goal for marketers when they plan a research design is whether the required data is already available. For instance, a fashion company that wants to enter the American market and who wants to identify the size of the apparel market in the US may realize that this information is already available through **secondary data** such as industry reports that have been gathered for a different objective than the one at hand. If this information is available, it saves the company the time and the cost of designing a study from scratch. Sometimes the data that fashion marketers are looking for is available through another firm's reports; earlier firm research studies; feedback collected from consumers, sales associates, or even stores.

Research with Primary Data

When the type of required information is not available through secondary data, fashion marketers need to collect data specifically for their objective. This is done by collecting primary data; information directly obtained from consumers for the specific research plan. Primary data includes demographic and psychological data about existing and potential consumers, customers' attitudes and opinions about existing products and competitive brands, and their awareness and perceptions of a brand.

There are different forms of designs to gather primary data. For example, this can be done through exploratory research to generate more information about opportunities or possibly to get a clear understanding of a problem that the company may be facing. As this form of research is usually less expensive, marketers may use this technique in order to identify what is happening without taking too much risk or incurring a lot of expense. For example, if the number of consumers purchasing from the brand has decreased, the fashion firm may decide to explore the reasons for this. Accordingly, the brand may examine the actions that competitors' brands may be taking, or it may interview a small number of customers in depth to better understand their responses.

In general, most exploratory research takes the form of *qualitative research*, which means that the outcomes of the research study involve in-depth verbal or visual insights of consumers' attitudes, opinions, perceptions, feelings, and purchase behaviours in words rather than numbers.

For example, Swarovski conducted in-depth interviews with female jewelry buyers in order to develop an external perspective of what different consumer segments might look like. The results indicated that there are numerous jewelry consumer types with diverse wants and needs.[62]

Focus groups are a common method that marketers use to conduct exploratory research. Focus groups consist of a group of five to nine consumers recruited to participate in a discussion about a certain product or service before its introduction to the market, or to gather some feedback on a given campaign, etc.

For example, in 2018, IKEA was looking for a way to develop a better understanding of "how people currently think and feel about climate change, what people are doing to take climate action in their daily lives, and how to motivate and enable them to do more". To do so, the company decided to recruit people from six countries around the globe such as China, Germany, India, Russia, UK and USA to join them in focus groups. The results helped "to inspire and enable IKEA co-workers and millions of customers to take positive action for the climate.[63]

Another qualitative approach is ethnographic research, where market researchers visit individuals' homes or partake in real-life consumer activities to better understand how people actually use the items they buy. For instance, P&G modified its products for emerging markets based on ethnographic research that indicated about 80% of individuals in India wash their clothing by hand. Because these individuals need to select an option that is gentler on the skin, P&G developed Tide Naturals, a detergent that cleans well without producing irritation.[64] An illustration of product development that L'Oréal created based on ethnographic research is L'Oréal Paris UV Perfect Matte & Fresh SPF 50/PA ++++, which offers maximum sunlight protection but which is also capable of avoiding make-up line marks around the hijab area.[65] L'Oréal did this by observing women who wear hijabs.

Another way to gather primary data is descriptive research that defines the characteristics of the population or phenomenon under examination. For example, a fashion company might want to describe the market potential of a new service it wants to introduce. This type of study thoroughly investigates the marketing issues and bases its findings on responses from a large sample of participants to survey questions. The findings are usually conveyed in quantitative terms—averages, percentages, or other statistical measurements.

Marketing researchers who use descriptive methods usually adopt a cross-sectional design. This method typically comprises the systematic assortment of responses from particular group of people, such as a questionnaire, at a defined time. In contrast, a longitudinal design involves repeated observations of the same sample of participants over a period of time.

Market researchers often rely on consumer panels to obtain data; this term describes a group of individuals that are representative of a larger market who agree to deliver information about products and services on a weekly or monthly basis. For example, in 2012, Unilever has used a customer panel that invites consumers to assist the firm in determining the future direction of its brands whereby respondents are expected to participate in at least one survey per month in return for loyalty points.[66]

The last form of primary data is causal research. Some fashion companies are interested in knowing for example what would happen if they offer a 50% discount to customers who purchase after 9:00 PM. In other words, they want to determine if changing something in the marketing mix would lead to another change, such as whether a specific price reduction will result in a sales increase.

Causal research seeks to determine the extent and nature of cause-and-effect relationships. Marketers choose this method when they want to assess whether a variation in something (e.g., placing a make-up display next to a facial wipes display) is accountable for a variation in something else (e.g., a large increase in facial wipes sales). The element that might cause such a variable is known as an independent variable and the effects are measured on dependent variables. They do their best to keep everything else the same, so that if they do observe a change, they can be reasonably confident it was due to the independent variable.

So, the idea is to find out if changes in the independent variable(s) cause some variation in the dependent variable(s). In the previous example, the make-up display is an independent variable, and sales data for facial wipes are a dependent variable—which means that this research is examining whether an upsurge in facial wipes sales "depends" on the proximity of the make-up display.

This type of causal research usually entails the implementation of experimental designs. Experiments seek to identify causality by eliminating alternative explanations. To preserve a high level of control, experiments may necessitate placing participants into a lab in order for researchers to control exactly what they want to test. For the facial wipes example, a group of women might be recruited and be asked to visit a "virtual store" on a computer screen. They would then be asked to select the items and fill their bag as they browse through the virtual aisles. The experiment might be designed in a way that half of the women—chosen at random—would be shown one location of facial wipes and the other half would be shown a different location. Everything else about their experience would be exactly the same. Thus, if the respondents in the first group on average were far more likely to choose the product, the experimenters could be reasonably confident that the placement of the display "caused" the increased preference.

Step 3: Selecting the Method to Gather Primary Data

Primary data can be collected in a lot of different ways. In the "old days," it was common for researchers to simply mail out questionnaires to consumers, go door-to-door with surveys, or perhaps to stop them as they shopped to answer some questions.

Another technique that is still common but starting to die out is contacting respondents by telephone. Due to fears about privacy and security—and the fact that a lot of people are simply fed up with being interrupted at dinnertime—it's increasingly rare to see these techniques in use. That is one reason why most survey research today is conducted online instead.[67] Respondents are sent invitations to participate, but they have more choice about whether or not to accept.

But marketing research continues to get more sophisticated. Some marketers even use brain scans to measure a consumer's physiological responses to different advertising messages. This practice is known as neuromarketing, which "studies the brain to predict and potentially even manipulate consumer behavior and decision making".[68] Most of this work to date has occurred for consumer packaged goods, rather than in the fashion and luxury industry. However, a few companies have tried it. For example, the fashion retail chain T.J. Maxx used neuromarketing in order to track consumers' brain activity as they browse the store. The company's unique selling point is to place luxury brands goods at low prices among more mass label items. The results of this experiment indicate that when shoppers identified a luxury brand item, an upsurge in brain activity was linked with astonishment, enjoyment and reward. This type of finding assists T.J. Maxx in designing its store layout by considering this 'treasure hunt' outcome and aiming to generate more instants of positive, purchase-inducing feelings.[69]

Step 4: Plan the Sample

After the researcher outlines the problem, chooses the appropriate research design, and decides how to gather the data, the subsequent stage is to plan from which population to get the required information. As the collection of data from a whole population is usually impossible, market researchers need to gather their data from a small proportion, or sample, of the population of interest. If the sample accurately reflects the larger group, they can confidently generalize their results to the overall population. But to do so, researchers need to identify the criteria that make up a representative sample. For example, just asking "people you know who wear Levi's jeans" probably is not the way to go about that.

Step 5: Collect and Analyze the Data

At this stage, the researcher has identified the nature of the problem, selected the appropriate research design and sample that states how to examine the problem at hand, and chosen the data collection and sampling techniques. Once all of this has been performed, the data are collected. Depending upon the method used, this process can take a few days or several months. Then the information has to be transferred to a format that will provide answers to the initially recognized problem. Analysis of data involves examining, cleaning, converting, and exhibiting data with the purpose of emphasizing worthwhile information, proposing conclusions, and supporting decision-making.

Step 6: Present the Research Report

The last stage in the market research process is to interpret the gathered data and draw conclusions from it by preparing a report. The research report must clearly and concisely communicate the research results for use in managerial decision making, and should include the following:

1. An executive summary of the report that emphasizes the main results of the whole report.

2. A clear explanation of the research techniques.

3. A comprehensive discussion of the research findings, involving all the statistical analysis.

4. Limitations of the research study.

5. Conclusions and managerial contributions based on the findings.

Chapter Summary

Now that you have read the chapter, you should understand the following:

1. How to analyze the marketing environment.

The marketing environment consists of the forces that affect a fashion and luxury brand's capability to function effectively in delivering products and services to its target market, and controls the brand's capability to create and maintain the flourishing relationships with its consumers. A variety of environmental external and internal factors influence a brand's marketing planning and fall under the macro and micro environments. The macro environment refers to all the actors that make up part of the larger society and impact the micro environment. It consists of the technological, political and legal, sociocultural, environmental and economic environments. The micro environment consists of the factors in the firm's immediate environment that impacts its abilities to function effectively in several ways in its selected markets. It involves the company and departmental structure, suppliers, competitors, marketing intermediaries, customers and publics.

Further to understanding the marketing environment, fashion brands also need to run a complete analysis of their firm's market situation by performing a SWOT analysis. **SWOT** stands for strengths, weaknesses, opportunities, and threats. Strengths and weaknesses refer to internal aspects, which are the resources, assets, processes and experience that have to do with the company. Opportunities and threats are external, rather uncontrollable aspects that can impact every fashion company.

2. How to gather market insights and trend forecasting.

Fashion companies refer to marketing information systems (MIS) to gather information. MIS is a tool that collects, categorizes, analyses and stores the type of information fashion marketers need to enable suitable marketing decision-making. Information can be collected from three different types of data: internal

(Continued)

company data, market intelligence, and market research. The internal company data consists of the assortment of information from within the firm's internal network (e.g. marketing department, finance department, purchasing department, customer service department...) to develop reports on the outcomes of sales and marketing activities. Market intelligence systems require the gathering and analysis of publicly available data related to consumers, competitors and changes in the marketplace that can be relevant to their firm, usually obtained from a companies' websites, Internet buzz, benchmarked competitors' products, industry trade publications, market share information, company's employees or direct field observations of the competitive marketplace. Finally, market research is the practice of gathering, analyzing, and interpreting data related to products or service offered to a market, to existing or potential customers, competitors, and the industry as a whole in order to improve marketing effectiveness. There are seven different stages in conducting marketing research. First, the company needs to clearly define the problem in order to understand the type of needed information. Next, it has to select the research design in order to identify the type of information that should be gathered and the type of research to perform. Research designs can be based on either primary or secondary data. Then, marketers need to choose the right method (e.g., surveys or observations) to gather primary data. After that, the subsequent stage is to plan from which population to get the required information to examine the problem at hand and choose the data collection technique. Once all of this has been performed, the market researcher should be ready to analyze the data and present it in a research report that clearly and concisely communicates the research results for use in managerial decision.

DISCUSSION QUESTIONS

1. Describe how the micro and macro environmental factors can affect a fashion brand.

2. How can the technological environment have an impact on luxury brands?

3. Explain how customers can negatively impact a firm's business. Why are marketers interested in satisfying customers?

4. Discuss a recent sociocultural change that may affect a fashion brand of your choice (e.g., sunglasses, apparel, make-up...). As a marketing manager, how would you react to this change?

5. Perform a SWOT analysis on a fashion company of your choice. Following the analysis, develop a strategy for growth based on the product-market grid.

6. Conduct a SWOT analysis for a mass fashion brand versus a luxury fashion brand. Indicate the reason why the competitors' marketing strategies have to be different for each type.

7. What is the main difference between internal data and marketing research? Which do you think fashion and luxury brands should refer to?

8. What do you predict will be in fashion for next season? How did you come up with these predictions?

9. How ethical is it to practice neuromarketing?

EXERCISES

1. Form a group and discuss where trends come from. Then, try to come up with new emerging trends and discuss the reason for their appearance.

2. Assess the marketing opportunities and threats for a fashion-brand of your choice, which may be posed by the increasing importance of a socially aware consumer.

3. Identify a lifestyle trend that is just surfacing in your locality. Describe this trend in detail and justify your prediction. What specific styles and/or products are part of this trend? How long do you think it will last? Why?

4. You are the Marketing Manager of Gucci. You were asking yourself about the future of the brand. What strategic decisions should you make to sustain the brand in the future? Explain.

CASE STUDY: THE PARADOX OF INCLUSIVE LUXURY

Dina Khalifa, University of Cambridge

The luxury industry is one of the most influential industries owing to its immense cultural power, global customer awareness and high visibility. The global luxury goods market is expected to increase from US$309.6 billion in 2021 to US$382.6 billion in 2025.[70] The true essence of the luxury strategy lies in inherent elitism, exclusivity and restricted accesses preserved for the "happy few". However, against a backdrop of rising socio-economic, gender and racial inequalities, luxury brand exclusivity may risk alienating large segments of society, thus creating social tensions that puts the industry under mounting pressure to become more inclusive. The proliferation of social media platforms coupled with shifts in societal norms and heightened consumer activism manifest in the recent anti-racism protests in the US and Europe, and the rise of the Black Lives Matter movement have further amplified the demand for inclusivity.

As such, the luxury industry has to rise to the challenge of balancing the seemingly contradicting imperatives of selling exclusivity and fostering inclusivity. In recent years, there has been an exponential rise in the number of industry initiatives aimed at promoting inclusivity and tackling the deeply rooted prejudices embedded within the fashion system. For example, the proportion of racially diverse, older, plus-size, or transgender models have significantly increased in fashion week runways in London,

(Continued)

New York, Paris and Milan. Additionally, there has been a wider representation of black and ethnic minorities in leadership roles. In 2017, Edward Enninful became the first black editor-in-chief of British *Vogue* and a year later Virgil Abloh became the first black man to become an artistic director at Louis Vuitton. Moreover, many brands including Gucci, Chanel and Burberry have hired Diversity and Inclusion Managers. However, as the appetite for luxury brands continues to grow in established and emerging markets in Asia, Latin America and Africa, an opportunity arises for brands to widen their access and cater to a broader and more diverse consumer. Yet the question remains: How can an industry that has historically operated on models of exclusivity, embed inclusivity in a way that preserves its elitist façade whilst driving real change?

The pandemic has further demonstrated the need to accelerate the transition towards an inclusive society with a stronger emphasis on social purpose. In particular, consumers are becoming less tolerant of unsustainable practices and are expecting businesses to align their mission, values and strategies to a purpose beyond profit maximization. Purpose-driven businesses serve not only shareholders but a wider range of stakeholders including employees, customers, suppliers, local communities, society at large and the planet.

With demand for corporate purpose expected to maintain momentum post-pandemic, especially among Millennials and Gen-Z, luxury brands have an opportunity to take on a role as driver for positive societal change. In embracing this opportunity, luxury brands could identify, and publicly share their central purpose, one that is embedded in their culture, and builds on their core values. Luxury brands are in a key position to lead business action in sustainability by leveraging their cultural authority and using their voice to communicate, advance, and debate socio-political challenges in the public sphere and thus accelerate behavioral change, and drive social change.

DISCUSSION QUESTIONS

1. Based on the arguments, do you think that the luxury sector could play a role in fostering social inclusion? Discuss the opportunities and challenges using SWOT analysis.

2. How can the shift to inclusivity impact luxury brands strategy development and future trends?

REFERENCES

D'Arpizio I. and Levato, F. (2019) 'Bain luxury goods worldwide market study—Spring 2019 update', Bain, June 01. www.bain.com/insights/luxury-report/ (accessed August 17, 2021).

Kent, S. (2019) 'Fashion's long road to inclusivity', *Business of Fashion*, October 7. www.businessof fashion.com/articles/news-analysis/fashions-long-road-to-inclusivity (accessed August 17, 2021).

Newbold, A. (2020) 'Will SS21 be a turning point for diversity?', *Vogue*, September 27. www.vogue. co.uk/fashion/article/diversity-fashion-ss21 (accessed August 17, 2021).

NOTES

1. Shatzman, C. (2020) 'Louis Vuitton's Paris atelier is now making hospital gowns', *Forbes*, April 15. www.forbes.com/sites/celiashatzman/2020/04/15/louis-vuittons-paris-atelier-is-now-making-hospital-gowns/#46b6aa8229a7 (accessed August 17, 2021).

   LVMH (2020) 'At the heart of the fight against Covid-19 is the manufacture of masks and gowns by our Maisons', *LVMH*, April 15. www.lvmh.com/news-documents/news/lvmh-maisons-repurpose-facilities-to-make-face-masks-and-gowns-for-hospital-staff-helping-battle-covid-19-in-france/ (accessed August 17, 2021).

2. Kohan, S. (2020) 'Apparel and accessories suffer a catastrophic 52% sales decline in March', *Forbes*, April 16. www.forbes.com/sites/shelleykohan/2020/04/16/apparel-and-accessories-suffer-a-catastrophic-52-percent-decline-in-march-sales/#7c0f22d41b5b (accessed August 17, 2021)

   Kestenbaum, R. (2020) 'LVMH converting its perfume factories to make hand sanitizer', *Forbes*, March 15. https://www.forbes.com/sites/richardkestenbaum/2020/03/15/lvmh-converting-its-perfume-factories-to-make-hand-sanitizer/#737a2feb4a9a (accessed August 17, 2021).

3. Bianchi, F., Dupreelle, P., Krueger, F. Seara, J., Watten, D. and Willersdorf, S. (2020) 'Fashion's big reset', BCG, June 1. www.bcg.com/en-us/publications/2020/fashion-industry-reset-covid (accessed August 17, 2021).

4. Rackham, A. (2021) 'Pandemic fashion: 'We went from selling sequins to sweatpants'', *BBC News*, February 2. www.bbc.com/news/newsbeat-55773751 (accessed October 17, 2021).

5. Pestle Analysis (n.d.) 'What is PESTLE Analysis? An Important Business Tool', pestleanalysis.com. https://pestleanalysis.com/what-is-pestle-analysis/ (accessed August 17, 2021).

6. Vonberg, J. (2018) 'Norway pledges to shut down all fox and mink fur farms by 2025', *The Independent*, January 16. www.independent.co.uk/news/world/europe/norway-fur-farm-ban-close-deadline-20225-mink-fox-animal-rights-erna-solberg-a8162196.html (accessed August 17, 2021).

7. Bogliari, A. (2020) 'Influencer marketing And FTC regulations', *Forbes*, December 2. www.forbes.com/sites/forbesagencycouncil/2020/12/02/influencer-marketing-and-ftc-regulations/?sh=28db76b11566 (accessed August 17, 2021).

8. Hall, C. and Suen, Z. (2020) 'China and the US signed a trade truce. Who now benefits?', *Business of Fashion*, January 16. www.businessoffashion.com/briefings/china/china-and-the-us-signed-a-trade-truce-who-now-benefits (accessed August 17, 2021).

9. Fernandez, C. (2020) 'As a global recession looms, quiet luxury returns', *Business of Fashion*, March 18. https://www.businessoffashion.com/articles/luxury/the-return-of-quiet-luxury (accessed August 17, 2021).

10. Financial Times (2020) 'Virus impact on fashion and luxury to be "worse than recession"', *Financial Times*, March 26. www.ft.com/content/4bee8020-5781-4658-839a-c8d56fc102e7 (accessed August 17, 2021).

11. Brooke, E. (2018) 'How the Great Recession influenced a decade of design' *Vox*, December 27. www.vox.com/the-goods/2018/12/27/18156431/recession-fashion-design-minimalism (accessed August 17, 2021).

12. Retail Dive Team (2021) 'The running list of 2020 retail bankruptcies', *Retail Dive*, February 5. www.retaildive.com/news/the-running-list-of-2020-retail-bankruptcies/571159/ (accessed August 17, 2021).

13. Arnett, G. (2019) 'What happens to luxury during a recession?', *Vogue Business*, August 16. www.voguebusiness.com/companies/luxury-recession-saks-bond-yield (accessed August 17, 2021).

14. Retail Dive Team (2021) 'The running list of 2020 retail bankruptcies', *Retail Dive*, February 5. www.retaildive.com/news/the-running-list-of-2020-retail-bankruptcies/571159/ (accessed August 17, 2021).

15. Selasky, S. (2020) 'Kroger, other retailers see "eye-popping profits" as workers reap little benefit', *Detroit Free Press*, April 12. www.freep.com/story/news/local/michigan/2020/12/04/kroger-walmart-amazon-profits-covid-19-pandemic/6458910002/ (accessed August 17, 2021).

16. Charuza, N. (2020) '26 Black fashion designers that should be on your radar, *Popsugar*, June 10. www.popsugar.com/fashion/black-fashion-designers-47524520 (accessed August 17, 2021).

17. Research and Markets (2019) 'Islamic clothing: Worldwide Market Size, Share & Trends 2018–2025 – Key Players are House of Fraser, Marks & Spenser, Aab, H&M, and Mango. Intrado Globe NewsWire, March 14. www.globenewswire.com/news-release/2019/03/14/1753024/0/en/Islamic-Clothing-Worldwide-Market-Size-Share-Trends-2018-2025-Key-Players-are-House-of-Fraser-Marks-Spenser-Aab-H-M-and-Mango.html (accessed August 17, 2021).

18. Danziger, P. (2018) '9 demographic trends shaping retail's future', *Forbes*, September 6. www.forbes.com/sites/pamdanziger/2018/09/06/9-demographic-trends-shaping-retails-future/?sh=7210e3f47b00 (accessed August 17, 2021).

19. Pollay, R.W. (1983) 'Measuring the cultural values manifest in advertising', *Current Issues and Research in Advertising*, 6 (1): 71–92.

20. Abrams, R. (2016) 'Barbie adds curvy and tall to body shapes', *The New York Times*, January 28. www.nytimes.com/2016/01/29/business/barbie-now-in-more-shapes.html (accessed August 17, 2021).

21. Chopra, K. (2019) 'Indian shopper motivation to use artificial intelligence', *International Journal of Retail & Distribution Management*, 47 (3): 331–47.

    Sohn, K., Sung, C.E., Koo, G. and Kwon, O. (2020) 'Artificial intelligence in the fashion industry: Consumer responses to generative adversarial network (GAN) technology', *International Journal of Retail & Distribution Management*, 49 (1): 61–80.

22. Craig & Karl (2018) 'The State of Fashion 2018', *The Business of Fashion/McKinsey*. www.mckinsey.com/~/media/mckinsey/industries/retail/our%20insights/renewed%20optimism%20for%20the%20fashion%20industry/the-state-of-fashion-2018-final.ashx (accessed August 17, 2021).

23. Schmelzer, R. (2019) 'The fashion industry is getting more intelligent with AI', *Forbes*, June 16. www.forbes.com/sites/cognitiveworld/2019/07/16/the-fashion-industry-is-getting-more-intelligent-with-ai/#4477cc9a3c74 (accessed August 17, 2021).

24. Martens, D., Provost, F., Clark, J. and de Fortuny, E.J. (2016) 'Mining massive fine-grained behavior data to improve predictive analytics' *MIS Quarterly*, 40 (4): 869–88.

25. Luce, L. (2019) 'Predictive analytics and size recommendations', in L. Luce *Artificial Intelligence for Fashion: How AI is Revolutionizing the Fashion Industry*. San Francisco, CA: Apress. pp. 107–121.

    Silva, E.S., Hassani, H. and Madsen, D.Ø. (2019) 'Big Data in fashion: Transforming the retail sector', *Journal of Business Strategy*, 41 (4): 21–7.

    Silva, E.S., Hassani, H., Madsen, D.Ø. and Gee, L. (2019) 'Googling fashion: Forecasting fashion consumer behaviour using Google trends', *Social Sciences*, 8 (4): 111.

26. Thomas, L. (2019) 'Nike acquires A.I. platform Celect, hoping to better predict shopping behavior', *CNBC*, August 6. www.cnbc.com/2019/08/06/nike-acquires-ai-platform-celect-hoping-to-predict-shopping-behavior.html (accessed August 17, 2021).

27. True Fit (2021) 'What we do', *True Fit*. www.truefit.com/About-Us/What-We-Do (accessed August 17, 2021).

28. Chung, M., Ko, E., Joung, H. and Kim, S.J. (2018) 'Chatbot e-service and customer satisfaction regarding luxury brands', *Journal of Business Research*, 117: 587–95.

    Rese, A., Ganster, L. and Baier, D. (2020) 'Chatbots in retailers' customer communication: How to measure their acceptance?', *Journal of Retailing and Consumer Services*, 56: article #102176.

29. Schmelzer, R. (2019) 'The fashion industry is getting more intelligent with AI', *Forbes*, June 16. www.forbes.com/sites/cognitiveworld/2019/07/16/the-fashion-industry-is-getting-more-intelligent-with-ai/#4477cc9a3c74 (accessed August 17, 2021).

30. Schmelzer, R. (2019) 'The fashion industry is getting more intelligent with AI', *Forbes*, June 16. www.forbes.com/sites/cognitiveworld/2019/07/16/the-fashion-industry-is-getting-more-intelligent-with-ai/#4477cc9a3c74 (accessed August 17, 2021).

31. Jung, J., Yu, J., Seo, Y. and Ko, E. (2019) 'Consumer experiences of virtual reality: Insights from VR luxury brand fashion shows', *Journal of Business Research*, 130: 517–24.

32. Hart, C. (2018) 'Balmain takes customers on a creative journey using virtual reality', *The Current Daily*, April 17. https://thecurrentdaily.com/2018/04/17/balmain-vr-experience/ (accessed August 17, 2021).

33. Phelps, N. (2020) 'Louis Vuitton', *Vogue*, October 6. www.vogue.com/fashion-shows/spring-2021-ready-to-wear/louis-vuitton (accessed August 17, 2021).

34. Baytar, F., Chung, T. and Shin, E. (2020) 'Evaluating garments in augmented reality when shopping online', *Journal of Fashion Marketing and Management: An International Journal*, 24 (4): 667–83.

35. Jiang, E. (2017) 'Virtual reality: growth engine for fashion?', *Business of Fashion*, February 28. www.businessoffashion.com/articles/technology/virtual-reality-growth-engine-for-fashion (accessed August 17, 2021).

36. Rewind (n.d.) 'Three Mobile: Augmenting London Fashion Week with 5G & MR', *Rewind*. https://rewind.co/portfolio/three-mobile-5g-mixed-reality-fashion-show/ (accessed August 17, 2021).

37. Dearborn, M. (2020) 'Ford to produce respirators, masks for Covid-19 protection in Michigan; scaling up production of gowns, testing collection kits', *Ford Media Center*, April 13. https://media.ford.com/content/fordmedia/fna/us/en/news/2020/04/13/ford-to-produce-respirators-masks-covid-19.html (accessed August 17, 2021).

38. Cohen, J.A. and Zendejas, A. (2019) 'Fashion brands making cloth masks you can buy now', *Harpers Bazaar,* December 2. www.harpersbazaar.com/fashion/trends/g32192171/fashion-brands-masks-coronavirus/ (accessed August 17, 2021).

39. Danziger, P. (2019) '6 global consumer trends for 2019, and the brands that are out in front of them', *Forbes,* January 13. www.forbes.com/sites/pamdanziger/2019/01/13/6-global-consumer-trends-and-brands-that-are-out-in-front-of-them-in-2019/?sh=7ca3f2434fe4 (accessed August 17, 2021).

40. Carrera, M. (2018) 'Gucci kicks off new training program', December 17. https://wwd.com/fashion-news/fashion-scoops/gucci-kicks-off-new-artisan-training-program-1202936955/ (accessed August 17, 2021).

41. LVMH (2021) 'Development & Transmission', *LVMH.* www.lvmh.com/talents/your-career-at-lvmh/development/ (accessed August 17, 2021).

42. Tyler, J. (2018) 'We visited H&M and Zara to see which was a better fast-fashion store, and the winner was clear for a key reason', *Business Insider,* June 15. www.businessinsider.com/hm-zara-compared-photos-details-2018-5 (accessed August 17, 2021).

43. Reuters Staff (2018) 'Richemont to buy Watchfinder as pre-owned watch market heats up', *Reuters,* June 1. www.reuters.com/article/us-watchfinder-m-a-richemont/richemont-to-buy-watchfinder-as-pre-owned-watch-market-heats-up-idUSKCN1IX5HQ (accessed August 17, 2021).

44. Bain, M. (2020) 'Amazon is said to be preparing a luxury fashion platform', *Quartz,* January 8. https://qz.com/1781553/amazon-said-to-be-launching-new-luxury-fashion-platform/ (accessed August 17, 2021).

45. Nanda, M.C. and O'Connor, T. (2020) 'How Dolce & Gabbana clawed its way back from cancellation', *Business of Fashion,* February 5. www.businessoffashion.com/articles/marketing-pr/dolce-gabbana-racism-gay-rights-outrage (accessed August 17, 2021).

46. Kent, S. (2019) 'What fashion can learn from a decade of disasters', *Business of Fashion,* December 14. www.businessoffashion.com/articles/professional/end-of-the-decade-fashion-moral-sustainability-climate-labour (accessed August 17, 2021).

47. Kent, S. (2019) 'What fashion can learn from a decade of disasters', *Business of Fashion,* December 14. www.businessoffashion.com/articles/professional/end-of-the-decade-fashion-moral-sustainability-climate-labour (accessed August 17, 2021).

48. Newburger, E. (2020) '"Clothing designed to become garbage" – Fashion industry grapples with pollution, waste issues', *CNBC,* February 8. www.cnbc.com/2020/02/07/new-york-fashion-week-how-retailers-are-grappling-with-sustainability.html (accessed August 17, 2021).

49. Gayle, D. (2011) *The River that DID Run Red: Chinese Waterway Turns Scarlet after Illegal Factories Dump Dye Stocks.* Mail Online. www.dailymail.co.uk/news/article-2074671/Chinese-Jian-River-flows-blood-red-illegal-dye-factories-dump-stock.html (accessed August 17, 2021).

50. BBC (2019) 'Katy Perry "saddened" by blackface claims about her shoe range', *BBC News,* February 13. www.bbc.com/news/newsbeat-47211111 (accessed October 17, 2021).

51. Kelly, K. (2019) 'Garment workers have organized strikes for over 100 years as they pay the human cost of fashion', *Teen Vogue,* March 8. www.teenvogue.com/story/garment-workers-strikes-human-cost-of-fashion (accessed August 17, 2021).

52. Rein, S. (2010) 'Where Barbie went wrong in China', *Forbes* January 22., www.forbes.com/2010/01/22/barbie-mattel-china-leadership-managing-rein.html?sh=11513efc1f1d (accessed August 17, 2021).

53. Hawkins, L. (2019) 'Flannels opens first London flagship, designed like a prismatic puzzle', *Wallpaper,* September 5. www.wallpaper.com/fashion/flannels-opens-first-london-flagship (accessed August 17, 2021).

54. Business of Fashion Team (2018) 'Farfetch's first major post-IPO move: what does it mean?', *Business of Fashion,* December 14. www.businessoffashion.com/articles/news-analysis/farfetch-major-ipo-move-stadium-goods-recommerce (accessed August 17, 2021).

55. Davis, D.-M. (2020) 'Gucci is opening a Beverly Hills outpost of its Michelin-starred restaurant in Florence – here's a look inside', *Business Insider,* February 11. www.businessinsider.com/gucci-osteria-first-american-restaurant-in-beverly-hills-2020-2 (accessed August 17, 2021).

56. Momentum Worldwide (2019) '76% of consumers prefer to spend on experiences than on material items, new study finds', *PR Newswire,* October 14. www.prnewswire.com/news-releases/76-of-consumers-prefer-to-spend-on-experiences-than-on-material-items-new-study-finds-300937663.html (accessed August 17, 2021).

57. Doepke, K. (2015) 'Zara – customer data as competitive advantage', *Open Forum, Harvard Business School,* April 14. https://web.archive.org/web/20191226041031/https://www.hbs.edu/openforum/openforum.hbs.org/goto/challenge/understand-digital-transformation-of-business/zara-customer-data-as-competitive-advantage.1.html

58. Color Marketing (2018) 'What is color forecasting', *Color Marketing,* June 6. https://colormarketing.org/2018/06/06/what-is-color-forecasting/

59. Pantone (2020) *Pantone Color of the Year 2020.* www.pantone.com/articles/color-of-the-year/color-of-the-year-2020 (accessed August 17, 2021).

60. Abdul, G. (2020) 'Pantone's new color joins a movement to destigmatize menstruation: Period red', *The New York Times*, October 1. www.nytimes.com/2020/09/30/business/pantone-color.html (accessed August 17, 2021).

61. WGSN (2021) 'From design to delivery', *WGSN.* https://www.wgsn.com/en/members/ (accessed August 17, 2021).

62. Kittinger-Rosanelli, C. (2012) 'Creating Crystal Experiences: MIR talks to Alexander Linder, director corporate consumer and market insights (CCMI), Daniel Swarovski Corporation AG', *GfK-Marketing Intelligence Review*, 4 (2): 52–57.

63. Inter IKEA Systems B.V. (2018) Climate action starts at home, *Ikea.* www.ingka.com/wp-content/uploads/2020/01/IKEA-Climate-Action-Report-20180906-002.pdf (accessed March 4, 2022).

64. Brown., B and Anthony, S.D. (2011) 'How P&G tripled its innovation success rate', *Harvard Business Review,* June. https://hbr.org/2011/06/how-pg-tripled-its-innovation-success-rate (accessed August 17, 2021).

65. Bukalapak (2021) 'Hijab muslim LOreal UV Perfect Matte Fresh SPF 50 PA LOREAL Sunblock, *Bukalapak.* www.bukalapak.com/p/perawatan-kecantikan/perawatan-wajah/pembersih-wajah-wanita/36qo4ms-jual-hijab-muslim-loreal-uv-perfect-matte-fresh-spf-50-pa-loreal-sunblock (accessed October 17, 2021).

66. Baker, R. (2012) 'Unilever readies new customer insight panel', *Marketing Week,* February 2. www.marketingweek.com/unilever-readies-new-customer-insight-panel/ (accessed August 17, 2021).

67. Nunan, D., Malhotra, N.K. and Birks, D.F. (2020) *Marketing Research: Applied Insight.* Pearson UK.

68. Herrell, E. (2019) 'Neuromarketing: What you need to know', *Harvard Business Review*, January 23. https://hbr.org/2019/01/neuromarketing-what-you-need-to-know (accessed August 17, 2021).

69. Abnett, K. (2015) 'Can neuroscience unlock the luxury mind?', *Business of Fashion,* April 22. www.businessoffashion.com/articles/luxury/can-neuroscience-unlock-the-luxury-mind (accessed August 17, 2021).

70. Statista (2021) *In-depth: Luxury Goods 2021.* www.statista.com/study/61582/in-depth-luxury/ (accessed August 17, 2021).

CHAPTER 6
Segmentation, Targeting and Positioning

LEARNING OBJECTIVES

After you read this chapter, you will understand the answers to the following:

1. What are the different ways to segment markets?

2. What are the different forms of target marketing strategies?

3. How can fashion brands position themselves in the market?

We hear a lot these days about "body positivity," an attitude that encourages women in particular to feel good about their shape—even if it doesn't resemble the super-skinny and often airbrushed models they see in fashion magazines. As companies like Victoria's Secret—who built their brand on the promise that women who wear their scanty lingerie and underwear will feel sexy and catch the eye of men—fall out of favor, new companies are springing up with a range of garments that are specifically designed for larger, "full-bodied" women. Some of these new entries are Adore Me, American Eagle's Aerie and True & Co.[1]

One of the big winners thus far is ThirdLove. The idea for the company began in 2011, when Heidi Zak, a woman who worked for a Silicon Valley tech firm had an unpleasant experience when she tried to buy a bra at a Victoria's Secret store. The retailer's flimsy garments appealed to her when she was younger, but at this point in her life she didn't think that image suited her any longer. In fact, she was so embarrassed by the process that she hid the trademark pink bag in her backpack on the way out.

(Continued)

This traumatic episode prompted Heidi and her husband (also a techie) to start a new company that would allow women to avoid going into a store altogether when they wanted to get fit for a bra. Their ideal customer was a woman who felt she had moved on from being a Victoria's Secret shopper and was looking for a new option.

The couple turned to technology to solve the problem. They developed a smartphone app that used computer vision (similar to technology employed by NASA) and complex algorithms to determine the correct bra size, based upon photos the customer uploaded. ThirdLove also offered half sizes, an innovation in the bra category.

As the concept took off, the company expanded to offer larger sizes, as it realized that many plus-size women also feel intimidated by the shopping experience. Evidently this touched a nerve; the expanded range completely sold out three weeks after the company introduced it.

Today ThirdLove offers over 80 sizes and continues to target a diverse range of women who believe they are excluded from a market that targets stereotypically "hourglass" body shapes. The CEO observed, "We believe the future is building a brand for every woman, regardless of her shape, size, age, ethnicity, gender identity, or sexual orientation. This shouldn't be seen as groundbreaking, it should be the norm."[2] As demand grows for these diverse options, the company is setting its sights on other categories such as swimsuits and athletic wear.[3]

Obviously, not every woman is a 22-year-old with a body like a Victoria's Secret "Angel." The reality is that fashion marketers can't please all consumers at the same time and in the same way. For this reason, companies need to identify one or more **market segments** composed of buyers who are good prospects for what they make. They may be newer groups who aren't satisfied with what they currently find, such as ThirdLove's customers. Or it may be that customers have different incomes or preferences; that's why it's common for larger companies to offer separate brands that appeal to different types of people. Think

The segmentation, targeting and positioning process

Nattee Sriyant / Shutterstock.com

for example of the cosmetics giant L'Oréal brand that sells under a variety of names including L'Oréal Paris, Maybelline, Yves Saint Laurent, Lancôme, and Urban Decay.

In this chapter, we'll review the three-step process that marketers commonly used to be sure that what they sell aligns with what their customers want. The shorthand for this sequence is STP: segmentation, targeting, and positioning.

Step 1: Segmentation

Most companies engage in a process of **market segmentation**, where they divide the larger marketplace into different parts based on one or more significant attributes, such as gender, lifestyle, or age. The segments they identify ideally are made-up of consumers who will react to the company's marketing strategies in a similar way and who will usually share characteristics such as common interests, needs, or geographic locations (like women who have aged out of slinky underwear styles). Think for example of Marriott's set of hotel brands, that range from the value-oriented Courtyard chain to the luxury Ritz-Carlton Hotel.

How can fashion marketers identify likely segments? In this section, we'll take a look at how marketers segment their customers, starting with the different forms of segmentation variables that they can adopt to divide a bigger market.

As you can imagine, there are numerous ways to slice up this pie. We divide these up into three broad categories—and keep in mind that they are not necessarily mutually exclusive.

Demographic Segmentation

Demographic segmentation is defined as a market segmentation process based on variables such as age and family life cycle, gender, income and social class, and ethnicity. These are dimensions that are relatively easy to measure (although some like gender and ethnicity are getting more complicated).

Age and Lifecycle

Individuals do not stick with the same products over their lifetimes. Age is one of the most important demographic factors for fashion marketers. Individuals of different age groups possess distinct needs and wants. Consumers who belong to the same generation usually share a lot of similarities in terms of their outlook on life, their values, and their brand preferences. And, as family needs and expenditures change over time, it's often valuable to segment the consumer market by considering the stage of the family life cycle they occupy. Shoppers who are at different life cycle stages are unlikely to require the same type of fashion products, or they may not need it in the same amount or form. For example, a single person might prefer a racy Porsche Spyder, while her older brother with kids might opt for a larger Cayenne SUV so he can fit his family in the car as well.

Generational marketing describes an approach that divides consumers in terms of the generation to which they belong. For example, many apparel retailers and brands target teenage girls with their trendy new fashion lines, including jeans, tops and accessories. The kids' segment makes up another worthwhile buying group in the fashion industry. A number of luxury brands have been lately targeting the upscale children's clothing segment, given its growing appeal in the fashion market. The rental online retailer Rent the Runway expanded its market by adding new kids' labels available through its monthly rental service; these include Chloé, Fendi, Stella McCartney and Little Marc Jacobs. Other brands also followed this trend, such as Givenchy, Gucci and Balenciaga and online retailers such as MyTheresa and Net-a-Porter.[4]

Generation Z (or iGen) is the demographic cohort of those who were born between 1997 and 2010.[5] This is the first generation of the 21st century. It consists of individuals who are Digital Natives and tech addicts, who therefore expect brands to engage with them through digital conversations.[6] These individuals are more likely to buy and look for smartphones, tablets or wearable technology instead of apparel.[7]

This cohort has values that are completely different from those of previous generations and have had a huge impact on the fashion industry. It has been accused of killing some fashion retailers such as Abercrombie & Fitch, J. Crew, Aéropostale, American Eagle, and Gap, since they are not as much concerned about buying products as they are with buying an experience with the product as a bonus.[8] This generation highly values comfort and function. Many value the freedom to wear comfortable garments that make them feel relaxed all day.

Generation Z are better informed about how to make effective decisions with all of their financial resources than the previous generations—lessons possibly taught by their Generation X parents, many of whom experienced disrupted careers following the Global Recession of 2008 and the coronavirus crisis. Gen Z has also experienced this, some of them were hard-hit by disrupted education and the closure of many workplaces where they could have been employed.

This group is more likely to explore brands through their devices before they purchase, and they look for fashion retailers that provide in-store technologies, such as smartphone self-checkout, interactive shopping screens, and virtual try-on for apparel shopping. They research new styles and trends through social media, and they might seem to care less about fitting in, on the contrary, they might choose to make decisions that reveal their personal identity.[9] Further to this, many members of this generation care a lot about sustainability.[10] A 2019 report revealed that around 62% of Generation Z prefer to purchase from sustainable brands and 54% will pay an additional 10% on sustainable products.[11]

Primark flagship store, Boston

Image courtesy of Wikiklrsc, via WikiMedia Commons. Shared under the CC BY-SA 3.0 license

One of the fashion brands that was able to understand this cohort is Primark. The brand was able to engage teenagers by converting its stores into a shareable experience. Customers are motivated to upload their photographs taken while shopping to the brand's website with the hashtag #Primania, with a chance to be featured on a rolling feed in specific stores, as well as its US flagship. The brand has also equipped its stores with free WIFI access and have designed changing rooms in a way to fit two consumers, to be more selfie friendly.

A Gen Z consultant with the Center for Generational Kinetics stated that "Gen Z really is different; they aren't a more extreme version of Millennials but are different—and that's mostly because of parenting.[12]" So a good question would be: who are the Millennials?

Generation Y, usually known as **Millennials** or "Echo Boomers," comprises those who were born between the years 1981 and 1996. Millennials are the children of the baby boomer generation. This age segment is the first cohort to grow up with e-commerce. The oldest Millennials were teenagers at the time the Internet became a mass medium, and the youngest were 11 when Apple introduced its iPhone back in 2007.

Millennials represent the most important and most dominant consumer demographic group that influences fashion markets today.[13] They have transformed the way fashion brands do business. The most preferred apparel brands/retailers for millennial women in the USA are Forever 21, Target, Macy's, H&M, Amazon, American Eagle and Old Navy. For men, it's Amazon, Macy's Nike, Adidas, and Levi's. And, as we've seen, overall Millennials are a very concerned generation when it comes to environmental sustainability and social issues.[14] Some Millennials are starting to look for apparel that is practical, heavy-duty, and long-lasting. That helps to explain why some outdoor retailers such as North Face have exploded in popularity as well.[15] Some luxury brands such as Gucci decided to go anti-fur in response to young consumers' widespread concerns about sustainability and animal welfare.[16]

Millennials are also impacting the food industry.[17] They look for more healthy food choices; nearly nine out of 10 Millennials are concerned about what they eat.[18] They expect food companies to be transparent about revealing their ingredients and sources in addition to food being natural, organic and locally sourced. They also want customization when it comes to the food they eat.[19] For example, Chipotle does this by allowing customers to completely customize their online orders; they can select different portion sizes, light versus normal options and side dishes.

Generation X is the demographic cohort born between the mid-1960s and the early 1980s. This generation is a profitable target market for luxury brands since many of them have higher earnings than other generations, in addition to high brand loyalty.[20] While this cohort grew up without the digital boom, they still spend a lot of their time browsing the web and searching online for new and distinguished products. Gen X also look for honesty and trustworthy communication from brands and are equally comfortable using both traditional and digital media channels.

Baby Boomers is a term used to describe the demographic group that was born between 1946 and 1964. A lot of fashion brands tend to ignore Baby Boomers although they make up almost 42% of spending in the US, versus 13% for the other generations such as Millennials and Gen Z.[21] These brands instead focus on a much younger audience.

This is a mistake because this age cohort has both the money and the interest in apparel, travel and other lifestyle pursuits. For example, (at least before the pandemic) baby boomers typically planned to take four to five leisure trips a year with an average of $6,600 spent, which is 20% to 50% more than travelers from Gen X or Millennial cohorts.[22]

Gender

Numerous products, ranging from perfumes to fashion clothing and accessories, are specifically marketed to different genders. This distinction begins early on—parents who still value a traditional gender dichotomy can even buy pink diapers for baby girls and blue diapers for baby boys.

Today, however, there is a new perspective on the binary definition of gender. Fashion marketing companies are trying to shift their strategies to appeal to a gender-free society. "According to Pew research, 35% of Generation Z knows someone who identifies as non-binary and prefers gender neutral pronouns," states an article in *Fortune*.[23] ASOS, the online fashion retailer, is focusing on increasing the number of sales from a new generation that doesn't want to be classified according to a specific gender.[24] Adidas and Beyoncé recently launched a gender-neutral collection, a collaboration between Adidas and Beyoncé's Ivy Park label.[25]

This trend has affected the kidswear segment as well. According to Stacia Andersen, Brand President of Abercrombie & Fitch and Abercrombie Kids, "…parents and their kids don't want to be confined to specific colors and styles, depending on whether shopping for a boy or a girl." Given this changing sentiment, Abercrombie & Fitch launched a unisex kids line as its first gender-neutral collection in 2018.[26] Other companies followed suit. For instance, the fashion retailer John Lewis removed the "Boys" and "Girls" labels from its kidswear apparel in order to avoid reinforcing gender stereotypes in addition to launching a new unisex apparel line for kids, featuring dinosaur print dresses and spaceship tops.[27] Further to this, a number of beauty brands have also moved from relying on heavily gendered marketing into more gender-neutral ones. An example is Panacea, a gender-neutral skin-care brand.

Ethnicity

Marketers cannot ignore the stunning diversity of cultures that comprise mainstream society. An **ethnic subculture** consists of a group of consumers who are held together by common cultural ties and is identified both by its members and by others as a distinguishable category.

The multicultural demographic that comprises "Hispanics, African-Americans, Asian-Americans and all other multiculturals already makes up 38% of the American population"[28] and the purchasing power of this segment is rising at a quicker speed than the country's average. Ramen noodles, hip-hop/rap music and hip-hop fashion are only some examples of products and trends propelled by ethnic backgrounds and tastes that have been embraced by the general American consumer.

More and more companies today are aiming to tap opportunities in the **multicultural** beauty market. Over the recent couple of years, the demand for multicultural beauty products has increased as a consequence of a growing middle class in emerging markets and multi-ethnicity in the West. The market for multicultural beauty is thought to be more diverse, given the evolution of interethnic couples and families.[29]

According to Garuba-Okelarin (2016) "Companies that previously only provided limited foundation ranges have expanded their spectrum of shades in their catalogues and a few brands such as Tom Ford with Betty Adewole, YSL with Jordan Dunn and Charlotte Tilbury with Tiara Young are now including darker skinned models in their advertising".[30] Christian Louboutin appealed to different skin tones by extending "his Nude Collection of women's shoes from five to seven skin tones, adding "porcelain" and "deep chocolate"".[31] For her shapewear collection, Kim Kardashian launched a collection called SKIMS that comes in nine different skin tones instead of the general three adopted by other brands. The purpose is to make sure that women have options to match their skin color as closely as possible.[32]

Also, rising demand for *halal* beauty and personal care products in some markets is worth noting. This interest parallels the growing demand for "modest fashion" we discussed earlier. Companies must obtain a certification showing that these brands are following the Islamic standards (some companies offer vegan choices, guaranteeing that no animal derivatives are used).[33]

One of the first Korean companies to obtain halal certification from the Malaysian government is Talent Cosmetics.[34] SimplySiti, another halal brand launched by singer Siti Nurhaliza, offers cosmetic, perfumes and beauty care products that are halal-certified. Conventional retailers such as Clara International, Ivy Beauty Corporation, and Saaf Skincare have also joined the halal market trend, launching products that are "free from alcohol, blood and parts or substances from animals that have not been slaughtered according to Islamic practices".[35] Amara Halal Cosmetics offers an extensive selection of halal-certified cosmetic goods such as nail polish, lipstick, and liquid foundation.

Income and Social Status

The dissemination of wealth is of great interest to marketers since it identifies what groups have the highest buying power and market potential. But income *per se* often is not a very good predictor of what specific items people will buy. That is because people from different social classes (as we will discuss in Chapter 9) may choose to spend their money differently due to variations in values and priorities. For example, a middle manager at a financial services company and a successful hairstylist may make roughly the same income, but one may spend their money on gourmet food while the other would rather buy a Mercedes.

Still, consumers obviously rely on money to allow them to acquire the goods and services that they need to express their tastes, so clearly income is still crucially important. Is social class or income a better indicator of a person's consumption behavior? The answer is mainly related to the types of products the market offers. The following general conclusions can be made regarding the relative value of social class (place of residence, occupation, cultural interests, and so on) versus income in predicting consumer purchase behavior:

- Social class appears to be a better indicator of products that have symbolic features but range in price from low to moderate (e.g., cosmetics, wine, fashion).

- Income is a better indicator of major purchases that do not have status or symbolic features (e.g., basic appliances).

- Both social class and income data are needed to forecast buying of expensive and symbolic goods such as homes and automobiles (unless of course a person splurges and leases a high-end car or home!).

Some consumers rely upon the display of **status symbols** to broadcast their social status (for more on status symbols see[36]). As we saw in Chapter 2, within the last century or two, the quest for status was at work when wealthy women commissioned designers to adorn them in unique and expensive gowns – and then they made sure that others saw them wearing this finery in public.

Christian Dior logo bag

Image courtesy of Patrick Sawaya Photography

In those days, a "designer label" didn't exist so people had to use other means to discern which woman had just spent a sizeable portion of her husband's income to impress them. Today, in some cases fashion brands make things a bit easier because they prominently display their labels on the exterior of clothing, accessories, luxury cars, and so on. Designer labels, initials, logos and trademarks are emblazoned on our clothing, shoes, bags and even sheets and towels. For example, luxury brands are using a lot of big logo or monogram logo T-shirts that are easily recognized by consumers. Take the example of the Fendi monogram T-shirt or the big Dior logo or Valentino logo for both women and men.

There are two problems with this "look at my label" strategy:

1. The profusion of "knockoffs" and counterfeit products that flood the world's market and diminish the value of the originals.

2. The increasing number of "entry-level" products that allow less-affluent consumers to flash the same labels. For example, in recent years, luxury automobile makers such as Mercedes, BMW, and Audi have created new versions that list at less than half the price they charge for one of their traditional models. When Tesla launched a "low-end" Model III the company could barely handle the demand after getting bombarded with preorders.[37]

Targeting Affluent Consumers   Some marketers appeal to high-income consumer markets. This is understandable, since more expensive items typically offer higher profit margins. Nevertheless, marketers cannot assume that individuals who earn the same income should belong to the same segment group. As we discussed in the previous section, social class includes more than income. It is also related to a way of life, and various aspects—including how someone has acquired their money, where they have got it from, and the amount of time they had it for—significantly impact affluent consumers' interests and spending patterns.[38]

One emerging strategy—that became especially attractive due to the pandemic—is to offer "affordable luxuries" to people who cannot afford to purchase the designer's typical product range. For example, a woman who lost her job due to the virus might no longer (or at least temporarily) be able to spend over $500 on a Fendi T-shirt, but she might be able to splurge on a $26 bar of Chanel soap. **Affordable fashion** is emerging as a compromise to keep consumers engaged with the marketplace even though their incomes may have taken a hit due to the pandemic.

The SRI consultancy firm classifies luxury consumers based on three different attitudes towards luxury:

1. Luxury is utilitarian: individuals will purchase items that will last for a long period of time. They are likely to engage in considerable pre-buying search and make rational rather than affective decisions.

2. Luxury is a status signal: these individuals are more likely to be younger than those who consider luxury as utilitarian but older than those who consider luxury as a gratification. Their possession of luxury goods reflects a sense of achieving something. The need to achieve and show success to others drives this group to buy more status consumption related luxury goods like luxury cars and houses in selective residences.

3. Luxury is gratification: this segment forms the tiniest group and is likely to involve younger, male individuals. These individuals consider luxury to be highly extravagant and pleasant. They are also ready to spend high amounts on items that reflect their uniqueness and enable them to attract the attention of those around them. These individuals are more likely to make impulsive buying and are rather affective by nature.[39]

Targeting Low Income Consumers   Over 2.5 billion individuals—making-up almost half the world's population—live below the poverty threshold, and many marketers disregard this group.[40] Still, while poor individuals clearly have less money to consume goods and service than rich ones, they have basic needs like everyone else in society.

Many companies now focus on targeting low income consumers given their big numbers. Companies are creating less expensive products and services around their very specific needs. In order to sustain a low profit margin, this is compensated by high sales volumes obtained from this segment. This is known as a **bottom of the pyramid** approach.

Unilever Global for example was faced with the problem of wanting to increase rural sales of Rexona deodorant in the Philippines. While the normal package sizes were too expensive for these consumers, Unilever created a cream version of the deodorant that comes in a single-use-sized packet that costs about 10 cents, which turned out to be a successful strategy.[41]

In order to target the poor segment in developed countries, a **frugal innovation** strategy was recommended. This strategy suggests that companies do not need to do more with less, but they are requested to make things in a different way than what they have been used to in the past. This involves the following:

*   *"Good enough"*: Basic, functional goods that can perform their actual job without any embellishments or improved functionality/design.

*   *Partnerships*: Collaborating to combine the intellectual property and resources of firms that have market entrance and the consumer insights of not-for-profits, charities and local or small firms.

- *Affordability*: Inexpensive goods without compensating the main functionality or quality.

- *Quality and performance*: Products should maintain their quality and their main functionality equivalently to more premium products.

- *Usability*: Easy to use, requiring no special information and understanding of how it should function.

- *Sustainable*: Goods should be economically sustainable, but meanwhile offer social value.

A great example of a company that has implemented this strategy is the automobile brand Renault with its launch of the Logan. The carmaker created a no-frills car by using its available parts and technologies. The developed model was mainly designed based on the basics, ignoring all optional additions. It allowed consumers who previously only had the option to buy a secondhand car to get their hands on a brand new one.[42]

Geographic Segmentation

Geographic segmentation is a segmentation strategy whereby a marketer divides the marketplace based on geographic locations. Other factors related to differences in geographic segments may involve climate, cultural preferences, populations, and more. Savvy fashion marketers recognize that fashion consumers have preferences for items that vary from one region to the other and across different geographical locations.

In warmer locations, shoppers are more likely to purchase shorts and swimwear for longer periods of time. Calzedonia targets these warmer areas with beaches and resorts by offering a wide assortment of swimwear apparel and accessories. However, the same retailer might be merchandising thermal leather effect leggings for a different region or area. North Face and Canada Goose, which generally sell winter outfits will market their products in cold areas all year long. Another example is the luxury car company Porsche that chooses to target customers who live in warm climates, e.g. the southwest regions of the US, with a higher percentage of convertible vehicles. Consumers in Asia are more likely to favor white cars.[43] This preference drives marketers to provide a greater number of white cars produced for this specific area.

Fashion retailers also understand cultural preferences when it comes to colors across

Canada Goose winter outfit

Image courtesy of José Francisco Salgado via WikiMedia Commons. Shared under the CC BY-SA 3.0.

different regions. Think of Indian weddings, where brides traditionally wear a red dress, a color associated with purity in India. Marketers can also segment the market geographically by considering the density of population or the population of a particular area. For example, a retailer selling the most luxurious fashion products may only want to place itself in very exclusive markets like New York City, Los Angeles or London where its elite target market is present.

Fashion marketers also rely on geodemographic segmentation when they want to select the best locations for their new stores. **Geodemographic segmentation** refers to an analytical tool that combines data on consumer expenditures and other socioeconomic factors with geographic information about the areas in which people live in order to identify consumers who share common consumption practices. This approach is based on the assumption that "birds of a feather flock together"; people who have similar needs and tastes tend to live near one another, so it should be possible to locate "pockets" of like-minded people who can be reached in more direct ways. For example, premium fashion retailers would open in more up-market socio-economic residential areas such as Sloane Street in London, Fifth Avenue in New York, Rue Saint-Honoré in Paris or Via Manzoni in Milano.

Psychographic Segmentation

Consider a marketer who wishes to target a student population. The ideal consumer is identified as someone who is 21 years old, a senior business major living on a large university campus and whose parents make between $40,000 and $80,000 per year. You may know a lot of people who fit this description. Do you think they are all the same? Would they all be likely to share common interests and buy the same products? Probably not, since their lifestyles are likely to differ considerably.

Demographic and geographic information are beneficial; however, they don't give marketers complete information about how to divide the marketplace into significant segments. While marketers can refer to demographic characteristics, when it comes to fashion markets, savvy marketers understand that preferences are more complicated than just demographic (e.g., gender) or geographic (e.g., climate) characteristics. Successful marketers benefit from different segmentation tactics, by referring to one of the most valuable and more refined technique known as psychographic segmentation.

Psychographic segmentation involves "the use of psychological, sociological and anthropological factors... to determine how the market is segmented by the propensity of groups within the market—and their reasons—to make a particular decision about a product, person, ideology, or otherwise hold an attitude or use a medium".[44] Psychographics can help a company fine-tune its offerings to meet the needs of different segments. Demographics allow us to describe *who* buys, but psychographics allow us to understand *why* they buy.

Conducting a Psychographic Analysis: Using AIOs

Most contemporary psychographic research attempts to group consumers according to some combination of three variables—activities, interests, and opinions—which are known as **AIOs**. Using data from large samples, marketers create profiles of customers who resemble each other in terms of their activities and patterns of product usage.

Activities   **Activities** involves work, hobbies, social events, vacation, entertainment, community, club memberships, shopping, sports, and social event of consumers. Such activities enlighten marketers about the things that a person or group does or has done, where they are involved and the way they amuse themselves. This dimension provides marketers with information on the individuals' daily journey.

For example, recent research shows that there is a boom in women participating in sports activities. In 2016, during the Rio Olympics, fully 45% of the 11,000 athletes who participated in the running events were women. Also, more and more women today classify themselves as sports fans. "On average, across 24 major countries representing the Americas, Europe and Asia, nearly half of all women now declare themselves either interested or very interested in sport compared to 69 per cent of men," says Paul Smith, founder and chief executive of Repucom, a sports research firm.[45]

Based on this activity dimension of women's lifestyles, a lot of fashion retailers are taking notice. Mainstream sportswear brands such as Nike, Adidas and Under Armour currently embrace women in their marketing campaigns and they have created specific collections for women. Also, there are other fashion activewear brands that are interested in this segment such as Lululemon and Sweaty Betty.

Under armour women's activewear

Creative Commons Zero – CC0

Many fashion and luxury brands are nowadays appealing to the segment of pet lovers. For instance, brands like Versace, Louis Vuitton, Burberry, Moncler, Elisabetta Franchi, and Tiffany have all provided apparel or accessories to dogs.

Opinions   **Opinions** refer to how people think about social issues, politics, business or economics, education, products, and the future. Fashion marketers should also consider consumers' opinions when they describe specific market segments. For instance, fashion brands that sell jackets are now moving to the production of jackets with *faux*-fur instead of real fur, given consumers' increasing sensibilities towards animal welfare.

The luxury brand Tiffany detected an important change in their customer's opinions about the political and social issues related to *conflict diamonds*. The brand instituted a zero-tolerance policy for acquiring diamonds from countries with human rights infringements. Tiffany went one step ahead by developing a charitable foundation working on awareness for responsible mining.[46]

Uses of Psychographic Segmentation

Psychographic segmentation can be used in a variety of ways:

- *To define the target market*: This information allows fashion marketers to go beyond simple demographic or product usage characteristics (such as young females or recurrent users).

- *To create a new perspective of the market*: Fashion marketers may develop their strategies with a "typical" consumer in mind. This stereotype can be misleading since the actual customer may not be congruent with these assumptions. For instance, a marketer of a beauty skin care creams for female consumers was shocked to find that its key market was made more of mature rather than the younger females they were appealing to.

- *To position the product*: Psychographic information permits marketers to highlight the product aspects that match an individual's lifestyle. Products targeted at people whose lifestyle profiles show a high need to be around other people might focus on the product's ability to help meet this social need.

- *To better communicate product attributes*: Psychographic information can offer very useful input to advertising creatives who must communicate something about the product. The creative designer of a certain luxury brand should get a much richer mental image of the target consumer than that gathered through dry statistics, and this insight improves their ability to "talk" to that consumer.

Lifestyle

Lifestyle represents an important factor that fashion marketers rely on when they want to select their product lines. Consumers often choose products, services, and activities over others because they are associated with a certain lifestyle. For this reason, lifestyle marketing strategies attempt to position a product by fitting it into an existing consumption pattern. Because a goal of lifestyle marketing is to allow consumers to pursue their chosen ways to enjoy their lives and express their social identities, a key aspect of this strategy is to focus on product usage in desirable social settings. The goal of associating a product with a social situation is a long-standing one for advertisers, whether the product is included in a round of golf, a family barbecue, or a night at a very glamorous club.

An important part of lifestyle marketing is to identify the set of products and services that seems to be linked in consumers' minds to a specific lifestyle. Marketers who pursue co-branding strategies intuitively understand this; that is why Hermès and Apple teamed up for a co-branding deal. Other examples of co-branding are Target (e.g. with Victoria Beckham), H&M (e.g. with Balmain, Comme des Garçons, Moschino) and Uniqlo, which all had partnerships with designers on capsule collections.[47] To boost its comeback in 2017, Levi's unveiled 50 collaborations with worldwide influencers asking them to customize or style their personal trucker jacket. Some of these collaborators were G-Dragon, Justin Timberlake, Diplo, Justice and Tinie Tempah, and the designers Virgil Abloh and Jun Takahashi.[48]

A related concept is **product complementarity**, which occurs when the symbolic meanings of different products are related to each other.[49] These sets of products, termed **consumption constellations**, are used by consumers to define, communicate, and perform social roles.[50] For example, the American "yuppie" of the 1980s was defined by such products as a Rolex watch, an Armani suit, a BMW car, a Gucci briefcase and shoes.

Our recent study on constellations suggested that "it would be effective to place Fossil or Tory Burch wearables in Macy's or Nordstrom stores in the active sections of the stores, next to Under Armour and Lululemon Athletica, respectively".[51] This strategy can help fashion brands to decide on product-licensing decisions. For example, brands can form licensing agreements with other fashion companies, brands or retailers that fit in a similar consumption constellation. A fashion/health-oriented brand such as Tory Burch can consider giving a license for a wearable to a fashion/health-oriented apparel brand like Lululemon.

Consumption constellations can also allow fashion marketers to track the best co-branding deals. In one of our studies, we suggested that Fossil and Under Amour brands can collaborate together to create an exceptional line of accessories that would adopt technology enabled by sensors inserted in the textiles. These brands might also launch a new version of smartwatches that would appeal to both stylish and energetic consumers.[52]

How to Create a Pen Portrait of Your Consumer

Fashion marketers usually use lifestyle segmentation to create profiles, or **personas**, of the typical consumer they want to target so that they can get a more vivid picture. Some create a **mood board** that enables them to compile a set of images that personify the look they hope to sell. This is also done through a technique known as a **pen portrait** (sometimes referred to as a **persona** or **customer avatar**), an informal written and illustrated description of a person or specific customer segment that can help marketers get a better understanding of who will be using or wearing a certain product, how they will be using it and for which occasions.

The focus in the pen portrait is to provide a real description of the person's demographics (e.g., age, gender, ethnicity), lifestyle, social status, stage of life, appearance, attitude, and fashion style. You can make one by using a collage of pictures that you can gather from free and inexpensive sources (Creative Commons/Wikimedia, stock photos) or from your own drawings. You need to make sure that you are collecting pictures that clearly and factually represent the consumer's lifestyle, preferred activities, and social status. You can see an illustration of a pen portrait in Figure 6.1.

User Personalities

Personality refers to a person's unique psychological makeup and how it consistently influences the way a person responds to their environment. One of the approaches to personality is to focus on traits or the identifiable characteristics that define a person. For example, people can be distinguished by the degree to which they are socially outgoing (*the trait of extraversion*) or as the degree to which they are open to new experiences (*the trait of openness*).

Some specific traits that are relevant to marketers include *innovativeness* (the degree to which a person likes to try new things), *materialism* (the amount of emphasis placed on acquiring and owning products), *self-consciousness* (the degree to which a person deliberately monitors and controls the image of the self that is projected to others), and *need for cognition* (the degree to which a person likes to think about things and by extension expend the necessary effort to process brand information).[53] Since large numbers of consumers can be categorized in terms of their possession

Chloe
Age 25 years old

Lives in Le Marais

Works at Vogue France

Shops at Claudie Pierlot, Maje, and Sandro

Her regular workout is a stroll along the
Seine

Her favorite artist is Monet

She plays the piano

Window Shops at Rue Saint Honoré

Weekly girls night out at Quartier Latin

Always orders a gin martini

Enjoys historic travels; is independent and
cultured

Reads Le Monde every morning

Enjoys people-watching during her afternoon
cup of tea

FIGURE 6.1 A pen portrait

Images courtesy of Flickr, Pixabay, Public Domain Pictures, Wikimedia Commons, Pickpik, Pexels, Le Monde and Flickr

of various traits, these approaches can in theory be used for segmentation purposes. If a manufacturer, for example, could determine that individuals who fit a trait profile are more likely to prefer a product with certain features, this match could be used to great advantage.

Imagine that one day your favorite Creed fragrance magically came to life as a person (bear with us). How would you describe that person? Would it be male or female? Young or old? Stodgy or daring? Would they listen to country music, opera or hip-hop?

The notion that individuals purchase items that are extensions of their personalities makes sense.[54] This idea is endorsed by many marketing managers who try to create brand personalities that will appeal to different types of consumers. A **brand personality** refers to the set of traits people attribute to a product as if it were a person. These inferences about product's personality are an important part of **brand equity**, which describes the extent that a consumer holds strong, favorable and unique associations about a brand in memory.[55]

Behavioral Segmentation

Behavioral segmentation refers to the process of dividing the marketplace into smaller groups and classifying homogeneous groups together based on their buying behavior. This can be done through usage rate, usage occasions and brand loyalty.

Usage Rate

It is important for fashion marketers to understand which segment group is producing the bulk of customers for a particular product. According to a very general rule of thumb frequently used in marketing research, the **80/20** rule, only 20% of a product user's account for 80% of the volume of product sold.

Researchers attempt to determine who uses the brand and try to isolate heavy, light and non-users. They also look for patterns of usage and attitudes toward the product. Marketers primarily target these heavy users, even though they may constitute a relatively small number of total users as they are incredibly profitable over the long-term and may make up the bulk of profits to a specific item's bottom line. These heavy users may be good candidates to become **brand ambassadors**, who are so enthusiastic about the brand that they advocate it to others.

After the heavy users are identified and understood, the brand's relationship to them is considered. Heavy users may have quite different reasons for using the product; they can be further divided in terms of the benefits they derive from using the product or service. For instance, marketers at the beginning of the walking shoe craze assumed that purchasers were basically burned-out-joggers. Subsequent psychographic research showed that there were actually several different groups of "walkers", ranging from those who walk to get to work to those who walk for fun. This realization resulted in shoes aimed at different segments such as Nike Healthwalkers.

The Long Tail   While the 80/20 strategy still remains valid in most contexts, the suitability of the Internet to offer an indefinite selection of items to billions of people has shifted fashion retailers' strategies when it comes to segmentation. Some e-commerce retailers benefit from the so-called **long tail** approach to merchandising. This refers to a business strategy that helps them to make noteworthy profits by selling low volumes of hard-to-find items to a larger number of consumers, instead of only selling bigger volumes of a lower number of prevalent fashion goods. Online retailers – especially Amazon – can sell you, say, a vintage *Vogue* issue that a traditional bookstore would find difficult to stock.[56.]

Usage Occasions

A different way to segment a market on the basis of behavioral segmentation is to consider usage occasions. This segmentation factor recognizes that our needs change, depending upon the specific occasion or situation for which we need the product. Some fashion brands build their marketing campaigns around specific usage or occasions (e.g., holidays, events, times of the day…) rather than a set of unique product qualities. Think of Rent-The-Runway, the online retailer that offers one-off dress rentals for special occasions and events such as black-tie galas, cocktail parties, prom, date night, or just another day at the office.

Brand Loyalty and Affiliation

A loyal customer is someone who has developed a strong emotional attachment to a given brand to the extent that this person will continuously purchase it over a period of time. This type of customer is extremely valuable, as you might imagine, because they have a long **lifetime customer value**. This term describes the amount of revenue a company can expect from a buyer over a period of years rather than just due to a one-off purchase.

Brands often work hard to retain their loyal consumers. In the hospitality industry for example, airlines, hotels and restaurants do whatever they can to provide consistently good customer experiences and where possible to "delight the customer" at every opportunity.

And it's increasingly common for marketers to institute some kind of loyalty or a **frequency marketing program** that rewards customers every time they make a purchase. American Airlines launched the first such program way back in 1981, when it enrolled passengers who earned frequent flyer miles.[57] Today, consumers are accustomed to earning miles or points (or perhaps free coffee at Starbucks), so this incentive motivates them to patronize the same company over time. In the fashion space, for example, Nordstrom has been significantly investing in its loyalty programs to beat back competition from other upmarket retailers and e-commerce competitors and retain its customers.[58]

Step 2: Targeting

As we've seen, the first stage in a target marketing strategy is segmentation, whereby the company divides the marketplace into smaller groups that possess similar characteristics. The second stage is targeting, where the company assesses the attractiveness of each possible segment and selects the most profitable segments. A key targeting decision focuses on how fine-tuned the target should be: Should the firm appeal to a larger segment or should it focus on satisfying the needs of a smaller one? There are four different target marketing strategies that marketers can select from.

Undifferentiated Targeting

A retailer like Walmart that chooses to implement an undifferentiated target market strategy caters to a more extensive range of individuals. This approach can be very efficient because manufacturing, research, and promotion costs can profit from **economies of scale**—it's simply less expensive to create one product or one advertising campaign than to select numerous targets and spend the time and money to develop specific goods or messages for each. As tempting as this may be, unfortunately unless you run a very large mass-market operation like Walmart does, it's very hard to be all things to all people.

Differentiated Targeting

A **differentiated targeting strategy** is when a fashion brand launches products and services that appeal to multiple target groups, with a different marketing mix for each. This usually happens when a company has a portfolio of separate brands with unique images, and it can identify one or more segments that have different needs for distinct types of products. For example, a fashion brand can appeal to both males and females with separate product lines, or it can appeal to females with at least two different forms of lifestyles. Think of Rimowa, the luggage company. This brand is able to satisfy the needs of multiple customer groups such as those who are professionals and Generation X and Y status seekers. Recently, Rimowa decided to target a new market, the Millennials, with a new line.[59] It went after this new customer by partnering with other brands that also appeal to this age cohort such as Christian Dior, Moncler, Off-White, and Supreme.

Concentrated Targeting

When a fashion company launches one or more products to a specific segment, it adopts a **concentrated marketing strategy**. Here, a product is created for a very well defined and specific segment of the marketplace. A great example is Whole Foods, the retailer that goes beyond general groceries to appeal to nutritionally conscious individuals who are willing to pay more expensive prices for organic food. Differentiating itself from other beauty care brands on the market, Lush promotes the ethical purchasing and purity of handmade goods. This brand appeals to a specific segment in the market, those who are environmental and animal friendly consumers.

Lush handmade soap

canbedone / Shutterstock.com

There are so many brands out in the market that sell products that are sweet. However, not everyone can satisfy their craving because some people may be facing allergies such as lactose intolerance or nut allergies. Divvies took advantage of this niche market and developed cookies and cupcakes that are vegan and nut free, allowing the brand to stand out in the market.[60]

Customized Targeting

Customized marketing is a strategy that allows the producer or the brand to create products that are tailored for specific individuals or locations. Although this approach can be complicated and expensive, ironically, it's the way the whole process started. A trend that still continues today but started hundreds of years ago is when wealthy women hired designers to make one-of-a-kind gowns for them. We can think of that as the origin of customized targeting!

There is a difference between local marketing and individual marketing. **Local marketing** comprises tailoring fashion products, promotion and communication messages to the needs and wants of local customers, e.g., a country, a city or a particular store. For example, Levi's sells T-shirts that appeal to different destinations in the world, such as a Levi's London graphic for the British market or Levi's Tokyo for the Japanese market.[61]

Individual marketing refers to tailoring fashion products, promotion and communication messages to the needs and wants of individual consumers. This can be adopted by referring to a *one-to-one marketing* whereby a consumer may request a custom-made wedding dress that is designed only for her (e.g., Elie Saab, Christian Dior, Vera Wang, Giambattista Valli, Jenny Packham, or Ralph and Russo).

More commonly, we see this approach in the context of **mass customization**. This term describes a strategy adopted by fashion marketers whereby they modify a mass and common good or service to meet an individual's specific needs.

To understand how this works, think about the program that Levi Strauss first introduced in 1999. Every jeans wearer's body is a bit different and (believe it or not) many people have one leg that is slightly longer than the other. It's not financially viable for a high-volume company like Levi Strauss to tailor a one-off pair of jeans for every person's unique measurements. However, a garment like blue jeans is made up of several components such as pants legs, a button fly, etc. Rather than literally sew a unique pair of jeans for each customer, the company can combine different components in a unique way. So, if your left leg measures 30" and your right leg is 30.5", all the in-store tailor has to do is to grab a 30" leg piece and a 30.5" leg piece and combine them in one garment. Voilà—mass customization in action.[62]

Nike and Converse have developed 'mass customization' services, which offer shoppers the opportunity to create their own designs through a digital customization platform where they can select from an extensive range of colors and materials. Mass customization has also been embraced by luxury brands such as Burberry Bespoke, a service that allows customers to customize luxury trench coats (priced from about $1,800 to $8,800). In addition, you can customize your scarf at the Burberry Scarf Bar, where you choose your initials on scarves (priced from about $475 to $995) that come in different colors, materials and patterns[63]. Christian Dior also offers the option to personalize your bags, bracelets, and mitzvah scarves with "My ABCDior" letters and symbols[64].Louis Vuitton offers the "Mon Monogram" service, allowing you to personalize your favorite Louis Vuitton leather

Burberry Scarf Bar[65]
Ugis Riba / Shutterstock.com

goods with your initials and the colorful stripes of your choice.[66] Envying this form of customization? All you need to do is to show up into any Louis Vuitton store and let the salesperson know that you want to add a personal touch by hot stamping your initials on your wallet or luggage tag.

Step 3: Positioning

The final step in the STP process is **positioning**. Here the marketer uses elements of the marketing mix (product design, price, distribution, and marketing communications) to influence the consumer's interpretation of its meaning—especially vis-a-vis the competition.

Positioning Dimensions

Many dimensions can be used to establish a brand's position in the marketplace:

- Lifestyle: A Chanel purse is "high class."

- Price leadership: Primark and Walmart set the standard for low prices.

- Attributes or benefits: Nutella is a "good breakfast option." TKMaxx is about "Big Labels, Small Prices."

- Product class: Lyft is about improving "people's lives with the world's best transportation."

- Competitors: An ad campaign by Philip Plein states: "Don't Be a Puma, Be a Tiger."[67]

- Occasions/situations: *Vogue* prints different covers for different markets such as Vogue New York, Vogue Arabia, Vogue China, and Vogue India.

- Users: "Just do it" by Nike or "Impossible is nothing" by Adidas.

- Quality: Clive Christian perfumes "are made using the finest ingredients from around the globe."[68]

Repositioning

Repositioning occurs when a brand's original market position is modified. In some cases, a marketer may decide that a brand is competing too closely with another of its own products, so sales are being **cannibalized** (that is both brands are taking sales away from each other, rather than competing companies).

Another reason for repositioning crops up when too many companies stress the same attribute. For example, quality tends to be an attribute most apparel companies emphasize, whether they are high-end or low-end products. Certainly, they all cannot have the highest quality, so an attribute like this may lose its meaning over time.

Finally, repositioning can occur when the original market evaporates, is unreceptive to the offering or needs something different. For instance, eBay Fashion was relaunched in a campaign entitled "Wear It Your Way," that targeted young Millennials and Gen-Z shoppers. E-bay Fashion now strives to be a leading player during the Amazon era.[69]

Perceptual Mapping

The technique of **perceptual mapping** helps companies to determine just how their products or services appear to consumers in relation to competitive brands on one or more relevant characteristics. It enables them to see the gaps in the positioning of all brands in the product or service class and to identify areas in which consumer needs are not being adequately met.

The easiest way to create a perceptual map is simply to ask consumers what attributes are important to them, and how they feel competitors rate on those attributes. Figure 6.2 is an example of a perceptual map for fashion brands.

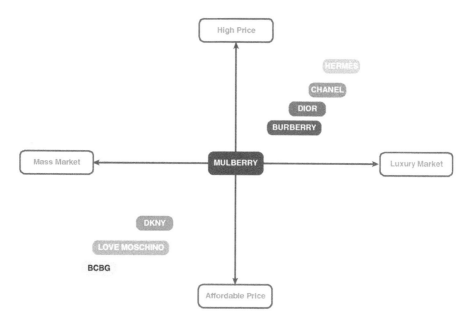

FIGURE 6.2   An example of a perceptual map

Chapter Summary

Now that you have read the chapter, you should understand the following:

1.   What are the different ways to segment markets?

Segmentation refers to dividing the larger marketplace into different parts based on one or more significant, mutual traits. The formed segments are made-up of consumers who will react in a similar way to the company's marketing strategies and who will usually share characteristics such as common interests, needs, or geographic locations. A fashion market can be segmented based on demographic, geographic, psychographic

(Continued)

and behavioral segmentation. Demographic segmentation refers to segmenting the market based on variables such as age and family life cycle, gender, income and social class, and ethnicity. Geographic segmentation is a segmentation strategy whereby a marketer divides the marketplace based on geographic locations and groups potential customers by country, state, city... Psychographic segmentation involves the division of the market based on consumers' shared personality traits, beliefs, values, attitudes, interests, and lifestyles. Psychographics can help a company fine-tune its offerings to meet the needs of different segments. Finally, behavioral segmentation refers to the process of dividing the marketplace into smaller groups and classifying homogeneous groups together based on their buying behavior. This can be done through, usage rate, usage occasions and brand loyalty.

2.   What are the different forms of target market strategies?

The next step after segmentation is targeting, in which marketers assess the attractiveness of each prospective segment and select the most profitable segments to whom it wants to sell its products and services. A key targeting decision focuses on how exceptionally tuned the target should be: Should the firm appeal to a larger segment or should it focus on satisfying the needs of a smaller one? There are four different target marketing strategies that marketers can select from: *Undifferentiated, Differentiated, Concentrated* and *Customized* marketing. Undifferentiated marketing strategy takes place when the marketer disregards the obvious segment differences and adopts a strategy that is thought to appeal to the largest number of people. A differentiated marketing strategy is when a fashion brand launches products and services that appeal to multiple target groups with different marketing mix elements. Concentrated marketing is a strategy whereby a product is created and communicated with a very well defined and specific segment of the marketplace. Customized marketing is a common strategy that allows the producer or the brand to create products that are tailored for specific individuals or locations. There is a difference between local marketing and individual marketing. Local marketing comprises tailoring fashion products, promotion and communication messages to the needs and wants of local customers, e.g., a country, a city or a particular store while individual marketing refers to tailoring fashion products, promotion and communication messages to the needs and wants of individual consumers.

3.   How can fashion brands position themselves in the market?

A positioning strategy is a fundamental part of a company's marketing efforts, as it uses elements of the marketing mix such as product design, price, distribution, and marketing communications to impact the consumer's interpretation of its meaning. Positioning is what differentiates a company's product from competitive brands that offer similar products and services in the mind of the customer. There is a number of dimensions that can be used to establish a brand's position in the marketplace such as lifestyle, price leadership, attributes or benefits, product class, competitors, occasions/situations, users and quality. When firms realize that their brands are not precisely reflecting what they want and is not keeping up with consumers' needs and demands, a repositioning strategy may be adopted. Repositioning occurs when a brand's original market position is modified in order to change the way people think about a brand, product, or service.

DISCUSSION QUESTIONS

1. Suppose you want to launch a new luxury watch brand. Select a geographic market you are familiar with. Use psychographic segmentation in order to identify the market segments. Which target market would you select for this product, and why?

2. Is there any difference between positioning and repositioning? What do you think are the advantages and challenges for repositioning a fashion brand?

3. How can fashion companies cultivate and reward loyal customers?

4. What are some of the positives and negatives of targeting people with specific needs? Identify some specific marketing strategies that you feel have been either successful or unsuccessful at appealing to this segment. What characteristics distinguish the successes from the failures?

5. Why have Millennials had such an important impact on consumer culture? How has this affected fashion over the last few years?

6. In what situations is demographic information likely to be more useful than psychographic data and vice versa?

7. If you are a fashion company with limited company resources such as low investment capital, which target market strategy would you choose and why?

8. What is the impact of counterfeiting on luxury brands?

9. You are about to open a new fashion apparel business. Discuss the major market segments for the fashion industry that you will consider. Explain your selection.

EXERCISES

1. Select a brand and put together a pen portrait for the customer you think that this brand is targeting. Write a description of who your target customer is by referring to the different forms of segmentation the chapter discusses. Which strategy would you use to target this market?

2. Search for brands that are applying co-branding strategies. What do you think are the advantages and challenges related to this?

3. Visit a retailer website (e.g., Harrods, Neiman Marcus...) and investigate the different brands of jeans at different price levels (e.g., Levi Strauss, Frame, Valentino, J Brand, Paige, Gucci, Citizens

(Continued)

of Humanity...) and so on. Analyze their positions in the marketplace relative to fashion, price and other factors that you might identify. Select one brand and identify how this brand repositioned itself lately.

4. Generate a perceptual map for a fashion category of your choice.

5. Locate one or more consumers who have immigrated from another country or are studying or working in another country. Interview them about how they have adapted to their host culture? In particular, what changes did they make in their consumption practices, especially fashion purchases over time?

6. Find good and bad examples of ads targeted to ethnic backgrounds. What elements of ads or other promotions appear to determine their effectiveness in reaching and persuading this group?

7. Compile a set of recent ads attempting to link consumption of a fashion product with a specific lifestyle.

8. Using media targeted to the group, construct a consumption constellation for the social role of college students. What set of products, activities or interests tend to appear in ads depicting "typical" college students? How realistic is this constellation?

CASE STUDY: SMART ADAPTIVE CLOTHING

Nancy Connor, Founder, Smart Adaptive Clothing

"There has to be a better way."

Smart Adaptive Clothing founder Nancy Connor has repeated these words at critical breakthrough moments in her life.

In 2014 Nancy's Father, "Bo," needed additional care and moved into an assisted living community. Shortly after this, Bo broke his hip twice and his hand all in about 12 months. This meant that Bo no longer could wear his signature style of button-down shirts paired with pressed slacks—his "power uniform" he wore every day during his previous life as an executive.

Now, Bo was dressed daily in sweatpants and sweatshirts—mainly due to the convenience and ease for the caregivers of putting on and taking off this type of clothing. Dressing this way, though, had a negative impact on Bo's feelings about himself and his life.

Nancy wondered, "What if Bo had access to clothing that looked great *and* was easy to put on and take off?" She realized that how we dress directly impacts how we feel. Our confidence is directly linked to the way we perceive ourselves. When we look good, we feel better.

So, Nancy began to dig deeper into the problem. She discovered that a wide variety of people encounter difficulties with everyday tasks like dressing, whether due to Parkinson's Disease,

MS, ALS, Alzheimer's, loss of fine motor skills, paralysis, neuropathy, post-cancer treatment, chronic illnesses, post-surgery, age-related infirmities, or other problems. And these difficulties also present problems for caregivers who may struggle to help their patients or loved ones with the demands of daily life. Even something as "simple" as fastening buttons on a shirt or blouse can be a real challenge.

This is a highly specialized market segment, but increasingly an important one. These people can benefit from **adaptive clothing**, which is constructed to make it easier to get dressed. This new category represents a booming market; it is forecasted to grow to $400 billion globally by 2026.[ii] But after researching the available adaptive clothing options, Nancy found that there weren't many appealing alternatives for people who had difficulty getting dressed because they have trouble manipulating buttons and other closures. Most of the available options looked "medical" and were hardly flattering to the wearer.

Nancy believed that it wasn't necessary for people to sacrifice style for convenience. She was so convinced that she left her career of 20 plus years in corporate America to start Smart Adaptive Clothing. She was managing three business units in the medical device industry that sold internationally and domestically. Nancy knew how to run a business, so it was "just" a matter of learning everything about the apparel business...

She envisioned a line of adaptive clothing based on universal designs, meaning anyone can wear it, dress it up or go casual. When she started, she carefully selected fabrics that are soft, easy care, flattering, classic designs with trendy twists. Nancy and her team tested their designs, including fabrics, Velcro, buttons, and labels on consumers with different disabilities to be sure every garment would be not only attractive, but useable. Smart Adaptive Clothing's blouses and shirts closely resemble "regular" garments because they retain the buttons on the front closure (placket) and cuffs, and they strategically sew Velcro fasteners behind each button for easy on | off. Currently, the company sells blouses and shirts for women and men, with plans to expand into jeans, slacks and kids wear.

But of course, it's one thing to build a better mousetrap, and quite another to reach the audience for it. Smart Adaptive Clothing currently has a hybrid business model; it sells directly to clients and also to wholesale customers in the USA and the UK. In 2019, the company expanded into the United Kingdom market when an Instagram colleague opened an online store. This partnership brought Smart Adaptive Clothing to London Fashion Week 2020. Additionally, the company advertises on Instagram and Facebook, and it exhibits at trade shows that target the disabled and their caregivers.

The company is off to a good start, but as is the case with any startup, there are serious challenges ahead. For one, more competitors are jumping into the market—including some major players like Tommy Hilfiger, Kohl's and Lands' End.[ii] And of course, the pandemic didn't make life any easier for Nancy and her team.

Nancy feels her biggest challenge now is an overall lack of awareness among consumers that adaptive clothing can enhance their lives. Many people have created "home hacks" and learned how to "make do" because they don't know that options like Smart Adaptive Clothing's line exist. The best way to reach these people is unclear: Should the company stick to its current e-commerce

(Continued)

model, or try to partner with bricks-and-mortar retailers? Some people with disabilities are sensitive to being labeled as such, so buying "adaptive clothing" may be a turnoff for them. Still, Nancy is determined to bring a workable and stylish solution to millions of struggling consumers—one Velcro fastener at a time.

DISCUSSION QUESTIONS

1. Velcro fasteners, snaps, and so on are *attributes* of the unique apparel products the company manufactures. But what are the *benefits* that consumers buy? What is the best way to communicate these benefits to wearers and caregivers?

2. What is the best way to distribute these products—online, mass-market retailers, specialized merchants, etc.?

3. As our population ages, we can expect to see a big increase in the market for adaptive clothing. Which segment(s) of consumers should Smart Adaptive Clothing prioritize, and what is the best way to reach these people?

REFERENCES

i. Centers for Disease Control and Prevention (CDC) (2018) 'Disability impacts all of us', *CDC*. www.cdc.gov/ncbddd/disabilityandhealth/infographic-disability-impacts-all.html (accessed August 23, 2021).
ii. Gaffney, A. (2019) *The $400 Billion Adaptive Clothing Opportunity. Vogue Business*. www.vogue business.com/consumers/adaptive-clothing-differently-abled-asos-target-tommy-hilfiger (accessed August 23, 2021).

NOTES

1. Lunden, I. (2019) 'ThirdLove, the direct-to-consumer lingerie startup, gets a $55M boost', *Tech Crunch*, February 26. https://techcrunch.com/2019/02/26/thirdlove-the-direct-to-consumer-lingerie-startup-gets-a-55m-boost/ (accessed August 23, 2021).

   Ryan, R. (2019) 'To get online bra-fitting right, ThirdLove is going physical', *Forbes*, August 1. www.forbes.com/sites/retailwire/2019/08/01/to-get-online-bra-fitting-right-thirdlove-is-going-physical/?sh=2de5294d2661 (accessed August 23, 2021).

   Robehmed, N. (2018) 'Next billion-dollar startup: Entrepreneurs create $750m bra business by exposing Victoria's weakness', *Forbes*, October 18. www.forbes.com/sites/natalierobehmed/2018/10/18/next-billion-dollar-startup-entrepreneurs-create-750m-bra-business-by-exposing-victorias-weakness/?sh=3a475a914d03 (accessed August 23, 2021).

2. O'Connor, C. (2014) 'Want a bra that fits perfectly? this billionaire-backed app helps with just your iPhone', *Forbes*, February 10. www.forbes.com/sites/clareoconnor/2014/02/10/want-a-bra-that-fits-perfectly-this-billionaire-backed-app-helps-with-just-your-iphone/?sh=4a58aefe36b0 (accessed August 23, 2021).

3. Bump, B. (2019) '7 Brands that got inclusive marketing right', *HubSpot, November 12*. https://blog.hubspot.com/marketing/inclusive-marketing-campaigns (accessed August 23, 2021).

4. Chen, C. (2019) 'Rent the Runway to expand into kids' clothing', *Business of Fashion,* April 5. www.businessoffashion.com/articles/finance/rent-the-runway-expands-into-kids-clothing (accessed August 23, 2021).

5. Dimock, M. (2019) 'Defining generations: Where Millennials end and Generation Z begins', *Pew Research Center*, January 17. www.pewresearch.org/fact-tank/2019/01/17/where-millennials-end-and-generation-z-begins/ (accessed August 23, 2021).

6. Djafarova, E. and Bowes, T. (2021) '"Instagram made me buy it": Generation Z impulse purchases in fashion industry', *Journal of Retailing and Consumer Services*, 59: article #102345.

    Smith, K.T. (2019) 'Mobile advertising to Digital Natives: Preferences on content, style, personalization, and functionality', *Journal of Strategic Marketing*, 27 (1): 67–80.

7. Pike, H. (2016) 'Tapping Generation Z', *Business of Fashion*, February 2. www.businessoffashion.com/articles/retail/tapping-generation-z (accessed August 23, 2021).

8. Schlossberg, M. (2016) 'One sentence reveals how teen Generation Z is killing Gap, Abercrombie, and J. Crew', *Business Insider,* February 5. www.businessinsider.com/generation-z-is-killing-gap-abercrombie-and-j-crew-2016-2 (accessed August 23, 2021).

9. Qasem, Z. (2021) 'The effect of positive TRI traits on centennials adoption of try-on technology in the context of E-fashion retailing', *International Journal of Information Management*, 56: article #102254.

10. Gazzola, P., Pavione, E., Pezzetti, R. and Grechi, D. (2020) 'Trends in the fashion industry. The perception of sustainability and circular economy: A gender/generation quantitative approach', *Sustainability*, 12 (7): article #2809.

    Shrivastava, A., Jain, G., Kamble, S. S. and Belhadi, A. (2021) 'Sustainability through online renting clothing: Circular fashion fueled by instagram micro-celebrities', *Journal of Cleaner Production*, 278: article#123772.

11. Petro, G. (2020) 'Sustainable retail: How gen z is leading the pack', *Forbes,* January 31. www.forbes.com/sites/gregpetro/2020/01/31/sustainable-retail-how-gen-z-is-leading-the-pack/?sh=6bb9f0242ca3 (accessed August 23, 2021).

12. Bloomberg (2019) 'Reality bites back: To really get Gen Z, look at the parents', *Business of Fashion,* July 29. www.businessoffashion.com/articles/news-analysis/reality-bites-back-to-really-get-gen-z-look-at-the-parents (accessed August 23, 2021).

13. Launchmetrics Content Team (2018) '5 brands winning over millennial fashion consumers', *LaunchMetrics,* September 19. www.launchmetrics.com/resources/blog/the-battle-for-millennial-mindshare (accessed August 23, 2021).

14. Su, J., Watchravesringkan, K.T., Zhou, J. and Gil, M. (2019) 'Sustainable clothing: Perspectives from US and Chinese young Millennials', *International Journal of Retail & Distribution Management*, 47 (11): 1141–62.

15. Russell, J. (2018) 'Millennial brand preferences: A 2018 update', *The Robin Report,* December 3. www.therobinreport.com/millennial-brand-preferences-a-2018-update/ (accessed August 23, 2021).

16. Financial Times (2018) 'Gucci unveils plan to become fur-free from 2018', *Financial Times*. www.ft.com/content/9b36505c-af1b-11e7-aab9-abaa44b1e130 (accessed August 23, 2021).

17. Lerro, M., Raimondo, M., Stanco, M., Nazzaro, C. and Marotta, G. (2019) 'Cause related marketing among millennial consumers: The role of trust and loyalty in the food industry', *Sustainability*, 11 (2): 535.

    Oh, H.J., Chen, R. and Hung-Baesecke, C.J.F. (2017) 'Exploring effects of CSR initiatives in strategic postcrisis communication among millennials in China and South Korea', *International Journal of Strategic Communication*, 11 (5): 379–94.

18. Coughlin, J. (2019) '3 food trends inspired by millennials that older consumers are eating up', *Forbes*, June 9. www.forbes.com/sites/josephcoughlin/2019/06/09/3-food-trends-inspired-by-millennials-that-older-consumers-are-eating-up/?sh=50bc78ab7b96 (accessed August 23, 2021).

19. Rosenbloom, C. (2018) '9 ways millennials are changing the way we eat', *The Washington Post*, February 21. www.washingtonpost.com/lifestyle/wellness/9-ways-millennials-are-changing-the-way-we-eat/2018/02/20/6bb2fe60-11eb-11e8-8ea1-c1d91fcec3fe_story.html (accessed August 23, 2021).

20. Lamb, R. (2011) 'Brand loyalty highest in Gen X consumers: eMarketer', *Retail Dive*. www.retaildive.com/ex/mobilecommercedaily/brand-loyalty-highest-in-gen-x-consumers-emarketer (accessed August 23, 2021).

21. Berezhna, V. (2018) 'Meet fashion's next generation: Over 60s', *Business of Fashion*, April 13. www.businessoffashion.com/articles/luxury/meet-fashions-next-generation-senior-citizens (accessed August 23, 2021).

22. Partner, P. (2019) '9 Travel trends and habits of baby boomers', *Intrado Globe News Wire*, October 10. www.globenewswire.com/news-release/2019/10/10/1927954/0/en/9-Travel-Trends-and-Habits-of-Baby-Boomers.html (accessed August 23, 2021).

23. Benveniste, A. and Bloomberg (2019) 'Someday there might not be a menswear department', *Fortune*, December 8. https://fortune.com/2019/12/08/gender-neutral-clothing-brands-gen-z/ (accessed August 23, 2021).

24. Bloomberg (2018) 'ASOS focuses on growing its genderless offering', *Business of Fashion*, October 17. www.businessoffashion.com/articles/news-analysis/asos-focuses-on-growing-its-neutral-fashion (accessed August 23, 2021).

25. Harper's Bazaar (2020) 'Beyoncé's new Ivy Park x Adidas gender-neutral collection is here', *Harpers Bazaar*, January 18. www.harpersbazaar.com/uk/fashion/fashion-news/a30575175/beyonce-ivy-park-adidas-collection-gender-neutral/ (accessed August 23, 2021).

26. Howland, D. (2018) 'Abercrombie & Fitch launches unisex kids line', i January 22. www.retaildive.com/news/abercrombie-fitch-launches-unisex-kids-line/515232/ (accessed August 23, 2021).

27. Hosie, R. (2017) 'John Lewis gets rid of 'boys' and 'girls' labels in children's clothing', *The Independent*, September 02. www.independent.co.uk/life-style/john-lewis-boys-girls-clothing-labels-gender-neutral-unisex-children-a7925336.html (accessed August 23, 2021).

28. Gil, M. and Rosenberg, S. (2015) *The multicultural edge: rising super consumers*. Nielsen. www.nielsen.com/wp-content/uploads/sites/3/2019/04/the-multicultural-edge-rising-super-consumers-march-2015.pdf (accessed August 23, 2021).

29. Abnett, K. (2015) 'Sixty-six shades of skin: Tapping the multicultural beauty market', *Business of Fashion*, February 17. www.businessoffashion.com/articles/global-markets/sixty-six-shades-skin-tapping-multicultural-beauty-market (accessed August 23, 2021).

30. Garuba-Okelarin, S. (2016) 'Beauty and diversity: A note on diversity in the UK cosmetics market', *HuffPost*, February 26. www.huffingtonpost.co.uk/segun-garubaokelarin/beauty-and-diversity-cosmetics_b_9301652.html (accessed August 23, 2021).

31. Booker, L. (2016) 'Christian Louboutin unveils nude shoes in seven skin tones', *CNN*, March 31. https://edition.cnn.com/2016/03/31/living/nude-shoe-christian-louboutin-feat/index.html (accessed August 23, 2021).

32. Marinelli, G. (2019) 'Everything we know about skims, Kim Kardashian West's solutionwear line', *Glamour*, September 10. www.glamour.com/story/skims-kim-kardashians-solutionwear-line (accessed August 23, 2021).

33. Szalai, I. (2015) 'Market focus: beauty growth dynamics in the Middle East and Turkey', *Euromonitor*, April 29. https://blog.euromonitor.com/market-focus-beauty-growth-dynamics-in-the-middle-east-and-turkey/ (accessed August 23, 2021).

34. Chitrakorn, K. (2015) 'Can halal cosmetics outgrow their niche?', *Business of Fashion*, November 18. www.businessoffashion.com/articles/beauty/can-halal-cosmetics-outgrow-their-niche (accessed August 23, 2021).

35. Strugatz, R. and Chitrakorn, K. (2019) 'Fenty Beauty vs. Kylie Cosmetics: The race to a billion dollar brand', *Business of Fashion*, February 5. www.businessoffashion.com/articles/beauty/fenty-beauty-vs-kylie-cosmetics-the-race-to-a-billion-dollar-brand (accessed August 23, 2021).

36. Fisher, J.E. (1987) 'Social class and consumer behavior: the relevance of class and status', *ACR North American Advances*, 14: 492–496.

   Schaninger, C. M. (1981) 'Social class versus income revisited: An empirical investigation', *Journal of Marketing Research*, 18 (2): 192–208.

   Eastman, J.K. and Eastman, K.L. (2015) 'Conceptualizing a model of status consumption theory: An exploration of the antecedents and consequences of the motivation to consume for status', *Marketing Management Journal*, 25 (1): 1–15.

   Giovannini, S., Xu, Y. and Thomas, J. (2015) 'Luxury fashion consumption and Generation Y consumers', *Journal of Fashion Marketing and Management*, 19 (1): 22–40.

Grotts, A.S. and Johnson, T.W. (2013) 'Millennial consumers' status consumption of handbags', *Journal of Fashion Marketing and Management*, 17 (3): 280–93.

O'Cass, A. and Siahtiri, V. (2013) 'In search of status through brands from Western and Asian origins: Examining the changing face of fashion clothing consumption in Chinese young adults', *Journal of Retailing and Consumer Services*, 20 (6): 505–15.

37. Rauwald C. Clothier, M. (2014) 'Luxury car makers bet on lower-priced ride', *Bloomberg*, January 16. www.bloomberg.com/news/articles/2014-01-16/luxury-car-makers-bet-on-lower-priced-rides (accessed August 23, 2021).

38. (1987) 'Reading the buyer's mind', *U.S. News & World Report*, March 16: 59.

39. Gardyn, R. (2002) 'Oh, the good life', *American Demographics*, November 1. https://adage.com/article/american-demographics/good-life/44684 (accessed August 23, 2021).

40. Prabhu, J., Tracey, P. and Hassan, M. (2017) 'Marketing to the poor: An institutional model of exchange in emerging markets', *AMS Review*, 7 (3/4): 101–22.

41. Mahajan, V. (2016) 'How Unilever reaches rural consumers in emerging markets', *Harvard Business Review*, December 14. https://hbr.org/2016/12/how-unilever-reaches-rural-consumers-in-emerging-markets (accessed August 23, 2021).

42. Angot, J. and Plé, L. (2015) 'Serving poor people in rich countries: The bottom-of-the-pyramid business model solution', *Journal of Business Strategy*, 36 (2): 3–15.

43. Thomas, S. (2019) 'Which of these colours will help retain your car's resale value?', *Gulf News*, December 17. https://gulfnews.com/auto/auto-care/which-of-these-colours-will-help-retain-your-cars-resale-value-1.1576594399104 (accessed August 23, 2021).

44. Alpert, L. and Gatty, R. (1969) 'Product positioning by behavioral life-styles', *Journal of Marketing*, 33 (2): 65–69.

45. Chitrakorn, K. (2017) 'Global sportswear brands making a play for women', *Business of Fashion*, September 20. www.businessoffashion.com/articles/marketing-pr/how-sportswear-brands-are-making-a-play-for-women (accessed August 23, 2021).

46. Tiffany (2021) 'The Tiffany & Co. Foundation', *T&Co*. www.tiffanyandcofoundation.org/ (accessed August 23, 2021).

47. Sherman, L. (2019) 'High-Low collaborations democratised fashion. But what did they do for the designers?', *Business of Fashion*. www.businessoffashion.com/opinions/news-analysis/high-low-collaborations-democratised-fashion-but-what-did-they-do-for-the-designers (accessed August 23, 2021).

48. Fernandez, C. (2017) 'Levi's unveils 50 collaborations to boost comeback', *Business of Fashion*. www.businessoffashion.com/articles/retail/levis-unveils-mega-scale-trucker-jacket-collaborations-to-boost-comeback (accessed August 23, 2021).

49. Solomon, M.R. (1983) 'The role of products as social stimuli: A symbolic interactionism perspective', *Journal of Consumer Research*, 10 (3): 319–29.

50. Solomon, M.R., and Assael, H. (1987) 'The forest or the trees? A gestalt approach to symbolic consumption', in J. Umiker-Sebeok (ed.), *Marketing and Semiotics: New Directions in the Study of Signs for Sale*. Berlin: De Gruyter. pp. 189–218.

Nieroda, M.E., Mrad, M. and Solomon, M.R. (2018) 'How do consumers think about hybrid products? Computer wearables have an identity problem', *Journal of Business Research*, 89: 159–70.

Solomon, M.R. (1988) 'Mapping product constellations: A social categorization approach to consumption symbolism', *Psychology & Marketing (1986–1998)*, 5 (3): 233–58.

51. Nieroda, M.E., Mrad, M. and Solomon, M.R. (2018) 'How do consumers think about hybrid products? Computer wearables have an identity problem', *Journal of Business Research*, 89: 159–70.

52. Nieroda, M.E., Mrad, M. and Solomon, M.R. (2018) 'How do consumers think about hybrid products? Computer wearables have an identity problem', *Journal of Business Research*, 89: 159–70.

53. Goldberg, L.R. (1990) 'An alternative "description of personality": The big-five factor structure', *Journal of Personality and Social Psychology*, 59 (6): 1216–29.

Goldsmith, R.E. (2002) 'Some personality traits of frequent clothing buyers', *Journal of Fashion Marketing and Management: An International Journal*, 6 (3): 303–16.

Mulyanegara, R.C. and Tsarenko, Y. (2009) 'Predicting brand preferences: An examination of the predictive power of consumer personality and values in the Australian fashion market', *Journal of Fashion Marketing and Management: An International Journal*, 13 (3): 358–71.

54. Sun, L., Li, J. and Hu, Y. (2020) 'I cannot change, so I buy who I am: How mindset predicts conspicuous consumption', *Social Behavior and Personality: An International Journal*, 48 (7): 1–10.

   Solomon, M., Russell-Bennett, R. and Previte, J. (2012) *Consumer Behaviour*. Pearson Higher Education AU.

55. Keller, K.L. (1993) 'Conceptualizing, measuring, and managing customer-based brand equity', *Journal of Marketing*, 57 (1): 1–22.

56. Anderson, C. (2004) 'The long tail', *Wired,* October 1. www.wired.com/2004/10/tail/ (accessed August 23, 2021).

57. Winship, T. (2011) 'Airline frequent flyer miles, 30 years later', *abc News,* May 17. https://abcnews.go.com/Travel/airline-frequent-flyer-miles-30-years/story?id=13616082 (accessed August 23, 2021).

58. Reuters (2019) 'Nordstrom reports better than expected results', *Business Of Fashion,* August 21. www.businessoffashion.com/articles/news-analysis/nordstrom-reports-better-than-expected-results (accessed August 23, 2021).

59. Financial Times 'Case study: Why Rimowa rules the luggage carousel', *Financial Times,* January, 29. www.ft.com/content/3583dbf6-e0d7-11e7-a0d4-0944c5f49e46 (accessed August 23, 2021).

60. Divvies (2021) 'Divvies' https://divvies.com/ (accessed August 23, 2021).

61. Levi's (2021) 'Levi's', levi.com (accessed March 4, 2022).

62. MW (2015) *Levi's second attempt at mass customization, The M Ways,* May 1. https://mwe4eva.wordpress.com/2015/05/01/levis-second-attempt-at-mass-customization/ (accessed August 23, 2021).

63. Burberry (2021) 'Personalised gifts for her', burberry.com. https://us.burberry.com/personalised-womens/ (accessed August 23, 2021).

64. Dior (2021) 'My ABCDior', dior.com. www.dior.com/en_int/womens-fashion/my-abcdior (accessed August 23, 2021).

65. Skinner, P. (2015) 'Burberry opens the scarf bar', *Asia Tatler,* November 4. https://sg.asiatatler.com/style/burberry-opens-the-scarf-bar (accessed August 23, 2021).

66. Louis Vuitton (2021) 'Mon Monogram', louisvuitton.com. https://us.louisvuitton.com/eng-us/stories/personalization-mon-monogram (accessed August 23, 2021).

67. Manning, C. (2018) 'Philipp Plein declares war on Puma with new marketing campaign', *Fashion Week Daily,* January 11. https://fashionweekdaily.com/philipp-plein-sport-puma/ (accessed August 23, 2021).

68. Clive Christian (2021) 'Clive Christian: Discover the extraordinary', clivechristian.com. https://www.clivechristian.com/usa/welcome-to-clive-christian/ (accessed August 23, 2021).

69. Biron, B. (2018) 'With new digital campaign, eBay Fashion aims to reposition in the face of competition', *Glossy,* March 30. www.glossy.co/ecommerce/with-new-digital-campaign-ebay-fashion-aims-to-reposition-in-the-face-of-competition (accessed August 23, 2021).

SECTION III

How Consumers Think About and Choose Fashion

This or that? As with any other type of product or service, the decision to buy a fashion product often is not as simple as it appears. Even if something on the shelf just "grabs you," there are many factors that led up to your choice. And, of course many decisions are a lot more complicated because they're influenced by other things you have learned about the world, your motivation to choose a product, not to mention the other people you have in mind who will see you consuming the product! We'll discuss these important factors in the chapters to follow.

CHAPTER 7

Micro Factors:
Perception, Learning and Attitudes

LEARNING OBJECTIVES

After you read this chapter, you will understand the answers to the following:

1. Why is perception a three-phase process that transforms raw stimuli into meaningful information?

2. How do fashion companies and brands use principles of learning to change consumers' behavior?

3. How do fashion consumers form attitudes?

Dexter returns home from his grocery shopping trip, clutching all the ingredients he needs to cook dinner tonight in order to celebrate his one-year anniversary with Courtney. As he plops the bags down on the kitchen table, he sees a brand new bright blue sweatshirt from Uniqlo sitting there, adorned with a big gold bow. Suddenly, Courtney jumps into the kitchen and yells, "Happy anniversary!". She goes on to explain that she knows how excited he'll be, now that he no longer has to wear that ratty old blue thing all the time. Dexter tries to keep his cool, as he absorbs the fact that his wife wants him to throw out his lucky U.C.L.A. sweatshirt. True, it is starting to disintegrate—but he always has such fond memories of his partying college days whenever he wears it.

Perception

As Dexter knows, many objects hold important meanings—though not necessarily to others. Indeed, we live in a world overflowing with sensations. Wherever we turn, we are bombarded by a symphony of colors, sounds and odors. Some of the "notes" in this symphony occur naturally, such as the loud barking of a dog, the shades of the evening sky, or the heady smell of a rosebush. Others come from people; the person sitting next to you in class might sport tinted blonde hair, bright pink pants, and perhaps enough perfume to make your eyes water. The fashion industry adds new colors to new lines each season to keep the fashion marketing machine continually working.

Marketers certainly contribute to this stimulating environment of colors, sounds, and odors. Consumers are never far from advertisements, product packages, radio, television and online commercials, and traditional and electronic billboards, all clamoring for our attention. Each of us copes with this bombardment by paying attention to some stimuli and tuning out others. And the messages to which we do choose to pay attention often wind up differing from what the sponsors intended, shaped by our own unique experiences, biases, and desires.

Sensation refers to the immediate response of our sensory receptors (eyes, ears, nose, mouth, fingers) to such basic stimuli as light, color, and sound. Perception is the process by which the sensations are selected, organized, and interpreted. The study of **perception**, then, focuses on what we add or take away from these raw sensations as we choose which to notice, and then go about assigning meaning to them.

Sensory Systems

External stimuli, or sensory inputs, provide sensations that can be received on a number of channels. We may see a billboard or a man in a formal suit, hear a jingle, feel the softness of a cashmere sweater, taste a new flavor of ice cream or smell a leather jacket. The inputs our five senses pick up constitute the *raw data* that begins the perceptual process. As stated earlier, we receive stimuli through our five senses: vision, smell, sound, taste and touch.

Today, we are living in an era of **sensory marketing**, where companies need to pay extra attention to the impact of sensations on our product experiences.[1] In the following sections, we will take a close look at how smart marketers use our sensory systems to create a competitive advantage.

Vision

Marketers rely heavily on visual elements in displays, advertising, store design, and packaging. Meanings are communicated through a product's color, size, and styling.

Color

Color, as an important element of vision, may influence our emotions more directly. Color is an important element for the development of brand names, symbols, logos and packages[2] (See also[3]). Studies suggest that some warm colors (particularly red) create feelings of arousal, whereas cool colors (such as blue) are more relaxing. Colors such as green, yellow, cyan, and orange are considered the best hues to capture attention, but extensive use of these hues can overwhelm people and cause visual fatigue.[4]

Sensory system

Kolonko / Shutterstock.com

Color Responses

Some reactions to color come from learned associations. Black is the color we generally associate with mourning in the United States and most of Europe, whereas for some Asian people the color white serves this purpose.[5] In addition, we associate black with power and it may even have an impact on people who wear it. In the context of fashion, black gives a sense of modernism. Think of Yohji Yamamoto who has used a lot of black in his collections. Yohji considers black to be a combination of modesty and arrogance, and of laziness, practicality and mysteriousness.[6]

Different skin colors offer growth opportunities in the cosmetics market. For example, the demand of skin whitening products is mainly driven by Arabs and Asians given that a lighter skin rather than a darker tone is usually associated with a beauty in their communities.[7] Nevertheless, as the globe suffers a racial reckoning as an outcome of the death of George Floyd, a number of brands have made significant alterations to address the enduring dispute of retailing and marketing of skin-whitening items in Asian, African, and Middle Eastern markets. For instance, Johnson & Johnson stated that it will stop retailing some Neutrogena and Clean & Clear product lines in Asia, which were marketed as products that help remove dark spot and whiten skins. Also, L'Oréal decided to eliminate the terms "white," "fairness," and "light" from its Garnier brand in South Asia, words mainly used to communicate the act of skin whitening.[8]

As people grow older, their vision is likely to have a yellow cast.[9] For this reason, color looks less bright to older people. This is the reason why older people usually gravitate toward white and bright tones, and why the luxury car brand Lexus produces approximately 60% of its cars in white given its older customer base.[10] As for gender, women are usually drawn to brighter tones and are more sensitive to subtle shadings and patterns. Some researchers associate this with biology; claiming that women can see more colors than men do, while more men have the tendency to be colorblind.[11]

The **hue** (the color, red versus blue) is not the only determinant in the impression we get from color. **Value** (light versus dark) and **intensity** (brightness versus dullness) are also important elements. A dull or grayed red creates a different impression from a bright red. Similarly, a light blue and a dark blue create different feelings or perceptions.

Since the use of colors provoke robust emotional reactions, the selection of a **color palette** is essential to design product packages. Pantone, originally a manufacturer of color cards for print makers, is a leading developer and marketer in communicating a universal language of color.[12] It enables a number of industries such as textiles, apparel manufacturers, graphic designers and digital technologists to choose precise colors through every stage of their workflow. International designers and manufacturers "[...] rely on Pantone products and services to help define, communicate and control color from inspiration to realization."[13] Their original product, the Pantone Matching System, has become a worldwide standard language for accurate color reproduction.

Pantone currently offers a number of services such as the Pantone Color Institute, a consulting service that forecasts global color trends and guides businesses on color during the development of a product and in creating a certain brand identity and product development. This Institute collaborates with international brands to leverage the power, psychology and emotion of color in their design strategies. Pantone forecasts are massively influential. These color predictions are like a "self-fulfilling prophecy". Many designers conform to the forecasts and use the new color palette in their collections. V*oila!* It looks like Pantone got it right again...

Tiffany Blue color as a registered trademark for Tiffany & Co.

TY Lim / Shutterstock.com

Color as Trade Dress

Some color combinations come to be so strongly associated with a corporation that they become known as the company's **trade dress**, similar to a trademark, and the company may even be granted exclusive use of these colors. For example, Tiffany & Co. has an exclusive right to the use of the Tiffany Blue color as its *registered trademark*.

As a rule, however, trade dress protection is granted only when consumers might be confused about what they are buying because of similar coloration of a competitor's packages.[14]

Tommy Hilfiger attempted to secure exclusive use of red, white and blue for his label, an act that seems particularly audacious in the United States, given the colors of the American flag.[15]

Smell

Odor can stimulate our emotions or generate a comforting feeling. Smells can generate memories or release stress. One study even determined that our olfactory system is the most sensitive of all of our senses in terms of its ability to discriminate among odors.[16] Humans are able to remember around 10,000 distinct smells, which can activate important memories and can take individuals back to nostalgic feelings and childhood memories.[17]

Some of our responses to scents result from early associations that call up good or bad feelings, and that explains why businesses are exploring connections among smell, memory or mood. Many manufacturers and retailers today pay close attention to **scent marketing**.[18] This term refers to techniques that help to boost sales by focusing upon the scents that are pumped into stores.[19]

Fragrance is processed by the **limbic system**, the most primal part of the brain and the place where we first experience emotions. Smell is a direct line to feelings of happiness and hunger and even to memories of happy times. An industry executive explains that vanilla "evokes memories of home and hearth, warmth and cuddling."[20] This explains why "plain" vanilla has been widely used in scented products, from perfumes and body creams to cake frosting, and coffees. While scientists are still exploring the impact of smell on people's behavior, marketers are doing their best to creatively exploit these associations.

Businesses have discovered the economic clout of the ancient tenets of **aromatherapy**, by offering the public tools to "transform their environments" by creating, altering, or masking scents such as these:

- Sea breeze for calm

- Lavender for relaxation

- Green tea for introspection

- Pine for energizing

- Jasmine for sensuality

Scented environments have been shown to influence consumers' buying intention, how long they stay in a store, and even their willingness to pay a higher price.[21] Brands like Victoria's Secret use scents to increase store traffic, and department stores locate beauty and fragrance departments on the ground floor to fully awaken the senses upon entry.

The hotel industry relies on the power of scent to communicate a distinctive story and reinforce brand recognition. Some hotels also integrate their "signature scent" into linen sprays in guest rooms and even into their business cards.[22] The fashion retailer Stradivarius sprays a "Girl's Perfume" scent to appeal to its female customers, while its sister company Zara sprays perfume with more of a spicy scent to appeal to both genders.[23]

In 2013, Abercrombie & Fitch faced a lot of complaints from shoppers because of the strong fragrance the company pumped into its stores. Although the company reduced the intensity of its signature smell by 25%, the problem remained. Researchers discovered the cause of shoppers' discomfort: it turns out that Abercrombie chose a perfume made from musk, which is linked to making people feel nervous and cramped when it is sprayed in enclosed places.[24]

Take this as a warning: retailers should be cautious about the fragrance they use. Some of them hire specialized companies to advise them on these choices, such as Scent Air.[25] Scent Air has created distinctive scents for many fashion brands. For example, for Hugo Boss, the consultants used a smooth, woody scent to communicate the minimal store design. For Bloomingdale's, the company produced different fragrances for different departments: a "powdery" smell for newborns, a lilac smell for lingerie, and a coconut smell for swimwear. In Chapter 12, we will further discuss the different types of scent marketing that companies can use to shape their stores' atmospheres.

Sound

Music and sound are also important tools in the marketer's arsenal. Many aspects of sound affect people's feelings and behaviors, so companies pay a lot of attention to **sound symbolism** when they create their brand names. This term describes how the sound of a word affects people's perceptions about what it describes and the feature they infer it possesses, such as its size, speed, and weight.[26] A study on phonetics indicated that consumers are more likely to recall and recognize brand names that start with the letters *k, p, t, b, d,* and *g*. It also claimed that firmer sounds may be associated with harder or more durable product features such as work boots, but this may backfire for a "soft" product such as shampoo.[27]

Another study also found that front vowels, produced in the front of the mouth, such as "I" in "KIKI" gives a sense of something that is "small, feminine, fast, light, and angular". Back vowels, produced in the back of the mouth, such as the "ou" in Bouba is associated with items that are "large, masculine, slow, dark, and round". For example, for cars, participants selected names stressing back vowels such as "Bromley" for larger vehicles like SUVs.[28]

Touch

"Touch me" or "Try me" is a request we often encounter in retail stores. Moods are usually stimulated and relaxed on the basis of sensations of the skin, whether from a luxurious massage or the bite of a winter wind. Marketers recognize the importance of the sense of touch in consumer behavior. Researchers have also found that touch can impact sales. We are more confident about what we perceive when we can touch it. Individuals who score high on a "Need for Touch" scale are especially influenced by this dimension. **Haptic information** is the information we obtain while using the touch sense.[29] Haptic marketing is a somewhat recent discipline that emphasizes the practice of tactile sensations to impact consumer buying behavior.[30]

Research supports the power of touch in boosting feelings of perceived ownership and impacting the price the consumer is willing to pay.[31] For this reason, retailers like Apple encourage shoppers to touch the products in the store. Mass retailers such as Primark, Zara, Gap and Banana Republic drive their customers to touch their products through the placement of items on tables that are positioned at an easy-to-touch height. Fragrance and cosmetic brands have long applied the strategy of touch by offering free trials and samples, giving consumers the chance to try items before purchasing them.

Recent studies indicate that shoppers prefer to touch and see a product before they buy it online.[32] As touch is ultimately becoming a sense that brands want to incorporate, some online retailers such as Macy's, ASOS and Nordstrom among others are offering free item deliveries and returns, hoping to allow consumers to touch the products. And subscription services for fashion and beauty products, such as StitchFix and SpandexBox (where you get a new pair of leggings each month to fuel your workout) allow customers to experience small samples of new items before they commit to buying larger quantities.[33]

Taste

This sense is not normally associated with apparel fashion marketing, but flavors do enter into the cosmetics industry. Consider the fruit-flavored lip gloss and lipstick options today. The Lük Beautifood Lip Nourish is a natural lipstick produced with natural food based elements, which comes in several flavors such as Zesty Lime and Ginger and Pink Grapefruit, which taste yummy enough to eat (but don't!).[34]

Taste perceptions link to our other senses.[35] Our brains essentially arrive at a taste sensation by merging a food's taste, smell and touch into one experience. In one study, researchers demonstrated how taste and vision link together. When they dyed some white wine with a red odorless color, a panel of wine experts used descriptors they usually use for red wine, even though the taste was unchanged.[36] Other studies show that sounds also affect what we taste. For example, a lot of background noise and loud music can impair an individual's ability to sense some food tastes such as sweet and sour.[37]

The Stages of Perception

In this section, we will focus on the types and process of **perception,** in which the consumer absorbs sensations, and then uses them to make sense of what is going on in the world.

This process is trickier than it sounds, especially because a lot of these sensations never get noticed in the first place. If consumers do not pay attention to the message, whatever the marketer tried to communicate will be lost. To increase the chance that the individual will pay attention and interpret the message correctly, it is essential for marketers to understand the three stages that correspond to this process: *exposure, attention*, and *interpretation* (see Figure 7.1).

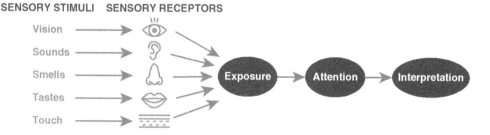

FIGURE 7.1   An overview of the perceptual process

Exposure

Exposure occurs when a stimulus comes within the range of a person's sensory receptors. Generally, the more exposure a stimulus (or message) gets, the more consumers will become aware of it. Outdoor advertising such as billboards, ads on buses and bus shelters, and even mobile billboards are getting heavy use by the fashion industry as the competition to reach customers intensifies.

Sensory Thresholds

If you have ever blown a dog whistle and watched pets respond to a sound you cannot hear, you know there are some stimuli that people simply are not capable of perceiving. Of course, some of us are better able to pick up sensory information than are others, whose sensory channels may be impaired by disabilities or age. The science that focuses on how the physical environment is integrated into our personal, subjective world is known as **psychophysics**.

When we define the lowest intensity of a stimulus that can be registered on a sensory channel, we speak of a threshold for that receptor. The **absolute threshold** refers to the minimum amount of stimulation that can be detected on a sensory channel. The absolute threshold is an important consideration in designing marketing stimuli. A billboard might have the most entertaining copy ever written, but this genius is wasted if the print is too small for passing motorists to see it from the highway.

The **differential threshold** refers to the ability of a sensory system to detect changes or differences between two stimuli. The minimum difference that can be detected between two stimuli is known as the **JND** (just noticeable difference).

The issue of when and if a difference will be noticed by consumers is relevant to many fashion marketing situations. Sometimes a marketer may want to ensure that a change is observed, as when a merchandise is offered at a discount. In other situations, the fact that a change has been made may be downplayed, as in the case of price increases or when a product is downsized.

A consumer's ability to sense a difference between two different stimuli is *relative*. A whispered talk that might be inaudible on a noisy highway can unexpectedly become public and awkward in a quiet seminar. It is the *relative difference* between the designated level of the discussion and its environments, rather than the loudness of the discussion itself that defines whether the stimulus will be noted. Ernst Weber, a 19th century psychologist, discovered that the size of the difference threshold seemed to be associated with the initial stimulus intensity, suggesting that the stronger the initial stimulus, the greater a change must be for people to notice it. This effect is known as **Weber's Law**.

How does this law apply to fashion? For example, if a River Island store believes that a price reduction should be at least 20% for it to motivate buyers to purchase a sale item, then according to Weber's Law the retailer should cut the price for a lipstick from $10 to $8, thus reducing $2 from the total price. However, if the same retailer is trying to sell a pair of jeans for $100, it cannot benefit from $1 discount only as this will not make an appealing difference for the consumer. River Island should instead reduce the denim by $15.

Attention (Shock Tactics)

While you are attending a lecture, sometimes you fully concentrate while other times you find yourself daydreaming. Suddenly, maybe you hear the professor call out your name. That will wake you up, and quickly! **Attention** refers to the magnitude to which processing activity is assigned to a particular stimulus—such as hearing your name.

Today consumers are bombarded with a huge amount of information, so they often experience states of **sensory overload.** This means that their sensory organs are exposed to far more stimulation from the environment than they can process. As consumers are usually exposed to around 3,500 or more pieces of advertising information per day[38], marketers continue to look for strategies to guarantee that they can grab consumers' attention.

How can you as a marketer get consumers' attention?

While the humans' brain ability to process information is restricted, consumers tend to be selective about the things they may want to pay attention to. The process of **perceptual selection** means that people attend to only a small portion of stimuli to which they are exposed. In general, consumers are more likely to be aware of the stimuli that relate to their current needs. For example, a consumer who rarely notices clothing ads for babies will become very much aware of them if they are expecting a baby.

In general, stimuli that differ from others around them are more likely to be noticed. Some aspects that impact consumers' chances of devising processing activity to a stimulus can be created through **contrast.** Contrast can take the following forms:

Size: Larger stimulus sizes are more likely to grab consumers' attention than smaller ones. For this reason, some companies place very large billboards with some animation to draw consumers' attention and drive them to nearby stores. In cities, sides of whole buildings are covered with images printed on vinyl.

Color: As we mentioned earlier in this chapter, color can have a powerful impact on consumers' attention. Marketers try to create contrast in colors, making them easily stand apart from each other.

Position: Stimuli that are in places where consumers are more likely to see them have a better chance of being noticed. For this reason, suppliers usually compete against one another to have their items placed at the right locations in the store. Items should usually be placed at eye level and toward the center of the display as this is where consumers' attention will be centered. Some fashion jewelry brands display one single ring with brighter lighting on top of it, placing a visual emphasis on the product and immediately drawing consumers to shelves. Zara uses this strategy

Nike X Off White employ color contrast

kudryavtsev dmitriy / Shutterstock.com

Patagonia Campaign using shock tactics

by locating its most fashionable and expensive clothing at the entrance of its store, in a way to capture your attention and drive you inside to browse.

Expectations: Stimuli that present something that is unexpected are more likely to grab our attention. One of these strategies is to place ads in unconventional places, where there is less competition for attention. This can include places like the back of loyalty cards, floors and escalators in shopping malls, mirrors in toilets or changing rooms.

Harvey Nichols launched a campaign in an unexpected way, showing one of its models suffering bladder malfunctions.

Patagonia, the sustainably conscious outdoor clothing brand, implemented the same strategy with the campaign called "Don't Buy This Jacket", which asked shoppers not to buy the brand's product, producing the opposite effect and attracting consumers.

Interpretation

Interpretation refers to the process of assigning meaning to a sensory stimulus based on the previous connotations that the individual has in addition to the assumptions this person makes about it. Two consumers can see the same fashion product, but they can interpret it in a different way based on what they were expecting to see. The Diesel brand decided to secretly open a

Diesel Limited Edition campaign

Solarisys / Shutterstock.com

'fake' store selling limited edition items on Canal Street in New York ahead of New York Fashion Week in 2018. The shop looked exactly like any other store in that neighborhood that sells a lot of counterfeit items. Named "Deisel", shoppers could not believe that this was an authentic Diesel outlet, because this definitely was not the right location for a real fashion brand to place itself.[39]

Learning

How do we "know" that Levi's jeans are durable, or that a Yves Saint Laurent coat is chic? **Learning** is a reasonably long-lasting change in behavior triggered by information or experience. Two main theories explain the learning process and how companies and brands "teach" shoppers to buy their products: behavioral and cognitive theories.

Behavioral Learning

Have you ever wondered why a company seems to repeat the same advertisement for a brand over and over again? **Behavioral learning theories** considers that learning happens as a consequence of experience and the associations individuals form between events. For learning of this sort to occur, it may be necessary to repeat the same message—even to the point where we wince when we see it again! Behavioral learning can take the form of classical conditioning or operant conditioning.

Classical Conditioning

Classical conditioning refers to the process of learning to respond to a given situation through repetition. This takes place when a stimulus that causes a response is paired with another stimulus that originally does not provoke a response alone, but which will cause a parallel response over time because of its association with the initial stimulus.

For example, if you usually tune into a fashion runway show, and you treat yourself to a piece of chocolate every time you start to watch, eventually the sound of the start of the show may make you crave chocolate even though you are not actually hungry.

Classical conditioning theory was first proposed by the Russian scientist Ivan Pavlov, who was doing research on digestion in animals. Pavlov observed that when his lab assistants came around to unlock dogs' cages at feeding time, their keys made a jangling sound. Over time the dogs learned to associate the sound of the keys with a yummy meal, so just hearing them at other times caused the animals to salivate in anticipation.

The food in this case was an **unconditioned stimulus**; this means it naturally causes a response (salivation). As this stimulus occurs together with something else that is initially neutral (like keys jangling or a bell ringing), over time that second stimulus becomes associated with whatever first caused the response—it is a **conditioned stimulus**. When the animal (or person) later displays the same reaction to the conditioned stimulus as to the unconditioned stimulus, this is a **conditioned response**.

The same process works when we shop. Marketers frequently rely upon classical conditioning techniques to create connections between messages and products with some other stimulus. When these cues are repetitively paired with conditioned stimuli, such as brand names, shoppers learn to experience different sensations such as contentment, hunger, or excitement when they interact with these cues later on.

For example, in a typical advertising execution the Lancôme brand started with a stimulus it knew would make its customers experience positive feelings: the celebrity Julia Roberts. After repetitively pairing the movie star with images of Lancôme's La Vie est Belle perfume, the perfume alone became a conditioned stimulus that would cause positive emotions, even when people saw Lancôme perfume without images of the celebrity. This can be viewed in Figure 7.2.

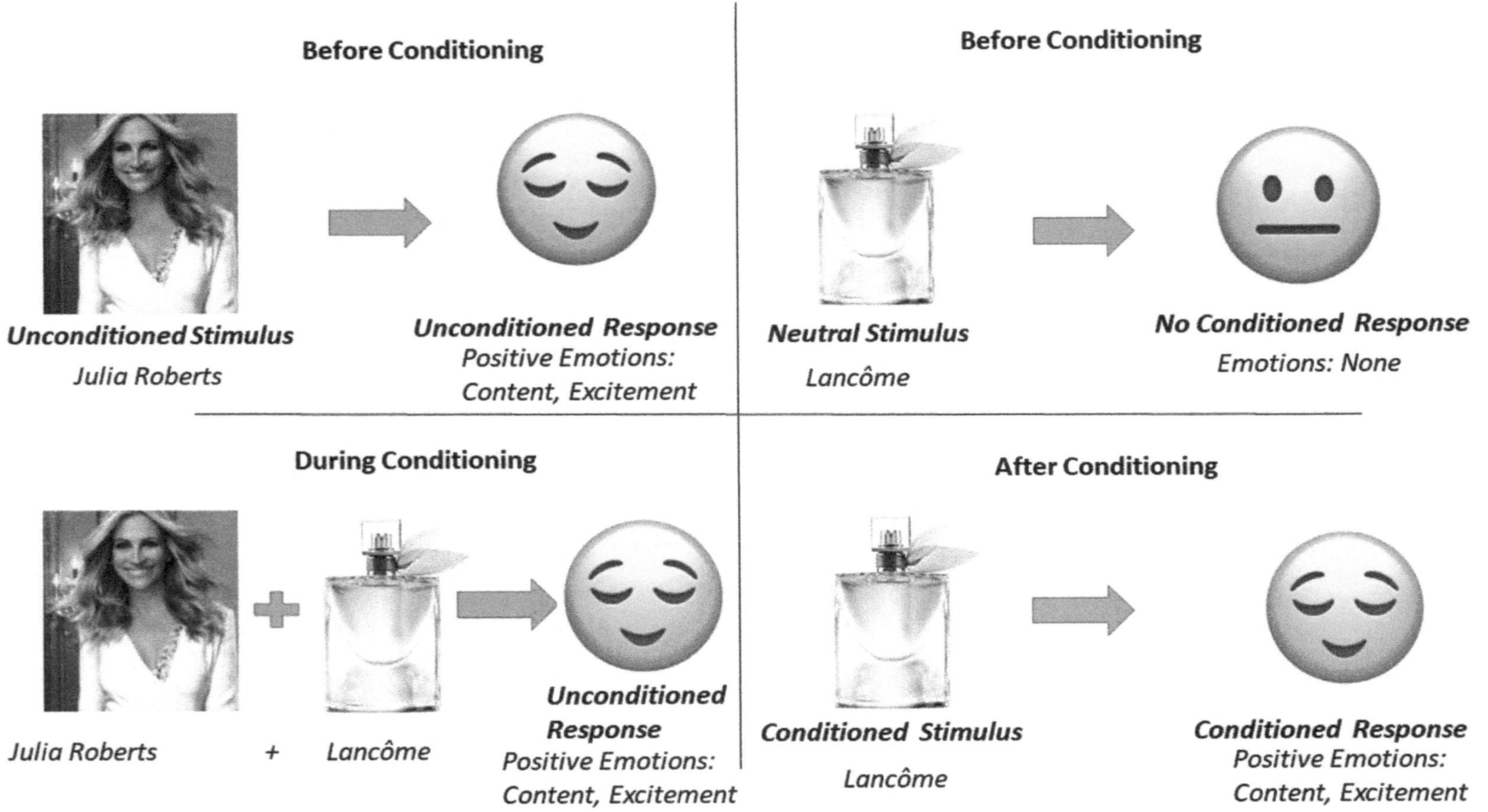

Before Conditioning

Unconditioned Stimulus
Julia Roberts

Unconditioned Response
*Positive Emotions:
Content, Excitement*

Before Conditioning

Neutral Stimulus
Lancôme

No Conditioned Response
Emotions: None

During Conditioning

Julia Roberts + *Lancôme*

Unconditioned Response
*Positive Emotions:
Content, Excitement*

After Conditioning

Conditioned Stimulus
Lancôme

Conditioned Response
*Positive Emotions:
Content, Excitement*

FIGURE 7.2   An example of the use of classical conditioning

In order for classical conditioning to happen, **repetition** is the key to developing associations between brands and consumers' response. Some studies show that the intervals between exposures may impact the usefulness of this strategy in addition to the medium form the marketer is adopting; the most effective repetition strategy is a mixture of interval exposures that rotate across different media types such as TV ads supplemented by printed media.[40]

Fashion brands usually use their signature logos throughout their products' design and while launching their campaigns. For example, Coach repeatedly uses the "C" while Louis Vuitton uses the "LV" monogram. The idea is to keep repeating the logos over and over again until they are etched in consumers' minds.

But be careful if you plan to use this strategy. Research indicates that there is a limit to the number of repetitions that can help retention. As we sometimes find in the case of those constantly playing TV spots, at some point we may no longer pay attention to a stimulus we've seen or heard too many times, and we'll place our attention elsewhere.

In some classical conditioning situations, **extinction** may take place. This happens when a conditioned response is no longer reinforced and the association between the stimulus and the response ceases. For example, sometimes a marketer overexposes its brand to consumers to the extent that its unique appeal disappears. The Lacoste polo shirt, with its differentiated crocodile logo, is a good example of this problem. When the once unique crocodile started to show up on kids' apparel and a lot of other products, it lost its impact. Another example is when the Burberry checkered pattern started to be worn *en masse* by the British working class in the early 2000s, though the label has since recovered from this perceived negative brand association.[41]

Stimulus Generalization

Stimulus generalization refers to the inability to distinguish between slightly dissimilar stimuli. For instance, in his research, Pavlov realized that when his dogs heard sounds similar to the original conditioned stimulus, they would sill salivate.

In marketing, stimulus generalization explains why some "me too" products prosper in the market. Shoppers have the tendency to confuse these products with the original ones. This describes the reason why some companies that own store brands usually design their packages similarly to leading brands.

How Can Marketers Benefit from Stimulus Generalization?

Product line and form extensions   Brands that own a number of product lines also rely on the concept of stimulus generalization. Marketers adopt a **product line and form extensions** strategy by introducing supplementary items to the same product category that go under the same brand name. For instance, these additions might include new essences, flavors, forms, colors, added ingredients, or package sizes. Launching new products with an existing brand name can increase the probability of acceptance as consumers have the tendency to positively associate the new products to the existing brand name. For instance, Lindt Chocolate does this when it launches additional flavors.[42]

Zara Home

Image courtesy of muammerokumus via Flickr. Shared under CC BY-SA 2.0 license.

Benefit package design

Image taken by the authors

Family branding   **Family branding** refers to the practice of selling a group of products or services under the same brand name. One familiar example is Apple. Apple uses the same brand name and logo on all of its products such as iPad, iPod, and iPhone, which makes it easier for customers to identify its products. Another example is Zara Home; its home furnishings and loungewear products were incorporated into the Zara brand.

Licensing   **Licensing** is a contractual arrangement that permits an established company brand or designer (*licensor*) to give an authorization to another company to manufacture products under its name and distribute the new product lines (*licensee*). Fashion designers and brands usually benefit from licensing by taking the opportunity to expand into different markets such as housewares, accessories, and cosmetics. For instance, in 2018, L'Oréal obtained the license to sell Valentino Perfume and Beauty products that was formerly held by the Puig company.[43]

L'Oréal also produces licensed fragrances and cosmetics for both Armani and Saint Laurent. Safilo, the Italian eyewear creator, has licensed a number of brands such as Fendi, Givenchy, Jimmy Choo, Dior, Boss, Missoni, Moschino, Elie Saab, Marc Jacobs, Juicy Couture, and Tommy Hilfiger.[44]

Stimulus Discrimination

Stimulus discrimination refers to the ability to select and differentiate a specific stimulus that is *not* associated with an unconditioned stimulus. The consumer's ability to differentiate among similar stimuli is mainly linked to the brands' positioning strategies, which aim to create a distinctive image in the consumer's mindset. Reputable brand names try to persuade customers not to buy the imitation brands, making them feel that their selection may not meet their expectations. Some fashion brands make sure to design their packages in a way that they stand out from their competitors. For example, Benefit make-up uses a range of practices that allows its brand and products to stand out from the crowd. It uses different printed designs products, very unique package shapes and distinctive ads to promote the brand.

Operant Conditioning

Consumers usually learn to keep buying the same fashion brands over and over again whenever they receive some rewards. However, obviously they avoid buying brands that they find to be defective or disappointing in some way. **Operant conditioning** (also known as **instrumental conditioning**) refers to learning that occurs due to a process of trial and error. The learner gets rewarded or punished in some way for making a response, and this reinforcement makes it more or less likely that he or she will make the same response the next time the situation arises.

For example, a man who needs a new polo shirt may try Brand A but finds that it fits too loosely, while Brand B is too short, and Brand C is too long. Finally, he tries Brand D. If the fit is good and he is happy with it (and especially if his girlfriend compliments him on it!), then he will learn to continuously buy polo shirts from Brand D.

Reinforcement schedules   It is very important for marketers to decide on the most effective **reinforcement schedule** that they will adopt by determining when and how often a behavior is to be rewarded or punished.

- In a **continuous reinforcement ratio**, the desired behavior is reinforced after every single transaction takes place. A fragrance shop for example may offer a free gift to its customers every time they buy an item from Elie Saab.[45]

- In a **fixed reinforcement ratio**, the reward is given to individuals every nth time a specific transaction takes place. For example, some retailers such as Selfridges and Harvey Nichols offer a credit voucher after a customer accumulates a specific number of points.

- In a **variable reinforcement ratio**, the reward is given to individuals on a random basis. Some of these examples might be companies that run contests, where only a few people actually win a prize.

Observational Learning

Humans, unlike most other animals, don't necessarily have to directly experience a reward or punishment in order to learn from it. **Observational learning** occurs when the individual looks at other people's behaviors and notes what happens to them. In these cases, learning happens due to an indirect, rather than a direct experience.

For example, if your friend or someone you see in a movie gets a compliment on that new Balenciaga sneaker they are wearing, this reinforcement may be sufficient for you to figure out if you like this brand as well. This helps to explain why stores like to employ attractive staff and encourage them to wear their most up-to-date fashion items to work.

Cognitive Learning

Of course, not everything we learn resembles the way that dogs, pigeons or other animals figure out simple connections between stimuli and responses! In order to explain these higher-order processes, we turn to cognitive **learning** theory; this approach focuses on the problem-solving process whereby individuals need to search for information in order to make the right decision. Consumers tend to use cognitive learning strategies once they are in the process of searching for products that represent their own personalities (such as finding a new handbag or pair of shoes), or when making a significant purchase (such as buying a home, a new luxury car, or going on a honeymoon).

Attitudes

The term attitude is widely used in popular culture. You might be asked, "What is your attitude towards the new Louis Vuitton collection?" An **attitude** is a lasting, general evaluation of people, brands, products, issues, or even advertisements. This evaluation is the result of what we have learned about things, whether they are good or bad, desirable or undesirable, etc.

An attitude is *lasting* because it tends to endure over time. It is *general* because it usually relates to more than a one-time occurrence. Consumers form various attitudes towards an extensive assortment of objects ranging from product-specific behaviors (such as shopping at Harrods rather than Primark) to more general consumption-related behaviors, such as if someone is a *fashionista* who lives for the latest collections, or if they go out of their way to recycle their old garments.

To measure consumers' attitude, marketers differentiate among three components: affect, behavior and cognition. We refer to these elements as the **ABC Theory of Attitudes**. **Affect** refers to the way a consumer feels about an attitude object; for example, if a favorite fragrance makes you happy. **Behavior** involves the person's intentions to do something with regard to an attitude object. In marketing situations, this component refers to a consumer's plan to purchase a product or if he or she actually buys repeatedly. **Cognition** refers to the beliefs a consumer has about an attitude object. For example, a shopper who prefers Nike shoes may do so because they think that they are more durable than other brands in the category.

The Hierarchy of Effects

Although the three components of an attitude are important, their relative importance will vary depending on a consumer's level of motivation with regard to the attitude object. Attitude researchers have developed the concept of a hierarchy of effects to explain the relative impact of the three components. Each hierarchy specifies that a fixed sequence of steps occurs *en route* to an attitude. Three different hierarchies are summarized in Figure 7.3.

It's obvious that some purchases are more important to us than are to others. However, even though we can generalize—for example, all things equal, more expensive items tend to attract a lot more thought before we buy them—we still find differences among consumers in terms of how important things are to them and thus how much "hard work" they will put into thinking about them.

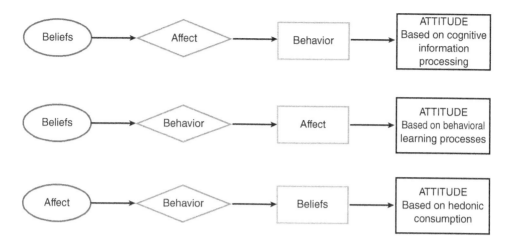

FIGURE 7.3 Three hierarchies of effects

SOURCE: Solomon, M.R. (2009) *Consumer Behavior* (8th ed.), Upper Saddle River, NJ: Pearson Education, p. 259. Reprinted by permission of Pearson Education.

For example, we may assume that items like pantyhose or underwear are relatively unimportant choices for the average consumer. But even here we can see that—partly through marketing campaigns—it's possible to turn a mundane purchase into an important one. Lingerie has become a fashion-oriented product due to extensive promotions by companies such as Victoria's Secret and these items often can be quite expressive of a woman's identity. Similarly, both men and women ramped up their engagement with underwear choices partly due to the Calvin Klein #mycalvins ad campaigns.

The standard learning hierarchy[46]   A consumer approaches a product decision as a problem-solving process. First, they form beliefs about a product by accumulating knowledge regarding relevant attributes (for example, Diesel jeans are durable). Next, the consumer evaluates these beliefs (durability is important to me) and then forms a feeling or affect about the product (Diesel jeans are perfect for me; I love them). Finally, based on this evaluation, the consumer engages in a relevant behavior, such as buying the product. This careful choice process may (if the marketer is lucky) create **brand loyalty**: the consumer "bonds" with brands toward which he or she holds highly favorable attitudes and buys them repeatedly.

The low involvement hierarchy   However, the simple truth is that we often just don't put that much effort into evaluating the things we buy. In these cases, a consumer can form an attitude via the *low-involvement hierarchy of effects*. Here, the consumer initially does not have a strong preference for one brand over another. Instead, they act on the basis of limited knowledge and then form an evaluation only after the fact.

For these situations, the attitude is likely to come about through behavioral learning, where the consumer's choice is reinforced by good or bad experiences with the product after purchase. The possibility that consumers simply don't care much about many decisions is important, because it implies that all of the concern about influencing beliefs and carefully communicating information about product attributes may largely be wasted. Some consumers are not necessarily going to pay attention anyway; they may be more likely to respond to some simple stimulus-response connections when making purchase decisions, such as noticing that an item is on sale and making a quick decision to buy it. This results in what we might call the **involvement paradox**: The *less* important the product is to consumers, the *more* important are many of the marketing stimuli (such as point-of-purchase displays, packages and jingles) that must be devised to sell it.

The experiential hierarchy   Researchers have begun to focus more on the significance of emotional response as a central aspect of an attitude. According to the **experiential hierarchy of effects**, consumers act primarily on the basis of their emotional reactions. This perspective highlights the idea that attitudes can be strongly influenced by intangible product attributes, such as package design, and by consumers' reactions toward accompanying stimuli, such as advertising and brand names. The resulting attitudes will be affected by consumers' hedonic motivations, such as how the product makes them feel or the fun its use will provide. That helps to explain why some fashion marketing campaigns focus so much on fantasy appeals, where they encourage buyers to use their imaginations and construct stories in their minds about the "wild" or "sensual" experiences they will have if they purchase these products.

Chapter Summary

Now that you have read the chapter, you should understand the following:

1. Why is perception a three-phase process that transforms raw stimuli into meaningful information?

Perception is the process by which physical sensations such as sights, sounds, taste, touch and smells are selected, organized and interpreted. We make judgments about people and objects based on stimuli presented to us. The eventual interpretation of a stimulus allows it to be assigned meaning. Thus, we perceive people as having certain attributes based on their appearance; similarly, we perceive conceptions of products based on their packaging.

2. How do fashion companies and brands use principles of learning to change consumers' behavior?

Learning is a reasonably long-lasting change in behavior triggered by information or experience. Two main theories explain the learning process and how companies and brands "teach" shoppers to buy their products: behavioral and cognitive theories.

Behavioral learning theories consider that learning happens as a consequence of experience and the associations that individuals form between events. Behavioral learning can take the form of classical conditioning or operant conditioning. While classical conditioning takes place when there is an association between two stimuli, operant conditioning happens when a certain response to a stimulus results in a reward. Extinction takes place when a conditioned response is no longer reinforced and the association between the stimulus and the response ceases.

Contrary to behavioral theories, cognitive learning is a problem-solving process that requires individuals to search for the proper information.

3. How do fashion consumers form attitudes?

An attitude is a lasting, general evaluation of people, brands, products, issues, or even advertisements. To measure consumers' attitudes, marketers differentiate among three components: affect, behavior and cognition, the so-called *ABC Theory of Attitudes*. Affect refers to the way a consumer feels about an attitude object. Behavior involves the person's intentions to do something with regard to an attitude object. Cognition refers to the beliefs a consumer has about an attitude object.

DISCUSSION QUESTIONS

1. With consumers being bombarded with advertising campaigns, how can fashion marketers get their attention?

2. Why is consumers' perception of interest to marketers?

3. A lot of studies indicate that our sensory detection abilities weaken as we grow older. Discuss the implications of the absolute threshold for fashion marketers attempting to appeal to the senior market.

4. Select a fashion brand's product of your choice. How can the brand use classical and operant conditioning in its advertising with the aim of creating positive feelings among its consumers?

5. How would you use reinforcement to encourage people to try a new make-up product?

6. Do you believe in aromatherapy? Do you feel that essential oils have a therapeutic benefit to the body? Survey consumers regarding their awareness and use of these products.

EXERCISES

1. Collect a set of current ads for one type of product (for example fragrances, cosmetics, fashion jeans or athletic shoes) and analyze the colors employed. Describe the symbolism conveyed by different colors and try to identify any consistency across brands in terms of the colors used in product packaging or other aspects of the ads.

(Continued)

2. Look through a current fashion magazine and select one ad that captures your attention over others. Give the reasons why.

3. Find ads that use the techniques of contrast and novelty. Give your opinion of the effectiveness of each and whether the technique is likely to be appropriate for the consumers targeted by the ad.

4. In a small group, find two different fashion advertisements: one that uses classical conditioning and another that uses instrumental conditioning. Identify the unconditioned stimulus, conditioned stimulus and conditioned response. Report your findings to your classmates.

5. Select a reputable fashion brand. How would you use stimulus generalization to develop strategies for a product line and form extensions, licensing, or family branding?

6. Select a fashion product of your choice. Specify the three components of your attitude and identify the sequence through which the steps occurred.

CASE STUDY: IT'S BEEN EMOTIONAL – THE NEUROSCIENCE OF IRRATIONAL CONSUMER DECISION-MAKING IN LUXURY FASHION

Edel Moore, University of Leeds

Think about the last time you went shopping for a fashion item or consumer goods. Whether you shopped alone or with friends, online or in a physical store, with purpose for a specific item or leisurely for a random find, you will have moved through a variety of emotional based states. From feelings of anticipation, belonging, desire to the euphoria of success when you found what you were looking for. A rollercoaster of emotions that many of us repeat, without reason, on a regular basis.

The study of consumer decision-making for most of the twentieth century was dominated by theories of rational processing. An understanding that consumption, led by the human mind, originates from conscious thought, and follows a think-feel-do pattern. We, too, when asked, would say that we have an awareness of the decisions involved in our fashion purchases. However, newer dual-process theories question the exclusivity of rational approaches and propose that emotions, instinct and nonconscious responses also play a role. In 2002, Kahneman was awarded a Nobel Prize in economics for demonstrating that human decision-making deviates from the optimal and is influenced without awareness. It is hypothesized that as much as 95% of purchasing decision-making exists at the nonconscious level. Cognitive neuroscience, through the analysis of brain activity, shows that millions of neurons associated with thought and behavior are automatically activated without or prior to the intervention of conscious thought. Neuroscientific evidence also suggests that even rational decision-making depends on nonconscious prior emotional processing. As pioneered by Damasio (1994), humans are not best demarcated as thinking machines but rather as feeling machines that think. Fashion and luxury retail are dependent on creating permanent nonrational connections between brand and purchase choice. Luxury fashion brands rely on deep emotional relationships with consumers to elevate a desire for their products above all other alternatives. Although Lajante and Ladhari (2019: 307) wrote that emotions are "episodic, dynamic, and recursive process, physiologically rooted, that cannot be reduced to its conscious dimension". This definition could easily be applied to luxury purchase decisions. Christian Louboutin exemplifies this bond when he states that for his products "The shiny red color of the soles has no function other than to identify to the public that they are mine." (Collins, 2011). Academics and research agencies are now looking to neuromarketing to understand, from a neural perspective, how fashion brands override rationality to create a want and reward for products that are not necessary.

Neuromarketing or Consumer Neuroscience is an emerging interdisciplinary research field linking the study of consumer psychology, marketing and cognitive neuroscience. The Neuromarketing Science and Business Association (NMSBA; www.nmsba.com) states that the purpose of neuromarketing is to examine brain and biometric responses, as well as behavior, to understand and shape how customers feel, think and act. When we shop, we produce involuntary chemical and physical reactions that determine our emotional response to marketing triggers, such as branding or advertisements. These in turn dictate feelings, preferences and decisions. However, consumers are not always consciously aware of automatic processing, so are unable to articulate these through traditional self-report market research methods such as surveys and focus groups.

Neuromarketing is harnessing newly accessible, non-invasive tools to measure neural functions to understand and predict human behavior within marketing contexts. Although a growing list, the main techniques involve recorded brain scans (EEG/FMRI) and biometric tracking of biological underpinnings of emotions through eye-tracking, pupil dilatation, galvanic skin response (GSR) and electrocardiograms (ECG). EEG (electroencephalogram) measures changes in electrical activity in response to external stimuli. Sensors are placed on the scalp and readings are taken at a rate of 2,000 times per second to identify the exact instance a function occurs. While highly accurate in timing, currently EEG has limitations in predicting locations of activity and accessing information deep within the brain. FMRI (functional magnetic resonance imagining) calculates differences between oxygenated and deoxygenated blood in the brain during active and rest states. It is extremely good at mapping the location of activity, allowing researchers to accurately represent what is happening in the brain while a subject is thinking. Though one of the most insightful neuroscientific tools, it is also the costliest. It does not have the timings accuracy of EEG and is limited in its ability to reflect true retail environments or interaction as experiments are conducted under clinical conditions. Research specific to luxury fashion is still in its infancy, but both of these methods have shown exciting findings in many retail and marketing areas including the impact of unconscious exposure to brands. Lab-based experiments show promotional material

(Continued)

from Gucci and H&M triggering emotional neural responses with less than 50 milliseconds of exposure (Romsoy, 2015). Subsequent experiments (Goto et al., 2019; Yen and Chiang, 2021) have discovered that neural activity registered at 200 milliseconds post exposure to a brand visual can be linked as a predictor to subsequent purchases. These highlight the instant connection between brand and purchase choice prior to any subjective awareness of selection.

Neurophysiological based techniques according to authors such Cerf and Garcia (2017) and Harrell (2019) are widely employed to investigate fashion consumers' emotional state in relation to issues such as website design, packaging, advertising and branding. These tools are less costly, allow for more natural consumer interactions and require less specialist training. Eye-tracking has been used to measure attention, pupil dilation to appraise attraction, and GSR and ECG to monitor changes in skin conductivity and heart rate relating to excitement and desire.

Academics and market researchers from disciplines including behavioral economics, management and marketing have been greatly aided in their investigations of consumers' emotional and cognitive responses through advancements in neuroscience techniques. By combining neuroimaging and biometric applications with traditional marketing, research consumer neuroscientists can now study complex brain functions through non-invasive methods, methods to gain insights into how and where involuntary chemical and physical reactions concur to determine consumers' emotional response to marketing stimuli. Although not yet specific to luxury fashion behavior, the insights neuromarketing will uncover when aligned with the sector are extremely exciting.

DISCUSSION QUESTIONS

1. From your own personal perspective, reflect on how your last five fashion purchases were governed by rational thinking or irrational decision-making processes.

2. Explain the main neuromarketing research methods used by consumer scientists.

3. Discuss the importance of neuroscientific tools to the study of consumer behavior in the fashion sector.

REFERENCES

Cerf, M. and Garcia-Garcia, M. (2017) *Consumer Neuroscience*. Cambridge, MA: MIT Press.

Collins, L. (2011) Sole Mate. *The New Yorker*. www.newyorker.com/magazine/2011/03/28/sole-mate (accessed August 30, 2021).

Damasio, A.R. (1994) *Descartes' Error: Emotion, Reason and the Human Brain*. New York, NY: Grosset/Putnam.

Goto, N., Lim, X.L., Shee, D. Hatano, A., Khong, K.W., Grüdtner Buratto, L., Watabe, M. and Schaefer, A. (2019) 'Can brain waves really tell if a product will be purchased? Inferring consumer preferences from single-item brain potentials', *Frontiers in Integrated Neuroscience*, 13: 19.

Harrell, E. (2019) 'Neuromarketing: What you need to know', *Harvard Business Review*, January 23. https://hbr.org/2019/01/neuromarketing-what-you-need-to-know (accessed August 30, 2021).

Lajante, M. and Ladhari, R. (2019) 'The promise and perils of the peripheral psychophysiology of emotion in retailing and consumer services', *Retailing and Consumer Services*, 50: 305–313.

Ramsoy, T. (2015) *Introduction to Neuromarketing and Consumer Neuroscience*. Rørvik: Neurons.

The Neuromarketing Science and Business Association 'What is Neuromarketing?' www.nmsba.com/neuromarketing/what-is-neuromarketing (accessed August 30, 2021).

Yen, C. and Chiang, M.C. (2021) 'Examining the effect of online advertisement cues on human responses using eye-tracking, EEG, and MRI', *Behavioural Brain Research*, 402, Article 113128.

NOTES

1. Lund, C. (2015) 'Selling through the senses: Sensory appeals in the fashion retail environment', *Fashion Practice*, 7 (1): 9–30.

   Chae, H., Baek, M., Jang, H. and Sung, S. (2021) 'Storyscaping in fashion brand using commitment and nostalgia based on ASMR marketing', *Journal of Business Research*, 130: 462–72.

   Nghiêm-Phú, B. (2017) 'Sensory marketing in an outdoor out-store shopping environment – an exploratory study in Japan', *Asia Pacific Journal of Marketing and Logistics*, 29 (5): 994–1016.

2. Hynes, N. (2009) 'Colour and meaning in corporate logos: An empirical study', *Journal of Brand Management*, 16 (8): 545–55.

3. Baxter, S.M., Ilicic, J. and Kulczynski, A. (2018) 'Roses are red, violets are blue, sophisticated brands have a Tiffany Hue: The effect of iconic brand color priming on brand personality judgments', *Journal of Brand Management*, 25 (4): 384–94.

   Hynes, N. (2009) 'Color and meaning in corporate logos: An empirical study', *Journal of Brand Management*, 16 (8): 545–55.

   Labrecque, L.I. and Milne, G.R. (2012) 'Exciting red and competent blue: The importance of color in marketing', *Journal of the Academy of Marketing Science* 40 (5): 711–27.

   Labrecque, L.I., Patrick, V.M. and Milne G.R. (2013) 'The marketers' prismatic palette: A review of color research and future directions', *Psychology & Marketing* 30 (2): 187–202.

   Tavassoli, N.T. (2001) 'Color memory and evaluations for alphabetical and logographic brand names', *Journal of Experimental Psychology: Applied*, 7 (2): 104–11.

4. Wright, A. (n.d.) 'What exactly is colour psychology?', *Colour Affects*. www.colour-affects.co.uk/how-it-works (accessed August 30, 2021).

5. Reich, H. (2010) *Don't You Believe It!: Exposing the Myths Behind Commonly Believed Fallacies*. New York, NY: Skyhorse.

6. Menkes, S. (2000) 'Fashion's Poet of Black: YAMAMOTO', *The New York Times*, September 5. www.nytimes.com/2000/09/05/style/IHT-fashions-poet-of-black-yamamoto.html (accessed August 30, 2021).

7. Szalai, I. (2015) 'Market focus: Beauty growth dynamics in the Middle East and Turkey', *Euromonitor*, April 29. https://blog.euromonitor.com/market-focus-beauty-growth-dynamics-in-the-middle-east-and-turkey/ (accessed August 30, 2021).

8. Ramirez, R. (2020) 'Beauty companies are changing skin-whitening products. But the damage of colorism runs deeper', *Vox*, July 1. www.vox.com/first-person/2020/6/30/21308257/skin-lightening-colorism-whitening-bleaching (accessed August 30, 2021).

9. Seltman, W. (2020) 'Slideshow: A visual guide to cataracts', *WebMD*, June 15. www.webmd.com/eye-health/cataracts/ss/slideshow-cataracts (accessed October 18, 2021).

10. Solomon, R., Bamossy, G., Askegaard, S. and Hogg, M. (2016) *Consumer Behaviour: A European Perspective*, 6th ed. Harlow: Pearson.

11. Letzter, R. (2016) 'Here's why men are much more likely to be colorblind', *Insider*, August 1. www.insider.com/why-are-more-men-than-women-colorblind-2016-7 (accessed August 30, 2021).

12. Pantone (2021) 'About Pantone', www.pantone.com/about-pantone (accessed August 30, 2021).

13. Pantone (2021) 'About Pantone', www.pantone.com/about-pantone (accessed August 30, 2021).

14. (2017) *Trade Dress: The Forgotten Trademark Right.* FindLaw. https://corporate.findlaw.com/intellectual-property/trade-dress-the-forgotten-trademark-right.html (accessed August 30, 2021).

15. Wilson, E. (2010) 'Tommy Hilfiger replants his American flag', *The New York Times,* May 14. www.nytimes.com/2010/05/16/fashion/16TOMMY.html (accessed August 30, 2021).

16. Bushdid, C., Magnasco, M.O., Vosshall, L.B. and Keller, A. (2014) 'Humans can discriminate more than 1 trillion olfactory stimuli', *Science*, 343 (6177): 1370–2.

17. Stafford, T. (2012) 'Why can smells unlock forgotten memories?', *BBC Future*, March 13. www.bbc.com/future/article/20120312-why-can-smells-unlock-memories (accessed August 30, 2021).

18. Grybś-Kabocik, M. (2018) 'The scent marketing: Consumers perception', *The Business & Management Review*, 9 (4): 483–6.

Madzharov, A.V., Block, L.G. and Morrin, M. (2015) 'The cool scent of power: Effects of ambient scent on consumer preferences and choice behavior', *Journal of Marketing*, 79 (1): 83–96.

19. ScentAir (2021) 'Scent marketing for retail', *ScentAir*. https://scentair.com/industries-clients/scent-marketing-retail (accessed August 30, 2021).

20. Collin, C. (1994) 'Everything's coming up vanilla', *The New York Times*, June 10: D1: (2).

21. Minsky, L., Fahey, C. and Fabrigas, C. (2018) 'Inside the invisible but influential world of scent branding', *Harvard Business Review*, April 11. https://hbr.org/2018/04/inside-the-invisible-but-influential-world-of-scent-branding (accessed August 30, 2021).

22. Air Scent (2019) 'A scent branding guide to hotel air fresheners & fragrances', *Air Scent*, November 19. www.airscent.com/scent-branding-guide-hotel-air-freshener-fragrances/ (accessed October 18, 2021).

Meyer-Delius, H. (2017) 'Sensory marketing: What can your brand learn from it?', *Printsome*, January 13. https://blog.printsome.com/sensory-marketing-small-brands/ (accessed October 18, 2021).

23. Meyer-Delius, H. (2017) 'Sensory marketing: What can your brand learn from it?', *Printsome*, January 13. https://blog.printsome.com/sensory-marketing-small-brands/ (accessed October 18, 2021).

24. Young, K. (2014) 'How shoppers find the scent of Abercrombie & Fitch stressful', *The Telegraph,* June 3. http://fashion.telegraph.co.uk/beauty/news-features/TMG10872620/How-shoppers-find-the-scent-of-Abercrombie-and-Fitch-stressful.html (accessed August 30, 2021).

25. 12.29 (2021) '12.29 ...only scent remains', *12.29.* https://1229scent.com/ (accessed August 30, 2021).

ScentAir (2021) 'Scent marketing for retail', *ScentAir*. https://scentair.com/industries-clients/scent-marketing-retail (accessed August 30, 2021).

26. Klink, R. R. (2000) 'Creating brand names with meaning: The use of sound symbolism', *Marketing Letters*, 11 (1): 5–20.

Ketron, S. and Spears, N. (2021) 'Sound-symbolic signaling of online retailer sizes: The moderating effect of shopping goals', *Journal of Retailing and Consumer Services*, 58: article #102245.

Sidhu, D.M., Deschamps, K., Bourdage, J.S. and Pexman, P.M. (2019) 'Does the name say it all? Investigating phoneme-personality sound symbolism in first names', *Journal of Experimental Psychology: General*, 148 (9): 1595–1614.

27. Lowrey, T.M. and Shrum, L.J. (2007) 'Phonetic symbolism and brand name preference', *Journal of Consumer Research*, 34 (3): 406–14.

28. Klink, R.R. (2003) 'Creating meaningful brands: The relationship between brand name and brand mark', *Marketing Letters*, 14 (3): 143–57.

29. Rodrigues, T., Silva, S.C. and Duarte, P. (2017) 'The value of textual haptic information in online clothing shopping', *Journal of Fashion Marketing and Management: An International Journal*, 21 (1): 88–102.

Silva, S.C., Rocha, T.V., De Cicco, R., Galhanone, R.F. and Manzini Ferreira Mattos, L.T. (2021) 'Need for touch and haptic imagery: An investigation in online fashion shopping', *Journal of Retailing and Consumer Services*, 59, 102378.

30. Magnarelli, M. (2018) 'The next marketing skill you need to master: Touch', *Forbes*, September 14. www. forbes.com/sites/margaretmagnarelli/2018/09/14/haptic-marketing/?sh=277da5597a3f (accessed August 30, 2021).

31. Peck, J. and Shu, S.B. (2009) 'The effect of mere touch on perceived ownership', *Journal of Consumer Research*, 36 (3): 434–47.

32. Skrovan, S. (2017) 'Why many shoppers go to stores before buying online', *Retail Dive*, April 26. www.retaildive.com/news/why-many-shoppers-go-to-stores-before-buying-online/441112/ (accessed August 30, 2021).

33. Scarano, G. and Gibson, B. (2021) 'The best clothing subscription boxes', *BuzzFeed*, February 11. www. buzzfeed.com/genevievescarano/the-best-clothing-subscription-boxes (accessed August 30, 2021).

34. Nourished Life (n.d.) 'Edible makeup good enough to eat', *Nourished Life*. www.nourishedlife.com.au/ article/2117372/edible-makeup-good-enough-eat.html (accessed August 30, 2021).

35. Stone, H. and Pangborn, RM. (1968) 'Intercorrelation of the senses', in W. Danker (ed.), *Basic Principles of Sensory Evaluation*', West Conshohocken, PA: ASTM International. pp. 30–46.

36. Small, D. (2008) 'How does the way food looks or its smell influence taste?', *Scientific American*, April 2. www.scientificamerican.com/article/experts-how-does-sight-smell-affect-taste/ (accessed August 30, 2021).

37. Spence, C. (2014) 'Noise and its impact on the perception of food and drink', *Flavour*, 3 (1): 1–17.

38. Gibson, O. (2005) 'Shopper's eye view of ads that pass us by', *The Guardian*, November 19. www. theguardian.com/media/2005/nov/19/advertising.marketingandpr (accessed October 18, 2021).

39. Richards, K. (2018) 'Why Diesel opened a deceptive NYC pop-up store selling knockoffs of its own clothes', *Adweek*, February 12. www.adweek.com/brand-marketing/why-diesel-opened-a-deceptive-nyc-pop-up-store-selling-knockoffs-of-its-own-clothes/ (accessed August 30, 2021).

40. Janiszewski, C., Noel, H. and Sawyer, A.G. (2003) 'A meta-analysis of the spacing effect in verbal learning: Implications for research on advertising repetition and consumer memory', *Journal of Consumer Research*, 30 (1): 138–149.

41. Day, J. (2004) 'Burberry doffs its cap to "chavs"', *The Guardian*, November 1. www.theguardian.com/ media/2004/nov/01/marketingandpr (accessed October 18, 2021).

   Brennan, S. (2018) 'Burberry finally shakes off its "chav check" reputation as millennials re-embrace the iconic print (and even Gigi Hadid is a fan)', *The Daily Mail*, August 18. www.dailymail.co.uk/femail/ article-6071585/Burberry-finally-shakes-chav-check-reputation.html (accessed October 18, 2021).

42. Lindt (2022) www.lindtusa.com/new-flavors--sc4#facet:&productBeginIndex:0&facetLimit:&orderBy:&p ageView:grid&minPrice:&maxPrice:&pageSize:& (accessed March 1, 2022).

43. Reuters (2018) 'L'Oréal Wins Valentino perfume and beauty licence', *Business of Fashion*, May 28. www. businessoffashion.com/articles/beauty/loreal-wins-valentino-perfume-and-beauty-licence (accessed August 30, 2021).

44. Safilo Group (2021) 'Elie Saab', *Safilo*. www.safilogroup.com/it/prodotto/marchi/elie-saab (accessed October 18, 2021).

   The fragrance shop (n.d.) 'Free gifts for her*', thefragranceshop.co.uk. www.thefragranceshop.co.uk/ womens-free-gifts/l (accessed August 30, 2021).

45. *Safilo Group*. (2021). 'Elie Saab', *Safilo*. www.safilogroup.com/it/prodotto/marchi/elie-saab (accessed October 18, 2021).

46. Solomon, M.R. (2021) *Consumer Behavior: Buying, Having and Being*, 13th ed. Hoboken, NJ: Pearson Education.

CHAPTER 8
Individual Consumer Dynamics: Motivation and the Self-Concept

LEARNING OBJECTIVES

After you read this chapter, you will understand the answers to the following:

1. Why are consumers motivated to buy fashion items?

2. Why do consumers get involved with fashion products?

3. How do the self-concept affects fashion consumer behavior?

Giselle is trying to concentrate on the report her client expects by five o'clock. She has worked hard to maintain this important account for the firm, but she can't help but be distracted by her date with Claude last night. Although they had a good time at that fashionable new poké place, Claude seemed to treat her more as a new friend than as a potential lover. As she procrastinates by looking through **L'Officiel,** Giselle starts to feel depressed as every page seems to feature beautiful women who seem to do nothing but diet, exercise and wear skin-baring clothes. Surely these models have gone under the knife to attain these features—do real women look like that? Although Claude is not exactly a hunk like Pio Marmaï or Nicolas Duvauchelle, still it would be nice if he acted a bit more interested. Giselle starts to wonder if it's worth investing some money in a Sandro dress. Maybe then—after a few glasses of red wine—she'd have the courage to upload her photo on that Meetic.fr dating app her friends have been talking about.

Theories of Fashion Motivation

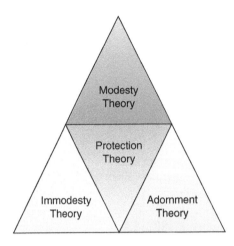

FIGURE 8.1 Theories of motivation to purchase fashion items

Giselle's dilemma is not very unusual. Almost everyone at one point or another is insecure or dissatisfied with their appearance. And one common solution is to look to fashion brands to bolster what we see in the mirror. Whenever we try to explain why a consumer makes a choice, we always have to consider their[a] motivation: What drives that selection over others?

Why do we wear clothes? The answer may seem obvious, but actually there are many reasons—beyond the fact that we don't want to get arrested for indecent exposure! Early theorists, such as Elizabeth Hurlock and Knight Dunlap[1], explored several of them, but most agreed on the following four main functions:

1. modesty
2. immodesty
3. protection
4. adornment.

Modesty Theory

This theory suggests that people wear clothing to conceal the private parts of their bodies.[2] Moralists believe that one's innate feeling of guilt and shame from being naked led to finding ways to clothe the body. This approach, often called the **Biblical Theory**, stems from the story of Adam and Eve and the fig leaf.

However, modesty is not universal, that is, the same in all cultures. A part of the body covered in one culture is left exposed in another without shame. In Muslim cultures, Hijab is "the principle of modesty and includes behaviour as well as dress for both males and females. The most visible form of hijab is the head covering that many Muslim women wear. Hijab however goes beyond the head scarf. In one popular school of Islamic thought, hijab refers to the complete covering of everything except the hands, face and feet in long, loose and non-see-through garments".[3]

And our definition of modesty of course changes over time. For example, the swimsuit of the 1920s is quite different from today's in terms of acceptable exposure.

As we discussed in Chapter 3, we're seeing to some extent a shift toward modesty as fashion targets women who choose to dress conservatively for religious or cultural reasons. In 2016, the first hijab-wearing model, Halima Aden, signed a contract with IMG Models and made her runway debut during New York Fashion Week, walking in Kanye West's Yeezy Season 5 show. She also appeared as the first hijab-wearing *Vogue* cover girl on the covers of British and Arabian Vogue.[4]

Fast-fashion retailers like H&M and Uniqlo are styling their photoshoots with models wearing veils. The sportswear brand Nike has also launched an athletic head covering designed for hijabi women.[5] Lately, Nike introduced its first collection for modest swimwear.[6]

A few luxury brands such as Dolce and Gabbana, Oscar de la Renta, and Carolina Herrera have also followed this trend by creating modest clothing for Middle Eastern women.[7]

Immodesty Theory

In contrast to a modesty motivation, sometimes people wear certain kinds of clothing because they *want* to draw attention to certain parts of the body. The words "decent" or "proper" are frequently used to refer to the "appropriate" amount of body exposure according to the speaker. A tight sweater and jeans cover the body, but they also

Swimsuit of the 1920s

Everett Collection / Shutterstock.com

Nike launches hijab for female Muslim athletes

"Nike Hijab" by dnai miller

Kim Kardashian

Sky Cinema / Shutterstock.com

draw attention at the same time. Sex appeal is not solely what fashion is about but sexuality and dress throughout the ages have undoubtedly been intertwined.

Almost since the beginnings of *Keeping Up with the Kardashians* in 2007, this entrepreneurial family has been a catalyst for the expansion of immodest fashion in many parts of the world with a lot of "sexy" or "hot" fashion trends.[8] As the new generation is influenced by the "**Kardashian Effect**", a new fast-fashion industry has emerged, driven by social media and copycatting these influencer trends, such as PrettyLittleThing, Boohoo, Nastygal, and Fashion Nova.

Protection Theory

Some theorists argue that clothing was first used to protect us from elements such as the cold, or from insects and animals. Still others argue that clothing was used as protection against enemies or to ward off supernatural forces.[9]

Apparel functions as a barrier between the body and the environment. We wear clothes to protect our bodies from the sun, wind, rain and cold by wearing parkas, gloves, hats, and so on. Some people wear clothing or accessories as amulets to bring good luck or protection from harmful spiritual powers; this might be called psychological protection as opposed to physical protection. Superstitions, fear from the unseen, belief in evil spirits, and luck have all been responsible for the use of certain garments, jewelry, and other adornments.[10] Here are some interesting examples:

- Cowrie shells protect women from sterility in many Pacific cultures.

- Bridal veils protect the bride from evil spirits.

- Evil-eye beads protect children and animals from unseen powers in Southeast Asia.

- Lucky charms, jewelry, coins, clothing, shoes and hats are believed to bring good luck. Four-leaf clovers in Ireland, Chinese golden toads, Egyptian Ankhs, are all examples of luck charms.[11]

Adornment Theory

One of the prevalent forms of clothing and accessories is adornment, personal decoration, or aesthetic expression. Adornment shows status and identity and raises one's self esteem.[12] Adornment is achieved through clothing and accessories (external adornment) or by making permanent changes to the body (bodily adornment).[13]

External adornment can be wrapped around the body (shawls), suspended from the body (necklaces), preshaped to fit the body (jackets), clipped to the body (earrings), applied to the body (false eyelashes), and handheld (purses). Bodily adornment includes such modifications as tattooing, piercing, scarification, or plastic surgery. Temporary bodily adornment that many of us practice includes changes to our hair, wearing make-up and artificial eyelashes, shaving body hair, or using tanning spray.

These original functions of clothing may be thought of as intrinsic reasons or motivations for clothing choices. Social-psychological or hedonic bases, also primary reasons for today's fashion choices, are discussed in the next section.

The Motivation Process

Motivation refers to the processes that lead people to behave as they do. It occurs when a need (something that is lacking) is aroused that the consumer wishes to satisfy. Once a need has been activated, such as protection, a state of tension exists that drives the consumer to attempt to reduce or eliminate the need. Once the goal is attained, tension is reduced, and the motivation recedes (for the time being). Motivation can be described in terms of its *strength*, or the pull it exerts on the consumer, and its *direction*, or the particular way the consumer attempts to reduce motivational tension.

Theories of Motivation

The degree to which a person is willing to expend energy to reach one goal as opposed to another reflects their underlying motivation to attain that goal. Many theories have been advanced to explain why people behave the way they do. Most share the basic idea that people have some finite amount of energy that must be directed toward certain goals.

Drive Theory

Drive theory focuses on biological needs that produce unpleasant states of arousal. We are motivated to reduce the tension caused by this arousal. Tension reduction has been proposed as a basic mechanism governing human behavior.

In a marketing context, tension refers to the unpleasant state that exists if a person's consumption needs and wants are not fulfilled. A person may be grumpy if they haven't eaten, or they may be dejected or angry if they cannot afford that new fashion item they want. This state activates goal-oriented behavior, which attempts to reduce or eliminate this unpleasant state and return to a balanced one, called **homeostasis**. Behaviors that are successful in reducing the drive by eliminating the underlying need are strengthened and tend to be repeated.

Drive theory, however, runs into difficulties when it tries to explain some facets of human behavior that run counter to its predictions. People often do things that increase a drive state rather than decrease it. For example, people may delay gratification. If you know you are going out for a lavish dinner, you might decide to forgo a snack earlier in the day even though you are hungry at that time.

Expectancy Theory

Most current explanations of motivation focus on cognitive factors rather than biological ones to understand what drives behavior. Expectancy theory suggests that behavior is largely driven by expectations of achieving desirable outcomes—positive incentives—rather than pushed from within.[13] We choose one product over another because we expect this choice to have more positive consequences for us. For example, a teenager may choose to wear specific clothes in anticipation of acceptance by the "in" group at school.

To understand how expectancy theory works, consider a privately-owned jewelry store that has the choice to pay employees on salary, hourly, or on a commission basis. If an employee expects to earn a fixed rate, such as $15 an hour, or $120 a day, expectancy theory says she might not be motivated to be overly charismatic when presenting the jewelry because the reward is the same whether or not she closes the sale. This is where commission can be the game changer in a company's sales. If the employee knows that the amount of money she makes is within her control, according to this theory she will more likely to be friendly, helpful, and an overall effective salesperson.

Taking its cue from Amazon, another example would be shopping at Selfridges where customers know that if they are online and want to order a certain item, all it takes is one click to make the order. The effort that the customer has put in to order the item is directly rewarded by receiving a message confirming that the order has been successfully placed.

Motives

When you ask a man why he just paid $2000 for an Armani suit, he's unlikely to explain, "I feel very insecure about myself and I want to impress other people." Sometimes consumers are unwilling or even unable to share the "real" reasons for their choices. Motives can sometimes be conscious, in which case the consumer is fully aware of what they are looking for and the reason for that, or unconscious, generally unknown to the consumer as these motives may either be suppressed, dormant or unidentified. There are two different types of motives: rational or emotional.

Rational motives indicate that consumers choose certain goals based on entirely objective measures such as durability, versatility, quality, price, safety, convenience and comfort. This motive is linked with a conscious and logical reason for buying. For instance, fashion retailers such as Amazon and Zalando focus more on the rational approach to motivate consumers to purchase.

Emotional motives indicate that consumers choose certain goals based on entirely subjective measures such as brand name, pride, status, luxury, and exclusivity. There are several buying motives for emotional products:

- *Fashion or imitation*: Some emerging brands may use this strategy to advertise for their products by featuring popular celebrities. For example, Jennifer Lopez completed her look with YEPREM jewelry for the release of her latest #PaTiLonely video.

- *Sexual attraction:* Marketers benefit from consumers' desires to appeal to romantic partners to sell some fashion products and services such as fragrances, deodorants, apparel, body/hair lotions and creams, cosmetics, eyewear, shoes, spa services, and couples travel packages. For instance,

Tom Ford and Gucci both use the promise of sexual attraction to motivate consumers to buy their products.

- *Comfort*: The desire to feel relaxed is very important to some consumers. Therefore, this criterion is crucial to motivate consumers who desire a comfortable experience, such as upholstered interiors in luxury cars or all of those sweatpants people have been wearing at home during the pandemic.

- *Care for loved ones:* People have an innate desire to constantly care for their families; be it a childless couple, a nuclear or an extended family. Consumers can be motivated to buy fashion products as a result of their love for their partners, families, societies and even countries. For instance, Tiffany, for valentine's celebrations, tapped into men's emotional motives toward their lovers by telling them, "Make her heart skip a beat".

- *Status insecurity*: People may feel insecure about their standing in society, or even resent others because of their preeminence in a certain field. Chivas Regal Scotch proclaims, "What the rich give the wealthy."

Tom Ford Eyewear

Cineberg / Shutterstock.com

Tiffany campaign tapping into emotional motives

Grzegorz Czapski / Shutterstock.com

Motivational Conflicts

A goal has **valence**, which means that it can be positive or negative. A **positive value** goal is one toward which consumers direct their behavior; they are motivated to *approach* the goal and will seek out products that will be instrumental in attaining it.

However, not all behavior is motivated by the desire to approach a goal. Consumers may instead be motivated to *avoid* a negative outcome. They will structure their purchases or consumption activities to reduce the chances of attaining this end result. For example, many consumers work hard to avoid rejection, a negative outcome. They will stay away from products that they associate with social disapproval. Perhaps last year's fashion is a product for some to stay away from since that would bring on social disapproval from peers. Not everyone, of course, reacts that way, as many consumers feel last season's styles on sale are good bargains. We also buy products, like deodorants and mouthwash, to avoid negative results such as onerous social consequences of underarm odor or bad breath.

Because a purchase decision may involve more than one source of motivation, consumers often find themselves in situations in which different motives, both positive and negative, conflict one another. Since marketers are attempting to satisfy consumers' needs, they can also be helpful by providing possible solutions to these dilemmas. There are three general types of conflicts can occur: approach-approach, approach-avoidance, and avoidance-avoidance.

Approach-Approach Conflict

In an **approach-approach conflict**, a person must choose between two desirable alternatives. A student might be torn to having to choose between two fashion items to wear to a club, or they might have to decide between going home for the holidays or going on a skiing trip with friends.

The theory of **cognitive dissonance** is based on the premise that people have a need for order and consistency in their lives and that brings "a tension between a person's actions and their mental model of the world". For example, "clothes should not end up in landfills" versus "this £4 dress looks cute, so what if I only wear it once". Individuals are motivated to reduce their inconsistency (or dissonance) and, thus, eliminate unpleasant tension.[14]

A state of dissonance occurs when there is psychological inconsistency between two or more beliefs or behaviors. It often occurs when a consumer must make a choice between two products when both alternatives usually possess both good and bad qualities. By choosing one product and not the other, the person gets the bad qualities of the chosen product and loses out on the good qualities of the unchosen one. This loss creates an unpleasant, dissonant state that the person is motivated to reduce. People tend to convince themselves, after the fact, that the choice they made was the smart one by finding additional reasons to support the alternative they chose, or perhaps by "discovering" flaws with the option they did not choose.[15] A marketer can resolve an approach-approach conflict by bundling several benefits together. For example, a message that encourages readers to find a compromise and reduce dissonance might imply that you "can have your cake and eat it, too" because our latest fashions are now on sale for a limited time, so you don't have to sacrifice on either trendiness or price.

Approach-Avoidance Conflict

An **approach-avoidance conflict** exists when a person desires a goal but wishes to avoid it at the same time. Many of the products and services we desire have negative consequences attached to them as well. We may feel guilty or ostentatious when buying a status-laden product or a fur coat. Some solutions to these conflicts include the proliferation of fake furs, which eliminate guilt about harming animals to create a beautiful fashion item. Many marketers try to overcome guilt by convincing consumers that they do deserve the luxury product they are getting, for example, L'Oréal cosmetics ads had a long-running tagline: "Because you're worth it!".

Avoidance-Avoidance Conflict

Sometimes consumers find themselves caught "between a rock or a hard place." They may face a choice with two undesirable alternatives; for instance, the option of either paying a high price for a new fashion item or buying last season's styles, which are on sale and affordable, but will be seen as out of style. Marketers frequently address an **avoidance-avoidance conflict** with messages that stress the unforeseen benefits of choosing one option (for example, you'll get 10% off if you open a charge account, to ease the pain of an expensive new fashion purchase). Some marketers may also allow customers to make installment payments over extended periods. Other marketers have also adopted the buy now and pay later strategy. A host of new **Buy Now Pay Later (BNPL)** companies such as Afterpay, Zip Pay, and Klarna allow consumers to get whatever they want now and pay over time.[16]

Needs

A **need** refers to the discrepancy between the consumer's present state and some ideal state. This gulf creates a state of tension. The magnitude of this tension determines the urgency the person feels to reduce the tension. One thing marketers do is to try to create products and services that will provide the desired benefits and permit the consumer to reduce these tensions.

Needs versus Wants

People may assume that needs and wants refer to the same thing, but this is not accurate. A basic need can be satisfied in any number of ways, and the specific path a person chooses is influenced both by a person's unique set of experiences and by the values instilled by the culture in which the person has been raised. These personal and cultural factors combine to create a **want,** which is the manifestation of a need.

For example, protection and hunger are basic needs that must be satisfied. The lack of protection can be satisfied by a $10 coat from Primark that gives adequate coverage and keeps the person warm enough. A $1,500 coat from Balmain can also satisfy this need for protection (as well as needs for status and self-actualization).

Types of Needs

People are born with a need for certain elements necessary to maintain life, such as food, water, air, and shelter. These are called **biogenic needs**. People have many other needs, however, that are not innate.

We acquire **psychogenic needs** as we become members of a specific culture. These include the need for status, power, and affiliation. Psychogenic needs reflect the priorities of a culture.

Needs can also be thought of as utilitarian versus hedonic. **Utilitarian needs** are desires to achieve some functional or practical benefit (such as comfort or protection as we discussed earlier). The satisfaction of utilitarian needs implies that consumers will emphasize the objective, tangible attributes of products, such as the durability of a pair of blue jeans, or a comfortable car.

Hedonic needs are subjective and experiential; they involve emotional responses.[17] Consumers may rely on a product to meet their needs for excitement, self-confidence, fantasy and perhaps to escape the routine aspects of life. Of course, we may be motivated to purchase a product because it provides both types of benefits. For example, an Hermès bag may be bought because of the luxurious image it portrays. (For more on hedonic and utilitarian needs in fashion, see also.[18])

Classifying Consumer Needs

A lot of research has been done to classify human needs. Some psychologists have tried to define a universal inventory of needs that could be traced systematically to explain virtually all behavior. One such effort, developed by Henry Murray, delineates a set of 20 psychogenic needs that result in specific behaviors. These needs include such dimensions as *autonomy* (being independent), *defendance* (defending the self against criticism), and even *play* (engaging in pleasurable activities).[19]

Specific Needs

Other approaches have focused on specific needs and their ramifications for behavior. Table 8.1 summarizes some personal needs that are relevant to consumer behavior.

TABLE 8.1   Needs that are relevant to marketers

Type of need	Marketing Relevance	Example
Need for achievement (desire for personal accomplishment)	Those with this need place a premium on products and services that signify success or evidence of their achievement.	Working women in senior positions interested in professional attire. Individuals who are interested in getting more fashion certifications to bolster their careers.
Need for affiliation (desire for belongingness and social acceptance)	Relevant to products and services that are consumed in groups and alleviate loneliness, such as team sports, shopping, and visiting bars.	Teenagers often shop for clothing together. Holiday packages for family and friends.
Need for power (desire to control one's environment)	Many products and services allow consumers to feel that they have mastery over their surroundings, ranging from muscle cars and loud boom boxes imposing one's musical tastes on others) to power clothes.	Individuals who are attracted to fast cars with greater horsepower. For example, a male wearing formal business attire may feel more powerful, a perfect example of "dress for success".
Need for uniqueness (to assert one's individual identity)	This need is satisfied by products that pledge to accentuate a consumer's distinctive qualities.	For example, Lady Gaga prefers to use creative products that show she is a nonconformist.

Maslow's Hierarchy of Needs

One influential approach to motivation and needs was proposed by the psychologist Abraham Maslow. Maslow's approach is a general one originally developed to understand personal growth and the attainment of "peak experiences." Maslow formulated a hierarchy of biogenic and psychogenic needs, in which levels of needs are specified. A hierarchical approach implies that the order of development is fixed—that is, a certain level must be attained before the next higher one is activated. This perspective has been adapted by marketers because it (indirectly) specifies certain types of product benefits people might be looking for, depending on the different stages in their development on their environmental conditions.

These levels are summarized in Figure 8.2. At each level, different priorities exist in terms of the product benefits a consumer is looking for. Ideally, an individual progresses up the hierarchy until his or her dominant motivation is a focus on "ultimate" goals, such as justice and beauty. Unfortunately, this state is difficult to achieve (at least on a regular basis); most of us have to be satisfied with occasional glimpses or **peak experiences**.

This implication of Maslow's hierarchy is that one must first satisfy basic needs before progressing up the ladder (that is, a starving man is not interested in status symbols, friendship, or self-fulfillment). This hierarchy is not set in stone. Its use in marketing has been somewhat simplistic, especially since the same product or activity can satisfy a number of different needs. For example, clothing can satisfy needs at nearly every level of the hierarchy:

- *Physiological:* Clothing covers the body and protects us from the elements.

- *Safety:* Clothing sold in the United States must pass flammability standards so that it won't burst into flames when close to an ignition source.

MASLOW'S HIERARCHY OF NEEDS

FIGURE 8.2   Level of needs (based on Maslow's hierarchy)[20]

- *Social:* Fashion is something to share with and be seen in by others.

- *Esteem:* Wearing the latest fashion or an art-to-wear piece makes us feel good about ourselves and gives us a sense of status among our peers.

- *Self-actualization:* "My clothes are an expression of the total me."

Another problem with taking Maslow's hierarchy too literally is that it is culture-bound. The assumptions of the hierarchy may only apply to Western culture. People in other cultures (or for that matter, in Western culture) may question the order of the levels as specified. A religious person who has taken a vow of poverty would not necessarily agree that physiological needs must be satisfied for self-fulfillment to occur.

Similarly, many Asian cultures value the welfare of the group (belongingness needs) more highly than needs of the individual (esteem needs). The point is that this hierarchy, while widely applied in marketing, is helpful to marketers because it reminds us that consumers may have different need priorities in different consumption situations and at different stages in their lives rather than because it *exactly* specifies a consumer's progression up the ladder of needs.

Fashion Product Involvement

Do consumers form strong relationships with products and services? A respondent in a study that looked at the attachments we form with what we buy had this to say[21]: She "[...] feels connection with this brand as if you're connected to a certain family that is external to your [usual] comfort zone, not your parents, not your family, it's a community you're connected to."

This example illustrates that people can become pretty attached to certain products or even brands. Of course, that doesn't mean that we're equally smitten with everything we buy; indeed, the fast-fashion business model assumes that in many cases buyers want to consume a garment for the short-term, then set it aside quickly when the next trend comes along. Still, on the other hand, we all own products that we're extraordinarily attached to—maybe because they remind us of something good that happened in our lives.

A consumer's motivation to attain a goal influences their desire to expend the effort necessary to attain the products or services believed to be instrumental in satisfying that objective. However, not everyone is motivated to the same extent—one person might be convinced they can't live without the latest style or modern convenience, while another is not interested in this item at all.

Involvement is defined as "a person's perceived relevance of an object based on their inherent needs, values, and interests".[22] The word *object* is used in the generic sense and refers to a product (or a brand), an advertisement, or a purchase situation. Consumers can find involvement in all the just mentioned "objects". For instance, consumers may be so highly involved with limited edition Supreme sneakers that they may be willing to queue for few hours to be able to purchase the new product. Involvement can be viewed as the motivation to process information.[23]

When relevant knowledge is activated in memory, a motivational state is created that drives behavior (such as shopping). As involvement with a product increases, the consumer devotes more attention to ads related to the product, exerts more cognitive effort to understand these ads, and focuses attention on the product-related information in them.[24]

On the other hand, a person may not bother to pay any attention to the same information if it is not seen as relevant to satisfying some need. A person who prides themself on their knowledge of exercise equipment may read anything they can find about the subject, spend their spare time in athletics stores, and so on, while another person may skip over this information without giving it a second thought. So it is with fashion; many people are extremely involved with fashion; they spend considerable time and money shopping for the latest styles, whereas others find shopping for clothes only slightly preferable to a trip to the dentist.

A person's degree of involvement can be conceived as a continuum, ranging from absolute lack of interest in a marketing stimulus at one end to obsession at the other. Consumption at the low end of involvement is characterized by **inertia,** when decisions are made out of habit because the consumer lacks the motivation to consider alternatives. At the high end of involvement, we can expect to find the type of passionate intensity reserved for people and objects that carry great meaning to the individual.

For example, the passion of some consumers for famous people (living like Drake, Kylie Jenner, Ariana Grande and Cristiano Ronaldo or dead like Michael Jackson and Marilyn Monroe) demonstrates the high end of the involvement continuum. For the most part, however, a consumer's involvement level with product falls somewhere in the middle, and the marketing strategist must determine the relative level of importance to understand how much elaboration of product information will occur.

The Many Faces of Involvement

Involvement can take many forms. It can be cognitive, as when someone is motivated to learn all he or she can about the latest specs of a new Tesla car, or emotional as when the thought of a new pair of Balenciaga sneakers gives some fashionista goosebumps. And the very act of *buying* the Balenciaga shoes may be very involving for people who are passionately devoted to shopping. To complicate matters further, advertisements, such as those produced for Nike or Adidas, may themselves be involving for some reason (for example, because they make us laugh, cry, or inspire us to work harder).

It seems that involvement is a fuzzy concept because it overlaps with other things and means different things to different people. Indeed, the consensus is that there are actually several broad types of involvement related to the product, the message, the perceiver, or the process.[25]

Product Involvement

Product involvement is associated with a consumer's level of interest in a specific product. The more involved consumers are in a product, the more likely they are to purchase it or purchase it sooner than others. They also may encourage others to do the same.

Smart marketers know that their most avid fans are a great resource—rather than ignoring their suggestions, they know they need to take them seriously. For example, Rebecca Minkoff found a different way to engage her fans. She asked her Instagram followers to select which designs should be on the runway fashion show for Spring/Summer 2015 in New York. Followers were later able to see their selected designs during the fashion show.[26]

Perhaps the most powerful way to enhance product involvement is to invite consumers to play a role in designing or personalizing what they buy. As we discussed in Chapter 6, **mass customization** refers to the personalization of products and services for individual customers at a mass-production price.[27] Improved manufacturing techniques in many industries allow companies to produce made-to-order products for many customers at a time. Customers love the idea of mass customization as it allows them to get unique products and it deepens their emotional engagement with both products and brands.[28]

Many fashion brands today have adopted the concept of customization:

Christian Dior: My ABCDior

Papin Lab / Shutterstock.com

- Louis Vuitton created its Mon Monogram service in 2008, giving its customers the chance to add their initials, colored stripes to core styles and choose among an assortment of heritage travel stickers.

- Dior allowed customers to personalize the Lady Dior bag with up to three badges of their selection.

- At the Tommy Hilfiger store, customers can pick any product, and have it directly customized in store while they wait.

- The luxury company Fendi believes that mass customization is the wave of the future, so it collaborated with the ecommerce retailer Farfetch to develop customization software.[29]

Not only fashion apparel brands are trying to engage their customers, but chocolate brands are also following the same strategy. For instance, Nestlé launched a made-to-order luxury bar in 2019.[30]

Message-Response Involvement

Message-response involvement refers to getting consumers involved with a particular product through the use of different media vehicles to impact consumers' motivation. Although consumers differ in their level of involvement with respect to a product message, marketers do not have to sit back and hope for the best. By being aware of some basic factors that increase or decrease attention, they can take steps to increase the likelihood that product information will get through to the consumer. A marketer can boost consumers' motivation to process relevant information by using one or more of the following techniques:

- **Appeal to the consumers' hedonic needs**. For example, some fashion brands such as Dolce & Gabanna use puppies, babies, and grandparents in their ads to trigger positive emotional needs.

- **Use interactive technology**. For example, the color matching feature on the Sephora Virtual Artist bot for mobile applications gives shoppers the option to find and try on a variety of product shades.

- **Use innovative stimuli**, such as uncommon cinematography, unexpected silences or unforeseen movements in ads.

- **Use prominent stimuli** such as loud music or fast action to grab attention in commercials. For printed commercials, a large size increases attention. People tend to pay more attention to colored pictures than to black and white ones.

- **Include celebrity endorsers** to generate higher interest in commercials. For example, Kaia Gerber is the latest It Girl to collaborate with Karl Lagerfeld on a new line.

- Personalize the product as we discussed earlier.

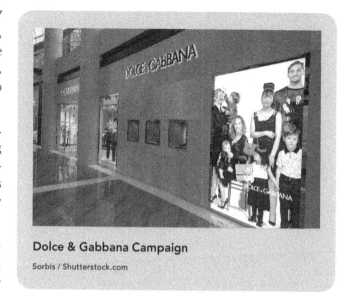

Dolce & Gabbana Campaign

Sorbis / Shutterstock.com

Sephora Virtual Artist augmented reality app

Sephora.com

Perspectives on the Self

Many products, from apparel and perfume to automobiles, are bought because the individual is trying to emphasize or hide some parts of their self. An important question to marketers is how consumers' thoughts and feelings about themselves shape their appearance and fashion consumption practices, mainly as they attempt to be in line with their society's expectations about how people should look and behave.

Is There a Self?

Although it seems natural to think about each consumer as having a self, this concept is actually culture bound. Western societies tend to emphasize the unique nature of the self.[31] Many Eastern cultures instead highlight the idea of a **collective self**[32], where the person's identity is hugely affected by their social group. In both cultures, the self is considered to be segregated into an inner, private aspect of the self-versus the outer, public aspect. Where cultures vary is in terms of which part they perceive as the "real you"; the West is more likely to endorse a liberal understanding of the self, which focuses upon the inherent distinctiveness of every person. In contrast, non-Western cultures tend to emphasize an interdependent self where individuals construct their identities in their relationships with others.

Clothing is a way to announce one's identity.[33] Fashion becomes inseparably involved in the construction and the reconstruction of our identity (see[34]). It can validate and help establish this identity: "Whenever we clothe ourselves, we dress 'toward' or address some audience whose validating responses are essential to the establishment of our self."[35] Previous researchers stated that the things we own reflect who we are. This is one of the most basic and dominant aspect of consumer behavior.[36]

Self-Concept

Self-concept refers to the beliefs an individual forms about their qualities and the way this person evaluates these qualities. While in general, individuals have positive views of their self-concept, there definitely are some parts of the self that we evaluate in a more positive way than others. For instance, a woman may sometimes feel much better about her professional identity than she does about her feminine identity.

Components of the Self-Concept

The self-concept is a complex construct. It is analyzed by scholars in different ways, using different typologies. Kaiser[37] discusses self-concept in the following ways:

- *Self as structure or self-schema:* structured thought processes that organize qualities of self. Clothing can be thought of as "like me" or "not like me"; studies have found that people quickly can decide what clothing falls into each category.

- *Self as process:* a symbolic interactionist view of the development of self through social interactions. Responses to our appearance or to our clothes affect the feelings about the self; social interaction causes us to continually examine and refine our perceptions of self.

- *Self-perception or self-image:* based on observations of our own behavior, we make self-attributions. We also receive feedback from others to help us in forming a self-image. We choose clothing to be consistent with how we want to appear to others and how we see ourselves.

- *Social comparison or self-evaluation*: our comparison with others in society. Our appearance is so visual that it is natural for people to compare themselves to others.[38]

- *Self-definition or symbolic self-completion:* statements about the self; self-definitions can also be thought of as goals or roles, such as career, religious, or gender self-definition, where an individual uses symbols to build and retain these parts of self. After evaluation with a resulting sense of incompleteness, one may take action to reduce this tension by finding a suitable symbol, which might be clothing or fashion, to complete one's self-definition.

- *Self-esteem:* feelings of self-worth; the positivity or negativity of self. Often we evaluate our-selves; we evaluate the self as we would any object. Those with high self-esteem think highly of themselves.

Self-Esteem and Clothing

Self-esteem describes the degree of positivity of an individuals' self-concept. Individuals who have a low level of self-esteem do not presume that they will do very well, and they are motivated to escape embarrassment, defeat, or rejection. On the other hand, individuals who have high self-esteem expect to perform well and be successful, are more likely to take risks, and are keener to be the center of attention.[39]

Cultural symbols such as fashion and the act of appearance management can function to express one's self-esteem—that is, when people feel good about themselves, they may pay a great deal of attention to their appearance. On the other hand, people who have low self-esteem may ignore their appearance or overcompensate by being obsessive about how they look. Creekmore calls this latter case *adaptive functioning* as people use clothing as a means to obtain social approval.[40]

Self-esteem is influenced by a process where the consumer compares their actual standing on some attribute to some ideal. A consumer might ask, "Am I as attractive as I would like to be?", "Do I make as much money as I should?", and so on. The **ideal self** is our conception of how we would like to be, while the **actual self refers** to our more realistic appraisal of the qualities we have and don't have.[41] The ideal self is partly molded by elements of the consumer's culture, such as heroes or people depicted in advertising, who serve as models of achievement or appearance. We may purchase products because we believe they are instrumental in helping us achieve these goals. We choose some products because we perceive them to be consistent with our actual self, while we use others to help us reach the standard set by the ideal self.

Self-esteem advertising attempts to change product attitudes by stimulating positive feelings about the self. One strategy is to challenge the consumer's self-esteem and then show a linkage to a prod-uct that will provide a remedy. L'Oréal launched a new program to empower young people with the goal of "turning self-doubt into self-worth". This program consists of confidence courses that will highlight issues related to body language, communication, employability and relationships.[42]

Another example of companies using self-esteem and positive advertising is Dove. Dove launched its "Real Beauty" campaign following research that indicated that only 2% of women par-ticipants believed that they were "beautiful".[43] The main purpose of this campaign was to encour-age women to embrace their appearances instead of denouncing themselves. So, instead of creating an impressive campaign, Dove communicated a personable image that reinforced women, provid-ing them with more self-confidence, which they link with the brand, resulting in intense emotional connection with Dove.

The Body as Product

An individual's perceptions of their physical appearance are an important characteristic of their self-concept. **Body image** is defined as an individual's subjective valuation of their physical self.

Body image is not always necessarily accurate. A man may believe that he is much fitter than he is, while a woman might perceive herself as being fatter than she really is. Unfortunately, it is not uncommon to find marketing strategies that exploit consumers' tendencies to distort their body images by preying upon insecurities about appearance. They try to create a gap between the real and ideal physical self, and then encourage the desire to buy products and services to close the gap.

In real life, clothing can be used to extend the body and change its perceived shape. Certain styles of clothing are often chosen to camouflage parts of one's body due to a negative body image. Many consumers are skilled at applying principles of design to create illusions of a slimmer or taller body and de-emphasizing parts with which they are unhappy.

Nowadays, social media is highly affecting the way people think and feel about their appearance. "Health and wellness, fitness, and plant-based food accounts can all be inspirational models for some users. Through these frameworks, social media users can maintain a healthy and positive outlook on their body image".[44] While social media can have a positive impact on individual's mental health, studies indicate that it can also negatively influence our perceptions of our bodies. One study found that "...young women who spend more time on Facebook may feel more concerned about their body because they compare their appearance to others (especially to peers)."[45] Therefore, this is causing serious psychological outcomes for women's body image when they try to compare the way they look with others.

Ideals of Beauty

A person's satisfaction with the physical image they reveal to other people is affected by how closely that image matches the image valued by their culture. An **ideal of beauty** is an *archetype*, or *exemplar*, of appearance. Ideals of beauty may comprise physical characteristics (such as men are, in general, more muscular than women and women are curvier), in addition to apparel styles, beauty and cosmetics, skin tone (light versus dark), and body shape (round or oval, athletic, pear, etc.). Consumers, desires to be congruent with these ideal images motivate them to make many different buying decisions. What's more, the influence to display these traits happens earlier and earlier: For example, the fashion retailer Abercrombie was highly criticized for selling push-up tops to little girls.[46]

Every society anoints certain people as aesthetic ideals, and it motivates emulation of these exemplars as it rewards attractive people (however a culture defines this quality). We characterize periods of history by a specific "look," or ideal of beauty. Often these relate to broader cultural trends, such as today's emphasis on fitness and toned bodies. Our language provides phrases to sum up these cultural ideals. We may talk about a "bimbo," a "girl-next-door," or an "ice queen," or we may refer to specific women who have come to embody an ideal, such as J-Lo, Gwyneth Paltrow, the late Princess Diana, and before her, the late Princess Grace.[47] Similar descriptions for men include "jock," "pretty boy," and "bookworm," or a "Brad Pitt type," a "Wesley Snipes type," and so on.

A look at US history reveals a succession of dominant ideals. For example, in sharp contrast to today's emphasis on health and vigor, in the early 1800s it was fashionable for women to appear delicate to the point of looking ill. Other past looks include the voluptuous, lusty woman that Lillian Russell made popular; the athletic Gibson Girl of the 1890s; and the small, boyish flapper of the 1920s exemplified by the silent movie actress Clara Bow. More recently, Kim Kardashian's ample behind "broke the internet" and inspired legions of young women to sign up for buttocks enhancements due to what one plastic surgeon dubbed "the Kardashian Effect."[48]

While some claim this is an unfortunate symptom of our modern consumer culture, in reality there *always* have been idealized standards of beauty for the masses to idolize. Throughout history, cultural elites and rulers meticulously edited the impressions they communicated to their peers and followers. It's hard to imagine that Julius Caesar, George Washington, or the British royal family (past and present) didn't have strong opinions about which of their images would adorn currency or portraiture.[49]

Beautiful: Compared to Whom?

All of this effort, money and yes, heartache for many begs a very basic question: Who gets to decide that this face or body is beautiful, while that one...not so much?

What cues lead us to view some faces as beautiful or handsome as opposed to others? Specifically, people appear to favor features we associate with good health and youth, because these signal reproductive ability and strength. These characteristics include large eyes, high cheekbones, and a narrow jaw.

Men also use a woman's body shape as a sexual cue; an evolutionary explanation is that feminine curves provide evidence of reproductive potential. During puberty, a representative female puts almost 35 pounds of "reproductive fat" on the hips and thighs area that supply the roughly 80,000 extra calories she will need to maintain a pregnancy.[50] Most fertile women have waist-to-hip ratios of 0.6 to 0.8, an hourglass shape that also happens to be the one men rank highest. Even though preferences for overall weight change over time, waist-to-hip ratios tend to stay in this range. Even the super thin model Twiggy (who pioneered the "waif look" decades before Kate Moss) had a ratio of 0.73.

How do women infer that a potential male mate has desirable characteristics of strength and health? They tend to favor men with heavy lower faces (an indication of a high concentration of androgens that impart strength), those who are slightly above average in height, and those with prominent brows.[51]

In one study, women viewed a sequence of male headshots that had been digitally modified to overstate or lessen masculine traits. They saw men with square jaws and well-defined brow ridges as good short-term partners, whereas they preferred those with feminine traits, such as rounder faces and fuller lips, for long-term mates. Overwhelmingly, participants said those with more masculine features were likely to be risky and competitive and also more apt to fight, challenge bosses, cheat on spouses, and put less effort into parenting. They assumed that men with more feminine faces would be good parents and husbands, hard workers, and emotionally supportive mates.[52]

Still, those findings pertain primarily to basic structural features of the face. They still don't explain why for example the stick-thin Kate Moss is the darling of one generation, while the ample Kim Kardashian rules another. High cheekbones aside, it's clear that the standards we use to decide whether we're shaping up or not vary across time and cultures.

Psychologists refer to this process as **social comparison**.[53] The basic message is that we don't arrive at judgments like these in isolation. Instead, we choose a comparison standard that is lower, the same or higher than where we perceive ourselves to be. If someone asks you to rate your ability to shake your booty on the dance floor, your response will depend on whether you're comparing yourself to professional dancers or to ungainly novices. The standard you use is a yardstick, and obviously your choice of which yardstick to use influences the measurement you take.

The notion of social comparison is tremendously important when we try to answer the question, "What is beautiful?". Like the distorted mirrors in a funhouse, our appraisal of who we are depends upon whose (imagined) perspectives we take. We also calibrate these sonar readings to the external standards we adopt: Studies show that young women alter their perceptions of their own body shapes and sizes after they watch as little as 30 minutes of TV programming, leaf through the pages of a typical fashion magazine brimming with thin, airbrushed models, or in some cases even by checking out Instagram posts.[54]

Working on the Body

As many individuals experience a gap between their real and ideal physical selves, they often go to great lengths to change aspects of their appearance. From cosmetics to plastic surgery, tanning spas to low calorie food, a huge assortment of products and services are directed toward altering and maintaining aspects of the physical self in order to present a desirable appearance. It is very hard to overemphasize the importance of understanding the physical self-concept (and consumers' wishes to improve their physical appearance) to many fashion marketing activities and decisions.

Although people perceive a strong link between self-esteem and appearance, some consumers exaggerate this connection even more and sacrifice greatly to reach what they consider to be a desirable appearance. Women tend to be taught to a greater degree than men that the quality of their bodies impacts their self-worth, so it is not surprising that most major body image distortions occur in women. These psychological disorders cause the patient to believe that their body literally is bigger or smaller than others see it. Despite the current cultural movement that celebrates Body Positivity where we are encouraged to love the skin we're in, there is still a stigma attached to obesity or even relatively larger body types in many places.[55]

A distorted body image has been linked with the rise of eating disorders that are especially prevalent among young women. Individuals who suffer from anorexia have a distorted view of their body and perceive themselves as fat or even obese to the extent that they become willing to starve themselves in order to become thinner.

Eating disorders affect mostly women, but some men as well. They are common among male athletes who also conform to various weight requirements such as boxers and male models.[56] In general, though, most men who have distorted body images consider themselves to be too light rather than too heavy: Society has taught them that they must be muscular to be masculine. Men are more likely than women to express their insecurities about their bodies by becoming addicted to exercise. In fact, striking similarities have been found between male compulsive runners and female anorexics.

Cosmetic surgery, as we discussed in Chapter 4, is another very popular way for people to modify their bodies in pursuit of a more pleasing appearance. Consumers are increasingly electing to have cosmetic surgery to rectify a poor body image.[57] It has been lately reported that for the sake of selfie love, a lot of individuals who are as young as 19 are resorting to plastic surgery in order to get the perfect filtered look.[58]

Although the highest five countries in the ranking of plastic surgery (e.g., America, Brazil, Japan, Italy and Mexico) make up almost half of all known surgeries in the world, this does not mean that plastic surgery is not very common in other countries as well. In the United states, 13 people per thousand engage in plastic surgeries, which is lower than the other countries such as in South Korea where 20 people per thousand undergo plastic surgery, followed by Taiwan and Belgium with a number of 17 per thousand, and finally Lebanon and Italy with a number of 16 per thousand.[59]

Other companies and institutions also contribute to the surgery craze. In some countries, banks offer loans to prospective patients. For example, the Lebanese bank Credit Libanais provides a surgery loan with convenient repayments that can be extended over up to 36 months.[60] In Caracas, Venezuelan banks run billboard advertisements for bank loans to pay for breast lifts.[61] South Korea, which claims to have the highest rate of plastic surgery worldwide, is becoming a hub for Chinese consumers who fly there to get double eyelid surgery that makes them look more like Caucasians, or for V-shaped facial surgery. The Korean government decided to support this sector[62] and to fund the rapidly growing medical tourism business that motivates individuals to travel to countries where it's relatively inexpensive to obtain elective surgeries.

Another popular type of body adornment is tattoos. Today these are a form of adornment for both men and women. This body art can be used to communicate aspects of the self. Tattoos may also serve some of the same functions that other types of body painting reflect in primitive cultures. Tattoos (from the Tahitian tatau) are related to folk art.

In addition to tattoos, the practice of body piercing—decorating the body with various kinds of metallic inserts—also has evolved from a practice associated with some fringe groups to become a popular personal or fashion statement. Piercings can take the form of a hoop protruding from a navel to scalp implants, where metal poles are implanted in the skull.

Chapter Summary

Now that you have read the chapter, you should understand the following:

1.   Why are consumers motivated to buy fashion items?

There are many reasons why consumers buy fashion items. Most researchers agree on the following four main functions as motivations for buying fashion today: modesty, immodesty, protection and adornment. *Modesty theory* suggests that people wear clothing to conceal the private parts of their bodies; *immodesty theory* suggests that individuals wear clothing to draw attention to certain parts of the body. *Protection theory* suggests that clothing functions as a barrier between the individual's body

(Continued)

and the environment, protecting the person from the sun, wind, rain, and cold. Finally, according to the *adornment theory*, people wear clothing for personal decoration or aesthetic expression.

So how does motivation work? Motivation occurs when a need is aroused that the consumer wishes to satisfy. Once a need has been activated, a state of tension exists that drives the consumer to attempt to reduce or eliminate the need. Once the goal is attained, tension is reduced, and the motivation recedes.

Many theories have been advanced to explain why people behave the way they do such as the *drive theory*, which focuses on biological needs that produce unpleasant states of arousal and *expectancy theory*, which suggests that behavior is largely pulled by expectations of achieving desirable outcomes—positive incentives—rather than pushed from within.

2.   Why do consumers get involved with fashion products?

Fashion products inspire a lot of passion, at least for some people. *Involvement* refers to "a person's perceived relevance of an object based on their inherent needs, values, and interests". Involvement can be viewed as the motivation to process information. A person's degree of involvement can be conceived as a continuum, ranging from absolute lack of interest in a marketing stimulus at one end to obsession at the other. Consumption at the low end of involvement is characterized by inertia when decisions are made out of habit because the consumer lacks the motivation to consider alternatives. At the high end of involvement, we can expect to find the type of passionate intensity reserved for people and objects that carry great meaning to the individual. Marketers design specific strategies to get consumers involved either in a product or in a message. *Product involvement* is associated with a consumer's level of interest in a specific product. The more involved consumers are in a product, the more they are apt to purchase it or purchase it sooner than others. *Message-response involvement* refers to getting consumers involved with a particular product through the use of different media vehicles to impact consumers' motivation and behavior.

3.   How does self-concept affect fashion consumer behavior?

Positive statements about a certain product/brand strengthens both perceptions of a product and a consumer's self-concept. *Self-concept* refers to the beliefs an individual forms about his or her qualities and the way this person evaluates these qualities. *Self-esteem* is the degree of positivity of an individuals' self-concept. Fashion and the act of appearance management can function to express one's self-esteem—that is, when people feel good about themselves, they may pay a great deal of attention to their appearance. Some fashion brands rely upon *self-esteem advertising*, which is a way to change product attitudes and drive consumers to positively behave towards a brand by stimulating positive feelings about the self. An individual's perception of their physical appearance is an important characteristic of their self-concept. Body image, which is linked to an individual's subjective valuation of their physical self, can greatly impact consumers' desires to buy products and services. An individual's satisfaction with their image is affected by how closely that image matches the image valued by their culture. In order to attain an ideal beauty, some individuals engage in different acts such as eating disorders, cosmetic surgeries, tattooing, and body piercing.

DISCUSSION QUESTIONS

1. Do you think modesty is an important driver in today's fashion? How does it differ across cultures and geographical regions? These are important questions that international brands have to tackle head on in a globalized fashion industry.

2. Identify ideals of beauty in two different countries—how are they the same or different?

3. Describe the three types of motivational conflicts, citing an example of each from current marketing campaigns.

4. How do you think consumers have changed in terms of their fashion buying motivations since the start of the Covid-19 pandemic?

5. Is it ethical for marketers to encourage infatuation with the self?

6. Which top level of needs does fashion clothing address? Explain why.

7. The long-standing cultural emphasis on razor-thin fashion models diverges from the growing body positivity movement that discourages the practice of criticizing different body types. But can this new focus go too far if it encourages consumers to no longer worry about their weight?

EXERCISES

1. Describe how a man's level of involvement with fashion would affect how he is influenced by different marketing stimuli. How might you design a strategy for a line of suits for a segment of low-involvement consumers, and how would this strategy differ from your attempts to reach a segment of men who are very involved with their appearance in the workplace?

2. Compare and contrast the real and the ideal self. List three fashion products for which each type of the self is likely to be used as a reference point when a purchase is considered.

3. Analyze fashion ads from several fashion magazines and ads from other types of magazines (home, men's, sports, and so on). Count and compare the number of super-thin female models versus average female body types, and super-muscular male models versus average male body types.

4. Locate additional examples of self-esteem advertising and evaluate the probable effectiveness of these appeals—is it true that "flattery gets you everywhere"?

5. Devise separate promotional strategies for an article of clothing each of which stresses one of the levels of Maslow's hierarchy of needs.

CASE STUDY: SOMETHING WICKED – EMBODIED FEMALE EMPOWERMENT

Edel Moore, University of Leeds, UK
Claire Evans, University of Huddersfield, UK
Dr. Karen Dennis, University of Leeds, UK

The mood is sultry, the music rhythmic, female bodies encased in strategically placed leather and lace glide in a seductive manner around carefully constructed landscapes. The promotional material for Something Wicked at first glance appears to conform to all we know about how sex sells. Stereotypical depictions of 'sexy' women generating comparison conflict built on insecurities between a current and desired state. It is hard to imagine how the potential for discrepancies between a consumer's subjective valuation of self and those depicted through the idealised models tallies with female empowerment in the 21st century. Scratch below the surface, however, and an alternative reading of self-esteem emerges where clothing becomes inextricably linked with the construction and reconstruction of the private elements of the inner self.

Something Wicked is an independent British luxury lingerie brand who pride themselves on producing garments and accessories of the highest quality, manufacturing in the UK and producing their lingerie in-house from start to finish. Their made-to-order wholesale and direct-to-customer online retailing strategy has seen sales quadruple in recent years. The company's product portfolio has expanded to include bridal ranges and product personalisation through a bespoke engraving service. They continue to see growing global demand, with 50% of current sales emanating from the United States of America. Specialists in leather, they create bespoke pieces, using mindfully sourced luxury materials, which are hand crafted at their establishment in the historic textile mills of Leeds, United Kingdom. Their brand values are centred around supporting local makers and championing the historical heart of British industry. The provenance of every detail of the product offering is meticulously evaluated to comply with the company's core business values. Leather components are crafted by a female saddler, the wax polish is handmade in London by an award-winning beekeeper using 100% natural ingredients, even the luxury gift wrapping is ethically produced by an English packaging company. Quality and high-level production values underpin the business supply chain. A key future challenge is ensuring the brand ethos is not compromised whilst developing the capacity to deliver more product against increasing market demand.

Something Wicked's brand statement is 'run by women, made by women, for the empowerment of women.' Their female led team of managers, makers and seamstresses are passionate about keeping production and manufacture in-house from beginning to end, ensuring that women are not being empowered in one country whilst being exploited in another. They are proud of the ethos behind the brand of being made by women for women. For the company, female empowerment is central to all business practices. Managing Director, Steff McGrath strongly believes that a consumer can buy a t-shirt saying "girl-power," but if the predominantly female workforce behind its production are not fairly treated, it cannot be empowering to the wearer.

Empowerment is more than just a tag line for the company, it is at the heart of everything they do. Something Wicked's lingerie encourages the wearer 'to be who you truly are'. Their 'never-off-the-rack' production values reflects their customers' motivations to own a luxury fashion item, which can accommodate and positively emphasise the consumers individualism and multifaceted actual and ideal self-concepts. Lingerie is an intimate product used for adornment, which may result in conspicuous or inconspicuous consumption. There is symbolic meaning for the wearer and/or viewer, as well as consumption integration as a means to express aspects of self that may outweigh functional benefit. The marketing message is that a piece of Something Wicked's lingerie inspires the wearer to be true to themselves. That 'you', the consumer, through the products can 'indulge yourself whether you are rolling in the sheets or working the room'. Here Something Wicked are asking women to reclaim the body, connect with social-psychological or hedonic needs, and achieve enablement through being subject as well as object.

The 'erotic' ethically produced pieces adorning the models derive from an authentic commercial philosophy of female equality embedded in business ownership, management, design, manufacturing, marketing and promotion. By drawing heavily on traditional, and in places, patriarchy's depictions of female sexuality Something Wicked are in danger of only furthering stereotypes. The overemphasis on the importance of sex in our daily lives and the acquisitions of products can distort the valuation of self in many cultures. However, by reclaiming the erotic and positioning female empowerment in the company narrative, Something Wicked is reframing how a brand can utilise hedonic messages to create involvement and ownership for female customers. Through depicting women in active control situations, the promotional campaigns stress freedom for the wearer to make their own lifestyle decisions. The clothing becomes inextricable linked with the construction and reconstruction of the private elements of the inner self. The strategy attempts to move typical advertising in the lingerie sector from objectifying to portraying females who are confident and independently taking control of their identity and consumption choices.

Something Wicked as a luxury handcrafted UK lingerie and accessories brand embodies female emancipation and empowerment through all elements of luxury clothing design and experimentation as their core U.S.P. It provides one cohesive corporate philosophy of transparent authenticity of female empowerment, which links to the self-concept and purchase motivations of consumers where "you wear what you stand for."

DISCUSSION QUESTIONS

1. Discuss the strengths and weaknesses of the business's 'brand value' strategy and consider how it could be exploited/developed to further customer appeal.

2. Explain the success Something Wicked has experienced in relation to the concepts of self-identity, and fashion brand involvement. How can authenticity of business model and promotional message leverage positive brand attitude, and emotional connection among female lingerie consumers?

3. Drawing on a range of readings of femininity and sexuality, discuss how exploitation and emancipation can be reconciled within the luxury lingerie sector.

(Continued)

REFERENCES

Beaty, C. and Evans, C. (2020) Exploring product development possibilities within Something Wicked to create a more streamlined production process, FFF Summary Report.

Drake, V.E. (2017) 'The impact of female empowerment in advertising (femvertising)', *Journal of Research in Marketing*, 7 (3): 593–599.

Kilbourne, J. (2003) 'Advertising and disconnection' in T. Reichert and J. Lambiase, *Sex in Advertising: Perspectives on the Erotic Appeal*. Mahwah, NJ: Lawrence Erlbaum. pp. 175–81.

Something Wicked website www.somethingwicked.co.uk/ (Accessed: 14 January 2021).

NOTES

1. Dunlap, K. (1928) 'The development and function of clothing', *The Journal of General Psychology*, 1 (1): 64–78.
   Hurlock, E.B. (1929) *The Psychology of Dress: An Analysis of Fashion and its Motive*. New York, NY: Ronald.

2. Jamal, A. and Shukor, S.A. (2014) 'Antecedents and outcomes of interpersonal influences and the role of acculturation: The case of young British-Muslims', *Journal of Business Research*, 67 (3): 237–45.
   O'Cass, A., Lee, W.J. and Siahtiri, V. (2013) 'Can Islam and status consumption live together in the house of fashion clothing?', *Journal of Fashion Marketing and Management: An International Journal*, 17 (4): 440–59.
   Sobh, R., Belk, R.W. and Gressel, J. (2012) 'Modest seductiveness: Reconciling modesty and vanity by reverse assimilation and double resistance', *Journal of Consumer Behaviour*, 11 (5): 357–67.

3. BBC (2009) 'Hijab', September 3. www.bbc.co.uk/religion/religions/islam/beliefs/hijab_1.shtml (accessed October 18, 2021).

4. Vogue Arabia (2018) 'All of Halima Aden's runway moments', *Vogue Arabia*, February 25. https://en.vogue.me/fashion/hijab-halima-aden-nyfw-runway-debut-kanye-west-yeezy-season-5/ (accessed September 1, 2021).

5. Guardian Staff (2017) 'Nike launches hijab for female Muslim athletes', *The Guardian*, March 8. www.theguardian.com/business/2017/mar/08/nike-launches-hijab-for-female-muslim-athletes (accessed September 1, 2021).

6. Binkley, C. (2019) 'Nike takes the plunge into modest swimwear', *The New Yorker*, December 9. www.newyorker.com/culture/on-and-off-the-avenue/nike-takes-the-plunge-into-modest-swimwear (accessed September 1, 2021).

7. Rushforth, S.H. (2017) 'Carolina Herrera Launches Her First Abaya Collection', *Harpers Bazaar Arabia*, April 26: www.harpersbazaararabia.com/fashion/the-style/carolina-herrera-launches-first-abaya-line (accessed September 1, 2021).

8. Kale, S. (2019) 'They can sell anything': how the Kardashians changed fashion', *The Guardian*, January 28. www.theguardian.com/fashion/2019/jan/28/they-can-sell-anything-how-the-kardashians-changed-fashion (accessed September 1, 2021).

9. Abu-Rabia, A. (2005) 'The evil eye and cultural beliefs among the Bedouin tribes of the Negev, middle east', *Folklore*, 116 (3): 241–254.
   Apostolides, A. and Dreyer, Y. (2008) 'The Greek evil eye, African witchcraft, and Western ethnocentrism', *HTS Teologiese Studies/Theological Studies*, 64 (2): 1021–1042.

10. Marshall, S.G. (2000) *Individuality in Clothing Selection and Personal Appearance*. Hoboken, NJ: Prentice Hall.

11. Conant, E. (2020) 'From evil eyes to sacred hearts, a look at lucky charms around the world', *National Geographic*, June 9. www.nationalgeographic.com/travel/article/evil-eyes-and-other-good-luck-charms-around-the-world (accessed September 1, 2021).

12. Venkatesh, A., Joy, A., Sherry Jr, J.F. and Deschenes, J. (2010) 'The aesthetics of luxury fashion, body and identify formation', *Journal of Consumer Psychology*, 20 (4): 459–70.

13. Batten, A.J. (2010) 'Clothing and adornment', *Biblical Theology Bulletin*, 40 (3): 148–59.

    Loren, D.D. (2015) 'Dress (clothing and adornment)', in P. Whelehan and A. Bolin (eds), *The International Encyclopedia of Human Sexuality*. Hoboken, NJ: Wiley. pp. 317–20.

14. Festinger, L. (1962) *A Theory of Cognitive Dissonance*. Stanford, CA: Redwood.

15. Brehm, J.W. (1956) 'Postdecision changes in the desirability of alternatives', *The Journal of Abnormal and Social Psychology*, 52 (3): 384.

16. Klarna US (2021) 'The shortcut to shopping', *Klarna.com*. www.klarna.com/us/aus18/ (accessed September 1, 2021).

17. Hirschman, E.C. and Holbrook, M.B. (1982) 'Hedonic consumption: emerging concepts, methods and propositions', *Journal of Marketing*, 46 (3): 92–101.

18. McCormick, H. and Livett, C. (2012) 'Analysing the influence of the presentation of fashion garments on young consumers' online behaviour', *Journal of Fashion Marketing and Management: An International Journal*, 16 (1): 21–41.

    Parker, C.J. and Wang, H. (2016) 'Examining hedonic and utilitarian motivations for m-commerce fashion retail app engagement', *Journal of Fashion Marketing and Management: An International Journal*, 20 (4): 487–506.

    Yim, M.Y.C., Yoo, S.C., Sauer, P.L. and Seo, J.H. (2014) 'Hedonic shopping motivation and co-shopper influence on utilitarian grocery shopping in superstores', *Journal of the Academy of Marketing Science*, 42 (5): 528–44.

    Yoo, J. and Park, M. (2016) 'The effects of e-mass customization on consumer perceived value, satisfaction, and loyalty toward luxury brands', *Journal of Business Research*, 69 (12): 5775–84.

19. Costa Jr, P.T. and McCrae, R.R. (1988) 'From catalog to classification: Murray's needs and the five-factor model', *Journal of Personality and Social Psychology*, 55 (2): 258–65.

20. Maslow, A. H. (1943) 'A theory of human motivation', *Psychological Review*, 50 (4): 370.

    Maslow, A. H. (1954) 'The instinctoid nature of basic needs', *Journal of Personality*, 22: 326–347.

21. Cui, C.C., Mrad, M. and Hogg, M.K. (2018) 'Brand addiction: Exploring the concept and its definition through an experiential lens', *Journal of Business Research*, 87: 118–27.

22. Zaichkowsky, J. L. (1985) 'Measuring the involvement construct', *Journal of Consumer Research*, 12 (3): 341–52.

23. Andrews, J.C. (1988) 'Motivation, ability, and opportunity to process information: Conceptual and experimental manipulation issues', *Advances in Consumer Research*, 15: 219–225.

    Dholakia, U. (2001) 'A motivational process model of product involvement and consumer risk perception', *European Journal of Marketing*, 35 (11/12): 1340–62.

24. Dholakia, U. (2001) 'A motivational process model of product involvement and consumer risk perception', *European Journal of Marketing*, 35 (11/12): 1340–62.

25. Richins, M.L., Bloch, P.H. and McQuarrie, E.F. (1992) 'How enduring and situational involvement combine to create involvement responses', *Journal of Consumer Psychology*, 1 (2): 143–53.

26. Mau, D. (2014) 'Rebecca Minkoff's latest social media experiment: Video app Keek', *Fashionista*, April 11. https://fashionista.com/2014/02/rebecca-minkoff-keek (accessed October 19, 2021).

27. Tiihonen, J. and Felfernig, A. (2017) 'An introduction to personalization and mass customization', *Journal of Intelligent Information Systems*, 49 (1): 1–7.

28. O'Connor, T. (2018) 'Cracking luxury's customisation challenge', *Business of Fashion*, February 20. www.businessoffashion.com/articles/news-analysis/cracking-luxurys-customisation-challenge (accessed September 1, 2021).

29. O'Connor, T. (2018) 'Cracking luxury's customisation challenge', *Business of Fashion*, February 20. www.businessoffashion.com/articles/news-analysis/cracking-luxurys-customisation-challenge (accessed September 1, 2021).

30. Picheta, R. (2019) 'Nestlé launches luxury KitKat bars—but they're not cheap', *CNN*, September 4. https://edition.cnn.com/2019/09/23/business/kit-kat-luxury-bars-scli-gbr-intl/index.html (accessed September 1, 2021).

31. Markus, H.R. and Kitayama, S. (1991) 'Culture and the self: Implications for cognition, emotion, and motivation', *Psychological Review*, 98 (2): 224–53.

32. Gaertner, L., Sedikides, C., Luke, M., O'Mara, E.M., Iuzzini, J., Jackson, L.E. and Wu, Q. (2012) 'A motivational hierarchy within: Primacy of the individual self, relational self, or collective self?', *Journal of Experimental Social Psychology*, 48 (5): 997–1013.

33. McNeill, L.S.(2018) 'Fashion and women's self-concept: A typology for self-fashioning using clothing', *Journal of Fashion Marketing and Management: An International Journal*, 22 (1): 82–98.

34. Gupta, S. and Gentry, J.W. (2016) 'Construction of gender roles in perceived scarce environments – Maintaining masculinity when shopping for fast fashion apparel', *Journal of Consumer Behaviour*, 15 (3): 251–60.

     Loussaïef, L., Ulrich, I. and Damay, C. (2019) 'How does access to luxury fashion challenge self-identity? Exploring women's practices of joint and non-ownership', *Journal of Business Research*, 102: 263–72.

     Titton, M. (2015) 'Fashionable personae: Self-identity and enactments of fashion narratives in fashion blogs', *Fashion Theory*, 19 (2): 201–20.

35. Perinbanayagam, R. S. (1974) 'The definition of the situation: An analysis of the ethnomethodological and dramaturgical view', *Sociological Quarterly*, 15 (4): 521–541.

36. Belk, R.W. (1988) 'Possessions and the extended self', *Journal of Consumer Research*, 15 (2): 139–68.

37. Kaiser, S.B. (2012) *Fashion and Cultural Studies*. London: A&C Black.

38. Solomon, M. R., White, K., Dahl, D. W., Zaichkowsky, J. L. and Polegato, R. (2017) *Consumer Behavior: Buying, Having, and Being*. Boston, MA: Pearson.

39. Kernis, M.H. (2003) 'Toward a conceptualization of optimal self-esteem', *Psychological Inquiry*, 14 (1): 1–26.

40. Creekmore, A.M. (1974) *Clothing Related to Body Satisfaction and Perceived Peer Self* (Research Report No. 239). East Lansing, MI: Michigan State University Agricultural Experiment Station.

41. Kaur, H. and Anand, S. (2021) 'Actual versus ideal self: An examination of the impact of fashion self-congruence on consumer's fashion consciousness and status consumption tendencies', *Journal of Global Fashion Marketing*, 12 (2): 146–60.

     Kressmann, F., Sirgy, M.J., Herrmann, A., Huber, F., Huber, S. and Lee, D.J. (2006) 'Direct and indirect effects of self-image congruence on brand loyalty', *Journal of Business Research*, 59 (9): 955–64.

     Sirgy, M.J. (1982) 'Self-concept in consumer behavior: A critical review', *Journal of Consumer Research*, 9 (3): 287–300.

42. Roderick, L. (2017) 'L'Oréal looks to have a "bigger purpose than selling product" with e-mentorship programme', *Marketing Week*, February 23. www.marketingweek.com/loreal-mentorship-programme/ (accessed September 1, 2021).

43. Entrepreneur Middle East (2017) 'The self-esteem movement: Why marketers want you to love yourself (and how they sometimes fail)', *Entrepreneur Middle East*, October 26. www.entrepreneur.com/article/303355 (accessed September 1, 2021).

44. King University Online (2019) 'The link between social media and body image', *king.edu*, October 9. https://online.king.edu/news/social-media-and-body-image/ (accessed September 1, 2021).

45. Fardouly, J. and Vartanian, L.R. (2015) 'Negative comparisons about one's appearance mediate the relationship between Facebook usage and body image concerns', *Body Image*, 12: 82–8.

46. CNN Wire Staff (2011) 'Abercrombie criticized for selling push-up tops to little girls', *CNN*, March 27 http://edition.cnn.com/2011/BUSINESS/03/26/abercrombie.bikini.controversy/index.html (accessed September 1, 2021).

47. Vacker, B. and Key, W.R. (1993) 'Beauty and the beholder: The pursuit of beauty through commodities', *Psychology & Marketing*, 10 (6): 471–94.

48. Hershkovits, D. (2014) 'How Kim Kardashian broke the internet with her butt', *The Guardian*, December 17. www.theguardian.com/lifeandstyle/2014/dec/17/kim-kardashian-butt-break-the-internet-paper-magazine (accessed September 1, 2021).

49. Solomon, M.R. (2021) *The New Chameleons: How to Connect with Consumers Who Defy Categorization*. London: Kogan Page.

50. Solomon, M.R (1994) *Buying, Having and Being*. London: Prentice Hall.

51. Kościński, K. (2014) 'Assessment of waist-to-hip ratio attractiveness in women: An anthropometric analysis of digital silhouettes', *Archives of Sexual Behavior*, 43 (5): 989–97.

     Whiteman, H. (2014) 'Women more attracted to masculine mates during ovulation', *Medical News Today*. www.medicalnewstoday.com/articles/272697, (accessed October 27, 2021).

52. Kruger, D.J. (2006) 'Male facial masculinity influences attributions of personality and reproductive strategy', *Personal Relationships*, 13 (4): 451–63. doi.org/10.1111/j.1475-6811.2006.00129.x (accessed September 1, 2021).

53. Festinger, L. (1954) 'A theory of social comparison processes', *Human Relations*, 7 (2): 117–40.

54. Brooks, K.R., Mond, J.M., Stevenson, R.J. and Stephen, I.D. (2016) 'Body image distortion and exposure to extreme body types: Contingent adaptation and cross adaptation for self and other', *Frontiers in Neuroscience*, 10: 334.

55. BBC. (n.d.) 'From New York to Instagram: The history of the body positivity movement', *BBC*, www.bbc.co.uk/bitesize/articles/z2w7dp3 (accessed September 1, 2021).

56. Stephen, E.M., Rose, J.S., Kenney, L., Rosselli-Navarra, F. and Weissman, R.S. (2014) 'Prevalence and correlates of unhealthy weight control behaviors: Findings from the national longitudinal study of adolescent health', *Journal of Eating Disorders*, 2 (1): 16.

57. Yazdanparast, A. and Spears, N. (2018) 'The new me or the me I'm proud of?: Impact of objective self-awareness and standards on acceptance of cosmetic procedures', *European Journal of Marketing*, 52 (1–2): 279–301.

58. De Graaf, M. (2017) 'How selfies are driving plastic surgery boom among Millennials seeking a "natural filter"', *Daily Mail*, February 15. www.dailymail.co.uk/health/article-4228914/How-Instagram-selfies-driving-plastic-surgery-boom.html (accessed September 1, 2021).

59. Twigg, M. (2017) 'Where plastic is fantastic: The world's cosmetic surgery capitals', *Business of Fashion*, July 5. www.businessoffashion.com/articles/beauty/where-plastic-is-fantastic-the-worlds-cosmetic-surgery-capitals (accessed September 1, 2021).

60. Beirut (n.d.) 'Surgery Loan at Credit Libanais'. www.beirut.com/l/5266 (accessed October 19, 2021).

61. Romero, S. (2011) 'Chávez tries to rally Venezuela against a new enemy: Breast lifts', *The New York Times*, March 14. www.nytimes.com/2011/03/15/world/americas/15venezuela.html (accessed September 1, 2021).

62. Stevenson, A. (2014) 'Plastic surgery tourism brings Chinese to South Korea', *New York Times*, December 23. www.nytimes.com/2014/12/24/business/international/plastic-surgery-tourism-brings-chinese-to-south-korea.html (accessed October 19, 2021).

CHAPTER 9

Macro Factors:
Group and Social Influence, and
Fashion Opinion Leadership

LEARNING OBJECTIVES

After you read this chapter, you will understand the answers to the following:

1. What is the role of reference groups in fashion decision-making?

2. How can opinion leaders impact consumers' fashion decisions?

3. How does social class affect fashion adoption?

How exciting can it get? Amanda can't believe it—she scored an invitation to the hottest party of the year at that glam new club, Luxe. All the coolest people will be there; she'll be forever grateful to her friend Alex for getting her on the list.

But now, what to wear? As she and Alex look through the racks at FashionNova in Los Angeles, her friend pulls out an item and snorts: "Look Amanda, how about a pair of these cage trousers? You'll certainly be the center of attention if you show up in these!"

They have gained popularity amongst provocative dressers; the "pants" consist of a few thin strips of faux leather sewn together in the shape of a cage from the waist down—with plenty of flesh revealed. Amanda and Alex have a good laugh about the types of girls who would stoop so low to be stylish. Amanda eventually buys a more modest outfit for the big night. When she meets Alex at the entrance to the club, Amanda can't believe what she sees: There's her BFF, decked out in a tight bodysuit and a pair of the very same cage trousers she was making fun of a few days before! Alex looks a bit sheepish, but as they make their way into the soirée she whispers in Amanda's ear: "Hey, if you can't beat 'em, join 'em." It's certainly funny how the pressure to be *au courant* can change your opinions in a hurry.

All humans need to belong to groups. We want to try to please others. Our choices about what to eat, drink, watch, listen to, drive, wear, and so on, are all learned and are highly impacted by our culture, family, friends, groups, and social environment. In fact, our desire to integrate or be part of a group is the primary motivation for many of our purchases and activities. All of these are macro-external factors that influence the way we behave.

Reference Groups

A reference group is defined as "an actual or imaginary individual or group conceived of having significant relevance upon an individual's evaluations, aspirations, or behavior".[1] Reference groups influence our fashion clothing choices in three ways.

1. *Informational:* A reference group that can improve a person's knowledge about their surroundings. For example, when an individual is seeking to gather information from opinion leaders who are experts in a certain product category.

2. *Utilitarian:* Motivates an individual to conform because s/he expects a reward or punishment based upon this behavior. For example, marketers creating expectations about the kind of coffee that people expect one to serve to guests.

3. *Value-expressive:* For individuals who seek to express themselves or boost their self-esteem. Think of the "young generation" that is advertised by the Pepsi brand.[2]

This section focuses on how other people, whether co-workers, friends and family, or just casual acquaintances, influence our purchase decisions. It considers how our preferences are shaped by our group memberships, by our desire to please or be accepted by others, or even by the actions of famous people whom we've never met. Finally, it explores why some people are more influential than others in affecting fashion and other product preferences, and how marketers go about finding people and enlisting their support in the persuasion process.

Types of Reference Groups

Although two or more people are generally essential to create a group, the term "reference group" often is used a bit more loosely to refer to any external entity that delivers social cues.[3] The referent may be a well-known figure like Bella Hadid or someone whom you know personally like your room-mates. Reference groups that affect consumption include *primary reference groups* such as parents and close friends, and *secondary reference groups* such as co-workers, schoolmates, sororities or fraternities, fellow *fashionistas*, technology and car enthusiasts, or simply casual acquaintances.

Obviously, some groups and individuals exert a greater influence than others, and they impact a broader range of consumption decisions. For example, parents may play a main role in forming our values toward any important issues, such as attitudes about marriage or where to go to university. This type of influence is termed **normative influence**—that is, the reference group helps set and enforce fundamental standards of conduct as they provide reinforcement and criticism to the individual. Normative influence may result in conformity to the fashion norms of a particular group as individuals attempt to gain acceptance by group members. Many studies have found that fashion conformity is related to peer acceptance.[4]

In contrast, a Porsche club might exert **comparative influence**, where decisions about specific brands or activities are affected as individuals compare themselves to group members. So, friends may exert a normative impact on whether or not it's cool to buy a high-performance car, while sportscar geeks might exert a comparative impact due to their informed opinions about which specific vehicle is the one to get.

Formal versus Informal Groups

A formal reference group may exist as a large, official association that has a particular structure and roles, complete with a formal contract, systematic meeting times, and officers. An example of that would be the *Fédération Française de la Couture,* which is the leading trade organization for the French fashion industry.[5] A group can also be relatively small and informal, such as people who follow the work of the designer Sandra Mansour. The main difference between this group and the formal one is that the connection among members is based on personal rather than on professional relationships.

In general, informal groups influence our opinions to a greater extent. That is because these groups are more involved in our day-to-day activities and gaining their approval tends to be more important to us, since they are high in normative influence. Larger, formal groups tend to be more product- or activity-specific and, thus, exert more comparative influence.

Membership versus Aspirational Reference Groups

Although some reference groups are formed of individuals that the consumer already knows (**membership reference groups**) others are created of individuals that consumers can iden-

tify with or whom they aspire to be like (**aspirational reference groups**). Not surprisingly, fashion brands usually focus on highly recognizable and famous celebrities such as actors, football players, musical artists, and sports stars and celebrities who receive a lot of media attention such as Kim Kardashian, Chiara Ferragni, Gigi and Bella Hadid, Christiano Ronaldo, Michael Jordan, Kobe Bryant as these luminaries represent what many consumers would ideally like to be.

Many luxury and sportswear brands have focused on launching collaborations with celebrities, as a win-win situation for both parties. The celebrity can increase their popularity and the fashion brand can receive more buzz and achieve higher sales figures. For example, Cardi B, an American rapper, signed a deal with Reebok to promote the Aztrek sneaker. In 2019, the luxury brand Balmain and the celebrity Cara Delevingne teamed up with Puma for a special edition of a 35-piece collection.

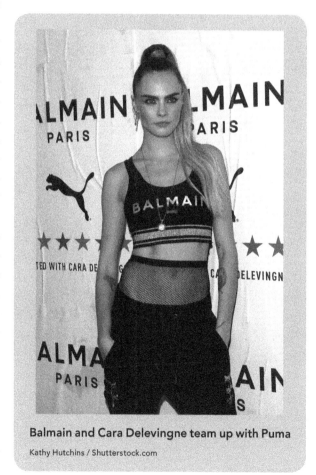

Balmain and Cara Delevingne team up with Puma

Kathy Hutchins / Shutterstock.com

Marketers really want to identify the reference groups that matter to their customers. These connections offer marketers insights into what their customers may need and want at every phase of the buying journey. This also gives them guidance as to the type of messages to design to communicate with the target audience and to select the right figure to represent the brand to the aspirational group.

Since individuals have the tendency to compare themselves to others who are similar, they are often swayed by knowing how people like them conduct their lives. For this reason, a lot of novel brand campaigns are drifting away from using famous faces. Instead, they feature "normal" people whose consumption activities provide comparative social influence. Some fashion companies such as Sephora, for example, employ everyday people such as their own employees in their advertising to extol their brands.[6]

Positive versus Negative Reference Groups

Reference groups may have either a positive or a negative impact on a consumer's behavior. In most cases, consumers model their behavior to be consistent with what they think the group expects of them. However, reference groups also give us clues about which brands to reject.[7] In some cases, consumer may try to distance himself or herself from other people or groups that function as *avoidance groups*. Some people may deeply examine and research the dress of certain disliked groups such as "nerds" and deliberately avoid products they associate with these stigmatized people. For example, a shopper who values sustainability might refuse to buy a certain fashion brand because they think of its typical wearers as people who are oblivious to environmental concerns.

When are Reference Groups Important?

Reference group influences are not equally powerful for all types of products and consumption activities. For example, generally products that are not very complex, that are low in perceived risk, and that can be tried prior to purchase are less susceptible to personal influence.[8] Although we can try on clothing (unless we're shopping online), a lot of decisions are driven by what we anticipate others' reactions to our choices will be. For this reason, they tend to be highly susceptible to reference group influence.

In addition, the specific impact of reference groups may vary. At times they may determine the use of certain products rather than others (such as owning or not owning a computer, or eating junk food versus health food), while at other times they may have specific effects on brand decisions within a product category (such as an Off-White versus Philip Plein T-shirt).

Two dimensions that influence the degree to which reference groups are important are whether the purchase is to be consumed publicly or privately and whether it is a luxury or a necessity. As a rule, reference group effects are more robust for purchases that are:

1. *Luxuries* (such as diamonds) rather than necessities, since products that are purchased with discretionary income are subject to individual tastes and preferences.

2. *Socially conspicuous or visible to others* (such as fashion apparel or living room furniture), since consumers tend to be swayed more by the opinions of others if their purchases will be observed.[9]

The Power of Reference Groups

Why are reference groups so persuasive? When another person or group has the ability to influence what happens to us, we say that they possess social power.[10] **Social power** refers to "the ability to influence others".[11] To the degree that you are able to make someone else do something, whether they do it willingly or not, you have power over that person. Fashion used to be associated with social power in the past, which became a prevailing means to assign and structure social relations as well as to impose social class differences. "In the ancient Roman Empire, the visual representation of fashion was so ingrained within the society that the ruling government decreed the models and colours of shoes worn by the members of each social class".[12]

In their classic work, French and Raven (1959) proposed five different forms of power: coercion, reward, legitimacy, reference, or expertise.[13] The following sections will discuss the difference among all the types of powers.

Referent Power

If a person admires the qualities of a person or a group, they are more likely to try to imitate those qualities by copying the referent's behaviors (such as choice of clothing, cars, or leisure activities) as a guide to forming consumption preferences. **Referent power** refers to the ability to command the respect and affection of others.[14] Prominent people in all walks of life can affect people's consumption behaviors by virtue of product endorsements (such as Michael Jordan for Air Nike, or Fenty for Rihanna), distinctive fashion statements (such as Jenifer Lopez displays for high-end

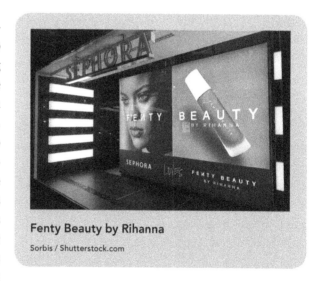

Fenty Beauty by Rihanna

Sorbis / Shutterstock.com

designer clothing such as Versace). Referent power is important to many marketing strategists because consumers voluntarily change behaviors to please or identify with a referent.

Information Power

A person can have power simply because he or she knows something others would like to know. Editors of trade publications in the fashion industry such as *Vogue* and *Woman's Wear Daily* often

Jenifer Lopez

"GLAAD 2014 - Jennifer Lopez - Casper-28" by DVSROSS is marked with
CC BY 2.0.

possess power due to their ability to compile and disseminate information that can make or break individual designers or companies.[15] People with **information power** are able to influence consumer opinion by virtue of their (assumed) access to the "truth." In 2007, Imran Amed founded the *Business of Fashion* and became its editor-in-chief. By 2011, Amed was named one of the 100 most influential men in Britain by *British GQ*[16]

Legitimate Power

Sometimes people are granted power by virtue of social agreements, such as the power given to police officers and university professors. The **legitimate power** conferred by a uniform is recognized in many consumer contexts, including teaching hospitals, where medical students are ceremoniously awarded white coats to enhance their aura of authority with patients, and banks, where tellers' uniforms communicate trustworthiness.[17] This form of power may be "borrowed" by marketers to influence consumers. For example, an ad featuring a model wearing a white doctor's coat can add an aura of legitimacy or authority to the presentation of the product.

Expert Power

Fashion designers possess **expert power** since they are the makers of fashion and they have the skill to develop new apparel lines each season. But fashion is notoriously fickle; some designers are *hot* one season, and *not* the next. For example, Hedi Slimane was celebrated for his signature androgynous style when at Yves Saint Laurent but his first collection for Celine in 2018 was panned by critics. Thus, designers' influence is only as good as their last success (not unlike movie makers and actors). Expert power is derived from possessing a specific knowledge or skill. Another idea to deliberate on here is the emergence of creative directors as the newest up and coming influencers. From Virgil Abloh to Olivier Rousteing, creative directors nowadays have certain influence over the fashion industry as a whole, with their exclusive insight into the brand's upcoming seasons and their lavish networking and Instagrammable events[18]!

Reward Power

When a person or group has the means to provide positive reinforcement, that entity will have **reward power** over an individual to the extent that this reinforcement is valued or desired.[19]

The reward may be tangible, as occurs when an employee is given a raise. Or the reward may be intangible: Social approval or acceptance is exchanged in return for molding one's behavior to a group or buying the products that are expected of group members. Often fashion items fall into this category. For instance, facial masks used to make people feel uneasy. However, with the Coronavirus pandemic outbreak, things have changed. Wearing a mask today is a sign of care rather than a sign of fear. According to a *New York Times* article, masks have become "the real must-have accessory, both in terms of utility and coolness, of the 21st century.[20]"

Coercive Power

Although a threat often is effective in the short term, it does not tend to produce permanent attitudinal or behavioral change. **Coercive power** refers to influencing a person by social or physical intimidation. Fortunately, coercive power is rarely employed in marketing situations. However, elements of this power base are evident in fear appeals, intimidation in personal selling, and some campaigns that emphasize the negative consequences that might occur if people do not use a product such as deodorant or the right kind of make-up.

Virgil Abloh, Creative Director at Louis Vuitton

lev radin / Shutterstock.com

Virtual Communities

Before the Internet was widely accessible most membership reference groups consisted of people who had face-to-face contact. Now, it's possible to share interests with people whom you've never met—and probably never will. A **virtual community of consumption** is a collection of people whose online interactions are based on shared enthusiasm for and knowledge of a specific consumption activity.[21] These anonymous groups grow up around quite a diverse set of interests; everything from Barbie dolls to fine wine. Virtual communities come in many different forms:

- *Video Game Communities:* The most common communities are connected with MMORPGs (Massively multiplayer online role-playing game, e.g. World of Warcraft). *Multi-User Dungeons (MUDs)* were an early form of gaming communities, which "allowed multiple players to connect and adventure with one another in real time... MUDs are text-based games not unlike a chat room. Most often connecting through telnet clients, users take on the roles of their character in a virtual world where every room, object, and creature is described as one might find in their favorite novel".[22]

- *Chat rooms, Slack, Discord and mailing lists:* Internet Relay Chat (IRC), otherwise known as *chat rooms*, is a text-only medium that is steadily declining. Slack and Discord are platforms that allow small groups of people to exchange text and images. Mailing lists are groups of people on a single mailing list who share information.

- *Social networks*: these are platforms like Facebook, Instagram, WeChat, TikTok and Twitter. They are the most public social networking cores, which allow individuals to form smaller groups based on their common interests, activities and backgrounds. Other communities in this category, such as Pinterest and YouTube focus on media sharing.

- *Blogs:* The fastest-growing form of online community. This term derives from a *weblog*. Bloggers can fire off thoughts on a whim, click a button, and quickly have them appear on a site. Personal blogs frequently look like online diaries, with brief musings about the day's events, and perhaps a link or two of interest. Fashion blogs play a very central role in influencing choices today.[23] Fashion blog are blogs related to fashion content, where bloggers do post news and photographs taken from the most up-to-date runway trends or photographs featuring them posing with different fashionable outfits. Among the trendiest blogs are *The Blonde Salad, Who What Wear, and The Fashion Advocate.*

The Blonde Salad

Chiara Ferr Chiara Ferragniagni

Virtual Communities have a big impact on individuals' product preferences. These loyal consumers essentially network together to form their tastes, and evaluate product quality. They place great weight on the judgments of their fellow members.

Although consumption communities are largely a grassroots phenomenon founded by consumers for other consumers, these community members can be reached by marketers—if they are careful not to alienate members by being too aggressive or "commercial." Using tracking data, companies can create a detailed profile of any individual consumer who has posted information.

Fashion Conformity and Individuality

Many of us have experienced this common dilemma: How can I fit in with others and still be an individual? How can I look similar to my friends and still stand out? There is a tension between dressing to fit in and dressing to be unique.[24] Sorority/Fraternity members' appearance, school uniforms, and formal and informal workplace dress codes are all areas where forces of conformity and individuality clash.

Conformity describes a change in beliefs or actions as a response to real or imagined group pressure. For the society to function, its body of individuals adopt **norms**, or informal rules that govern behavior. Conformity in dress can be thought of as acceptance or adherence to a clothing norm, which represents the typical or accepted manner of dressing shown by a specified group.[25] We use the term **mode** to mean the most common form of clothing worn among a given group of people, or the greatest frequency of a **style** (a characteristic or distinctive form of dress). As we've already seen, fashion represents the popular, accepted, prevailing style at any given time. **Individuality** in dress refers to a desire to set oneself apart from the norm.

Information from reference groups can result in conformity to group norms. This is especially prevalent when groups such as bank or hotel employees adhere to strictly defined fashion norms. Dress codes in the workplace act to create or maintain a unified look or image. They are sometimes explicit—that is, clearly explained to the employee (perhaps written)—but more often they are implicit, where clothing norms are "understood" and followed. Fellow employees thus serve as a comparative reference group that provides information on how to appropriately conform.

Factors that Influence the Likelihood of Conformity

Conformity is not an automatic process, and many factors contribute to the likelihood that consumers will pattern their behavior after others. Among the factors that affect the likelihood of conformity are the following:

- *Cultural pressures:* Different cultures exert different degrees of pressure on members to conform. For example, in 1960s, there was a famous slogan in the USA: "Do your own thing."

- *Fear of deviance:* Group members are sometimes scared that they will be *sanctioned* by the group in case their behavior differs from that of the group. For example, **cyberbullying** of teens who don't conform to their peers is a huge problem.[26]

- *Commitment:* The more an individual is engaged with a group and wants to belong to it, the more this person will be motivated to obey the principles of the group. For example, students who are members of a university fashion group or individuals who are members of a celebrity fan group may do anything their idols ask of them.

- *Group unanimity, size, and expertise:* The more power a group has, the more likely the members will comply. It is usually tougher to repel the demands of a big number of people than just a small one.

- *Susceptibility to interpersonal power:* This trait is linked to those who usually feel the need to identify or improve their image in the views of significant others. This is usually complemented by the possession of products the individual thinks will impress his or her surrounding, and by the inclination to learn more about products while observing others.[27] Research in early adolescents found that those who were more susceptible to interpersonal influence placed more importance on the display aspects of clothing. The reason is that these individuals usually refer to dress as a significant normative and informational cue to get social acceptance.[28]

Opinion Leadership: The Role of Influencers

Although consumers get information from personal sources, they do not tend to ask just *anyone* for advice about purchases. If you decide to buy a new fashion item, you will most likely seek advice from a friend who has a reputation for being stylish, who spends their free time reading *Vogue, GQ,* or perhaps *Business of Fashion,* who doggedly follows well-known fashion bloggers, or who shops at main fashion capitals and trendy boutiques.

Fashion opinion leadership   Everyone knows people who are knowledgeable about products and whose advice is taken seriously by others.[29] These individuals are **opinion leaders;** today they are often called **influencers**.[30] An opinion leader is a person who is frequently able to influence others' attitudes or behaviors. A fashion influencer's adoption of a new style gives it prestige among a group. That helps to explain why expenditures on influence marketing total almost $14 billion per year.

Fashion opinion leaders tend to buy fashions early in the fashion season. Like other opinion leaders, they take the risk and others then follow the lead. Opinion leaders in some fields may or may not be purchasers of the products they recommend. Those who are the first to use a new product are known as *innovators.* Opinion leaders who also are early purchasers have been termed *innovative communicators.*

Fashion theorists use the term **fashion leader**, which is similar to a fashion opinion leader.[31] One early theorist stated this of fashion leaders: "The leader of fashion does not come into existence until the fashion is itself created [...] a king or person of great eminence may indeed lead the fashion, but he leads only in the general direction which it has already adopted.[32]" Thus, the leader may "head the parade" or further the trend toward a new fashion.

True fashion leaders constantly seek distinction and, therefore, are likely to launch a succession of fashions rather than just one, as perhaps a celebrity might do at the height of their popularity. In the past, fashion opinion leaders used to be the editors-in-chief of top fashion magazines and highly noticeable fashion consumers, such as movie and music celebrities.[33] Currently, fashion bloggers and influencers who share their distinctive tastes, photographs, outfits or product reviews through social media are considered fashion opinion leaders.[34]

In addition to this, there are professional shoppers, interior designers, and other types of consultants we can think of as **professional influencers**. Whether or not they actually make the purchase on behalf of the consumer, their recommendations can be enormously influential. The consumer in essence relinquishes control over several or all decision-making functions, such as information search, evaluation of alternatives, or the actual purchase. For example, a client may commission an interior designer to redo her house, or a personal shopper may make decisions on behalf of their clients.

Many retail stores have their own personal shoppers, sometimes called **client specialists**, whose service customers can utilize. These super salespeople keep a client book with individual customers' preferences, measurements, and other pertinent information. They may do the majority of the "shopping" for clients before calling them to come into the store to try on items, and sometimes they even go to the client's home with possible choices. For example, luxury retailers like Harrods employ personal shoppers whose job is to provide clients with a **bespoke shopping service**. Individuals who are interested in getting this service can directly book an appointment. Lately, even airports have been adopting this strategy. For example, Heathrow airport allows travelers to allocate a personal shopper who can help clients select items while they wait for their flights.

In addition to this, individuals can hire personal shoppers to help them out. Lately, personal shoppers are available not only face-to-face but also on Instagram. Such shoppers are known to search the world for limited edition valuable pieces, whether handbags, jewelry pieces, and more, and recommend them to their client.

Influencers and social media.   **Social media influencers (SMIs)** "represent a new type of independent third-party endorser who shapes audience attitudes through blogs, tweets, and the use of other social media".[35] It refers to those who have created a certain market reputation based on their knowledge and expertise in a given context. Influencers post regularly on social media platforms, building trust and driving a large number of followers to engage with them.[36]

Fashion and luxury brands rely today on social media influencers in order to motivate followers to purchase specific products. Influencers can promote a brand and improve a brand's reputation, thus making up a part of the brand's social media strategy.[37] Marketers should be cautious as to which type of influencer to use as a communication tool given that their level of engagement and interaction, credibility and perceived trust will vary. Influencers are either offered free items from brands in return for mentioning or recommending a brand on their social media platforms (e.g., TikTok, Instagram or YouTube) or they are paid for making posts with hashtags like #ad or #sponsored. This sponsored content can be extremely influential and may impact consumers' brand preferences.[38]

Marketers differentiate among four types of influencers[39]:

1. **Mega-influencers** refer to those who have millions of followers across different social media platforms, with at least more than one million followers on one social media platform.[40] They are generally celebrities who have been highly recognized offline such as movie stars, sports celebrities, musicians, and reality television stars.[41] Examples include Justin Bieber, Selena Gomez,

Kendall Jenner, a Mega Influencer

Andrea Raffin / Shutterstock.com

Ariana Grande, Kendall Jenner, Kim Kardashian, Beyoncé, Jennifer Lopez, Taylor Swift, and Miley Cyrus. However, some mega-influencers have gained their fame online such as Chiara Ferragni, Huda Kattan, Kristina Bazan, and Camila Coelho. In general, only large-scale brands approach mega-influencers given that their services are very pricey; they may receive up to $1 million per post![42] Mega influencers are great for major brands that want to generate awareness of a new product launch among a large number of followers.

2. **Macro-influencers** are usually followed by a number ranging between 200,000 and 900,000 followers. Examples include Suzy Menkes, Imran Amed, Shiva Safai, and Susie "Bubble" Lau. They are in general experts in one particular product category.

3. **Micro-influencers** refer to those who have a number of followers ranging between 10,000 and 200,000. While the number of followers for each micro influencer is smaller as compared to mega and macro influencers, these influencers have a higher level of engagement with their audience since they can establish stronger relationships with a smaller community.[43]

Susie "Bubble" Lau, a Macro Influencer

Mauro Del Signore / Shutterstock.com

4. **Nano-influencers** have less than 10,000 followers.[44] Ironically, these influencers with smaller numbers of followers may actually be *more* effective than the big guys. That's because their fans tend to be more highly engaged with them, and they may have more credibility because people see them as more sincere. That is why some experts suggest the best strategy is to use a combination of mega and micro influencers to maximize effectiveness; this may involve a mixture of celebrities and amateur fashion bloggers for example.[45]

Virtual influencers   Over the past few years, another form of influencer has emerged. Although they may have followers numbering in the millions, they aren't actually real people.[46] They are **virtual influencers**, and several of them have found great success by collaborating with real-life celebrities.[47] Miquela Sousa, better-known by her Instagram account name @lilmiquela, is the first fashion virtual influencer who boasts more than two million followers. This Mega influencer has partnered with many brands such as Prada, Diesel, Moncler, Chanel, Proenza Schouler, Supreme, Vetements, and Vans.

Other virtual influencers have arrived on the scene more recently, such as Blawko, Shudu, Brenn and Bermuda. Blawko is the male virtual influencer who is Miquela's best friend and Bermuda's ex. Brenn is an influencer who has a curvier shape and noticeable stretch marks on her body. She was created to symbolize a more inclusive side of the fashion industry.[48] Although the jury is still out, early results indicate that virtual influencers are quite effective due to their popularity among younger shoppers.[49]

Social Class

Economic conditions and social status often determine the type of clothing we select. All societies can be roughly divided into the "haves" and the "have-nots" (though sometimes "having" is a question of degree). The United States is a place where "all men are created equal," but even so some people seem to be more equal than others. A consumer's standing in society, or **social class**, is determined by a complex set of variables, including income, family background, education, and occupation. Today, the term *social class* is commonly used to refer to the socio-economic status of individuals in a given society. Individuals who belong to the same social class are somewhat equal in terms of their standing in the society. They have similar occupations, and they tend to have similar lifestyles because of their income levels and shared tastes. These individuals are more likely to mingle with each other and to have common values concerning how they want to live. Indeed, "birds of a feather flock together," research shows that more often than not, people choose to marry those who belong to a similar social class.

Miquela Sousa, computer generated influencer

Lil Miquela via Instagram

Blawko, male virtual influencer

Blawko via Instagram

When we think about a person's social class, we may consider a number of components. Two major ones are occupation and income. A third important one is educational achievement, which is strongly related to income and occupation.

Occupational prestige is defined to a greater extent by what the person does for living. Hierarchies of occupational prestige tend to be quite stable over time, and they also tend to be similar in different societies. A typical ranking includes a variety of professional and business occupations at the top, such as the CEO of a large corporation, physician, professor at a prestigious university, while those jobs hovering near the bottom include fast food operators, cleaners and garbage collector. Because a person's occupation tends to be strongly linked to their leisure time, allocation of family resources, and so on, this variable is often considered to be the single best indicator of a social class.

In the context of fashion choices, Kaiser describes an even broader concept of **social location**, referring to an abstract point of intersection of these and other variables, including one's sex and age, in a certain time and place with its own belief and value configuration. Through the socialization process, where individuals learn what is expected of them, most of the time people want to obey the rules or "dress the part" within their social location. The place one occupies in the social structure is an important determinant not only of how much money is spent. It also influences how it is spent.

A Universal Pecking Order

For many kinds of animals, a social group is established whereby the most insistent or aggressive animals exert power over the others and receive the best selection of food, living space, and even coupling partners. Chickens, for instance, have a clear **dominance-submission hierarchy**. Within this ladder, each hen takes a position in which she is obedient to all of the hens above her and controls all of the ones below her (this is the source of the term *pecking order*).[50]

We also follow a pecking order where we are ranked based on our relative position in a community. This standing determines their access to education and consumer goods including housing and consumer durables. Consumers try to improve their social ranking by moving up from one social level to the other whenever possible. This eagerness to enhance their lots in life, and often making others know that they have done so, is fundamental to many marketing strategies.

Clothing Used to Regulate Distinction between Classes

The power groups throughout history have been able to maintain class distinctions; clothing was once a means of that control. Although hard to imagine today, dress was controlled by law in many societies. **Sumptuary laws** were restrictions that regulated style of dress and personal expenditures on clothing and accessories by regulating dress. They functioned in Western Europe to separate the royal class from others. As the merchant or business classes gained wealth and were able to afford opulent apparel similar to the royal courts, laws were enacted to prevent these non-elites from resembling royals. In Elizabethan England, laws prohibited commoners from wearing gold or silver cloth, velvet, or furs;

and they specified the colors, motifs, and styles a person could wear depending upon his or her designated rank, class, and position within society.

Sumptuary laws have been part of the history of Korea, Japan, and China as well, with regulation of ornamentation of robes indicating social and political position dating back to 200 B.C. In Korea up until the 1900s, commoners were forbidden to wear long, flowing sleeves—a sign of dissociation from manual work.[51] The Japanese kimono was regulated by prescribed laws for the various working classes in the late 1600s after merchants became wealthy and outshone the local leaders in terms of kimono designs, which had become bold and flowing. In the nineteenth century, wealthy Chinese women had their feet bound (literally, broken) so they could not walk—this mutilation signified that their husbands were so wealthy they could afford to be carried from place to place. During the Chinese Cultural Revolution, the Mao suit, composed of a jacket with a high-rounded collar that buttoned down the center and baggy pants, became the uniform for most men.

Chinese Tunic Suit

Image courtesy of Chrislb via WikiMedia Commons. Shared under the CC BY-SA 3.0 license.

The *qi pao*, a traditional women's dress, was outlawed as decadent, so a version of the Mao suit was prescribed for women also. The goal was to use clothing to reinforce the idea of one common social class in a Maoist society, as opposed to the earlier pattern of using dress to distinguish between social classes.[52]

Social Class Affects Taste and Lifestyle

Although social class still matters, it's getting more difficult to clearly link certain brands or stores with a specific class. That's because a lot of "affordable luxuries" now are within reach of many consumers who could not have managed to acquire them in the past. The driver of this global change is income distribution.

In many countries, traditionally there has been a huge gulf between the rich and the poor—you were either one or the other. Today, rising incomes in many economically developing countries such as South Korea and China, coupled with decreasing prices for quality consumer goods and services, are leveling the playing field so that there are many more opportunities for people making modest incomes to get a taste of the good life. For example, sophisticated cell phones, computers, and LCD and high-definition televisions now have significantly lower prices from not too long ago.

H&M x Giambattista Valli

Andrea Raffin / Shutterstock.com

The Rise of Mass Class

This change is fueling demand for mass-consumed products that still offer some degree of *panache* or style. Think about the success of companies such as H&M, Zara, TopShop, Gap, Nike, and L'Oréal.

They cater to a consumer segment that analysts have labeled **mass class**: the hundreds of millions of global consumers who now enjoy a level of purchasing power that's sufficient to let them afford high-quality products—except for big-ticket items like college educations, housing, and luxury cars.

This trend is also known as **masstige**, a combination of "mass" and "prestige."[53] Several collaborations were created between the Swedish fast-fashion retailer Hennes & Mauritz (H&M) and a number of designer luxury brands. This started with Karl Lagerfeld in 2004 and thereafter brought a series of collaborations (e.g. Stella McCartney, Roberto Cavalli, Comme des Garçons, Jimmy Choo, Versace, Marni, Balmain, Kenzo, Erdem, Giambattista Valli).

Fashion may not be one of life's little luxuries anymore since everyone can afford to be stylish, whether they shop at Gap, Target, H&M, or Saks Fifth Avenue. Consumers are mixing and matching, saving money on a Costco T-shirt, and mixing it with a high-end item from Saks. Another example is the luxury retailer Selfridges, which sells selected items from mass brands such as TopShop and Primark.

Social Mobility

To what degree are consumers likely to change their social classes? In some societies, such as India with its caste system, one's social class is very difficult to change. In contrast, Denmark ranks first on the Social Mobility Index.[54] **Social mobility** refers to the "passage of individuals from one social class to another".[55]

This passage can be upward, downward, or even horizontal. *Horizontal mobility* refers to movement from one position to another roughly equivalent in social status, such as becoming a nurse instead of an elementary school teacher. *Downward mobility* is, of course, not very desirable, but this pattern is unfortunately quite evident in recent years as farmers and other displaced workers have been forced to go on welfare or have joined the ranks of the homeless.

Regardless of the unfavorable trend, demographics in fact decree that there should be *upward mobility* in our society. The middle and upper classes have fewer children per family than the lower classes (*differential fertility*), and they tend to restrict family size below replacement level (often having only one child). Consequently, positions taken by people from higher social status over time should be occupied by those of lower social status. Generally, though the off-spring of blue-collar consumers tend also to be blue-collar, whereas the offspring of white-collar consumers also tend to wind up as white-collar. People tend to improve their positions over time, but these increases are not usually dramatic enough to catapult them from one social class to another.[56]

How Social Class Affects Fashion Diffusion

Fashion has been explained as members of one class imitating those of another, who in turn are driven to ever new expressions of fashion. Quentin Bell and other sociologists considered the history of fashion as inexplicable without relating it to social class; one class always is striving to reach the next level or at least to imitate the look of that level.[57]

As we saw in Chapter 3, we can describe three different kinds of diffusion: Trickle-up, trickle-down and trickle across. Let's get into a bit more detail about each.

Trickle-Down Effect

The relationship between product adoption and class structure was first proposed in 1904 by the sociologist Georg Simmel. The trick-le-down effect theory has been an approach often used to understand fashion, especially as it applies to fashion history. It states that there are two conflicting forces that drive fashion change. First, subordinate groups try to adopt the status symbols of the groups above them as they attempt to climb up the ladder of social mobility. Dominant styles thus originate with the upper classes and *trickle down* to these below.[58]

This is where the second force kicks in: People in the subordinate groups are constantly looking below them on the ladder to ensure that they are not imitated. They respond to the attempts of lower classes to

Lady Diana Wearing Lady Dior

Tim Graham Photo Library / Getty Images

"impersonate" them by abandoning the fashion and adopting even newer fashions. These two processes create a self-perpetuating cycle of change—the machine that drives fashion.

As a notable example of how the trickle-down process works, consider the impact of the late Princess Diana as a fashion trendsetter. When Christian Dior named one of its bags the "LADY DIOR" to honor the Princess, the line completely sold out within mere moments from its arrival to stores in 1996.[59] Since then, this bag became a signature piece of the French fashion house, which has still kept its place in the fashion scene today.

Kate Middleton, the Duchess of Cambridge, has followed Princess Diana, as the new royal trendsetter since her royal wedding in 2011. Many brands enjoyed an increase in their sales after she was seen wearing one of their items, to the extent that their whole stock also would sell out within minutes.[60]

The trickle-down effect theory is grounded on the traditional process of mimicking and adapting innovative trends from main fashion capitals such as Paris, Milan, London, and New York designers. While the products of luxury designers are expensive and not affordable to everyone in the society, mass fashion brands can highly benefit from this effect by producing less expensive adaptations of these items. These items are usually imitated over and over again until they are accessible at very low prices, until they become accepted by even late adopters.[61] Zara, H&M, and Shein are among the fast-fashion companies that adopt a trickle-down approach, reproducing the hottest designs from the fashion runway very quickly for a fraction of their price.[62]

Trickle-Across Effect

The tickle-down process was quite useful to explain fashion changes when applied to a society with a stable structure that permitted the easy identification of lower versus upper-class consumers. This task is not so easy in modern times. A perspective based on class structure cannot account for the wide range of styles that are simultaneously made available in our society. In contemporary Western society, then, this approach must be modified to account to new developments in mass culture; thus **trickle-across theory** was developed.[63]

Modern consumers have much greater degrees of individualized choices than in the past because of advances in technology and distribution. All classes generally have access to the same information at the same time. Thus, we see many of the same styles in a variety of types of retail venues at all different prices. Due to the Internet, **knockoff artists** (those who copy designer styles) can produce their versions of what they see on the runway very fast and can in some cases literally deliver their goods to the stores before the original designer can.

Thus, the upper classes are not necessarily getting new style information first. Consumers tend to be influenced more by opinion leaders who are similar to them. As a result, each social group has its own fashion innovators who determine fashion trends. It is probably more accurate to speak of this trickle-across today, where fashion diffuses horizontally among members of the same social group, than the trickle-down effect.

Trickle-Up Effect

Current fashions often originate with cultural subgroups or the lower classes and trickle up to higher classes. The **trickle-up effect theory** postulates that information starts at the bottom of a social structure and flows upward. Jeans are a classic example. The original Levi Strauss jeans were first worn by miners during the Gold Rush and by farmers and blue-collar workers who needed sturdy, functional clothes. With the addition of a logo or designer initials on the back pocket, designer jeans were born, along with a higher price tag, and marketed to those with plenty of discretionary income. In the 1950s, Levi's

Gold Miners wearing Levi's jeans, 1882

Horace Herbert Draper: English: Ike Williamson and crewmen from the Porcupine Gold Mining Company standing in front of a donkey engine, Porcupine, Alaska, circa 1907. Shared under the public domain.

became a symbol of youth rebellion when the iconic actor James Dean wore them in the movie *Rebel Without a Cause*. After that, denim became much more mainstream, especially as labels like Levi Strauss and Wrangler became part of the uniform that defined college students in the 1960s and 1970s.[64]

Here are other examples of the trickle-up effect:

- Leg warmers; an item borrowed from ballet dancers and other classic dancers.

- The T-shirt, originally worn by laborers as a functional and convenient undergarment.[65] Now, many luxury brands sell the humble T-shirt at very high prices. For example, a Philip Plein T-shirt can go for around $900.

Lately, with social media and the Internet, many trends have started at street level, and then trickled up to impact the luxury designers' creations.[66] One example of this is Comme des Garçons Play x Converse, whereby the Japanese designer adapts and embellishes the affordable Chuck Taylor shoe for a fashionable consumer at a higher price point. According to a womenswear buying manager at Selfridges, "…designers used to dictate the fashion agenda, which would eventually trickle down to the man or woman on the street; today it's all about the 'trickle-up' effect. Designers are looking at what's happening on the street and building from that".[67] Recently, the vintage trends that are being adopted by many brands such as Chanel, Gucci and many others are all influenced by the trickle-up approach.

Chapter Summary

Now that you have read the chapter, you should understand the following:

1.   What is the role of reference groups in fashion decision-making?

Consumers usually admire various groups. The term reference group refers to any external effect that delivers social cues. The referent may be a well-known figure who has an impact on people or a person or a group whose influence is confined to the consumers' immediate environment. Groups can take two forms: formal and informal ones, with the main difference being that the relationship among members is based on personal rather than on professional relationships. Consumers' preferences are usually shaped by group memberships, and by their desire to please or be accepted by others, or even by the actions of famous people whom they have never met. Some people are more influential than others in affecting fashion and other product preferences and this is hugely driven by the social power that these groups may have: information power, referent power, legitimate power, expert power, reward power, and coercive power are all forms of social power.

2.   How can opinion leaders impact consumers' fashion decisions?

When consumers decide to buy a fashion item, they are most likely to seek advice from a person who has created a certain market reputation based on their knowledge and expertise in the fashion and luxury context. Fashion opinion leaders are those who buy fashions early in the fashion season and who have the ability to influence others' attitudes or behaviors by recommending certain brands, products or services and highly engaging individuals.

   In the past, fashion opinion leaders used to be the editors-in-chief of top fashion magazines and highly noticeable fashion consumers, such as movie and music celebrities. Currently, fashion bloggers and influencers who share their distinctive tastes, photographs, outfits or product reviews through social media are considered fashion opinion leaders. Over the past few years, another form of influencer has emerged, the virtual influencers who are skilled in influencing the new generations.

3.   How does social class affect fashion diffusion?

Social class refers to the overall rank of individuals in a given society. Individuals who belong to the same social class are somehow equal in terms of their social standing in the society; they are more likely to have similar lifestyles and dress in similar ways. Social mobility refers to the passage of individuals from one social class to another. A certain change in social class such as the emergence of a class with a higher income fueled the demand for mass-consumed products. There are three primary effect theories of fashion adoption: Trickle-down, trickle-up, and trickle across. Trickle-down means that fashion starts at the higher level and then those styles are gradually adopted by lower social classes. Trickle-up means that fashion trends start with street fashion and move gradually up the fashion ladder. Trickle-across means that fashion moves across socioeconomic levels somewhat quickly, with apparel styles becoming available at all price points at roughly the same time.

DISCUSSION QUESTIONS

1. As a consumer, do you feel affected by any reference group? How can fashion influencers affect your buying decision?

2. Who are your avoidance groups? How do they impact on your behavior?

3. What are some of the obstacles to measuring social class in today's society? Discuss some ways to get around these obstacles.

4. What differences in fashion purchases would you expect to observe between a family characterized as underprivileged versus one whose income is average for its social class?

5. How do you assign people to social classes, or do you at all? What consumption cues do you use (clothing, speech, cars and so on) to determine social standing?

6. Some people argue that social status symbols are dead. Do you agree? What fashion shows high status?

7. Virtual influencers are quite effective due to their popularity among younger shoppers. Do you believe that these influencers will replace people? How ethical is it to motivate people to interact with computers?

EXERCISES

1. Think of a fashion product that you have recently bought. What roles did others play in the purchase of this item and how were they able to affect your selection?

2. Write down all of the groups you belong to. How many are there? How do they differ? What are their implications for your fashion choices?

3. Compile a collection of ads depicting consumers of different social classes. What generalizations can you make about the reality of these ads and about the media in which they appear?

4. Explain the difference between the three different processes of fashion adoption: Trickle-up effect theory, trickle-down effect theory and trickle-across effect theory. For each theory, provide a respective example and explain it.

5. Identify a lifestyle trend that is just surfacing in your universe. Describe this trend in detail and justify your prediction. What specific styles and/or products are part of this trend? How long do you think it will last? Why?

CASE STUDY: BURBERRY

Linda Welters, University of Rhode Island

Burberry is a quintessentially British luxury brand with a long and storied history. The story begins in 1856 when Thomas Burberry opened an outfitter's shop in Basingstoke, Hampshire, England where he sold outerwear. He later developed a tightly-woven cotton twill fabric called gabardine that resisted rain; he patented the fabric in 1888. Burberry's gabardine earned high marks for water resistance, durability, and breathability and was well suited to Britain's damp and rainy climate.

The company opened a store in London in 1891 and Paris in 1909, and began using an equestrian knight logo. Soon explorers, adventurers, and the military—including British explorer Sir Ernest Shackleton—outfitted themselves in Burberry products. In 1912 Thomas Burberry designed a belted gabardine raincoat with a collar that fastened high at the neck called the Tielocken. When the British military issued a call for an officers' coat during World War I, Burberry and Aquascutum, another British outerwear firm, responded. The Burberry "trench-warm" featured a double-breasted closure, convertible collar, storm shield, epaulettes, belt, and D-rings to suspend equipment. With its detachable wool lining, the so-called trench coat became the outerwear of choice among officers engaged in trench warfare in France. After the war, admiration for the officers led to widespread adoption of the trench coat for civilian use on both sides of the Atlantic. It became a standard offering for men's outerwear along with the Mackintosh, polo coat, and chesterfield. In the 1920s, the company trademarked the Burberry check—a black, camel, and red plaid design—for use as a lining in its rainwear, and they sold their products to stockists in New York, Buenos Aires, Montevideo, and Japan.

In the 1940s, the trench coat started appearing on the silver screen. Humphrey Bogart wore trench coats as a private detective in *The Maltese Falcon* (1942) and *The Big Sleep* (1946), and in his role as an ex-patriot nightclub owner in *Casablanca* (1942). The trench coat became a symbol of the tough, honorable, private detective with its ability to disguise, protect from inclement weather, and hide a revolver and cigarettes in roomy pockets. Bogart wore trench coats off screen as well. Trench coats vacated the cinema for a short period, but returned in two very different guises. Audrey Hepburn wore one in a downpour at the climax of *Breakfast at Tiffany's* (1961) while Peter Sellers donned a trench coat as the bumbling Inspector Clouseau in *The Pink Panther* (1963).

Fashion designers such as Yves Saint Laurent co-opted the style, creating trench coats out of novel materials such as ciré and gilded leather. Burberry experimented with its classic coat by using the check on the outside. Traditional trench coats regained traction after John Molloy published his *Dress for Success* books in the 1970s. His research showed that men wearing beige trench coats created a better impression than men wearing black raincoats because of the beige raincoat's association with the upper middle class. Women in business began wearing trench coats too. Burberry raincoats signaled financial success, but other companies, such as London Fog, made good-quality trench coats at lower price points.

In the 1990s, heritage companies began expanding and improving their product lines with the goal of becoming luxury brands. Gucci, Prada, and Louis Vuitton, for example, revamped their business models by appointing creative directors to oversee product development and brand image. Meanwhile, Burberry was suffering a substantial drop in profits due to excessive licensing and overexposure in the mass market. Considered an "aging British icon," the company's owners considered selling it. Instead, they decided to transform Burberry's into a global luxury brand. Rose Marie Bravo took over as chief executive in 1997; she was charged with updating the brand image, regaining control over product development and licensing, and attracting a newer, younger client base. The company focused on innovation around core heritage products, including the trench coat and the iconic check. British models Kate Moss and Stella Tennant appeared in Burberry ads in the late 1990s and early 2000s. A new store opened on Bond Street in 2000 near those of other luxury brands, and Christopher Bailey was appointed design director in 2001. A 2002 IPO on the London Stock Exchange provided an infusion of cash to grow the brand. The Burberry brand trenchcoats and checked scarves became a hot commodity, and their clothing, bags, and fragrance followed suit.

However, the company hit a snag when its more affordable lines allowed Burberry products to be co-opted by subcultural groups in England. Rowdy football (soccer) fans and the "chav" subculture wore its check pattern—some of it counterfeit—as a uniform, damaging its exclusive positioning. To further tarnish the image, paparazzi snapped Danniella Westbrook, a soap opera actress with drug problems, in head-to-toe Burberry in 2002. Soon several prestigious London stores dropped Burberry from its offerings.

A new CEO, Angela Ahrendts, righted the ship in 2006. She reduced product lines and raised prices, making them more exclusive. Manufacturing returned to the UK, most notably at the company factory in Castleford, Yorkshire. Consequently, all trench coats bore the "Made in England" label. Christopher Bailey was promoted to Chief Creative Officer in 2009. He brought fashion shows back to London from Milan and developed legendary advertising campaigns with high-profile models and actors such as Cara Delavigne, Naomi Campbell, Eddie Redmayne, and James Corden among others. Emma Watson, star of the *Harry Potter* series, became the face of Burberry in 2009/2010. Bailey produced a fashion video in 2016 showcasing the company's legendary history.

The company fully embraced digital technology early on. Burberry sold products in selected markets through a company website beginning in 2005. Burberry was the first to live stream a fashion show in 2010, and the first to sell direct-to-consumer immediately following a fashion show in 2016. Burberry tapped into consumers' love for the brand in 2009 by launching "The Art of the Trench," a website where people could post photographs of themselves in Burberry trench coats. Burberry had become Britain's largest luxury brand by the mid 2010s.

Ahrendts left the company for Apple in 2014, and Bailey assumed the role of CEO in addition to his design director duties. Rare is the company where the design function and the business function is successfully managed by the same individual. Bailey left Burberry in 2018, and Riccardo Tisci took over as Chief Creative Officer. Since then, the company has endured negative publicity for burning unsold products in 2018, and for showcasing a hoodie that featured a noose around the neck in 2019. Burberry is currently collaborating with artists and designers for projects, notably Vivienne Westwood.

(Continued)

DISCUSSION QUESTIONS

1. How did reference groups affect the image of Burberry products, both positively and negatively, across time?

2. In what way did Burberry employ opinion leaders to enhance brand image?

3. What is the relationship between Burberry products and social class? In other words, what social class associations are projected by Burberry products?

SELECTED REFERENCES

Ahrendts, A. (2013) 'Burberry's CEO on turning an aging British icon into a global luxury brand." *Harvard Business Review*. https://hbr.org/2013/01/burberrys-ceo-on-turning-an-aging-british-icon-into-a-global-luxury-brand (accessed September 6, 2021).

Church Gibson, P. (2012) *Fashion and Celebrity Culture*. London: Berg.

Faiers, J. (2013) *Dressing Dangerously: Dysfunctional Fashion in Film*. New Haven, CN: Yale University Press.

Hill, D.D. (2011) *American Menswear: From the Civil War to the Twenty-First Century*. Lubbock, TX: Texas Tech University Press.

Molloy, J.T. (1975) *Dress for Success*. New York, NY: Warner Books.

Moore, C.M. and Birtwistle, G. (2004) 'The Burberry business model: Creating an international luxury fashion brand', *International Journal of Retail & Management*, 32 (8): 412–22.

The New York Times (1917) 'Trench coats in demand', *The New York Times*, August 29, p. 15. Available from www.nytimes.com/1917/08/29/archives/trench-coats-in-demand.html (accessed September 6, 2021).

NOTES

1. Park, C.W. and Lessig, V.P. (1977) 'Students and housewives: Differences in susceptibility to reference group influence', *Journal of Consumer Research*, 4 (2): 102–10.

2. Lessig, V.P. and Park, C.W. (1978) 'Promotional perspectives of reference group influence: Advertising implications', *Journal of Advertising*, 7 (2): 41–7.

3. Escalas, J.E. and Bettman, J R. (2003) 'You are what they eat: The influence of reference groups on consumers' connections to brands', *Journal of Consumer Psychology*, 13 (3): 339–48.

4. Kim, H., Rhee, E.Y. and Yee, J. (2008) 'Comparing fashion process networks and friendship networks in small groups of adolescents', *Journal of Fashion Marketing and Management: An International Journal*, 12 (4): 545–64.

    Valaei, N. and Nikhashemi, S.R. (2017) 'Generation Y consumers' buying behaviour in fashion apparel industry: A moderation analysis', *Journal of Fashion Marketing and Management: An International Journal*, 21 (4): 523–43.

5. Fédération de la Haute Couture et de la Mode (2021) 'Fédération de la haute couture et de la mode', fhcm Paris. https://fhcm.paris/en/the-federation/ (accessed September 6, 2021).

6. Himawan, D. (2018) 'New campaigns stray away from famous faces', *L'Officiel*, March 2. www.lofficielusa.com/fashion/new-campaigns-stray-away-from-famous-faces (accessed September 6, 2021).

7. Law, K.M., Zhang, Z.M. and Leung C-S. (2004) 'Fashion change and fashion consumption: The chaotic perspective', *Journal of Fashion Marketing and Management*, 8 (4): 362–74.

8. Clark, R.A. and Goldsmith, R.E. (2005) 'Market mavens: Psychological influences', *Psychology & Marketing*, 22 (4): 289–312.

9. O'Cass, A. and McEwen, H. (2004) 'Exploring consumer status and conspicuous consumption', *Journal of Consumer Behaviour: An International Research Review*, 4 (1): 25–39.

10. Magee, J.C., Milliken, F.J. and Lurie, A.R. (2010) 'Power differences in the construal of a crisis: The immediate aftermath of September 11, 2001', *Personality and Social Psychology Bulletin*, 36 (3): 354–70.

11. Lammers, J., Stoker, J.I. and Stapel, D.A. (2010) 'Power and behavioral approach orientation in existing power relations and the mediating effect of income', *European Journal of Social Psychology*, 40 (3): 543–51.

    Kim, J., Kang, S. and Lee, K.H. (2018) 'How social capital impacts the purchase intention of sustainable fashion products', *Journal of Business Research*, 117: 596–603.

12. Okonkwo, U. (2007) *Luxury Fashion Branding*. London: Palgrave Macmillan, London.

13. French, J.R., Raven, B. and Cartwright, D. (1959) 'The bases of social power', *Classics of Organization Theory*, 7: 311–20.

14. Magee, J.C., Milliken, F.J. and Lurie, A.R. (2010) 'Power differences in the construal of a crisis: The immediate aftermath of September 11, 2001', *Personality and Social Psychology Bulletin*, 36 (3): 354–70.

15. Hays, K. (2018) 'What's the role of today's magazine editors?', *Women's Wear Daily*, August 31. https://wwd.com/business-news/media/role-of-modern-fashion-beauty-magazines-editors-1202780616/ (accessed September 6, 2021).

16. Heaf, J. (2017) 'The business behind the Business of Fashion', *GQ*, April 12. www.gq-magazine.co.uk/article/the-business-of-fashion (accessed September 6, 2021).

17. Lammers, J., Galinsky, A.D., Gordijn, E.H. and Otten, S. (2008) 'Illegitimacy moderates the effects of power on approach', *Psychological Science*, 19 (6): 558–64.

18. Yotka, S. (2019) 'Go viral, post #Spon, get #Canceled: How social media transformed fashion in the 2010s', *Vogue*, July 18. www.vogue.com/article/2010s-fashion-social-media-impact (accessed September 6, 2021).

19. Lammers, J., Galinsky, A.D., Gordijn, E.H. and Otten, S. (2008) 'Illegitimacy moderates the effects of power on approach', *Psychological Science*, 19 (6): 558–64.

20. Friedman, V. (2020) 'The mask: The surgical face mask has become a symbol of our times', *The New York Times*, March 17. www.nytimes.com/2020/03/17/style/face-mask-coronavirus.html (accessed September 6, 2021).

21. Fang, Y.H. and Chiu, C.M. (2010) 'In justice we trust: Exploring knowledge-sharing continuance intentions in virtual communities of practice', *Computers in Human Behavior*, 26 (2): 235–46.

    Pan, Y., Xu, Y.C., Wang, X., Zhang, C., Ling, H. and Lin, J. (2015) 'Integrating social networking support for dyadic knowledge exchange: A study in a virtual community of practice', *Information & Management*, 52 (1): 61–70.

22. Lopez, C.E. and Tucker, C.S. (2019) 'The effects of player type on performance: A gamification case study', *Computers in Human Behavior*, 91: 333–45.

    Williamson, F. (2020) 'Multi-user Dungeons (MUDs): What are they? And how to play', *Medium*, July 4. https://medium.com/@williamson.f93/multi-user-dungeons-muds-what-are-they-and-how-to-play-af3ec0f29f4a (accessed October 20, 2021).

23. Halvorsen, K., Hoffmann, J., Coste-Manière, I. and Stankeviciute, R. (2013) 'Can fashion blogs function as a marketing tool to influence consumer behavior? Evidence from Norway', *Journal of Global Fashion Marketing*, 4 (3): 211–24.

    Titton, M. (2015) 'Fashionable personae: Self-identity and enactments of fashion narratives in fashion blogs', *Fashion Theory*, 19 (2): 201–20.

    Esteban-Santos, L., Medina, I.G., Carey, L. and Bellido-Pérez, E. (2018) 'Fashion bloggers: Communication tools for the fashion industry', *Journal of Fashion Marketing and Management: An International Journal*, 22 (3): 420–37.

24. Kim, H. and Markus, H.R. (1999) 'Deviance or uniqueness, harmony or conformity? A cultural analysis', *Journal of Personality and Social Psychology*, 77 (4): 785–800.

Chan, C., Berger, J. and Van Boven, L. (2012) 'Identifiable but not identical: Combining social identity and uniqueness motives in choice', *Journal of Consumer Research*, 39 (3): 561–73.

25. Chaney, D. and Goulding, C. (2016) 'Dress, transformation, and conformity in the heavy rock subculture', *Journal of Business Research*, 69 (1): 155–65.

26. Unicef (n.d.) 'Cyberbullying: What is it and how to stop it', www.unicef.org/end-violence/how-to-stop-cyberbullying (accessed September 6, 2021).

Anderson, M. (2018) 'A majority of teens have experienced some form of cyberbullying', *Pew Research Center*, September 27. www.pewresearch.org/internet/2018/09/27/a-majority-of-teens-have-experienced-some-form-of-cyberbullying/ (accessed September 6, 2021).

27. Kahle, L. R. (1995) 'Observations: Role-relaxed consumers: A trend of the nineties', *Journal of Advertising Research*, 35 (2): 66–72.

28. Khare, A. (2014) 'How cosmopolitan are Indian consumers? A study on fashion clothing involvement', *Journal of Fashion Marketing and Management*, 18 (4): 431–51.

Gentina, E., Shrum, L.J. and Lowrey, T.M. (2016) 'Teen attitudes toward luxury fashion brands from a social identity perspective: A cross-cultural study of French and US teenagers', *Journal of Business Research*, 69 (12): 5785–92.

29. Youssef, C. and Lebdaoui, H. (2020) 'How fashion influencers contribute to consumers' purchase intention,' *Journal of Fashion Marketing and Management*, 24 (3). www.emerald.com/insight/content/doi/10.1108/JFMM-08-2019-0157/full/html (accessed October 27, 2021).

Santora, J. (2021) '100 Influencer Marketing Statistics For 2021', https://influencermarketinghub.com/influencer-marketing-statistics/ (accessed October 27, 2021).

30. Djafarova, E. and Bowes, T. (2021) '"Instagram made Me buy it": Generation Z impulse purchases in fashion industry', *Journal of Retailing and Consumer Services*, 59: 102345.

31. Rahman, S. U., Saleem, S., Akhtar, S., Ali, T. and Khan, M.A. (2014) 'Consumers' adoption of apparel fashion: The role of innovativeness, involvement, and social values', *International Journal of Marketing Studies*, 6 (3): 49.

32. Bell, Q. (1947) *On Human Finery*. London: Hogarth Press.

33. Crane, D. (1999) 'Diffusion models and fashion: A reassessment', *Annals of the American Academy of Political and Social Science*, 566: 13–24.

34. Casaló, L.V., Flavián, C. and Ibáñez-Sánchez, S. (2018) 'Influencers on Instagram: Antecedents and consequences of opinion leadership', *Journal of Business Research*, 117: 510–19.

35. Freberg, K., Graham, K., McGaughey, K. and Freberg, L.A. (2011) 'Who are the social media influencers? A study of public perceptions of personality', *Public Relations Review*, 37 (1): 90–2.

36. Britt, R.K., Hayes, J.L., Britt, B.C. and Park, H. (2020) 'Too big to sell? A computational analysis of network and content characteristics among mega and micro beauty and fashion social media influencers', *Journal of Interactive Advertising*, 20 (2): 111–18.

SanMiguel, P. and Sádaba, T. (2018) 'Nice to be a fashion blogger, hard to be influential: An analysis based on personal characteristics, knowledge criteria, and social factors', *Journal of Global Fashion Marketing*, 9 (1): 40–58.

37. Jin, Y. and Liu, B.F. (2010) 'The blog-mediated crisis communication model: Recommendations for responding to influential external blogs', *Journal of Public Relations Research*, 22 (4): 429–55.

38. De Veirman, M., Hudders, L. and Nelson, M.R. (2019) 'What is influencer marketing and how does it target children? A review and direction for future research', *Frontiers in Psychology*, 10: 2685.

39. Adegeest, D. (2019) 'Fashion brands are turning to influencers with fewer followers', *Fashion United*, April 30. https://fashionunited.uk/news/fashion/fashion-brands-are-turning-to-influencers-with-fewer-followers/2019043042918 (accessed October 20, 2021).

Cohen, J. (2019) 'Why are micro influencers so popular?' *Launchmetrics*, September 9. www.launchmetrics.com/resources/blog/micro-influencers (accessed October 20, 2021).

Hosie, R. (2019) 'Why brands are turning away from big Instagram influencers to work with people who have small followings instead', *Insider*, April 9. www.businessinsider.com/brands-turning-to-micro-influencers-instead-of-instagram-stars-2019-4 (accessed September 6, 2021).

40. Ladhari, R., Massa, E. and Skandrani, H. (2020) 'YouTube vloggers' popularity and influence: The roles of homophily, emotional attachment, and expertise', *Journal of Retailing and Consumer Services*, 54: 102027.

41. Britt, R.K., Hayes, J.L., Britt, B C. and Park, H. (2020) 'Too big to sell? A computational analysis of network and content characteristics among mega and micro beauty and fashion social media influencers', *Journal of Interactive Advertising*, 20 (2): 111–18.

42. Britt, R.K., Hayes, J.L., Britt, B C. and Park, H. (2020) 'Too big to sell? A computational analysis of network and content characteristics among mega and micro beauty and fashion social media influencers', *Journal of Interactive Advertising*, 20 (2): 111–18.

43. Launch Metrics (2019) '3 Predictions about the future of influencer marketing', *Launch Metrics*, February 26. www.launchmetrics.com/resources/blog/predictions-influence-marketing (accessed September 6, 2021).

44. Ladhari, R., Massa, E. and Skandrani, H. (2020) 'YouTube vloggers' popularity and influence: The roles of homophily, emotional attachment, and expertise', *Journal of Retailing and Consumer Services*, 54: 102027.

45. Wissman, B. (2018) 'Micro-influencers: The marketing force of the future?', *Forbes*, March 2. www.forbes.com/sites/barrettwissman/2018/03/02/micro-influencers-the-marketing-force-of-the-future/?sh=16f0cbc96707 (accessed September 6, 2021).

46. Thomas, V.L. and Fowler, K. (2021) 'Close encounters of the AI kind: Use of AI influencers as brand endorsers', *Journal of Advertising*, 50 (1): 11–25.

47. Dodgson, L. (2019) '13 computer-generated influencers you should be following on Instagram', *Insider*, September 22. www.insider.com/cgi-influencers-you-should-be-following-instagram-2019-9 (accessed September 6, 2021).

48. Dodgson, L. (2019) '13 computer-generated influencers you should be following on Instagram', *Insider*, September 22. www.insider.com/cgi-influencers-you-should-be-following-instagram-2019-9 (accessed September 6, 2021).

49. Dodgson, L. (2019) '13 computer-generated influencers you should be following on Instagram', *Insider*, September 22. www.insider.com/cgi-influencers-you-should-be-following-instagram-2019-9 (accessed September 6, 2021).

50. Zimbardo, P.G. and Ruch, F.L. (1975) *Psychology and Life* (9th ed.). Glenview, IL: Scott, Foresman.

51. Sjoberg, G. (1960) *The Preindustrial City: Past and Present*. Glencoe, IL: Free Press.

52. Garrett, V.M. (1994) *Chinese Clothing: An Illustrated Guide*. Hong Kong: Oxford University Press.

53. Paul, J. (2015) 'Masstige marketing redefined and mapped: Introducing a pyramid', *Marketing Intelligence & Planning*, 33 (5): 691–706.

    Kumar, A., Paul, J. and Unnithan, A.B. (2020) '"Masstige" marketing: A review, synthesis and research agenda', *Journal of Business Research*, 113: 384–398.

54. Hutt, R. (2020) 'These are the 10 countries with the best social mobility', *World Economic Forum*, January 20. www.weforum.org/agenda/2020/01/these-are-the-10-countries-with-the-best-social-mobility/ (accessed September 6, 2021).

55. Turner, J.H. (1981) *Sociology: Studying the Human System*. Santa Monica, CA: Goodyear.

56. Beeghley, L. (2015) *The Structure of Social Stratification in the United States*, New York, NY: Routledge.

57. Stone, E. and Farnan, S.A. (2018) *The Dynamics of Fashion*. New York, NY: Bloomsbury.

58. Bellezza, S. and Berger, J. (2020) 'Trickle-Round signals: When low status is mixed with high', *Journal of Consumer Research*, 47 (1): 100–27.

59. Leigh, T. (2019) 'Lady Diana and Lady Dior: A love story', *Forbes*, April 29. www.forbes.com/sites/tiffanyleigh/2019/04/29/lady-diana-and-lady-dior-a-love-story/?sh=16cbd6fdcbb6 (accessed September 6, 2021).

60. Vogue (2011) *The Kate Middleton Effect on What We Buy*. www.vogue.com.au/fashion/news/the-kate-middleton-effect-on-what-we-buy/news-story/9619d2b7bf78851dde88cd8638876831 (accessed September 6, 2021).

61. Dahlén, M. (2012) 'Copy or copyright fashion? Swedish design protection law in historical and comparative perspective', *Business History*, 54 (1): 88–107.

    Seivewright, S. (2012) *Basics Fashion Design 01: Research and Design* (Vol. 1). London: A&C Black.

62. Hanbury, M. (2018) 'Zara and Forever 21 have a dirty little secret', *Insider*, March 6. www.businessinsider.com/zara-forever-21-fast-fashion-full-of-copycats-2018-3 (accessed September 6, 2021).

    Pike, H. (2016) 'The copycat economy', *Business of Fashion*, March 14. www.businessoffashion.com/community/voices/discussions/what-is-the-real-cost-of-copycats/fashions-copycat-economy (accessed September 6, 2021).

63. Atik, D. and Fırat, A.F. (2013) 'Fashion creation and diffusion: The institution of marketing', *Journal of Marketing Management*, 29 (7/8): 836–60.

McCracken, G. (1985) 'The trickle-down theory rehabilitated', in M.R. Solomon (ed.), *The Psychology of Fashion*. Lexington, MA: Lexington Books. pp. 39–54.

64. Kim, E., Fiore, A.M. and Kim, H. (2013) *Fashion Trends: Analysis and Forecasting*. Oxford: Berg.

65. Delong, M.R. (n.d.) 'Theories of fashion', *Love to Know*. https://fashion-history.lovetoknow.com/fashion-history-eras/theories-fashion (accessed September 6, 2021).

66. La Ferla, R. (2010) 'Fashion's military invasion rolls on', *The New York Times,* February 19. www.nytimes.com/2010/02/21/fashion/21military.html (accessed September 6, 2021).

67. Selfridges (2021) 'Selfridges loves: Streetwear? How about we just call it fashion…', *Selfridges.com*. www.selfridges.com/GB/en/features/articles/selfridges-loves/selfridges-lovesstreetwearhowaboutwejustcallitfashion/ (accessed September 6, 2021).

Image of Lil Miquela: Every effort has been made to trace the copyright holders and obtain permission to reproduce material. Please do get in touch with any enquiries or information relating to images or the rights holder.

Image of Blawko: Every effort has been made to trace the copyright holders and obtain permission to reproduce material. Please do get in touch with any enquiries or information relating to images or the rights holder.

Image of Chiara Ferragni: Every effort has been made to trace the copyright holders and obtain permission to reproduce material. Please do get in touch with any enquiries or information relating to images or the rights holder.

SECTION IV

Applying the Marketing Mix

CHAPTER 10

Product Development, Branding and Pricing

LEARNING OBJECTIVES

After you read this chapter, you will understand the answers to the following:

1. What are the layers of a fashion product?

2. What is the cycle of fashion adoption?

3. How can a company design the right fashion product and branding strategy?

4. What is the importance of designing an effective pricing strategy?

Marzena has a secret fantasy: for 10 years she has coveted a Birkin bag. But there's one small problem: the bags usually sell for anywhere from $10,000 to almost $200,000. When her wealthy old aunt dies and leaves her a nice sum of money, however, it's game on. Although Marzena certainly has plenty of other uses for her inheritance, she's working hard to rationalize her impulse to splurge on a bag. One day as she's ruminating about her dilemma at work, her friend happens to mention a new resale site called Rebag. This platform uses an algorithm to show bag owners the resale spot prices of their bags if they sell them to Rebag. They can track these prices over time to decide when to buy or sell. It turns out that some people who used to value luxury goods only for their intrinsic beauty, heritage—or perhaps bragging rights—now see them as solid investments that will gain in value over time.[1] Marzena thinks of her boyfriend Zach, who is an avid "sneakerhead." He can easily justify blowing $8000 on a pair of Nike Air Yeezy 2 Solar Red kicks, and then avidly track their "stock price" on StockX, which also follows the ups and downs of products including vintage sneakers, handbags, and watches. So, it's not about frivolously throwing away our hard-earned money after all—Marzena starts to think of herself as an investor. What's good for the gander is good for the goose.

Layers of the Product Concept

After analyzing the market and gaining marketing insights and trend forecasting data, fashion marketers should be ready to start designing the right fashion product and build the right branding strategy. In the context of fashion, the "Product" is the fundamental aspect of the marketing mix.

Obviously, you need to create a product that your customers want to buy. **A product** (like Marzena's Birkin bag) is a tangible item that is usually offered for sale for the sake of satisfying a customer need. A product can take the form of a good, a service, an idea, people, places, or even a mixture of these. A good consists of a **tangible product**, an item that people can see, feel, smell, hear, taste, or own, for example, a cupcake, a luxurious car, or a bangle from Hermès.

In contrast, **intangible products**—services, ideas, people, and places—are things that people can't constantly see, feel, taste, smell, or own. A fashion product consists of quality, design, style, brand name, package, features, values, color, size, material, logos, and trademarks etc., features that allow the actual product to be marketable.

The development, design, and launch of a fashion product requires a number of different decisions. These relate to the product features, branding and finally the product support-related services. As can be viewed in the picture of the Lady Dior Bag, there is a difference across the layers of the product—the core product, the actual product, and the augmented product. When designing their strategies regarding their products, fashion marketers should satisfy their customers' needs and wants at every level of the product.

- The **core product** refers to the benefits the product will offer to consumers. For example, a woman purchasing a set of make-up is buying more than make-up.[2] A research conducted by the University of the Basque Country indicated that consumers purchase make-up mainly for emotional reasons in order to strengthen the "perception of 'caring for oneself' and removing feelings of worry and guilt about not taking care of one's appearance". A teenager buying an iPhone is purchasing more than a normal phone, they are purchasing an item for entertainment for self-expression and a device to stay connected to the world.

- The **actual product** consists of a tangible good or the provided service that offered the necessary benefits relates to the physical quality, product features, and the design. For instance, when you purchase a pair of shoes, the core product is the need to protect your feet, while the actual product is a shiny, sexy, and fashionable leather good. The actual product consists of the sole elements of the product, such as its design, package, brand name, performance, quality.

- The **augmented product** refers to the supporting elements that allow the consumer to use the product, such as a warranty, credit card facility, home delivery, and after sale service. Did you know that you can do hands-free shopping when you buy from a Christian Dior Paris store? All you have to do is to pay and the brand will deliver it to your home.

Many studies have looked at criteria that consumers use when they decide on specific fashion products. Some of these dimensions are *extrinsic factors* (such as price, brand name, and store image) and others are *intrinsic factors* (such as comfort, style, color, fabric, care, fit, craftsmanship, and quality).[3] Here are some commonly used criteria that consumers use when they evaluate competing brands[4]:

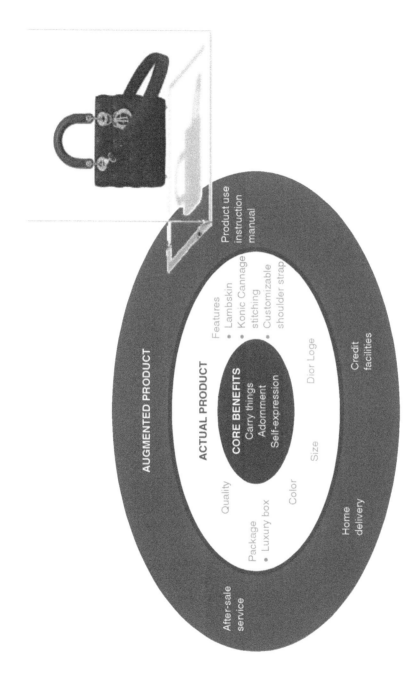

FIGURE 10.1 Layers of a fashion product

- *Appropriateness/personal styles*: Suitability to individual, good fit, appropriate for occasion, comfort, fabric type and quality, wardrobe coordination, suits my personality.

- *Economy/usefulness*: Price, good buy, ease of care, durability, versatility, matching, utility.

- *Attractiveness/aesthetics*: Beautiful, fashionable, color/pattern, styling, good fit, pleasing to others.

- *Quality:* Quality of construction, fabric or material type, fiber, durability.

- *Other-people-directed/image*: Prestige, sexy, brand and store name, label, fashionable.

- *Country of origin*: The place where it is made for example: Italy, France, China, United States.

- *Fiber/fabric*: Natural or synthetic, knits or woven.

- *Polysexuality* (primarily for luxury brands): "Pleasant to hear, smell, taste or touch" and therefore offer a "source of sensual pleasure".[5]

- *Exclusiveness* (also for luxury brands): Rarity, status, and country of origin.[6]

Fashion Product Classification

There are three basic types of fashion products, and it's important to understand what type you are dealing with because it helps you to define your strategy and also to identify your competition.

1. *Convenience products*: Inexpensive products that people buy frequently. These products are usually low priced and are bought impulsively with little effort made to compare across similar products. They are usually widely and massively available in the market. Examples include body lotions, hosiery, fashion magazines, and hair creams.

2. *Shopping goods*: These products are less frequently purchased. Consumers are more likely to do some comparisons among different products based on the quality, price, design, style, fit, and comfort. These products are usually selectively distributed across outlets. Examples include furniture, sleepwear, home furnishings, electronics, and fashion accessories that you would buy at a store like Uniqlo or H&M.

3. *Specialty goods*: A high price and a reputable brand image are crucial for these products. Consumers hold strong preferences for particular brands, so they are less likely to compare across brands. Consumers who purchase this type of products are usually less price sensitive. To use the terms we introduced earlier, in order to succeed in these markets, your brand must have a differentiation advantage rather than a cost advantage. Specialty fashion products are exclusively distributed in the market; often only a small number of stores carry them. Examples include Rolex, Mercedes, Apple electronics or designer clothing such as Balmain, Saint Laurent, Burberry, and Kate Spade.

The Diffusion of Innovations

The most important sociological theory that helps to explain how fashion works originally came from attempts to understand how farmers in the US Midwest decided to try different kinds of seeds or other new agricultural techniques. Other theorists (especially Everett Rogers, a communications expert) expanded upon those insights to explore how new ideas spread through populations including the fashion world. **Diffusion of innovations** refers to this process whereby a new product, service, or idea spreads through a population.[7]

An **innovation** is any product or service that is perceived to be new by consumers (even if it has long been used by others elsewhere). Innovations may take the form of a new clothing style, a new manufacturing technique (such as the ability to design your own running shoe at www.nike.com), or a novel way to deliver a service (such as a drone delivery service).

Lately, firms that are keen to speed up the pace of innovation have been integrating design thinking in order to get a competitive advantage over their rivals. **Design thinking** is a procedure that relies on rationality, imagination, insight, and complete reasoning to evaluate different options of what could be—and to generate positive results that create value to the consumer.

Design Thinking

The sensory experiences we receive from products and services play an increasingly key role when we choose among competing options—even in the case of things we don't normally associate with fashion. As manufacturing costs go down and the amount of "stuff" that people accumulate goes up, consumers want to buy things that will provide aesthetic value in addition to simply doing what they're designed to do.

That used to just mean that marketers thought a lot about issues like the **color palette** they used in their packages. And indeed, decisions that involve colors and shapes do play an important role in shaping our expectations about what is inside.

For example, when it launched a white cheese as a "sister product" to an existing blue "Castello" cheese, a Danish company introduced it in a red package under the name of Castello Bianco. They chose this color to provide maximum visibility on store shelves. Although taste tests were positive, sales were disappointing. A subsequent analysis of consumer interpretations showed that the red packaging and the name gave the consumers wrong associations with the product type and its degree of sweetness. Danish consumers had trouble associating the color red with the white cheese. The company relaunched it in a white package and named it "White Castello." Almost immediately, sales more than doubled.[8]

Today, many companies put as much effort into every aspect of a product's design as an *haute couture* artisan who painstakingly inserts every stitch into a new gown.

Design thinking

From Poise Design

In many categories (although brand managers don't like to admit it), the simple truth is that consumers don't see a lot of big differences among competing brands; they believe they all deliver the same basic functionality. What does distinguish among contenders is design—think about the cult following that Apple enjoys largely due to its simple and elegant phones and computers.[9] "Products have simple, clean lines, with even simpler, self-explanatory names. The core purpose of this simplicity is to make the products easy to use so they can be understood and easily adopted by non-experts".

A focus on distinctive and pleasing design has spelled success for companies that stand out from the pack. For example, for years, companies such as Procter & Gamble have plodded along, peddling boring boxes of soap powder to generations of housewives who suffered in silence, scrubbing and buffing, yearning for the daily respite of martini time. Then along came Method; a new brand that offered cleaners in exotic scents such as cucumber, lavender, and ylang-ylang in aesthetically pleasing bottles. Within two years after launch, Method was taking in more than $2 million in revenue. Shortly thereafter, they hit it big when Target contracted to sell Method products in its stores.[10] And there's a method to Target's madness. The store chain helped to make designers such as Karim Rashid, Michael Graves, Philippe Starck, Todd Oldham, and Isaac Mizrahi household names.

In fact, research evidence suggests that our brains are wired to appreciate good design: Respondents who were hooked up to a functional magnetic resonance imaging (fMRI) scanner showed faster reaction times when they saw aesthetically pleasing packages even compared to well-known brands such as Coca-Cola.[11] Mass-market consumers thirst for great design, and they reward those companies that give it to them with their enthusiastic patronage and loyalty. From razor blades such as the Gillette Sensor to the Apple Watch and even to the lowly trashcan, design *is* substance. Form *is* function.

Fashion innovation: Poise Design x Hussein Bazaza

From Poise Design

Slowly but surely, fashion is seeping into a wide range of industries. That's why it's so vital to think about fashion marketing in a holistic way—How do the basic drivers that determine whether a Rotate party dress made in Copenhagen will be a hit among young *fashionistas* also influence consumers' acceptance of a new Tesla electric car or a Sullivan Table Lamp?

Fashion Innovation

We can think of **fashion innovation** as a style, design, or look that consumers believe to be new. The apparel fashion industry offers the public new styles or variations of former styles with new creations and detail on an ongoing basis as it encourages us to replace last year's purchases.

This has long been a criticism of the fashion industry by those who view this process as wasteful and frivolous. Some companies have developed a more responsible perspective of "updating" and building wardrobes through a system of basics that serves as the backbone of a wardrobe, which can be augmented with new coordinating items each season. These companies are more likely to offer conservative, career-oriented apparel rather than young, cool, fashion-forward merchandise. But, regardless of how drastically they replenish their closets, consumers evaluate new offerings and decide whether to "indulge" in new purchases each season. Thus, adoption of fashion innovations is a continual process.

We saw earlier that today a lot of change actually starts with users, such as fashion-forward consumers who like to experiment with new styles—and post their experiments on social media. Thus, in modern times, fashion innovation may be completely out of the control of the fashion industry. For example, it's been popular for some time for young people to search thrift shops for new ideas and mix vintage styles in a new way. A mixed look is very hot nowadays: Young consumers combine looks from Zara or Uniqlo with an expensive Gucci watch, Louis Vuitton handbag, or Prada accessories.

If an innovation is successful (most real innovations are not), it spreads through a population. First, only a few adventurous people or customers buy or use it, and then more and more consumers decide to adopt it until, in some cases, it seems that almost everyone has bought or tried the innovation.

How fast and how far an innovation diffuses are influenced by many factors such as the communication and marketing channels used, the persuasive influence of consumers' leaders (see Chapter 8), the mobility and geographic location of consumers, and social norms. Some more daring styles, for example,

Vintage style
From Poise Design

A mix and match look

This image shows fashion blogger Wenwen Stokes dressed in a Louis Vuitton T-shirt and scarf, a Topshop suit and Miu Miu sunglasses.

Elena Rostunova / Shutterstock.com

may not be accepted in Italy but could be widely accepted in New York. With time (and perhaps some modifications of the style), the new style can diffuse throughout the world.

Cycles of Fashion Adoption

Although the longevity of a particular style can range from a month to a century, fashions tend to flow in a predictable sequence. The **fashion lifecycle** comprises the introduction, acceptance, culmination and the decline of the acceptance of a certain style as shown in Figure 10.2.

To illustrate how this process works and to show the similarities between other fashion products and apparel, consider how the fashion acceptance cycle works in the popular music business. In the "old days," (say, the middle part of the 20th century), a record label might sign a performer and promote an album to radio stations in the hope that the program directors will like what they heard and include a cut on their playlist. That could be a long process, and one that's not well-suited to today's rapidly changing tastes and the market's thirst for a constant flow of new material.

Fast forward to today: Let's take the case of the young superstar Billie Eilish. When she was 13 years old, she wrote a song for her dance teacher to use as part of a choreographed session. Billie and her older brother recorded her song, "Ocean Eyes"—and then uploaded it to SoundCloud, a music-streaming site. The song went viral—much to the artist's surprise.[12] This opened the door to a succession of hits, such as "Bury a Friend." The artist eventually became recognized by the mainstream market, and she even wrote the title song for the James Bond movie *No Time to Die*.

In the **introduction stage**, a small number of music innovators hear a song like the one Billie Eilish uploaded. During the **acceptance stage**, the song enjoys increased social visibility and acceptance by large segments of the population. In the **regression stage**, the song reaches a state of social saturation as it becomes overplayed, and eventually it sinks into decline and obsolescence as new songs rise to take its place.[13]

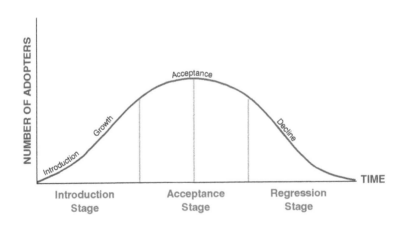

FIGURE 10.2 A normal fashion cycle

SOURCE: Reprinted with the permission of Macmillan College Publishing from Kaiser, S. (1985) *The Social Psychology of Clothing*. London: Macmillan.

Apparel fashions go through essentially the same process. The designer goods we described earlier may be the source of an innovation that is slowly adopted by fashion-forward, often young, people and found only at pricey boutiques. The look catches on and, unlike the music industry, is produced in lower-priced copies perhaps with lower-quality materials and eventually makes its way to mainstream department stores like Macy's. After the style saturates the market, and people tire of looking at it and wearing it, the style is found only at discount stores and, finally, as it disappears it is only found at thrift stores. But note that styles have a way of being reborn in slightly different forms: those discarded broaches that sell at thrift stores may be "rediscovered" and adapted by a later generation of fashion-forward shoppers. And so, the cycle continues...

Figure 10.3 illustrates that fashions are characterized by slow acceptance at the beginning, which rapidly accelerates, peaks, and then tapers off. Many retailers today feel that the fashion cycle is moving faster than ever before, going from one year or more down to five months. They see this change as being powered by the Internet and other technological innovations, the globalization of fashion, and savvy chains that produce instant knockoffs. The biggest task for retailers is figuring out which trends become fashion basics, which are flashes in the pan, and which looks will evolve. Although many fashions exhibit a moderate cycle, others are longer-lived or shorter-lived. Classics and fads can be compared to fashions by considering the relative length of the acceptance cycle (see Figure 10.3).

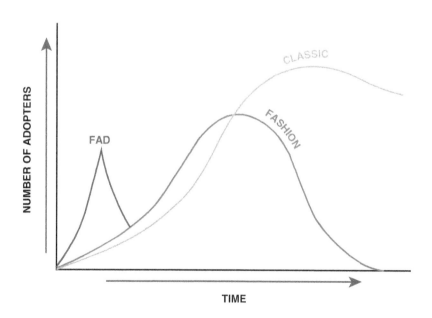

FIGURE 10.3 Fads, fashions and classics

Some styles become classics, those that seem to be acceptable or in good taste anytime, anyplace. They remain in general fashion for an extended period of time. They are in a sense "antifashion," since they guarantee stability and low risk to the purchaser for a long period of time.

Trench coat, a classic piece

Thomas Quack / Shutterstock.com

A **classic** is generally characterized by simplicity of design that keeps it from being dated. The "Little Black Dress" exhibit at the Victoria and Albert Museum in London in the 1980s exemplifies the concept of classic. Many of the dress designs throughout the decades look as appropriate for today as they did in their time. Blue jeans also have become a classic. Other examples include the Chanel suit, shirtwaist dress, turtleneck sweater, Oxford shirt, blazer, trench coat, a skirt length just below the knee, the pearl necklace, penny loafers, and pumps. Often classics are conservative and acceptable business dress. Can you think of others? How many of these items do you have in your wardrobe?

A **fad** is a short-lived fashion that suddenly becomes popular and quickly disappears. It generally affects only a specific group in the population. Adopters may all belong to a common subculture, and the fad "trickles across" members but rarely breaks out of that specific group. It may have an extreme design that does not appeal to the general population. Fads can be accompanied by a craze or mania by consumers resulting in retailers finding it difficult to keep the item in stock. Power bracelets, elastic bracelets made with semiprecious stones, was a recent New Age fad with young and not-so-young adults. They are modeled after Buddhist prayer beads and thought to have special powers such as increasing love (rose quartz), intelligence (amethyst), health (turquoise), and self-control (onyx).

Fads: Plastic shutter glasses

Dragon images / Shutterstock.com

There are many examples of fads over the years that you may or may not remember, including hula hoops and pet rocks. Check out www.badfads.com for an amusing look at past fads: bell-bottoms, Bermuda shorts, bouffant hairdos, body tattoos, conk hairdos, DA haircut, Farrah Fawcett hair, glassless glasses, go-go boots, granny glasses, hot pants, hair irons, jazzed-up jeans, leisure suits, Mickey Mouse items, miniskirts, Nehru jackets, pillbox hats, platform shoes, poodle skirts, short shorts, sideburns, tank top, taps on shoes, tie-dye T-shirts, turtleneck sweaters, Twiggy look, wraparound glasses, and zoot suits. Some of these have come back into fashion, such as the miniskirt, and some have been labeled classics, such as the turtleneck.

We can identify several important characteristics of fads:

- The fad is non-utilitarian—that is, it does not perform any meaningful function.

- The fad is often adopted on impulse; people do not undergo stages of rational decision making before joining in.

- The fad diffuses rapidly, gains quick acceptance, and is short-lived.

Is It a Fad, a Trend, or a Fashion?

The term **trend** often is also confused with fashion. A trend is a general direction or movement. As a style begins to be widely accepted, we think of it as a trend. If several designers are showing similar "looks," perhaps retro or a new skirt length, and fashion-forward consumers are adopting it, then this style might be labeled a trend.

Knowing if a style is a fad, trend, or fashion is difficult and comes only with time. Sometimes this judgment seems to be based solely upon 20-20 hindsight: If it quickly disappears, it was a fad. We might think something is a fad, but if its acceptance continues, it may turn into a trend. However, if a product doesn't connect to some deep-seated need like wellness or social status but is instead just a "novelty item" that is fun to try like a "shutter shades sunglasses" or a "pet rock", it's likely to be a fad that disappears quite quickly. And if it lasts for a while and has widespread acceptance, it becomes a fashion. When it peaks and begins to decline, it obviously ceases to be a trend and becomes an outdated fashion, or one that is over. Fashions, trends, and fads are like the stock market. You don't know when they've reached their peak until they're over, and only then can they be fully analyzed.

The trick for companies is to be the first to identify a trend (the other obvious trick is to know when it's over and not get stuck with merchandise no one wants). Companies that act on a new trend have an advantage, whether the firm is Starbucks (coffee), Nabisco (SnackWell's low fat cookies and crackers), Chrysler (retro cars), or a popular apparel designer. While nothing is certain, some guidelines help to predict if the idea or item will endure as a long-term trend or fashion, or if it will go the way of the hula hoop and pet rock:

- Does it fit with basic lifestyle changes? If a new hairstyle is hard to care for, it will not be consistent with women's increasing time demands. On the other hand, the movement to shorter-term vacations is more likely to last since they make trip planning easier for harried consumers.

- What are the benefits? The switch to poultry and fish from beef came about because these meats are healthier, so a real benefit is evident.

- Is it a trend or a side effect? An interest in exercise is part of a basic trend toward health consciousness, whereas the specific form of exercise that is "in" at any given time will vary (for example, Zumba versus Yoga).

- What other changes have occurred in the market? Sometimes the popularity of products is influenced by **carryover effects**. The miniskirt fad in the 1960s brought about a major change in the hosiery market: the development of pantyhose.

- Who has adopted the change? If the innovation is not adopted by Gen Z, Millennials, or some other important market segment, it is not likely to become a trend.

Creating and Adopting Innovations

The diffusion of innovation perspective focuses upon the adoption decisions of many people within and across groups.[14] An *individual consumer's* adoption of an innovation resembles the decision-making sequence as the person moves through each stage. The relative importance of each stage may differ depending on how much is already known about a product, as well as on cultural factors that may affect people's willingness to try new things.[15] Diffusions of innovation adoption includes five stages:[16]

1. *Knowledge:* The consumer obtains more insights about the innovation. They have awareness but have made no decision.

2. *Persuasion:* The consumer starts to create a favorable or unfavorable attitude towards the innovation. This phase is linked to the perceived risk of the new product (or service)—that is, the assessment of the consequences of adopting it.

3. *Decision:* The consumer chooses to either adopt or discard the innovation.

4. *Implementation:* The consumer essentially uses the product (or service).

5. *Confirmation:* The consumer pursues reinforcement for the innovation decision.

Types of Adopters

Do you know someone who stubbornly refuses to try new things? Even within the same culture, not all people adopt an innovation at the same rate. Some do so quite rapidly, such as fashion-forward consumers, and others never do it at all. We place consumers into approximate categories based upon their likelihood of adopting an innovation. The categories of adopters, shown in Figure 10.4, relate to phases of the product life cycle concept used widely by marketing strategists.

As we can see in Figure 10.4, roughly one-sixth of the population (**innovators** and **early adopters**) are very quick to adopt new products, and one-sixth of the people (**laggards**) are very slow. The other two-thirds, so called **early and late majority**, lie somewhere in the middle; these adopters represent the mainstream public. They are interested in new things, but they do not want them to be *too* new.

In some cases, people deliberately wait to adopt an innovation or new fashion because they assume that its price will fall after it has been on the market awhile or, in the case of technology, that

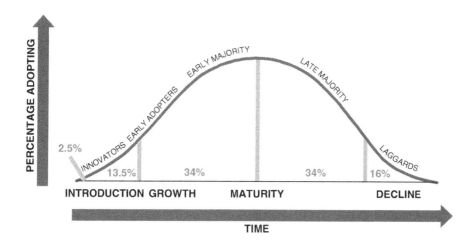

FIGURE 10.4 Types of adopters

its qualities or features will be improved. Keep in mind that the proportion of consumers who fall into each category is an estimate; the actual size of each depends on such factors as the complexity of the product, its cost, and how much risk is associated with trying it.

Even though innovators represent 2.5% (again, an approximation) of the population, marketers are keen to identify them. These are the brave souls who are always on the lookout for novel developments and will be the first to try a new offering. But remember that a person who is an innovator in one area may even be a laggard in another. For example, a woman who prides herself as being on the cutting edge of fashion may have no conception of new developments in sustainable cars. Despite this qualification, we can offer some generalizations regarding the profile of innovators.[17] Not surprisingly, for example, they tend to have more favorable attitudes toward taking risks. They are likely to have higher educational and income levels, and to be socially active.

Early adopters share many of the same characteristics as innovators, but an important difference is their degree of concern for social acceptance, especially with regard to expressive products such as clothing, cosmetics, and so on. Generally speaking, an early adopter is receptive to new styles because he or she is involved in the product category and also places high value on being in fashion.

What appears on the surface to be fairly high-risk adoption (for instance, wearing a skirt five inches above the knee when most women are wearing them below the knee) is actually not *that* risky if the style change has already been "field-tested" by innovators, who truly take the fashion risk. Early adopters are likely to be found in fashion-forward stores or in cities where fashion weeks are held featuring the latest "hot" designers. In contrast, true innovators are more likely to be found in small boutiques featuring as-yet-unknown emerging designers.

Branding the Fashion Product

A **brand** is a name, term, design, symbol or any other component that differentiates one retailer from others and identifies the producer or retailer of a fashion good or service. Branding is a marketing technique that includes the use of brand names and recognizable symbols and logos.

Brand Architecture

How can you brand several fashion products under one business? **Brand architecture** refers to the way big companies consolidate, manage and go to market with brands. Two of the most common of these philosophies are terms that sound quite similar to one another[18]:

House of brands: A conglomerate manages an assortment of ostensibly unrelated and independent brands that have no evident association to the master company. Each brand is marketed under an entirely different brand name and has a separate identity. Think for example of Maison LVMH, Kering, Richemont, Inditex, H&M group, Arcadia Group, and Capri Holding. Table 10.1 shows how Maison LVMH creates a house of brands.

This structure usually forms when a company has different target audiences for the same product category. For example, in the case of Maison LVHM, the conglomerate markets different brands of cosmetics that appeal to different target markets, for example KVD Vegan Beauty versus Fenty Beauty by Rihanna. The L'Oréal Group follows the house-of-brands strategy in the cosmetics and skin-care categories with distinctive brand promises, targeting the luxury market (such as Lancôme), the medical market (such as La Roche-Posay), and the lifestyle markets (such as Armani perfumes, Valentino perfumes).[19]

TABLE 10.1　Maison LVMH's house of brands portfolio

Maison LVMH					
Wines & Spirits		**Fashion & Leather Goods**	**Perfumes & Cosmetics**	**Watches & Jewelry**	
Clos des Lambrays	Cloudy Bay	Loewe	Marc Jacobs	Guerlain	Chaumet
Château d'Yquem	Chandon Australia	Moynat	Nicholas Kirkwood	Aqua Di Parma	Tag Heuer
Dom Pérignon	Belvedere	Louis Vuitton	Fenty	Parfums Christian Dior	Zenith
Ruinart	Bodega Numanthia	Berlutti		Givenchy Parfums	Bvlgari
Moët & Chandon	Cheval des Andes	Rimowa		Perfumes Loewe	Fred
Hennessy	Terrazas de los Andes	Patou		Benefit Cosmetics	Hublot
Veuve Clicquot	Woodinville	Loro Piana		Make Up For Ever	
Ardbeg	Chandon China	Fendi		Kenzo Parfums	
Château Cheval Blanc	Ao Yun	Celine		Fresh	
Glenmorangie	Chandon India	Christian Dior		KVD Vegan Beauty	
Krug	Clos19	Emilio Pucci		Maison Francis Kurkdjian	
Mercier	Volcan de mi Tierra	Givenchy		Marc Jacobs Beauty	
Chandon Argentina	Chandon Brazil	Kenzo		Cha Ling	
Cape Mentelle	Newton Vineyard	Pink Shirtmaker		Fenty Beauty by Rihanna	
Chandon California					

Branded house: In contrast to a house of brands, this strategy works for one master brand that usually has a chain of offerings that function with diverse sub-brand names. The sub-division of the brands usually adds clarity and further definition to the offering.

A branded house strategy usually applies in the case of **brand extensions** (the expansion of a recognized brand name for a new product or category) (for more on brand extension see[20]). Market leaders, such as Virgin, that strive to dominate entire markets and categories with the use of a sole, extremely significant and highly leveraged master brand will apply the same brand name to multiple categories, such as Virgin Air, Virgin Megastores, Virgin Mobile, Virgin Casino, and even Virgin Galactic.[21] Another example is the Armani brand, which applies the same brand name Armani to a range of sub-brands such Giorgio Armani, Emporio Armani, Armani Exchange, Armani Junior... Armani retains its branding through all of its sub-brands.

Types of Brands

Fashion brands can be classified under different types of brands as follows:

- *Manufacturer brand* refers to the brand that is usually marketed under the name of the producer or the designer of the goods. These types of brands are usually very common in the textile industry. An example of this type of brand is Levi Strauss. Another example is the international couture designer Elie Saab, who usually produces and markets the fashion apparel products under his name.

- *Private label brand* refers to fashion goods that are marketed by one retailer under its own name but produced by a third party. Examples include George by Asda, Alfani, American Rag, and Charter Club for Macy's.

- *Franchise brand* refers to an agreement between a franchisee and a given franchisor that offers the franchisor the exclusive right to sell the franchisee's goods in a specific territory. In return for having the franchise, the franchisee will pay the franchisor an initial payment and some

Manufacturer brand: International couture designer Elie Saab

FashionStock.com / Shutterstock.com

licensing fees on an annual basis. Common examples are Zara, Armani, Bottega Venetta, Coach, Jimmy Choo, and Versace. In the UAE, franchising partners are established luxury groups such as Al Tayer group representing Kering brands and Chalhoub group representing LVMH brands.

- *Licensed brand* refers to an agreement that gives the right to a company to produce or market a certain good or service from the owner for a specific fee. An example is the Ralph Lauren brand, which followed this strategy in order to expand its name and diversify into different product categories such as perfumes and home furnishings.[22] Fashion retailer Ted Baker signed a new product license agreement with Next to expand its collection of childrenswear.[23]

- We call merchants who only sell online **pure play retailers**. Some prominent examples include Boohoo, ASOS, Yoox, Net-A-Porter Group.[24] Pure play retailers either sell only private-labeled items such as Boohoo, giving them a competitive advantage in the market, or they sell a combination of private-labeled items in addition to other branded items such as ASOS.

- *Co-brands or partnership brands* form when two brands join together to create a new brand or perhaps to co-brand a new offering.[25] For example, Puma and Rihanna launched their latest collaboration, at a recent Paris Fashion Week. The fragrance founder Jo Malone is teaming up with the fast-fashion brand Zara to produce a new fragrance line. This form of partnership allows both brands to expand their presence in different markets.[26] For example, the two mega-brands Balenciaga and Gucci introduced a new partnership for the Autumn/Winter 2021 Aria collection.[27]

The Use of Colors in Branding

Color meanings can be powerful and can really influence the type of brand you choose. As we saw in Chapter 7, color can significantly affect the way we perceive brands. Fashion marketers should pay serious attention to the use of colors in branding to convey the right communication message to their target market. Table 10.2 details the meaning of different colors:

TABLE 10.2 The meaning of colors

Mental Associations	Color Type	Psychological Significance	Examples
Red			
Hot	Primary Color	Achievement	Christian Louboutin
Fire		Bold	Netflix
Heat		Passion	Target
Blood		Spontaneous	H&M
		Royalty	
Pink			
Feminine	Red and White Mix	Romance	PINK Victoria Secret
Soft		Refinement	Barbie
Floral		Empathetic	Dunkin Donuts
Peace		Gentleness	Hello Kitty

Mental Associations	Color Type	Psychological Significance	Examples
Purple			
Cool	Red and Blue Mix	Mysterious	Hallmark
Mist		Curious Royalty	Cadbury
Darkness			
Shadow			
Lavender			
Healing	Purple and White Mix	Mellow	Luxury Spa Chains
Relaxation		Sophisticated	Luxury Dry Cleaning Services
Cleanliness		Delicate	
Purity			
White			
Cool	Base of All Colors	Virtue	Apple
Snow		Purity	Abercrombie and Fitch
Winter		Cleanliness	
Yellow			
Sunlight	Primary Color	Lightness	Selfridges
Shine		Brightness	McDonalds
Nature		Luminosity	Ferrari
Orange			
Warm	Red and Yellow Mix	Energetic	Hermès
Metallic		Warm	Amazon
Autumnal		Vivid	
Brown			
Soil	Primary and Complementary Color Mix	Stable	Louis Vuitton Monogram
Earth		Natural	M&Ms
Nature		Sturdy	Magnum
Coffee			Moncler
Beige			
Cream	Brown and White Mix	Warm	Chloé
Sand		Dull	Nescafé
		Versatile	Gucci Monogram
Taupe			
Mole	Brown and Gray Mix	Neutrality	Georgio Armani Vector
Beauty Marks		Classic	
Neutral		Practical	
Relaxing			

(Continued)

TABLE 10.2 (Continued)

Mental Associations	Color Type	Psychological Significance	Examples
Green			
Nature	Blue and Yellow Mix	Natural	Starbucks Logo
Cool		Balanced	Heineken Logo
Leaves		Soothing	Rolex
Blue			
Cold	Primary Color	Calmness	Facebook
Sky		Serenity	Dell
Water		Stillness	Oreo
Ice			IBM
Teal			
Luxury	Blue and Green Mix	Assurance	Tiffany & Co.
Bold		Refinement	Cinnabon
		Cleanliness	
Gray			
Neutral	Black and White Mix	Mainstream	Nintendo Wii
Dull		Steady	Microsoft
Boring		Secure	Jeep
Black			
Natural	Negation of all Colors	Formal	Chanel
Night		Conformist	Valentino
Emptiness		Conservative	

The Logo

A **logo** refers to a symbol worked into a distinctive design to identify a company's goods and services. Common examples are the Swoosh sign for Nike, the green crocodile logo for Lacoste, Duc-carriage-with-horse for Hermès, and an apple for the Apple brand.

Logo shapes and colors used by fashion brands are not selected by chance. Your brand logo should communicate who the company is. It should provoke an emotional reaction that impacts the way current and potential consumers perceive your brand. Logos are very important as consumers rely upon them to define the brand's image and to easily identify the brand in a sea of goods. Luxury brands, in particular, use logos as a way to celebrate their product uniqueness and to communicate status. These marks are not just pretty images; they contribute to the value of a brand. For example, the chief merchant at The RealReal online resale website reported the site's sales data showed that consumers are 20% more likely to buy a brand with a visible logo rather than the same brand that doesn't explicitly show the logo.[28]

A lot of fashion brands lately, such as Balenciaga, Celine, Calvin Klein, Diane Von Furstenberg, Zara, Rimowa, and Balmain, have redesigned their logos, as they found the old ones were becoming boring, dated, or they failed to adequately define the brand personality.

Back in 2012, Hedi Slimane, the creative director of Yves Saint Laurent dropped the "Yves" from the brand to become known as Saint Laurent.

As for Burberry, the brand has redesigned its logo since it "ceases to be grounded in any typographic styling that is recognizably British or from a heritage of English type forms." As a change, the brand supplemented the logo with the words "London, England" underneath it, to reinforce the company's strong British origins. The whole impact of these strategies was to build a fresh slate for the creative director; a chance to rewrite the house's heritage and be able to move these brands into the global business.[29]

Marketers should think of designing a logo with the right colors and shapes. Shapes signify different things. For instance, a round shape means warmth, community, friendship, femi-

Zara's new logo

Funstock / Shutterstock.com

Saint Laurent's new logo

DELBO ANDREA / Shutterstock.com

ninity, unity and love. Think of the logo of Walt Disney. Squares and rectangle shapes express a sense of stability and balance, while triangles reveal more masculine and powerful meanings. Straight lines and precise logo shapes also convey power, competence, and efficiency.

Vertical lines are usually viewed as being masculine, powerful and aggressive, while horizontal lines are viewed as tranquil and calm. The effects of shape also cover the selected typeface. Sharp, angular typefaces give an aggressive or energetic impression; while soft, rounded typefaces reveal more of a youthful feeling. Curves of any kind are likely to be perceived as feminine in nature while strong and bold lettering are likely to be perceived as masculine.[30] Think for

Gucci GG interlocking letters

Creative Lab / Shutterstock.com

example of the Target logo, which has a circular shape. The circle shape delivers a sense of friendship, community, and durability—characteristics, which are all crucial to the Target brand.[31]

Sportswear brands usually design their logos based on movements and speed. Think, for instance, of the Nike Swoosh: the combination of curves terminating in a sharp point provides a solid feeling of movement.

Logos can also take the form of a full name such as Tommy Hilfiger, Ralph Lauren or Armani. They can also take the form of initials and letters such as DKNY, DVF or interlocking letters such as GG for Gucci or CC for Chanel.

The Trademark

A **trademark** is an identifiable emblem, phrase, word, or symbol that is associated with a particular product or brand and legitimately discerns it from all other brands. Trademark in fashion is when the designer's name or fashion brand name is completely associated with the particular fashion good. This involves attaching the trademark to the tag or incorporating it in a specific place on the product. For example, the Nike trademark is not only linked to the word 'NIKE', but it also refers to its symbol the "Swoosh". A registered trademark offers the fashion brand an exclusive right for the usage of its registered good through use of the ® symbol and allows it to differentiate its products from those of competitors, therefore lowering the risk of being copied or used without authorization.

In 2017, the sportswear brand Adidas has been unsuccessful in an effort to extend trademark protection to three parallel stripes in the European Union as competitors strive to get into the market for striped shoes and apparel. The General Court of the European Union administrated against Adidas' call for more trademark protection in the middle of mounting patent dilemmas in the sportswear sector.[32]

Packaging

Depending on the market positioning of the brand, the packaging of your fashion items sometimes is as or more important than the product itself. Packaging can act as a differentiator between one fashion brand and the other. When a package prominently features a name, logo or color related to a certain brand, consumers will easily be able to recognize and identify the brand among all competitors in the market. Think, for example, of Tiffany & Co. For the majority of consumers, the iconic robin's-egg blue box is more recogniz-able than the jewelry they'll find in the store. Also, think of the famous yellow bag of Selfridges & Co.

Product Support-Related Services

In fashion, customer service is cru-cial as the brand's representation of a product creates an image of value and utility in the consumer's mind. In the context of luxury, retailers or brands need to offer customers fantastic cus-tomer service to support their image. Employees are expected to be well

Tiffany & Co package

Sorbis / Shutterstock.com

educated about all existing and new products. They should also be allowed to receive free products for them to try and have prior knowledge about them.[33]

Employees should also be able to competently address consumer queries, whether face to face or on live chat, social media, and email. Employees must be able to smoothly handle complaints or products that customers want to return. A good salesperson should always act in a way that says, "the customer is always right" (even when they're not). For example, the company Rent the Runway decided to give refunds in addition to some extra cash to customers who faced some issues with cancelled orders due to supply chain complications.[34]

Some companies also provide in-store repair for some accessories. For example, the outdoor brand Patagonia is ready to take care of its customers' products: "We pay for repairs that we're responsible for and charge a fair price for repairs due to normal wear and tear".[35] To provide a premium customer service, some luxury brands provide customers who are buying in-store with a free home delivery option. For example, the houses of Chanel and Dior in Paris are ready to delivery your items straight to your home.

Fashion Pricing

What is a price? A **price** is an assignment of value, or the sum the consumer is willing to give in order to receive a good or a service. An effective strategy for the pricing of fashion products is one that you must justify based upon the brand name, quality of products, location, competition, and so many other factors.

In fashion, price doesn't only refer to the amount of cash that should be charged for a given product. It is also linked to the "value equation" that the brand builds in the consumer's mind. For a given amount of money to be paid, what kind of benefits and practical utility is the buyer receiving, such as style, quality, and convenience?[36] After all, in many cases you are selling something that the buyer doesn't really "need" so what he or she is willing to pay for it is somewhat arbitrary.

Marzena certainly convinced herself of that when trying to decide about a Birkin bag! Decisions regarding the right price depends on a number of factors such as the market demand and the environment.

Factors That May Affect Pricing

Product Cost

Pricing a fashion product is affected by its manufacturing costs such as the country of production, the quality and material used to produce the item, and the overhead costs (e.g., rental, employees...). For instance, Hermès sells its Diamonds Kelly Bracelet for $41,200 in comparison with its pure gold Kelly Bracelet that sells for $8,350. The difference in price is attributed to the diamonds that are additional to the normal bracelet.

Market Demand

While designing the right pricing strategy, marketers need to take into consideration the market demand and accurately estimate it. **Market demand** refers to the volume of products that consumers are willing to buy at a particular price. Demand for fashion products varies depending on whether the product is a mass or a luxury one. This can be viewed in Figure 10.5.

For instance, the demand for luxury **fashion goods** seems to be fairly **inelastic**. This means that the demand for products increases as its price increases. For status goods such as luxury automobiles, jewelry, apparel and accessories, a price increase may in fact result in a rise in consumer demand since they perceive these items to be more valuable. Therefore, a price increase does not discourage consumers from keeping on buying.

However, in the case of mass fashion, the demand curve is **elastic**. When the price of the mass fashion product goes up, the quantity that the consumer is willing to buy decreases. However, if the price goes down, the market will react differently by increasing its demand for the fashion items (see Figure 10.5).

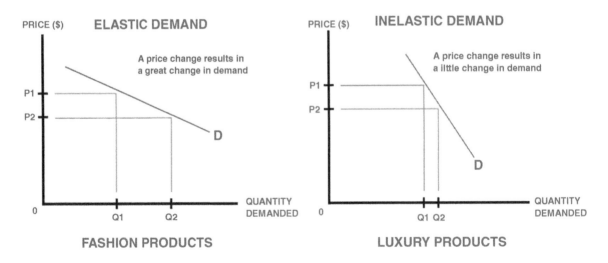

FIGURE 10.5   Demand curves for basic fashion products and luxury products

The Environment

Further to the estimated demand and the cost of the fashion product, when designing their pricing strategies, marketers should also consider the company's external environment such as the economic environment, competition, and consumer trends. Pricing fashion products can be a real challenge; the reason is that (like other kinds of products) a price may work well in one environment, while it might not be so competitive in other ones. Let's think about, for example, a cotton blouse for Massimo Dutti. What is it worth, and what should you charge?

- General economic trends such as inflation, recession, economic growth and consumer confidence may impact pricing decisions related to whether the company should increase its prices, reduce it or just keep it as it is. For instance, the coronavirus pandemic made fashion consumers become more price sensitive. A study indicated that 81% of US consumers think that the pandemic will cause a recession, triggering worries among individuals and making them less likely to purchase unnecessary goods such as fashion products. The results of this study revealed that consumers are more likely to focus on value; they expect companies to cut prices and offer additional promotions.[37]

- Fashion marketers must also predict how competitors will act to their pricing strategies. Sometimes companies should compete with other brands by decreasing their prices. However, a price war may affect consumers' perception of the brand's image. For this reason, some brands may rely on other elements than pricing to compete against competitors. For example, Massimo Dutti might want to actually raise the price of a blouse to make it look better than its competitor Mango.

- Consumer trends too can hugely impact prices. Culture and demographics have a big influence on all marketing decisions especially that both can shape the way consumers behave. According to Selfridges, "The sharing economy is the new black".[38] This model allows individuals to share items with one another. Uber, Airbnb, and Rent-the-Runway are all great examples of sharing goods and services. Now you can even rent your furniture from John Lewis.[39] Do you feel like shopping and wearing something nice but don't have enough money to spend? Just head to Selfridges and get your hands on a dress from their rental services.

Pricing Strategies

- *Cost-plus pricing*: Marketers usually select this method as it is easy to compute and is somewhat risk free. This technique requires the company to only calculate its cost per unit and add a mark-up to it. How to decide the markup percentage is often a matter of practice or a rule of thumb. A lot of brands mark-up apparel, accessories and other goods by adopting **keystone pricing**, a pricing strategy in which the brand doubles the cost of the product (100% markup) to set its price.[40] As for restaurants, they generally multiply the food cost by three (200% markup) and multiply their alcoholic beverages by four (300% markup).[41]

- *Competitive pricing:* Fashion brands may sometimes price their products similarly, more, or less than competitors' prices. For instance, think of the competitors Nike and Adidas; each company may use the other's prices as a benchmark to help it set its own.

- *New product pricing:* When introducing new products, fashion marketers may either adopt a skimming or a penetration pricing strategy. A **skimming price** is the process of setting a premium price during the introduction of a product and reducing it as the market progresses in response to market pressures. If a fashion product has a new style, is in demand and is exclusive, the fashion brand can set a high price during its introduction in order to cover all its development and promotional costs. When competitive products come into the market, the brand can reduce its price to stay competitive. Think of the strategy that Apple follows for the launching of its new iPhone on a yearly basis. The price of the iPhone is usually very high during launching stage and then becomes lower during the year. In contrast, **penetration pricing** is a technique where a brand sets low prices at the introductory phase in order to be able to enter the market and increase its market share.

- *Value based pricing:* This technique requires setting a price that provides optimum value to consumers. This strategy guarantees an acceptable product quality at affordable prices. A number of popular global retail chains such as Walmart, Home Depot, Target, George Clothing (ASDA), and Primark all implement this technique.

- *Multiple-products pricing:* Companies do offer a number of goods that consumers normally purchase all together. A consumer who purchases a Nespresso machine will need to continuously buy its capsules. The most used strategies for pricing multiple goods are product-bundle and captive-product pricing. **Product-bundle pricing** refers to offering two or more products in a sole package and for one price—a price that is usually cheaper than the total price of the products if purchased separately. Think of the cosmetic make-up kits that include a number of pieces for one price. Lancôme offers its La Vie Est Belle Perfume in a gift set along with two tubes of body cream for the price of $98. **Captive-product pricing** is a pricing approach a company adopts when it has two items that must be offered together for them to work. For instance, a wax warmer won't be able to work without wax sticks. The retailer sells the wax warmer at a low price and then makes its profit from the wax sticks that the consumer has to continuously buy. This technique also is commonly known as the **razor-and-blade model** because it was first used by shaving product companies that sold hand-held razors at a very low price (or even gave them away) in order to create ongoing demand for the blades the customer would need to use the device.[42]

- *Prestige pricing:* This strategy is a form of psychological pricing that requires the company to set a price exaggeratedly high to keep a favorable image of the brand. Some luxury brands follow this strategy to position themselves in the market. For instance, Chanel uses this strategy; the luxury brand also keeps increasing its prices in order to enhance the value of what it sells. For instance, during the pandemic, Chanel has even raised its prices by 6% more for some of its handbags such as Timeless Classic and Boy Chanel due to inflation and the rising costs of production and materials.[43] The strategy is that Chanel classic pieces do not depreciate in value. The more you wait, the more expensive it will be and the higher the value it will have in the future.

- Furthermore, fashion brands must take into account an important strategy in pricing known as **price architecture**. This term refers to a pricing structure that is designed in a way to serve the needs of different customers by maintaining different price points ranging from lower prices to more expensive ones. As Figure 10.6 shows, this strategy enhances the company's expansion and increases its value proposition. Accordingly, a fashion brand like TopShop can offer products at different price levels: for example, an introductory or low price point at $7, a medium price for $40 and a high price point of $150.

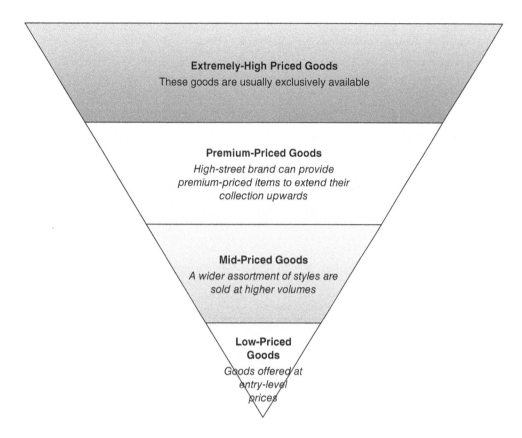

FIGURE 10.6 Price architecture

Chapter Summary

Now that you have read the chapter, you should understand the following:

1. What are the layers of a fashion product?

A product is a tangible item that is usually offered for sale for the sake of satisfying a customer's need. When designing strategies regarding their products, fashion marketers should satisfy their customers' needs and wants at every level of the product. The core product refers to the benefits the product will offer to consumers. The actual product consists of a tangible good or the provided service that offered the necessary benefits related to the physical quality, product features, and the design. The augmented product refers to the supporting elements that allows the consumer to use the product, such as a warranty, credit card facility, home delivery, and after sale service.

(Continued)

2.   What is the cycle of fashion adoption?

Fashion tends to follow cycles. The fashion cycle, or fashion life-cycle, comprises the introduction, acceptance, culmination, and the decline of the acceptance of a certain style. The fashion cycle is moving faster than ever before going from one year or more down to five months. The biggest task for retailers is figuring out which trends become fashion basics, which are flashes in the pan, and which looks will evolve. Although many fashions exhibit a moderate cycle, others are longer-lived or shorter-lived. Classics and fads can be compared to fashions by considering the relative length of the acceptance cycle. A classic is generally characterized by simplicity of design that keeps it from being dated. A fad is a short-lived fashion that suddenly becomes popular and quickly disappears. It generally affects only a specific group within the population.

3.   How can a company design the right fashion product and branding strategy?

A fashion product consists of quality, design, style, brand name, package, features, values, color, size, material, logos, and trademarks etc.; features that allow the actual product to be marketable. The development, design, and launch of a fashion product requires taking into consideration different decisions. These decisions are related to the product features, branding, and finally the product support-related services. The fashion product features consist of the appropriateness/personal styles, economy/usefulness, attractiveness/aesthetics, quality, other-people-directed/image, country of origin and fiber/fabric. Branding is a marketing technique which takes the form of brand names and recognizable symbols and logos.

How can companies brand several fashion products under one business? Brand architecture refers to the way big companies consolidate, manage and go to market with brands, which can either take the form of a house of brands or a branded house. House of brands is a strategy whereby one leading company manages an assortment of ostensibly unrelated and independent brands that have no evident association to the master company, whereas a branded house works for one master brand that usually has a chain of offerings that function with diverse sub-brand names.

Fashion brands can be classified under different types of brands: a manufacturer brand, which refers to the brand that is usually marketed under the name of the producer or the designer of the good; private label brand, which refers to fashion goods that are marketed by one retailer under its own name but produced by a third party; a franchise brand, which refers to an agreement between a franchisee and a given franchisor that offers the franchisor the exclusive right to sell the franchisee's goods in a specific territory; a licensed brand that refers to an agreement that gives the right to a company to produce or market a certain good or service from the owner for a specific fee; a pure play brand, which refers to a brand that focuses only on a specific product/activity or service; and a partnership brand which is formed when two brands join together to create a new brand or form partnerships.

Further to this, the use of colors in branding can be very powerful. Fashion marketers should pay serious attention to the use of colors in branding to convey the right communication message to their target market. They also need to select the right shapes and colors for their logos in a way that the brand logo should communicate who the company is and should provoke an emotional reaction that impacts the way current and potential consumers perceive the brand. The right selection of the trademark and package is also crucial as it legitimately discerns the brand from all competitive ones.

Finally, in fashion, customer service is fundamental as the brand's representation of a product creates an image of value and utility in a consumer's mind. In the context of luxury, retailers or brands should offer customers a dream customer service and should always be provided with careful assistance.

4.   How can a company design an effective pricing strategy?

A price is the consignment of value, or the sum the consumer is willing to give in order to receive a good or a service. An effective strategy for the pricing of fashion brands is linked to the brand name, quality of products, location, competition and other factors such as the market demand, economic situation, and the shift in market trends. There are a number of pricing strategies that brands can adopt in order to price their products such as cost-plus pricing, competitive pricing, new product pricing, value-based pricing, multiple product pricing, and prestige pricing. Fashion brands should consider adopting the price architecture strategy necessitating to offer customers different price points ranging from lower prices to more expensive ones.

DISCUSSION

1.   What makes a successful fashion brand?

2.   Think of five mass fashion brands and five luxury brands. To what extent do you think these brands are applying the elements of branding?

3.   What are the most important elements that fashion product designers should consider while developing a fashion product?

4.   Do you think that packaging is an important feature for fashion products? Explain your answer.

5.   How does prestige pricing become part of the value of such products such as Hermès scarves, Chanel suits, Tiffany diamond rings? Explain your answer.

6.   Identify a new fashion. Which leadership theory do you think best explains its origin?

7.   What is the difference among a fad, a fashion and a classic? Provide examples of each.

8.   Identify new fashions in areas other than apparel, such as electronics, toys, furniture, cars, music, and other entertainment, living arrangements, and other areas of popular culture. What stages of the fashion cycle do you think they are in?

9.   Some studies indicated that there are significantly more women in the innovator and early adopter categories, and more men in the late majority and laggard categories. Do you believe that this might vary by product categories? Explain.

10.   Are you an early adopter? Explain why or why not.

EXERCISES

1. In groups, design a new packaging idea for a brand of your choice whereby you want to position a new product or reposition an existing one in the market.

2. Evaluate the different pricing strategies. Go online and search for examples of brands that use each of the different pricing strategies.

3. Select a fashion brand of your choice. Assess the different strategies that the brand is using in relation to the product and price. Do you have any suggestions?

4. Select a fashion retailer and think of the types of consumers who would fall into each of the categories of fashion adoption. Provide a name for each category.

5. Form a group and search for recent examples of fashion, fad and trends. What is the basic difference between the three?

6. Go online and search for other examples of classic fashion styles. How many of these items do you have in your wardrobe?

CASE STUDY: HUNG-UP ON YOU – DESIGNING TO ELIMINATE SINGLE-USE PLASTIC IN FASHION RETAIL

Edel Moore, University of Leeds, Dr. Alana James, Northumbria University

Annually, the fashion sector utilizes large amounts of plastic in many different ways including the production of synthetic fibres (e.g., acrylic and polyester) employed in product manufacturing, product branding, in-store visual merchandising, and in the packaging of products for labeling and protection purposes. One of the largest, hidden sources of plastic in fashion however is in garment hangers.

Consumers are demanding that industry and retail revisit product development and supply chains to challenge and eliminate environmentally harmful components. Universally, awareness of the negative impact of single-use plastics on our ecosystems has gained heightened priority. Research by the Shelton Group stated that 65% of Americans polled were "very" or "extremely" concerned about ocean pollution due to plastic misuse as opposed to 58% who felt the same about climate change. Legislative and customer-led initiatives to remove single-use plastic items such as drinking straws have resulted in innovative replacement product design solutions.

The fashion industry is often perceived negatively in terms of environmental impact. However, one of the sector's greatest strengths is its ability to design creatively and implement quick-response, agile production solutions to meet customer requirements. The New Circular Design Guide by The Ellen MacArthur Foundation and IDEO places sustainability-orientated design thinking at the heart of developing alternatives to existing "take, make, dispose" manufacturing approaches. Stella McCartney, Patagonia, and Adidas were among the first to incorporate recycling and circularity of materials as significant components of product development and branding strategy. Luxury designers such as Roland Mouret are vocal in asserting that sustainability is core to any fashion brand, which opens up environmental and commercial opportunities. Although there is engagement for the design of environmentally friendly garments, less attention has been directed at eradicating plastics from hidden elements within the supply chain, such as labeling, packaging and hanger usage, composition and recycling.

When shopping in any fashion store, goods are displayed and hung on hundreds of plastic hangers, but what happens to these when items are sold? Are they reused? Does the consumer take them away? Or are they simply thrown away? It is not only bricks and mortar retail that use garment hangers, despite items not being hung, ecommerce also sends out garments with accompanying plastic hangers. In 2019, 82 million plastic hangers were sent out with items ordered online. Luxury fashion retailers are also reliant on temporary hangers. Over 23 million hangers every year are effectively single-use plastic products, with hangers replaced by better quality, often branded alternatives when the products reach the point of retail. Many of these in-transit hangers are made of lightweight plastics, which are so cheap to produce that they are more cost effective to discard to landfill and produce new rather than recycle.

A report into the environmental impact of plastic garments commissioned by Arch and Hook in 2020 found that many hangers are utilized only to transport garments from factories to the shop floor. Arch & Hook are heavily invested in designing environmentally friendly garment hangers as a solution to current practices. The Dutch company design solution—wooden hangers—results in a product that they feel is an ecological and economic solution to put an end to the production of harmful products. They are FSC® (Forest Stewardship Council) certified and any plastic used in production is 99% recycled or recyclable. In a similar manner, Brainform, one of the largest garment hanger suppliers in the world has radically redesigned their business model from a linear throughput approach to a circular system that achieves 80% re-use. In 2014, the company re-used over one billion hangers. This change in business ethos and practice at such a large scale has been recognized as a footprint model by The Carbon Trust. There are many other inventive suppliers responding to fashion's need to eliminate single-use plastics, which has led to exciting product developments in the use of paper, natural materials as well as novel managed recycle and regenerate services. However, it must be recognized that no material is without associated environmental impact.

The common consumer response to overcome the impact of plastic is recycling. Every day we recycle many household items to prevent them from going to landfill. However, recycling hangers is very difficult due to different components being made from a variety of materials. Many hangers have the arms made from either plastic, or for higher-end, luxury stores sometimes wood, with the functional hook being produced from metal. Furthermore, some hangers also include small rubber grips at the end of the arms to increase functionality, introducing yet another material component. To separate these different elements, the hanger would more than likely have to be broken, posing

(Continued)

safety risks to the consumer. Although recycling hangers is more challenging than first perceived, many companies are initiating radical design thinking to find commercially feasible recycling and reuse system solutions.

Garment hangers in both retail and domestic settings are commonplace products, but in the shadow of fashion garments their impact on the planet is rarely considered. 130.6 billion items of clothing were produced globally in 2019, resulting in over 954 million hangers being utilized throughout the fashion supply chain. Conscientious consumerism requires fashion to employ design thinking to revolutionize historic business models. Lessons learned from reversing the overproduction and underusage of plastic-based products such as single-use hangers in fashion are a small element of a bigger environmental battle. However, these changes in re-evaluating established approaches can be used as a starting point for the application of design thinking principles to tackle a wider culture of overconsumption and underuse that is detrimental to the environment.

DISCUSSION QUESTIONS

1. As recycling many plastic garment hangers is not an option due to the use of multiple materials, what else could a consumer do to prevent these items ending up in landfill?

2. How could the fashion industry begin to innovate in their ways of using plastic garment hangers?

3. How can the principles of design thinking be applied to generate initiatives around single-plastic elimination, reuse, and recycling to allow the fashion sector to refashion for a sustainable future?

REFERENCES

Arch & Hook (2020) *The Environmental Impact of Plastic Hangers in the UK*. Arch & Hook, November 11. Available from https://archandhook.com/exclusive-hanger-research-report/ (accessed September 8, 2021).

Ellen MacArthur Foundation (2017) 'Achieving re-use at scale in the fast moving consumer goods sector'. https://web.archive.org/web/20210619052248/https://www.ellenmacarthurfoundation.org/case-studies/achieving-re-use-at-scale-in-the-fast-moving-consumer-goods-sector (accessed September 8, 2021).

Gould, R.K., Bratt, C., Mesquita, P.L. and Broman, G.I. (2019) 'Integrating sustainable development and design-thinking-based product design', in A.H. Hu, Matsumoto, M., Kuo, T.S. and Smith, S. (eds) *Technologies and Eco-innovation Towards Sustainability I*. Singapore: Springer. pp. 245–59.

Thompson, L. and Schonthal, D. (2020) 'The social psychology of design thinking', *California Management Review*, 62 (2): 84–99.

Shelton Group (2019) 'Waking the sleeping giant. What middle America knows about plastic waste and how they're taking action', *Shelton Group*. https://sheltongrp.com/work/circularity-2019-special-report-waking-the-sleeping-giant (accessed September 8, 2021).

NOTES

1. Friedman, V. (2019) 'You too can play the handbag stock market', *The New York Times,* October 24. www. nytimes.com/2019/10/24/style/rebag-clair-handbag-stock-market.html (accessed September 8, 2021).

2. Barker, E. (2011) Here's the real reason women buy makeup', *Business Insider*, July 23. www. businessinsider.com/do-women-buy-cosmetics-because-theyre-useful-or-because-they-make-them-feel-good-2011-7 (accessed October 20, 2021).

3. Abraham-Murali, L. and Littrell, M.A. (1995) 'Consumers' conceptualization of apparel attributes', *Clothing and Textiles Research Journal*, 13 (2): 65–74.

    Jegethesan, K., Sneddon, J.N. and Soutar, G.N. (2012) 'Young Australian consumers' preferences for fashion apparel attributes', *Journal of Fashion Marketing and Management: An International Journal*, 16 (3): 275–89.

    Park, E.J., Kim, E.Y., Funches, V.M. and Foxx, W. (2012) 'Apparel product attributes, web browsing, and e-impulse buying on shopping websites', *Journal of Business Research*, 65 (11): 1583–9.

4. Forney, J.C., Pelton, W., Caton, S.T. and Rabolt, N.J. (1999) 'Country of origin and evaluative criteria: Influences on women's apparel purchase decisions', *Journal of Family and Consumer Sciences*, 91 (4): 57.

    Myers, J.H. and Shocker, A.D. (1981) 'The nature of product-related attributes', *Research in Marketing*, 5 (5): 211–36.

    Nieroda, M.E., Mrad, M. and Solomon, M.R. (2018) 'How do consumers think about hybrid products? Computer wearables have an identity problem', *Journal of Business Research*, 89: 159–70.

    Park, E.J., Kim, E.Y., Funches, V.M. and Foxx, W. (2012) 'Apparel product attributes, web browsing, and e-impulse buying on shopping websites', *Journal of Business Research*, 65 (11): 1583–9.

    Zhang, Z., Li, Y., Gong, C. and Wu, H. (2002) 'Casual wear product attributes: A Chinese consumers' perspective', *Journal of Fashion Marketing and Management: An International Journal*, 6 (1): 53–62.

5. Dubois, B., Laurent, G. and Czellar, S. (2001) 'Consumer rapport to luxury: Analyzing complex and ambivalent attitudes', (No. 736)., *HEC Paris*. Available from https://ideas.repec.org/p/ebg/heccah/0736. html (accessed September 8, 2021).

6. Godey, B., Pederzoli, D., Aiello, G., Donvito, R., Chan, P., Oh, H., Singh, R., Skorobogatykh, I., Tsuchiya, J. and Weitz, B. (2012) 'Brand and country-of-origin effect on consumers' decision to purchase luxury products', *Journal of Business Research*, 65 (10): 1461–70.

    Kawabata, H. and Rabolt, N.J. (1999) 'Comparison of clothing purchase behaviour between US and Japanese female university students', *Journal of Consumer Studies & Home Economics*, 23 (4): 213–23.

7. Beaudoin, P., Lachance, M.J. and Robitaille, J. (2003) 'Fashion innovativeness, fashion diffusion and brand sensitivity among adolescents', *Journal of Fashion Marketing and Management: An International Journal*, 7 (1): 23–30.

    Phau, I. and Lo, C.C. (2004) 'Profiling fashion innovators', *Journal of Fashion Marketing and Management: An International Journal*, 8 (4): 399–411.

8. Michael, S., Bamossy, G. and Askegaard, S. (2002) *Consumer Behaviour: A European Perspective*. London: Pearson.

9. Moorman, C. (2018). 'Why Apple is still a great marketer and what you can learn', *Forbes*, January 12. www.forbes.com/sites/christinemoorman/2018/01/12/why-apple-is-still-a-great-marketer-and-what-you-can-learn/?sh=5a3eb99115bd (accessed October 20, 2021).

10. Cadei, E. (2002) 'Cleaning up: S.F. duo putting a shine on its product line', *San Francisco Business Times,* December 8. www.bizjournals.com/sanfrancisco/stories/2002/12/09/smallb1.html (accessed September 8, 2021).

11. Reimann, M., Zaichkowsky, J., Neuhaus, C., Bender, T. and Weber, B. (2010) 'Aesthetic package design: A behavioral, neural, and psychological investigation', *Journal of Consumer Psychology*, 20 (4): 431–41.

12. Forrest, S. (2020) 'How Billie Eilish accidentally became famous', *Showbiz Cheat Sheet*, February 4. www. cheatsheet.com/entertainment/how-billie-eilish-accidentally-became-famous.html/ (accessed September 8, 2021).

13. Macdonald, K. (2020) 'No Time to Die soundtrack: What's the music in the new Bond film and when is it released?', *Classic FM*, October 2. www.classicfm.com/music-news/james-bond-no-time-to-die-trailer-soundtrack/ (accessed September 8, 2021).

14. Sproles, G.B. and Burns, L.D. (1994) *Changing Appearances: Understanding Dress in Contemporary Society*. New York, NY: Fairchild.

15. Arnould, E.J. (1989) 'Toward a broadened theory of preference formation and the diffusion of innovations: Cases from Zinder Province, Niger Republic', *Journal of Consumer Research*, 16 (2): 239–67.

16. Rogers, E.M. and Shoemaker, F.F. (1971) *Communication of Innovations; A Cross-Cultural Approach*. New York, NY: The Free Press.

17. Gatignon, H. and Robertson, T.S. (1985) 'A propositional inventory for new diffusion research', *Journal of Consumer Research*, 11 (4): 849–67.

18. Petromilli, M., Morrison, D. and Million, M. (2002) 'Brand architecture: Building brand portfolio value', *Strategy & Leadership*, 30 (5): 22–28.

    Yu, J. (2021) 'A model of brand architecture choice: A house of brands vs. a branded house', *Marketing Science*, 40 (1): 147–67.

19. Leijerholt, U., Chapleo, C. and O'Sullivan, H. (2019) 'A brand within a brand: an integrated understanding of internal brand management and brand architecture in the public sector', *Journal of Brand Management*, 26 (3): 277–90.

20. Chun, H.H., Park, C.W., Eisingerich, A.B. and MacInnis, D.J. (2015) 'Strategic benefits of low fit brand extensions: When and why?', *Journal of Consumer Psychology*, 25 (4): 577–95.

    Dall'Olmo Riley, F., Pina, J.M. and Bravo, R. (2015) 'The role of perceived value in vertical brand extensions of luxury and premium brands', *Journal of Marketing Management*, 31 (7–8): 881–913.

    Eren-Erdogmus, I., Akgun, I. and Arda, E. (2018) 'Drivers of successful luxury fashion brand extensions: Cases of complement and transfer extensions', *Journal of Fashion Marketing and Management: An International Journal*, 22 (4): 454–75.

    Phau, I., Matthiesen, I.M. and Shimul, A.S. (2020) 'Is HUGO still the BOSS? Investigating the reciprocal effects of brand extensions on brand personality of luxury brands', *Australasian Marketing Journal (AMJ)*. https://doi.org/10.1016/j.ausmj.2020.02.003

    Stankeviciute, R. and Hoffmann, J. (2020) 'The impact of brand extension on the parent luxury fashion brand: The cases of Giorgio Armani, Calvin Klein and Jimmy Choo. A retrospective commentary', *Journal of Global Fashion Marketing*, 11 (1): 90–97.

    Eren-Erdogmus, I., Akgun, I. and Arda, E. (2018) 'Drivers of successful luxury fashion brand extensions: Cases of complement and transfer extensions', *Journal of Fashion Marketing and Management: An International Journal*, 22 (4): 454–75.

21. Brexendorf, T.O. and Keller, K.L. (2017) 'Leveraging the corporate brand: The importance of corporate brand innovativeness and brand architecture', *European Journal of Marketing*, 51 (9/10): 1530–51.

22. Team, T. (2016) 'Why have Ralph Lauren's licensing revenues been declining in recent years?' *Forbes*, May 5. www.forbes.com/sites/greatspeculations/2016/05/05/why-have-ralph-laurens-licensing-revenues-been-declining-in-recent-years/?sh=6ab4d1ba7e6a (accessed October 20, 2021).

23. Reuters (2019) 'Next to replace Debenhams as Ted Baker's kidswear license partner', *Business of Fashion*, August 16. www.businessoffashion.com/articles/retail/next-to-replace-debenhams-as-ted-bakers-kidswear-license-partner (accessed September 8, 2021).

24. Ritchie, A. (2020) 'Pure play vs. Omnichannel Ecommerce: What's best for your store?', *Shogun*, September 3. https://getshogun.com/learn/pure-play-omnichannel-ecommerce (accessed September 8, 2021).

25. Mrad, M., Farah, M.F. and Haddad, S. (2019) 'From Karl Lagerfeld to Erdem: A series of collaborations between designer luxury brands and fast-fashion brands', *Journal of Brand Management*, 26 (5): 567–82.

26. O'Connor, T. (2019). 'Jo Malone founder is teaming up with Zara on new fragrance line', *Business of Fashion*, November 15. www.businessoffashion.com/articles/beauty/jo-malone-jo-loves-zara-emotions-fragrance (accessed September 8, 2021).

27. Chitrakorn, K. (2021) 'What Gucci's new look means for fashion', *Vogue Business,* April 16. www.voguebusiness.com/fashion/what-guccis-new-look-means-for-fashion-kering-balenciaga (accessed September 8, 2021).

28. Ahmed, O. (2017) 'As branding evolves, what's a Logo worth?', *Business of Fashion*, July 29. www.businessoffashion.com/articles/news-analysis/as-branding-evolves-whats-a-logo-worth (accessed September 8, 2021).

29. Stanley, J. (2018) 'Why do all new fashion logos look the same?', *Hypebeast*, September 20. https://hypebeast.com/2018/9/fashion-logo-balenciaga-celine-calvin-klein-burberry (accessed September 8, 2021).

30. Jiang, Y., Gorn, G.J., Galli, M. and Chattopadhyay, A. (2016) 'Does your company have the right logo? How and why circular – and angular – logo shapes influence brand attribute judgments', *Journal of Consumer Research*, 42 (5): 709–26.

    Pantin-Sohier, G. (2009) 'The influence of the product package on functional and symbolic associations of brand image', *Recherche et Applications en Marketing (English Edition)*, 24 (2): 53–71.

31. Paish, C. (2019) 'Top 10 of the world's most famous logos and what you can learn from them', *99designs*. https://99designs.com/blog/logo-branding/famous-logos/ (accessed September 8, 2021).

32. Bloomberg (2019) 'Adidas trademarked stripes can't go sideways, EU judges rule', *Business of Fashion,* June 19. www.businessoffashion.com/articles/news-analysis/adidas-trademarked-stripes-cant-go-sideways-eu-judges-rule (accessed September 8, 2021).

33. Chen, C. (2020) 'How to build the retail customer service dream team', *Business of Fashion*, January 8. www.businessoffashion.com/articles/retail/retail-customer-service-sales-associates/ (accessed September 8, 2021).

34. Bloomberg (2019) 'Rent the Runway pays angry customers $200 after service failures', *Business of Fashion*, September 27. www.businessoffashion.com/articles/retail/rent-the-runway-pays-angry-customers-200-after-service-failures (accessed September 8, 2021).

35. Patagonia (2021) Exchanges, returns and repairs. www.patagonia.com/repair-details.html (accessed September 8, 2021).

36. BoF Team (2013) 'The basics, part 8: Marketing', *Business of Fashion,* July 12. www.businessoffashion.com/articles/news-analysis/the-basics-part-8-marketing (accessed September 8, 2021).

37. Bianchi, F., Dupreelle, P., Krueger, F., Seara, J., Watten, D. and Willersdorf, S. (2020) 'Fashion's big reset', *Boston Consulting Group,* June 1. www.bcg.com/publications/2020/fashion-industry-reset-covid (accessed September 8, 2021).

38. Selfridges Rental (2021) 'Rent womenswear', *Selfridges.com*. https://www.selfridges.com/GB/en/features/project-earth/rent/ (accessed September 8, 2021).

39. Osborne, H. (2020) 'Never knowingly under-leased – John Lewis moves to rent out its furniture', *The Guardian,* August 15. www.theguardian.com/business/2020/aug/15/never-knowingly-under-leased-john-lewis-moves-to-rent-out-its-furniture (accessed September 8, 2021).

40. Solomon, M.R., Marshall, G. and Stuart, E. (2021) *Marketing: Real People, Real Choices* (10th edition), Hoboken, NJ: Pearson.

41. Ilvento, C. (1996) *Profit Planning and Decision Making in the Hospitality Industry*. Dubuque, IA: Kendall/Hunt.

42. McKenna, B. (2017) 'Razor-and-blade model: What is it? What companies have one?', *The Motley Fool,* January 13. www.fool.com/investing/2017/01/13/razor-and-blade-model-what-is-it-what-companies-ha.aspx (accessed September 8, 2021).

43. Baskin, B. (2018) 'Why Chanel is raising prices on its most popular bags', *Business of Fashion*, October 28. www.businessoffashion.com/articles/china/why-chanel-is-raising-prices-on-its-most-popular-bags (accessed September 8, 2021).

CHAPTER 11
Fashion Marketing Communications

LEARNING OBJECTIVES

After you read this chapter, you will understand the answers to the following:

1. What are the basic components of the communication process?

2. What determines whether the source of a promotional message will be effective?

3. What are the different ways that marketers can design their messages?

4. What are the different promotional mix tools a brand can use to communicate with fashion consumers?

Before the Internet opened the door for a legion of amateur fashion influencers, apparel companies relied upon emerging and established celebrities to promote their brands. Calvin Klein has a long history of provocative advertising campaigns. His most famous ad in 1981 helped to establish the brand's racy personality. It featured the 15-year-old actress Brooke Shields, who posed in a pair of super-tight jeans as she asked the flirtatious question: "Do you know what comes between me and my Calvins? Nothing." Since that time, we've seen a long series of attention-grabbing images of both male and female celebrities posing seductively in jeans, lingerie or tight-fitting underwear. Brooke Shields even made a second appearance thirty-seven years after her original iconic ad in a scanty lingerie shot.

In more recent years the #MyCalvins campaign has focused on social media-savvy celebs that are the darlings of the next generation, such as Kendall Jenner, A$AP Rocky and Shawn Mendes. The campaign tries to personalize the celebrities by picturing them in their underwear in domestic settings, intended to give viewers the feeling that they are alone with them in their private lives. A press release explained that the ad campaign intends to evoke a "… 'coming-of-age concept' focused

(Continued)

around 'universal truths of curiosity, companionship, sexual exploration and the spirit of rebellion.'"[1] These images have appeared on a range of platforms, including billboards, print ads, and on digital ads in Instagram, Facebook, YouTube, and TikTok.

The most recent wave of celebrities to appear expands the celebrity roster a bit more to include a more diverse set of stars. One of these is the supermodel Naomi Campbell, who had never modeled for Calvin Klein before. Others include Bella Hadid, Diplo, Odell Beckham Jr., Lay Zhang, Jelly Lin, and Hayley Foster. They pose for their webcams as they watch TV, eat snacks, and dance… almost like real people except for the amazing bodies they reveal in their Calvins. A 2019 press release stated, "The campaign brings to life the playful and pure perspective of sexy; one that encourages self-expression and underscores the idea that sexy is a state of mind."[2]

The Elements of Communications

Sexy may be a "state of mind," but it sure seems to sell a lot of underwear for Calvin Klein. Like this famous series of ads, most fashion communication is visual, or nonverbal. Consumers receive this information from impersonal sources such as the media (for example, magazines and the Internet), but they also gain a lot of information from personal sources such as people around them, including friends, family, salespeople and, sometimes more importantly—people on the street.

In this chapter, we'll begin with a discussion of the basic components of communication. We will also review some of the factors that help determine the effectiveness of communication devices. Then we will move on to discuss the different forms of promotional mix elements, a marketing technique to communicate with target audience.

Marketers and advertisers have traditionally tried to understand how marketing messages can change consumers' attitudes by thinking in terms of the **communications model**, which specifies that a number of elements are necessary for communication to be achieved. In this model, a *sender* must choose and encode a message (that is, initiate the transfer of meaning by choosing appropriate symbols that represent that meaning).

This meaning must be put in the form of a *message*. There are many ways to communicate something, and the structure of the message has a big effect on how it is perceived. The visual images of well-known designers and celebrities say a thousand words about the trendiness of today's fashions.

The message must be transmitted via a *channel* or *medium*, which for companies wanting to communicate with consumers could be television, radio, magazines, billboards, personal contact, or electronic communication channels such as email, websites, and social media platforms. The message is then decoded by one or more *receivers* (e.g., fashion consumers) who interpret it in light of their own experiences. Finally, *feedback* must be received by the source, who uses the reactions of receivers to modify aspects of the message. Many websites collect such information from its subscribers and visitors. The traditional communication process is depicted in Figure 11.1.

Chopard, the Swiss luxury watches and jewelry manufacturer, has launched the Happy Diamonds movie on its Instagram IGTV channel, directed by Xavier Dolan to communicate with fashion consumers regarding its diamond watch. The message includes "diamonds are happier when they are free!". To communicate this message, Julia Roberts was featured in the ad that was posted on the official Instagram account of Chopard.[3]

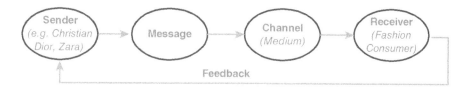

FIGURE 11.1 Communication model

In personal communications, the process is similar. The person sends a message, which can be verbal, such as a discussion about fashion trends, or nonverbal, through the medium of appearance or gestures. Another person receives this information, and then reacts to that message and consequently sends feedback to the sender. The sender may then adjust the message if the feedback dictates (for example, feedback such as, "You look tired today," in response to a nonverbal appearance message might precipitate the addition of make-up on the part of the sender).

Much of fashion communication falls within the realm of personal communication, both verbal and nonverbal. Fashion-oriented people talk to others about the latest trends or the best stores to shop at. An early study in this area emphasized the importance of opinion leaders (as we discussed in Chapter 9) in fashion decisions for online products and services. It is reported that 71% of people are more likely to purchase something online because it was recommended by others. This may be because Millennials distrust traditional advertising. This generation only tend to have faith in what individuals of their age or influencers they place trust in and social status say, generally seeking their opinions for validation.[4] As for Gen Zs, they believe that "I can take the concept of social media, but I can now filter. So I can listen to my friends and family when I feel like they're credible on the topic, but I also have means by which I can access influencers and experts that have points of view in this space that might align with mine."[5]

Visual observation is equally important in the communication of fashion. We consciously or unconsciously observe other people around us when we speak with them, or just see others around us. The mass media serve not only as direct persuasion, but as non-promotional communication through television programs, movies, and magazines by virtue of their visual content.

Hollywood's leading ladies have left their mark on fashion throughout the history of movies and TV. For example, "the

Audrey Hepburn, *Breakfast at Tiffany's*, playing Holly Golightly

Ralf Liebhold / Shutterstock.com

little black dress may have been introduced by Coco Chanel, but it was Audrey Hepburn who made the garment famous in the film *Breakfast at Tiffany's*".[6]

In 1934, the American actor Clark Gable single-handedly crashed sales of T-shirts at that time. In the comedy movie *It Happened One Night* he appeared bare-chested (a scandalous thing to do at that time). This fashion statement resulted in a reduction of 75% in T-shirt sales as American males tried to emulate the look.[7] Elizabeth Taylor ("The Queen of Diamonds"), exhaled a hint of magic wherever she appeared with "plunging necklines, furwraps, feather boas, and eye-catching headpieces".[8] Other silver screen icons from days past include Greta Garbo, Marlene Dietrich, Rita Hayworth with her strapless black satin gown, Esther Williams's bathing suits, Lucille Ball's shirtdress, Katherine Hepburn's trousers, Marilyn Monroe, Faye Dunaway's Bonnie and Clyde wardrobe, Diane Keaton's *Annie Hall* androgynous look, Mia Farrow's Great Gatsby femininity, Jennifer Aniston and Lisa Kudrow on *Friends*, Alicia Silverstone in Clueless, JLo, Madonna's cone bra, and so on and so on.

Changing Attitudes Through Marketing Communications

Marketing communication is more formalized than personal communication, and much effort, research, and expense is put into the process to ensure that consumers receive clear messages from senders. Consumers are constantly bombarded by messages inducing them to change their attitudes. These persuasion attempts can range from logical arguments to graphic pictures, and from intimidation by peers to exhortations by celebrity spokespeople. And communications flow both ways—the consumer may seek out information sources in order to learn more about these options.

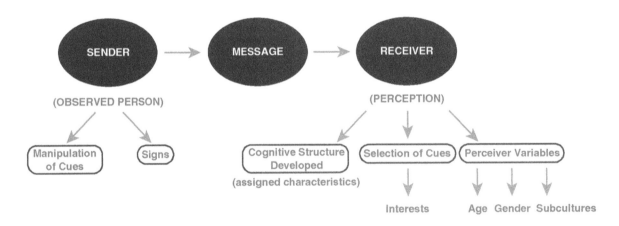

FIGURE 11.2   Appearance communication process

Tactical Communications Decisions

Suppose a high-profile apparel company wants to create an advertising campaign for a new fashion line targeted at young people. As it plans this campaign, it must develop a message that will create desire for the item by potential customers. To craft persuasive messages that might persuade some-one to purchase the product instead of the many other options available, we must answer several questions:

- Who will be shown wearing the fashion items in the ad? A well-known fashion model? A career woman? A K-Pop singer? The source of a message helps to determine consumers' acceptance of it as well as their desire to try the product.

- How should we construct the message? Should it highlight the negative consequences of being left out when others are wearing the garment, and you're still wearing last year's stuff? Should it directly compare itself with others already on the market or maybe present a fantasy in which a sexy young woman meets a dashing stranger on a romantic island?

- What media should transmit the message? Should it be depicted in a print ad? On television? On a billboard? On a website? On Instagram? On Tik Tok? If a print ad is produced, should it run in the pages of *Vogue*? *Cosmopolitan*? *Nylon*? Sometimes *where* something is said can be as important as *what* is said. Ideally, the attributes of the product should be matched to those of the medium.

- What features of the target market might impact the ad's acceptance? If targeted users are frus-trated in their daily lives, they might be more receptive to a fantasy appeal. If they're status ori-ented, maybe a commercial should show bystanders swooning with admiration as a famous actress walks by wearing the garment.

An Updated Model: Interactive Communications

Although the traditional communication model we discussed earlier is not wrong, it also doesn't communicate the whole story—particularly in our vibrant world of engagement, where consumers have a wide number of available options and greater control over which messages they will select to process.[9]

Actually, a popular strategy we call **permission marketing** is based on the idea that a marketer will be much more successful in persuading consumers who have agreed to see or hear about what they have to say. Consumers who "opt out" of listening to the message probably weren't good pros-pects in the first place.[10] On the other hand, those who say they are interested in learning more are likely to be sympathetic to marketing communications they have selected to see or hear. Consumers do not need to sit there and receive all communications; however, they have complete freedom in deciding what messages they may want to see and at what time.

The traditional model was developed to understand mass communications, where information is transferred from a producer (source) to many consumers (receivers) at one time—typically via print, television, or radio. This view basically perceives advertising as the process of conveying information to the consumer before performing a sales transaction. A message is seen as perishable—it is repeated (perhaps frequently) for a period of time and then it "vanishes" as a new campaign replaces it. In this view, the media exert direct and powerful effects on individuals and often are used by those in power to brainwash and exploit them. The receiver is basically a passive being—a "couch potato" who simply is the receptacle for many messages—who is often duped or persuaded to act based on the information they are 'fed" by the media.

Is this an accurate picture of the way we relate to marketing communications today? Proponents of **uses and gratifications theory** argue instead that consumers are an active, goal-directed audience that draws on mass media as a resource to satisfy needs. Instead of asking what media do for or to people, they ask what people *do* with the media.[11] The uses and gratifications approach emphasizes that media compete with other sources to satisfy needs and that these needs include diversion and entertainment as well as information.[12]

This also means that the line between marketing information and entertainment continues to blur, especially as companies are being forced to design more attractive retail outlets and websites in order to attract consumers. **Retailtainment** refers to the process of merging retail shopping and entertainment together, a mounting trend in fashion retailing where brands are tempted to offer in-store customer experiences.[13]

For example, the e-commerce luxury retailer Farfetch offers unique in-store experiences. In its retail store in London, Farfetch offers RFID-enabled apparel racks that identify the items a shopper looks at, and auto-populates these into the shopper's wishlist, touch-screen-enriched mirrors that allow the shopper to view the wishlist, and if s/he buys the garment s/he uses a mobile payment platform similar to the Apple Wallet. Farfetch has been called "The Retailer of the Future" because the retailer provides an easy, enjoyable experience that brings together the best parts of in-store shopping with the rapidity and convenience of online buying.[14] Similarly, the famous shoe brand TOMS placed VR headsets into 100 stores, allowing shoppers to virtually experience a trip to Peru and examine the influence on local people when they participate in the One for One giving campaign.[15]

The infusion of marketing images into daily life is illustrated by the popularity of the Hello Kitty characters, one of the most popular characters in Japan, that have popped up on everything from tofu dishes to telephones. This craze originated in Japan and then spread across and into the United States; the Sanrio company earns over a billion dollars from Hello Kitty products annually. When a Taiwanese bank put Hello Kitty on its credit cards, the lines to get these items were so long many people thought there was a banking crisis. In 2018, Japan's JR West train company unveiled its new Hello Kitty-themed Shinkansen bullet train that operates between Hakata and Shin-Osaka.[16] Clearly, marketing ideas and products serve as sources of gratification for many—even while others scratch their heads and try to figure out why!

Hello Kitty bullet train interior, Japan

ItzaVU / Shutterstock.com

Who's in Charge of the Remote?

Whether for good or bad, exciting technological and social developments certainly force us to rethink the picture of the passive consumer, with people becoming to a greater extent partners—rather than passive recipients—in the communications process. Their input is helping to shape the messages that they and others like them receive, and furthermore they may seek out these messages rather than sit home and wait to see them on TV or in the paper. This updated approach to interactive communications is illustrated in Figure 11.3. A web browser gives us the ability to request information about products, and even to give recommendations to product designers and market researchers.

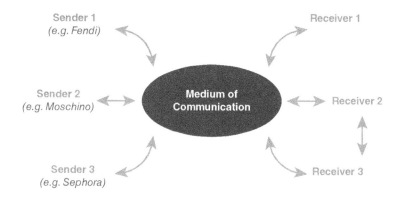

FIGURE 11.3 Interactive communication

The Message Source

Regardless of whether a message is sent by postal mail or email, if the same word is articulated or transcribed by different people it can have very different effects. Researchers have looked at **source effects** for more than 70 years. By ascribing the same message to different sources and assessing the degree of attitude change that happens after individuals listen to it, researchers can determine what aspects of a communicator will induce attitude change.[17]

A compelling source makes it more likely that the target audience will accept the message. This effect helps to explain the millions that celebrities earn when they decide to endorse products. The source can be selected because they are an expert, attractive, renowned, or even a "typical" consumer who is both likable and trustworthy. Two predominantly essential source features are *credibility* and *attractiveness*.[18]

Source Credibility

Source credibility refers to a source's perceived expertise, objectivity or honesty. This feature is linked to consumers' perception of a source's competence to provide the information they need to make a good decision.[19] If the product turns out to be shoddy or unattractive, consumers generate a negative attitude toward the brand and also the endorser.[20]

Recent studies indicate that Millennials don't trust endorsements or any of the more traditional, one-way communications techniques. They're even increasingly distrusting "influencers," and are starting to doubt their credibility. This skepticism is greatly due to the glut of fake posts that have plagued celebrities over the past few years.[21] For example, for the sake of becoming more credible, a number of influencers have been found sharing fake sponsored posts on their social media feeds just to give the impression that brands have sponsored them. These behaviors have made people trust them less.[22]

Building Credibility

Credibility can be enhanced if the source's qualifications are perceived as relevant to the product being endorsed. The #MyCalvins campaign includes young celebrities who are widely admired by Millennials and Gen Z consumers, so they create the desired impact for Calvin Klein. For some products, a salesperson may achieve credibility by dressing in the role of an expert. One study reported that a source appropriately dressed for the task demonstrated in an advertisement and pictured in an appropriate setting was assigned significantly higher credibility and intent-to-purchase ratings than for those not appropriately dressed.[23]

We often see sales associates wearing the clothing their store sells. In fact, displaying the clothes on a live person is perhaps the best way to help customers envision the product on themselves as opposed to viewing items on a rack, especially fashion items (e.g., outlandish and very trendy ones) that are not very appealing to a mass retail market. Retailers often encourage sales associates to wear their product by offering generous discounts; some actually have a garment program in which associates change into certain items set aside for them to wear during the hours they are on the sales floor working with customers.

Most glamorous celebrities are credible sources to sell expensive designer clothing; they may, in fact, be a large part of the limited market for such goods! Many of the actresses who attend the Academy Awards have had a gown made especially for them, and often the designers get invaluable publicity when famous people wear their clothes that night.

Mainstream luxury brands from Gucci to Dior have long relied upon the power of celebrity dressing (clothing, accessories and beauty) to construct their brands and improve their sales. According to Tamara Mellon, co-founder and former chief of Jimmy Choo, "A magazine feature [can] reach hundreds of thousands of potential customers for a fashion brand," but "The way to reach a billion? Dress the actresses competing for attention at a highly televised event."

Emerging brands can also benefit from celebrities and try to get to their stylists, who are driven to find fresh design talent to meet the constant demand for the type of new looks that allow celebrities to build their personal brands based on uniqueness and differentiation.[24]

Not only do celebrities give credibility to the designer's work and to the look, but also the designer confers credibility by virtue of their celebrity and reputation. For instance, the shoe brand Aquazzura, founded in 2011, is not a household name yet, but the brand became more famous since Meghan Markle became obsessed with the brand and wore it to several public occasions such as her engagement and wedding.[25]

Source Biases

A consumer's beliefs about a product's features can be diminished if the source is perceived to be biased in giving information.[26] **Knowledge bias** means that a source's knowledge about a given topic is not accurate. **Reporting bias** happens when a source has the necessary knowledge, but their readiness to express it truthfully is compromised, as when a star athlete is paid by a brand to consume its products, such as tennis shoes, exclusively. Although their credentials might be correct, the fact that the source is perceived as a "hired gun" compromises credibility. The reputation of the retailer who sells the product has a major influence on message credibility. Products sold by respected and well-known quality stores seem to carry the added endorsement (and implicit guarantee) of the store itself: "If Harrods carries it, it must be good."

The aura of credibility generated by reputable retail advertising reinforces the manufacturer's message as well. The reputation of the *medium* that carries the communication also enhances or diminishes the credibility of the advertiser. The image of a prestige fashion magazine such as *Elle* or *Vogue* confers added status to the product being advertised.

Source Attractiveness

Source attractiveness refers to a source's perceived social value. This quality can emanate from the person's physical appearance, personality, social status, or similarity to the receiver (we like to listen to people who are like us). Almost everywhere we turn, beautiful people are trying to persuade us to purchase or act in a certain way (for more on source attractiveness see also[27]).

Our society places a very high premium on physical attractiveness, and we tend to assume that people who are good-looking are smarter, cooler, and happier. Such an assumption is called a **halo effect**, which happens when individuals who rank high on one aspect are expected to outshine on others as well. This notion has been termed the "what is beautiful is good" stereotype.[28]

Star Power: Celebrities as Communications Sources

Celebrity endorsers don't come cheap, but many advertisers continue to believe in their effectiveness. One study found that famous faces capture attention and are processed more efficiently by the brain than "ordinary" faces.[29] Celebrities for whom people have positive attitudes, attract an audience's attention more easily than a normal ad, increase awareness of a firm's advertising and enhance both company image and brand attitudes.[30] Advertisements that use a celebrity, about whom many people already have positive feelings and impulses, grab an audience's attention more easily than a standard ad. In addition, a celebrity endorsement strategy can be an effective way to differentiate among similar products.

One reason for this effectiveness is that consumers are better able to identify products that are associated with a spokesperson. Some pop stars have a spokesperson or licensing deals with beauty companies such as Julia Roberts for Lancôme, Beyoncé for L'Oréal, and Katy Perry for Cover Girl. To celebrate Calvin Klein's fiftieth anniversary, the brand launched a campaign ad featuring Justin Bieber, the face of Calvin Klein, alongside his wife Hailey Bieber, in their first campaign together.[31]

Also, personal appearances by designers (who often are celebrities) can be effective advertising for their company **Trunk shows**—in which an entire line of merchandise is brought to a store and shown to its best customers who special order items—have become very successful for designers and retailers. These are often coupled with special appearances by the designer. For example, the renowned second youngest creative director in France, Olivier Rousteing has participated at several trunk shows at select retailers.[32]

Celebrities who scored very high in recent years according to Q Score Index

Tinseltown / Shutterstock.com

A market research company created one extensively used measure known as the **Q Score** (Q stands for "quality") to decide if a celebrity will make a good endorser. This rating considers two factors: consumers' level of familiarity with a name and the number of respondents who indicate that a person, program, or character is a favorite. The company evaluates approximately 1,500 celebrities each year.

Another instrument to measure consumers' perceptions of celebrities, the Davie-Brown Index (DBI), was developed in 2006 by Repucom and The Marketing Arm, a promotion agency known as the principal buyer of celebrity talent. This index is similar to the Q score, but it does more than assess awareness itself.[33] It is based on the following criteria: appeal, notice, trendsetting, influence, trust, endorsement, aspiration, and awareness.[34] Some celebrities who scored very high in recent years include (as you might expect) Taylor Swift, Justin Timberlake, Lady Gaga, Katy Perry, and Beyoncé.[35]

The Message

The most important feature when it comes to a message is to determine whether the communication differentiates the brand from others. In other words, did it stress a unique attribute of the product or perhaps elicit a certain kind of fantasy or mood?

In their advertisements, luxury brands differentiate themselves from mass-market and premium brands by creating desire based on enrichment and building dreams. **Enrichment** is a form of storytelling that takes consumers on a journey toward the destination of desire. An example is the Chanel brand, which offers its consumers the opportunity to listen and watch carefully curated, animated videos on its website, exposing different aspects of the brand's foundations, which all make up a part of Chanel's voice, and pride in the brand's heritage.[36]

Or think of the advertisement by Hermès that showed a lady living in Paris and walking through the streets with a horse, a main symbol for Hermès that refers to its heritage in saddlery. To generate desire, marketers need to drive their shoppers to dream and take them to an eccentric journey that only imagination can spark. Going back to Hermès, the brand usually displays the illustration of a tree and a butterfly, which is a repetitive motif for Hermès. A butterfly is a very delicate, temporary animal, while the tree is a rather eternal part of nature. A dialogue between endurance and ephemerality develops.[37]

The illustration of a tree and a butterfly, a repetitive motif for Hermès in its ads

Image Courtesy of The Advertising Archives

In order to design the right message, you should clearly think of how the message is said as well as what is said. Some of the issues facing marketers include the following:

- *Should the message be sent in words or pictures?* Visual stimuli can have a big effect (especially for fashion products of course!), particularly when the communicator wants to impact receivers' emotional responses.[38] Marketers usually focus on bright and creative images or photography.

Image ads from Benetton, Nike, Louis Vuitton, Balmain, and Ralph Lauren have no text other than the company name; however, they successfully convey powerful images. However, an image is not always the most effective at communicating actual information. The verbal form impacts ratings of the functional features of a product, while the visual form impacts aesthetic assessments. Verbal features are more effective when combined with a picture, especially if the image is **framed** (the message in the picture is highly linked to the copy).[39]

Verbal messages are most suitable for high-involvement contexts, such as in print forms where the receiver is driven to really pay attention to the ads. As verbal forms decay faster in memory, repeated exposures are required to attain the anticipated impact. Visual forms, however, permit the receiver to *chunk* information (gather slight pieces of information into larger ones) at the time of encoding. This process leads to a stronger memory trace that helps retrieval of information with time.[40]

- How many times should the message be repeated? Repetition can be a two-edged sword for marketers. As we saw in Chapter 7, multiple exposures to a stimulus are usually necessary for conditioned learning to happen. This is known as the **mere exposure phenomenon.**[41] Fashion magazines often repeat similar ads after a few pages, sometimes on the very next page. Positive effects for advertising repetition have been shown to boost consumers' awareness of the brand.[42] However, too much repetition can lead to **habituation**, whereby the consumer no longer pays attention to the stimulus out of exhaustion or boredom.

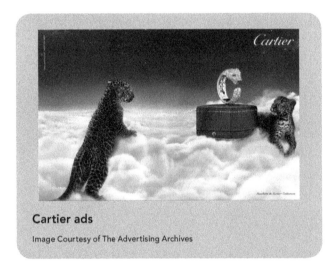

Cartier ads

Image Courtesy of The Advertising Archives

Too much exposure can result in **advertising wearout**, negatively affecting individuals' reaction to an ad.[43] The **two-factor theory** (repetition heightens familiarity but can also generate boredom) means that marketers can overcome this issue by reducing the amount of exposure time per repetition (such as using fifteen-second TV spots) (see also[44]). They can also preserve familiarity and relieve boredom by somewhat changing the content of ads over time for campaigns that have a common theme.[45] For example, Cartier keeps showing a panther, as one of the brand's signature motifs, in most of its ads but in different ways.

- *Should both sides of an argument be offered?* Most messages stress positive attributes about the product or motives to purchase; these are known as **supportive arguments**. An alternative is a **two-sided message**, in which both positive and negative information are offered. Studies revealed that two-sided ads can be effective under some circumstances—especially when the receiver is looking for a balanced presentation to be assured that a message is not overly biased, yet they are not widely used.[46]

- *How should the message be expressed?* The *way* something is said can be as significant as what is said—the same idea can be encoded in many different ways. It can tug at the heartstrings, scare you, make you laugh, make you cry, or make you want to know more. The major types of **message appeals** available to communicators are as follows:

○ **Emotional versus Rational Appeals** refers to where the appeal should be targeted, to the head or to the heart? When appropriately adopted, emotions can facilitate consumers' understanding and reception of an advertising message. Marketers should focus on whether the target consumer really needs an emotional appeal. For example, "an individual interested in a new in-home styling kit for her hair may simply need to be informed that L'Oréal has released a new product that works with ease. Put simply, a brand does not always need to elicit emotion in the consumer to produce a desired response". Therefore, the customer might be looking for a rational appeal. However, if the marketer realizes that the target market needs an emotional reason to choose a brand, the subsequent question might be whether to convey a positive or a negative one. If the brand decides to use a positive appeal, it needs to make sure that the message is authentic and true. Think of Google's "Parisian love" campaign, a love story through an evolution of Google searches: Studying overseas in Paris, translation of sentences, and locating a church. The campaign was very successful and amassed a lot of media attention.[47]

So, which is better, an emotional or a rational appeal? The answer depends upon the nature of the product and the relationship consumers have with the product/brand. The exact impact of rational versus emotional appeals is hard to estimate. Though recall of ad contents is more likely better for "thinking" ads than for "feeling" ads, traditional assessments of advertising effectiveness (e.g., day-after recall) may not be suitable to measure cumulative impacts of emotional ads. These open-ended measures are more focused toward rational responses, and emotional ads may be penalized since the reactions are not as easy to express.[48]

• **Sex Appeals:** Reflecting the widely-held belief that "sex sells": many marketing communications for products including fragrances, sunglasses, bags, clothing and automobiles present substantial doses of erotic suggestion that can vary from understated hints to obvious displays of skin. There are so many different brands in the market that are trying to stand out from the crowd, for this reason, fashion brands ranging from luxury ones to high street, resort to sex as a valuable selling tool.[49]

Some apparel retailers such as Victoria's Secret, Misguided, PrettyLittleThing, and Calvin Klein rely heavily on sexuality in their messaging.[50] Sexual appeals are also prominent for fragrances. This is understandable; a major reason that people wear perfume or cologne is to be attractive to others. Fragrance ads tend to use provocative photographs that resort to blatant sexuality. This is aggravated by the predominance of celebrity perfumes: Rihanna, Beyoncé, Lady Gaga and other renowned stars have popular fragrances that link to their highly sexualized identities.[51]

Many critics feel that objectification of women is degrading and inappropriate. Today we are witnessing a lot of pushback against overly sexualized advertising. An advertisement for the fashion retailer Pretty Little Thing that showed women wearing scanty lingerie has been banned by the Advertising Standards Authority (ASA) in the UK for being offensive.[52]

As many fashion consumers are becoming more sensitive about the abundant use of sexual imagery in advertising, some fashion retailers have started to scale back on these appeals. For instance, Abercrombie & Fitch made a major shift in the way they promote their fashion range, moving from conveying a sexual image with shirtless models into portraying an image of self-esteem and inner confidence.[53]

The motivation for retailers to remove the sexual appeal from their campaigns is perhaps the outcome of consumers voicing their concerns. While a number of fashion brands have changed their strategies over the last couple of years to adjust to consumers' change in attitudes, sex appeal is still being used as a marketing tool and may continue to be a sustainable strategy—if used appropriately. Think of how the online retailer Boohoo saw a rise in sales by only being the sole fashion partner for the reality TV show the *Love Island* edit in 2019.[54]

So, does sex appeal work? Although erotic content does appear to draw attention to an ad, its use may actually be counterproductive to the marketer. Ironically, a provocative picture can be *too* effective; it attracts so much attention that it hinders processing and recall of the ad's contents. Sexual appeals appear to be ineffective when used merely as a "trick" to grab attention. They do, however, appear to work when the product is *itself* sexually related—perhaps like that Calvin Klein lingerie we've mentioned. Overall, though, use of a strong sexual appeal is not very well received, especially among women.[55]

- **Humorous Appeals**: The use of humor can be very tricky, particularly since what is funny to one person may be offensive or incomprehensible to another. Specific cultures may have different senses of humor and also use funny material in diverse ways. Think of the Dolce & Gabanna ad that featured an Asian woman in an extravagant Dolce & Gabbana dress attempting to eat spaghetti with chopsticks. While the original video was attempting to convey a sense of humor, it was instead widely considered to be offensive, racist and disrespectful.[56] This resulted in a huge backlash in the Chinese marketplace with a number of celebrities and retailers vowing to boycott the brand, impacting sales.[57]

So, does humor work? In general, humorous advertisements do get attention. Apple Music partnered with Taylor Swift who was exercising while rapping with Drake and Future's "Jumpman". As the Apple Music is "distractingly good", Taylor faceplants off the treadmill. Pretty much anything that is featured with this artist is sure to attract eyeballs. Drake's song jumped in popularity since the campaign and Swift is yet again in the spotlight.[58]

Humor is more likely to be effective when the brand is clearly identified, and the funny material does not "swamp" the message. This danger is similar to that of beautiful models diverting attention from copy points. Subtle humor is usually better, as is humor that does not make fun of the potential consumer. Finally, humor should be appropriate to the product's image.

- **Fear appeals** focus on the negative outcomes that can take place unless the consumer alters a given behavior or an attitude. *Fear of deviance* may be important for adolescents as they believe that the group will apply sanctions to punish behavior that differs from the group. Skin care and anti-ageing beauty products often convey messages that stress the fear of growing older in order to motivate consumers to buy their products.[59]

So, does fear work? A number of studies reveal that negative appeals are usually most effective when only a moderate threat is used and when a solution to the problem is presented (else, people will disregard the ad as they think that will not be able to deal with the problem).[60] This approach also works better when source credibility is high. When a weak threat is unsuccessful, this may be linked to an insufficient understanding of the harmful outcomes of being involved in a given behavior. However, when a strong threat seems to be insufficient, it may be associated with *too much* elaboration to the extent that it may limit the processing of the suggested alteration in behavior—the consumer can be too taken by thinking why a certain message doesn't apply to them to notice the presented solution.[61]

The Promotional Mix

You might have designed a super creative and fashionable product, priced it very well, and placed it in the best possible location ever—but unless you're communicating the proper message and planting it in the minds of your target audience, all your marketing efforts will be useless.

A carefully crafted promotion strategy can mean the difference between market success or failure. Selecting the proper promotional mix elements allows the fashion company to drive sales and stand out in a crowded market. The **promotional mix** refers to the specific combination of the tools, channels, and processes a company uses to market its offerings. It consists of up to five components: advertising, sales promotion, personal selling, direct marketing and public relations. Each market is different, and there are different actors that may impact the fashion companies' promotional mix. The biggest challenge for fashion marketers is to identify the perfect combination of promotional elements to maximize the results of their marketing efforts.

Advertising

Advertising refers to any paid type of non-personal communication about a company, product, service or idea by an identified sponsor that appears in mass media.[62] It has been traditionally the main method of communicating a brand image. It enables marketers to raise awareness about a certain brand, goods or services through gaining customer attention.

The traditional forms of mass media advertising are as follows: Newspapers and magazines, radio, television, digital and social media, and outdoor. Each of these

H&M digital billboards at New York's Times Square

Raquel Rodr / Shutterstock.com

media forms has its advantages and disadvantages. For example, a mass-fashion brand such as H&M may choose to advertise via digital billboards in New York's Times Square and on Facebook and

Instagram sponsored ads, while more luxury brands such as Chanel may only choose to advertise via printed and online fashion magazines.

There are three different factors to consider when selecting the right fashion media advertising form:

1. *Determining reach, frequency, and impact*: **Reach** describes the fraction of individuals in the target market who are exposed to the ad campaign over a set amount of time. **Frequency** is the number of times a typical person in the target market is exposed to the communicated message. For example, Michael Kors would be interested to know how many customers will be exposed to its campaign and how many times they will see it during the same month. Finally, some media may have more **impact** than others given the size, colors used and movement of a typical advert; it may make a strong impression and be remembered longer. For example, a fashion product advertised in *Vogue* might be perceived differently from one that appears on Twitter.

2. *Selecting the proper media form and vehicle*: The marketer needs to consider the reach, frequency and impact of each of the media forms and match them to their needs. The most effective and efficient form of media is the one that best appeals to the brand's target market. In addition to selecting whether to advertise on social media or on TV, the fashion marketer must also decide on the best media vehicle, the precise media within each general media form. For example, if a fashion brand wants to reach teenagers, it has to do so through social media platforms such as Snapchat, TikTok, and Instagram, whereby if it wants to target Millennials it has to do so through Facebook, the top social media network used followed by Instagram.[63] If American Apparel wants to reach American Millennials, they can turn to Facebook or to Instagram. However, if a company chooses to target Chinese buyers, the dominant social media platforms there are Weixin WeChat and Sino Weibo.

3. *Deciding on media timing*: As fashion is seasonal in general, marketers need to carefully plan and design their **media schedule (**the pattern of timing, the duration and the frequency of advertisements over a specific period of time). They need to make sure to start advertising for their products, collections, and upcoming collaborations ahead of time in order to make consumers aware of their launch and create more hype. For example, for the H&M-Balmain collaboration with the Lebanese designer Sandra Mansour that was supposed to hit the market at the end of August, the partnership was announced by H&M at the end of July. Fashion brands should make sure to schedule ahead of time when to release news about a certain collection in order to create more buzz in the market.

Magazines

Fashion magazines are still considered as a major medium for fashion advertising campaigns, especially for luxury fashion brands that are established in main fashion capitals such as Paris, Milan, London, and New York. Brands that run fashion campaigns try hard to get the opportunity to be featured on the covers of major fashion magazines such as *Vogue* or *Harper's Bazaar*.

In fashion and luxury, however, the resources being assigned to print advertising are out of sync with how shoppers truly look for information. While consumers spend very little time on printed media versus the amount of time they spend on their mobiles and personal computers, a big portion of the fashion budget is still allocated to print. This disconnect is due to deep-rooted habits and a history of a favor for a favor relationship between brands and prevailing magazine editors. Furthermore, digital advertising still causes some concerns for the luxury industry, especially that luxury brands cannot control where or how their advertising will show up online.

That is why a big portion of digital ads are automated or "programmatic". **Programmatic advertising** permits brands to reach customers through a number of websites, following some criteria such as search history or shopping practices. But even here, the advertiser doesn't have total control because this technique may end up showing ads for luxury brands on sketchy websites that may show pornography, fake news—or even fanatic propaganda videos. During the Summer of 2020, Twitter users started to share comments about a Cartier campaign that was featured on Breitbart News Network, a famous site for its national populism and relations to white supremacists. Some users stated that this is "Not very classy" for Cartier.[64]

Print magazines still make up most of the advertising budget for high-end luxury brands. For Condé Nast, the publishing titan that functions the world's sleek fashion magazines such as *Vogue* (which has 24.6 million monthly readers), printed magazines still accounted for 36% of its revenue in 2019.[62] High-end luxury brands that emphasize watches, jewelry and *couture* fashion allocated 73% of their budgets to print ads in 2016.[65]

In contrast, the more accessible "broad luxury" category that consists of automobiles, cosmetics, and fragrances, spends about 30% of its allocated budgets on digital channels, and this figure is expected to keep rising over the coming years. Recently, some luxury fashion brands such as Gucci and Louis to Vuitton—conventionally huge magazine advertisers—are starting to move more and more of their budgets to digital advertising.[66]

Another challenge that hits fashion magazines was the coronavirus pandemic, when companies such as Kering and LVMH pulled back on budgets as their stores were closed for a period of time. But there is still some good news here: according to *Vanity Fair* Italia's Editor-in-Chief Simone Marchetti, "People are still buying magazines. They want information now more than ever."[67]

Radio Advertising

Radio advertising dates back to 1922, when a New York City radio station started to sell time for "toll broadcasting". The first radio ad was a 15-minute real-estate spot that offered flats in Queens.[68] One of the advantages of radio advertising is flexibility. It is an economical way to appeal to existing and potential customers. Of course, radio advertising for fashion can be challenging as fashion ads need to promote more of a visual rather than an auditory sensation. However, this medium is quite useful to create awareness related to a store's grand opening or discounts. A recent study performed by TagStation (done in partnership with the Radio Advertising Bureau) reported that automotive and fashion beauty care retailers can increase their store traffic by 32% when they promote their brands on the radio. Their study examined 1.5 million radio spot plays for 10 brands in the biggest 100 U.S. markets.[69]

Television

Television advertising is still an exceptional technique to reach a large audience and create brand awareness, and it remains the medium of choice for many regional and national firms. By appealing to millions of people around the world, large-scale broadcasts like the World Cup or the Super Bowl also provide a seamless platform for brands to promote their products, making television advertising a multi-billion-dollar industry.[70]

TV advertising is the most prominent and expensive medium. In 2020, the average cost of a 30-second Super Bowl commercial was a mind-boggling $5.6 million.[71] The luxury automaker Porsche bought its first Super Bowl ad in over 20 years to market the Taycan, its new all-electric car. With this ad, Porsche is trying to appeal to a new segment of potential customers.[72]

Nevertheless, the television environment is experiencing dramatic changes. Today, people are increasingly shifting to watch content online rather than on traditional television networks. Advertisers are changing accordingly as they continue to move more of their resources to these new media. In 2018, for the first time, online advertisers outspent TV advertisers globally.

Digital Media

As we have seen, fashion marketers are depending less and less on the conventional types of communication and are moving more toward digital or online media.[73] The common forms of digital media ads that are currently used comprise email, fashion retailers' own websites, social media platforms, and search engines, which are accessible through numerous devices.

If you are into fashion, you cannot ignore social media sites such as Facebook, YouTube, Instagram, Pinterest, Snapchat, WhatsApp, WeChat, TikTok, and Sino Weibo. A **social media platform** refers to the set of web-based technology that enables users to develop content and share it with millions of users around the world (see also[74]). These platforms continue to evolve; Facebook has even started to test *augmented reality* in advertising with fashion brands like Sephora, NYX, Urban Decay, Lancôme, Yves Saint Laurent and Michael Kors.

Fashion marketers recognize that they have to be available wherever their target markets are—and today's fashion consumers hang out in online social media communities. In 2020, about 3.08 billion people worldwide used social media, and that number is estimated to rise to almost 3.43 billion by 2023.[75]

Instagram alone has one billion monthly active accounts.[76] Paid ads pop-up as consumers scroll through their normal feeds, and companies can appeal to them based upon demographic and psychographic profiles. Social media networks became the biggest growth driver of Internet sales for L'Oréal in terms of attracting purchase traffic, although transactions are redirected to the L'Oréal brands' websites or third-party online websites for final checkout.[77]

Instagram advertising offers a sense of immediate delight—viewers see a post and they can directly purchase the items in their feed instead of clicking through to a brand's website by only using the in-app checkout. Some analysts estimate that consumers will spend $10 billion annually on Instagram shopping.[78] Google advertising is typically the next platform for brands after

Instagram and Facebook, but several brands are starting to promote on Amazon search as more users directly search for products on the marketplace.[79]

Luxury brands have lately rediscovered Twitter. However, this platform is not flooded with ads for apparel and jewelry brands. Luxury brands are trying to appeal to a more niche audience that is younger and more affluent than the typical Twitter user.[80] Some luxury brands are also broadcasting fashion shows on Twitter—such as Louis Vuitton, Gucci, Dior and Chanel. Hermès promoted a tweet to promote its Autumn/Winter 2020 fashion show, presenting a video of the Mondrian-inspired show and the hashtag #HermesFemme. Cartier also promoted its heritage series "L'Odyssee de Cartier" and publicized a new digital magazine, "Cartier News".[81]

Other social media platforms are trying hard to match Instagram's ease of use. To increase revenue through advertising, Pinterest permits users to purchase items they pin on its website. Consumers can use Apple Pay or a credit card to finalize a transaction, and retail partners consist of fashion retailers like Macy's, Nordstrom, and a number of boutiques and brands.[82] Nordstrom receives more than 10 million monthly views of its ad catalogs, according to its Pinterest page. Pinterest has also permitted furniture startups to achieve a considerable presence. For example, Room & Board has been using the promoted pins option to obtain new customers browsing for inspiration boards for contemporary furniture ideas. According to Pinterest's metrics, "Room & Board has seen 51 times return on ad spend on Promoted Pins campaign, as well as 33 times return on ad spend from their Shopping Ads campaign".[83]

Recently a number of fashion and luxury brands have started to consider the TikTok platform while planning their social media marketing mix, like Calvin Klein and Ralph Lauren. Other brands have jumped on this bandwagon such as Prada, Alice + Olivia, Dolce & Gabbana, Tory Burch, Burberry, Poshmark and Missoni.[84] MAV Beauty Brands was able to reach a 60% sales boost for its Marc Anthony True Professional line since its curly hair products were featured in a viral video challenge.[85]

Social media platforms also comprise the following:

- *Blogs*: a website that contains people's posted messages in diary form in which people share their thoughts about a particular subject with their audience. For example, Tao Liang is a fashion blogger who has built his online persona 'Mr. Bags' into one of China's most influential blogs. His impact has resulted in several partnerships with Givenchy, Burberry, Fendi, Chloé and Louis Vuitton, among others.[86]

- *Video blog (vlog):* a collection of videos instead of text to communicate with an audience. Today, many cosmetic brands are using YouTube vloggers to pitch a product on the brand's behalf, which is proving to be more organic than engaging people in a brand's channel.[87]

- *Podcasting:* creating a digital audio show people can listen to by downloading it to a computer or mobile device. Some fashion houses and designers have adopted the podcast trend, giving consumers an inside view into the fantasy world they build, beside the insightful analyses and nuanced observations of the industry as a whole. For example, 'Métier Class' by Chanel presents unique behind-the-scenes interviews with several Chanel muses, such as Marion Cotillard, Pharrell Williams, Keira Knightley and Karl Lagerfeld.[88]

Direct Marketing

Do you know that Tiffany & Co. still mails catalogs to their customers? **Direct marketing** is a type of one-to-one marketing communication that connects to a narrow target audience through telephone marketing, postal mail, email, or catalogs and brochures in order to generate a defined response. These responses can take the form of finalizing an order, requesting additional information, or even paying a visit to a brand's store. In spite of the profusion of "junk mail" that clogs up our mailboxes, direct marketing remains a popular technique for fashion brands: it provides fashion companies a cost-effective way to appeal directly to customers to take a certain action.

Direct-mail marketing involves sending letters, postcards, announcements, reminders or other promotional materials to a person at a precise address. Direct mail allows luxury and high-end fashion brands and retailers to get in front of a prosperous audience with the objective of encouraging prospective customers to go to retailer websites, stores, boutiques or events.[89]

For Porsche the Pfaff marketing agency developed 60 direct-mail pieces targeting homeowners in wealthy neighborhoods in Toronto with a very unusual approach. The agency placed an actual Porsche car outside the 60 different homes, took a picture, and converted it into a direct-mail postcard that showed the residents how their house would look with a remarkable new automobile parked in the driveway. Results indicated that 32% of the targeted individuals positively responded by booking a test drive through the website.[90]

As consumers often discard what they think of as "junk mail", BMW created an interactive technique to discourage that habit and engage consumers. The postcard they sent to customers can be opened by tearing down a seam that moves and interacts with the design. This allows the receiver to interact directly with the design, creating a better reaction to the message on the inside with clever involvement.[91] The BMW and Porsche mailers are examples of out of the box marketing; demonstrating that companies who differentiate themselves from the crowd will experience better performance of their direct marketing campaigns.

Catalog marketing is a communication form used by companies to combine several products together in a printed section or in an online store. For decades, fashion retailers relied upon catalogues to display their collections and promote their products through mail or telephone orders. Fashion retailers such as Victoria's Secret used printed catalogues to generate half of the company's overall sales in the 1980s.

However, with the development of e-commerce, catalogues became less popular. The quantity of catalogues sent in the US decreased by more than half between 2007 and 2017 to 9.4 billion, according to the Association of National Advertisers. But recently there has been a resurgence of catalogue marketing. For example, Naked Cashmere communicated with its customers through six paper catalogues sent via mail in 2019.[92] Amazon, the leader in ecommerce, have been distributing a physical catalogue in the US in 2018. A study indicated that catalogues are still able to reach 11 million viewers versus digital catalogues getting only to four million. So, if marketers only concentrate on digital channels, they are likely to miss out on millions of potential customers. Therefore, complementing the fashion company's marketing mix with printed catalogs permits it to develop deeper, longer lasting impressions with its customers.[93]

M-commerce (mobile commerce) refers to the marketing of products and services through a wireless device such as a mobile phone and tablets (see also[94]). It is rapidly becoming a main channel to encourage purchases as our smartphones alter our buying habits. People are depending more and more on digital devices now, and it is estimated[95] that m-commerce will increase by 25.5% compound annual growth rate (CAGR) from 2019 to reach $488 billion, or 44% of e-commerce, in 2024 to become consumers' favorite medium for online buying in the coming five years.

Given the rise in m-commerce, it makes sense that marketers would be interested in reaching out and touching this massive market. We have seen an explosion of fashion-oriented mobile apps for example, including FastAF, Depop and Drest.[96] Many retailers have turned to m-commerce via text messages **(SMS) marketing,** such as an ad for a store opening or a discount. M-commerce has the same likely challenges as other types of direct marketing in terms of "junk mails", such as snail mail and email whereby people do not get to see the message being sent. For example, during the coronavirus lockdown, a number of fashion brands sent i-messages and push notifications via SMS and brand apps to their customers hoping that they are safe and in good health. However, the challenge with SMS is that one is inundated with messages the person did not ask for and thus tunes them all out completely. There is also the problem of data privacy, that customers did not express consent to be contacted or have no way of preventing further contacts.

Sales Promotion

Sales promotion is a well-crafted program that fashion marketers implement to generate interest in or drive the purchase of a good or service during a specific period. It takes the form of an incentive such as a discount, contests, coupons, to encourage consumers to try a new product or encourage them to act on an offer in a specified time period. This can be an effective technique for fashion firms that want to achieve immediate objectives, such as creating buzz and boosting sales in the near term.

Sales promotion can take the form of price-based or value-based promotions. **The priced-based** technique focuses on short-term price cuts or rebates that motivate consumers to select a brand—at least during the promotional time—while the **value-based** technique focuses on stimulating interest in a retailer's products. If continuously used, price-based promotions can be challenging as consumers tend to become deal-prone and purchase from the brand only during limited promotion periods. The different forms of price and value-based techniques are shown in Table 11.1.

Personal Selling

Personal selling is a face-to-face communication technique where firms employ a representative to interact directly with potential shoppers by providing information about goods or services, answering consumers' questions and concerns in the hope of closing a sale organically while crafting a memorable experience for their customers.

This type of promotion is based on building closer relationships with consumers. When it comes to luxury selling, sales representatives need to connect with the shopper and engage with them in a very genuine way. That means viewing things from their customers' perspectives, paying attention to their wants and needs, and creating sincere delight in selling them luxury products.

TABLE 11.1 Types of sales promotions

Technique	Form	Description	Example
Price-Based Technique			
	Discounts	Reduced prices on goods and services. Discounts can be seasonal, based on holidays or on purchased quantity.	Tory Burch Outlets offer 20% discount on the first item purchased, 30% discount on the second item purchased and 40% discount on the third item purchased.
	BOGOFs (buy one, get one free)	Technique that allows customers to buy two items for the price of one.	Kiko make-up allows customers to choose and add 4 products to their shopping list from selected items: the least expensive product will be free.[1]
	Coupons	Document that confirms a consumer's right to receive a percentage or a fixed discount on selected products. Coupons can be found in newspapers, magazines, in-store, leaflets in mailboxes or on the Internet.	ASOS offers 15% off your first purchase + free standard shipping with promo code (ASOSNEW15).
	Rebates/refund	Consumers can get a cash return when they submit evidence of purchase.	Amazon gives a cash back to a consumer on selected items.
	Reward Loyalty programs	For regular purchases of goods or services customers are compensated through bonus points, which can be exchanged for some rewards or to pay for products.	At H&M customers are offered points for shopping: $1 = 1 point, for every 200 points they will receive a $5 reward. Customers with loyalty cards can also get exclusive offers and discounts, free online return and shop now and pay for items later.[2]
Value-Based Technique			
	Special/bonus packs	Added volume of the product is given away with every purchase.	Sunsilk Black Shampoo offers 20% additional quantity.[3]
	Contests/ sweepstakes	Offers consumers the chance to win cash or products. Sweepstakes winners are given rigorously by chance. Contests necessitate consumers to engage in some activity or competition.	Bohoo runs a competition whereby the winner will be offered a scholarship for a Master's degree from boohoo.com co-founder Carol Kane, who has collaborated with York St John University's London Campus. The competition is as follows: "Do you want to turn your side hustle into your dream career? Have you got a big business idea that's commercial, original AND socially responsible? If YES, this competition is for you".[4]
	Trial samples	Offering a real or trial-size product to consumers to make them try a new product.	At Hermès, customers are offered a free Hermès fragrance sample.
	Free premiums	Consumers receive a free gift or reward when they make a purchase.	Customers can receive a free Jean Paul Gaultier Classique clear tote bag with purchases of Classique 100ml fragrance.

[1]https://www.kikocosmetics.com/en-gb/promo-kiko/buy2-get2-2018-summer-sale/buy2-get2-2018-summer-sale-make-up.html
[2]https://www2.hm.com/en_us/member/info.html
[3]https://www.amazon.in/Sunsilk-Black-Shampoo-5-5ml-Sachet/dp/B00RH0ZPLU
[4]https://www.yorksj.ac.uk/news/2019/boocom-scholarships/

Customers today can get almost all the products they desire online and sometimes at a cheaper price. Only a personal relationship with the personal seller will set a luxury brand apart from a world of online resellers. The seller's main purpose should be to create an emotional response throughout the decision-making process instead of a rational cost-calculation. The salesperson's job should also be to associate the product with an additional value by suggesting additional goods that can add value to the initial purchase—this is called **upselling**.[97] To stay relevant, luxury sales representatives can't depend only on their general product information, nor on their supportive commitment. They should instead bring superiority and edginess to the customer experience by relying on today's technology to its fullest potential.

Technology and personal selling   Want a new pair of Chanel shoes? Believe it or not, you now can book an appointment through WeChat or WhatsApp and then all you have to do is walk to the Chanel store and head to the changing room where you can find the pair of shoes ready for you to try on.

Particularly after the pandemic, a good question is "How can fashion retailers reinvent the magic of the corner store and serve each consumer as if they have known them for a long time, reconnect in a special way and provide seamless and fast checkout?".

With the developments in mobile technology that are perfectly suitable for sales representatives, **"Clienteling"** (a method that aims to build stronger relationships with customers based on data about their preferences, activities and consumptions) can make this possible. If you walk into any Apple or Nordstrom store, this is the kind of experience you would expect to have. Many brands attempt to copy the Apple Store model and most of them fail to understand that all this success is not related to its products but to its people—the way they were recruited and trained to engage with their customers.

Retailers that have adopted this approach have become proficient at applying the three features of an effective clienteling strategy:

- *Information*: Information is power when it comes to retailing. Information assists sales representatives in further engaging with the customer and giving them more suggestions and guidance. Specialized apps give the salesperson access to shoppers' wish lists, usual buying size, previous buying history, apparel size, and likes and dislikes.[98] This technology gives sales representatives e-access to a "360-degree view" of their customer.

- *Personalized 1:1 communication*: Sales associates should try to have frequent communication with their customers. This isn't feasible by only sending random emails to inform the customer about a new collection or an added discount. Instead, sales associates can benefit from the functionality of the apps by automatically suggesting items based on consumers' previous purchases. These recommendations can be featured in a message sent on the app whereby the shopper will have the option to directly buy the item. Other forms of promotions and loyalty programs can also be sent to customers through these apps.[99] In addition, sales associates can now directly interact and serve consumers through WhatsApp conversations.[100] Burberry, Tamara Mellon, Reformation, and Christian Dior are among the brands who use this form of direct service to better serve their customers.

Sales associates of luxury brands should now "hold a mobile tablet with that white glove".[101] They need to know if their shoppers would like to have champagne while they are browsing. They should also identify opportunities to suggest purchases for special events or even pinpoint on a new purse in a color/style that matches the shopper's preferences.[102] Think of how the Ritz Carlton hotel masters this 1:1 VIP experience by keeping important information about their customers from previous visits. As one customer noted: "There were a few surprises. For example, in my guest room, there were cookies and a note. Not just any cookies. They knew, from our discussions prior to arrival, that my favorite cookies were the double chocolates. Nice touch! And, the note was signed, "From the Ladies and Gentlemen at the Ritz-Carlton (Ritz-Carlton's motto is 'Ladies and gentlemen serving ladies and gentlemen.')".[103]

- *Seamless checkout*: Research shows that consumers will drop out of a purchase after 2–3 minutes of waiting in the queue. In order to enhance the customer experience, retailers need to provide shoppers with a fast and safe checkout experience by adopting the proper technology. Remember your last visit to an Apple Store? You were probably welcomed by a very well-informed associate who could directly finalize your transaction from anywhere in the store (with the use of mPOS solutions) freeing you from standing in line. Studies demonstrate that sizeable numbers of consumers are happy with using digital wallets, like Apple Pay, Android Pay, and Samsung Pay. Accordingly, sales representatives should be well trained with the tools to provide seamless, safe and fast checkout for consumers, which is not anymore considered as a luxury but as a necessity (especially after the pandemic) in every retailer space.[104]

Persuasion Techniques in Selling

In the context of fashion, personal selling can take place in retail outlets and at the same time on television whereby the host can use persuasion techniques in order to drive the consumer to shop.[105] There are six persuasion strategies that salespeople can use to influence consumers to buy a particular product or service:[106]

- *Social proof* refers to the process of considering others in order to identify how someone must behave. For example, a salesperson in a fashion store tells the shopper that a lot of other people are buying the same product.

- *Scarcity*: If the shopper feels that a fashion good is limited rather than available in big amounts they are more likely to be driven to buy it directly. In this case, the salesperson makes the consumer feel that "I have to buy it now or never".

- *Authority*: Presenting consumers with people who are either real specialists with proficiency (for example three out of four dermatologists suggesting a facial cream) or who have the appearance of expertise.

- *Commitment and consistency*: A salesperson can use this strategy by letting the shopper indicate what kind of features they are looking for. For example, if the consumer says that she is looking for an A-line dress, the seller can then offer a dress that matches this feature. Once the seller shows the customer what she asked for, then the customer will be put in a situation whereby she will feel pressure to purchase the suggested dress.

- *Liking*: We tend to like people who are similar to us. To facilitate liking, salespeople are trained to carefully listen to what the consumer is saying and then mirror their communication style.

- *Reciprocation*: This technique refers to offering the shopper an in-store sample or something for free so that they feel obligated to buy an item from the retail shop.

Public Relations

Public relations (PR) is a form of promotion that focuses on cultivating good relationships with a company's publics; these comprise consumers, media, stockholders, legislators, and other stakeholders in the company. Nowadays fashion marketers refer to PR activities to impact the attitudes and perceptions of many groups by communicating positive messages to their targeted audience. Fashion brands can do so through several methods: press releases, sponsorships and special events, and guerrilla marketing activities.

A **press release** is a short, captivating news story written by a fashion company and shared with the media, hoping that it will be published for free. The objective is to pique the interest of a fashion journalist, or blogger.

Fashion brands have a long history of using Hollywood's red carpets to gain the attention of the press. Jimmy Choo, Marchesa and other fashion brands have effectively cashed in on the Academy Awards as a global PR platform.[107]

Brands are currently trying to find out new means to communicate, ways that resonate much more with the way the brand reaches or interacts with journalists, bloggers, influencers, consumers, and users.[108] Press releases or invitations to attend events remain the most highly used device to attract the press attention. For example, LVMH announced in a press release its partnership with Rihanna Fenty to relaunch the fashion line Fenty as "Luxury Maison".[109]

Sponsorships are PR activities through which fashion brands offer financial support to assist funding a particular event in return for recognition of the brand's contribution. These sponsorships are particularly effective because they allow marketers to reach customers during their leisure time; people often appreciate these efforts because the financial support makes the events possible in the first place. For example, since 2015, Nike has been the official sponsor for the NBA.[110] The Reebok brand sponsored New York Men's Fashion Week and supported the CFDA's Future Fashion Graduate Showcase since 2018.[111] In 2019 Christian Dior sponsored the exhibition *The Unexpected Subject: 1978 Art and Feminism in Italy*, which was attended by its creative director Maria Grazia Chiuri.[112]

A **fashion show** refers to an event organized by a fashion brand to display its collection of apparel and/or accessories during Fashion Week season. Fashion shows are important marketing events that allow fashion and luxury brands to communicate their upcoming collections, brand positioning and product assortments to the fashion press, buyers, and consumers. This tool is one of the most effective ways to get more media attention and press coverage. A number of fashion brands are trying to draw the audience attention to their shows by creating pre-show buzz with on-site countdown clocks and press releases. For example, in 2019, Jonathan Simkhai grabbed attention pre-show by running countdown clocks on social media feeds and websites.

Tribute to Gianni Versace reuniting the 1990s Supermodels Naomi Campbell, Cindy Crawford, Claudia Schiffer, Carla Bruni, and Helena Christensen

FashionStock.com / Shutterstock.com

Other brands try to create a buzz during and after their fashion show. For example, for Autumn/Winter 2018, Gucci presented a show featuring models carrying their own (fake) heads in their hands. As a result, mentions of Gucci across Facebook, Twitter, Instagram, and Reddit increased by more than 121% according to Brandwatch, while mentions of its creative director boomed 753%. During the time when fashion week news was flooding the media, and audience attention spans were short, Gucci was able to overcome all of this noise.[113] The luxury brand Versace ended up using Milan Fashion Week for a Bold Tribute to Gianni Versace with a reunion of the 1990s Supermodels Naomi Campbell, Cindy Crawford, Claudia Schiffer, Carla Bruni, and Helena Christensen who walked the runway at the end of the show holding hands. This show created huge buzz all over social media.[114]

Today, fashion shows are also increasingly live streamed, which allows brands to appeal to a larger audience. Facebook usually offers the most extended shelf life for a show, as it keeps the video on the brand's page. Instagram is quite effective at creating live engagement. Tory Burch follows a universal tactic to exhibit its show through common East Asian platforms such as Weibo, WeChat and Line. In 2020, a different form of fashion show took place. Due to the Covid-19 pandemic, worldwide fashion weeks including Milan, Paris, London and New York shifted to digital-only formats for their Spring/Summer 2021 programs.

Comme des Garçons at the Metropolitan Museum of Art's Costume Institute

Image courtesy of Rhododendrites via WikiMedia Commons. Shared under the CC BY-SA 4.0 license

Fashion exhibitions offer a great place for fashion brands who want to expose their heritage. Recently, this format has received a lot of renewed attention. Some notables examples include: Comme des Garçons at the MET (Metropolitan Museum of Art's Costume Institute), Musée Yves Saint Laurent Paris, or Balenciaga oeuvre at the Victoria & Albert Museum.

The *Christian Dior: Designer of Dreams* exhibition in the Victoria & Albert Museum in London, costing £3 million ($3.9 million) was its most popular exhibition to date and caught the interest of more than 480,000 visitors.[115] To celebrate the brand's 40th anniversary, Armani launched in 2015 the Armani/Silos, a fashion art space in Milan, which has its own standalone space dedicated to the Armani style through his exclusive designs.[116]

Guerrilla marketing techniques describe campaigns where a fashion brand can use surprise and/or unconventional interactions for the sake of capturing consumers' attention and promoting a product or service. This strategy comprises "ambushing" fashion consumers with promotional messages in locations where individuals don't expect to see them.

Ambient advertising is a common form of guerilla marketing. This notion refers to the assignment of messages in unconventional media forms such as the backs of garage and train receipts, screens attached to the back of supermarket carts, signs on elevator doors, or the ever-popular signs in toilets in bars and restaurants—the possibilities are endless.

To promote Rimmel's Quick Dry nail polish, the brand placed a huge attention grabber bottle of nail polish on the street that seemed to have been poured onto the floor from a height with the liquid drying in seconds, focusing on the quick drying aspect of the product.[117] Another great example is linked to the placement of a vending machine packed with mini bottles of Moët & Chandon champagne in the lobby of the Ritz-Carlton Philadelphia, which might be considered as one of the newest Instagrammable spots in the city center.[118]

Chapter Summary

Now that you have read the chapter, you should understand the following:

1.   What are the basic components of the communication process?

The communications model can be used by marketers as a mean to change consumers' attitudes and to allow them to make a purchase decision. For this communication to be achieved, a number of elements are necessary: a sender should initiate the transfer of meaning by choosing appropriate symbolic images that represent that meaning. This meaning must be put in the form of a message comprising what shall be said and in what way it will be said. The message must be transmitted via a channel or medium, such as television, radio, magazines, billboards, personal contact, or electronic communication channels such as email, Internet, websites, and social media platforms. The message is then decoded by one or more receivers who interpret it in light of their own experiences. Finally, feedback must be received by the source, who uses the reactions of receivers to modify aspects of the message.

2.   What determines whether the source of a promotional message will be effective?

Two predominantly essential features determine the effectiveness of a source: credibility and attractiveness. Source credibility refers to a source's perceived expertise, objectivity, or honesty while source attractiveness refers to the source's physical appearance, personality, social status, or similarity

(Continued)

to the receiver. While marketers think that hiring celebrities can be an effective technique, consumers are starting to doubt their credibility. For this reason, fashion marketers are starting to rely on means that are rather more authentic and consumer generated.

3.   What are the different ways marketers can design their messages?

Fashion marketers should think of how the message is delivered as well as what it contains. They should decide whether the message will be communicated in words or pictures. They should select how many times a message should be repeated and whether it should present both sides of an argument. Also, fashion marketers need to design what is to be communicated: is the message going to include humor, fear, rational or sexual appeal?

4.   What are the different promotional mix tools a brand can use to communicate with fashion consumers?

Fashion marketers need to select the proper promotional mix elements that allow their company to drive sales and stand out in a crowded market. Advertising, sales promotion, personal selling, direct marketing and public relations are all marketing tools that fashion firms can allocate. However, fashion marketers need to ensure they use the perfect combination of promotional elements in order to reach their target audience and maximize the results of their marketing efforts.

DISCUSSION QUESTIONS

1.   What are the main weaknesses of applying a direct marketing strategy?

2.   What are the benefits of implementing a public relations campaign when it comes to promoting fashion brands?

3.   What are the advantages and limitations of loyalty plans?

4.   Why do fashion companies launch exhibitions? What are the advantages and limitations?

5.   What are some of your favorite fashion ads? Why do you like them? Are there any that you don't like or that offend you? Which ones and why?

6.   Discuss the role of public relations in building a fashion brand. Use practical examples to support your arguments.

7.   What decisions should a fashion marketer consider while designing an advertisement?

8.   Discuss the role and importance of PR when it comes to a fashion brand.

EXERCISES

1. In a group, create a new communication campaign for a brand of your choice where you may want to position a new product in the market or reposition an existing product in the market.

2. Visit a fashion retailer and identity four different sales promotion techniques. What is the purpose of these promotions?

3. Collect a sample of fashion ads that appear to appeal to consumer values. What value is being communicated in each of them and how is this done? Is this an effective approach to designing a marketing communication?

4. Imagine that you are the marketing manager of a mass cosmetic brand. Your brand is currently not doing well. How can you increase store traffic and encourage customers to buy more products from the brand?

5. You are the marketing manager of a luxury fashion brand. As a fashion marketing consultant, determine the best promotional tools that you can use in order to communicate with your target market.

6. In groups, search for fashion brands that design marketing campaigns with socially responsible messages. Do you think that these campaigns are genuine?

CASE STUDY: #TFWGUCCI – COOL LUXURY AND INNOVATION IN FASHION MARKETING COMMUNICATIONS

Dr Ana Roncha, London College of Fashion, UAL; Professor Natascha Radclyffe-Thomas, British School of Fashion, GCU London; Dr Mirsini Trigoni, London South Bank University

Luxury marketing strategies and practices have changed in response to shifts in luxury consumer demographics. Kapferer and Bastien's 2009 "anti-laws of marketing" that proposed axioms such as: keep non-enthusiasts out; don't use celebrities in advertising; make it difficult for clients to buy and do not pander to consumers' wishes, seem to have little currency for today's most relevant luxury brands. A new luxury culture is emerging, one where taking a stand, being rebellious, more inclusive, celebrating diversity and creativity is key; subverting or dismantling formerly sacred brand codes is

(Continued)

seen as a fast-track to modernity (Baron, 2018). Italian luxury brand Gucci is a good example of how adopting a mindset of rebellious innovation and breaking the established rules of communication translates to increased brand awareness and business success.

#TFWGucci (That Feeling When Gucci)

To promote its 2017 watch collection, Gucci eschewed traditional luxury brand messaging and inverted the consumer-brand power structure. Instead of partnering with aspirational celebrity brand ambassadors, Creative Director Alessandro Michele worked with an internationally diverse group of emerging artists to produce a fashion meme-inspired campaign #TFWGucci. The word "meme", coined by Richard Dawkins in 1976 to mean an "imitated thing" refers to pieces of language and culture transmitted across time and space. Today, memes are both symptomatic of and integral to Web 2.0 culture where "sharing, imitating, remixing, and using popularity measurements have become highly valued pillars of participatory culture, part and parcel of what is expected from a 'digitally literate' netizen" (Shifman, 2014: 23).

#TFWGucci featured 30 memes—images or animated GIFs, often with text captions, created by a selection of international visual artists. Most memes directly or indirectly referenced fine art (e.g. surrealism) and used unusual and eye-catching imagery to arouse consumers' interest. Counterintuitive captioning created ambiguity, which offered multiple interpretations and humorous juxtapositions and captured audience attention, evoked enjoyment, and encouraged participation and reaction. For example, fashion designer and creator of the label Cult11AD William Ndatila used a Renaissance portrait of Eleonora de Toledo painted in 1560 by Agnolo Bronzino and inserted the text "When he buys you flowers instead of a Gucci watch". This "reaction meme" encouraged viewers to like and repost the meme to express their own feelings (this achieved close to 100k likes).

Despite some critiques of the campaign for appropriating meme culture and the apparent mismatch between product price points and online audience as captured in the comment 'rich ppl memes?' (Connolly, 2017), according to all measures of digital media engagement the 30 #TFWGucci memes resulted in high levels of reach, comments, engagement and positive sentiment (Connolly, 2017; Dhillon, 2017).

The #TFWGucci meme campaign created a curated collection of luxury "art pieces" intentionally designed to help viewers express themselves online in line with the principles of swarm creativity (Gloor, 2005). When viewed through Gloor et al.'s (2009) four-step framework for identifying and growing the "coolness" of new trends, it can be argued that Gucci's use of humor represents the new "cool" luxury. Cool trends should be fresh and new, show signs of redefining the market and be a leader, not a follower. Secondly, they should form part of a community, to promote a feeling of being with "people like us" (McPherson et al., 2001). The third characteristic is that cool trends need to be fun, the experience needs to appeal and create joy and contentment. Lastly, cool things should give meaning such as making people feel good and happier. Humor is often perceived as an effective technique to gain attention that can enhance liking and build strong brand recognition (Khan and Khan, 2013); however, humor is more often employed in low involvement-feeling products (e.g. food and drinks) instead of high involvement-feeling products (e.g. fashion and perfumes (Weinberger and Charles, 2013).

Lizzy Bowring, Catwalk Director for consumer and market intelligence agency WGSN, has stated that "Michele uses social media as a way of creating desire in an instant for the lens of social media"

(Bailey, 2017); the resulting media attention and online engagement generated by #TFWGucci demonstrated Gucci's creativity and competitive advantage in leveraging social media platforms such as Instagram for cementing its cool luxury identity whilst creating effective product advertising.

DISCUSSION QUESTIONS

1. Humor has been used as an effective technique to gain attention in advertising. What are the advantages of using humor as a component of communication for luxury fashion brands?

2. Using Gloor et al.'s "cool farming" innovation framework, analyze why the #TFW-Gucci meme campaign was so successful.

3. The luxury industry often appears to be the antithesis of "cool". Given luxury's associations with history, heritage and exclusivity and the concepts of ingroups and outgroups, outline the considerations for creating viral social media content for a luxury brand.

4. By using memes, Gucci is adopting a bottom-up approach as opposed to a top-down one in terms of brand communication. Consider other examples of brands that have used similar strategies to discuss how this connects to the concepts of brand community and brand engagement.

REFERENCES

Yotka, S. (2017) 'Gucci rewrites history in Florence's Pitti palace', *Vogue,* May 29. www.vogue.com/article/gucci-resort-2018-runway-show-news (accessed March 14, 2022).

Baron, K. (2018) 'Why Brandalism has become a luxury brand's new best friend', *Forbes.* www.forbes.com/sites/katiebaron/2018/06/04/why-brandalism-has-become-a-luxury-brands-new-best-friend/ (accessed September 9, 2021).

Connolly, K. (2017) 'Can brands be cool? Measuring the success of Gucci's ad campaign', *Anexine.* www.anexinet.com/blog/can-brands-cool-measuring-success-guccis-ad-campaign/ (accessed September 9, 2021).

Dhillon, K. (2017) 'The Very Best #TFWGucci memes', *High Snob Society.* www.highsnobiety.com/2017/04/12/gucci-memes-instagram/(accessed September 9, 2021).

Gloor, P. (2005) *Swarm Creativity.* New York, NY: Oxford University Press.

Gloor, P.A., Krauss, J.S. and Nann, S. (2009) *Coolfarming: How Cool People Create Cool Trends.* ICKN. www.ickn.org/documents/edumedia09_coolfarming.pdf (accessed September 9, 2021).

Kapferer, J-N. and Bastien, V. (2009) *The Luxury Strategy: Break the Rules of Marketing to build Luxury Brands.* London: Kogan-Page.

McPherson, M., Smith-Lovin, L. and Cook, J. M. (2001) 'Birds of a feather: Homophily in social networks', *Annual Review of Sociology,* 27 (1), 415–444.

Shifman, L, (2014) *Memes in Digital Culture.* London: The MIT Press.

NOTES

1. Arnold, A. (2017) '4 Ways social media influences millennials' purchasing decisions', *Forbes,* December 22. www.forbes.com/sites/andrewarnold/2017/12/22/4-ways-social-media-influences-millennials-purchasing-decisions/?sh=7791d707539f (accessed September 9, 2021).

2. Mau, D. (2019) 'Naomi Campbell stars in her first Calvin Klein campaign alongside Bella Hadid, Diplo and more', *Fashionista,* August 12. https://fashionista.com/2019/08/my-calvins-calvin-klein-ad-campaign-fall-2019 (accessed September 9, 2021).

   Bauck, W. (2019) 'New #MyCalvins campaign features Kendall Jenner, Noah Centineo and A$AP Rocky', *Fashionista,* February 19. https://fashionista.com/2019/02/my-calvins-ad-calvin-klein-ad-campaign (accessed October 20, 2021).

3. Chopard (n.d.) *@chopard* [Instagram profile] https://www.instagram.com/chopard/?hl=en (accessed September 9, 2021).

   Chopard (2021) 'The Happy Diamonds movie directed by Xavier Dolan starring Julia Roberts – presented by Chopard', *YouTube,* April, 20. www.youtube.com/watch?v=Oy2V1S-IIro (accessed October 20,2021).

4. Arnold, A. (2017) '4 Ways social media influences millennials' purchasing decisions', *Forbes,* December 22. www.forbes.com/sites/andrewarnold/2017/12/22/4-ways-social-media-influences-millennials-purchasing-decisions/?sh=7791d707539f (accessed September 9, 2021).

5. McKinsey & Company (2020) 'Meet Generation Z: Shaping the future of shopping', August, 20. www.mckinsey.com/industries/consumer-packaged-goods/our-insights/meet-generation-z-shaping-the-future-of-shopping (accessed October 20, 2021).

6. Brunker A. and Chilton, C. (2020) 'The evolution of the Little Black Dress', *Elle* February 11. www.elle.com/fashion/g8192/evolution-of-the-little-black-dress/ (accessed October 20, 2021).

7. Gellert, M. (2001) *The Fate of America: An Inquiry into National Character.* Dulles, VA: Potomac.

8. Boyd. S. (2016) '10 Fashion icons and the trends they made famous', *Forbes,* March 14. www.forbes.com/sites/sboyd/2016/03/14/10-fashion-icons-and-the-trends-they-made-famous/?sh=1f430c251268 (accessed September 9, 2021).

9. Schivinski, B. and Dabrowski, D. (2016) 'The effect of social media communication on consumer perceptions of brands', *Journal of Marketing Communications,* 22 (2): 189–214.

10. Godin, S. (1999) *Permission Marketing: Turning Strangers into Friends and Friends into Customers.* New York, NY: Simon and Schuster.

    Krafft, M., Arden, C.M. and Verhoef, P.C. (2017) 'Permission marketing and privacy concerns – Why do customers (not) grant permissions?', *Journal of Interactive Marketing,* 39: 39–54.

11. O'Donohoe, S. (1994) 'Advertising uses and gratifications', *European Journal of Marketing,* 28 (8/9): 52–75.

12. Athwal, N., Istanbulluoglu, D. and McCormack, S.E. (2019) 'The allure of luxury brands' social media activities: A uses and gratifications perspective', *Information Technology & People,* 32 (3): 603–26.

13. Alexander, B., Nobbs, K. and Varley, R. (2018) 'The growing permanence of pop-up outlets within the international location strategies of fashion retailers', *International Journal of Retail & Distribution Management,* 46 (5): 487–506.

    Deli-Gray, Z., Matura, T. and Árva, L. (2014) 'Children entertainment in retail stores', *International Journal of Retail & Distribution Management,* 42 (11/12): 1004–1007.

    Jahn, S., Nierobisch, T., Toporowski, W. and Dannewald, T. (2018) 'Selling the extraordinary in experiential retail stores', *Journal of the Association for Consumer Research,* 3 (3): 412–24.

    Klein, J.F., Falk, T., Esch, F.R. and Gloukhovtsev, A. (2016) 'Linking pop-up brand stores to brand experience and word of mouth: The case of luxury retail', *Journal of Business Research,* 69 (12): 5761–7.

    Watson, A., Alexander, B. and Salavati, L. (2018) 'The impact of experiential augmented reality applications on fashion purchase intention', *International Journal of Retail & Distribution Management,* 48 (5): 433–51.

14. Kansara, V.A. (2017) 'Inside Farfetch's store of the future', *Business of Fashion,* April 12. www.businessoffashion.com/articles/technology/inside-farfetchs-store-of-the-future (accessed September 9, 2021).

15. TOMS (2015) 'Experience the TOMS virtual giving trip' [Video]. *TOMS YouTube* channel, November 5. www.youtube.com/watch?v=jz5vQs9iXCs (accessed September 9, 2021).

16. Wong, M. H. (2018) 'First look at Japan's new Hello Kitty Shinkansen', *CNN,* June 27. https://edition.cnn. com/travel/article/hello-kitty-shinkansen-train-japan/index.html (accessed September 9, 2021).

17. Kang, Y.S. and Herr, P.M. (2006) 'Beauty and the beholder: Toward an integrative model of communication source effects', *Journal of Consumer Research,* 33 (1): 123–30.

18. Djafarova, E. and Rushworth, C. (2017) 'Exploring the credibility of online celebrities' Instagram profiles in influencing the purchase decisions of young female users', *Computers in Human Behavior,* 68: 1–7.

    Spry, A., Pappu, R. and Cornwell, T.B. (2011) 'Celebrity endorsement, brand credibility and brand equity', *European Journal of Marketing,* 45 (6): 882–909.

19. Chin, P.N., Isa, S.M. and Alodin, Y. (2020) 'The impact of endorser and brand credibility on consumers' purchase intention: The mediating effect of attitude towards brand and brand credibility', *Journal of Marketing Communications,* 26 (8): 896–912.

    Ismagilova, E., Slade, E., Rana, N.P. and Dwivedi, Y.K. (2020) 'The effect of characteristics of source credibility on consumer behaviour: A meta-analysis', *Journal of Retailing and Consumer Services,* 53: 101736.

    Loureiro, S.M., Cavallero, L. and Miranda, F.J. (2018) 'Fashion brands on retail websites: Customer performance expectancy and e-word-of-mouth', *Journal of Retailing and Consumer Services,* 41: 131–41.

20. Cheung, M., Luo, C., Sia, C. and Chen, H. (2009) 'Credibility of electronic word-of-mouth: Informational and normative determinants of on-line consumer recommendations', *International Journal of Electronic Commerce,* 13 (4): 9–38.

21. Fertik, M. (2019) 'How to get millenials to trust and respond to your advertising', *Forbes,* February 14. www.forbes.com/sites/michaelfertik/2019/02/14/how-to-get-millenials-to-trust-and-respond-to-your-advertising/?sh=2a9b32596c81 (accessed September 9, 2021).

22. Adegeest, D.A. (2018) 'Fashion is plagued by fake news and fake posts', *Fashion United,* December 20. https://fashionunited.com/news/fashion/fashion-is-plagued-by-fake-news-and-fake-posts/2018122025243 (accessed September 9, 2021).

23. O'Neal, G.S. and Lapitsky, M. (1991) 'Effects of clothing as nonverbal communication on credibility of the message source', *Clothing and Textiles Research Journal,* 9 (3): 28–34.

24. Pratt, R. M. (2014) 'For emerging designers, celebrity sells', *Business of Fashion.* www.businessoffashion. com/community/voices/discussions/are-celebrity-labels-good-for-fashion/emerging-designers-celebrity-sells (accessed September 9, 2021).

25. Rainey, S. and Cisotti, C. (2018) 'Forget Choos – we want pineapple shoes! How Italian brand Aquazzura became Meghan's go-to footwear – and now boasts a whole league of celebrity fans', *Daily Mail,* September 26. www.dailymail.co.uk/femail/article-6211301/Forget-Choos-want-pineapple-shoes.html (accessed September 9, 2021).

26. Eagly, A.H., Wood, W. and Chaiken, S. (1978) 'Causal inferences about communicators and their effect on opinion change', *Journal of Personality and Social Psychology,* 36 (4): 424–35.

27. McCormick, K. (2018) 'Impact of athletic star power on product consumption', *International Journal of Sports Marketing and Sponsorship,* 19 (3): 306–26.

    Santos, A.L., Barros, F. and Azevedo, A. (2019) 'Matching-up celebrities' brands with products and social causes', *Journal of Product & Brand Management,* 28 (2): 242–55.

    Van de Sompel, D. and Vermeir, I. (2016) 'The influence of source attractiveness on self-perception and advertising effectiveness for 6-to 7-year-old children', *International Journal of Consumer Studies,* 40 (5): 575–82.

28. Dion, K., Berscheid, E. and Walster, E. (1972) 'What is beautiful is good', *Journal of Personality and Social Psychology,* 24 (3): 285–90.

29. Buttle, H., Raymond, J.E. and Danziger, S. (2000) 'Do famous faces capture attention?', *Advances in Consumer Research,* 27: 245.

30. Crutchfield, D. (2010) 'Celebrity endorsements still push product', *AdAge,* September 22. https://adage.com/article/cmo-strategy/marketing-celebrity-endorsements-push-product/146023 (accessed September 9, 2021).

    Langmeyer, L. and Walker, M. (1991) 'A first step to identify the meaning in celebrity endorsers', *Advances in Consumer Research,* 18 (1): 364–71.

31. Mackelden, A. (2019) 'Justin and Hailey Bieber team up for steamy Calvin Klein campaign', *Harper's Bazaar,* October 5. www.harpersbazaar.com/celebrity/latest/a29374775/justin-hailey-bieber-calvin-klein-campaign-photos/ (accessed September 9, 2021).

32. Verner, A. (2018) 'Haute stuff: Olivier Rousteing shows off Balmain's edgy eveningwear', *Vogue*, July 1. www.vogue.com/article/balmain-44-francois-premier-evening-collection (accessed September 9, 2021).

    Moda Operandi (2021) 'Balmain for Women'. www.modaoperandi.com/balmain-mens-ss19 (accessed September 9, 2021).

    Solomon, M. R., Cornell, L. D. and Nizan, A. (2009) *Launch! Advertising and Promotion in Real Time*. Flat World Knowledge.

33. Lariviere, D. (2013) 'Lebron James outshines Tiger Woods in global celebrity measuring index', *Forbes*, June 18. www.forbes.com/sites/davidlariviere/2013/06/18/lebron-james-outshines-tiger-woods-in-global-celebrity-measuring-index/?sh=66803ff655e9 (accessed September 9, 2021).

34. Kang, M.Y., Choi, Y. and Choi, J. (2019) 'The effect of celebrity endorsement on sustainable firm value: Evidence from the Korean telecommunications industry', *International Journal of Advertising*, 38 (4): 563–76.

35. Stewart, R. (2016) 'Taylor Swift, Justin Timberlake and Beyoncé named "most marketable" musicians', *The Drum*, January 14. www.thedrum.com/news/2016/01/14/taylor-swift-justin-timberlake-and-beyonc-named-most-marketable-musicians (accessed September 9, 2021).

36. Cohen, J. (2019) 'The power of video content and storytelling in the luxury industry', *Launch Metrics*, October 14. www.launchmetrics.com/resources/blog/brand-story (accessed September 9, 2021).

37. Gurzki, H. (2019) 'Dreaming up a world – How luxury brands create desire', *Forbes*, November 20. www.forbes.com/sites/esmtberlin/2019/11/20/dreaming-up-a-world--how-luxury-brands-create-desire/?sh=6354d1b171af (accessed September 9, 2021).

38. Bulmer, S. and Buchanan-Oliver, M. (2006) 'Visual rhetoric and global advertising imagery', *Journal of Marketing Communications*, 12 (1): 49–61.

    Grass, R.C. and Wallace, W.H. (1974) 'Advertising communications: Print vs. TV', *Journal of Advertising Research*, 14 (5): 19–23.

39. Hirschman, E.C. and Solomon, M.R. (1984) 'Utilitarian, aesthetic, and familiarity responses to verbal versus visual advertisement', *Advances in Consumer Research*, 11 (1): 426–31.

    Roose, G., Vermeir, I., Geuens, M. and Van Kerckhove, A. (2019) 'A match made in heaven or down under? The effectiveness of matching visual and verbal horizons in advertising', *Journal of Consumer Psychology*, 29 (3): 411–27.

40. Childers, T.L. and Houston, M.J. (1984) 'Conditions for a picture-superiority effect on consumer memory', *Journal of Consumer Research*, 11 (2): 643–54.

41. Montoya, R.M., Horton, R.S., Vevea, J.L., Citkowicz, M. and Lauber, E.A. (2017) 'A re-examination of the mere exposure effect: The influence of repeated exposure on recognition, familiarity, and liking', *Psychological Bulletin*, 143 (5): 459–98.

42. D'Souza, G. and Rao, R.C. (1995) 'Can repeating an advertisement more frequently than the competition affect brand preference in a mature market?', *Journal of Marketing*, 59 (2): 32–42.

43. Chen, J., Yang, X. and Smith, R.E. (2016) 'The effects of creativity on advertising wear-in and wear-out', *Journal of the Academy of Marketing Science*, 44 (3): 334–49.

    Kronrod, A. and Huber, J. (2019) 'Ad wearout wearout: How time can reverse the negative effect of frequent advertising repetition on brand preference', *International Journal of Research in Marketing*, 36 (2): 306–24.

44. Lim, J.S., Ri, S.Y., Egan, B.D. and Biocca, F.A. (2015) 'The cross-platform synergies of digital video advertising: Implications for cross-media campaigns in television, Internet and mobile TV', *Computers in Human Behavior*, 48: 463–72.

    Schmidt, S. and Eisend, M. (2015) 'Advertising repetition: A meta-analysis on effective frequency in advertising', *Journal of Advertising*, 44 (4): 415–428.

45. Campbell, M.C. and Keller, K.L. (2003) 'Brand familiarity and advertising repetition effects', *Journal of Consumer Research*, 30 (2): 292–304.

46. Cornelis, E., Heuvinck, N. and Majmundar, A. (2020) 'The ambivalence story: Using refutation to counter the negative effects of ambivalence in two-sided messages', *International Journal of Advertising*, 39 (3): 410–32.

    Kim, K. (2020) 'Stealing thunder in negative political advertising: The persuasive impact of one-sided and two-sided negative messages on partisan individuals', *Journal of Creative Communications*, 15 (1): 7–18.

Eisend, M. (2006) 'Two-sided advertising: A meta-analysis', *International Journal of Research in Marketing*, 23 (2): 187–98.

Sawyer, A.G. (1973) 'The effects of repetition of refutational and supportive advertising appeals', *Journal of Marketing Research*, 10 (1): 23–33.

47. Rucker, D. (2017) 'Emotion in advertising: The difference between a spark and a backfire', *Forbes*, October 5. www.forbes.com/sites/derekrucker/2017/10/05/emotion-in-advertising-the-difference-between-a-spark-and-a-backfire/?sh=7821bc7431e5 (accessed September 9, 2021).

48. Zielske, H.A. (1982) 'Does day-after recall penalize "feeling" ads?', *Journal of Advertising Research*, 22: 19–22.

49. Winser, K. (2013) 'Why do we use sex to sell clothes?', *Forbes*, December 17. www.forbes.com/sites/kimwinser/2013/12/17/why-do-we-use-sex-to-sell-clothes/?sh=239933d34329 (accessed September 9, 2021).

50. Nazir, S. (2020) 'Does sex still sell in retail?', *Retail Gazette*, February 25. www.retailgazette.co.uk/blog/2020/02/sex-sells-still-case-for-retail-fashion-advertising-marketing-asa/ (accessed September 9, 2021).

51. Winder, K. (2013) 'Why do we use sex to sell clothes?', *Forbes*, December 17. www.forbes.com/sites/kimwinser/2013/12/17/why-do-we-use-sex-to-sell-clothes/#1869102f4329 (accessed September 9, 2021).

52. Smith, C. (2020) 'Pretty little thing: "overly sexualised" advert banned', *BBC*, February 5. www.bbc.com/news/business-51370851 (accessed September 9, 2021).

53. Nazir, S. (2020) 'Does sex still sell in retail?', *Retail Gazette*, February 25. www.retailgazette.co.uk/blog/2020/02/sex-sells-still-case-for-retail-fashion-advertising-marketing-asa/ (accessed September 9, 2021).

54. Burden, E. (2019) 'Boohoo on top after Asos honeymoon ends', *The Times*, June 28. www.thetimes.co.uk/article/boohoo-on-top-after-asos-honeymoon-ends-h9p69s29t (accessed September 9, 2021).

55. Huhmann, B.A. and Limbu, Y.B. (2016) 'Influence of gender stereotypes on advertising offensiveness and attitude toward advertising in general', *International Journal of Advertising*, 35 (5): 846–63.

56. McEleny, C. (2018) 'What brands can learn in the fallout from D&G's offensive Chinese ads', *The Drum*, December 3. www.thedrum.com/news/2018/12/03/what-brands-can-learn-the-fallout-dg-s-offensive-chinese-ads (accessed September 9, 2021).

57. Barr, S. (2018) 'Dolce & Gabbana: celebrities pledge to boycott designer amid racism backlash', *The Independent*, November 22. www.independent.co.uk/life-style/fashion/dolce-gabbana-racist-boycott-chopsticks-controversy-china-instagram-video-a8646216.html (accessed September 9, 2021).

58. McIntyre, H. (2016) 'Taylor Swift's Apple music commercial spurred a 431% jump in sales for Drake', *Forbes*, April 7. www.forbes.com/sites/hughmcintyre/2016/04/07/taylor-swifts-apple-music-commercial-spurred-a-431-jump-in-sales-for-drake/?sh=6b34b13349c0 (accessed September 9, 2021).

59. Davis, D.M. (2020) 'Gen Zers have a spending power of over $140 billion, and it's driving the frenzy of retailers and brands trying to win their dollars', *Insider*, January 28. www.businessinsider.com/retail-courts-gen-z-spending-power-over-140-billion-2020-1 (accessed September 9, 2021).

60. Sternthal, B. and Craig, C.S. (1974) 'Fear appeals: Revisited and revised', *Journal of Consumer Research*, 1 (3): 22–34.

61. Keller, P.A. and Block, L.G. (1996) 'Increasing the persuasiveness of fear appeals: The effect of arousal and elaboration', *Journal of Consumer Research*, 22 (4): 448–59.

62. Bachnik, K., Nowacki, R. and Szopinski, T.S. (2018) 'Determinants of assessing the quality of advertising services: The perspective of enterprises active and inactive in advertising', *Journal of Business Research*, 88: 474–80.

63. Insider (2018) 'Teens aren't using Facebook as much as millennials and Gen Xers – here's the social platform each generation uses the most', *Insider*, August 30. www.businessinsider.com/top-social-media-platform-by-age-group-2018-8 (accessed September 9, 2021).

64. BoF Team (2017) 'The trouble with digital advertising', *Business of Fashion*, October 20. www.businessoffashion.com/articles/marketing-pr/the-trouble-with-digital-advertising (accessed September 9, 2021).

65. Odell, A. (2020) 'The best-case, worst-case for fashion media', *Business of Fashion*, April 23. www.businessoffashion.com/opinions/media/the-best-case-worst-case-for-fashions-media-giants (accessed September 9, 2021).

66. Gallagher, K. (2017) 'Luxury fashion brands shift budgets to digital', *Business Insider*, June 12. www.businessinsider.com/luxury-fashion-brands-shift-budgets-to-digital-2017-6 (accessed October 20, 2021).

67. Fernandez, C. (2020) 'For fashion magazines, it's crunch time', *Business of Fashion,* March 25. www. businessoffashion.com/articles/media/fashion-print-magazines-coronavirus (accessed September 9, 2021).

68. Barnouw, E. (1990) *Tube of Plenty: The Evolution of American Television*. New York and Oxford: Oxford University Press.

69. Zaczkiewicz, A. (2018) 'Why beauty retailers might want to tap radio as ad platform', *Women's Wear Daily,* September 27. https://wwd.com/business-news/marketing-promotion/radio-marketing-report-1202850303/ (accessed September 9, 2021).

70. Guttmann, A. (2020) 'Global TV advertising – Statistics & facts', *Statista,* September 10. www.statista. com/topics/5952/television-advertising-worldwide (accessed September 9, 2021).

71. Su, R. and McDowell, E. (2020) 'How Super Bowl ad costs have skyrocketed over the years', *Insider,* February 2. www.businessinsider.com/super-bowl-ad-price-cost-2017-2 (accessed September 9, 2021).

72. Matousek, M. (2020) 'Porsche bought its first Super Bowl ad in over 20 years to promote the Taycan', *Insider,* January 28. www.businessinsider.com/porsche-buys-super-bowl-ad-to-promote-taycan-video-2020-1 (accessed September 9, 2021).

73. Liu, S., Perry, P. and Gadzinski, G. (2019) 'The implications of digital marketing on WeChat for luxury fashion brands in China', *Journal of Brand Management*, 26 (4): 395–409.
    Rocamora, A. (2017) 'Mediatization and digital media in the field of fashion', *Fashion Theory*, 21 (5): 505–22.

74. Kim, A. J. and Ko, E. (2012) 'Do social media marketing activities enhance customer equity? An empirical study of luxury fashion brand', *Journal of Business Research*, 65 (10): 1480–6.
    Chu, S.C., Kamal, S. and Kim, Y. (2013) 'Understanding consumers' responses toward social media advertising and purchase intention toward luxury products', *Journal of Global Fashion Marketing*, 4 (3): 158–74.

75. Tankovska, H. (2021) 'Number of global social network users 2017–2025', *Statista,* January 28. www. statista.com/statistics/278414/number-of-worldwide-social-network-users/ (accessed September 9, 2021).

76. Tankovska, H. (2021) 'Global social networks ranked by number of users 2021', *Statista.* www.statista. com/statistics/272014/global-social-networks-ranked-by-number-of-users/ (accessed September 9, 2021).

77. Reuters (2018) 'L'Oréal teams with Facebook on virtual makeup tests', *Business of Fashion.* www. businessoffashion.com/articles/beauty/loreal-teams-with-facebook-on-virtual-make-up-tests (accessed September 9, 2021).

78. Baskin, B. (2019) 'The week ahead: Instagram's checkout feature is already changing how we shop online', *Business of Fashion,* April 21. www.businessoffashion.com/articles/sustainability/the-week-ahead-instagrams-checkout-feature-is-already-changing-how-we-shop-online (accessed September 9, 2021).

79. Nanda, M. (2019) 'How to advertise in the digital age', *Business of Fashion,* November 1. www.business offashion.com/articles/professional/how-to-advertise-in-the-digital-age (accessed September 9, 2021).

80. Mondalek, A. (2020) 'Why are luxury brands advertising on Twitter?', *Business of Fashion,* March 6. www. businessoffashion.com/articles/professional/how-do-fashion-brands-use-twitter (accessed September 9, 2021).

81. Mondalek, A. (2020) 'Why are luxury brands advertising on Twitter?', *Business of Fashion,* March 6. www.businessoffashion.com/articles/professional/how-do-fashion-brands-use-twitter (accessed September 9, 2021).

82. Schlossberg, M. (2016) 'Instagram and Pinterest are killing Gap, Abercrombie, & J. Crew', *Business Insider,* February 15. www.businessinsider.com/social-media-is-killing-traditional-retailers-2016-2 (accessed September 9, 2021).

83. Barkho, G. (2020) 'How retailers are using Pinterest to drive e-commerce', *Modern Retail,* January 31. www.modernretail.co/platforms/how-retailers-are-using-pinterest-to-drive-e-commerce/ (accessed September 9, 2021).

84. Richards, K. (2020) 'Luxury brands go all in on TikTok', *Digiday,* February 7. https://digiday.com/ marketing/luxury-brands-go-tiktok/ (accessed September 9, 2021).

85. Lieber, C. (2020) 'How brands go viral on TikTok', *Business of Fashion*, February 31. www.businessoffashion. com/articles/professional/tiktok-viral-social-media-marketing-beauty (accessed September 9, 2021).

86. BoF Staff (2021) 'Tao Liang biography', *Business of Fashion.* www.businessoffashion.com/community/ people/tao-liang (accessed September 9, 2021).

87. BoF Staff (2016) 'YouTube is helping to sell a lot of makeup', *Business of Fashion*, October 31. www. businessoffashion.com/articles/news-analysis/youtube-is-helping-to-sell-a-lot-of-makeup (accessed September 9, 2021).

88. Chanel (2019) 'Podcast Métier Class', *Chanel*, March 2. www.chanel.com/gb/fashion/news/2019/03/podcast-metier-class-by-chanel-with-karl-lagerfeld.html (accessed September 9, 2021).

89. Rogers, J.L. (1996) 'Mail advertising and consumer behavior', *Psychology & Marketing*, 13 (2): 211–33.

90. Adage (2012) 'PFAFF Porsche', *AdAge*, July 26. https://adage.com/creativity/work/instant-direct-mail/28614 (accessed September 9, 2021).

91. Rhys (2018) '5 Inspirational direct mail marketing campaigns to get your creative juices flowing!', *Media Hut*, September 14. https://mediahut.co.uk/blog/5-inspirational-direct-mail-marketing-campaigns-to-get-your-creative-juices-flowing/ (accessed September 9, 2021).

92. Chen, C. (2019) 'How to use catalogues in a digital age', *Business of Fashion*, May 21. www.businessoffashion.com/articles/professional/how-to-use-catalogues-in-a-digital-age (accessed September 9, 2021).

93. Timmerman, U. (2019) 'Traditional marketing still has a role in an online world', *Retail Gazette*, July 1. www.retailgazette.co.uk/blog/2019/07/comment-traditional-marketing-still-role-online-world/ (accessed September 9, 2021).

94. Chu, S.C., Kamal, S. and Kim, Y. (2013) 'Understanding consumers' responses toward social media advertising and purchase intention toward luxury products', *Journal of Global Fashion Marketing*, 4 (3): 158–74.

Chi, T. (2018) 'Understanding Chinese consumer adoption of apparel mobile commerce: An extended TAM approach', *Journal of Retailing and Consumer Services*, 44: 274–84.

McLean, G., Osei-Frimpong, K., Al-Nabhani, K. and Marriott, H. (2020) 'Examining consumer attitudes towards retailers' m-commerce mobile applications: An initial adoption vs. continuous use perspective', *Journal of Business Research*, 106: 139–57.

95. Meola, A. (2020) 'Rise of m-commerce: Mobile ecommerce shopping stats & trends in 2021', *Business Insider*, December 30. www.businessinsider.com/mobile-commerce-shopping-trends-stats (accessed October 20, 2021).

96. Coscarelli, A. and Samaha, B. (2020) '15 fashion apps to download now', *Harper's Bazaar*, October 22. www.harpersbazaar.com/fashion/trends/a2713/best-fashion-apps/ (accessed September 9, 2021).

97. Phibbs, B. (n.d.) 'Closing the sale techniques for luxury retail', *Retail Doc*. www.retaildoc.com/blog/sales-closing-techniques-for-luxury-retail (accessed September 9, 2021).

98. Mangtani, N. (2017) 'Clienteling – defining the future in-store experience', *Forbes*, February 1. www.forbes.com/sites/nitinmangtani/2017/02/01/clienteling-defining-the-future-in-store-experience/#499f51133c2d (accessed September 9, 2021).

99. Mangtani, N. (2017) 'Clienteling – defining the future in-store experience', *Forbes*, February 1. www.forbes.com/sites/nitinmangtani/2017/02/01/clienteling-defining-the-future-in-store-experience/#499f51133c2d (accessed September 9, 2021).

100. Lieber, C. (2019) 'Why brands are sliding into your DMs', *Business of Fashion*, July 19. www.businessoffashion.com/articles/intelligence/why-brands-are-sliding-into-your-dms (accessed September 9, 2021).

101. Nix, K. (n.d.) 'Urgency for luxury brands to adopt mobile clienteling', *Retail Dive*. www.retaildive.com/ex/mobilecommercedaily/urgency-for-luxury-brands-to-adopt-mobile-clienteling (accessed September 9, 2021).

102. Nix, K. (n.d.) 'Urgency for luxury brands to adopt mobile clienteling', *Retail Dive*. www.retaildive.com/ex/mobilecommercedaily/urgency-for-luxury-brands-to-adopt-mobile-clienteling (accessed September 9, 2021).

103. Hyken, S. (2018) 'My Ritz-Carlton experience', *Forbes*, August 16. www.forbes.com/sites/shephyken/2018/08/16/my-ritz-carlton-experience/#1a74b5954d5e (accessed March 1, 2022).

104. Mangtani, N. (2017) 'Clienteling – defining the future in-store experience', *Forbes*, February 1. www.forbes.com/sites/nitinmangtani/2017/02/01/clienteling-defining-the-future-in-store-experience/#499f51133c2d (accessed September 9, 2021).

105. Fritchie, L.L. and Johnson, K.K. (2003) 'Personal selling approaches used in television shopping', *Journal of Fashion Marketing and Management: An International Journal*, 7 (3): 249–58.

106. Cialdini, R.B. (1993) *Influence: Science and Practice*, 3rd ed. New York, NY: HarperCollins.

107. BOF team (2012) 'Is the met ball becoming fashion's biggest PR platform?', *Business of Fashion*, May 8. www.businessoffashion.com/articles/intelligence/is-the-met-ball-becoming-fashions-biggest-pr-platform (accessed September 9, 2021).

108. Gulberti, G. (2018) '7 ways to make your press release visually stunning', *Launchmetrics*, August 28. www.launchmetrics.com/resources/blog/visual-press-release-tips (accessed September 9, 2021).

109. Vembar, K. (2019) 'Rihanna joins luxury group LVMH with Fenty launch', *Retail Dive,* May 13. www.retaildive.com/news/rihanna-joins-luxury-group-lvmh-with-fenty-launch/554630/ (accessed September 9, 2021).

110. NBC Sports (2015) 'Nike replace Adidas as official maker of NBA uniforms, apparel', *NBC,* June 11 www.nbcsports.com/northwest/nba/nike-replace-adidas-official-maker-nba-uniforms-apparel (accessed September 9, 2021).

111. Chen, C. (2018) 'Reebok to sponsor NYFW: Men's', *Business of Fashion,* June 11. www.businessoffashion.com/articles/news-analysis/reebok-to-sponsor-nyfw-mens (accessed September 9, 2021).

112. Zargani, L. (2019) 'Maria Grazia Chiuri's take on feminism: Still work to be done', *WWD,* April 3. https://wwd.com/eye/lifestyle/maria-grazia-chiuris-take-on-feminism-still-work-to-be-done-1203097850/ (accessed September 9, 2021).

113. Schiffer, J. (2019) 'How to turn a fashion show into an online 'moment'?', *Vogue,* September 19. www.voguebusiness.com/fashion/fashion-shows-social-media-moment-instagram-gucci-louis-vuitton (accessed September 9, 2021).

114. Okwodu, J. (2017) 'Versace just shut down Milan Fashion Week with an epic supermodel reunion', *Vogue,* September 22. www.vogue.com/article/versace-spring-2018-versace-supermodel-runway-reunion (accessed September 9, 2021).

115. Pinnock, O. (2019) 'The growing popularity of fashion exhibitions', *Forbes.* www.forbes.com/sites/oliviapinnock/2019/03/14/the-growing-popularity-of-fashion-exhibitions/#2269dd2dbbb1 (accessed September 9, 2021).

116. Armani/Silos (2021) 'Armani/Silos', *Armanisilos.com.* www.armanisilos.com/ (accessed September 9, 2021).

117. Ads of the World (2009) 'Rimmel', *Ads of the World,* January 3. www.adsoftheworld.com/media/ambient/rimmel_fast (accessed September 9, 2021).

118. Twinkle, T. and Zlotnick, S. (2019). 'Guys, there's now a champagne vending machine in center city', *Philadelphia,* January 7. www.phillymag.com/philadelphia-wedding/2019/07/01/champagne-moet-vending-machine-ritz-carlton/ (accessed September 9, 2021).

CHAPTER 12

Fashion Retailing and Distribution

LEARNING OBJECTIVES

After you read this chapter, you will understand the answers to the following:

1. What are the major fashion retail formats?

2. How can fashion marketers enhance the retail environment?

When Nike opened its Nike Town concept store in Chicago in 1992, heads turned. This wasn't just another shoe store! Visitors could interact with futuristic displays and learn about the basketball idol Michael Jordan. A visit to the store wasn't even necessarily about buying a new pair of shoes while you were there— Nike was confident you'd be so jazzed about the brand you'd purchase many of their styles down the road.

Nike Town was about presenting Nike's vision of a lifestyle that touted athleticism, a fierce competitive spirit— and of course different models of shoes and other merch to help you live the dream. If you did score a new pair of kicks while you were there, they flew through a two-story, clear pneumatic tube to reach you.

Fast forward to today. The original Nike Town store is just a distant memory. But there's a new vision to replace it (on the same site as the original) that was masterminded by Virgil Abloh, the creative director for Kanye West, and artistic director of Louis Vuitton, among other things.

Nike's newest creation is the NikeLab Chicago Re-Creation Center. You know it's also not just another shoe store right away—even the store's sign features an ironic statement on it: "for promotional use only." The store celebrates two of the biggest trends in retailing today: sustainability and experiences.

(Continued)

The recycling motif gets hammered home by walls that are lined in shoebox paper, while others feature bags of colorful shoe parts that came directly from the factory floor. There is colorful confetti all over the place that is actually what Nike calls Grind – ground-up shoes. When customers donate old shoes, those that are too worn to find a new owner journey on a conveyer belt to get ground up in a giant vat that spews out more Grind.

Nike involves customers in the experience of designing the next great pair of kicks – the store gives them free notebooks and markers they can use to sketch their dream shoe. Abloh says, "The footprint of this place is probably 20% retail on one of the most expensive retail streets in the country. The concept is valuable to me and the brand, but it's not about the exchange of dollars."[1]

Is this the future of retail?

What Is Fashion Retailing and Distribution

When you buy a fashion product, you often have a lot of options to consider regarding where you find it. Do you click on a website? Browse at a flea market? Perhaps you search the racks at your local department store. Let's dive into the last of The Famous Four Ps: Place.

Fashion retailing is the division that functions as an intermediary between the producers (e.g., brand or manufacturer) and customers. Fashion retailers belong to a **distribution channel**. They offer shoppers the luxury of time, place, and ownership value. A "place" refers to how and where the fashion product will be available and sold. Fashion brands follow different sales strategies in order to reach consumers. Some retailers allow their consumers to save time and money by offering a range of goods under one roof. Other fashion retailers search the world for the most glamorous delicacies to permit consumers access to items they would not see anywhere else.

Number of Channel Levels

Fashion companies manage their distribution channels to offer goods and services to their target markets in various ways. Every level of marketing intermediary that plays a role in bringing the product available to the end consumer is known as a **channel level**.

The number of **channel levels** between the producer and the final consumer varies in length from 0,1,2,3 or even more. Figure 12.1 identifies a number of business to consumer distribution channels. The first is known as the **direct marketing channel** in which the producer directly sells to the final consumer, meaning that all levels of the marketing channels are merged into a single ownership and under common control. Some fashion retailers appeal to the market through a **direct-to-consumer** (DTC) sales channel (exclusive physical store or a commerce-enabled website) in order to maintain a certain level of luxury image. Companies that conduct direct selling with consumers are more likely to control the environment and the customer experience. This offers the brand the opportunity to share the stories they want and to go beyond customers' expectations.

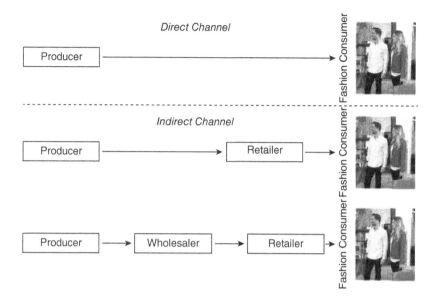

FIGURE 12.1   Fashion distribution channels

It is important to keep in mind that a lot of luxury brands such as Louis Vuitton sell their products only online or in stores in order to keep a unique and exclusive image. IKEA, the furniture retailer, manages the raw materials, supply, manufacturing, distribution and promotion of its goods all over the world, giving it a competitive advantage to offer products at very low cost. Another example is the fast-fashion brand Zara, which manages the whole supply chain all the way from raw materials to the finished fashion items that are placed on the shelves. Le Labo, Jo Malone and Diptyque have applied the direct marketing strategy to sell products to their consumers. Similarly, Louis Vuitton offers its perfume and sunglasses lines solely at 300 of its own stores.[2]

Other fashion brands may employ an **indirect marketing channel** that consists of having one or even more intermediaries in order to bring a fashion product to the final consumer. Think of all those fashion brands such as Self-portrait, Bash, Versus, Maje, Karl Lagerfeld, Moschino, DKNY, Calvin Klein, Pinko, Liu Jo, Tommy Hilfiger that you can find through intermediaries such as Selfridges, Harrods, Neiman Marcus, Bloomingdales or even online at ASOS, Farfetch, and Matchesfashion.

When it comes to beauty and cosmetics, most of the top luxury brands market their fashion goods through third-party department stores or at airport kiosks. Think of J'Adore or Sauvage from Dior, Chanel No. 5, Acqua Di Giò from Armani, or even cosmetics from Givenchy, Giorgio Armani, and Yves Saint Laurent.

However, some luxury brands realize that there is room for a direct retail driven model in beauty. Accordingly, the luxury brand Dior launched the Boutique Dior at 52 Avenue des Champs-Elysées. This store is like no other. It does not carry any of Dior's best-known fragrance items such as Miss Dior. However, the store promotes rare perfumes, lotions and white goods that cannot be found at any Dior airport or department store kiosk. For example, a bottle of Bois d'Argent perfume costs €395 per 450ml, while a body cream is priced at €90.[3]

While some fashion brands may either apply a direct or an indirect selling approach, others may follow a **multi sales-channel approach** that allows them to reach a wider audience and can take different forms. For example, the Twin Set brand can found either online or through the brand's physical stores, but it can also be found through department stores such as La Rinascente in Italy or even online on Giglio.com or Farfetch.com.

Major Bricks-and-Mortar Retailing Formats

Fashion companies need to decide on the form of retail store they would like to launch in order to appeal to their target market. Some brands may decide to open a stand-alone store; others may decide to open in a mall or even online. New store formats continue to evolve as customers and their environments change. For example, traditional department store layouts got a makeover after the pandemic to reduce customer traffic flows. Other new formats emerge, such as kiosks and **swishing parties** where consumers trade used clothing with one another. Below are the major retail formats in the context of fashion.

Department Stores

Department stores are businesses that sell a broad range of merchandise and present a wide selection of items scattered across various sections of the store according to product categories. The department store made an ostentatious appearance, from the mid-19th century, and has since redesigned buying habits and changed the meaning of service and luxury.

Le Bon Marché Rive Gauche in Paris was the world's first department store[4]. Several of the initial department stores, like John Lewis and Whiteleys in London, were established by drapers, apparel merchants who had more insights about the tastes and purchasing power of the emerging middle class that would propel the department store to affluent summits across Europe and the United States[5].

Traditionally, department stores used to include **nondurables** such as apparel, accessories, shoes, cosmetics, and bedding, and **durable goods** such as appliances, household textiles, furniture, and electrical appliances. The emergence of **category killers** (a huge retail shop that focusses on one specific form of discounted goods and becomes the main store in that specific category) has pushed department stores to focus mostly on non-durable goods. Some of the examples of luxury department stores are: Bloomingdale's, Nordstrom, Saks Fifth Avenue, Neiman Marcus, Harrods, Selfridges, Fenwick, Harvey Nichols, Au Printemps, Galleries Lafayette, and La Rinascente. Examples of middle market department stores include Macy's, Belk, Lord & Taylor, House of Fraser, and John Lewis.

Today, department stores have been hit hard with a noticeable drop in market share. Especially after the pandemic, managers of these stores are getting more and more worried about how to keep foot-traffic from further deterioration.[6] For example, Macy's Inc. and Kohl's Corp. all reported profit deterioration over the last several years.[7] The reason behind this challenge is that specialty stores are taking customers away from department stores by providing more selective and cutting-edge fashion assortments and improved customer service. For example, with more brands like Nike and Coach investing more in their own bricks-and-mortar stores and websites today, it decreases the need to have a department store to promote their items. And of course, shoppers' reluctance to reenter stores in large numbers due to the pandemic did not help.

Customers and more specifically many Millennials are looking for more experiences, they are trained to purchase on discount, and they are shifting toward apparel rentals rather than buying.[8] Department stores also face a decline in sales due to discount and outlet stores, catalogs, and online stores, which promote similar goods at cheaper prices as they don't have to shoulder the costs of expensive real estate, building sophisticated store atmospheres, and paying high salaries to professional salespeople.

Department stores have been under pressure as competition intensifies from online competitors such as Amazon, Boohoo, and ASOS. In line with all the difficulties, some one-time leaders haven't been able to sustain their presence in the market. For example, Sears and Neiman Marcus recently filed for bankruptcy (while declaring that their stores will still operate), while retail institutions including Debenhams and House of Fraser experienced similar difficulties.[9]

Galleries Lafayette

Image courtesy of Wouter Hagens via WikiMedia Commons. Shared under the public domain.

This hollowing out of middle-of-the market combined with the dominance of mass merchandising and niche specialty retailing stores is known as **bifurcated retailing**. To fight back against competitors, department stores are amassing more private label goods and exclusive domestic brand goods, expanding into online retailing, and trying to form better relationships with customers by offering enhanced customer service.

For instance, in order to fight against the pandemic, Neiman Marcus introduced Your Neiman's in July 2020—a digital center where individuals can obtain an assortment of offerings, comprising extended luxury services and experiences. Consumers can also get personalized services such as private appointments in-store, curbside pickup, accessing virtual events, or connecting online with an image consultant.[10]

To further engage its customers, Nordstrom allows online customers the option to search for merchandise that they can pick up during the same day from stores. The upscale department store chain also launched a new resale shop, which will not only allow consumers to buy used items, but to sell them in the store as well. With the popularity of the luxury second-hand market across the new generation, Selfridges launched its first permanent space dedicated to "pre-loved" fashion through a concession with Vestiaire Collective.[11]

Sephora, a specialty store

Faiz Zaki / Shutterstock.com

Specialty Stores

Specialty stores are shops that carry narrow and deep merchandise. They do not offer a big assortment of product lines, but they market a decent variety of brands within the lines they do provide. Specialty stores can appeal to the specific needs of a targeted consumer, and they usually have a great level of service. Think of Bed Bath & Beyond, Bodycare, Superdrug, and Sephora that have deep ranges but carry moderately few products compared to a department store. A specialty store often contains around 15,000 SKUs (stock-keeping units) and 200 brands.

Some specialty stores emphasize merchandise for a particular target market. For example, Evans is an online only brand that offers designs for plus size women. Flannels and Browns in London offers a range of apparel brands that focus upon the luxury market (e.g., Dolce and Gabanna, Balmain, and Moschino). One of the biggest specialty stores in the USA is Gap, which carries brands such as Gap, Old Navy, Banana Republic, and Athleta.

Convenience Stores

Convenience stores refer to shops with a limited range of recurrently purchased household goods and groceries, such as snacks, candies, over-the-counter drugs and toiletries. Convenience stores appeal to shoppers who are likely to pay a premium fee just for the convenience of buying merchandise that is close to home. One well-known example is 7-Eleven, which offers a range of beauty care and cosmetic products. Stores like this sometimes offer mass merchandised and cheap T-shirts, sunglasses and fashion magazines.

Supermarkets

Supermarkets are large stores that carry an extensive selection of edible and household goods. More and more supermarkets are complementing their merchandise assortment with apparel and they are enlarging their fashion spaces.

In the past, there was a stigma attached to purchasing apparel from supermarkets. Now, however, supermarkets are posing a growing threat to the high street fashion.[12] Think of the stylish, yet remarkably discounted merchandise at George by Asda that has been welcomed as leading the supermarket chic trend, followed by F&F by Tesco and Tu by Sainsbury's in the UK. Sainsbury's employs 30 fashion spotters to keep an eye on worldwide fashion runways and get inspired for the creation of the Tu apparel range.

Retailers like Walmart increasingly recognize that offering apparel and home is more profitable than just selling groceries. For this reason, the retailer re-introduced new fashion brands, in addition to relaunching the previously upscale fashion boutique Scoop as its elite brand for "fashion-forward customers."[13] Walmart also does big business when it comes to selling cosmetics. It is the biggest customer of the French L'Oréal label, accounting for just under 5% of its sales, while Coty, L'Oréal's competitor, creates 7% of its sales from Walmart supermarkets.[14] In order to face the competition of Amazon and Wal-Mart, the largest US supermarket chain Kroger also introduced a new apparel line.[15] Supermarkets also have jumped onto the bandwagon of the second-hand fashion world. For instance, Asda is the most recent supermarket to enter the second-hand market with the introduction of a 'Re-Loved' pop-up in its Milton Keynes store[16].

One form of a specialty store that is worth mentioning is the **category killer**. This term refers to a very large specialty store that carries a particular type of discounted goods and comes to be the leading retailer in that category. Think of Home Depot, Best Buy, Claire's, and Bed Bath & Beyond. Ikea is also a perfect example of a category killer in furniture retailing. The retailer focuses on efficiency and low cost to maximize its revenues without sacrificing quality and service.[17]

Contractual Retailers

Fashion retailers can make contractual agreements with producers, wholesalers or even other retailers and integrate their efforts in a way to attain more efficiency and marketing impact. The most typical contractual agreements in fashion may take the form of leased departments or franchises.

Franchises   A **franchise** is a contractual agreement between a franchisee and a given franchisor that offers the franchisor the exclusive right to sell the franchisee's goods in a specific territory. In return for having the franchise, the franchisee pays the franchisor an initial payment and some licensing fees on an annual basis. The franchise gets distribution at the retail level and through its dealers, but maintains control over how the merchandising will take place.

For example, the luxury Swiss Watchmaker Audemars Piguet aims to fully control the distribution of its luxury watches by removing third-party multi-brand retailers from its distribution channel within three to five years. The brand is planning to exert more control over its distribution by building sales through its monobrand stores that sell either proprietary or operated by franchise partners. When the brand

Audemars Piguet

Papin Lab / Shutterstock.com

Dolce & Gabbana, Milan

Casimiro PT / Shutterstock.com

directly sells to its customers, it will have the opportunity to keep a higher markup, better manage inventory levels, and collect data on its customers.[18]

Some luxury brands do not charge a royalty fee to the franchisee, but instead benefit from their sales revenues. Contrary to mass market brands, luxury brands do not sign any agreement before a store location is selected. They insist that all furnishings and fittings have to bought from the brand itself. Some luxury brands like Louis Vuitton do not grant franchises at all. Other brands grant franchises with the exclusion of key capital cities, such as Giorgio Armani, Dolce & Gabbana, Christian Dior, Tiffany's, Cartier, and Harvey Nichols.[19]

Leased Departments   **Leased departments** are departments within a larger retail store; an independent retailer who owns fashion merchandise rents its floor space. This arrangement permits bigger stores to provide a wider assortment of products than they would otherwise hold. Typical examples of leased departments include fine jewelry departments and boutique luxury spaces, optical centers, and watch and shoe repair within department stores.

Discount Stores

Discount stores refer to shops that market brand name goods at less than the normal retail price and offer clothing items at the mass price level. Think of Target, Kmart, and Walmart, which provide a wide variety of goods at cheap prices and with very minimal service and are the prevailing outlet for numerous products. Discounters upend the retail landscape because they cater to price-sensitive buyers who look for convenient access to mass merchandise. These retailers are progressively offering designer-name apparel at bargain prices. Did you know that Liz Claiborne designs ranges specifically for discount stores? This strategy may be harmful to luxury brands as it may cheapen the image of the brand.

Off-price Stores

Off-price retailers offer national brands, designer brands or promotional goods at cheap prices. Some discount stores buy irregular or leftovers from producers or other retailers in bulk and at very low prices and resell them at reduced prices. T.J. Maxx, T.K. Maxx (UK), Ross Stores, Marshalls, HomeGoods, and Burlington Coat Factory are examples of retailers that generally offer second-hand and off-the-season items. These retailers usually obtain numerous deliveries per week, with each one comprising thousands of goods. As such, they are able to offer new and diverse goods every couple of days. Such stores attract shoppers who constantly want to see new things on the racks. The success of off-price discounters in providing exciting items on a regular basis challenges traditional retailers that stock full line items to provide a similar experience.

Retailers offering second-hand and off-season items

Outlet Stores

A number of conventional retailers have opened **outlet stores** that sell slow moving and out-of-date goods. Nowadays factory outlets are brand- or retailer-owned brick-and-mortar or online stores that offer only a particular brand. They are usually located in an outlet mall along with other, similar stores or online.

Factory outlets increasingly sell goods that are purposely manufactured for the outlets; it's common for these products to be of lower quality than the company's other lines. An outlet store is usually operated by a retailer that seeks to sell the goods that are still in stock, while an off-price retailer usually buys large quantities from another retailer at a very low unit price.

Outlet malls are moving closer to city centers, often locating themselves in near proximity to normal stores and stimulating **cross-shopping** (a technique whereby shoppers buy from various retailers for the sake of obtaining better deals).[20] As a lot of buyers start to search more intensely for lower-priced merchandise, some mainstream retailers have found success in this part of the market. For instance, Nordstrom has spent the past few years reconsidering its merchandising strategy and the whole consumer experience, while at the same time heavily investing in digital. In order to increase foot traffic, Nordstrom has also considerably increased its discounted offerings, by opening a chain of discount stores known as Nordstrom Rack as part of a longer-term strategy to appeal to the increasing consumer demand for discounted items.[21] Another example of retailers that operate their own off-price stores is Saks Fifth Avenue, which launched its off-price division known as Saks Off Fifth.

Surprisingly, some outlet malls are starting to cater to wealthy shoppers as well. They actually are one of the fastest-growing channels in luxury[22]. However, these luxury outlet malls try to position themselves as toney destinations rather than as down-market shopping areas. Think of Woodbury Common in New York, Serravalle Outlet in Milan, Bicester Village near Oxford, Castel Romano Designer Outlet in Rome, McArthurGlen Designer Outlet Malaga in Spain, La Vallee Village Paris, or Shanghai Village in Shanghai.

Examples of world-class luxury brands located in Bicester Village near Oxford

For example, Bicester Villages, located in 11 sought-after destinations across Europe and China, are home to a combination of luxury boutiques from world-class international fashion and lifestyle brands such as Balenciaga, Gucci, Dior, Armani, Dolce & Gabanna, Jimmy Choo, Alexander McQueen, Valentino, Burberry, Manolo Blahnik, Fendi, Coach, Prada, Mulberry, Smythson, and Stella McCartney. Every boutique provides year-round savings on the recommended retail price of up to 60%—and sometimes more—in Europe, and up to 80% in China. To give customers a full luxury experience, the villages have a chauffeur service with pick-up places in selected cities, personal stylists to assist customers in attaining the best look, and a hands-free shopping feature that allows customers to shop without having to worry about carrying shopping bags. Each village is equipped with a VIP lounge, kids' playground, multi-faith prayer rooms, free Wi-Fi, and can organize worldwide home delivery.[23]

Popup Stores

Pop-up retail is a storefront space that is open only for a specific period of time in order to benefit from a faddish trend or seasonal demand. One of the advantages of a pop-up store is its low-cost to get up and running.

The goal of a pop-up store is to create consumer interest and generate buzz. This retail form has become a go-to marketing strategy for retailers looking to expand their brands, introduce and test new products, and test the desirability of new physical locations. This new format is a way for traditional retailers to respond to shoppers who clamor for novelty and stimulation. For this reason, the fashion products that you will find in these stores are usually short-lived or related to a specific collaboration, season, or theme. Effective pop-ups merge a right location and retail concept to develop a great customer experience and usually feature an engaging form and innovative design. Some seasonal pop-up stores sell Halloween costumes, Christmas gifts and decorations, and fireworks.

A number of traditional fashion retailers rely on pop-up stores to create more buzz in the market, such as Louis Vuitton, Christian Dior, Amazon, Chanel, and Bvlgari. In 2019, Gucci launched a series of global, themed pop-up stores intended to provide more reasons for customers to buy throughout the year, more specifically in places where the brand's corporate owner Kering doesn't have an actual physical footprint. Some of their target locations are Chengdu, Sao Paulo, Taipei, Bangkok, Moscow, Mexico City, Dubai and many more cities across Europe, Latin America, the US, Middle East and Asia Pacific regions. Known as the "Gucci Pin", the short-term stores focus on digital technology.[24]

Nordstrom has also applied this strategy by launching a series of "Pop-In@Nordstrom", displaying new pop-ups every four to six weeks and offering exclusive merchandise. The apparel brand Everlane and the luxury luggage company Away have both benefited from this format by launching their first pop-up with Nordstrom in 2017 and once again in 2019.[25] The fast-fashion retailer Zara also followed the trend by opening pop-up customization corners in its stores located in Amsterdam, Barcelona and Milan; customers can stitch words on 13 various denim designs from a €19.95 pair of shorts to a €39.95 jacket.[26]

Resale Stores

Have you ever thought that classic Chanel Boy or Hermès Birkin bags can have a second life? **Resale stores** refer to retailers that obtain secondhand goods for resale. This type of retailing can take the form of **thrift stores**, such as Goodwill and Cancer Research UK, and **consignment stores** in addition to a smaller number of antique stores.[27]

The profit from thrift shops is usually sent to charity, while consignment shops return a percentage to the main owner. Second-hand fashion used to be limited to thrift stores, hipsters, flea markets or eBay; however, this has recently changed with the shift in demand of the new generations for vintage items that drives them to this industry (e.g., 37% of Gen Z shop resale, compared to 27% of Millennials and 19% of baby boomers)[28].

A number of resale stores have lately emerged such as Thredup, Tradesy, Rebag, Depop, Poshmark, RealReal, Resee, and Vestiaire Collective, driving the global market of apparel resale to reach 24 billion U.S. dollars in 2018 and estimated to reach $51 billion by 2023.[29] The development of the resale market presents some challenges to the apparel sector. Imagine that the second-hand market was valued at $24 billion in the U.S. in 2018, as opposed to $35 billion for fast-fashion (e.g., H&M and Zara). Nevertheless, by 2028 the second-hand apparel market is predicted to outreach the fast-fashion market value, attaining $64 billion in the U.S. versus $44 billion for fast-fashion[30].

Gucci pop-up store

Image courtesy of Sikander Iqbal via WikiMedia Commons. Shared under the CC BY-SA 4.0 license.

Consumers are turning to the resale market for items that are lower in price and more environmentally friendly.[31] Purchasing from resale permits them to express themselves with exclusive vintage apparel, and it's entertaining because there is always something new and different that they can sometimes get at a bargain price. One of the most interesting expansions in the resale market is in the sneakers/trainers category. "By 2025, sales could reach $6 billion in the resale market. There is strong demand for athletic shoes like Nike's Air Jordan 1, Adidas' Yeezy Boost, Nike's Air MAX, Balenciaga's Triple S, Fendi's Multicolor, and Van's F.O.G. (Fear of God). Unlike many of the resale fashion categories, they often sell for many times their original high prices. For instance, Yeezy Boosts that originally cost $300 resold for $1,239".[32]

Some luxury fashion brands are trying to find ways to tap into the rapidly growing secondary market. For example, the luxury brand Burberry recently collaborated with the RealReal to appeal to the fast-emerging resale market by developing a pilot program that allows individuals who sell Burberry items on The RealReal to receive a private personal shopping experience at specific stores in the US.[33] The luxury department store Harrods initiated Fashion Re-told, a charity pop-up, which promotes pre-owned designer apparel from luxury brands such as Chloé and Stella McCartney. Other department stores are jumping onto this trend as well. Vestiaire Collective partnered with Selfridges to open its first off-line store in the luxury department, aiming to drive consumers to recycle items either through purchasing or reselling pre-owned fashion items in-store. Macy's has also started to sell secondhand apparel in its store with ThredUp.[34] The online retailer Farfetch is the latest company to get into this market, channeling its Second Life resale business as it encourages shoppers to sell their designer handbags in return for a credit reward.[35]

Rental Stores

Do you buy or rent your clothes? The sharing economy that has lately upset the taxi (e.g. Uber) and travel industries (e.g. Airbnb) is beginning to make its mark in apparel. Fashion rental is booming nowadays, and it is no more confined to occasion wear such as wedding gowns. A number of companies are giving shoppers the option of renting everyday items, from apparel and handbags to shoes and accessories. Luxury labels, kidswear, and, maternity wear are becoming widely popular among shoppers who are unwilling to spend a lot on items that they will not use for a long period of time or those who are eager to stay continuously fashionable.

Also, consumers who are environmentally conscious and price sensitive increasingly seek to rent rather than purchase new fashion items.[36] In 2019, the rental platform leader Rent the Runway attained unicorn rank (a privately detained startup company valued above $1 billion) as it closed a huge $125 million in funding; while other luxury brands and department stores, including Ann Taylor, Banana Republic (of Gap Inc) and Bloomingdales have set up their own rental services.[37]

To stay competitive in the market and be able to steal market share from department stores and many multi-brand retailers, Rent the Runway launched a series of exclusive apparel lines to the platform in collaboration with designers such Derek Lam, Prabal Gurung, and Jason Wu. Fashion rental companies are not only interested in the adult market; however, they also have started to seek new opportunities in the childrenswear market. For example, Rent the Runway decided to expand into the kids market through a monthly rental service that allows consumers to dress their kids in such upscale brands as Chloé, Fendi, Stella McCartney, and Little Marc Jacobs[38].

As the online apparel rental market is predicted to reach approximately $2 billion worldwide by 2023, this opportunity has enticed a number of start-up companies to start considering this market.[39] Examples are Flont, a company that rents out fine jewelry, Eleven James, a retailer that rents out luxury watches and Vivrelle or Villageluxe, an online retailer that allows you to rent luxury handbags, such as Chanel, Dior, and Hermès.

Rent the Runway launching a series of exclusive apparel lines in collaboration with fashion designers

Image courtesy of Ajay Suresh via wikiMedia Commons. Shared under the CC BY 2.0 license.

Mass fashion brands have also jumped onto this bandwagon. The fast-fashion retailer H&M launched a limited rental service presenting its premium-priced collection manufactured from recycled materials in a refurbished central Stockholm store. Levi Strauss & Co partnered with Rent the Runway to offer 29 items like skinny jeans and embroidered denim jackets to rent.

Direct Sellers

Direct selling takes place when sales associates offer a good to one consumer or a group, receive orders, and deliver the product. Direct selling is most common for home care items, cosmetics apparel and accessories, and services. Scentsy, Mary Kay, Avon, and Tupperware are among the main direct sellers.

One form of direct selling is at-home shopping parties also known as in-home selling. This technique involves a sales advisor doing a presentation in front of a group of individuals who have come together at a friend's home. While gathered, individuals usually purchase items that they do not usually intend to buy only because they are in a "group spirit". Avon, Mary Kay, Stella & Dot, Cabi, and W by Worth are some of the prominent fashion companies that use this business model.

E-commerce

When was the last time you bought something on your phone? For marketers, the growth of e-commerce is a sword that cuts both ways: on the one hand, they can reach consumers around the world even if they are physically located a hundred miles from nowhere. On the other hand, their competition now comes not only from the store across the street, but from thousands of websites spanning the globe. A second problem is that offering products directly to consumers has the potential to cut out the middleman—the loyal store-based retailers who carry the firm's products and who sell them at a marked-up price. The "clicks versus bricks" dilemma is raging in the marketing world.

E-commerce refers to the marketing and purchase of goods and services through an online exchange between companies and individual consumers. The largest segment in e-commerce is fashion (e.g., apparel, shoes, bags, and accessories), which has reached around US$620.6 billion in 2019 and is expected to expand at a rate of 12.2% per year to attain a global market value of US$991.64 billion by 2024.[40]

Why has e-commerce become so popular? Some e-retailers try to benefit from technological developments in order to offer additional value to customers that offline retailers cannot provide. For instance, Gucci allows you to virtually try on its Ace sneakers. Then a digital image is presented to you to see how the sneakers look on your feet.[41] The luxury website Moda Operandi offers exclusive styles by pushing brands to create limited edition runway pieces that could only be found on its website. Online formats are also convenient and time-efficient, and in many cases, they offer a level of price transparency that is hard to match as consumers compare prices on their phones or other mobile devices before they purchase. And, of course the pandemic added fuel to the fire as many shoppers who wanted to avoid public spaces discovered the joys of online shopping and delivery.

Normally, online buyers place a high significance on the following features of a website:

- The possibility to select a product and be able to get a pop-up window with more information about the item, including the price, material, colors, size, and stock.

- The possibility to click on a product and add it to your bag/shopping cart without having to close the page.

- The possibility to examine the products through improved images, additional product descriptions, and information.

- The possibility to enter all information linked to your consumption on one page, rather than having to scroll across different checkout pages.

- The possibility to mix and match item photos on one page to identify if the items go together.

- The possibility to share your potential purchases with others in your network in order to get their feedback *before* you make a fashion mistake.

Consumers increasingly use their mobile devices to make online purchases. As we saw in Chapter 11, m-commerce has become a very important channel for marketers. Social media platforms such as Facebook, Instagram, and Pinterest have created "buy buttons" that allow consumers to finalize their buying without having to exit the platform. A number of retailers went a step further; they added one-click checkout to their platforms to give consumers the convenience of making a purchase without re-entering their information.[42]

One of the limitations of e-commerce relates to the actual shopping experience. While it may be satisfactory to buy a computer or a book on the Internet, buying apparel and other items where touching the item or trying it on is essential, may be less attractive[43]. Even though most companies have liberal return policies, consumers can still get stuck with large delivery and return shipping charges for items that don't fit or simply aren't the right color.

Timing and delivery can also be a problem for companies. In order to overcome these issues, fashion brands and retailers are coming up with different strategies. For example, Amazon has added a 'try before you buy' fashion service for its Prime subscribers. Customers can choose between two and six items from a selection of apparel and shoes. Then, they can get the items delivered to their homes at no extra cost for a 7-day trial period. They can select the items they want to keep and only pay for these items while returning the unwanted ones for free.

New technology is enhancing the try before you buy strategy. In particular, as we saw in Chapter 2, augmented reality that superimposes a digital image over a physical one on your smartphone allows shoppers to get a good sense of what a product will look like without actually interacting with it. Here are a few recent examples of this tech in use:

- Dior used augmented reality to allow consumers to try on sunglasses using their smartphones.[44]

- Toyota introduced an innovative augmented reality program that allows consumers to test 10 of their automobiles without ever picking up the keys.

- The e-commerce retailer Alibaba uses Perfect Corp's virtual try-on technology to permit consumers to see how make-up will look on them before buying cosmetic products on its Taobao and Tmall online shopping platforms.[45]

- In order to deal with problems related to fit when it comes to online shopping, Amazon acquired the 3D body model startup Body Labs. The aim of this company is to develop true-to-life 3D body models to make virtual try-ons even more accurate.[46]

Nike introduced a new scanning solution known as Nike Fit that relies on a trademarked mixture of computer vision, data science, machine learning, artificial intelligence, and suggested algorithms. This feature allows the user to scan and measure the complete form of both feet within a few seconds, providing shoppers the ability to identify their perfect fit for every Nike shoe only by using a mobile device's camera. The scan of foot dimension can also be stored in the NikePlus member profile to make future online shopping easier.[47]

Also, fast delivery service has become essential as Millennials and Gen Z consumers prioritize **instant gratification**. In order to further satisfy customers, Farfetch provides same-day delivery in 18 key cities. Through a collaboration with Gucci, Farfetch can deliver hand-picked Gucci items within 90 minutes to its customers in 10 international cities.[48] Still want to have a faster delivery than 90 minutes?

Luxury's Internet Dilemma

The Internet Dilemma is a concept that defines the challenge luxury firms face as they strive to maintain the image of their brand, keep good relationships with customers, and preserve an exclusive aura and a fantasy component while offering goods and services to online customers.[49] Luxury brands face a huge dilemma when they try to appeal to young Internet-savvy consumers while keeping the sense of uniqueness that is a vital part of a luxury product. For this reason, some of these brands were quite slow to develop e-commerce sites. A typical example is the French label Chanel, which even today does not have an e-commerce presence for its apparel, shoes, handbags and accessories. However, the brand sells fragrances, eyeglasses, and beauty products online.[50]

In 2017, the LVMH group launched a multi-brand e-commerce website as a way to step up into the digital part of the fashion and luxury business. Named "24 Sèvres", the website offers a range of fashion, cosmetics and luggage goods from its own portfolio in addition to other brands. Some of the available brands are Louis Vuitton, Dior, and Fendi. This website aims to compete with more recognized online luxury websites such as Yoox, Net-a-Porter, MyTheresa, Matchesfashion.com, and Moda Operandi.[51]

The luxury group Richemont partnered in 2019 with Alibaba Group Holding Ltd. and agreed that the group's brands will be sold on the Tmall e-commerce site. Tom Ford, Brunello Cucinelli, and Jimmy Choo also participated by joining the Richemont brands Cartier, Piaget, and Vacheron Constantin on the site. Richemont decided to go this route to boost its online sales after the company acquired the online luxury retailers Yoox and Net-A-Porter and the pre-owned watch retailer Watchfinder. This is a great opportunity for the Swiss company to appeal to Chinese consumers— who are estimated to make up almost half of the global luxury market by 2025—without the cost of opening physical stores in Asia.

As companies continue to ramp up both their online and offline footprints, they need to design a proper **omnichannel marketing strategy.** This term describes a way to provide customers with a seamless shopping experience, regardless of whether they buy online through a tablet or mobile device, by telephone, or from a physical store (see[52]). Although many luxury brands were slow out of the gate to move into online sales, today numerous marketers such as Louis Vuitton and Nordstrom are catching up rapidly as they create new omnichannel experiences for customers.[53]

New technology allows the sales representatives to have access to a customer's preferences, amount and time of purchase, returns, and all the additional information they need to stay in touch with their shopping activities regardless of where they occur. As the customer shifts from a desktop to a tablet to a mobile device, it's important to have the ability to merge their search history and purchases regardless of where they occur.

The cosmetic brand Huda Beauty is one company that has properly implemented an omnichannel strategy. According to the Marketing VP for Huda Beauty, "An omnichannel experience is one that everybody wants to have. A physical experience needs to add something so that customers receive more than they would get online."[54] The brand, which mainly sells via social media, wanted to bring the experience of social media into real life, by offering an extremely strong and immersive encounter. Huda Beauty created a pop-up store to market its new eye-shadow palette, Mercury Retrograde, and the environment built around this very much focused on the cosmic and the magical. The whole exterior of the pop-up looked like a multi-faceted, metallic mass of geometrical forms. This was repeated inside with various 'galactic' features, "fractured" mirrored facades and shimmering fixtures and elements. Customers were able to take a seat on the same throne Huda used in her promotion material, sharing their experience through many images. This atmosphere moved them from the pop-up's physical environment into the empires of social media and the online world for others to see and experience[55].

Engineering the Physical Retail Environment

The growth of e-commerce doesn't mean that we're witnessing the end of brick-and-mortar stores.[56] Over the past few years, fashion retailers have taken a different approach to keep their footing in brick-and-mortar businesses by adapting and modifying the way they use their physical space. They are currently concentrating on the customer experience rather than only considering stores as an area filled with ever-changing items to be sold.[57] Below we will discuss how fashion marketers are rethinking the retail environment.

Store Atmospherics

Although e-commerce is currently booming, a study has demonstrated that most shoppers still favor the experience of shopping in bricks-and-mortar stores. The study indicated that music, visuals, and scents are crucial to shoppers; 79% of participants stated that they have the tendency to shop in a store rather than online as long as the atmosphere is enjoyable.[58]

Retailing as Theater

As mentioned previously in Chapter 11, retailtainment refers to the process of merging retail shopping and entertainment together, a mounting trend in fashion retailing whereby brands are tempted to offer in-store customer experiences. Think about Disney. It's like a theater. With competition becoming much stronger especially with the growth of Internet and TV shopping, companies need to come up with ways to differentiate themselves from others. So how can conventional stores compete? A lot of companies are trying to create entertainment centers. Think of M&M'S centered in Times Square, considered one of the hottest performances in town![59]

Retail theming refers to the process of entertaining consumers developing imaginative environments that takes them to fantasy worlds or deliver other forms of inspiration. One very common theming strategy is to transform a store into a **being space**. This type of environment looks like a kind of commercial living room, where people can sit and relax, have some entertainments, and connect with others. A perfect example is Starbucks. The coffee chain says its purpose is to develop into a so-called "third place," where people can spend most of their time if they are not at home or at work (or both, if they are still telecommuting after the pandemic). For this reason, the chain has placed in its stores more comfortable chairs and equipped it with free Wi-Fi.

Store Image

As discussed in Chapter 6, similar to people and brands, stores also have "personalities." Some of the significant features of **store image** are location, goods, and customer service. All of these factors usually merge together to produce an overall impression, and this is the reason why sometimes we may end up saying "oh it is so cool to purchase from this store" or "this store makes me feel nervous". We rapidly form an overall impression of a specific store, and our emotions are usually linked with intangible features like the interior of a store, the salespeople who assist us, or even the store's return policies.[60]

Since marketers identify the prominence of a store's image when it comes to retailing, fashion brands are trying to create unique and vibrant in-store atmospheres by emphasizing **atmospherics**, the conscious planning of space and its different dimensions to induce certain effects in shoppers. Atmospheric variables consist of five different characteristics: exterior variables, general interior, layout and design variables, point-of-purchase and decoration, and human variables.[61] Today, with e-commerce, there is a lot of emphasis on web atmospherics as well.[62]

Exterior Variables

The external variables of the retail shop comprise the building shape and features such as the architectural style, colors, and signage. **Outdoor signage** is central to physical retail because it's what drives foot traffic to a store. For example, luxurious and extravagant sign boards show that luxury products are sold inside the store. Some multi-brand retailers or off-price discounters use outdoor signs to communicate the types of brands they carry. In addition, the geographic location also affects consumers' image perceptions of the retail shop. Zara, for example carefully selects its location to be sure that its stores are located in the busiest upscale cities around the world such as the Champs-Élysées in Paris, places that affluent buyers are likely to visit. The chosen locations are usually in the most expensive places surrounded by luxury or more premium brands, reinforcing a sense of exclusivity and uniqueness.[63]

A **window display** is one of the most important marketing tools for a fashion retailer.[64] Inspirational and eye-catching store windows are also a crucial part of the exterior of the store, designed in a way to showcase the brand's products and services to the world with the objective of bringing customers in and tempting them to visit the store. Think of how Tiffany displays only a few pieces of jewelry in the window, underscoring the brand's uniqueness and exclusivity.

Recently, a few imaginative retailers have turned to **interactive window displays**. For instance, the Swedish hardware/homeware retailer Clas Ohlson grabs attention with an inno-

Gucci Window Display

tianalima / Shutterstock.com

vative motion-sensor-activated storefront. The retailer displays a screen on the stores' windows that becomes interactive when it senses someone standing in front of it. The screens are equipped with QR codes which, once scanned with a phone, allow shoppers to browse the retailers' catalog and finalize a purchase.[65] For its Hallucination campaign, Gucci used augmented reality for its window displays by placing classic artworks re-imagined with characters dressed in the brand's apparel and resembling an art gallery. A scannable QR code was available on the windows that allowed people who walk past the store to download the Gucci app and experience an animated version of the art.[66]

Interior Variables

The store's **interior decoration** has a major impact on the atmosphere. Many luxury brands invite consumers to linger on a sofa to express a sense of luxury while shopping and permit shopping partners to have a relaxed spot to rest and wait. The general interior dimension consists of the flooring/carpeting, lighting, aromas and music, temperature, cleanliness, wall textures, and color scheme.

These elements may be subtle (unless the air is thick with fragrance or the music is pounding), but they have a huge effect on shopping behavior. For example, a store soundtrack can turn people on (or off) because we listen to music to regulate arousal and mood, relate to others, or in some cases to help us remember events from the past.[67]

Previous studies show that store interiors can greatly impact the amount of time shoppers spend in a store, in addition to influencing sales.[68] Fashion and luxury retailers increasingly invest in **experiential retailing** to offer a distinctive retail experience and motivate shoppers to stay longer and spend more. For instance, the American retailer Abercrombie & Fitch sets its brand apart while providing an exceptional in-store experience with dim lighting and spotlights tending to remind one of a nightclub. The department store Selfridges in London designed "The Bowl" that allows customers to skate in the windows of Selfridges.

The Skate Bowl at Selfridges
Image courtesy of Ali

The right selection of in-store lighting is crucial since it can have a huge impact on a consumer's mood.[69] Research suggests that in-store lighting can help guide customers through a store, and potentially increase the average spend per customer. When it comes to lighting, retailers need to consider **color temperatures** as well as brightness. Cool color temperatures like a cool white make areas seem to be more spacious while warm color temperatures generate a feeling of intimacy and familiarity. Warm lighting makes consumers feel more relaxed and contented while brighter lighting allows them to clearly see products.

Think of the Louis Vuitton flagship store in New Bond Street in London, where the light highlights LV's iconic items in order to directly lead shoppers to these particular products.[70] Some retailers

Selfridges interior decoration

Image courtesy of Ali

are also making more use of natural light. For example, the luxury retailer Selfridges opened up the windows on its third-level womenswear section. Design experts recommend the use of natural light instead of spotlights that can cause lots of shadows and don't truly complement shoppers, an approach aimed to create the perfect lighting for social-media friendly experiences that are necessary for creating sharable content.[71]

A number of luxury fashion brands are currently using the recent green and organic movement as inspiration for interior color decoration, textures, and store fixtures. Green, steel, glass and wood materials typify the recent luxury retail environment. For example, in Salvatore Ferragamo's Fifth Avenue location in New York City, the store was designed with wood-bordered apparel racks, glass shelving, and taupe walls.

Fashion companies have always designed store environments intended to excite the eyes and ears. Recently retailers started to shift their attention to the importance of scent, and they are currently embracing the art of **olfactory branding,** or **scent marketing**. For example, the fashion retailers H&M and Calvin Klein use their identifiable branded fragrances to scent their spaces.[72]

There are four different forms of scent marketing:

- An **aroma billboard smell** is one that generates the most audacious scented statement—linking a brand to a scent. For example, all Ritz Carlton hotels have a similar smell regardless, of whether they are located in Paris or in London.

- A **thematic smell** is usually appropriate to the form of business. For example, a lavender scent in a spa.

- An **ambient smell** is more refined and is used to remove unpleasant smells. For example, restaurants usually use ambient smells for toilets.

- A **signature smell** is usually used in premium department stores or luxury fashion houses.[73] For example, Christian Dior used the services of Scent Company to tap into their customers' olfactory sense spreading their shops with a signature scent inspired by one of the most renowned Dior perfumes.[74]

Layout and Design Variables

Layout and design of the retail shop comprise the fixtures, allocation of floor space, product groupings, traffic flow, department locations, and allocations within departments. A carefully designed retail shop allows a retailer to make the best use of space by boosting the sales per square foot. Merchandise should be displayed in an efficient way to motivate shoppers to make additional purchases at the time they are browsing the shop. Retailers should be conscious not to overcrowd the shop floor with merchandise. Although this strategy can increase the assortment of items, it also reduces customer traffic flow space since a lot of shoppers do not feel comfortable with crowded stores but rather prefer to shop with less stress. Luxury brands usually display less merchandise on the retail floor while value-oriented retailers try to amass and pile more products. For example, stores like TJ Maxx, TK Maxx, or Ross tend to load up inventory to make the selling floor look more like a bargain hunt.

Fashion marketers also need to recognize that most of the people are right-handed, which means that they tend to turn right after entering a retail space and tend to grab products that are placed on the right. Accordingly, marketers need to take this into consideration when they plan the way people circulate in a store in order to allocate items on the most suitable tables or walls.[75] Retailers can locate their high-demand items or premium promotion in this specific location on the right known as the **power wall**.

There are mainly two floor plans that are used when it comes to merchandising fashion and luxury products. The **geometric plan** is convenient for apparel brands or retailers whereby an out of the ordinary store design is created at no cost by using racks and fixtures. Luxury specialty stores use **the angular floor plan** whereby the used angles and curves of furniture and walls reveal a premium image of the store. Meanwhile, the soft angles allow an easier traffic flow across the store.[76]

Think of the floor plans and fixtures structures of the fashion label Anthropologie (more can be viewed via the online resources). The style is ostensibly 'relaxed' in style with blueprints carefully planned to make sure that all racks, displays and furniture parts are placed at 40-degree angles. This symmetry generates a sense of flexibility that lures consumers further into the store, motivating them to explore more. Also, the segmented rooms in the store move consumers into the discounted sections where they can go through apparel and home assortments.[77]

Some fashion retailers use a mixture of floor plans. For example, Nordstrom includes several layouts to differentiate across the different branded shops that are placed within the store. The department store moves from a grid layout, which displays Nike and Adidas stores-within-a-store to a free-flow, premium brands set within the space. They skilfully combine various store layouts to generate different experiences for all the different labels that are placed under one retail shop.[78]

Point-of-Purchase and Decoration

Point-of-purchase and decoration includes product displays, point-of-purchase displays, posters, cards, interactive displays, and wall decorations. Previous research indicates the effectiveness of product displays on a company's sales.[79] For instance, fashion marketers think of how to group items together. The **visual merchandising strategy** must take into consideration placing products based on their usage—all items related to a certain occasion or of a given color displayed together.

Interactive displays such as augmented reality are being used more and more in-store to enrich the retail experience and grow a brand's reach (see[80]). For example, the tech company Ombori introduced its smart mirror to the Max Fashion Store of the Future at the Ibn Battuta Mall in Dubai. When shoppers are inside the store, a smart voice-controlled mirror with a camera permits them to browse items and promotions only by talking to the mirror either in English or in Arabic. The mirror can also take amusing pictures that customers can share on different digital platforms.[81]

Nike has been trying to merge in-person experiences with digital capabilities in its stores. At the brand's flagship store in Manhattan, shoppers can refer to the Nike app to reserve items for in-store pickup, scan QR codes on dummies to look over for existing colors and sizes, pay directly for goods, and take in-store appointments with Nike consultants. At their store in Soho in New York, Nike displays an athletic atmosphere—such as a basketball half-court and a treadmill—boosted with cameras and digital screens to offer customers an immersive experience and real-time feedback. As convenience is becoming very important to consumers, fashion retailers are trying to come up with creative ways to make in-store shopping much easier. For example, the fashion retailer Everlane permits shoppers who have an online registration to "shop walletless" in-stores. Reformation, an apparel retailer, allows customers to use digital screens to choose the merchandise they would like to try on, which sales representatives put later on in fitting rooms.[82]

Further to this, fashion retailers are relying more on digital instore signage. They are using these signs in fitting rooms in order to reveal accessories and complementary articles to the products that customers have selected. Fashion retailers need to provide informational signage (e.g., womenswear, menswear or kidswear departments) to aid the shopper navigate the store more conveniently. Directional signage is also crucial as it guides the shopper where to go next. Retailers also design persuasive signage in order to shape consumers' behavior regarding otherwise unnoticed goods. Signs which exhibit a certain item provide an opportunity for brands to communicate precise information of new, seasonal, or featured products.[83] For example, Topshop always uses the tag "As seen on *Vogue*" to promote their unique items in-store. Other retailers also use messages such as "Touch me" or "Try me" or "last chance to buy".

Human Variables

Human variables involve the density, characteristics and appearances of salespeople. Research shows that the number of employees in a store affects shoppers' perception of the store's service quality.[84] Fashion retailers usually manage the density of salespeople in their stores. In general, a higher number of employees are needed in stores where a high level of service is provided. Think of the premium apparel brands or retailers that usually hire sales associates to advise on fit and items selections and to assist them throughout the shopping experience. When the number of employees in a store is perceived to be lower than required in order to operate properly, this is known as **understaffing** and may negatively influence consumers' perceptions and responses.

Further to this, the appearance of employees plays a very important role. A previous study indicated that when salespeople are dressed professionally and appropriately to fit their job, the service is perceived more positively.[85]

The Future of Fashion Retailing: Are Stores Dead?

Despite all the worldwide changes, brick-and-mortar stores will not be dead in the near future, though they might look quite different. Customers still want to have in-store shopping experiences and they still want to experience the gratification of that particular feeling of holding a brand they love in their hands. A rising number of retailers are changing their strategy from stuffing their spaces with merchandise to using these spaces in order to display products, provide additional services and form stronger relationships with customers. Fashion retailers are turning to digital transformation strategies to enhance their in-store experiences and this trend will probably accelerate. Think of Nordstrom Local stores that don't offer any product merchandise orders, but only allow people to get apparel tailored and enjoy a spa treatment.[86]

By the time the world resolves the severe issues of Covid-19, physical stores will once again become dynamic, but not as much as for the supply of items as much as for the communication of the retailer with its target market. According to Doug Stephens, author of *Reengineering Retail: The Future of Selling in a Post-Digital World*, there will be a decrease in the number of needed shops and also a reduction of 25% to 30% in the square footage assigned to physical stores. Stephens predicts that "brick-and-mortar stores will be used more as galleries, showrooms and event spaces[87]". This means that, for the predictable future, the bulk of sales will still happen in physical retail shops. However, those stores that continue to innovate and to take advantage of the latest technologies will emerge as the winners in the race to success. For example, in 2019, Timberland opened a new purpose-led flagship store that spotlights the company's sustainability qualifications and brings a unique experience to shoppers. The space displays a "natural but urban materiality–juxtaposing timber and greenery with concrete to bring nature into the city and encourage interaction and exploration[88]".

Chapter Summary

Now that you have read the chapter, you should understand the following:

1. What are the major fashion retail formats?

There are different channel levels that a fashion brand can use in order to offer its product to the end consumer. This can vary in length and it can take the form of 0,1,2,3 or even more. Fashion brands can reach their target markets either directly or indirectly. A direct marketing channel means that the producer sells directly to the final consumer, whereby all levels of the marketing channels are merged into a single ownership and are under common control. Other fashion brands may follow an indirect marketing channel, which consists of having one or even more intermediaries in order to bring a fashion product to the final consumer.

Fashion companies need to decide about the form of retail store they would like to launch in order to appeal to their target market. The main store formats are as follows: 1) convenience stores refer to shops with

(Continued)

a limited range of recurrently purchased household goods and groceries; 2) department stores are businesses that sell a broad range of merchandise and present a wide selection of items scattered across various sections of the store according to product categories; 3) supermarkets are large shops that carry an extensive selection of edible and household goods; 4) contractual retailers such as a) a franchise takes the form of a contractual agreement between a franchisee and a given franchisor with exclusive rights to sell the franchisee's goods in a specific territory or b) leased departments, which are departments within a larger retail store whereby an independent retailer who owns fashion merchandise rents its floor space; 5) category killers refer to a very large specialty store that specializes in a particular type of discounted goods and comes to be the leading retailer in that category; 6) discount stores refer to shops that market brand name goods at less than the normal retail price and offer clothing items at the mass price level; 7) off-price retailers emphasize offering national brands, designer brands or promotional goods, selling high quality goods at cheap prices; 8) outlet stores refer to stores that sell slow moving and out-of-date goods at discounted prices; 9) pop-up stores refer to a storefront space that is opened only for a specific period of time in order to benefit from a faddish trend or seasonal demand; 10) resale stores refer to retailers that obtain secondhand goods for resale; 11) rental stores refer to stores that lease items for a share in the revenue; and finally 12) e-commerce refers to the marketing and purchase of goods and services through an online exchange between companies and individual consumers.

2.   How can fashion marketers enhance the retail environment?

In order to improve the retail environment, fashion marketers are devising good in-store atmospheres in order to appeal to consumers' senses and to differentiate their brands from those of competitors. The atmospheric variables consist of five different characteristics: 1) exterior variables such as good architectural style, colors, and signage; 2) general interior such as the flooring/carpeting, lighting, aromas and music, temperature, cleanliness, wall textures, and color scheme; 3) layout and design variables such as fixtures, allocation of floor space, product groupings, traffic flow, department locations, and allocations within departments; 4) point-of-purchase and decoration such as product displays, point-of-purchase displays, posters, cards, interactive displays, and wall decorations, and 5) human variables such as the density, characteristics and appearances of salespeople. All of these atmospheric variables may impact consumers' perceptions of the store's service quality and can greatly affect the amount of time spent in a certain store in addition to the amount of a company's generated sales.

DISCUSSION QUESTIONS

1.   Discuss your experiences of buying online.

2.   As a fashion marketer, discuss the advantages and disadvantages of pop-up stores.

3.   What do you think of companies who require their employees to look a certain way, e.g., Abercrombie & Fitch has been sued for keeping minorities off the sales floor, Hooters only hires buxom women who wear skimpy outfits? Discuss.

4.   As a fashion marketer for a luxury brand, which fashion channel would you select? Explain why.

5. Do you think that luxury outlets are a good way to sell luxury brands merchandise? Explain why or why not.

6. As a fashion marketer, on which basis would you select your intermediaries?

7. How will changes and developments in technology affect the way a fashion brand distributes its items?

CASE STUDY: INTANGIBLE LUXURY SERVICES – THE CASE OF AMAZON'S ALEXA

Zahy Ramadan & Norma Al Rahbany, Lebanese American University

The idea of modern luxury is shifting towards a new meaning; it is now based on the proposition of being an exclusive medium of self-expression that reflects the person's internal desires. This is embodied by Amazon's Echo Look, a device that is powered by an interactive voice assistant called "Alexa". The device features a camera that enables it to take pictures and videos of the user, and consequently giving them feedback on the acquired style. This intangible luxury service is driven by the functional and relational value that is created from the usage of artificial intelligence (AI).

Indeed, this "AI fashioned" generation consider Alexa as their "friend" who is capable of winning their trust through a deep understanding of their needs. Users also receive a personalized experience,

(Continued)

as Amazon is collecting data about users' styles and is customizing their products to target users' exact needs and wants. After the successful launch testing of the Echo Look, Amazon discontinued the device by the end of 2020[89] and embedded its features in all of its Amazon Echo products that use a camera in order to increase the range of its fashion-related services.

However, growing concerns related to the security and privacy of such services are making headlines. Since a lot of personal pictures are linked to this device, along with the background of the pictures that are taken, the pertaining risks are sizeable. Potential users are voicing their concerns[90] that their camera-enabled Echo devices might be hacked. Furthermore, consumer protection agencies are worried[91] that the pictures' background might be used by Amazon to scan for relevant products and consumption contexts that they might use to build highly-targeted product recommendations.

Accordingly, the dilemma for users will be whether having a customized fashion consultant at their service would outweigh security and privacy concerns. Indeed, the luxury-like experience and the perceived value of such a unique service might not be enough to negate the potential risks for consumers. Nonetheless, it is believed that the anthropomorphization of Alexa and its friendly voice might help users overcome these concerns and help Amazon to extend luxury fashion services.

Such a direction would be expected to fuel the growth of e-commerce for fashion-related products alongside showrooming (customers checking the actual product in a physical store, only to then buy it online). As Covid-19 already had accelerated the migration towards e-commerce, Amazon with its Alexa solution is expected to entice customers into that digital environment and even increase the frequency of purchases. Amazon's strategy and interest in the luxury sector is obvious with their latest new dedicated luxury stores on their site. While some brands might shy away from such an initiative, others will take advantage of these new tools in order to increase their market penetration and appeal towards younger, connected generations.

DISCUSSION QUESTIONS

1. How can fashion marketers take advantage of such a retailer-driven solution?

2. How is Amazon redefining fashion retailing? Will Alexa supersede physical stores?

NOTES

1. Wilson, M. (2019) 'Virgil Abloh's new Nike store is a peek at the future of retail', *Fast Company,* May, 31. www.fastcompany.com/90357179/virgil-ablohs-new-nike-store-is-a-peek-at-the-future-of-retail (accessed September 13, 2021).

2. Guilbault, L. (2019) 'Why Dior and Chanel are launching direct retail for beauty', *Business of Fashion,* July 4. www.businessoffashion.com/articles/professional/why-dior-and-chanel-are-launching-direct-retail-for-beauty (accessed September 13, 2021).

3. Guilbault, L. (2019) 'Why Dior and Chanel are launching direct retail for beauty', *Business of Fashion,* July 4. www.businessoffashion.com/articles/professional/why-dior-and-chanel-are-launching-direct-retail-for-beauty (accessed September 13, 2021).

4. LVMH (2021) 'Le Bon Marché Rive Gauche'. www.lvmh.com/houses/selective-retailing/le-bon-marche/ (accessed September 13, 2021).

5. Glancey, J. (2015) 'A history of the department store', *BBC,* March 26. www.bbc.com/culture/bespoke/ story/20150326-a-history-of-the-department-store/index.html (accessed September 13, 2021).

6. Bloomberg (2019) 'Stores scramble to bolster foot traffic', *Business of Fashion,* December 6. www. businessoffashion.com/articles/news-analysis/department-stores-scramble-to-bolster-foot-traffic (accessed September 13, 2021).

7. Bloomberg (2019) 'Stores scramble to bolster foot traffic', *Business of Fashion,* December 6. www. businessoffashion.com/articles/news-analysis/department-stores-scramble-to-bolster-foot-traffic (accessed September 13, 2021).

8. Saiidi, U. (2016) 'Millennials are prioritizing experiences over stuff', *CNBC,* May 5. www.cnbc. com/2016/05/05/millennials-are-prioritizing-experiences-over-stuff.html (accessed September 13, 2021).

    Hanbury, M. (2019) 'Millennials' attitudes towards clothing ownership are bringing about a major change in the fashion industry', *Insider,* May 26. www.businessinsider.com/millennials-renting-more-clothes-threatens-hm-zara-forever-21-2019-5 (accessed September 13, 2021).

9. Meyersohn, N. and Isidore, C. (2020) 'J.Crew declared bankruptcy. Three other famous stores may follow it', *CNN,* May 4. https://edition.cnn.com/2020/05/04/business/j-crew-bankruptcy-jcpenney-sears-neiman-marcus-retailers-coronavirus/index.html (accessed September 13, 2021).

10. The Neiman Marcus Group (2020) 'Neiman Marcus unveils exciting new ways for customers to access renowned services', *Cision PR Newswire,* July 21. www.prnewswire.com/news-releases/neiman-marcus-unveils-exciting-new-ways-for-customers-to-access-renowned-services-301097258.html (accessed September 13, 2021).

11. Mariott, H. (2019) 'Selfridges opens secondhand clothing concession with Vestiaire Collective', *The Guardian,* October 31. www.theguardian.com/fashion/2019/oct/31/selfridges-opens-secondhand-clothing-concession-with-vestiaire-collective (accessed September 13, 2021).

12. Bloomberg (2017) 'Britain's Sainsbury's looks to fashion instead of food', *Business of Fashion,* May 15. www.businessoffashion.com/articles/news-analysis/supermarket-sainsburys-looks-to-fashion-instead-of-food (accessed September 13, 2021).

13. Cheng, A. (2020) 'Walmart is a growing grocery power, but it's still nowhere near the fashion giant it promised it'd be', *Forbes,* February 18. www.forbes.com/sites/andriacheng/2020/02/18/walmarts-bid-to-be-fashionable-remains-a-work-in-progress/#148a2ea4c0a0 (accessed September 13, 2021).

14. Bloomberg (2018) 'Walmart asks beauty suppliers to look beyond China for sourcing', *Business of Fashion*, August 17. www.businessoffashion.com/articles/news-analysis/under-new-tariffs-walmart-asks-beauty-suppliers-to-look-beyond-china-for-sourcing

15. Bloomberg (2017) 'Supermarket chain Kroger launches fashion line', *Business of Fashion,* November 3. www.businessoffashion.com/articles/news-analysis/supermarket-chain-kroger-launches-fashion-line (accessed September 13, 2021).

16. Hughes, H. (2019) 'Asda trials resale with second-hand clothing pop-up, "Re-Loved"', *Fashion United,* September 3. https://fashionunited.uk/news/retail/asda-trials-resale-with-second-hand-clothing-pop-up-re-loved/2019090345054 (accessed September 13, 2021).

17. Wileman, A. and Jary, M. (1997) *Retail Power Plays: From Trading to Brand Leadership.* New York, NY: New York University Press.

18. Reuters (2018) 'Swiss watchmaker Audemars Piguet to boost revenue by taking sales inhouse', *Business of Fashion,* September 6. www.businessoffashion.com/articles/news-analysis/swiss-watchmaker-audemars-piguet-to-boost-revenue-by-taking-sales-inhouse (accessed September 13, 2021).

19. CPP Luxury (2009) 'All about franchising an international luxury brand', *CPP Luxury,* December 1. https:// cpp-luxury.com/all-about-franchising-an-international-luxury-brand/ (accessed September 13, 2021).

20. Skallerud, K., Korneliussen, T. and Olsen, S.O. (2009) 'An examination of consumers' cross-shopping behavior', *Journal of Retailing and Consumer Services,* 16 (3): 181–89.

21. Hoang, L. (2017) 'Is Nordstrom's off-price strategy hurting its mainline business?', *Business of Fashion,* February 25. www.businessoffashion.com/articles/news-analysis/is-nordstroms-off-price-strategy-hurting-its-mainline-business (accessed September 13, 2021).

22. Shannon, S. (2016) 'How Bicester Village retail outlet became a new luxury destination', *Financial Times,* November 11. www.ft.com/content/c6bafc88-895a-11e6-8cb7-e7ada1d123b1 (accessed September 13, 2021).

23. The Bicester Village shopping collection (2021) 'Your visit'. www.tbvsc.com/en/visit (accessed September 13, 2021).

24. Fernandez, C. (2019) 'Gucci rolls out new pop-up concept', *Business of Fashion,* November 5. www.businessoffashion.com/articles/news-analysis/gucci-rolls-out-new-pop-up-concept (accessed September 13, 2021).

25. David, D-M. (2019) 'Glossier's new partnership with Nordstrom proves the luxury department store remains a favorite for e-commerce brands looking to dabble in brick-and-mortar, even as other high-end retailers flounder', *Business Insider,* December 14. www.businessinsider.com/nordstrom-remains-popular-partner-for-ecommerce-brands-glossier-popups-2019-12 (accessed September 13, 2021).

26. Reuters (2019) 'Zara to roll out denim customisation pop-up', *Business of Fashion,* March 13. www.businessoffashion.com/articles/news-analysis/zara-to-open-denim-customisation-pop-ups-in-three-stores (accessed September 13, 2021).

27. NARTS (2021) 'Industry statistics & trends', *NARTS, The Association of Resale Professionals.* www.narts.org/i4a/pages/index.cfm?pageid=3285 (accessed September 13, 2021).

28. Loeb, W. (2019) 'The resale fashion industry is bigger and more disruptive than you think', *Forbes,* May 15. www.forbes.com/sites/walterloeb/2019/05/15/resale-fashion-industry-bigger-and-more-disruptive-than-you-think/#3fd59608609b (accessed September 13, 2021).

29. Shahbandeh, M. (2021) 'Retail and apparel resale market value worldwide from 2017 to 2019, with a forecast until 2024', *Statista,* January 11. www.statista.com/statistics/826354/retail-and-apparel-resale-market-value-forecast-worldwide/ (accessed September 13, 2021).

30. Stein, S. (2019) 'Secondhand could supplant fast fashion in a decade, ThredUp & The RealReal are leading the way', *Forbes,* March 26. www.forbes.com/sites/sanfordstein/2019/03/26/resale-revamp-thanks-to-thredup-and-the-realreal/?sh=307d75451f3e (accessed September 13, 2021).

31. (2019) 'The rise and rise of the designer resale market', *Financial Times,* July 24. https://www.ft.com/content/a7e5d5f8-7c91-11e9-8b5c-33d0560f039c (accessed September 13, 2021).

32. Loeb, W. (2019) 'The resale fashion industry is bigger and more disruptive than you think', *Forbes,* May 15. www.forbes.com/sites/walterloeb/2019/05/15/resale-fashion-industry-bigger-and-more-disruptive-than-you-think/#3fd59608609b (accessed September 13, 2021).

33. Kent, S. (2019) 'Burberry partners with the RealReal to tap fast-growing resale market', *Business of Fashion,* October 7. www.businessoffashion.com/articles/news-bites/burberry-partners-with-the-realreal-to-tap-fast-growing-resale-market (accessed September 13, 2021).

34. Howland, D. (2019) 'Macy's debuts secondhand apparel sales with ThredUp', *Retail Dive,* August 14. www.retaildive.com/news/macys-debuts-second-hand-apparel-sales-with-thredup/560879/ (accessed September 13, 2021).

35. (2019) 'The rise and rise of the designer resale market', *Financial Times,* July 24. www.ft.com/content/a7e5d5f8-7c91-11e9-8b5c-33d0560f039c (accessed September 13, 2021).

36. Little J. (2019) 'Hire calling: why rental fashion is taking off', *The Guardian,* July 29. www.theguardian.com/fashion/2019/jul/29/hire-calling-why-rental-fashion-is-taking-off (accessed September 13, 2021).

37. O'Connor, T. (2020) 'Three strategies for brands entering the rental market', *Business of Fashion,* January 24. www.businessoffashion.com/articles/professional/how-to-do-fashion-rental-as-a-brand-rent-the-runway-white-label (accessed September 13, 2021).

38. Chen, C. (2019) 'Rent the runway to expand into kids' clothing', *Business of Fashion,* April 5. www.businessoffashion.com/articles/news-analysis/rent-the-runway-expands-into-kids-clothing (accessed September 13, 2021).

39. Reuters (2019) 'Rental apparel brings new wrinkles for retail stores', *Business of Fashion,* September 18. www.businessoffashion.com/articles/news-analysis/rental-apparel-brings-new-wrinkles-for-retail-stores (accessed September 13, 2021).

40. Statista (2020) 'Fashion e-commerce report 2020', *Statista.* www.statista.com/study/38340/ecommerce-report-fashion/ (accessed September 13, 2021).

41. Lee, A. (2020) 'Gucci reveals Snapchat AR shoe try-ons', *WWD,* June 29. https://wwd.com/business-news/technology/gucci-reveals-snapchat-ar-shoe-try-ons-1203661812/ (accessed September 13, 2021).

42. Meola, A. (2020) 'Rise of m-commerce: Mobile ecommerce shopping stats & trends in 2021', *Insider,* December 30. www.businessinsider.com/mobile-commerce-shopping-trends-stats (accessed September 13, 2021).

43. Skrovan, S. (2017) 'Why most shoppers still choose brick-and-mortar stores over e-commerce', *Retail Dive*, February 22. www.retaildive.com/news/why-most-shoppers-still-choose-brick-and-mortar-stores-over-e-commerce/436068/ (accessed September 13, 2021).

44. Roger, S. (2020) 'Is immersive technology the darling of the fashion world?', *Forbes*, February 19. www.forbes.com/sites/solrogers/2020/02/19/is-immersive-technology-the-darling-of-the-fashion-world/#68b5a4672256 (accessed September 13, 2021).

45. Bloomberg (2019) 'Alibaba leads investment in Taiwanese augmented reality start-up', *Business of Fashion*, September 19. www.businessoffashion.com/articles/news-analysis/alibaba-leads-investment-in-taiwanese-augmented-reality-start-up (accessed September 13, 2021).

46. Hanbury, M. (2018) 'Amazon is reportedly scanning people's bodies so it can sell you clothes', *Business Insider*, May 3. www.businessinsider.com/amazon-3d-body-scanning-for-clothes-2018-5 (accessed September 13, 2021).

47. Nike (2019) 'What is Nike Fit?', *Nike*, May 9. https://news.nike.com/news/nike-fit-digital-foot-measurement-tool (accessed September 13, 2021).

48. Cheng, A. (2018) 'What Farfetch's IPO filing says about the $300 billion luxury fashion industry', *Forbes*, August 21. www.forbes.com/sites/andriacheng/2018/08/21/what-farfetchs-ipo-filing-says-about-the-300-billion-luxury-fashion-industry/#3361541ebb1f (accessed September 13, 2021).

49. Baker, J., Ashill, N., Amer, N. and Diab, E. (2018) 'The internet dilemma: An exploratory study of luxury firms' usage of internet-based technologies', *Journal of Retailing and Consumer Services*, 41: 37–47.

Chandon, J.L., Laurent, G. and Valette-Florence, P. (2016) 'Pursuing the concept of luxury: Introduction to the JBR Special Issue on "Luxury Marketing from Tradition to Innovation"', *Journal of Business Research*, 69 (1): 299–303.

Okonkwo, U. (2009) 'Sustaining the luxury brand on the Internet', *Journal of Brand Management*, 16 (5/6): 302–10.

50. Reuters (2017) 'Online sales? Maybe one day, says Chanel', *Business of Fashion*, November 24. www.businessoffashion.com/articles/news-analysis/online-sales-maybe-one-day-says-chanel (accessed September 13, 2021).

51. Reuters (2017) 'LVMH confirms launch of multi-brand fashion site', *Business of Fashion*, May 10. www.businessoffashion.com/articles/news-analysis/lvmh-confirms-launch-of-multiple-brand-website (accessed September 13, 2021).

52. Aiolfi, S. and Sabbadin, E. (2019) 'Fashion and new luxury digital disruption: The new challenges of fashion between omnichannel and traditional retailing', *International Journal of Business and Management*, 14 (8): 41–51.

Lynch, S. and Barnes, L. (2020) 'Omnichannel fashion retailing: Examining the customer decision-making journey', *Journal of Fashion Marketing and Management: An International Journal*, 24 (3): 471–93.

Silva, S.C., Duarte, P. and Sundetova, A. (2020) 'Multichannel versus omnichannel: A price-segmented comparison from the fashion industry', *International Journal of Retail & Distribution Management*, 48 (4): 417–30.

53. Berthiaume, D. (2020) 'The top five most "competent" premium omnichannel retailers are…' *Chain Store Age*, February 10. https://chainstoreage.com/top-five-most-competent-premium-omnichannel-retailers-are (accessed September 13, 2021).

54. Cuff, S. (2020) 'Creating a stir in Covent Garden, Huda Beauty's first pop up', *The Store Front*, February 17. www.thestorefront.com/mag/huda-beauty-pop-up-covent-garden/ (accessed September 13, 2021).

55. Cuff, S. (2020) 'Creating a stir in Covent Garden, Huda Beauty's first pop up', *The Store Front*, February 17. www.thestorefront.com/mag/huda-beauty-pop-up-covent-garden/" www.thestorefront.com/mag/huda-beauty-pop-up-covent-garden/ (accessed September 13, 2021).

56. Maloney, G. (2019) 'No, online shopping did not overtake brick-and-mortar store sales last month', *Forbes*, April 8. www.forbes.com/sites/gregmaloney/2019/04/08/correction-online-shopping-did-not-overtake-brick-and-mortar-store-sales-last-month/#4fd0144a3e79 (accessed September 13, 2021).

57. Wertz, G. (2018) 'How brick-and-mortar stores can compete with e-commerce giants', *Forbes*, May 17. www.forbes.com/sites/jiawertz/2018/05/17/how-brick-and-mortar-stores-can-compete-with-e-commerce-giants/#bebef4d3cc0a (accessed September 13, 2021).

58. Clarke, D.W., Perry, P. and Denson, H. (2012) 'The sensory retail environment of small fashion boutiques', *Journal of Fashion Marketing and Management*, 16 (4): 492–510.

Spence, C., Puccinelli, N.M., Grewal, D. and Roggeveen, A.L. (2014) 'Store atmospherics: A multisensory perspective', *Psychology & Marketing*, 31 (7): 472–88 (2021) 'M&Ms New York', *M&Ms*. www.mms.com/en-us/mms-store-new-york (accessed September 13, 2021).

60. Spiggle, S. and Sewall, M.A. (1987) 'A choice sets model of retail selection,' *Journal of Marketing*, 51: 97–111.

61. Turley, L.W. and Milliman, R.E. (2000) 'Atmospheric effects on shopping behavior: a review of the experimental evidence', *Journal of Business Research*, 49 (2): 193–211.

62. Kim, H., Choi, Y.J. and Lee, Y. (2015) 'Web atmospheric qualities in luxury fashion brand web sites', *Journal of Fashion Marketing and Management*, 19 (4): 384–401.

    Jain, S. (2021) 'Examining the moderating role of perceived risk and web atmospherics in online luxury purchase intention', *Journal of Fashion Marketing and Management*, 25 (4): 585–605.

    Brun, A., Kluge, P.N., Königsfeld, J.A., Fassnacht, M. and Mitschke, F. (2013) 'Luxury web atmospherics: An examination of homepage design', *International Journal of Retail & Distribution Management*, 41 (11/12): 901–16.

63. Kent, A., Dennis, C., Cano, M.B., Helberger, E. and Brakus, J. (2018) 'Branding, marketing, and design: Experiential in-store digital environments', in Information Reso Management Association (ed.) *Fashion and Textiles: Breakthroughs in Research and Practice*. Hershey, PA: IGI Global. pp. 275-298

    Nazir, S. (2019) 'How does Zara survive despite minimal advertising?', *Retail Gazette*, January 22. www.retailgazette.co.uk/blog/2019/01/how-does-zara-survive-despite-minimal-advertising/ (accessed September 13, 2021).

64. Nobbs, K., Foong, K.M. Baker, J. (2015) 'An exploration of fashion visual merchandising and its role as a brand positioning device', *Journal of Global Fashion Marketing*, 6 (1): 4–19.

65. Schaverien, A. (2018) How retailers are making their storefronts more interactive with Ombori', *Forbes*, November 21. www.forbes.com/sites/annaschaverien/2018/11/21/interactive-storefronts-ombori-window-shopping/#71684f9116e7 (accessed September 13, 2021).

66. Wisenthal, M. (2018) '10 unique window displays to inspire retailers to build their own eye-catching design', *Shopify*, May 8. www.shopify.com/retail/10-innovative-window-displays-that-you-should-consider-stealing (accessed September 13, 2021).

67. Schäfer, T., Sedlmeier, P., Städtler, C., and Huron, D. (2013) 'The psychological functions of music listening', *Frontiers in Psychology*, 4: 511. doi.org/10.3389/fpsyg.2013.00511

    North, A.C., Sheridan, L.P., and Areni, C.S. (2016) 'Music congruity effects on product memory, perception, and choice', *Journal of Retailing*, 92 (1): 83–95. doi.org/10.1016/j.jretai.2015.06.001

68. Donovan, R.J., Rossiter, J.R., Marcoolyn, G. and Nesdale, A. (1994) 'Store atmosphere and purchasing behavior', *Journal of Retailing*, 70 (3): 283–94.

    Ward, J.C., Bitner, M.J. and Barnes, J. (1992) 'Measuring the prototypicality and meaning of retail environments', *Journal of Retailing*, 68 (2): 194–220.

69. Soars, B. (2009) 'Driving sales through shoppers' sense of sound, sight, smell and touch', *International Journal of Retail & Distribution Management*, 37 (3): 286–98.

70. Ufford, L. (2017) 'Let there be light: Retail lighting designs to encourage sales', *Shopify*, August 22. www.shopify.com/retail/let-there-be-light-lighting-strategies-to-boost-store-sales (accessed September 13, 2021).

71. Ahmded, O. (2018) 'Lights, camera, selfie!', *Business of Fashion*, October 17. www.businessoffashion.com/articles/intelligence/lights-camera-selfie (accessed September 13, 2021).

72. Johnson, R. (2013) 'Olfactive branding: retail's fragrant frontier', *Business of Fashion*, August 1. www.businessoffashion.com/articles/intelligence/olfactive-branding-retails-fragrant-frontier-hm-calvin-klein-bloomingdales-nike-scent-air-1229 (accessed September 13, 2021).

73. Sendra-Nadal, E. and Carbonell-Barrachina, Á.A. (eds.) (2017) *Sensory and Aroma Marketing*. Wageningen: Wageningen Academic Publishers.

74. Scent Company (2017) 'Dior branding its flagships with a signature scent', *Scent Company*, November 4. http://blog.scentcompany.info/dior-branding-signature-scent/ (accessed September 13, 2021).

75. Brown, S. (2018) '9 tips for mastering the in-store experience', *Business of Fashion*, August 8. www.businessoffashion.com/articles/professional/8-tips-for-mastering-the-in-store-experience (accessed September 13, 2021).

76. Mathur, U.C. (2010) *Retail Management: Text and Cases*. Delhi: IK International.

77. Helen Katharine (2018) 'Luxury strategy: Visual merchandising'. February 28. www.helenkatharine. com/visual-merchandising/ (accessed September 13, 2021).

78. Damen, A. (2021) 'The ultimate guide to retail store layouts', *Shopify*, June 2. www.shopify.com/retail/ the-ultimate-guide-to-retail-store-layouts (accessed September 13, 2021).

79. Tulipa, D., Gunawan, S. and Supit, V.H. (2014) 'The influence of store atmosphere on emotional responses and re-purchase intentions', *Business Management and Strategy*, 5 (2): 151–64.

Park, H.H., Jeon, J.O. and Sullivan, P. (2015) 'How does visual merchandising in fashion retail stores affect consumers' brand attitude and purchase intention?', *The International Review of Retail, Distribution and Consumer Research*, 25 (1): 87–104.

80. Boardman, R., Henninger, C.E. and Zhu, A. (2020) 'Augmented reality and virtual reality: New drivers for fashion retail?', in G. Vignali, L.F. Reid, D. Ryding and C.E. Henniger (eds), *Technology-Driven Sustainability*. Cham: Palgrave Macmillan. pp. 155–172.

Javornik, A. (2016) 'Augmented reality: Research agenda for studying the impact of its media characteristics on consumer behaviour', *Journal of Retailing and Consumer Services*, 30: 252–61.

Perannagari, K.T. and Chakrabarti, S. (2019) 'Factors influencing acceptance of augmented reality in retail: Insights from thematic analysis', *International Journal of Retail & Distribution Management*, 48 (1): 18–34.

Watson, A., Alexander, B. and Salavati, L. (2018) 'The impact of experiential augmented reality applications on fashion purchase intention', *International Journal of Retail & Distribution* Management, 48 (5): 433–51.

81. Ombori (2018) 'Ombori Grid – Max Fashion Dubai' [Video]. *Ombori YouTube channel,* November 15. www.youtube.com/watch?v=mBAreA8BIeQ (accessed September 13, 2021).

82. Mckinsey (2019) *Perspectives on Retail and Consumer Goods*. www.mckinsey.com/~/media/McKinsey/ Industries/Retail/Our%20Insights/Perspectives%20on%20retail%20and%20consumer%20goods%20 Number%207/Perspectives-on-Retail-and-Consumer-Goods_Issue-7.ashx (accessed September 13, 2021).

83. (2018) '5 types of signage no retailer can afford to ignore', *Shopify*, May 10. www.shopify.com/retail/ retail-signage

84. Baker, J., Grewal, D. and Parasuraman, A. (1994) 'The influence of store environment on quality inferences and store image', *Journal of the Academy of Marketing Science*, 22 (4): 328–39.

Hu, H. and Jasper, C.R. (2006) 'Social cues in the store environment and their impact on store image', *International Journal of Retail & Distribution Management*, 34 (1): 25–48.

85. Baker, J., Parasuraman, A., Grewal, D. and Voss, G.B. (2002) 'The influence of multiple store environment cues on perceived merchandise value and patronage intentions', *Journal of Marketing*, 66 (2): 120–41.

86. Morgan, B. (2019) 'Fashion of the future: what retail customer experience will look like in 5 years', *Forbes*, May 10. www.forbes.com/sites/blakemorgan/2019/05/10/fashion-of-the-future-what-retail-customer-experience-will-look-like-in-5-years/#64b3070569e0 (accessed September 13, 2021).

87. Howland, D. (2021) 'Brick and mortar's next chapter', *Retail Dive*, June 1. www.retaildive.com/news/ brick-and-mortars-next-chapter/578768/ (accessed September 13, 2021).

88. Dalziel & Pow (2019) 'Timberland opens new purpose-led flagship', *Dalziel & Pow*, November 14. www. dalziel-pow.com/news/timberland-opens-iconic-new-purpose-led-flagship-on-carnaby-street (accessed September 13, 2021).

89. Caman, A. (2020) 'Amazon will no longer support the Echo Look, encourages owners to recycle theirs', *The Verge*, May 29. www.theverge.com/2020/5/29/21274805/amazon-echo-look-discontinue-gadget-shopping-recycle-fashion-camera (accessed December 9, 2021).

90. Ramadan, Z. (2019) 'The democratization of intangible luxury, *Marketing Intelligence & Planning*, 37 (6): 660–673. https://doi.org/10.1108/MIP-11-2018-0490 (accessed December 9, 2021).

91. Barrett, B. (2017) 'Amazon's "Echo Look" could snoop a lot more than just your clothes', *Wired*, April 28. www.wired.com/2017/04/amazon-echo-look-privacy/ (accessed December 9, 2021).

Index

Page numbers followed by *f*, *i* and *t* indicate figures, images and tables